THE CONCISE ENCYCLOPEDIA OF
WESTERN PHILOSOPHY AND PHILOSOPHERS

THE CONCISE ENCYCLOPEDIA OF

Western Philosophy
and Philosophers

EDITED BY J. O. URMSON

THE CONTRIBUTORS

J. L. ACKRILL

H. B. ACTON

A. HILARY ARMSTRONG

A. J. AYER

ERROL BEDFORD

ISAIAH BERLIN

KARL BRITTON

JOSEPH G. DAWSON

M. A. E. DUMMETT

DOROTHY M. EMMET

A. C. EWING

MARVIN FARBER

J. N. FINDLAY

THOMAS GILBY

ROLAND HALL

R. M. HARE

R. HARRÉ

H. L. A. HART

D. J. B. HAWKINS

P. L. HEATH

RONALD W. HEPBURN

EDMUND HILL

WALTER KAUFMANN

I. G. KIDD

G. S. KIRK

STEPHAN KÖRNER

J. D. MABBOTT

ALASDAIR MACINTYRE

D. M. MACKINNON

D. G. C. MACNABB

PHILIP MERLAN

ERNEST NAGEL

P. H. NOWELL-SMITH

JAMES O'CONNELL

D. J. O'CONNOR

R. S. PETERS

ANTHONY QUINTON

RICHARD ROBINSON

ERWIN I. J. ROSENTHAL

GILBERT RYLE

RUTH LYDIA SAW

P. F. STRAWSON

F. A. TAYLOR

IVO THOMAS

J. O. URMSON

JAMES WARD SMITH

G. J. WARNOCK

ALAN R. WHITE

B. A. O. WILLIAMS

HAWTHORN BOOKS, INC.

Publishers

New York

CONTENTS

ILLUSTRATIONS

Acknowledgments

We should like to thank Dr. Arthur E. Murphy, of Texas University, Austin, Texas, and Dr. Emerson Buchanan, Editor of the *Journal of Philosophy*, Columbia University, New York, for their great assistance in reading the text.

We are indebted to the following for their help with and their permission to reproduce the plates listed below:

4, 9, 60 The Trustees of the British Museum, London

7 The Syndics of the Fitzwilliam Museum, Cambridge

12, 17, 50, 64 The Trustees of the National Portrait Gallery, London

14 The Governing Body of The Queen's College, Oxford

20 Dr. H. St. J. Atkins, President, University College, Cork

21 *A Life of Bernard Bosanquet* by Helen Bosanquet, Macmillan and Co. Ltd., London

22 The Warden and Fellows of Merton College, Oxford

24, 61, 65, 92, 94 The Master and Fellows of Trinity College, Cambridge

25 The President and Fellows of Magdalen College, Oxford

28 The Master and Fellows of Pembroke College, Oxford

35 The Trustees of the National Gallery, London

36 The Trustees of Columbia University, New York, who are the owners of the painting

51, 78 The Trustees of the National Galleries of Scotland

53 The University Court of the University of Glasgow

59 The Governing Body of Christ Church, Oxford

75 Sir Ian Forbes-Leith of Fyvie, Bt, Fyvie Castle, Aberdeenshire

NOTE: **Bold type** within any article denotes that there is a separate entry on the person or philosophical term which should be referred to for further reference.

INTRODUCTION

BY THE EDITOR

It is likely that there are fields of inquiry in which the happy compiler of an encyclopedia would have as his main task the collection of a set of impartial accounts of the main agreed results; this would seem to be true of the sciences except on the very frontiers of recent research and speculations on the fringes. But in philosophy, for reasons which will be set out later in this introduction, there is no set of agreed results to which all experts would subscribe; "there is not a single matter within its sphere which is not still in dispute", said Descartes in his *Discourse on Method*, and that statement is as true in the twentieth as it was in the seventeenth century. Therefore any set of answers to the main problems of philosophy, however eminent their authors, would either represent but one of countless viewpoints and constitute a party manifesto or would constantly contradict one another. It follows that an encyclopedia of philosophy cannot set out to give authoritative answers to philosophical problems without either deceiving its readers by representing as the agreed answer what is in reality a contending opinion or confusing them with a series of inconsistent answers; this being so it has seemed better not to try to answer these questions at all.

This encyclopedia will therefore be searched in vain for a key to the riddle of the universe or even for pronouncements on the reality or otherwise of matter, the objectivity or subjectivity of moral standards or the relation of mind and body; but there remain many useful tasks which an encyclopedia of philosophy can perform. First, it is possible to give explanations of the key technical terms used by philosophers of all shades of opinion; such terms as "analytic", "category", "universal", "dialectic" and "sense datum" are in constant use in philosophical texts and cannot be adequately explained by even the best dictionary. Secondly some account can be given of the main answers to philosophical questions, those standard positions held so frequently as to be given a name such as realism, idealism, monism, dualism, nominalism, conceptualism, rationalism, and empiricism; these "isms" are rather skeletons of positions than full answers and no philosopher worthy of consideration can be adequately described as holding any combination of these "isms", for he always has his own peculiar contribution to make; but no reading of philosophy is possible without some understanding of these terms, dangerous and misleading though many of them are.

Thirdly the work and opinions of individual philosophers can be summarily described, certainly not as an adequate substitute for a reading of the philosopher himself but either to provide background information or as a preliminary guide to the reading of his works.

Finally some indication can be given of what the main fields of philosophical investigation are by articles on logic, metaphysics, epistemology, ethics and aesthetics which attempt to explain what problems exercise philosophers within those fields. It is within one or other of these four groups – explanations of technical terms, descriptions of well-known "isms", accounts of individual philosophers and general descriptions of the main fields of philosophical inquiry – that most of the articles in this encyclopedia fall. Even in such articles the most honest and unprejudiced writer must to some extent be partial since he must select, explain and interpret; but, if he bears in mind this inevitable proviso, the reader may confidently expect to receive accurate information rather than partisan expressions of opinion.

This encyclopedia is concise. To be concise certainly demands the omission of all superfluous material, but still the editor is faced with hard decisions. Is he to attempt to include articles on every subject on which a reader might reasonably expect or hope to obtain information? The attempt would be doomed to failure, but even so it could only be made at the price of making all the articles very short. Moreover this procedure suffers from the decisive disadvantage that there are many subjects on which nothing worth saying could be achieved within the compass of a brief article. The dates of Kant's birth and death and a list of his more important works might be given in an article of a hundred words; but if any account of Kant's views is to be given it is certain that anything said in one or two brief paragraphs would be worse than useless for it would be largely unintelligible and where intelligible misleading. In fact the article on Kant in this encyclopedia contains about six thousand words; the informed reader will readily see, and the uninformed reader must be asked to accept, that it is as simple and as clear an account of Kant's philosophy as is compatible with accuracy and that nothing it contains could be omitted in any account of Kant which sought to do him justice; six thousand words is in this case the minimum length compatible with accuracy and intelligibility.

Thus extreme brevity in the individual articles is not a reasonable method of attaining an over-all brevity. The total number of articles included has been restricted on the principle that it is better to have a fair number of useful articles than to have a large number of useless ones, though selection has its drawbacks. Apart from the obvious effort to include the important rather than the unimportant and to anticipate what the reader is most likely to look for, various principles of selection have played a part of which the reader may be usefully informed.

First, and most importantly, a fairly narrow interpretation of what constitutes philosophy has been chosen, one conforming rather to the usage of professional philosophers in the western tradition than to popular usage. In popular thought a philosopher is a man of high principle immune so far as is humanly possible to the shorter-term interests and problems of ordinary mortals, calm and unruffled in the face of adversity, who has a message for human beings about how they may best and most wisely live, a message which is called "a philosophy of life". But it is not for such traits as these, even when they had them, that the great philosophers of the western tradition have achieved their fame; Plato, Aristotle, Aquinas, Descartes, Locke, Berkeley, Hume, Kant and the other great ones of western philosophy achieved their greatness in quite other ways than this and it would be in general beside the point to ask for their "philosophy of life". Perhaps only for a short period around the time of the birth of Christ when Stoic and Epicurean sages contended about how life should be lived has philosophy in the west conformed at all to the popular picture. With a few striking excep-

tions eastern philosophy has traditionally been more in accord with this popular conception; in deciding to limit our scope to philosophy as practised by the great western philosophers we have therefore excluded traditional eastern philosophy. There is in this decision no suggestion that the Buddhist and Confucian sages are unworthy of attention; the simple truth is that their achievement is not closely related to that of the western philosophers and it is not possible to include two subjects within the limits of one concise encyclopedia. The decision how to live is no doubt more important than any intellectual struggle for theoretical understanding; but this latter is the aim of western philosophy.

A second principle of selection has been that the needs of non-specialist readers have been given priority and articles on very technical problems and the philosophers who specialized in them have therefore been kept to a minimum; thus the more abstract speculations of logic have been omitted – there is, for example, no article on Lord Keynes, whose sole contribution in print to philosophy was an important but very abstruse treatise on probability. Readers who can usefully tackle such subjects and authors will not need the guidance of this encyclopedia.

Thirdly it has been assumed that the reader will not be an expert linguist; therefore philosophers whose works are not available in translation into English have been omitted or given treatment shorter perhaps than their merits. This encyclopedia therefore does not claim to be a comprehensive guide to modern philosophy, though it endeavours to range beyond the confines of contemporary British and American philosophical fashions.

But it would be idle to pretend that for every inclusion and exclusion some rational reason can be given; apart from the mere oversights attributable to the human errancy of the editor some decisions about the contents have inevitably been marginal and arbitrary. The editor here and now expresses his regrets to those who would have chosen differently; he would have added much if he could, but in fact every addition to what there is would have involved the exclusion of something which is included.

In the choice of articles the most difficult decision has been with regard to living philosophers whose work is still in progress. Many living philosophers have been included, but those whose work is still in progress have been treated with a brevity not indicative of their merits and those whose writings are readily accessible in book form have been given preference over those who have written mainly in learned journals. In this particular field it has been impossible to regard merit as the sole principle of selection.

The reader will perhaps recollect our earlier statement that articles which attempt to answer directly the great problems of philosophy have been avoided because there are no agreed answers in philosophy and therefore any answers here given would inevitably be partisan and in a way unsuitable for the contents of an encyclopedia. This statement might well sound like a hostile attack on philosophy and give ground for the view, not infrequently expressed, that the study of philosophy is an idle folly and vexation. Does it not seem that philosophy is a vain waste of words to be shunned by the man with his feet firmly on the ground? It would be as well for us to look into the reasons for this lack of agreed results in philosophy to see whether it is a good ground for the remainder of the harsh reproaches to which philosophy is subject.

"Philosophy" is a transliteration of a Greek word which is usually translated "love of wisdom" but which is perhaps better translated as "love of knowledge". All knowledge has never been counted as within the field of philosophy; particular pieces of practical information that have no theoretical bearing have never been counted as within the special province of the philosopher; he may know the name of his neighbours and how to mix a cocktail, but this would not count as part of philosophical erudition. But originally, it must be emphasized, philosophy included many fields of inquiry which are now counted as right outside the competence of the philosopher, including all that we would now call science; even geography was claimed as part of philosophy by the great Greek geographer Strabo; generally, any investigation prompted by theoretical curiosity rather than by immediate practical needs was counted as philosophical in the original acceptance of the word.

Gradually, as what we now call the sciences began to develop, it became convenient to distinguish various special interests within philosophy as "na-tural philosophy", "mental philosophy" and "metaphysical philosophy". But even as late as the seventeenth century, in Newton's time, natural philosophy was thought of merely as a special interest within a single subject; for Newton natural philosophy, in which he specialized, was far from being so narrow a discipline as modern physics, as is well indicated by his saying in the *Principia*: "And thus much concerning God, to discourse of whom from the appearances of things does certainly belong to natural philosophy". But as the knowledge first of pure mathematics, then of the physical nature of the world, then of its chemical nature advanced these studies became full-time specialist pursuits with well-tried methods of their own and technical vocabularies; from being a mere province in the interest of the philosopher they became disciplines on their own. Biology, the field of philosophy to which Aristotle had early made such great contributions, was the next to split off; even in the middle of the nineteenth century Herbert Spencer could write a system of philosophy which started with metaphysical first principles, ended with a treatise on ethics, and included a volume on biology in the middle, but it was already becoming a separate discipline. Psychology, which used to be called mental science or mental philosophy, has become a special discipline only within living memory and at Oxford and Cambridge is still taught normally in conjunction with philosophy. Logic, though included in this encyclopedia as philosophy, is now becoming so technical that in some universities it is taught more in the departments of mathematics than those of philosophy.

Thus we see that the field of philosophy has gradually contracted. All theoretical studies are, in their infancy, part of philosophy; they cease to be part of philosophy only when they become established disciplines with technical methods of their own and agreed results. Thus one explanation of why there are no agreed results in philosophy lies ready to hand; it is that whenever within any field of philosophy (or what has hitherto been counted as philosophy) we find a sure method of procedure and an agreed way of testing hypotheses we cease to call that field philosophy any longer. Philosophy is thus the fissiparous mother of all the sciences; they were all part of her, she gave birth to them and tended them in their feeble infancy; now grown older they assert their independence in the way natural to children.

Already we have here a sufficient justification of the pursuit of philosophy as the original source of all theoretical understanding of the world and hence, indirectly, of our mastery of our environment. It would be hasty, moreover, to assume that there are no further new sciences still being nursed by philosophy in their infant stage of development. If part of the activity of philosophers is still the first crude tentatives in new sciences, this will go some way, at least, to explain the continuing lack of agreed results in philosophy; for until a science is well established no one can be sure what the valid methods for approaching it are or even quite what we may expect to achieve by its pursuit; there can only be intelligent groping at a method until the genius with luck arrives to put the science on a firm basis – and this genius will be known thereafter not as a philosopher but as the first ". . . ologist".

How many new sciences will be thrown off by philosophy in the course of time no one can tell, though it would be rash to suppose that the process is at an end. But the question now arises whether we should suppose that this is the sole function of philosophy, whether we are to see philosophers solely as the midwives to embryonic sciences. We must ask whether all that philosophers now work on will one day be converted into a set of special sciences or else be recognised as vain and useless like astrology and divination; or is there some distinctive province of philosophy different in kind from that of the sciences, so that guardianship of young sciences will be but a part-time occupation for the philosopher.

There have been many claims in the history of philosophy to have established special fields of philosophical inquiry in which the results could be counted as the results or discoveries of philosophy. Sometimes philosophy has been regarded as itself a science, but as distinguished from other sciences by its special subject-matter; while the other sciences, the so-called empirical sciences, – physics, biology and psychology and the like – have the task of investigating the sensible world, philosophy on this view has the task of investigating the intelligible world underlying the appearances to which the other sciences are confined, an investigation which must proceed by pure intellectual argu-

ment and cannot rely at all on the senses. Sometimes again philosophy has been assigned the task of bringing to light the very general principles alleged to be common to and to underlie all the sciences, or of giving an all-embracing account of the world based on the findings of all the special sciences, or of providing a general critique of the sciences (a dangerous and pretentious claim this), or of bringing to light the ultimate presuppositions of all our thinking. Some of these tasks, though suggested, have scarcely been attempted; when others have been attempted they have usually seemed mere speculation, perhaps unintelligible, certainly unjustified, to almost all save their authors. It is not on the basis of such claims as these that we can hope to find a further justification for philosophy and a special field of philosophical inquiry, though many philosophers who have made such claims have made great contributions to philosophy which we cannot afford to neglect.

We have seen that one explanation of the lack of special philosophical results is that when results are obtained they are counted as the beginnings of some autonomous science and cease to count as belonging to philosophy. We must now go on to see that there are other areas of philosophy in which progress is made when what was a problem ceases any longer to be a problem. There are here no positive results to be set down as part of the discoveries of philosophy simply because the progress consists in causing men to cease to be perplexed, to cease to think that they are confronted with a problem, where once they were perplexed. Perhaps in this matter of making apparent problems disappear we have at least one of the characteristic functions of philosophy. A simple illustration will perhaps help the reader to grasp what is here in question, though in the very nature of the case it must seem a trivial illustration: in the earlier part of the fifth century B.C. a number of very intelligent men began to be perplexed about the possibility of making negative statements; for, as they argued, if we say "The cat is not white" the first part of what we say is "The cat is not"; but if the cat is not, then there is no cat, there is nothing to say anything about and we must be silent; it is permissible to speak only of what is. These intelligent men were, of course, as aware as we are that this argument is revolting to common-sense or, as

Parmenides put it, to opinion; but they were intent on following the argument out wherever it might lead them without fear of ridicule from respectable people. Plato solved this difficulty by pointing out that to say that the cat is not white is not to deny that there is a cat but rather to say that the cat is other than white; in technical language, the existential and predicative uses of the verb "to be" were distinguished. Here, then, we have the removal of a simple, though not stupid or simple-minded, confusion; but we have no positive results, not even the result of establishing the nature of negation, for, as later history showed only too clearly, it remained possible to be confused and perplexed about negation in novel ways which Plato did not foresee. Negative statements are very perplexing to anyone who reflects about them and there will never be an end to puzzles about them; when each puzzle is removed then philosophical progress is made, a progress towards clarity; but there are hardly any positive results to count as philosophical knowledge. The history of philosophy is full of similar examples, some of them much more complex than that just described; the great philosophers may not have found the final solutions to the problem of this and the problem of that, but as a result of their work there are some ways of being perplexed by some problems into which no student who has read their work need ever fall again. Perhaps, indeed, there is no such thing as a final solution to these problems but only a continual struggle not to be baffled and blinded, not to fall into conceptual confusion.

It is probable that all philosophers would agree that some achievements in philosophy are best described as the banishment of some confusion and not as a positive discovery. Some modern philosophers, indeed, have wished to claim that all genuinely philosophical problems are rather puzzles to be dissolved than questions to be answered; those philosophers who have been influenced by Wittgenstein are particularly associated with this view, which is strikingly expressed in Wittgenstein's *Philosophical Investigations*. In making this claim they in part wish to exclude from philosophy some questions which they recognize are not of the "puzzle" variety – questions of psychology and judgments of value, for example, and to this extent the question is only one of how widely we would be well advised to extend our use of the terms "philosophy". But they also wish to claim that many of the central problems of philosophy, such as the question of free-will and the problem of the justification of induction, are, contrary to appearances, of this kind – puzzles which arise only from our conceptual confusion which will merely vanish if we can clear our minds of these confusions. About this all that can be usefully said in an impartial introduction is that for none of these central questions is there an agreed method or agreed answer and that we therefore cannot know whether they are of one nature or of another; they may turn out to be answerable by some new science yet to be invented, they may turn out to be conceptual confusions, or they may turn out to require some new and specifically philosophical treatment, or they may remain for ever unsolved, or some may turn out to be of one kind and some of another; we cannot now say because we have not yet even succeeded in making clear what sort of an answer to them would be satisfactory, but we certainly cannot agree with the facile counsel of despair which urges us to forget about them.

But one further thing can be said in answer to the charge that philosophy achieves no results. Even with regard to such problems which any impartial person must admit to remain unanswered by philosophers in any conclusive way, there has been great progress; all the possible methods of approach yet thought of have been continuously improved, questions previously confused with each other are continually being distinguished, new difficulties in old views are continually being discovered. To imagine that philosophy stands still would be to fall into a great error; it is continually changing, and changing for the better, even if it never reaches its goal.

We would not be justified in going further into the question of the nature of philosophy and the reasons for the paucity of any "results of philosophy". Enough has been said to make it clear that in such an encyclopedia as this we cannot provide authoritative answers to philosophical questions but must limit ourselves to explaining the various technical terms used by philosophers in their attempts to answer these questions, to describing the answers given by various great philosophers to them and to describing some of the stock ways of trying to answer them. The reader must then read further for himself – a bibliography is provided to enable him to find some books for further reading on most of the central questions of philosophy – and above all he must then think further for himself. There are not only no stock answers in philosophy, there are no authorities who can be treated as arbiters of debates; every man must in the end make up his own mind on philosophical questions in accordance with what seems to him to be the weight of the various arguments which others can put up for his consideration.

But if the final answers to philosophical questions are not to be expected from an encyclopedia nor from any other book, the beginner in philosophy might reasonably ask what his best plan of campaign for improving his philosophical capacity might be. While it is hoped that this encyclopedia will be a useful reference book for him it is reasonable to try here to give him some guidance on how best to approach the immense literature of philosophy. Probably most people who make up their minds to study philosophy start by reading some text-book put out for beginners or some general history of philosophy, and this may well seem the logical thing to do. But such a course of reading on its own is liable to be very dull and unrewarding, and there is much to be said for starting with a quite different plan. We would advise the philosophical beginner to make his start by reading some of the simpler of the great classics of philosophy, such as Berkeley's *Dialogues between Hylas and Philonous*, Descartes' *Discourse on Method*, Hume's *Enquiry concerning the Human Understanding*, Plato's *Republic*, Mill's *Utilitarianism* and Russell's *The Problems of Philosophy*. Such books are not recommended because the editor of this encyclopedia agrees with them or because he believes that the reader will agree with them; indeed no one could agree with them all because they disagree among themselves. They are recommended as excit-

ing and daring products of some of the greatest intelligences that have ever played on philosophical subjects and as simple in the sense that their general intention will be immediately plain to any attentive reader, though he will never exhaust them. Any reader of such books as these (the books and not merely selections from them) who remains uninterested may safely assume that philosophy is not for him. Having made such a start the beginner should find himself well able to proceed further with the aid of this encyclopedia under the guidance of his own interests. No suggestion that textbooks and histories of philosophy should never be read is, of course, intended by these recommendations, but only advice to the solitary beginner not to make them his exclusive diet at the beginning of his studies.

The reader has been thoroughly warned that there are no authorities in philosophy who can give us the accepted and authoritative answer to the problems of philosophy. But there are, needless to say, more and less able philosophers; there are philosophers who are able and willing to speak simply and clearly and those whose words are as obscure as their thought; there are philosophers who have carefully studied what others have to say and those whose historical knowledge is less secure. Both the editor and the reader may count themselves lucky that many of the most eminent and most able philosophers of the day have agreed to contribute to this volume and have accepted the task of speaking as simply and as clearly as the requirement of accuracy would permit. The reader must, of course, expect some variation in the level of difficulty, and philosophy is never easy; it would be impossible and pointless to attempt to make an article on, say, a medieval logician as simple as the basic article on logic; but, though many of the articles will interest the most advanced expert, the interests of the intelligent layman have always been given the first consideration.

A

Abelard, Peter, (*c.* 1079–1142) born in Brittany, France. The details of his stormy life are to be found in the autobiographical letter known as the *Historia Calamitatum.* Most famous of all the events of Abelard's life is his seduction of Héloise, niece of the Canon Fulbert of Notre Dame; when their child was born they married secretly but Héloise's brothers broke into Abelard's room at night and castrated him. Consequently Héloise became a nun and Abelard a monk.

Abelard is noted in the history of philosophy for his ability as a **dialectician** and for his contribution to the solution of the problem of **Universals**. He studied **logic** under Roscellinus, a nominalist master, and later disputed with the realist theologian William of Champeaux in Paris. The details of this debate, together with an account of the successive positions taken up, are to be found in Abelard's logical treatises *Concerning Genera and Species* and the *Glosses on Porphyry.*

Abelard stands firmly by the principle that only individuals exist and that universal terms, being more than mere names, get their content of meaning from the abstractive power of the mind. The famous formula that the mind may consider factors separately without considering them as separate from one another gave a convenient dialectical answer to the question as it was raised by **Boethius** and left the way open for the fuller explanation provided later by the Aristotelian psychology.

Abelard also wrote an ethical treatise, the *Scito Te ipsum*, which emphasizes the subjective element in human conduct and stresses the importance of intention in the moral qualification of an action.

Plate 1, page 33.   (J.G.D.)

Aesthetics. Though the division of philosophy into a number of departments has little theoretical value, aesthetics has long been regarded as one of the main departments of philosophy alongside of logic, metaphysics, the theory of knowledge and ethics; though it must be admitted that it has never had the degree of attention given to these other branches. The word "aesthetics" itself is little over a century old and results from a German coinage by the philosopher Baumgarten; thus though the word is ultimately derived from the Greek word

aesthesis which means "perception", no weight can be put on this etymology. Where we now speak of aesthetics earlier writers would have spoken of the theory of taste or criticism of taste. The *Hippias Major* of **Plato**, in which the sophist Hippias vainly attempts to provide **Socrates** with a satisfactory definition of beauty, is the oldest surviving work in the field of aesthetics and there is a continuing literature from that period.

Aesthetics gains its subject-matter from the fact that people are constantly judging things, whether natural objects, products of the "fine arts" or other man-made articles, to be beautiful, sublime, charming, ugly, ridiculous or uncouth; moreover, they attempt to support or question such judgments and fall into argument about them. The philosophical problems of aesthetics arise from reflection on these data; it will be helpful to list some of them without discussion. What have these terms like "beautiful", "sublime", "charming", "ugly", got in common with each other that they do not share with "worthy", "useful", "wicked" and "right"? what is the difference in meaning of the terms "beautiful" and "sublime"? how, if at all, can we show such judgments of aesthetic merit to be true and how justify one view rather than another? how does aesthetic appraisal differ from ethical and economic appraisal? what is a work of art? can we have the same aesthetic attitude to works of art as to natural phenomena? Such questions as these sufficiently indicate the general character of philosophical aesthetics, though by no means all philosophers would agree that we have mentioned the most important problems or formulated them in the best possible way. There are certainly other questions; one of these is about where the boundary of philosophical aesthetics lies – whether, for example, a discussion of the distinction between classical and romantic art is philosophical or wholly within the field of art criticism. It is certainly necessary to make some distinction between aesthetics and criticism; thus to give reasons for thinking a certain work of art a good one is no part of philosophy, and the philosopher has no special competence in regard to such questions.

It is natural to find a close parallel between the problems of aesthetics and those of **ethics**. Some would indeed regard it as a mistake, however natural; others would maintain that to speak of a parallel is an understatement and hold that we should start with a general theory of value, a single theory which can be applied with slight modifications to the field of ethics, aesthetics and economics. But certainly the most important question of ethics is naturally expressed in some such way as: "Is there any standard of morality beyond the conventions of a group and, if so, what is it?". We can equally naturally ask whether there is any standard of aesthetic judgment and, if so, what it is. This being the case, it is not surprising to find a close parallel between the most common aesthetic and ethical theories. As the ethical relativist claims that moral beliefs hold only for an individual or a group so it is claimed that there is no criterion of good taste save that conventionally accepted within a group; as the ethical hedonist finds moral worth solely in the production of pleasure, so the aesthetic hedonist claims that the production of pleasure is the sole criterion of aesthetic merit; as some moralists say that goodness is an ultimate moral quality objectively present in things of value, so some have claimed that beauty is an objective quality; similarly we have subjectivist and emotivist theories of meaning in both fields.

The most influential classical discussion of aesthetics was that of **Kant** in his *Critique of Judgment*, especially through his insistence on the preconceptual level of the aesthetic judgment and the formal character of the criteria of aesthetic merit; the precise form of his discussion depends on his view that judgments differ in quantity, quality, relation and modality, so that the problem of aesthetics is mainly to say how aesthetic judgments differ in these four ways from others. In modern times the best-known theory is that of **Croce** in his *Aesthetics*, to which that of **Collingwood** in his *Principles of Art* is essentially similar; for Croce the work of art is a sensuous intuition of some emotion of which it is also an adequate expression, the canvas, the written words or the sounds being mere causal aids to others to have the same intuition. The view put forward in **Cassirer**'s *Philosophy of Symbolic Forms*, especially as restated in S. K. Langer's *Feeling and Form*, has also been very influential. It is common to these views to see aesthetic experience as essentially expression, or symbolism, of feeling, and to connect it as such with all use of language and other symbolism;

Croce indeed regards general linguistics and aesthetics as one and the same thing. These theories, idealist in tendency, have not gained much support from more empirical and analytic philosophers, but these have notably failed to provide any alternative. The immense difficulty with all aesthetic theories is to give any clear meaning to the terms which it seems natural to use; symbolism, expression, intuition and significant form are constantly recurring notions which could well be given far more rigorous analytic examination and explanation than they have yet received.

Some philosophers, indeed, deny the possibility of any general aesthetic theory; aestheticians, they say, assume that there is some common feature of experience of all the diverse arts and of natural beauty, and that there is some general criterion of judgment to be found which will be applicable in all these fields; but this assumption they consider to be without any justification. We can say, they hold, what makes us admire this painting, that painting, this landscape and that symphony, but we must not expect there to be anything common to all these cases. Whether this extreme scepticism is justified or not, it must be admitted to these critics that aesthetics, more than any other branch of philosophy seems doomed either to a pretentious vagueness or to an extreme poverty which make it a poor step-sister to other main fields of philosophical inquiry. In recent years in the United States, however, there has been a considerable growth of work on aesthetics which, we must hope, may bear some fruit in the near future.

(J.O.U.)

Albert the Great (1206–1280), also known as Albertus Magnus, Albert of Lauingen and Albert of Cologne; canonized in 1931. Born at Lauingen in Swabia, Albert studied at Padua, where he joined the Dominicans; later he became Bishop of Ratisbon. He taught at Cologne, where he died, and Paris. Traveller, administrator, theologian, he was an indefatigable experimentalist, especially in botany and zoology. His temper was not unlike that of his contemporary, Roger **Bacon**, who held him in grudging respect. He cleared the sources of thirteenth-century speculation, and wrote of **Aristotle** with great sympathy and sure instinct for his meaning. With his pupil Thomas **Aquinas**, he led the movement which installed in Christian thought an Aristotelianism specifically new to the patristic tradition. But he was the less synthetic and impersonal thinker of the two, though he was more encyclopaedic and syncretic. He wrote on Aristotle in the older style of paraphrase and digression, and is closer to **Avicenna** than to **Averroes**. His feeling for the Neoplatonism of Dionysius and Proclus descends through his disciples – Ulrich of Strasbourg, who died in 1277, and Dietrich of Freiburg, who died in 1310 – to Master Eckhart, John Tauler and the Dominican mystics of the Rhineland. (T.G.)

Plate 2, page 34.

Alexander, Samuel (1859–1938), an Australian by birth. As an undergraduate at Oxford he was brought up in the **idealist** tradition of that period. But he became one of the most noted **realist** metaphysicians of his time. He was for many years Professor of Philosophy at Manchester University.

Alexander's great work was his *Space, Time and Deity*, which appeared in 1920. The basic stuff of the universe is space-time or pure motion, and everything in it develops out of the primary stuff by a process of emergent evolution. Things or substances are volumes of space-time with a determinate contour; low in the scale of evolution is matter, whence emerges life and finally, so far as we are concerned, mind; but no one can say what will emerge in the future in the evolutionary process. The next stage to which the universe is striving is at that stage deity; God is in the making but never actual. On this metaphysical foundation, which the reader may well find obscure, Alexander built a realist theory of knowledge. Knowledge occurs when two finite existences are compresent and one (the knower) is aware of this compresence; even memory is a case of compresence of a knower with an event characterised by pastness. There can be knowledge, contemplation, only of a compresent object; the knower is said by Alexander to enjoy himself only, without self-knowledge. (J.O.U.)

Analysis is a Greek word, meaning the resolution of a complex whole into its parts. It is opposed to **synthesis**, which means the construction of a whole out of parts.

Philosophers have always had two main aims, the construction of systems of **metaphysics, logic** or **ethics** (synthesis) and the clarification of important ideas (analysis). These cannot always be sharply distinguished, since what is synthesis from one point of view is analysis from another. **Plato's** *Republic*, for example, may be considered as the construction in thought of a perfectly just society or as the analysis of the idea of a just society. Large parts of **Aristotle's** *Ethics* are concerned with the analysis of such important ideas as "voluntary action", "virtue and vice", "pleasure", etc.

In recent times continental philosophy has tended to be synthetic (**Kant** is an important exception) and British philosophy to be analytic. For **Descartes** the analysis of concepts was only a preparation for the construction of a system of knowledge based on the "clear and distinct ideas" obtained by analysis; and **Spinoza** sought to construct a view of the world deduced, on the geometrical model, from a small number of definitions and axioms. British philosophers, on the other hand, have tended to be suspicious of constructive metaphysics and to be more concerned with the analysis of thought and experience into their fundamental elements.

Since the beginning of this century the view that analysis is either the whole, or the most important part, or the distinguishing feature of philosophy has been widely accepted in English-speaking countries. Philosophers who follow this trend often have little in common with each other except the use of the word "analysis" to describe their various activities. All that can be said about their view of the function of philosophy – and even this is not wholly true – is that they take it to be, not the acquisition of new knowledge (which is the function of the special sciences), but the clarification and articulation of what we already know. Three main stands can be detected in the practice of analysis:

(1) G. E. **Moore** questioned an assumption that metaphysicians have been prone to make and which was certainly made by the **idealists** who at that time dominated British philosophy. This was that we do not know all the ordinary humdrum things about the world that we claim to know. Some had said that these things are actually false; others, that even if they were true we could not know them to be true. The world, as it appears to the plain man, is mere appearance; reality is

something recondite, wholly unlike what we take it to be, and to be discovered only by profound researches conducted in some new technical language. Against this, Moore held that for the thinker such truisms as that he has a body, that he was born some years ago and that he has existed ever since, are not only true but can be known for certain to be true. Nevertheless he had no wish to assert that metaphysical theories which contradicted these assertions were merely outrageous falsehoods. They were certainly that; but they were also mistaken attempts to answer very genuine and puzzling questions. Briefly, though we cannot seriously doubt the truth of such ordinary statements and though we know, in a sense, what they mean, we may not be able to state clearly and precisely *what* they mean. We do not, in his words, "know their proper analysis" and almost all his philosophical activity was devoted to discovering the proper anlysis of propositions whose truth cannot seriously be doubted.

To give the proper analysis of a concept or proposition is to replace the word or sentence which is normally used to express it by some other expression which is exactly equivalent to it and at the same time less puzzling. An analysis, therefore, is a sort of definition, a kind of equation with the puzzling expression, the *analysandum*, on the left-hand side and the new expression, sometimes called the *analysis*, sometimes the *analysans*, on the right. Now most of the ideas that seem to need this sort of clarification are highly complex and the very word "analysis" implies the splitting of a complex form or replacing an expression that stood for a complex concept by a longer expression that laid bare its hidden complexity. Moore seems to have used this technique with no other aim than that of clarifying our concepts; he had no metaphysical theory and did not suppose that the things mentioned in the analysis were in any sense more real or fundamental than those mentioned in the analysandum. How, indeed, could they be, if the analysandum and the analysis were to refer, as they must, to exactly the same things?

(2) At the same time, Bertrand **Russell**, was led to the practice of the same sort of definitional analysis as Moore, but for very different reasons and with very different aims. Where Moore sought only clarity and never wished to depart from com-

mon sense beliefs, Russell sought metaphysical truth and was quite willing to say with the Idealists that common sense beliefs can be false and ordinary language wholly inadequate as a means of discovering and expressing truth. As a metaphysician, his aim was to give a general account of the universe. His account was the exact opposite of that of the Idealists. They had claimed that only reality as a whole (the absolute) was wholly real; particular things were abstractions from this totality and, as such, only partially real or not real at all. Russell's picture of the world was that of a world composed of "atomic facts", corresponding to each of which there would be a true "atomic statement".

Consider the statement "it is either raining or snowing". This is not made true by correspondence with a complex alternative fact, either-rain-or-snow. It is true if either of the atomic parts of which it is composed ("it is raining" and "it is snowing") is true. Thus compound or "molecular" statements do not correspond or fail to correspond to compound facts; they can be broken down into atomic statements which do, when true, correspond to atomic facts. The aim of analysis was to be the breakdown of complex facts into their atomic components, the method the analysis of complex statements into theirs. Russell's conception of analysis was influenced in two main ways by the fact that he came to metaphysics from the study of mathematics and formal logic. As a mathematician, he regarded all defined terms as theoretically superfluous. Thus if "two" can be defined as "one plus one" and "three" as "two plus one" it is clear that arithmetical operations could be carried on with no numerals other than "one". He had himself claimed to "eliminate" in this way even the notion of "number" by defining it in terms belonging to logic. As a metaphysician, Russell held that if the word "number" could be eliminated by being defined, then numbers are not part of the ultimate constituents of the world which it was his aim to discover. These constituents, whatever they turned out to be, would be only such things as would be named in a language in which all defined terms had been replaced by ultimately indefinable terms. For Russell, therefore, though the technique of analysis was, as it was for Moore, the replacing of an analysandum by an analysis, the aim was very different: Moore sought clarification, Russell metaphysical truth.

Secondly, Russell's study of logic had convinced him that the *grammar* of all natural languages is radically misleading. "Horses do not bellow" and "chimaeras do not exist" have the same grammatical form; but, while the first denies that certain objects (horses)| have a certain property (bellowing), the second does not deny that chimaeras have the property of existing. Rather it says that nothing in the world has the property of being a chimaera. Russell's aim here was that of replacing expressions whose grammatical form was misleading by expressions of "proper logical form", in which the grammatical structure would properly reflect the form of the fact stated. Confronted by the statement "the average plumber earns ten pounds a week", one might be puzzled by the question "Who is this average plumber?" and perhaps led into wild metaphysical speculation. The remedy was to see that the statement could be translated into "the number of pounds earned each week by plumbers divided by the number of plumbers is ten", a statement from which "the average plumber" has been eliminated. No one is likely to be bemused in such a simple case; but serious consequences, both theoretical and practical, had certainly followed from making the same mistake about more important objects such as "the State" or "Public Opinion". It is clear that in some sense these, like armies, governments, schools and other institutions are abstractions and that to say something about them is to say something, though not the same thing, about the people who make them up. In technical language they were said to be "logical constructions" out of the more concrete objects (people) who compose them. Russell and his followers had high hopes that analysis could be carried to yet deeper metaphysical levels by showing that the things, including people, that we normally treat as being on the "ground-floor level" of experience, were logical constructions out of more fundamental entities.

(3) Russell's views on logic and techniques of analysis were taken up by the **logical positivists**, but used with a very different aim. Where Russell sought a true metaphysical theory, the positivists held *all* metaphysics to be nonsensical and were mainly concerned to establish a sharp line between metaphysics and natural science. Analysis was to be used first for the elimination of metaphysics and secondly for the clarification of the language of science. The word "elimination" here is to be taken in a much more straightforward sense than in connection with Russell. Russell had not claimed that the objects which his analytical method "eliminated" did not, in the ordinary sense, exist; only that they were not metaphysically ultimate. Water exists; but because it is composed of oxygen and hydrogen it is not part of the "ultimate furniture of the Universe"; and this is shown by the fact that the word "water" can be replaced by "H_2O". The positivists, on the other hand, used analysis to show that certain words used by metaphysicians and, in consequence, the theories in which those words appear were literally nonsensical.

Since all metaphysics, including Russell's atomism, was to be eliminated, a new aim had to be found for analysis; for metaphysical truth was not merely impossible for us to attain, it was an absurd goal to aim at. It had never been agreed just *what* was to be analysed. Was it to be concepts and propositions, as Moore said? Or facts, as Russell usually said? In practice this had made less difference than might be expected, since the actual technique of analysis had always been the replacement of one *expression* (word, phrase or sentence) by another. The method was linguistic, though both Moore and Russell have always repudiated linguistic aims. With the positivists, aim and method come closer together; for both "concepts" and "facts" come under the ban of being metaphysical, thought is identified with language, and the analysis of linguistic expressions is an end in itself. The clarification and articulation of the language of science can hardly be regarded as an extrinsic aim.

The name "linguistic analysis" is often now used for a general approach to philosophy that is widespread in the English-speaking world and has some adherents on the continent, particularly in Scandinavia. These philosophers differ widely among themselves, for example in their degree of affection towards metaphysics. Their method is certainly linguistic, since it involves paying careful, even minute attention to the actual usage of words, phrases and sentences in a living language; but it cannot, in any clear or strict sense, be called "analysis". What is common to all the linguistic analysts is the belief that the first step towards the solution of a philosophical problem is to examine the key words in the area that generates the problem and to ask how they are in fact used. Thus problems of perception are to be solved, not by condemning ordinary language wholesale and inventing a new vocabulary (impressions, sensations, sense-data), but by asking what precisely we are claiming when we claim to see something. This is the sort of question which Moore asked; but whereas Moore jumped, almost without argument, to the conclusion that the answer must be given in terms of "sense-data", the linguistic analysts try to answer it by exploring the locutions in which the verb "to see" and kindred words actually occur. There is nothing here to which we can point as being "analysis" as we can point to definitional substitution in Moore and Russell. Perhaps the survival of the name "analysis" is only a just tribute which some philosophers pay to those who have greatly influenced them and from whose work their own work stems. (P.H.N.-S.)

Analytic. The terms "analytic" and "synthetic" were introduced by **Kant**, who defined an analytic judgment as one in which the idea of the predicate is already contained in that of the subject and therefore adds nothing to it. Thus "all bodies are extended in space" is analytic, since the idea of extension is contained in that of body. On the other hand "all bodies have some weight" is synthetic since the idea of weight is not so contained. Kant's distinction has been criticized for being too metaphorical – it is not clear what is meant by saying that one idea is "contained in" another – and for being insufficiently general – it applies only to propositions of subject-predicate form.

Various attempts have been made to make the distinction more precise. An analytic proposition is sometimes said to be one the denial of which would be self-contradictory; or it is said to be a covert tautology, on the grounds that, if we define "body", as "extended thing", "all bodies are extended" means "all extended things are extended". It should be noted that on this view the analyticity of a proposition depends on our choice of definitions which is, according to some philosophers, arbitrary. Thus if we defined "body" as "that which

has extension and weight", "all bodies have weight" would be analytic. If this is so, we cannot determine from the form of a *sentence* whether or not it expresses an analytic proposition, but must appeal to what the speaker means by it. If these or similar definitions of "analytic" are adopted, it will be seen that analyticity can be extended to propositions other than those of subject-predicate form.

Analytic propositions, though they may inform us of the meanings of words, can give no knowledge of matters of fact. The philosophy of **logical positivism** was based on a sharp distinction between analytic and synthetic and on the view that all **a priori** propositions must be analytic. Many philosophers now doubt whether this sharp distinction can be maintained. It has been most thoroughly examined by Waismann in *Analysis* (1949–53) and by **Quine** in *From a Logical Point of View.* (P.H.N.-S.)

Anaxagoras of Clazomenae in Ionian Greece, flourished *c.* 450 B.C. He was prosecuted for impiety (for describing the sun as a white hot lump of stone) while working in Athens, partly because he was a friend of Pericles. His book *On Nature*, which was probably short (3,000–8,000 words?), seems to have been written later than **Empedocles'** *On Nature* and tries to overcome the **eleatic** dilemma in another way. In the beginning all the natural substances (not merely a limited number of basic substances like Empedocles' roots) were mixed together; then Mind, "finest of all things and purest", started a rotation which brought the heavier parts to the centre, by vortex-action, to form earth, and the lighter to the circumference. This was a traditional, non-cyclical cosmogony; the production of a plural cosmos did not destroy the initial unity, since still "there is a portion of everything in everything, except Mind". Apparent coming-to-be, as for Empedocles, was caused by mixture. Objects were made up of "seeds", perhaps meaning constituent pieces having the nature of the whole; each seed contained a portion of every natural substance, including the substantial opposites and the main world-masses, but had the appearance of that substance whose portion predominated. Changes, as for example in nutrition, were presumably caused by an interchange of portions so as to alter the predominance in different seeds. Anaxagoras insisted that matter could be theoretically divided *ad infinitum*, and is indeed, what **Zeno** of Elea had denied, "both great and small". He did not attempt to reconcile this with the idea of the predominance of one substance in every seed. In most other details of cosmology and epistemology Anaxagoras was more conservative, often reviving Milesian views. See also **Pre-Socratics**. (G.S.K.)

Anaximander of Miletus, a Greek seaport in Asia Minor, flourished *c.* 560 B.C. His scientific activities included making a famous map of the world. Like **Thales** he tried to name a single substance out of which the world originated: for him this was "the indefinite", probably implying a material of indefinite extent to which no precise name could be given because it did not exist within the developed world. From the Indefinite was somehow separated off a nucleus which produced fire and dark mist. The mist solidified at its centre into earth, while the surrounding flame burst to form the heavenly bodies – wheels of fire, each showing through a single aperture in a tegument of mist. The earth is cylindrical, and stays still because of its equidistance from everything else. Physical change within the world occurs through the mutual encroachments and reactions of opposed materials like the hot and the cold, ultimate regularity being assured because these "pay penalty and retribution to each other for their injustice according to the assessment of time". There was a zoogony to parallel the cosmogony: the first living creatures, generated out of primeval slime by the heat of the sun, emerged out of prickly husks on to dry land. Men originally grew up inside a kind of fish, for otherwise they could not have survived their long period of helplessness in childhood. See also **Pre-Socratics**. (G.S.K.)

Anaximenes of Miletus, a Greek seaport in Asia Minor, flourished *c.* 545 B.C. He reverted to **Thales'** idea of a definite world-component as originative material, but said that this was *aer*, air or rather mist. For the first time he gave some account of how a single substance could turn into a diversified world: *aer* changed its appearance according to its degree of concentration. Rarefied, it became fire; condensed, water and earth. This

was an important new idea; and Anaximenes behaved unusually methodically in citing a specific indication that density can affect, for example temperature – when the lips are compressed in exhalation. He seems to have chosen air/mist as the basic substance not only because of its apparent meteorological connexion with fire (in the sky) and also with rain, but also because it appeared to fulfil in the world the function of soul, commonly envisaged as breath, in living creatures; soul being motive, directive, and in some way divine. In cosmology Anaximenes was less imaginative than his older contemporary **Anaximander**, often merely elaborating the popular world-picture as exemplified in Homer. The flat earth rode on air; the fiery heavenly bodies went round, not under, the earth, driven by winds; among them were invisible bodies that caused eclipses. See also under **Pre-Socratics**. (G.S.K.)

Anselm of Canterbury (1033–1109), canonized 1494. He was born at Aosta, Italy. In 1033, Anselm joined the Benedictine Abbey of Bec in Normandy under Lanfranc. He subsequently became Archbishop of Canterbury.

Apart from **Erigena** Anselm was the first systematic thinker of the Middle Ages. Meeting the difficulties occasioned by the **dialecticians** of his day with the celebrated formula "a faith seeking understanding", he was not prepared to substitute dialectic for theology but at the same time he insisted upon a reasoned presentation of traditional Christian belief.

His philosophical writing came in response to a request by some of his monks for a rational meditation on the existence and nature of God which would dispense with reference to scriptural authority. The *Monologion* and *Proslogion* are his reply.

In the former he begins with the experienced occurrence of differences in degrees of value, of goodness and of being in the objects around us. From this he argues to the necessary existence of an absolute standard, an absolute good, an absolute being in which the relative participates. And this absolute we call God. The argument follows a familiar Platonic method already used by **Augustine** and would later be more fully elaborated by Thomas **Aquinas**.

In the *Proslogion*, Anselm presents us with the famous "ontological argument" with which his name is so closely linked. We may, he says, start with no more than the commonly accepted idea of what we mean when we use the term God, namely a being than which no greater can be thought. This, he says, is a point of departure available even to the fool who, according to scripture, denies the existence of God. Such a being, then, can be said to exist in the mind. But to exist actually is more perfect than to exist in the mind. To deny the actual existence of God, then, is both to affirm actual existence – because it is of God, than whom there is nothing more perfect, that we are speaking and to deny it is to fall into foolish contradiction. If God then is to be truly the being than which nothing greater can be thought, he must exist in reality as well as in the mind.

The argument of the *Proslogion* at once aroused controversy and to this day philosophers have not ceased to be sharply divided in their acceptance or rejection of its validity. The monk Gaunilo wrote a *Book on behalf of the Fool* attacking the validity of the conclusion and pointing out that by similar argument one might establish the "existence" of anything, for instance of a most perfect island. Anselm in his reply pointed out that only in the unique case of the most excellent of all beings does the argument conclude and that only an infinite being can be conceived necessarily to exist.

In the Middle Ages the Franciscans tended to accept the argument, though **Scotus** required that it be shown that the nature of God is not self-contradictory. Aquinas on the other hand rejected it. In modern times **Descartes** accepted the argument; **Leibniz**, like Scotus, required the possibility of God to be accounted for; and **Kant** rejected it. (J.G.D.)

Plate 3, page 35.

Antisthenes (*c.* 444 B.C. – *c.* 366 B.C.) was the son of an Athenian father and a Thracian mother, pupil of the rhetorician Gorgias, close friend of **Socrates**, critic of **Plato**, and later held to be one of the prototypes of the **Cynics**. From the few fragments that survive from numerous writings, we see the intertwinings of three threads: the **Sophistic**, the Socratic, and what was later to become Cynic. He held virtue to be self-sufficient for

happiness. As knowledge necessitating moral action it could be taught, and once gained was unshakeable. Education begins with the study of the meaning of words. Words correspond directly with reality, and a proposition is either true or meaningless, contradiction and false statement being impossible. But practical **ethics** are stressed rather than great learning. Although not an ascetic, Antisthenes especially condemned luxury (wealth and external goods being unimportant), for a man should be rich in his soul. Virtue should be combined with exertion, which yielded the only important pleasure. Hercules was the ideal example of this. Established laws, convention, birth, sex, race, were unimportant in comparison with the law of virtue, by which the state should be governed. Although many of his views are clearly Socratic, the ancients asserted that his importance lay in giving the impulse through **Diogenes** to the way of life later called Cynic, and it is likely that **Stoicism** too was influenced by his practical ethics. (I.G.K.)

A posteriori, *see* A priori.

A priori is a Latin phrase meaning "from what comes before", contrasted with *a posteriori*, "from what comes after". These terms were introduced in the late scholastic period to translate two technical phrases in **Aristotle**'s theory of knowledge. Aristotle distinguished what is prior in the order of nature or more fundamental from what is prior in the order of discovery or known to us first. There are many truths, such as that fire burns or that water will not flow uphill, that we know from experience before we are able to explain why they should be so. Until we discover their causes our knowledge of them must be said to be empirical and not truly scientific. An *a posteriori* argument was an argument from observed effects to unknown causes; for, though the effects are known to us first, the causes are logically prior. An *a priori* argument was an argument from causes to effects or, since the relation of cause and effect was not sharply distinguished by Aristotle from that of logical ground and consequent, from ground to consequent. *A priori* arguments were held to provide certain scientific knowledge as opposed to probable belief.

From the seventeenth century, for example in

Descartes and **Leibniz**, *a priori* came to mean "universal, necessary and wholly independent of experience". The term *a posteriori* fell into disuse and *a priori* is now usually contrasted with "empirical" i.e. depending on experience. The term *a priori* is now used of (1) arguments, (2) propositions and (3) ideas.

(1) An *a priori* argument is one in which the conclusion follows deductively from the premises, as for example in a mathematical proof. If the premises are true and the argument valid, no experience is needed to confirm the conclusion and no experience could refute it. By contrast, an argument from experience (empirical, inductive, or probable argument) is one in which the conclusion, however strongly supported by the premises, is not necessitated by them. For example, if we argue that it will rain somewhere in England next January, on the grounds that no January has been known to pass without some rain, this argument, though weighty is not conclusive. There might be a January without rain even though there never has been one. Since **Hume** it has been generally believed that all natural science contains an empirical element and therefore cannot be *a priori*.

(2) An *a priori* proposition is one which (it is claimed) is independent of experience, except in so far as experience is necessary for understanding its terms. Thus we know *a priori* that a whole is equal to the sum of its parts; for, once we understand the terms involved, we see that this is universally and necessarily true and that no experience could refute it.

(3) Empiricist philosophers – so called because they tend to emphasise the role of experience in knowledge at the expense of *a priori* elements – have sometimes held that all *ideas* are derived from experience. We can (they say) have no idea unless we have either come across an instance of it, as in the case of "red" or "horse", or fabricated it, as in the case of "dragon", out of elements that we have come across. There are, however, some ideas of great importance in philosophy, the origin of which it is difficult to explain in this way. Among them are the ideas of substance (thing), cause, existence, equality, likeness and difference. Of these it is claimed that, so far from their being derived from experience, we could have no experience without them. This is not to say that we are born equipped with these ideas, but rather that they are presupposed by our being able to have any experience at all. (**Plato**'s *Meno* and **Leibniz**'s *New Essays on the Human Understanding* are classic expositions of this doctrine, sometimes called the doctrine of Innate Ideas. For the empiricist view see **Locke** and **Hume**.)

Synthetic *a priori* propositions: it is clear that all **analytic** propositions are *a priori*. If "bachelor" means "unmarried man" we need investigate no particular cases to satisfy ourselves of the truth of the proposition "No bachelor is married". But the question whether any **synthetic** proposition can be known *a priori* is one of the most important and difficult in philosophy. The **Rationalists** believed that the fundamental principles of science could, like those of logic and pure mathematics, be known *a priori*. Hume argued (in effect) that the principles of logic and pure mathematics were indeed *a priori*, but only because they were analytic. But all knowledge of matters of fact, both common sense and scientific, depended, he argued, on such causal principles as that every event must have a cause and that like causes must have like effects. He claimed to show that these principles are synthetic, cannot be known *a priori* and must be derived from experience.

Kant saw the force and the sceptical tendency of Hume's argument and devoted his most important book, the *Critique of Pure Reason*, to establishing the possibility and scope of *a priori* knowledge. He held that such knowledge was possible in mathematics (which he did not regard as analytic) and in physics. With regard to metaphysics he agreed substantially with Hume, but he also undertook to show how it is that men necessarily continue to ask metaphysical questions which it is impossible for them to answer.

In this century the **logical positivists** and many philosophers influenced by them follow Hume in denying the possibility of synthetic *a priori* knowledge. The most difficult problem for them concerns the status of pure mathematics. Mathematical statements are usually regarded as analytic; very few philosophers would now follow J. S. **Mill** in regarding them as synthetic generalizations from experience which have exceptionally good backing but might, nevertheless, not be universally true. Recently, however, the possibility of synthetic *a priori* knowledge has been much discussed, partly owing to doubts about the validity of the distinction between analytic and synthetic, and the issue cannot be regarded as closed. Although they do not use this terminology, something akin to synthetic *a priori* knowledge plays an important part in the philosophy of the **Phenomenologists**. (P.H.N.-S.)

Aquinas, Thomas (*c.* 1225–1274), canonized 1323. He was born about 1225 at Roccasecca near Aquino on the northern border of the ancient Kingdom of Sicily, of a Lombard family kin to Frederick II and distinguished in his service. He proceeded from Monte Cassino to the University of Naples where he entered the Dominicans, studied under **Albert the Great** at Cologne and at Paris where he graduated and lectured for two periods as Master before and after a nine years' appointment as adviser to the Papal Court. A large man, decided and calm, patrician yet modest, he enjoyed the affection even of his adversaries. He died at Fossanova, not far from his birthplace, on his way to the Second Council of Lyons, 1274. Ninety-eight items are listed in the catalogue of his works; some run into several folios. Proclaimed Doctor of the Church in 1567, he is the classical systematic theologian of Catholicism.

In 1879, Leo XIII inaugurated the revival of Thomist philosophy, now an important intellectual movement, not narrowly clerical. It has to be lifted out of his wider interests expressed in his two testaments of theological synthesis, the earlier *Summa contra Gentiles* and the *Summa Theologica* (or *Theologiae*) of his maturity. To what extent the result can be appreciated without reference to the witness of Christianity is a matter of some dispute: the Dominicans, who can be presumed to be his genuine heirs, insist that it is rationally consistent and sufficient, also not committed to a medieval reading of the world, though determined by the period when the main body of **Aristotle**'s writings was entering western Europe, at first across the Spanish frontier with Islam, afterwards from Byzantium.

According to tradition he set his colleague, the Flemish Dominican, William of Moerbeke (1215–1286), to provide fresh translations from the Greek into Latin. His effort was to get back to the

original. Aristotle's philosophy could otherwise scarcely be separated from the contributions of the great Arab thinkers, notably **Avicenna** and **Averroes**. It was mingled with Neo-Platonist strains inherited from **Augustine**, Proclus, Dionysius, and **Boethius**. His expositions *De Divinis Nominibus* and *De Causis* and his treatise *De Substantiis Separatis* show that he was critically aware of these; his polemical pieces *De Unitate Intellectus* and *De Aeternitate Mundi* do the same with the opposite tendency of making Aristotle uncongenial to Christian convictions.

The so-called baptism of Aristotle, however, was no mere surface reconciliation. Aquinas meant to take the philosophical arguments to their deepest level, not to amass materials which might be fitted into the existing theological framework. He pressed the distinction between potentiality and actuality to the core of reality itself, and the old problem of the One and the Many turned into the creation by *esse subsistens* of all existents. He showed that a universal and particular Providence followed from knowing and loving at their best. He defended immortality without diminishing the doctrine that the soul is essentially embodied. If he borrowed from Aristotle he certainly made capital gains.

His predecessors and most of his contemporaries, such as the Franciscan **Bonaventura** and the English Dominican Robert Kilwardby, though well capable of sustained scientific inquiry, drew no clear distinction between their reflections on a historical and revealed religion and a philosophy which could be its own warrant. He himself calls for careful interpretation on the relations between Reason and Faith – or, let us say, any extra-rational way of knowledge. There are two extremes, neither of which do justice to the balance he struck. On the one hand he was not a special pleader who treated rational investigation as merely ancillary to religious belief; on the other he never countenanced a practical separation between them, indeed he fought such a split when it widened into the celebrated Double Truth theory associated with **Siger of Brabant** and the Latin Averroists. He was a thoroughgoing rationalist who was also a saint in love with God; yet he was an integrated character and the two went together. He was not content with his rationalism, but never thought that the appeal to authority could serve as a substitute.

The clue is found in his notion of subordination without subservience. The world is composed of real things which act as true causes, that is, principles and goals of activity, not merely instruments or occasions. All the same, because they are in themselves they are not of themselves, because they are complete so far as they go they are not exclusive. Hence to be truly wise about them, and more than narrowly scientific, we must see them in the light of the First Cause. Their own proper interest is not thereby suppressed; their value is more than relative and symbolic. Creatures are real; according to his terminology, they are at once secondary and principal. Moreover they interact and are dependent on one another. By a judicious use of analogy, which is treated as a law of being rather than an artifice of logical classification or literary metaphor, the mind can range at large and from its environment discover truth beyond its experience. His Hellenic spirit of disinterested inquiry, his quality of looking at things both in themselves and as connected makes his philosophy so comprehensive and rich: it may be compared to his picture of the commonwealth where parts are not subjected like slaves but converse together in true polity.

The patterning of meanings is an idle exercise unless rooted in reality, and his power of detailed analysis does not make him lose sight of individual and personal substance. This is particularly evident in his psychological and moral philosophy. Science is the tested knowledge of conclusions in principles, of effects in causes, and the philosophical sciences differ from the particular sciences in that they do not stay with the proximate causes at work but seek reasons more universal, yet not on that account more summary. He does not fall into the philosophism of deducing facts from reasons, or of treating the specialist sciences as applications of metaphysics.

His exposition of **Boethius'** *De Trinitate* distributes the philosophical disciplines. Logic, which runs through them all, is directly the study, not of real objects, but of scientific method and the mental constructions, *entia rationis*, we place on our experience. The bent towards truth considered in itself or towards the doing or making of something differentiates theoretical and practical philosophy. Theory isolates what is general and constant in individual and changing facts, and theoretical philosophy may be conveniently grouped according to the three degrees of abstraction. First, Natural Philosophy engages objects which not only exist in material processes but cannot be understood without reference to them. Second, Mathematical Philosophy, while considering the implications of quantity, needs no such appeal to the sensible world. Third, Metaphysical Philosophy reaches beyond the material world because its objects are either non-material, for instance, God, or not of necessity material, for instance, substantial unity. His Natural Philosophy treats of inanimate and of animate bodies, and corresponds to the topics of Aristotle's *Physics* and *De Anima*. Mathematical Philosophy is treated only in passing. His Metaphysical Philosophy covers what is now called **Epistemology**, General Metaphysics, and Natural Theology. So much for theory. As for practice, the chief science is Moral Philosophy, which includes personal ethics, economics (in the Aristotelean sense), and politics.

These headings may serve for a general outline of the parts of his philosophy, remembering that they are not set in separate compartments. A poet and on occasion a writer of distinguished prose, the general run of his expository style is curt and repetitive: sometimes the sparse vocabulary conceals the variety of the ideas and the delicacy of the distinctions. Many of his works were dictated to or written up by secretaries.

He completed a commentary on the *Posterior Analytics* and began one on the *De Interpretatione*. He observed the Aristotelian logic which had been worked acutely for a century or more. Typical examples of his discourse are found in his academic debates. These fall into two classes, the *Quaestiones Disputatae* (the chief being *De Potentia*, *De Malo*, *De Spiritualibus Creaturis*, and *De Veritate*) which in the main report his serialised discussions during a teaching-course, and the *Quaestiones Quodlibetales*, or chosen questions for special occasions. His general dialectic begins from induction and proceeds deductively either **a posteriori** for discovery (*via inventionis*) or **a priori** for assessment (*via judicii*).

It was his welcome to Aristotle's natural and metaphysical philosophy which scandalised some of his contemporaries. Declining the Neoplatonism, so attractive to a religious thinker, of contemplating the Ideas apart from this shadow world, he saw them embodied here and now about us. His thought, like Aristotle's, was stamped by the existing reality of Nature, and it would be impossible to enumerate here all the issues where his stand is not that of an other-worldling.

Substance and accidents (not to be confused with *noumenon* and phenomena) are the first categories of the material world. Substance is being able to exist in itself, the accidents are inhering realities, such as being quantified, qualified, related. Material processes are shaped by the four causes – final, efficient, material and formal. All activity has a purpose or end, *finis*, but Thomas's teleological reading of the universe is not the eighteenth-century Argument from Design writ large: the finality within the acting thing is immanent, not imposed. The efficient cause, *agens*, is the producer; he maintains that things are true originators, not merely conditions of action. The material cause, the basic potential subject, and the formal cause, the actual determinant, are intrinsic and essential to the effect. All material substances are composed of matter, *materia prima*, and form, *forma substantialis*. Bare matter so conceived is not the ultimate atomic or infra-atomic point which can be calculated or recorded by scientific apparatus, but the substantial potentiality common to all material things which are formed differently in number, degree, and kind under the action of secondary causes. He wrote commentaries on the *Physics* and *De Coelo et Mundo* of Aristotle and a treatise *De Principiis Mundi*. Like Aristotle he accepts both being and becoming, and refuses to say with **Parmenides** that reality is immobile or with **Heraclitus** that all is flux.

He commented on *De Anima*, *De Sensu et Sensato*, and *De Memoria et Reminiscentia*. The tang of reality infuses his psychology, which is less a study of consciousness than of living, and chiefly human, substance and activity. The Matter-Form distinction is uncompromisingly applied: the soul is the substantial form of the body. By one and the same actuality man is a bodily, vegetative, sensitive, and intellective being. He is not a spirit inhabiting a body, but a single substance with it, and this psychophysical unity is hardly defended despite the difficulties it raises against the immortality of the soul. This is but one example of the continuity which enables Thomas to move so readily from one level to another. By his constant recognition of the individual he avoids the artificiality of treating the psychological faculties as mannikins when he structurally classifies the human abilities, habits, and activities.

These are twofold, cognitive and appetitive. As regards the psychology of knowledge, he adopts the Aristotelean dynamism; a power of abstraction, *intellectus agens*, works on images developed by the senses and makes them actually intelligible; he differs from the Averroists in treating this as a power personal to each one of us. The foundations of knowledge are experimental. He does not accept innate ideas; evidence is lacking and Aristotle's doctrine of ideas acquired from sensation meets the bill even for those who hold that the spring of intelligence is non-material. Similarly the operations of will are fused with emotion. That function of the will called free will, *liberum arbitrium*, corresponds to our deliberation when we are not confronted with an irresistible object. The phase of voluntary activity called choice, *electio*, is concerned with means to ends, not ends as such; in other words, liberty is not a creative absolute, but rather a versatility within limits.

With respect to the so-called Problem of Knowledge as presented from the days of **Descartes**, one is tempted to call Thomas a critical realist. The problem is by-passed rather than solved. Since he does not regard human concepts as objects of direct knowledge he never asks what are the tests to show their correspondence with extra-mental reality. That is given, not found by projecting the structure of our language and logic. We may reflect on our concepts, but as such they are not set terms, but relations opening out to real objects. Truth and error come only with the judgment and its existential implication. Though our particular associations may be at fault, the fundamental affirmation of being, together with its necessary derivatives, cannot be validly contradicted.

Let it be said at the outset of his general metaphysics, for which some texts are his exposition on Aristotle's *Metaphysics* and on Boethius' *De Hebdomadibus* and his tract *De Ente et Essentia*, that we are not offered an elaboration of quiddities or a systematisation on the mathematical model. We are past matter and form, and the distinction between potentiality and actuality becomes that between essence and existence in finite things. This, his central thesis, does not mean that real existence is just an adventitious predicate to a constituted meaning, but that, within a real thing, that by which it is what it is does not itself achieve complete reality. Only with God is such act-of-being, *esse*, identical with essence.

Had he done nothing else but write a natural theology he would still have been among the giants. God is not the object of an intuition, but from a deeply considered acceptance of the world about us and without putting into our premises more than they contain, we can arrive at conclusions, first, that God is, and next, that we can think profitably about him.

The celebrated five ways, *quinque viae*, sometimes called the proofs for the existence of God, follow some general themes running through the universe, namely, change, dependence, contingency, limited perfection, and utility. Were they to extend to the whole or reality we should have no explanation of their presence. (He is well aware that a series of incidents can be indefinitely prolonged, indeed he sees no rational demonstration against the world's stretching endlessly into the past and future, but this does not detract from the need of transcending the series.) Hence he infers the changeless changer, the uncaused cause, the necessary being, the completely perfect, and the ultimate end – notions all of which combine in the nominal definition of God.

He Who Is exceeds our classification of sorts of being, nevertheless we can say what he is not by a process of elimination, *via negationis*. Furthermore, Thomas advances past the traditional negative theology by showing that we can think positively when we are dealing with unmixed values: to say that God is good means more than that he is not evil, even more than that he is the cause of the goodness we see about us. Goodness is more properly his than ours, being taken to its highest strength, *via eminentiae*. The treatise on the Divine Names in the *Summa Theologica* (1a. xiii) steers an exacting logical course between the extremes of agnosticism and anthropomorphism.

If he did not start with a sense of God's presence

neither did he start with an ethical insight. Human activity is for the sake of happiness. In reality this *beatitudo* is God, but he has to be discovered. If we are to find him then we should act appropriately. From this hypothetical imperative Thomas's moral philosophy follows, which, since "ought" supposes "can", is unintelligible apart from his psychological and theological teaching. He is an intellectualist in that he holds that happiness is grasped by an act of knowledge, and that prudence plays a paramount role in reaching it. Acting for pleasure, or even for love and for joy, is criticised as not getting to the philosophical heart of the matter.

Moral acts, *actus humani*, are our deliberate adjustments of means to an end itself beyond morals. Morality in the abstract is determined by what kind of act is performed, good, bad, or indifferent; in the concrete the personal intention will be either right or wrong. Circumstances must also be taken into account. Merely as a moral philosopher he may seem to add little to the eudemonianism and the typology of the virtues set forth in Aristotle's *Nicomachean Ethics* on which he wrote a commentary. Here he was but on the threshold of his heroic ideal of theological perfection, which makes his criticism of the Stoic standard of passionless virtue all the more impressive.

His synthesis on the nature and divisions of Law dominates his social philosophy. Law is a rational ordinance, not directly a manifestation of might; it is for the common good, and this means a communion of persons, not totalitarian advantage; in the human community it comes from the ruler who is the representative, not the owner of the people; and it must be promulgated. The Eternal Law in the mind of God is the exemplar of all law. It is impressed on human minds as the Natural Law, which is immutable in its principles though its derivative precepts may be variously developed according to region and period. Some deeds are good, therefore commanded; some evil, therefore forbidden – that is the test of where it applies. In contrast, though not in contradiction, stands the Positive Law; its precepts may sometimes reinforce the Natural Law, but as such they are not conclusions from it but rather pragmatic supplements to make the good life easier or safeguard the public order. They oblige in conscience, but here the test is reversed; some deeds are commanded, therefore good; some forbidden, therefore evil. Thomas was the first to depart from the traditional view, formed by the Stoics and Augustine, that the civil power, like private property, was *propter peccatum*, a remedy against our anti-social appetites. He recovered Aristotle's idea of the State meeting the essential demands of human nature, which, he says, using two terms, is both social and political. "Social" may be taken to mean the moral requirements of living together in community and society, "political" the constitutional forms that are chosen. Human legislation should know its limits, and not seek to cover the whole field of morality. (T.G.)

Plate 4, page 36.

Aristippus of Cyrene in North Africa (*c.* 435–356 B.C.) was one of the Socratic circle, a **sophist**, and the traditional founder of the **Cyrenaic** school of philosophy. While his life and views are in harmony with its tenets, it is possible that these tenets were first systematically formulated by his grandson, also named Aristippus.

He made the goal of his life the enjoyment of present pleasure, eschewing regret for the past and toil for the future. But happiness consisted in the prudent, intelligent control or mastery of such pleasure, not in slavery to it, nor in abstinence. Hence his famous remark on his association with his expensive mistress Lais: "I have Lais, not she me." All acts were indifferent except in so far as they produced pleasure for the doer. Aristippus made his life the art of adapting himself to place, time and person, and playing his part appropriately whatever the circumstances, a virtuosity he displayed especially at the court of Dionysius of Syracuse. It was said of him that he alone could play the dandy or go in rags. He had in fact an extraordinary capacity for enjoyment combined with a great freedom from wants, a combination later to raise a difficult choice of ideals for his successors. (I.G.K.)

Aristotle, (384–322 B.C.) was the son of a doctor of Stagira in northern Greece. For twenty years, from 367, he was a member of **Plato**'s Academy. When Plato died and **Speusippus** became head of the Academy, Aristotle left Athens and went first to Assos (on the coast of Asia Minor) and then to Lesbos. About 342 he was invited by King Philip of Macedonia to go there to supervise the education of the King's son, Alexander. A few years later he returned to Athens to found a new school, which became known as the Lyceum or Peripatos. The school flourished; but in 323 Aristotle left Athens for political reasons and retired to Euboea. There he died in 322.

Aristotle's early writings were mostly intended for a general public. Written in a polished style (some in dialogue form), they were largely Platonic in outlook. These works were well known in antiquity but only fragments survive. The works which we possess are systematic treatises intended for serious students. These works had only a limited circulation in antiquity until texts were edited by Andronicus in the first century B.C.; our text of Aristotle is based ultimately on Andronicus' edition, and so were all translations into Latin and Arabic. Aristotle's treatises have a rather peculiar character, for they are in essence notes of or notes for lectures. A lecturer rehandles his material many times over the years and introduces second thoughts and new ideas, and his notes in their final form may contain parts written at very different dates and not always integrated into a smooth unity. Thus an Aristotelian treatise is not to be thought of as a work written, revised and published in a certain year, but rather as something that has been added to and altered over a period of years without perhaps ever receiving a final re-writing. Moreover what we count as a single treatise may really consist of several originally separate courses strung together by Andronicus or an earlier editor. All this makes the problem of the chronology of Aristotle's writings very complicated and hence makes it difficult to give an account of how his thought changed or developed. These questions have been the subject of much valuable research in recent years but cannot be discussed here. This article will aim only at giving brief accounts of some of Aristotle's ideas and providing a guide to some of his main works.

It is worth saying a word about Aristotle's approach to philosophy. His very name suggests to some people the idea of a dogmatic system of rigid doctrines. This is a misleading idea. Aristotle's manner is far from dogmatic: he is always reopening questions and admitting difficulties. Nor is his method dogmatic. He does not argue arrogantly from premises laid down by him as self-evident. He considers carefully what his predecessors have said and what ordinary men say, he assumes that their divergent views will all have some element of truth in them, and he seeks to elicit reasonable solutions to problems by clarifying the issues and qualifying or refining the various inconsistent solutions that have been offered. Finally, it is a mistake to think that the philosophical value of his work must reside in his conclusions (or "doctrines"); it is his skill in analysis and his acuteness in argument quite as much as his positive conclusions which make him a very great philosopher.

The following notes, necessarily superficial, will introduce some of the ideas which recur constantly in Aristotle:

(1) *Categories*. Aristotle's categories classify reality: everything that exists falls under one of them – is either a substance or a quality or a quantity or a relation etc. (Aristotle sometimes lists ten categories, usually fewer). It is because items in different categories have irreducibly different sorts of being that terms like "is" and "one" which are applicable in all categories are in an important way ambiguous (compare the scholastic doctrine of *transcendentalia*). Inattention to this type of ambiguity and to categorial distinctions had led, Aristotle argued, to philosophical paradoxes.

Substance is prior to all the other categories because substances exist "separately" while qualities, etc., exist only as the qualities *of* substances. Individual substances (for example Socrates or this table) are the subjects to which predicates belong and are not themselves predicates of anything else. Aristotle places in the category of substance not only individual substances but also their species and genera (man, animal). For to say that Socrates is a man is not to mention some quality etc. which he has, but to say *what he is*. Moreover science, which studies reality and above all substance, defines and studies species not individuals. Yet of course species do *not* exist separately as individuals do. There is a deep difficulty in Aristotle's thought here, which may be expressed by saying that his word *ousia* (literally "being") does duty both for our "substance" and for our "essence"; Aristotle assigns to

ousia incompatible characteristics, some of which really belong to individual substances, others to species or essences.

(2) *Form and Matter*. A table is wood and glue put together in a certain way. Aristotle distinguishes as separate aspects of the table its matter (the wood and glue) and its form (how it is put together, its structure). Many of his central ideas – and of his puzzles – are connected with this distinction. (*a*) Form is *immanent*: the form of table exists only as the form of this table or that table, that is, as the form of certain matter. There is no separately existing transcendental Platonic Form of Table (or indeed of Man or Justice). (*b*) Form or structure is normally determined by function. It is because of what it has to do that a table has a flat top and four legs. Form may in fact be identified with function: to say what a table *is* is to say what it does or is for. (*c*) Matter is "for the sake of" form, not *vice versa*. If you want an axe – something for cutting down trees – you must of course use iron to make it; but there can be iron without there being an axe. So to state the form or function of something explains it far more than stating what it is made of; the form implies the appropriate matter in a way in which the matter does not imply the form. (*d*) Wood and glue, the matter of a table, are not matter in an absolute sense. In a piece of wood we can again draw a distinction between form and matter, since wood, like everything else, is made of earth, air, fire and water (or of some of these) combined in a certain way. Nor are these four elements pure matter. They can change into one another. This implies a persistent underlying stuff capable of receiving the form of earth, air, etc. but in itsels without any form or definite character. This if what Aristotle calls *first* (or "*prime*") *matter*, a characterless substrate which never actually exists on its own but only in the form of earth, air etc. (*e*) Besides pressing the distinction of matter and form to the extreme concept of prime matter, Aristotle also uses it by analogy in quite different problems. Thus in the definition of a species he treats the genus as the matter and the differentia as the form: the genus is relatively indeterminate, the differentia gives its definite character to the species. This is typical of Aristotle's way of extending the application of key concepts, – which adds a certain unity to his thought at the cost of some ob-

scurity. (*f*) So far form has been the correlative of matter, the form *of* some matter. Aristotle raises the question whether there can be form without matter and says that there can. But his form-without-matter is very different from a Platonic Form. *God* is form without matter.

(3) *Actuality and Potentiality.* A block of wood is potentially a statue, an acorn is potentially an oak; the completed statue and the mature oak are the actualisations of those potentialities. (*a*) There is a close connection between the antithesis form-matter and the antithesis actuality-potentiality. Matter is what has the potentiality of receiving form; form is what actualises the potentiality. So Aristotle sometimes uses the two antitheses interchangeably. (*b*) It is not any and every material that is capable of receiving a given form: an acorn *cannot* become an elm, wood *cannot* be made into an axe. What oaks come from and what axes are made of are particular questions to be answered by separate investigations. Aristotle does not think that they and all similar questions can be adequately answered simply by saying that actual so-and-so's come from potential so-and-so's; *this* is part of a quite general philosophical analysis of the notions of growth and change. (*c*) Aristotle argues that actuality is prior to potentiality in definition, value and time. The actuality has to be mentioned in a definition of the potentiality, but not *vice versa*. The actuality is the end for the sake of which the potentiality exists. And although an acorn exists before the oak it grows into, it is itself the product of some already existing mature oak: "for from the potentially existing the actually existing is always produced by an actually existing thing, for example, man from man, musician by musician; there is always a first mover, and the mover already exists actually". (A table of course is not produced by a table; but it *is* produced by someone who already has the *form* of a table "in his mind"). (*d*) Since a potentiality implies the possibility of change to the actuality, which is better, there can be no element of potentiality in a perfect changeless being.

(4) *The Four "Causes".* Aristotle holds that the full explanation of anything should say what it is made of (material cause), what it essentially is (formal cause), what brought it into being (efficient cause) and what its function or purpose is (final

cause). The oddity of describing all these as *causes* is not to be held against Aristotle; "cause" is the traditional translation in this context of a Greek word of wider meaning.

Aristotle holds that in a way the formal, efficient and final causes are identical. It is the essential nature of a table (formal cause) to subserve certain purposes (final cause), and it was the thought of those purposes in the carpenter's mind that brought the table into being (efficient cause). It is the essential nature of a horse to perform certain characteristic functions and exercise characteristic powers, and to do this, to live the life of a mature horse, is just what horses are for; and a horse is produced by horses, that is, creatures already exercising the functions of mature horses.

It should be noticed that the notion of explanation by the four causes applies to things rather than events, is derived from reflection on the process of production (natural and articial), and implies a kind of universal teleology.

(5) *Classification of Sciences.* A survey of Aristotle's work in special fields can conveniently be prefaced by an account of how he classifies the various branches of inquiry, a classification of considerable historical importance. His basic division is into theoretical, practical and productive sciences. Theoretical science studies "what cannot be otherwise" and aims simply at truth. It can be subdivided into three main parts, distinguished by subject-matter: physics deals with things that exist separately but are liable to change, mathematics with things that are changeless but have no separate existence, "first philosophy" (metaphysics) with what both exists separately and is changeless. Practical sciences are to do with "what can be otherwise" and are ultimately aimed at action; the most important practical sciences are ethics and politics. Productive sciences are concerned with making things.

Logic is regarded by Aristotle not as a substantive part of philosophy but as ancillary to all parts. For it studies forms of reasoning and expression common to various subject-matters, and a grasp of it is pre-requisite for the student of any topic. This view of logic is reflected in the traditional name of Aristotle's logical works – the "Organon" (that is, tool or instrument).

(6) *Logic.* The *Prior Analytics* contains Aristotle's great contribution to formal logic, his theory of

the syllogism. This is a purely formal system of remarkable rigour but limited scope. The limitations are that it handles only certain kinds of statement and that the inferences it studies are all inferences from two such statements to a third. The statements in a categorical syllogism all have one or other of the following forms: all A is B, no A is B, some A is B, some A is not B. Modal syllogisms bring in such forms as "all A *may be* B" and "all A *must be* B". Aristotle works out all possible combinations of premises and conclusions, determines which syllogisms are valid, and investigates some of the logical relations between different syllogisms.

The *Posterior Analytics* contains Aristotle's "logic of science". His account of the form a completed science should take is much influenced by the model of geometry and rests on the view that there are in nature "real kinds" whose essence we can know. A given branch of science is about some limited class of objects. It starts from principles and axioms – some common to all sciences, some peculiar to this one – and from definitions of the objects being studied. It then demonstrates by syllogisms that certain properties necessarily belong to the objects in question. This seems remote from what scientists do, and indeed from what Aristotle does in his scientific works; but it must be remembered that it expresses an ideal for the exposition of a completed science rather than a programme for investigators.

Two further points: (*a*) Aristotle is rejecting the notion, which he ascribes to Plato, of one grand comprehensive science; different sciences require different premises. (*b*) Aristotle uses the term translated "induction" to explain how we get indemonstrable starting points from which to make our deduction; but this is not induction in our sense. We are said, for example, to grasp the truth of the principle of contradiction (one of the principles common to all sciences) by "induction"; this means simply that we are led on ("induced") to recognise it as evidently true by noticing one or more instances of it. Aristotle gives a somewhat similar account of how we acquire concepts; having seen a number of men we are able to seize upon the nature common to them all. Grasping the universal, like grasping a universal truth, is a matter of direct apprehension not of inference.

(7) *Physics*. The study of *physics*, or nature, includes the study of living things, but it will be convenient to treat Aristotle's biology and psychology separately from his more general physical works. The *Physics* and connected works contain discussion and analysis of such concepts as nature, change, chance, time, place, continuity, infinity, growth; proofs that movement is eternal and that there is an eternal Prime Mover; and much doctrine as to the actual constitution and workings of the universe. What Aristotle has to say on this last subject is naturally out-of-date (and would not now be regarded as in a philosopher's province). His analyses of concepts are often subtle and illuminating but cannot be usefully summarised. His treatment of movement and continuity led him to reject as senseless, questions about the velocity (or direction) of a moving body at a given *point* (of space or time); this had unfortunate effects on the study of dynamics.

The argument for a Prime Mover starts from Aristotle's conception of change and causation. There could not be an absolutely first (or last) change. For since change implies pre-existing matter (or potentiality) and a pre-existing efficient cause to impose form on the matter (to actualise the potentiality), there must have existed before a supposed first change something capable of being changed and something capable of causing change. But then to explain why these potentialities (for being changed and for causing change) were actualised at a certain time, and not before, we must assume some actual change just prior to that time, that is, a change before the supposed first change. Change therefore, or movement, must be eternal. But how is eternal change to be explained? Not by the assumption that there is something eternally *self-moving*. The very term "self-mover" is misleading. For the concept of movement or change demands that we distinguish in a "self-mover" one part which causes change and another which undergoes it. We must therefore assume the existence of a being itself *unmoved* which can somehow cause eternal movement. This Prime Mover, eternal, changeless and containing no element of matter or unrealised potentiality, keeps the heavenly bodies moving and maintains the eternal life of the universe. Theology will have something more to say about its nature and mode of operation.

(8) *Biology*. If Aristotle's work on physics suffers from a lack of experiment and observation, the same cannot be said of his biology. He collected a vast amount of information about living creatures and, in spite of some fundamental errors, was better informed on the subject than most of his successors until comparatively recent times. He recognised that theories must wait upon facts; after giving a theory about the generation of bees he says: "the facts have not been sufficiently ascertained". And if at any future time they are ascertained, "then credence must be given to the direct evidence of the senses more than to theories".

Two of Aristotle's important contributions are connected with classification and with teleological explanation. He achieved valuable systematic classifications of animal life, rejecting what he regarded as an inadequate Platonic method – the method of dichotomy – and employing multiple differentiae to distinguish the main classes of creature. He thought of the various species as eternal and not evolved from other species, but as capable of being arranged in a scale leading from the lowest and least developed to the highest and most complex.

Aristotle regards teleological explanation as the essence of the biologist's work: the explanation of material structure in terms of function. Nature, the perfect craftsman, does nothing in vain; and the true explanation of the characteristics of a species must show how they serve some purpose in relation to the life of the members of the species. Aristotle's teleology is nothing to do with one species subserving the interests of another, it is to do with each species in itself. The job of an embryo is to become a mature animal, live its proper life and reproduce itself; and its parts and characteristics are to be explained as contributing to these ends. "For any living thing that has reached its normal development . . . the most natural act is the production of another like itself, an animal producing an animal, a plant a plant, in order that, as far as its nature allows, it may partake in the eternal and divine. That is the goal towards which all things strive, that for the sake of which they do whatsoever their nature renders possible."

(9) *Psychology*. The word "*psyche*", commonly translated "soul", really has a wider meaning; plants as well as animals have *psyche*, they are *living*.

Living things can be ordered according to the complexity of their powers. Some (plants) have only the power of nutrition and reproduction; others have also the power of perception, desire and movement; men have in addition the power of thought. Aristotle's main discussion of these various psychical functions is in the *De Anima*, which also contains his general account of soul and its relation to body.

A dead man, a body without a soul, is not strictly a man at all, for it lacks just those powers the possession of which defines what it is to be a man. A man (and any animal or plant) is a body-with-soul; and the relation between body and soul is the relation of matter to form. Soul is the form of body, as sight is the form of the eye ("when seeing is removed the eye is no longer an eye, except in name – it is no more a real eye than the eye of a statue"). Soul, the power of life, cannot exist in any and every body (form requires appropriate matter); it is only a body with suitable organs which can possess life. Such a body is *potentially* a living animal or plant; soul is the *actuality* of such a body. This important conclusion (which is closer to **Ryle** than to **Descartes**), enables Aristotle to dismiss the question whether soul and body form a unity: "this is as meaningless as to ask whether the wax and the shape given to it by the stamp are one, or generally the matter of a thing and that of which it is the matter. Unity has many senses . . . but the most proper and fundamental sense . . . is the relation of an actuality to that of which it is the actuality". On this general view to talk of a psychological activity is to talk not of the activity of an immaterial substance inside a body but of the actual functioning of a living body; and Aristotle's accounts of psychological concepts always bring in the relevant physical and physiological facts.

Aristotle allows one exception to the rule that soul is the form or actualisation of body. The activity of *nous* (pure intuitive thought) does not depend on body and may therefore exist separately from it. His doctrine on this point is exceedingly obscure, and it is disputed whether he attributes some sort of immortality to the *nous* in the individual human soul. In general his account of soul dissolves the question of personal immortality as effectively as that of the unity of body and soul.

(10) *Metaphysics*. Aristotle expresses two views

[*continued on p. 49*

PLATE I. ABELARD, Peter (*c.* 1079–1142): Abelard taught for some time at the School of Notre Dame and his lectures must have looked very much like this thirteenth-century scene shown in relief on the south door of Notre Dame, Paris.

Photo: Mella

PLATE 2. ALBERT THE GREAT (1206–1280), painting by Justus
van Ghent (fl. 1446–1480/5). (Ducal Palace, Unbino)

PLATE 3. ANSELM of Canterbury (*c.* 1033–1109) with other saints: altarpiece by the della Robbias (Luca 1390/1400–1482; Andrea 1435–1525). (*Galleria della Collegiata, Empoli*)

35

Photo : John R. Freeman and Co.

PLATE 4.   AQUINAS, Thomas (c. 1225–1274): page from a manuscript of *De ente et essentia* written in England, c. 1300.   (*British Museum, London*)

PLATE 5. ARISTOTLE (384–321 B.C.): ninth/tenth-century manuscript page from the third book of the *Meteorologica*. (*Austrian National Library, Vienna*)

PLATE 6. ATHENS was the centre of Greek civilization and many of the Greek philosophers. including Aristotle, Plato and Socrates, lived and taught there.

PLATE 7. AUGUSTINE (354–430) Saint, painting by Simone Martini (*d.* 1344).
(*Fitzwilliam Museum, Cambridge*)

PLATE 8. AUSTIN, John Langshaw (1911–1960), photographed at the Joint Session of the Aristotelian Society and the Mind Association at Birmingham University, August 16, 1952.

Photo: John R. Freeman and Co.

PLATE 9. AVERROES, (1126–1198): manuscript page from a translation, by one of the Toledo school of translators, of *De substantia orbis*, written in Germany, early sixteenth century.
(*British Museum, London*)

AUICENNA

ostendam uobis in isto primo libro de rebus unī salibus necdicine tam theorice quam practice

Photo : Bibliothèque Nationale

PLATE 10. AVICENNA, (980–1037) teaching: page from a twelfth-century illuminated manuscript. (*Bibliothèque Nationale, Paris*)

PLATE 11. AYER, Alfred Jules (1910–), photographed in 1959.

PLATE 12. BACON, Francis (1561–1626), portrait by the Studio of Paul van Somer
(c. 1576–1621). (National Portrait Gallery, London)

IIIIW senescuit senescunt stoici non propter innata senectutem si multiplica͞t vmeraut nisicent͞u ipm acron qui nos circundat z neuligencia regis z igno͞rancia z͞t͞e͞r ͞pecauimus que regis defeni suplent. er quoz infectone necligencia z ignorancia calor naslis post temp͞ consistendi mmuu mapit z cuis zimuo z zistempancia magis arcelerat͞ er cum debilitate actiua preuiut senectutis ͞su temp͞ consistendi prt auferri z post illud cor arcelerato potest retardari. z rapidus ͞ursus que sit m flore a tempe consistendi ac senectute z de senectute ac semu z ex semo ad decrepita etatem non festinet. ͞Qz cursus etatis plus currt de senectute ad semu m vna die ͞qm facit de iuuentute ad senectute m trib͞z z pl͞s de semo ad decrepita etatem ͞qm de senectute ad semu. ͞Que discrepancia z debilitas calone naslis fit duob͞z modis. ͞p resolutoem ͞uidit naslis z augmentu͞ extree. Calor iuuatis m siniditate cristit naslis et ad augmento extree ͞uidiss extinguit͞ que preuint er debilitate digerendi vt Auicen. m p͞ canone de complexionib͞z. Sed cae resolutoie naturalia s͞uuos͞t z augmenta[18] extree ͞p quas calor naslis debilitat͞ sint multe vt

[Medieval manuscript text, Latin, largely illegible abbreviated hand]

PLATE 13. BACON, Roger (*c.* 1214–1292) with a pupil. Page from a fifteenth-century manuscript of *De retarda-tione senectutis*. (*Bodleian Library, Oxford. Ms. Bodl. 211 p. 5*)

Photo: *University Press*

45

PLATE 14. BENTHAM, Jeremy (1748–1832), portrait by Andrew Geddes (1783–1844).
(*The Queen's College, Oxford*)

Photo: Exclusive News Agency

PLATE 15. BERDYAEV, Nicolas (1874–1948), photograph.

Photo : Exclusive News Agency

PLATE 16. BERGSON, Henri Louis (1859–1941), photograph.

about "first philosophy" (the name "metaphysics" was given by an editor to the treatise on first philosophy because it came after – *meta* – the *Physics* in his edition). One view, already mentioned, is that it is the study of changeless, separable substance, that is, theology. The other is that it is not a departmental science dealing with a particular kind of being, but that it studies *being as such*, together with concepts (for example, unity, identity) and principles (for example, the law of contradiction) which are common to all departmental sciences. Aristotle is not very successful in reconciling these two views. Most of the *Metaphysics* is metaphysics in the wider sense – as a brief synopsis of the work will show.

In Book I Aristotle surveys and criticises the views of his predecessors on the ultimate principles of reality in order to confirm his own view that there are four and only four different kinds of "cause". Book III develops a number of problems further discussed later. Book IV discusses the law of contradiction and the law of excluded middle (without trying to *prove* them). Book V is a lexicon of important philosophical terms, various senses of each being discriminated. Books VII and VIII discuss substance and wrestle with the notions of essence, genus, universal, substrate, form, etc. The next books treat of actuality and potentiality, unity, plurality and similar notions. Book XII contains Aristotle's theology. Books XIII and XIV discuss and reject certain views held in the Academy about immaterial substance: there are no such things as Platonic Ideas or Ideal Numbers, and mathematical objects are not substances.

Only Book XII can be further discussed here. In it Aristotle argues again (as in the *Physics*) that there must be an eternal, immaterial Prime Mover – which he now calls "God". God, himself not susceptible of movement, causes movement as an object of desire and love. His life is perpetual activity – activity being perfect and complete in every moment and not, like movement, a process. The only sort of activity which can be ascribed to God is pure thought, uninterrupted intuitive knowledge of the highest object of knowledge, God himself. "It must be of itself that the divine thought thinks (since it is the most excellent of things), and its thinking is a thinking about thinking".

The outer heavens and the planets are animate beings moved by a desire to imitate the eternal activity of God; the outer heaven comes nearest by its single continuous spatial movement. In nature as a whole there is something similar: the processes of birth, growth and reproduction maintain forever the life of the various species. But of course plants and animals are not *consciously* imitating God (except that man, possessing reason, may do so), nor is God aware of or concerned about them.

10) *Ethics*. The *Nicomachean Ethics* is certainly one of the best books ever written on the subject. It is rich in analysis of moral and psychological concepts, and in ingenious arguments. The following account will indicate the main lines of the work:

(i) The good life. "Good" is not, Aristotle argues, the name of a single quality. Different kinds of thing are called good for different reasons: an axe is a good one if it *cuts* efficiently, eyes are good if they *see* well. To decide what is the best life for man one must ask what are the proper functions of a man (as cutting is the function of an axe); a good man will be one who performs those functions excellently, and his will be the good life. Now the function of something is what it alone can do or what it can do better than anything else. Man is distinguished from other animals by his power of thought. So the functions of a man – the effective performance of which will make him a good man – are those of his activities which involve thought and which therefore he does not share with other animals. Man's possession of reason shows itself not only in his ability to think, but also in his ability to control by thought and principle his desires and conduct; so the virtues of the good man will be not only intellectual but also moral or ethical (that is, virtues of character, *ethos*).

(ii) Moral virtue. Moral virtues, like skills, are acquired by practice. A man becomes generous by being trained or habituated to do the things a generous man would do. He has himself become generous when he has acquired a settled disposition of character so that he now does such things regularly, gladly and without ulterior motive. The "gladly" is important; it helps Aristotle to argue that the virtuous life is pleasant. His ideal is the man who always does what he ought because he wants to; the presence of a moral struggle, the need to conquer desires – these are signs of imperfection.

Moral virtue is concerned with feelings and actions, and in these there can be too much, too little, or the right amount, "the mean". Virtue is a matter of striking the mean between opposite vices: generosity lies between meanness and prodigality. The mean involved is not an arithmetical average, it is the mean "relative to us", that is, it is what is appropriate to a man. There are no simple rules for deciding what *is* appropriate; it is the possession of *phronesis* ("practical wisdom") which enables a man to hit the mean. This doctrine of the mean is more famous than it deserves to be. Aristotle admits to difficulty in bringing *all* virtues and vices into his scheme. More important, that virtue is not just a matter of the right amount is implied by Aristotle's own words: "... anger and pity ... may be felt both too much and too little, and in both cases not well; but to feel them at the right *times*, with reference to the right *people*, with the right *motive*, and in the right *way*, is what is intermediate and best, and this is characteristic of virtue". The doctrine of the mean, in fact, contains little positive moral teaching and is inadequate if considered as simply analysis of vice-virtue concepts.

Supplementary discussions consider responsibility and choice. Aristotle acutely analyses the conditions under which responsibility can be disclaimed, and reduces these to two – duress and ignorance of material facts. Choice he finds to involve deliberation and desire: our desires and character determine our *ends*, we deliberate about the *means* by which we may reach these ends.

(iii) Intellectual virtue: practical wisdom. This intellectual virtue enables a man to get the right answers to practical questions of conduct. It involves skill in deliberation but also presupposes the possession of moral virtue. For to have the right aims is a matter of moral virtue – character determines ends. Moral goodness and practical wisdom are in fact inseparable, each involving the other in its definition.

Three further points about practical wisdom may be noted. Firstly, Aristotle no longer concentrates exclusively on the means-end kind of deliberation. One may see something to be right not as being a means to a future goal but as falling under some moral principle. The means-end terminology common in Aristotle is indeed inadequate

to his own account of the good life: the aim of the good man is not to achieve some future goal but to live well all through his life. Secondly, though Aristotle gives simple examples of deliberation, he does not underestimate the complexity of practical questions or suppose they can be settled easily. To appreciate all the factors in a situation and to weigh their various claims one must have an experienced eye for what matters. Age and training are what count here, not mere cleverness. Thirdly, Aristotle does not suppose that deliberation precedes every action (or every right action). But the man of practical wisdom would be able afterwards to justify what he did by reference to ends or principles. Before passing from practical to theoretical wisdom Aristotle has important discussions of *akrasia* (knowing what one ought to do but not doing it) and of pleasure, its nature and value.

(iv) Intellectual virtue: theoretical wisdom. This intellectual virtue is wisdom about "what cannot be otherwise". It involves intuitive knowledge of unprovable starting-points (concepts and truths) and demonstrative knowledge of what follows from them. This virtue, Aristotle argues, is the highest that man can have: it is to do with the highest objects and it is the virtue of the divine part of man's soul (for no activity but that of pure thought can be attributed to God). The life of theoretical philosophy is the best and happiest a man can lead. Few men are capable of it (and they only intermittently). For the rest there is a second-best way of life, that of moral virtue and practical wisdom.

It is striking how Aristotle, starting from the question what is man's nature and his function *as a man*, ends by finding his highest and most proper activity in the *imitation of God* through the exercise of pure reason, the spark of divinity in him.

(12) *Politics*. In the *Politics* Aristotle seeks to explain the nature and purpose of a state (a city-state) and so to discover what constitution and laws would be the best. Further, since politics is a branch of *practical* inquiry, Aristotle not only expounds an ideal constitution but also makes sensible suggestions as to how actual cities of various kinds could best be run. The main philosophical interest of the work is in its analysis of political concepts ("state", "citizen", "law" etc).

(13) *Poetics*. This work must just be mentioned

(though it cannot be discussed) because of the enormous – not wholly beneficial – influence it has had in the past both on the writing of drama and on theories of aesthetics. (J.L.A.)

Plate 5, page 37.

Atomism. The atomic theory of the nature of the world was first stated by **Leucippus** and was elaborated by his associate **Democritus** in the fifth century B.C.; it was restated by **Epicurus** in a slightly modified form; the fullest ancient version still available is that of **Lucretius** in his poem *De Rerum Natura* which is based on Epicurus. It is common to regard ancient atomism as a metaphysical speculation, in contrast with modern science; but if we distinguish the general atomic hypothesis from its application by the ancients to particular problems we see that its main significance is as the first conceptual scheme making possible the pursuit of empirical science.

In stating the theory of atomism Leucippus and Democritus were continuing the tradition of the Ionian philosopher-scientists; but they were acquainted with the criticisms urged by **Parmenides** and **Zeno** of Elea against earlier physical speculation and their theory was designed to meet this criticism. They started from the principle that nothing comes into existence from nothing or is reduced to nothing – the equivalent of a denial of creation and affirmation of the conservation of matter; Democritus, though probably not Leucippus, also maintained that everything happens from some cause and in accordance with immutable principles, being the first man of whom we know to state this basic presupposition of scientific inquiry.

The world consists both of what is, the solid, the atoms, and of what is not, the empty, the void; in saying that what is not *is* the atomists are merely stating the reality of the void in technical language. The void is infinite in extent; the atoms are also infinite in number; according to Democritus the atoms are also infinite in variety of shapes and sizes, though all are too small to be perceptible, whereas Epicurus held that the variety of shapes and size is inconceivably great but not infinite. The atoms are of finite size, they are not geometrical points; they are called atoms because they are physically indivisible though from a geometrical

point of view they have parts. Solidity, size, shape and, in some versions, weight, are the only properties of atoms; they do not differ in quality and they have no colour, smell, taste, warmth or cold. It should be noted that so conceived they have only the measurable, mechanically relevant properties which **Locke** was to call primary qualities.

Beyond the atoms and the void there is nothing, and these are eternally changeless except in their spatial relationships. "Sweet and bitter, warmth and cold are appearance; in reality there are the atoms and the void" said Democritus. In more modern language, everything has to be explained in terms of atoms – their relative positions and arrangements, their shape, their size and their motions. Thus the apparent coming into being and annihilation of objects is to be explained in the terms of the forming and dissolution of groups of atoms. Many of the attempts to provide such explanations were inevitably crude, but we must not confuse the crudity of the attempt with the sophistication of the methodological principle; thus white colour was explained in terms of the smoothness of the atoms composing the object and an acrid smell in terms of the jagged shape of the atoms given off to reach the nose. It is interesting to note that Democritus was fully aware of the philosophical difficulties that are raised by rejecting the apparent evidence of the sense in favour of a theoretical world-picture; in a notable fragment (Diels-Kranz 125) he represents the senses as saying to the reason: "Wretched mind, are you trying to overthrow us with proofs obtained through us? Then our overthrow is your fall."

The senses could speak of proofs obtained through them because empirical evidence was offered for the existence of the atoms. Thus Lucretius urged that the force of the wind could be explained only if the wind consisted of invisible particles and pointed to the slow and imperceptible wearing away of stones by water. Direct empirical evidence was not offered for the void, but it was argued (fallaciously) that reason requires us to recognize it if we are to explain the phenomenon of motion, for a body can only move if there is an empty space for it to move into.

The existence of universes and bodies within them was variously explained. There is some doubt about the view of Democritus: most probably he started with atoms in spontaneous random motion as a brute fact; through their collisions whirls or vortices were set up on a huge scale and universes were formed from these vortices; since there were an infinite number of atoms in infinite space there would be an infinite number of essentially similar universes coming into existence, existing or breaking up. Epicurus started with a continual rain downwards of atoms moving with inconceivable speed; in the void they would all move with equal velocity; therefore he posited the famous *clinamen* or divergence from course of a few atoms to set up the side motions and interactions necessary for the formation of universes.

The atomic theory was all-embracing and not merely a physical hypothesis. The soul was corporeal, consisting of very fine fast-moving atoms dispersed through the body and disintegrating with the body at death. Sense-perception was explained as the emission of atoms from the body perceived to the appropriate sense-organ; thus when we see something a thin shell of atoms moves from its surface to the pupil of the eye. Even thought was conceived, it appears, as the reception of specially fine atoms, imperceptible to the senses, from the body thought of; sometimes, as in dreams, such atomic images came unbidden; at other times, and always in the case of the most subtle conceptions, the atoms were mentally perceived only by a special act of attention.

The ancient atomists were not atheists, but it is hard to be sure of their theological views. Certainly they recognized that we perceive the gods in dreams and thought, and this appears to have been regarded as a proof of their existence. But certainly they recognized no divine intervention in or control of the universe and human affairs; the gods as recognized in religion were repudiated by them.

The atomic view was never widely accepted in the ancient world. This was partly because of the scientific rejection of atomism by **Aristotle** in spite of his admiration for and interest in Democritus' work, partly because atomism was associated with moral views which were unpopular and frequently misrepresented, and partly because of the incompatibility of Christianity and the other mystery religions with the materialism of the atomists, their denial of an after-life and their denial of the conventional "interventionist" gods.

Consequently the atomic hypothesis was almost forgotten in later antiquity and in the Middle Ages.

Atomism was first revived on a significant scale in the seventeenth century, mainly because of the researches of **Gassendi** into the surviving texts of Epicurus and the poem of Lucretius. It cannot be too strongly stated that the atomism of Gassendi, Boyle, Locke and Newton was directly derived from ancient atomism; thus the famous doctrine of primary and secondary qualities they all shared is simply a restatement of the ancient atomic theory. The only fundamental changes made were such as were required by Christian orthodoxy; the soul was now stated to be immaterial and God was conceived as having created the atoms and originally put them in motion according to laws of his devising. The scientific progress of the seventeenth century consisted rather in making new and better hypotheses to explain particular phenomena in terms of the atomic hypothesis than in its fundamental modification, which was to come in the eighteeth century. It is therefore a mistake to stigmatize Greek atomism as purely rationalistic speculation in contrast to an empirically based modern atomism. The Greeks were technically unequipped to confirm special applications of the atomic theory by experiment as was increasingly achieved in modern times; but the provision of the conceptual framework had to come before experiment and this the Greeks successfully achieved.

(J.O.U.)

Augustine (354–430), Saint, also known as Aurelius Augustinus and Augustine of Hippo. He was born at Thagaste in Numidia (Souk-Ahras in Algeria on the Tunisian border). His mother was a Christian, his father a pagan. Augustine received a thorough education in rhetoric, a discipline over which the spirit of Cicero presided. Before he was twenty he had turned his back on Christianity, intellectually repelled less by the strangeness of its doctrines than by the crudity, in style and content, of its Scriptures. Its canons of behaviour were also uncongenial to him, and as a very young man he was already established in Carthage with a mistress and a professorial chair of rhetoric.

His energetic and curious mind had been fired with a love of philosophy by Cicero's *Hortensius*, now lost, which he read at the age of eighteen. This started him on an intellectual adventure that led him first to Manichaeism, then to the thorough-going **scepticism** of the Academics; next, about the time he was appointed to a chair of rhetoric at Milan, to **Neoplatonism**; and finally, at the age of thirty-two, to what he himself used to call Catholic Christianity. He was baptized in Milan at Easter 387, about nine months after his conversion.

In 391 he was ordained priest and in 395 bishop of the city of Hippo Regius (Bône, on the Algerian coast). His native genius and his strenuous devotion to his pastoral duties soon made him the intellectual leader of African Catholicism. After an episcopate of over thirty years, during which he won an Empire-wide reputation, he died at Hippo on 28 August, 430, as the Vandals were besieging the city.

It would be a great mistake to suppose that Augustine's philosophy can be scientifically assessed in isolation from his theology. His thought is always concrete, always the expression of his personal experience, and this was an experience of conversion to Christianity followed by a life spent in teaching it. For him Christianity was the true philosophy, and pagan schools of philosophy were so many false or defective theologies.

Truth is one, it is divine (it is indeed what God is), and its possession is happiness, *beatitudo*. Augustine defines beatitude as *gaudium de veritate*, enjoying Truth. Under the pull of Truth his life had a certain splendid simplicity about it; first the quest for Truth, then at his conversion the discovery of it, and after that a life spent in its exploration.

It is wisdom that gives knowledge of Truth, so the quest for Truth is a quest for wisdom. One of the first philosophical problems to engage Augustine was how a man can pass from being unwise to being wise. To do this he must desire the wisdom he lacks. But desire implies knowledge of the thing desired. Desire of wisdom therefore implies lack of wisdom and possession of wisdom, that is knowledge of it, at the same time. This conundrum was posed for Augustine by the Academics, for whom wisdom consisted in knowing that we can know nothing, and he made use of it in his *De Utilitate Credendi* against his Manichee friends, who thought they had all the answers. Dialectically he extricated himself from the *impasse* of scepticism by what has been called the Augustinian *Cogito*: *Si fallor, sum* (if I am wrong, I am). But his real method was the most un-Cartesian one of what could be described

as systematic faith. "Unless you believe, you shall not understand", Isaiah 7, 9, xx was one of his favourite texts. (He thought naturally in texts. The older he got, the more biblical his thought and its expression became). Faith alone can provide the base from which the quest for wisdom must start, because it is both a knowing, which makes love of the thing known possible, and a not knowing, so that love is still desire, not yet enjoyment. Augustine's conversion was his discovery of wisdom by faith, and the beginning of his exploration of it by understanding.

This method is deployed most conspicuously in the *De Trinitate*. In this work too we can assess the extent and the bearing of Augustine's Platonism. His cosmos is constructed on a Platonic dialectic; there is the outer and the inner world, the lower and the higher, the sensible and the intelligible, and the carnal and the spiritual. Progress in wisdom is a movement of the mind inwards and upwards to God at the apex and the centre, an opening of the mind to the illumination of incommutable truth, which is there within and above, always available for its inspection, provided the mental vision has been purified by faith. But this progress is, so to speak, a feeling one's way backwards along the channel of influence which comes downwards and outwards, causing the participating or imaging of the higher order in the lower, Creator in the creature.

The word "Creator" suggests the limits of Augustine's Platonism. His crucial theme of the divine image in the world and in man is more biblical than Platonic, and depends on the wholly biblical doctrine of creation. In virtue too of this doctrine Augustine could regard the material world with a reverence impossible for a thorough Platonist. The goal of his vision was the resurrection of the body, not the soul's release from the prison of the body. His doctrine of evil as no-thing, as a privation, a lack of due order, marks his easy independence of Platonism as much as his emancipation from Manichaeism.

The Incarnation is a doctrine which accords ill with the ultra-spiritualism and intellectualism of the Platonists, but fits smoothly into Augustine's God-imaging world. The divine image in man has been defaced by sin, which upsets the divine order, ruffles the clear surface. It is restored by a transcendent manifestation of divine order, in which the Word, the image *par excellence*, makes up for pride by humility, disobedience by obedience, restores life by enduring death, and innocence by taking the consequences of guilt. The dialectical statement of the Incarnation by St Paul or St John plucks an immediate response from Augustine the trained rhetorician.

The Word incarnate is the Way back for man to the Word who is Truth, and the Way on to the risen Christ who is Life. Restoration must come from above just as creation comes from above. All the initiatives are God's. Hence Augustine's teaching on grace. Human freedom is only fully vindicated when its unconditional derivation from the divine freedom is accepted. Divine grace is shown us in divine charity – "God so loved the world ..." and the human response is a response of charity, which Augustine would almost say is as natural as falling off a log. *Amor meus pondus meum* ("My love is my weight"), he said. Since, then, his ethic stems from grace before will-power, and from the personal relationship of love before abstract principle, it is quite free from the harsh Puritanism which has often been ascribed to it, and which was far more characteristic of the Pelagianism which he fought so strenuously.   (E.H.)

Plate 7, page 39.

Aurelius, *see* Marcus Aurelius.

Austin, John Langshaw (1911–1960), English philosopher. He was White's Professor of Moral Philosophy in the University of Oxford. His writings are few, but he has had a very considerable influence on recent analytic philosophy. His work consists mainly of close examinations of the way words are ordinarily used, without any direct reference to the traditional problems of philosophy. Austin gives an admirable brief account of his reasons for this procedure in his "A Plea for Excuses"; in short, he maintains that the distinctions enshrined in the ordinary use of language are more subtle than is usually realized and are likely to be intrinsically of interest and importance, and he would further add that it is in principle a mistake for a philosopher to proceed further in a conceptual inquiry before he has carefully assessed what resources are at his disposal – if this investigation of existing language is not the end-all of philosophy

it is at least the begin-all. He makes no claim that his activities exhaust all that a philosopher might legitimately wish to do.

The best known and most influential of Austin's papers is his examination of the concept of knowledge entitled "Other Minds". It is here that he first explained his notion of a "performative" or "performatory utterance"; performatives are speech-acts which are in themselves the performance of an action, as saying "I promise" is in itself the making of a promise and not a mere statement about a promise.   (J.O.U.)

Plate 8, page 40.

Averroes (1126–1198); his name is latinized from Ibn Rushd. Philosopher, jurist, judge and physician, he was born at Cordova, Spain, and died at Marrakesh. To the West, Averroes is best known as the commentator of **Aristotle**. The Latin version of Aristotle's complete works usually contains Averroes' Commentaries – often made from a Hebrew translation of the (lost) Arabic original. On many Aristotelian writings he wrote three different kinds of Commentaries: *Summaries* in his own words, and *Middle* and *Long Commentaries* quoting portions of the text and adding explanatory and critical comments, in the light of classical commentators like Themistius, Alexander of Aphrodisias, and of Fārābī, **Avicenna** and Avempace (Ibn Bājja). He shows penetrating insight; his exposition is lucid and concise adhering more closely to Aristotle than any of the earlier *Falāsifa*. (Muslim religious philosophers). Not having Aristotle's *Politics* Averroes commented on **Plato**'s *Republic*, which he treated as the second, practical part to supplement Aristotle's *Nicomachean Ethics*, the first, theoretical part of the science of politics. His refutation of Ghazālī's attack on the *Falāsifa* (the *Tahāfut al-tahāfut* or *The Incoherence of the Incoherence*) deserves special notice, together with three polemical religious-philosophical treatises of which the *Faṣl al-maqāl* is the most important. His Aristotelian commentaries haves furthered understanding of the master, spread his influence in the West among Jews and Christians, and have given rise to *Averroism*.

His significance as a religious philosopher lies in his polemical treatises, his spirited rebuttal of Ghazālī's attack and his Commentary on Plato's

Republic. After Ghazālī, philosophy was on the defensive, under constant fire from jurists and theologians. Hence the polemical nature of much of Averroes' writing. He set out to prove the essential agreement between the religious law (*Sharīʿa*) and philosophy (*falsafa*) by claiming identity of aim for both in the *Faṣl* (*Decisive Chapter on the Agreement between Religious Law and Philosophy*) and in the Commentary on the *Republic*: one is "the companion and foster-sister" of the other. Truth is one and indivisible, only sought and explained in different ways. The theory of the double truth is wrongly fathered on him; it belongs to the Latin Averroists. Averroes asserts the philosopher's exclusive ability, right and duty to expound the inner meaning of the prophetically revealed Law by demonstrative argument. The theologians use dialectical arguments and confuse the masses. With Plato he distinguishes the few elect philosophers from the masses. With Aristotle he distinguishes three classes of arguments (demonstrative, dialectical and rhetorical or poetical), which he assigns to three classes of believers: philosophers, theologians and the masses. The masses must accept the stories, parables and metaphors of Scripture in their plain meaning. But Scripture contains the whole truth even though its inner meaning is only accessible to the metaphysician. All three classes must accept certain statements in the *Qurʾan* (*Koran*) in their literal meaning as religious truth inaccessible to human reason, because they are God's revelation. On these grounds, he maintains and justifies the superiority of the *Sharīʿa* over the *Nomos* (secular law). He agrees with Avicenna that this Law teaches true beliefs and convictions in a form accessible to all believers and obligatory on all. The *Nomos* is only concerned with the happiness of the élite, the *Sharīʿ* guarantees every believer his share of happiness.

Averroes' vindication of the *Sharīʿa* as the constitution of the ideal Muslim state is combined with a sustained critique of the Muslim state of his time, on the basis of Plato's imperfect constitutions. He adheres to the traditional explanation of prophecy against the theory of the *Falāsifa* and insists, like Avicenna, on the superior and exceptional character of Muhammad as the divinely sent prophetic lawgiver. (E.I.J.R.)

Plate 9, page 41.

Avicenna (980–1037), Persian philosopher and physician; his name is latinized from Ibn Sīnā. The most original of the *Falāsifa* (Muslim religious philosophers', he achieved a philosophical monotheism which approaches as closely as possible a synthesis between the tenets of Islam and the teachings of **Plato** and **Aristotle**. Persian zest for life combined with a restless quest for truth produced a philosophical system which mirrors a creative, critical intellect imbued with deep religious feeling.

Unlike Fārābī to whom he is greatly indebted, and **Averroes**, whose original contribution is largely contained in his Commentaries, Avicenna succeeded in formulating a *Summa* of philosophy out of a critical study of Aristotle, helped by **Neoplatonic** commentators and the **Stoics**. His *Shifā* exerted a strong influence on Muslims, Jews and Christians, though, together with his other philosophical writings, it aroused the hostility of the theologians. Ghazālī's *Incoherence of the philosophers* was mainly directed against Avicenna. It forced creative philosophical speculation in Islam on the defensive and even Averroes could not restore it to its former position.

In **logic** Avicenna's strict adherence to Aristotle's concept of cause and effect brought him into conflict with the theologians. His logical determinism clashed with their theological determinism.

In psychology he combined Aristotle with **Plotinus** in his widely accepted idea of the immortality of the rational soul which as form is substance.

More far-reaching is his contribution to **metaphysics**. Like all *Falāsifa* he was helped by Plotinus and Porphyry who tried to harmonize Plato and Aristotle and, by giving Plato's thought a turn towards religious **monism**, enabled Muslims to blend traditional beliefs and convictions with Greek thought. Avicenna's concept of God in whose Being existence and essence are identical, gained wide currency in the West, expecially with the Jew **Maimonides** and the Christian Thomas **Aquinas**. So did its corollary that in all created beings essence is separate from existence which is only an accident. Accepting Aristotle's concept of the Universe, especially the eternity of matter, Avicenna clashed with the theological axiom of the "Creation out of Nothing". Moreover, creation is a necessary consequence of God's existence as an absolute, simple unity in whom knowledge, will and power are one with his essence. He is the uncaused First Cause, hence necessarily the Creator. Maimonides and Aquinas are opposed to the Avicennian concept and maintain the Scriptural position of the creation in time by God's free-will out of nothing.

To close the gap between revelation and reason Avicenna escaped into an intellectual mysticism (in his *Ishārāt, Indications*). The speculative mystic (*ārif*) who attained the highest degree of knowledge, gains intellectual union with God in intuitive perception. Practical philosophy is part of Avicenna's *Metaphysics* because the attainment of human happiness is only possible in society. Prophecy and *Shari'a* (prophetically revealed Muslim Law) are indispensable for human survival and happiness. The prophetic lawgiver brings mankind a divine law guaranteeing welfare in this world and bliss in the hereafter. Fārābī identified the prophetic lawgiver with Plato's philosopher-king; Avicenna does not and grants to the prophet spontaneous, intuitive knowledge, thus placing him above the philosopher. The ideal Muslim state with Muhammad's law as constitution is the counterpart to Plato's *Republic* which, together with his *Laws*, illustrated for the *Falāsifa* the political significance of the *Shari'a* and supplied in the concept of Justice and Law, that common ground which enabled them to attempt their blending of Islamic fundamentals with Greek concepts. Therein consists their originality as religious philosophers with the superior *Shari'a* as basis and centre of their system.

Plate 10, page 42. (E.I.J.R.)

Ayer, Alfred Jules, F.B.A. (1910–), born in London. He was educated at Eton and Oxford, where he later held academic posts as Research Student of Christ Church and Fellow of Wadham College. From 1946–59, he was Grote Professor of the Philosophy of Mind and Logic in the University of London, and in 1959 was appointed to the Wykeham Chair of Logic at Oxford. He is well known as a broadcaster and has appeared on television.

Ayer achieved early fame as the author of *Language, Truth and Logic* (1936), a work which did much to familiarize the English-speaking world with the philosophy of **Logical Positivism**. Based on first-hand acquaintance with the **Vienna Circle**,

it ranks among the clearest and most forthright expositions of the subject in any language. In some respects, also, it represents a synthesis of British and Continental versions of **empiricism**. Ayer agrees with the latter in rejecting **metaphysics** and confining philosophy to **analysis**; but his conception of the analytic method – the translation of problematic expressions into a logically more explicit terminology – is not very different from that of the "Cambridge school"; and he typically makes use of it to resolve traditional cruxes in the theory of knowledge. Material objects, for instance, are not "constructed" out of **sense-data**, but statements mentioning the one can be logically "reduced" to statements mentioning only the other. This linguistic **"phenomenalism"** is put forward as a truth already glimpsed in the writings of **Berkeley** and **Hume**. Apart from its controversial treatment of ethical propositions (as "emotive" rather than factual), the other main feature of Ayer's discussion is his proposal to distinguish a weaker form of the verification principle, designed to exclude metaphysics while preserving the significance of other propositions supposedly more useful to science. Difficulties of formulation have proved greater than expected, and are reviewed, with other matters, in Ayer's introduction to the second edition (1946).

Ayer's later writings have been largely devoted to retrenchment of his position in the light of subsequent criticism. The same epistemological problems are repeatedly attacked, and with substantially the same weapons; but there is less disposition to claim finality for the results. The common sense claims to knowledge of the external world, the past, the self and other people are now scrutinized, not in order to "reduce" or repudiate them, but in order to elucidate the logical grounds for their acceptance. In pursuit of this inquiry, Ayer has been increasingly led to doubt the possibility of analysing claims about material objects into claims about the actual or possible occurrence of sense-data; and he has at length forsaken phenomenalism. His present position seems best described as that of an analytically-minded empiricist, dubious of the current claims made for "ordinary language", and without commitments to any really definable school. (P.L.H.)

Plate 11, page 43.

B

Bacon, Francis (1561–1626) was born in the shadow of the English Court which dominated his whole life. He was educated at Cambridge and admitted to the Bar in 1575. In 1584, through the help of his uncle, Lord Burghley, he obtained a seat in the House of Commons. He was befriended by Essex, the favourite of Elizabeth, who tried unsuccessfully to get him made attorney-general in 1593, in preference to Sir Edward Coke.

Under James I Bacon's fortunes improved. In 1607 he was made solicitor-general and in 1613 attorney-general; in 1617 Lord Keeper and in 1618 Lord Chancellor. He was also created Baron Verulam of Verulam and in 1621 Viscount St Albans. Three days after this final honour Bacon was accused of bribery, found technically guilty, and deprived of office. He had accepted presents from litigants, the usual practice of the time. To quote his own words: "I was the justest judge that was in England these fifty years. But it was the justest censure in Parliament that was these two hundred years." He died in 1626, in retirement, working on his scientific projects.

Bacon had always held that his aim in seeking political advancement was to improve man's estate and to use his wealth and influence to forward the cause of a new science that might contribute to this end. But in spite of repeated attempts he obtained neither a college nor a royal foundation. He lived lavishly, and debts which he accumulated prevented him spending much on the advancement of science during his lifetime; after his death they also prevented the implementation of his will, in which he provided for lectureships in natural philosophy at Oxford and Cambridge.

His actual contributions to learning and science were similarly incomplete – programmatic aspirations rather than concrete pieces of work. In 1603 he laid the foundation for his Great Instauration in his *Valerius Terminus* and in his *De Interpretatione Naturae Proemium*, which were followed by his *Cogitata et Visa*. He announced that he had constructed a new method of scientific discovery. Large natural histories and collections of facts had to be amassed, preferably within a college, and carefully interpreted. The same stress on natural history and a new method of interpretation runs through his *Advancement of Learning* (1605), together with a criticism of previous thinkers and passionate pleas for the use of knowledge to better man's earthly estate.

This was a preliminary to the Great Instauration itself, which was to consist of six parts, the *Advancement of Learning* forming a major section of the first part. The plan consisted in six parts as follows:

(1) A classification and review of existing sciences which would make the gaps in them obvious. He fulfilled this portion of his plan in his *De Dignitate et Augmentis Scientiarum* (1623).

(2) A new inductive method for putting all human minds on a level in the interpretation of nature. (This he sketched in his *Novum Organum*, 1620).

(3) Natural history or a collection of data and experiments arranged in accordance with the principles laid down in Part 2.
(This was extremely fragmentary consisting of his *Parasceve ad historiam naturalem et experimentalem*, 1620; his *Historia Naturalis et experimentalis ad condendam philosophiam: sive phenomena universi*, 1622; and his *Sylva Sylvarum*, 1627, which was a strange collection of facts and fables).

(4) The Ladder of the Intellect, which was meant to consist of fully worked out examples of his method. (There is none of this extant save a preface called *Scala Intellectus sive filum labyrinthi*).

(5) Generalisations reached from natural history without the use of Bacon's special method of interpretation. (Only a preface to this exists called *Prodromi sive Anticipationes Philosophiae Secundae*).

(6) The New Philosophy or Active Science, consisting of the complete science of Nature. This was to be built on the facts of Part 3, established by the methods of Part 2.
(None of this is extant – perhaps significantly).

Bacon wrote many other works which do not fall into his Great Instauration and which are not easily regarded as anticipations or offshoots of it. Most famous are his *New Atlantis* (his contribution to the ideology of Utopia), *De Sapientia Veterum* (1609), and *De Principiis atque Originibus* (1623–4), which was his attempt to supplant the Platonic and Aristotelian traditions by a more materialistic type of theory deriving from Democritus. Also in refutation of earlier philosophers he wrote his *Redargutio philosophiarum* (1608) – his treatise on "the idols of the theatre". There are also several other fragments like his *Temporis partus masculus* and his *Delineatio et argumentum*, both of which were anticipatory of his Great Instauration.

Bacon's main contribution to philosophy was in the sphere of scientific method. He was one of the most powerful and articulate rebels against the Aristotelian and Platonic traditions; in many respects he attempted to revive a materialism akin to that of **Democritus**. He claimed that Aristotelian logic was a useless tool for discovery. It forced assent, but revealed nothing new and dragged experiment along like a captive. Also the final causes which it employed in its explanations had wonderfully corrupted philosophy. They were only appropriate in explaining human affairs. The alternative school of thought, **Rationalism**, deriving from **Plato**, was equally useless. No trust was to be placed in the abstract axioms of the geometric method. Definitions could not remedy the evil in nature or material objects, because they consisted themselves of words and these words produced others. "Words are but the images of matter; and except they have life of reason and invention, to fall in love with them is to fall in love with a picture". Rationalists are like spiders spinning ideas out of the recesses of their mind. The brute empirics, on the other hand, are no better. For they are like ants, aimlessly collecting data. The bees provide the proper model for scientific procedure. Order is the secret – the amassing of data or natural history, storing it, and interpreting it judiciously according to definite canons.

In his endeavour to replace rash anticipations of Nature by orderly interpretations the inquirer is brought up against certain deep-seated limitations of the human mind. These Bacon called the Idols of the Tribe. Men tend to generalise too readily, to find instances which suit their purposes and to believe more readily that which they prefer. Bacon therefore stressed the importance of looking for the negative instance, of seeking systematically for exceptions to generalisations. Idols of the tribe are also due to other limitations such as the dullness of

our perceptual apparatus. But there are also Idols of the Den, which are defects due not so much to human nature generally as to individual differences and idiosyncrasies, both innate and acquired. Then there are Idols of the Market Place, which are due to words and phrases that corrupt and muddle our thinking – especially vague words and words that describe nothing. Finally there are the Idols of the Theatre which arise from systems of philosophy. The remedy for these obstacles was not simply to expose the faulty reasoning of others, but to set out the new method of inquiry clearly for all to use.

This method consisted of accumulating data and dealing with it in a certain manner. Suppose the cause of heat was sought. A table of *presence* had first to be compiled containing all the known instances in which heat was present. A table of *absence* had then to be constructed with instances corresponding to these in the table of presence, but differing in that the simple nature, heat, was absent. A table of *degrees* had also to be compiled containing instances in which heat was present in varying degrees. By examining the tables a generating nature might be found which was co-present, co-absent, and co-variant with the effect or generated nature. An interpretation or "first vintage" could then be made – for example, that motion is the cause or "form" of heat. (These tables are very similar to J. S. **Mill**'s joint methods of agreement and difference and the method of concomitant variations.)

One of the most vexed questions of Baconian scholarship is the status of these "forms" which it was the natural philosopher's business to discover. He distinguished physics which investigates efficient and material causes but "does not stir the limits of things which are much more deeply rooted" from **metaphysics**, which investigates "forms". These are both generic and generating "natures". Heat, for instance, is a limitation of a more generic nature "motion"; and it is also in some way *produced* by motion. Such "forms" do not seem like Aristotelian formal causes because they are generators of other natures and not just correlative with matter. It is often suggested that Bacon had in mind some primitive atomic theory akin to that of Democritus; for he praised Democritus. Yet these "forms" are observables to be discovered by compiling tables. Atoms are not observable.

Whatever doubts there may be about the status of these forms, there can be no doubt about Bacon's enthusiasm for projects of a practical sort which a knowledge of the laws of the combination of these forms might permit. He was one of the first to stress that knowledge gives man power over nature and has been heralded as a forerunner of both **Utilitarianism** and **Marxism** in this respect. Bacon thought that the aim of his Great Instauration was "knowledge of the causes and of the secret motion of things, and the enlarging of the bounds of human empire, to the effecting of all things possible". He subscribed to the alchemist's ideal of transmuting substances of one kind into substances of another. But he thought that such an undertaking must be based on a thorough understanding of "what is constant, eternal, and universal in nature."

Bacon met with little concrete success either in developing his fundamental science or in inaugurating a college to house it. But he inspired many with his dream of improving man's estate by the employment of scientific method. The Royal Society, which was founded in 1662, was Baconian in spirit. It combined his emphasis on observation and experiment with a concern for inventions of practical use. It was founded by Puritans who believed, like Bacon, that science could reveal the wonders of God's creation and be used to improve man's estate.

Bacon's thought influenced not only the development of science but also the typically British conception of knowledge and scientific method as exemplified by **Locke, Berkeley, Hume,** J. S. **Mill,** and **Russell**.

Bacon's account of scientific method has been criticized by later thinkers in at least four major respects. First of all he was mistaken in thinking that there is any "inductive" method which could put all men on a level in the matter of arriving at well-founded generalisations. There may be methods for testing generalisations once they have been made, but there are no recipes for arriving at them.

Secondly Bacon failed to distinguish between rash "anticipations" of nature and working hypotheses. Data cannot be collected without some sort of hypothesis, let alone a theory developed. The nineteenth century logician **Whewell** made much of this defect in Bacon's account.

Thirdly Bacon was profoundly ignorant of mathematics and overlooked its great importance in the development of theories. He rejected the Copernican hypothesis, ridiculed Gilbert's speculations about magnetism, and failed to see the importance of Harvey's work. He understood little of the work of continental thinkers like Kepler and Galileo. This failure to grasp the importance of mathematics led him to overlook the role of deduction in science. For often, when a theory has to be tested, there is a long deductive journey, made possible by mathematics, between postulates and their consequences which are observationally testable.

Finally Bacon ignored problems connected with the *justification* of inductive reasoning, which have troubled philosophers since Hume.

His importance in the history of thought is his stress on the observational basis of science and the search for the negative instance.   (R.S.P.)

Plate 12, page 44.

Bacon, Roger (*c.* 1214–*c.* 1292), born in England. Bacon's long career which was spent partly at Oxford and partly at Paris covers the whole of the vital period in the thirteenth century when Greek and Arabic science and philosophy were being finally assimilated into western thought.

In many respects he appears as conservative and traditional as his fellow Franciscan, **Bonaventura,** being no less observant of religion and equally convinced of the supremacy of theological knowledge. Yet he differs profoundly from the latter in his reaction to the new science.

Where Bonaventura was able to see a new, perhaps interesting, field for human investigation, but one which in the long run could only distract men from that contemplative activity to which all men should aspire, Bacon saw, not new material, but a new method. A method which would radically transpose the approach to learning and to knowledge by applying the new mathematical and experimental techniques to the study of philosophy and theology.

His most characteristic writing is to be found in

his *Opus Majus* which, together with the shorter *Opus Minus* and *Opus Tertium* elaborates his views on how to engage in the urgent task of reforming the teaching of Christian wisdom. These works were written at the request of Pope Clement IV and urged in view of the political hegemony which would fall to the West as a result of the advance of science. But Clement died and Bacon remained frustrated. It was his misfortune to be convinced of the practical importance of positive and scientific studies long before they became a practical possibility. (J.G.D.)

Plate 13, page 45.

Beauty, *see* Aesthetics.

Being, *see* Metaphysics, Existentialism, Realism, Idealism, Monism, Dualism.

Bentham, Jeremy (1748–1832), the leader of the English **Utilitarians**. He was born in London, the son of a wealthy attorney, and was educated for his father's profession. But Bentham's interest in the Law was of a different sort: and in reading Helvetius at the age of twenty he was particularly impressed by the "Greatest Happiness Principle" which Helvetius had taken from Joseph Priestley. From this time onwards Bentham devoted his life to the building of a scientific foundation for legislation and jurisdiction. His first task was to repudiate the basis of Natural Law and historic precedent upon which Blackstone had based his defence of the British Constitution. His interest in the theory of punishment led him to design a model prison or Inspection House – a plan accepted by the Government though never carried out. In 1785 Bentham went to Russia to visit his brother Samuel, a government engineer. Back in England he took up every kind of legal, social, economic and educational reform, applying to each one his tireless "method of detail". After 1808 the influence of James **Mill** led him to become an advocate of representative institutions and of the Radical reform of Parliament. By this time he had formed a circle of friends and disciples, to whom in many cases he entrusted the editing, rewriting, or translation of his manuscripts: Dumont's French versions earned Bentham a European reputation and

he became the inspiration and mentor of liberals throughout the world. He died during the Reform Bill agitation and his embalmed body is to be seen in University College London, of which he was a principal founder.

The fundamental theory of Utilitarianism is given in *An Introduction to the Principles of Morals and Legislation* (1789). Bentham holds that what moves a man to action is always a desire to secure his own pleasure or to avoid his own pain. "Nature has placed mankind under the governance of two sovereign masters, *pain* and *pleasure* ... They govern us in all we do, in all we say, in all we think." This is a psychological or metaphysical principle. The moral principle is that actions are to be approved or disapproved according to the tendency they appear to have to increase or diminish the happiness, advantage, pleasure or good of the parties concerned in the actions; if the whole community is affected, then the happiness of all must be considered. Bentham's view distinguishes between judgments of approval or disapproval and mere liking and disliking. A man must *like* what he takes to be for his own advantage: he considers an action *right* when he sees or believes that it will bring the maximum advantage or happiness to all those affected; that is, the greatest possible pleasure *however distributed* amongst persons. To make a moral judgment it is necessary to measure pains and pleasures, and to compare one person's pains and pleasures with another's. Bentham gives seven "circumstances" to be considered: the intensity of the pleasure (or pain), its duration, its certainty, its nearness, its fecundity (or tendency to produce further pleasures), its purity (or tendency not to be followed by pains) and its extent – the number of persons affected by it. There are many different sorts of pleasures: there are pleasures in poetry, in pushpin and in the vile crimes of malefactors. An impartial judge will not discount a pleasure merely because he does not happen to relish it himself. Bentham rejects tradition, religious authority and personal "intuition" of moral truth. The only general rules he accepts are those of the law, and for these he offers a Utilitarian test: Does the general observance of this law promote human happiness to the greatest practicable degree? In private conduct Bentham would dispense with rules altogether. A man should choose the action which maximises pleasure, not one prescribed by any rule.

How can men, who are moved only by the prospect of their own advantage, be led to act in such a way as to promote the general happiness? Bentham's answer is: (1) the law by its punishment, and public opinion by its rewards and penalties, constrain men from acting against the general interest. (2) Enlightened self-interest shows men that in most cases the general good is also their individual advantage. The law *produces* an artificial harmony between individual interest and the general interest: a man who would otherwise stand to gain by crime finds that, where a punishment is attached, the balance is one of misery. Education *reveals* an unsuspected harmony of interests: in particular, the doctrines of political economy seemed to offer novel scientific proofs of the efficacy of co-operation.

Bentham inherited and adapted the doctrines of **Locke**, **Hume**, Priestley, and Locke's French disciples. His philosophical influence comes down chiefly through J. S. **Mill**, Henry **Sidgwick** and G. E. **Moore**: it provoked a violent reaction in F. H. **Bradley**, *Ethical Studies* 1876. The principal object of criticism is the doctrine that men seek only their own pleasure. This is not true if pleasure is understood in an ordinary sense: and can be accepted only as the tautology that men seek after what they want or what they think will be (in some sense) good for them. If "good", "pleasure", "advantage" means whatever men aim at, then it is pointless to advise men to seek their own good – this advice offers no guidance whatever. But in fact Bentham did not advise men to seek their own good. He offered the particular advice that they should do so in such a way as to allow all men indifferently as much as possible of *their* own good (which means "of whatever *they think* will do them good" since it is left to them to judge.) That this is the best way to secure one's own greatest happiness, is not a tautology; and the arguments by which Bentham tried to commend his maxim have (in some cases) to be supplemented by an appeal to force – but force which itself might contribute to a change of mind.   (K.B.)

Plate 14, page 46.

Berdyaev, Nicolas (1874–1948) was born in Russia; he remained there until his expulsion in 1922, when he settled first in Germany and then in France. A faithful member of the Russian Orthodox Church, Berdyaev, in most of his work, should be classed as a religious thinker and as a social and political propagandist rather than as a philosopher in the narrower sense of the word; his aim was a practical one – to bring about a Christian social system – rather than theoretical. His fundamental philosophical thesis was a distinction between the material world, subject to natural law and necessity, of which man as an animal is a part, and the higher world of freedom of which man as spirit is a part, a position reminiscent of **Kant**'s distinction of the phenomenal and noumenal worlds.   (J.O.U.)

Plate 15, page 47.

Bergson, Henri Louis (1859–1941), French philosopher. He was Professor of Philosophy first at Clermont-Ferrand in Auvergne and later at the Collège de France in Paris, and produced a philosophy of "creative evolution" which made a considerable impression in literature as well as thought during the early years of the twentieth century (see, for example, the Preface to G. Bernard Shaw's *Back to Methuselah*). This was not only a romantic para-biological theory of a "Life-Force" invoked to counteract materialistic or mechanistic notions of the evolution of life in nature. It was an ingenious speculative theory of the relation of life and matter, correlated throughout with a particular theory of knowledge. Indeed, Bergson's work could either be interpreted idealistically, in which case the theory of knowledge is prior, and we have a certain kind of concept of matter because our minds work in a certain way; or it could be interpreted as an evolutionary realism in which our minds have come to think in a certain way because of the natural history of their evolution. In any case, Bergson's originality lay in the way in which he interpreted a theory of evolution and a theory of knowledge in terms of each other. The theory of knowledge was presented first, in *Essai sur les données immédiates de la conscience* (1889), (the English translation is entitled *Time and Free-will*), and in *Matière et Mémoire* (1896). Here Bergson draws a sharp distinction between the character of our conceptual knowledge of the external world and consciousness as known from within. The intellect in its scientific study of the external world proceeds by analysis and classification. For analysis, the world must be considered as composed of isolatable objects externally related to each other; for classification these must be regarded as repeatable instances of similar kinds. So the world is interpreted in terms of limited kinds of discrete units, undergoing repeatable rearrangements in space. Hence the intellect thinks naturally of static objects in *spatial* juxtaposition; it does not grasp fundamental changes through time, but imagines change as a succession of static states of affairs, spread out in a succession of instantaneous spaces – a limitation which was brought out by **Zeno** of Elea in his paradoxes about motion, and which, Bergson thought, is never transcended by mere concepts, although it may be met practically by devices such as the infinitesimal calculus, where a succession of very small intervals are considered as though they formed a continuous movement. The intellect therefore, Bergson says, "spatializes", and its ideal form of thinking is geometry.

Sharply contrasted is our own self-consciousness. Here change in time is experienced from within; we are aware not of a succession of distinct states, but of our present as arising out of our past and turning into a not clearly envisaged future. The "time" of this inner experience is not external clock time, which is "spatialized time", measured for instance by noting successive positions of the hands of a clock. It is an actual experience of change, in which stages of "before" and "after" interpenetrate each other; this kind of time Bergson calls "duration" (*durée*), and he claims that it is not merely a way of measuring a changing reality, but is the changing reality itself. The state of mind in which we are aware of the quality and flow of inner consciousness is called Intuition. It is a non-conceptual kind of awareness; Bergson even says that it dispenses with symbols; what he here means by "symbol" is not clear, and indeed his own attempts to express and describe Intuition are couched, perhaps inevitably, in metaphors. For a form of consciousness which used neither concepts nor imaginative metaphors would presumably not be explicit thought at all, but *feeling*. Indeed Bergson speaks at times of Intuition as "sympathy", and as "integral experience". In the essay *Introduction à la Métaphysique* (1903), published in the *Revue de*

Métaphysique et Morale, he speaks of metaphysics as "the science which claims to dispense with symbols". If this were the whole truth, it is hard to see how it could become articulate knowledge, since any expression must presumably use some form of symbolism. Bergson does not, however, present Intuition as able to work apart from intellect, although he describes these as if they were polar opposites. Intuition is compared with the creative inner excitement which enables a writer to fuse his mass of materials into a unity, which he cannot do unless he has first gathered the materials by intellectual effort. "Any one of us, for instance, who has attempted literary composition, knows that when the subject has been studied at length, the materials all collected, and the notes all made, something more is needed in order to set about the work of composition itself, and that it is an often very painful effort to place ourselves directly at the heart of the subject, and to seek as deeply as possible an impulse, after which we need only let ourselves go ... Metaphysical intuition seems to be something of the same kind. What corresponds here to the documents and notes of literary composition is the sum of observations and experience gathered together by positive science. For we do not obtain an Intuition from reality – that is, an intellectual sympathy with the most intimate part of it – unless we have won its confidence by a long fellowship with its superficial manifestations." (*Introduction to Metaphysics*, E.T. pp. 89–91). In neither case, however, can the "impulse" produce a synthesis out of the materials apart from an integrating idea. Bergson's description of "intuition" seems to be not so much an account of such integrating ideas as of the underlying state of mind out of which they may come. This is a form of feeling intensely concentrated on the present task, but which has behind it the resources of the person's whole past experience. Here Bergson's particular view of *Memory* should be taken into account. He holds that consciousness contains implicitly the whole of one's past experience, but the function of the brain of the animal organism is to act as a "filter", letting through selectively into immediate awareness such memories as may be relevant in attending to the situations in which one is placed. But by reversing the practical habits of the intellect (always to Bergson primarily a way of thinking shaped by practical needs), it may be possible through contemplative Intuition to draw on a wider range of the resources of consciousness. Bergson was here impressed by the work of Charcot on amnesia, and by experimental work on hypnotically recovered memories. He was writing before Freud's theory of the unconscious mind had been put forward, and he uses the word "consciousness" broadly and not only for such experiences as are within the focus of attention. Indeed he imagines a rudimentary form of consciousness in all living organisms, and is prepared to interpret them by what he calls an "inverted psychology".

Bergson's theory of knowledge, drawn in terms of the contrast between Intellect and Intuition, is correlated with a view of the function of these within the process of Evolution. Intelligence, Bergson holds, begins with the making of tools. "Instinct" he describes as an innate power of using natural instruments, either parts of the organism itself, or materials directly found in the environment. Intelligence is first of all a power of making tools as artificial instruments: *homo faber*, the smith, rather than *homo sapiens*, would describe man at the dawn of intelligence. So intelligence starts from the interest in practical construction; it always bears the stamp of this practical interest, and finds its model of intelligibility in artefacts, which are discontinuous, isolatable systems, repeatable as specified types. Instinct on the other hand is continuous with the organizing power of life; but it is unreflective and unadaptive. When it can become disinterested and self-conscious, it is Intuition, and then it can carry forward the original impetus of life into the creation of new forms. Bergson interprets evolution as the outcome of an impulse of life (*élan vital*) manifesting itself in innumerable forms. This is not finalist teleology in the classical sense, which Bergson calls "inverted mechanism", development tied to the realisation of predetermined ends. Nor is it vitalism as ordinarily understood, since no "vitalist principle" is invoked over and above the physico-chemical components of organisms. Rather, the whole of nature is said to be the outcome of a force which thrusts itself forward into new and unforeseen forms of organised structure. These store and utilize energy, maintaining their power of growth and adaptive novelty up to a point, and then relapse into repetitive routine,

and ultimately into the degradation of energy. The universe, Bergson says, shows two tendencies: there is "a reality which is making itself in a reality which is unmaking itself". The laws of the tendency to repetition and the dissipation of energy are the laws of "matter"; the counter tendency is the thrust of "life". Here, in *L'Evolution Créatrice*, "matter" is represented as a real tendency in nature, inverse to life, and representing the running down of life into uniformity. Bergson also speaks of "matter" as the picture formed by the artificial fixing of a system of spatialized concepts by the intellect. Possibly the link is to be found in the belief that the more things display the tendency inverse to life, the more they are amenable to this kind of intellectual treatment. But the notion of pure matter, and indeed the notion of a purely free and creative life impulse, would be abstractions. What is routine and mechanical and what is living and creative are never in fact, as Bergson often acknowledges, found in complete separation from each other. But his concern to bring out the difference between them underlies his whole work; and it finds a special application in *Les deux sources de la morale et de la réligion* (1932). Here Bergson turns from biology to moral and religious sociology. He describes the "closed" morality and religion based on social custom as the conservative force of a limited society making for the solidarity and preservation of a social group. His analysis follows closely that of the French sociological school of Durkheim. The demand for solidarity and stability stops at the cohesion of limited groups. Groups cohering by closed morality are always limited groups, not just by definition, but because their way of life is maintained through real or possible conflict with other groups. Humanity as a whole does not therefore form a group of this kind; and those persons, prophets and saints, who are charged with an outgoing love towards humanity, are drawing on a different source. The analogy of closed morality to the repetitive mechanisms studied by the intellect is apparent; the "open" morality and religion are forms of intuition, and their source is a direct contact with the springs of life in the *élan vital*. In this last book Bergson is prepared to call it "love" which is "either God or from God". Whether he was received into the Roman Catholic Church is not publicly known; he is reported to have held back until just before his death in order to maintain his solidarity with the Jewish people in their time of troubles.

Bergson's works are written in a non-technical, flowing and persuasive style. They show wide knowledge of the biology and psychology of his day, and an enthusiastic, sometimes visionary, power. Other philosophers have, however, remarked on his tendency to write in unexplained metaphors, and on the lack of rigorous exposition of his central concepts, notably those of *durée* and the *élan vital*, and of the case for their supposed identity. (D.M.E.)

Plate 16, page 48.

Berkeley, George (1685–1753), was born in Ireland, in the neighbourhood of Kilkenny. His ancestors were English and Protestant, but Berkeley passed his early and later years entirely in Ireland, and, though he was always of the Anglican faith, appears to have regarded himself as decidedly an Irishman. He was excellently educated, first at Kilkenny College, and, from 1700, at Trinity College, Dublin, of which he was subsequently a Fellow for many years. He was ordained in 1707, became Dean of Derry in 1724, and Bishop of Cloyne ten years later. He married in 1728. He died in 1753, while supervising the introduction of his son George to Christ Church, in Oxford and his grave is in the Cathedral there.

Berkeley's life is noteworthy, apart from his philosophical writings, chiefly for his curious attempt in middle life to introduce a university to Bermuda. The aim of this scheme was mainly missionary. Berkeley hoped to attract to his college not only the colonial settlers of America, but also some of the indigenous Indians, there to be trained as ministers of religion and apostles of culture. Berkeley, whose energies, powers of persuasion, and ingenuous charm were remarkable, succeeded in securing much public and official support for his project. He obtained a charter, a large sum of money by private subscription, and the promise from Parliament of a subvention from public funds. But his scheme was really impracticable, and was in the end seen to be so. Bermuda – as he was perhaps not clearly aware – is far too distant from the American mainland to have been a suitable site for his purposes; and after he had left for America

in 1728, hesitations and doubts began to prevail at home. Berkeley waited abroad almost three years for his grant to be paid over, but in 1731 the Prime Minister, Walpole, let it be known that his hopes were not to be gratified. The house at Newport, Rhode Island which Berkeley built and inhabited is still preserved.

The works on which Berkeley's fame chiefly rests were written when he was a very young man. By the time he first visited England in 1713, being then twenty-eight, he had already published his *Essay towards a New Theory of Vision* (1709) and his *Principles of Human Knowledge* (1710), and the *Three Dialogues between Hylas and Philonous* were published in that year. In his later philosophical writings he did little more than defend, explain, and at certain minor points amend, the views thus early developed. It is, in fact, clear from his correspondence that for long periods of his later life he did not occupy his thoughts with philosophy at all. In this respect he differs strikingly from Locke, whose main work did not appear till he was nearly sixty; and in fact the young Berkeley, who was early acquainted with Locke's writings, is apt to refer to Locke's thoughts as those of a very old man – as admirable, indeed, for one so advanced in years.

Berkeley is a most striking, and indeed a unique, phenomenon in the history of philosophy. There have been many philosophers who have constructed bold and sweeping, and often extraordinary, metaphysical systems. There have been some also, particularly in the English tradition, employed in the clarification and defence of "common sense". There have been thinkers, again, devoted to the defence of religious faith. It is the peculiar achievement of Berkeley that, with astonishing ingenuity and skill, he contrived to present himself in all these roles at once. This achievement exactly suited his temperament, in which a taste for ambitious metaphysical doctrine was combined with strong religious beliefs and with a solid respect for ordinary good sense; but it was of course due only to his insight and intellectual power that he was able so to frame his theories as to yield him rational satisfaction also. His synthesis of these usually incompatible roles is doubtless unstable, and few of his readers have been able to follow him in it. At first, to his great chagrin, he was seen *merely* as a fantastic metaphysician; more recently, he has found occasional defenders as being *merely* the advocate of "common sense". But if one is to feel the full force of his theories, it is essential to see how in them three diverse aspects are combined.

Berkeley's position is best understood by contrast with **Locke**'s – this course following, in fact, its actual historical development. The picture of the world which, in his student reading, Berkeley found in Locke was roughly as follows: The universe is really, according to Locke, a mechanical system of bodies in space. It is *made*, as it were, of Matter; and material bodies really possess just those qualities required for their mechanical mode of operation – "solidity, figure, extension, motion or rest, and number". These bodies operate on, among other things, the sense-organs of human beings, who possess minds – "immaterial substances" – as well as bodies. When this occurs, the mechanical stimulation of the sense-organs and brain causes "ideas" to arise in the mind, and these are the objects of which the observer is really aware. In some respects these ideas faithfully represent the actual character of the "external world", but in others not; ideas of, for instance, sound, colour, and smell have no real counterparts in the world, but are only modes in which an observer so constituted is affected by the appropriate mechanical stimuli.

Now Berkeley soon came to regard this picture of the world as at once ridiculous, dangerous, and detestable. It was ridiculous, he thought, because it clearly entailed a fantastic scepticism, in manifest conflict with good common sense. For how could an observer, who was aware of nothing but his own ideas, know *anything* about Locke's "external world"? Locke himself had asserted, absurdly enough, that colour, for instance, is only an apparent, not a real, feature of that world; but how could he know that, in *any* respect, contemplation of our own ideas apprises us correctly of the world's actual character? A **sceptic** has only to suggest the possibility that our ideas mislead us, not only in some ways, but in every way, as to the character of objects, and it is evident that Locke could in no way counter this suggestion. Locke is thus committed to the ridiculous view that, for all we can *know*, objects in the world may be utterly unlike what we take them to be – and perhaps that, for all we can *know*, there may be no such objects. This is surely repugnant to any man of good sense.

But Locke's doctrine, he believed, was also exceedingly dangerous. For, apart from its offering a general pretext for scepticism, its tendency was towards **materialism** and atheism, and therefore, in Berkeley's view, towards the subversion of morals. God was brought in by Locke as the designer, creator, and starter of the great Machine; but how could he show that Matter itself was not eternal? And if it were, would his system not make it possible, and even rational, to deny the existence of God altogether? Again, Locke himself had held that consciousness belonged to "immaterial substances", which doubtless he would have regarded as immortal souls. But he had confessed that he could not disprove the counter-suggestion that consciousness might be just one of the properties of matter, and so, presumably, wholly dependent on the maintenance of certain material, physical conditions. His theory was thus in some danger of permitting – if it did not actually encourage – denial of the existence of God and of the immortality of the soul; and with this denial, in Berkeley's opinion, religion fell, and dragged morality after it.

Finally, it is clear, though it is less explicitly asserted, that Berkeley was utterly oppressed and repelled by the notion that the Universe is really a vast machine. Those metaphors of clocks and engines, wheels and springs, in which Locke delighted, inspired in Berkeley the utmost detestation. The world, he felt, *could not* be really like this – particularly if, in order to maintain that it is, we have to assert that its actual appearance is delusive; that, in fact, the "visible beauty of creation" is to be regarded as nothing but a "false imaginary glare". Why should we deny the evidence of our senses, in order to believe that the Universe is so repulsive?

Now Berkeley perceived – and it struck him as a revelation – what seemed to be a bold but beautifully simple means of eliminating, at one blow, all these horrors and absurdities. It was necessary only to *deny the existence of Matter*. For what would be the consequences of this? First, the actual course of our everyday experience would be quite unaffected. On Locke's own admission, we are never actually aware of anything but our own ideas; to deny the existence, then, of his "external objects", material bodies, is not to take away anything that has ever entered into our experience, and is indeed to leave quite undisturbed the opinions of un-philosophical men. But not only so; it must also put an end to all sceptical questioning. For Locke was obliged to concede to the sceptic that our ideas might mislead us as to the character of things, precisely because he had regarded things as being something *other* than our ideas. But if instead we adopt the view that things – the ordinary objects of experience – are just "collections of ideas", it will then be manifestly impossible to suggest that things may not be as they appear to us, and even more so to suggest that their very existence is doubtful. If an orange is not an "external" material body, but a collection of ideas, then I may be – as of course any man of good sense actually is – entirely certain that it exists, and that it really has the colour, taste, texture, and aroma that I find in it. Doubts on so simple a point could only seem to arise as a result of the needless assertion that things exist, *distinct* from and in addition to the ideas we have.

We may next see how Berkeley counters two serious objections. First, must it not be admitted that our ideas have *causes*? We do not simply produce our ideas ourselves; they plainly come to us from some independent source; and what could this be, if not the "external objects" of Locke's theory? Now Berkeley admits that our ideas are caused; but to take them to be caused in the way supposed by Locke is, he holds, both needless and impossible. It is needless, for we can suppose them to be caused by God; we can suppose that it is directly by the will of God that ideas occur in our minds as they do, with such admirable order and regularity. And it is in fact impossible, he holds, that they should be caused otherwise; for to *cause* is to *act*, and nothing is genuinely active but the *will* of an intelligent being.

But, it may secondly be objected, if Matter is denied, what becomes of physics? It is plainly impossible to dismiss the discoveries of Newton and his fellows as mere moonshine; but Matter, in the form of particles or "corpuscles", is precisely that of which they have discovered and proved so many of the properties. What is there for the laws of physics to hold true of, if there are really no material bodies?

Berkeley's earliest reflections on this objection were rather evasive; but later, notably in the *De Motu* of 1721, he devised a strikingly ingenious reply in which, though running hopelessly against the main tendency of his age, he anticipated the ideas of many of our own contemporary philosophers of science. He answered, in effect, that scientific theories are not true of anything at all. Certainly, if correct, they *apply* to the world of our experience, in that they enable us both to predict and in some degree to control its course; but their function is no more than that of predictive devices. The theory of the corpuscular structure of matter, for example, makes possible the exact mathematical expression of formulae, by the use of which we can make invaluable predictions; but there is no need to make the supposition that the corpuscles and particles of that theory actually exist. That there are such corpuscles is a theoretically useful supposition; so long as it proves useful it should ocntinue to be made; but it should never be re-garded as a literal truth. Thus, the practice of science need not be disturbed by Berkeley's doc-trines; it is necessary only for the scientist to own that he is not investigating "the nature of things", but rather perfecting the formulation of predictive devices.

It ought to be mentioned here also that, in the belief that the errors of earlier thinkers, notably of Locke, had been due in part to linguistic unclarity, Berkeley devoted the Introduction of his *Principles* to an investigation of language. In that passage he rather unfairly interprets Locke's vague expres-sions always in their least favourable, most vulner-able sense. But his own insistence that the essence of language lies in its use, and on the concrete understanding of expressions in definite contexts, makes this one of his most original and stimulating contributions to philosophy.

Two of Berkeley's later works may be mentioned briefly. His *Alciphron* is a long work in dialogue form, in which the tenets of Anglican orthodoxy are defended against various current types of "free-thinking" and **deism**. Though able enough, it suffers from the artificiality of the convention, and has little interest now that the controversies which prompted it are dead. Berkeley's last work was *Siris*, a very extraordinary production, in which a strangely rambling, ponderous, and speculative statement of some part of his earlier opinions leads on to an enquiry into the virtues of tar-water, a medicine which Berkeley made popular, and for the promotion of which he worked in his later years with almost eccentric zeal.

Berkeley's main work was slow to exert any influence on philosophy, though his limited first work on vision became fairly well known. His criticisms of Locke were for the most part powerful and well-taken; and the transition to his own remarkable doctrine of a theocentric, non-material universe, whose *esse* was *percipi* (which existed because it was perceived), and in which human beings were conceived of as conversing directly with the mind of God, was at least a triumph of ingenuity. But this doctrine was too extraordinary to be taken seriously; the fact that, so far as actual experience went, he could represent it as coinciding with the customary views of ordinary people was felt, rightly, to be not enough to make it actually the same; and Berkeley was not welcomed as the defender of common sense. Even his criticism of Locke was deprived of much of its effect, since it appeared to lead straight into a position still less defensible; and his philosophy of science was then much less acceptable than it would be, if it were propounded today. It was then generally accepted that physical theory was merely a kind of extension of ordinary observation, revealing truths of just the same kind as those of common experience. Today this has become somewhat difficult to believe; but to deny it then was probably felt, rightly enough in Berkeley's case, to constitute a veiled attempt to undermine the physicist's prestige. There is no doubt that this was Berkeley's intention; he had the bad luck to detest the "scientific worldview", at a time when that view was in the first flush of its ascendancy.

Today the ordinary student of Berkeley is most likely to regard him as a pioneer of **phenomenalism**. It is certainly true that it was part of his doctrine to maintain that material objects were – could be reduced to, or analysed as sets or collections of ideas as he said, of sense-data as his successors would say. This is, moreover, the classic rejoinder to theories of "indirect" perception, such as Locke had classically expounded. It must, however, not be forgotten that Berkeley, unlike his recent successors, was not engaged in cool and neutral philosophical analysis. His phenomenalism was, in his hands, primarily an ontological thesis;

he genuinely wished to deny that matter exists that there are any really material things. He was happy, indeed, to believe that ordinary opinion, could be so analysed as to conform with his ontology, and he believed that they *ought* to be understood in that way. He was, however, consciously and deliberately, as Locke had been almost inadvertently, a metaphysician, not merely an analyst.

It was remarked above that the result of Berkeley's ingenious attempt to unify metaphysics and common sense is unstable. This instability may be located in his use, adopted from Locke, of the term "idea". Berkeley's use of this term (like Locke's) is not so much ambiguous as insufficiently determinate. When he wishes to bring out the common sense aspect of his doctrine, he stresses that he means by "ideas" the *things* that we perceive; when he speaks as an ontologist, affirming that *esse* is *percipi* and that matter does not exist, he insists that ideas are "only in the mind". It seems likely that, if his use of this term were more closely scrutinized and made more precise, his theory would become not so much less plausible, as almost impossible to state. In so far as it depends on fluidity at this key point, it does not stand firm. (G.J.W.)

Plate 17, page 97.

Black, Max (1909–). He was born in Russia but obtained his formal education in England, and since 1940 has been teaching philosophy in the USA. He is at present Professor of Philosophy at Cornell University. Black's major professional interests are in the foundations of logic and mathematics, the theory of knowledge, and the philosophies of language and of science. The temper of his thought is empirical and analytical, and he has been a vigorous defender of both common sense and scientific knowledge against various forms of hostile criticism. Although his outlook has been influenced by **Russell**, **Moore** and the **Logical Positivists**, he has nonetheless been an acute critic of various doctrines advocated by these thinkers. Moreover, while he has been a prominent exponent of the linguistic method of philosophic analysis associated with **Wittgenstein**, he has not been an orthodox follower of this approach, either in his use of the method of linguistic analysis or in his choice of problems to which he has applied the method. On the contrary, Black has been a philosophical free lance, and has made judicious use of a variety of intellectual techniques in his discussions of a wide range of specific issues.

Black has stressed the importance of examining philosophical questions with attention carefully fixed on the context that determines the meanings of the terms entering into the formulation of those questions. He has tried to show that many traditional philosophical puzzles (such as the problem whether one can know that other minds exist, or the problem of demonstrating in wholesale fashion the validity of inductive inferences) are spurious, largely because the statements of these questions violate this requirement of contextual analysis. However, he has not yet published any systematic treatment either of the philosophy of language or of science, although he has made important constructive analyses of a number of concepts fundamental to these subjects. In particular, he has not only produced searching critiques of various traditional and recent philosophies of **induction**; he has also outlined an inductive procedure for validating principles of inductive reasoning without invoking question-begging assumptions.   (E.N.)

Blanshard, Brand (1892–). He is the most prominent American exponent of a viewpoint developed from the absolute **idealism** which flourished in Oxford in the earlier part of this century. His most important work is *The Nature of Thought* (1939); here he describes, partly in psychological, partly in logical terms the development of human thought. Thought can, and must, be described in psychological terms, but we will not understand its development unless we see it as guided by a logical ideal. The logical ideal is a system, such as is conceived in the coherence theory of **truth**, in which all thoughts are necessarily connected with each other. We must seek necessity everywhere, and attempts to reduce it to the empirical, as in **Hume**'s theory of causation, or to the trivial, as in conventionalist or linguistic theories of the **a priori**, are subjected by Blanshard to sustained attack.
                                        (J.O.U.)

Boethius, Anicius Manlius Severinus (*c.* 480– *c.* 524), born in Rome, into one of the great senatorial families, the *Gens Anicia*. Boethius accepted public service under Theodoric, the Ostrogoth ruler of Italy, and rose to high office. Later,

as a result of political intrigue by his enemies he was disgraced and was executed. His most celebrated work, the *De Consolatione Philosophiae*, was composed while he was in jail.

Boethius's importance in the history of philosophy, however, rests not only upon his authorship of the *Consolation*, but perhaps even more upon his effort to translate and transmit to the Latin West the collected wisdom of the Greeks.

His declared intention was to translate and comment on all the works of **Plato** and **Aristotle**, but of this he achieved no more than the translation of the Aristotelian logical writings together with Porphyry's introductory *Isagoge*. For centuries, however, these remained the only sources of direct access to Aristotle's philosophy available to western thought.

It is in his commentary on Porphyry's *Isagoge* that Boethius, though he elsewhere gives Aristotle's solution, allows his own platonising sympathies to lead him into the famous formulation of the problem of **Universals**, "whether *genera* and *species* actually subsist or are found in the mind and intellect alone". This formulation proved both a starting point and a stumbling block in the controversy which played so large a part in early medieval philosophizing.

Boethius was further instrumental in transmitting a knowledge of Greek scientific methodology by his translations and classification of the four mathematical disciplines, Arithmetic, Music, Geometry and Astronomy. This *quadrivium* of study which follows upon the *trivium* of Grammar, Rhetoric and Dialectic provided a systematic approach by way of the "Seven Liberal Arts" to education. Elaborated later by Cassiodorus and by Isidore of Seville, this arts curriculum survived the Dark Ages in the monastic and court schools of the West, to become fully established in the medieval university system.

The authenticity of his theological writings is now fully accepted. In these Boethius again sets before his heirs a pattern of theological method and of the rigorous application of **logic** to the analysis of Christian doctrine which became a paradigm for subsequent theologians.

Lastly, it would be hard to exaggerate the importance of the *De Consolatione Philosophiae* in the history of European thought. No book was more widely read and it was early translated into the vernacular.

The opening sections give, through the mouth of the lady Philosophy, the conventional answers, **Stoic** and Platonic, of pagan wisdom in reply to Boethius's account of his misfortunes. Thereafter the Christian convictions of the author give a positive direction to the argument and true goodness is found on analysis to consist only in union with God. There follows a discussion of the problem presented by the existence of evil in a world governed by a benevolent providence and of the difficulty of establishing a relationship between the free human agent and the foreknowledge of God.

The *Consolation* was both a vehicle for the transmission of ancient wisdom and a model for philosophizing for the next thousand years.

Plate 18, page 98. (J.G.D.)

Bonaventura (1221–1274) was the name given to John of Fidanza, canonized in 1482. Born in Italy, Bonaventura joined the Franciscan order and studied under Alexander of Hales in Paris. Here he later held the Franciscan Chair of Theology contemporaneously with his Dominican counterpart, Thomas **Aquinas**. He died in 1274 while taking part in the Council of Lyons.

His philosophical doctrines are to be found mainly in his commentary on the *Sentences* of Peter Lombard and in the two short treatises, the *Itinerarium Mentis in Deum* and the *De Reductione Artium ad Theologiam*.

Bonaventura's work in Paris coincided with the debates occasioned by the impact of the full **Aristotelian** corpus of scientific writings upon the West and the rising importance of **Averroism** in the Universities. His philosophical position can best be understood as a relatively conservative reaction on the part of a man who was primarily a theologian and a return to a systematic elaboration of the Platonising philosophical content which is to be found in the writings of **Augustine**. So we find the explicit and formulated presentation in Bonaventura of the typical Augustinian theses concerning man's knowledge of God, the seminal reasons, the soul as a substance, and an illuminationist theory of knowledge.

Bonaventura regards all true speculation as a search for God. This may begin with investigation of the physical world which bears the imprint of its Creator, the *vestigia Dei*. It is only in the study of himself, however, and in acquaintance with his own soul which is an image of God, *imago Dei*, that man can begin to achieve true knowledge. Exercising his memory, his understanding and his will, under the influence of divine illumination, man is led to the contemplation of God, not as a cause through His effects but immediately and ecstatically.

Though Duns **Scotus** later became the official Doctor of the Franciscans, Bonaventura, the *Doctor Seraphicus*, is perhaps more truly characteristic of the deeply religious outlook of the Order.

Plate 19, page 99. (J.G.D.)

Boole, George (1815–1864), was born in Lincoln, England. Though entirely self-educated, he became a mathematician of distinction and in 1849 was appointed to the Chair of Mathematics at Queen's College, Cork. Two years earlier, he had published a short book, *The Mathematical Analysis of Logic*, which has come to be regarded as the first substantial step towards modern mathematical logic. *An Investigation of the Laws of Thought*, published in 1854, though better known, is important chiefly for its application of Boole's logical algebra to the theory of probability.

Earlier mathematicians, in particular Gregory and Peacock, had shown that algebraic methods can be used to represent relations between entities other than numbers. The basic idea of Boole's logic is the use of methods, substantially equivalent to those of ordinary algebra, to operate on variables, x, y, z, ... standing for classes and the symbols 1 and 0 standing respectively for the universal class and the empty class (though the use of these terms was not introduced by Boole himself.) In Boole's symbolism, if "x" represents a class, say, the class of red things, "$(1 - x)$" or "$\bar{x}$" for short, stands for the complementary class of things that are not red. Operations corresponding to addition, subtraction and multiplication in ordinary algebra are introduced. If "x" stands for the class of red things and "y" for the class of square things, then "xy" stands for the product of the two classes, the things that are both red and square. And "$x + y$" stands for the class of things that are either red or square but not both. (This exclusive sense of "+" distinguishes Boole's algebra from most later versions.)

With this notation we can represent a limited class of statements of logical importance. For example:

All men are mortal

becomes:

$$x(1 - y) = 0 \text{ or } x\bar{y} = 0$$

(that is, "the class of men who are not mortal is empty".)

Moreover, we can combine these expressions and operate on them in accordance with the rules of the algebra to derive other expressions from them and so solve problems involving logical relations between classes. These include the simple syllogism of classical logic as well as other much more complex problems.

In another application of the algebra to hypothetical propositions, Boole came near to discovering the truth-table technique later developed by C. S. **Peirce** and modern logicians. Boole's ideas were developed by later workers, in particular, by Schröder, and the study of Boolean algebra is a recognized branch of modern mathematics.

Plate 20, page 100. (D.J.O'C.)

Bosanquet, Bernard (1848–1923), born in Alnwick, England. He gave up his Oxford teaching in 1881 to devote the rest of his life to writing and to social work. He was the last British philosopher to work out a complete system of philosophy covering all types of human experience. His work was influenced mainly by **Hegel** and was based on the conception of individuality understood as the harmony of a variety of differences, the individual as "concrete universal", in contrast with the "abstract universal" found in scientific reasoning operating by general laws and the elimination of differences. This notion of individuality he found expressed in human persons, in works of art, in the State, and supremely in the Absolute as the final ideal transcending and unifying all these subordinate "concrete universals".

Late in his life he fell more under the influence of F. H. **Bradley** and became more doubtful about the power of reason, to grasp the unities met with in experience. The individuality of a person or picture required the conception of a type of unity in which the variety could not be so clearly distinguished nor the elements so rationally related as Hegel had supposed. (J.D.M.)

Plate 21, page 101.

Bradley, Francis Herbert (1846–1924), English philosopher. A research Fellow of Merton College, he lived the whole of his adult life at Oxford. He suffered from poor health and was naturally retiring and reserved, and he devoted himself completely to philosophical thinking and writing. He wrote in a brilliant and trenchant style, with a force and vigour seldom equalled in English philosophy.

He was influenced in his youth by **Hegel** and the German logicians who followed him, but his philosophy was uniquely his own.

In his first book, *Ethical Studies*, he criticizes utilitarian theories from a Hegelian angle and works out a theory of self-realisation which is also Hegelian in its general design. The self is to be realised in self-conscious membership of the state (which is understood as an organic unity of spiritual beings) and not in isolated self-cultivation. The essay in this volume entitled "My Station and its Duties" is indeed the best short statement in English of the Hegelian conception of morality. But in the next essay "Ideal Morality" Bradley passes beyond these Hegelian concepts of rational unity and of moral right as supremely embodied in Law and the State. Many fields such as science and art and philosophy itself provide moral ends and fields of self-realisation independent of national frontiers and civic allegiance; and in the last resort morality itself is unintelligible and internally incomplete and attains its completeness only by moving on into religion.

In *Principles of Logic* Bradley next worked out a complete survey of logical forms shewing how each finds its place in the hierarchy of human reason. But he emphasized at every point that all these forms arise from a basic experience of immediate feeling whose unity they all fail to express. They all therefore involve an element of unavoidable subjectivity and error.

Appearance and Reality, which followed the *Logic* is Bradley's greatest work. Here, in the first part, he subjects to a relentless dialectical criticism all the general categories of human thought and experience. In arguments reminiscent of **Zeno** of Elea and of **Kant's** antinomies, he shows that quality and relation, substance and cause, space and time, self and object, are all of them, if taken as real, beset by insoluble contradictions and must therefore be dismissed as "appearance". The absolute reality must have a nature which transcends all these categories. Relations are grounded in the nature of their terms, and no term can be understood apart from its relations. Whether relations are regarded as completely external (in an atomism such as **Russell**'s) or as completely internal (as in the monadology of **Leibniz**), they fail to satisfy the demands of reason. Thus the whole relational mode of thinking – and in the end all modes of thinking are in one way or another relational – cannot claim to attain knowledge of reality. Reality must have a type of unity unlike anything in our worlds of rational thought, a unity above and beyond relations, a unity to whose nature only the undifferentiated unity of feeling gives any clue. This absolute reality differentiates itself into finite centres of experience which however cannot be identified with human persons because of the element of time which infects all human life. In the second part of *Appearance and Reality* it is argued that each category of human experience, whose final inadequacy had been demonstrated in the first part, must somehow find a place in the real, though taken up and transmuted in it; and each of them has a degree of reality corresponding to the extent to which it is comprehensive and self-consistent.

In his later work Bradley did not go back on his fundamental metaphysical position and the suprarational and even mystical or religious view of the real to which it leads. At the time of his death he was working on a long essay on relations, of which the incomplete draft published in the posthumous volume of his *Collected Essays* gives the best exposition available of this central part of his philosophy. But he developed steadily the positive argument of the second part of *Appearance and Reality* by emphasizing more strongly the partial truth to be found in the various logical and epistemological categories which many of his readers thought he had intended totally to destroy, and by elaborating his theory of degrees of truth. Each of these categories is now justified in its own sphere and degree; what is resisted is the claim of any one of them to be (or to be the model for) the whole truth. At the same time, and no doubt for similar reasons, his work became less

polemical and his style more mellow and tolerant.

Bradley's position in the history of philosophy is thus a curious one. He was probably the only first-rank philosopher England produced in the nineteenth century; and in brilliance and acuteness his only previous rival was **Hume**. Yet his influence was slight and his followers few. This was partly because he came at the end of the idealist movement, and partly because he was a very unorthodox representative of it, so that the few later idealists looked back not to him but to Hegel for their inspiration. There are indeed strands in recent theology which recall his metaphysical position, but they do not seem to have had any links with his work. Though his main tenets have won little acceptance he can still be read with profit for three reasons: first for the vigour and effectiveness of his style; secondly, because his devastating criticisms of utilitarian, associationist, individualist, and pragmatist theories remain of use against such tendencies, which are liable to tempt each new generation of philosophical students; thirdly because his work in philosophical psychology on such subjects as memory, imagination, and introspection has permanent importance. (J.D.M.)

Plate 22, page 102.

Braithwaite, Richard Bevan (1900–), English philosopher, Knightbridge Professor of Moral Philosophy in the University of Cambridge since 1953; since 1924 a Fellow of King's College, Cambridge, where he studied first physics, then mathematics, and then philosophy. Though mainly a philosopher of science, he has also been interested in giving an account of religious belief which would make it tenable for the thoroughgoing empiricist, and in putting moral choice on a rational basis by applying the mathematical theory of games to conflict-situations. This use of the theory of games developed by statisticians is the chief innovation in his main work *Scientific Explanation*, where he draws on it for "the prudential policy" for making choices between statistical hypotheses; this provides a rejection procedure, and so guarantees that probability statements have an empirical meaning, by allowing them to be *provisionally* refutable by experience, the rejection being subject to revision after each new series of tests. This procedure is unnecessary for the limiting case, that of universal statements, which are of course open to *conclusive* refutation (by a single counter-instance). In the same book he explains the use of "models", theoretical concepts, and mathematical reasoning in scientific theories, and also discusses the status of laws of nature. (R.HALL)

Plate 23, page 103.

Brentano, Franz, (1838–1916), German-Austrian philosopher, who made important contributions to philosophical psychology. Born in the Rhineland, Brentano became a Professor of Philosophy at the Catholic University of Würzburg, but resigned his chair and his priesthood after the declaration of Papal Infallibility in 1871. He accepted a philosophical chair at Vienna, but resigned it in 1880, returning later as an instructor. His last years were spent in Florence. His two most important works are *Psychology from the Empirical Standpoint* (published 1874, second edition 1911), and *The Origin of Ethical Knowledge* (published 1889), which influenced **Moore** in writing *Principia Ethica*. His posthumously published work is considerable and valuable.

In his *Psychology* Brentano is out to provide a "psychognosy", that is a logical geography of mental concepts, which will serve as an indispensable preliminary to an empirical psychology. He assumes without question that the world contains *two* sorts of "phenomena", the physical and the "psychical", and seeks to find (a) some feature or features which will be *distinctive* of "psychic phenomena"; (b) certain "basic classes" into which psychic phenomena may be divided.

As regards the differentiae of the psychical, Brentano holds these to be (a) "intentionality" or directedness to objects; (b) direct and inerrant revelation to an "inner perception", which is one with the act perceived. By the term "intentionality" (derived from the Scholastic *esse intentionale*) Brentano means what is revealed by the fact that most mental verbs are senseless (or only elliptically significant) in the absence of appropriate *object*-expressions, which state *what* the mental activity expressed by the verb is concerned with. Thus if I am said to observe, my observation is for example *of* a house or a tree; if I am said to doubt, my doubt is, for example *about* the equality of 2 + 2 to 4; if I am said to be pleased, there must be something I am

pleased *with*, etc. etc. In his second edition Brentano makes the all-important point that intentionality is not a relation between the mind and an object: it is merely *relational* or *relationlike (relativlich)*. A relation to an *X* would entail that an *X* existed, whereas a mental directedness to an *X* usually does not. What is distinctive of Brentano's position is that he thinks this "relationlikeness" is ultimate and needs no further analysis.

In his classification of Mental Phenomena Brentano admits only three Ground-Classes: (a) Presentations (*Vorstellungen*) in which some object is simply present to mind; (b) Judgments, in which something is *accepted* as real or factual, or *rejected* as the reverse; (c) Phenomena of Love and Hate, that is cases of affective-conative acceptance or rejection. In the case of (a) there is no distinction of correctness or incorrectness, but in the case of (b) there is such a distinction, the criterion of which is an inward self-evidence (*Evidenz*). In regard to (c) Brentano holds that certain acts of liking, disliking or preferring have an inwardly self-justifying character which mediates the knowledge of what is absolutely good, evil or better. Pleasure, for example, is absolutely good. (J.N.F.)

Broad, Charlie Dunbar (1887–), English philosopher, Fellow of Trinity College, Cambridge, and Knightbridge Professor of Moral Philosophy 1933–53. Earlier, after lecturing at St Andrews and Dundee, he was Professor of Philosophy at Bristol. Strongly influenced by many previous Cambridge philosophers, including **Russell** and **Moore** as well as W. E. Johnson and **McTaggart** (whose main work he subjected to an intensive three-volume examination), he owes little to foreign influences, and nothing at all to **Wittgenstein**, who influenced most Cambridge philosophers profoundly. His original training in the physical sciences, combined with a cool and cautious temperament, has governed his whole approach to philosophy, in which he never expects or claims to reach conclusions that have certainty, but only those that have the balance of probabilities in their favour; indeed he often avoids committing himself to *any* particular conclusion, being content to set out the relative merits and demerits of competing theories. Broad claims for himself neither the task of construction nor of demolition, but "at most the humbler (yet useful) power of stating difficult things clearly and not too superficially". While admitting that speculative philosophy, which reaches general conclusions about the nature of the universe, has value, especially if like British Idealism it takes in social, moral, aesthetic, and religious considerations, he has regarded it as not for him. Not only has he denied finality even to future speculative systems, but he doubts that any attempt to construct one can be profitable without there first being a considerable advance in critical philosophy, the two main tasks of which are (1) "to analyse and define the concepts which are used in daily life and in the special sciences", such as place, person, cause, matter, change and perception, and having done this (2), to criticise the fundamental propositions which contain them. This type of philosophy makes progress, according to Broad, in so far as it replaces vague and instinctive beliefs by clear and analysed beliefs which have stood up to criticism. In carrying out parts of critical philosophy in this sense in a series of large books, some giving particular attention to the concepts of physics, his actual procedure has been for the most part the careful dissection of existing theories and possible alternatives and of the arguments for and against them, as for example in *The Mind and its Place in Nature*, where seventeen different theories of the relation between mind and matter are considered, the one most favoured being one type of "emergent materialism". In this book and other writings Broad takes an interest in psychical research: though not prepared to accept the possibility of immortality in the sense of survival (which he considers at length), he regards the alleged paranormal phenomena as due to the persistence after death of a "psychic factor", which had previously formed with the brain and nervous system a compound of which mentality was an emergent quality. Broad has also written on ethics, though here his interpretations of some great philosophers and the importance he ascribes to the work of H. **Sidgwick** are highly questionable. His greatest achievement, and the most difficult to follow, is his monumental work on McTaggart.

Plate 24, page 104. (R.HALL)

Butler, Joseph, (1692-1752), Bishop, holds a lastingly important place in English moral philosophy and philosophy of religion. His ethical thought is contained primarily in his *Fifteen Sermons* (1726) and his *Dissertation upon the Nature of Virtue*: his philosophy of religion in *The Analogy of Religion* (1736), to which the *Dissertation* was an appendix. These two sides of Butler's thought are most closely interconnected; for conscience is not only the crucial concept of his **ethics**, but it also provides an impressive disclosure of the being and nature of God. Virtue, to Butler, is natural to man, vice a violation of our nature, a kind of self-mutilation. Human nature is a complex structure that Butler likens to a watch with intricately co-operating parts, to a political constitution, and to a body with its component members. The full realising of this nature (and the attainment of virtue) involve the hierarchial subordination of its various elements under conscience. The promptings of hunger and thirst, appetition of all kinds, form the base of the hierarchy, as Butler conceives it. This group of "particular passions" is disciplined and regulated by benevolence – concern for the good of others – and by self-love – thought of not as the indulging of the passions, but as the control and management of them with a view to one's long-term, total well-being. Butler denied that self-love and benevolence were mutually antagonistic principles; indeed, the policies they initiate tend to coincide – for the most part in this world, and perfectly hereafter. Conscience is an essentially reflective and rational principle. It refuses to reduce all duties to one alleged supreme duty such as the production of the general happiness; our duties are multiple; and only God, with his synoptic and omniscient view, could afford to play the utilitarian. A measure of agnosticism pervades Butler's thought on account of his strong sense of human ignorance (the *Fifteenth Sermon* is devoted to this theme). Perhaps the most memorable features of his ethical thought, however, are the many shrewd analyses that make up his moral psychology; analyses of such concepts as forgiveness, resentment, self-deceit, compassion. Particularly effective among these are his arguments against **Hobbes'** egoistic interpretation of pity.

The Analogy of Religion was conceived as an answer to **deism**. The deists held that a natural and rational religion escaped a great many intractable difficulties that beset a religion based on alleged revelation. But Butler maintained that analogous difficulties belong to *both* spheres, although they are decisive against neither. "The design", he wrote, "of the following treatise will be to show, that the several parts principally objected against in this moral and Christian dispensation . . . are analogous to what is experienced in the constitution and course of Nature, or Providence; that the objections themselves which are alleged against the former, are no other than what may be alleged with like justice against the latter, where they are found in fact to be inconclusive . . ." As this suggests, Butler does not claim *a priori* certainty for his apologetic, but a probability high enough, he believes, to satisfy faith. (R.W.H.)

Plate 25, page 105.

C

Cajetan, Thomas de Vio, (1468–1534), born at Gaeta, Italy, died in Rome. He was Dominican Master-General, later Cardinal. The classical commentator on the *Summa Theologica* of Thomas **Aquinas**, he combined scholasticism and humanism, an extraordinary ability to pursue detailed abstraction and a robust common sense. His criticism of Scotism brought him to the problem of analogy, the use of the same name for different objects in more than a purely equivocal or metaphorical sense. He distinguished two proper types. The first is the analogy of attribution based on a causal connection; here the concept is attributed formally and intrinsically to the primary analogate, and to the others by an external designation, *denominatio extrinseca*. The second is analogy of proportionality; a pair of concepts proportionately similar are attributed formally to all the analogates. Only this, he held, meets the requirements of metaphysical thinking, and most Thomists have agreed with him, including the influential John of St Thomas (1589–1644). But not Francis Sylvester of Ferrara (1474–1528), his successor as Master-General and the author of the classical commentary on the *Summa Contra Gentiles*, who now leads a growing minority who would vindicate the dignity of attributional analogy in the light of causality. (T.G.)

Cambridge Platonists. A group of English philosophical theologians, for the most part centred on Cambridge and predominantly Puritan, they wrote and preached in the later seventeenth century. Best known among them are Ralph **Cudworth**, Richard Cumberland, Henry More, Benjamin Whichcote, John Smith and Joseph Glanvill.

Their writings contain a mass of erudition, philosophical, mystical, ancient and "modern", often uncritically employed and on the whole lacking in rigorous logical coherence. The thought of **Plato**, in particular, is seldom accurately differentiated from the speculations of **neoplatonists**. Nonetheless, the Cambridge Platonists made a considerable impact on the history of ideas, in **epistemology** and **ethics** as well as in theology. They attempted to disengage theological thinking from the polemics of the reformation and the earlier seventeenth century: to restore the emphasis upon religion as above all else a way of living, to give primacy to religious experience – often to mystical experience – instead of to doctrinal and credal controversy or to priest and ritual. To Henry More, who was most in sympathy with mysticism, the path to knowledge of God was not chiefly by the way of learning but by way of moral purification, a view that carries echoes of **Plotinus**. Joseph Glanvill's *The Vanity of Dogmatizing* is in the main a repudiation of intellectual pretention and arrogance, whether among the over-revered Ancients, in the scholastics or in moderns infected with the same vice. Real understanding, to Glanvill, starts only from a wholesome scepticism. The Platonists had themselves, however, a humble confidence in reason. Whichcote repeatedly reminded his reader that reason is "the candle of the Lord". Irrationalisms indeed, were as much part of their target as scholasticism; and the reconciling of reason and revelation – as distinct from the sacrificing of either in favour of the other – was the dominant aim of their work. The controversial issue to which they were most single-mindedly devoted was undoubtedly the refutation of the philosophy of **Hobbes**. Against his claim that matter and motion were adequate concepts for a philosophy of nature, Cudworth protested: ". . . as if there were not as much reality in fancy and consciousness as there is in local motion". The *activity* of mind, the reality of noncorporeal spirit, were thus strenuously argued for by the Platonists against all brands of materialism. More insisted that spirit must be thought of as extended, for otherwise it seemed to lack full reality. In pursuit of this view, he made infinite extension an attribute of God. Also against Hobbes, the Platonists denied that moral obligation was created by divine or by human authority. Moral right and wrong, good and bad, they claimed, are "eternal and immutable", the products of no decrees, orders or agreements. (R.W.H.)

Carnap, Rudolf (1891–), born in Germany. He taught philosophy at the University of Vienna and later at the German University in Prague, but left Europe in 1936 for the USA, where he has been Professor of Philosophy at the University of Chicago and since 1954 at the University of California in Los Angeles. He is generally acknowledged to be the leading living exponent of logical empiricism (or positivism), the internationally influential philosophical movement that originated with the **Vienna Circle.** This was an informal discussion group of scientifically oriented thinkers, who combined a sympathy for the anti-metaphysical positivism of the Viennese physicist-philosopher **Mach** with the cultivation of logical analysis as practised by **Russell** and the early **Wittgenstein.** Carnap was a member of this group for some years; and eventually he served as co-editor of *Erkenntnis,* the semi-official organ of logical empiricism, until it became a casualty of the Second World War. He still continues to be an editor of the *International Encyclopedia of Unified Science,* an incompleted series of monographs designed by the late Otto Neurath, another member of the Vienna Circle, to exhibit the essential methodological unity of the major scientific disciplines and to expound their foundations from the perspective of logical empiricism.

Carnap has been a prolific contributor to the theory of knowledge, mathematical logic, the philosophy of science, and the foundations of probability and induction. His writings are a large storehouse of ingenious technical analyses and innovations, they reveal an uncommon gift for architectonic construction, and they are models of formal precision and clarity. They also exhibit Carnap's readiness to revise his ideas repeatedly. For although the basic scientific and anti-metaphysical temper of his thought has not changed over the years, his detailed views on many issues have undergone important alterations.

One of Carnap's long-standing concerns has been the construction of an adequate criterion of cognitively meaningful discourse. He first adopted and developed a stringent form of what is commonly called "the verifiability theory of meaning". He maintained, in effect, that the meaning of a statement consists in the sensory or introspective data which establish the statement directly and conclusively. However, although it can readily be shown that on this criterion metaphysical utterances whose alleged content transcends the domain of possible experience are nonsensical (and not even false), Carnap soon recognized that the criterion also rules out as meaningless most if not all scientific statements. For various technical reasons he also came to view as unpromising the task he had set for himself (in his first major book, *Der Logische Aufbau der Welt,* 1928) of indicating in detail how every purportedly factual statement may be translated into statements about sense-data; and he eventually came to doubt the feasibility of such translations even into the language of everyday affairs and experimental physics. He has since sought to develop a more liberal version of the verifiability criterion of cognitive significance, one which could be a guide in constructing symbolic systems that are required in theoretical science but which would also help to demarcate metaphysical vagary from genuine scientific hypothesis. The general import of Carnap's currently proposed criterion is that a statement is meaningful if, and only if, the statement itself or some of its logical consequences can be tested by sensory observation.

Carnap's ideas on the province of philosophy have undergone an analogous liberalization. In his important *The Logical Syntax of Language* (1934), in which he formulated some of his characteristic views on logic, mathematics and the philosophy of science in rich detail, he defined logical syntax as the study of how the signs in a language are related to one another in virtue of their purely structural properties. He maintained that the laws of logic and mathematics make no assertions about any subject matter, but are simply linguistic structures whose *a priori* necessity within the language in which they occur is derived entirely from the conventionally instituted syntactical rules governing the use of that language. Moreover, he declared that philosophical controversies are usually generated by the confusion of "pseudo-object" statements (such as the claim that time extends infinitely in both directions, which he held equivalent to the syntactical statement about signs that any positive or negative real-number expression can be used as a time-coordinate) with genuine statements about some non-linguistic subject matter. He therefore concluded that philosophy should be identified with the logical syntax of the language of science. This recommendation apparently made illegitimate any consideration of the relations of signs to what they represented, and in particular outlawed any analysis of what is meant by factual truth. However, as was made evident by the work of Alfred Tarski, it is possible to develop a precise theory of semantics, which is concerned with the relations of signs to what they signify; and indeed, Carnap eventually made important contributions to this branch of logical analysis. In any event, he now enlarged his earlier conception of the scope of philosophy, and identified the latter (using the terminology of Charles **Morris**) with the semiotical analysis of the structure of cognitive discourse.

Carnap's main preoccupation during the past decade has been with the technical development of the logic of inductive inference. On his view, statements such as "It is highly probable on the available evidence that Smith is guilty as charged" cannot be explicated in terms of empirically ascertainable relative frequencies in some class of repeatable events, as can be done for a statement like "The probability of obtaining heads with a fair coin is one-half" (which in effect asserts that in a long series of tosses a coin falls uppermost about half the time). In statements of the first type, Carnap believes, the word "probable" refers to a logical relation between the evidence and the hypothesis based upon it. Since it is this logical sense of probability that Carnap thinks is the relevant one in evaluating the weight of the evidence for some conclusion in inductive inquiries, he has attempted to construct an explicit symbolism for this logical relation, and has also devised a variety of numerical measures for degrees of logical probability. However, although Carnap has already erected an imposing structure of ideas and theorems on this subject, the

structure is not completed, and its eventual value for scientific practice remains an open question.

(E.N.)

Cartesianism, *see* Descartes.

Cassirer, Ernst (1874–1945) built up his original reputation as an historian of philosophy, especially of that of the seventeenth century, and as a philosopher of science; but in his last years, which he spent in the United States, his original philosophical work came to be highly valued there and his influence can be traced in the writings of American philosophers such as S. K. Langer and C. W. Hendel. He was a product of the famous neo-Kantian school of Marburg and spent most of his teaching life at Berlin and Hamburg; but on the advent to power of the Nazis he moved first to England, then to Sweden and finally to the United States. He never rejected the Kantian philosophy which he learnt at Marburg, though he developed it. **Kant** had taught that human experience was conditioned by the categories, the forms of thought under which all phenomena were subsumed; in his *Philosophy of Symbolic Forms* Cassirer maintained that in addition to the Kantian categories informing scientific thought there are also forms of mythical thinking, historical thinking and everyday practical thinking, which could be brought to light by the study of the forms of expression in language. Each of these kinds of thinking is valid in its own right, and though scientific thought is a later development than mythical thought the latter is not merely primitive science. Cassirer's thought is difficult and expressed at very great length; his works all contain long and learned discussions of the linguistic, anthropological and philosophical work of his predecessors. (J.O.U.)

Categories. Aristotle borrowed "categoria" from legal parlance, where it meant "accusation", and stretched it to mean anything that could be asserted truly or falsely of anything. If we complete "Socrates is . . ." with any noun or adjective, or "Socrates. . ." with a verb, we ascribe a predicate to Socrates. Aristotle saw that predicates are of different types. To say of what kind Socrates is, for example a man or an animal, is very different from saying merely where or how heavy he is. Aristotle distinguished several ultimate predicate-types or Categories.

1. Kind, for example ". . . a man".
2. Quality, for example ". . . pale".
3. Quantity or size, for example ". . . six-foot".
4. Relation, for example ". . . older than Plato".
5. Location, for example ". . . in Athens".
6. Time or date, for example ". . . in the fifth century B.C.".
7. Action, for example ". . . argues".
8. Undergoing, for example ". . . being prosecuted".

Aristotle called several of his predicate-types after ordinary interrogatives, like What? Where? How big? and When? Any answer to "What is Socrates?" specifies a Kind, any answer to "Where" a Location, and so on. All predicates of one type will answer, truly or falsely, one interrogative and will not answer any other interrogative.

To most predicates, for example ". . . laughs" or ". . . shrewd", there correspond abstract nouns, like "Laughter" or "Shrewdness". If we ask What, ultimately, is Laughter? or Shrewdness? or Slavery? the answer names the appropriate category. "Laughter is an Action"; "Shrewdness is a Quality"; "Slavery is a Relation". But not all abstract nouns correspond to predicates. "Possible" is not a predicate, for example, of Socrates, so we cannot ask to what category possibility belongs. Predicates of Kind, like ". . . a man" and "gold" do not naturally yield abstract nouns. We speak of the brightness or remoteness of Venus, but not of her "heavenly bodihood". Her brightness or remoteness might alter or cease, but Venus could not become less or more of a body. If she ceased to be a body she would cease to be at all.

Moreover, to find a particular instance of brightness we have to find a particular *bright star* or *bright torch*, etc. An instance of brightness can be found only in a member of a Kind. But we find a specimen of *star* or *torch*, just in finding a star or torch. Brightness is something that for example, *this star* possesses. But being a star is not something extra that *this star* also possesses – else the question "Of what Kind is it?" would arise again about the possessor of this postulated property of being a star.

What made Aristotle want to discriminate predicate-types was perhaps partly this. When a thing alters, it ceases to be what it was. So, apparently,

Socrates, who is getting warm, being no longer what he was, cannot still be a man or Xanthippe's husband; which is absurd. To resolve this paradox it is helpful to be able to say that Socrates has changed from having one quality to having another, but this is not a change from one to another Kind, or from one to another Relation. We specify the general field of a change by specifying the category of the predicates between which the transition is. Though Socrates is never continuously the same age, he is continuously a human being. Not everything is in flux.

Kant gave to the word "category" a different philosophical use. For him a category is a structural principle exemplifiable in scientifically ascertainable facts. Thus all facts of the form "X's happening was due to Y's happening" come under the category of Cause and Effect. We know, before we find out the actual explanation of X, that there has to be an explanation with this structure.

Today the word "category" is used by philosophers, if at all, for any supposedly ultimate type, without any settled convention about what it is a type of. Without *ad hoc* elucidations the word is therefore nowadays a vague one.   (G.R.)

Chance, *see* Probability, Libertarianism.

Chrysippus, of Soli, Cilicia (*c.* 280–207 B.C.). He succeeded Cleanthes in 232 as third head of the Stoa. On coming to Athens about 260, he became a pupil in the Academy of Arcesilaus, from whom he acquired an extreme virtuosity in logic and dialectic. When converted to the Stoa, the School was suffering from divergent theories in the unorthodox systems of Ariston and Herillus, and from a severe attack from Academic **scepticism**. Chrysippus, in an enormous literary output which displayed his dialectical power, repelled attacks and formulated in great detail what became the definitive system of **stoicism**, justly winning the title of Second Founder. He was not an original thinker; he exercised his skill in refurbishing the fundamental doctrines of **Zeno** of Citium. "Give me the doctrines", he said with characteristic dry humour, "and I shall supply the proofs". But his relentless logic led to differences of detail most noticeable in his psychology and theory of knowledge. And as his logic drove him towards extreme positions, so the paradoxes inherent in Stoicism were spotlighted. To his boast "Without Chrysippus, there would have been no Stoa", Carneades, the most formidable opponent of Stoicism, could answer, "Without Chrysippus, there would have been no Carneades". (I.G.K.)

Cicero, Marcus Tullius (106–43 B.C.), Roman lawyer, politician and writer. Trained in philosophy from youth up, auditor and friend of the leading professors of the Academy, Stoa and Epicurean School, he maintained his interest and reading during his busiest years in public life. In 45, personal distress and political helplessness unleashed his full energies on making Greek philosophy accessible in Latin literary form. Within the next two years appeared a long series of works in dialogue form which covered the various departments of contemporary philosophy by expounding and criticising the doctrines of the three leading Schools. By temperament and training an Academic **sceptic**, in **ethics** he followed and widened the eclecticism introduced to the Academy by Antiochus. He admired the noble ideals of **stoicism**; to **Epicurus** he was unsympathetic. He thought of himself as a translator (in some cases his source books can be traced, for example, to Clitomachus, Philo, Antiochus, Panaetius, Posidonius), but he claimed the right of independent presentation and criticism. His aim was perhaps to naturalize Greek philosophy, as his predecessors, beginning with translations, had naturalized Greek literature; he thought with reason that the impact of his mastery of language and style could initiate the process. The creator of a Latin philosophical vocabulary which was to become current, his influence was immense, and he remains invaluable as a source for the three dominant Schools of his time. (I.G.K.)

Plate 27, page 107.

Clarke, Samuel (1675–1729), English philosopher who championed a Newtonian philosophy in opposition to the prevailing Cartesian climate of thought in the Cambridge of his day. In a famous correspondence with **Leibniz**, he maintained that space and time were infinite homogeneous entities, as against Leibniz's claim that they were ultimately relational. In *A Discourse Concerning the*

Being and Attributes of God (the Boyle lectures, 1704–5), he contended against "deniers of natural and revealed religion", **Hobbes** and **Spinoza** being notable targets. Morality to Clarke is based, not on the sheer power or the command of God, nor upon "contracts" brought into being by human communities, but on independent and self-evident relations between situations and the kind of actions they demand. A mistaken moral judgment is of the same logical order as a contradiction in mathematical reasoning. Joseph **Butler** found this rather too abstract a presentation of moral philosophy. But the most powerful criticism came from **Hutcheson** and **Hume**, who denied that moral judgment lay in the perceiving of relations, or in the activity of reason alone. Clarke had neglected the crucial role of the feelings or passions, or, in the language of more recent approaches to morals, he failed to see that decisions about what ought to be the case cannot be logically deduced from statements about what *is*. (R.W.H.)

Cohen, Morris R. (1880–1947), born in Russia. He emigrated to the United States as a boy, and from 1912 until his retirement in 1938 taught philosophy at The College of the City of New York. He was one of the most acute and learned philosophical minds of his generation, and wrote extensively on logic, the philosophy of science, social and legal philosophy, and intellectual history. Many of his students whom he influenced eventually established careers for themselves not only as teachers of philosophy but also as distinguished members of the American bar and bench.

Cohen was an outspoken **naturalist** in his general outlook, was a vigorous exponent of liberalism conceived as a faith in rational analysis, and he rejected every variety of supernatural and authoritarian interpretation of the universe and man's place in it. He was a sharp critic of *a priori* rationalism, whether of the **Leibnizian**, **Kantian** or **Hegelian** variety; and he carried on a life-long polemic against influential tendencies (especially in social and legal philosophy) to settle issues of concrete fact or policy on the basis of purely formal considerations. Nevertheless, he subscribed in essentials to a philosophical realism that had been advocated by the early **Russell**, maintaining with the latter that philosophy, like the sciences, succeeds in making significant intellectual advances only when it grapples in piecemeal fashion with limited and clearly formulated problems. He was indefatigably critical of sensationalistic (or **Humean**) empiricism, which he identified with positivism, partly on the ground that its implicit nominalism is incompatible with the ostensible fact that objective relational structures are discoverable in the flux of existence, and partly because it misconceives the nature and role of abstractions (or theoretical constructions) in scientific inquiry.

Cohen believed that the truths of logic are about neither physical nor psychological processes, but that they formulate the absolute invariants exhibited by all possible objects. On the other hand, he construed the laws of the positive sciences to be expressions of relations which are invariant only under special types of changes and only in certain specialized domains. He therefore maintained that factual statements are at best only contingently true, and are inherently incapable of a purely rational demonstration. Accordingly, he recognized a fundamental polarity between what he called the rational and the empirical elements in existence; and his writings contain spirited criticisms of philosophies that ignore these as well as other polar aspects of nature. He expounded this principle of polarity in his major book, *Reason and Nature* (1931), which contains, in addition to an uncompromising critique of anti-rational currents in contemporary philosophy, a generalized account of scientific method, and numerous analyses of philosophic issues that are raised by the substantive materials of mathematics, physics, biology, the social sciences, and ethical theory.   (E.N.)

Coherence, *see* Truth.

Collingwood, Robin George (1889–1943), English philosopher. He spent all his working life at Oxford, first as an undergraduate, then as a Fellow of Pembroke College and finally as Professor of Metaphysics. In addition to his main life's work in philosophy he was a very eminent authority on the archaeology and history of Roman Britain.

He was a very original philosopher, and the bold, fresh style in which he argues out his position makes him an unusually stimulating and exciting author even for readers who are not in agreement with him. Contrary to his own statement in his *Autobiography*, his views appear to have undergone considerable change (on this point see the excellent Editor's Preface to the *Idea of Nature*); this fact, together with his originality, makes it difficult to give a summary account of his views. Brought up in the Oxford realist school, led by Cook **Wilson** and **Prichard**, he early reacted to a position more nearly in sympathy with **Idealism**; in his *Essay on Philosophical Method* (1933), perhaps the best of his earlier writings, he took the view that philosophy was essentially rational and systematic, an attempt to set forth human knowledge in systematic form. But he insisted that this system was but a transmutation into a higher form of knowledge already possessed in a less developed form – thus moral philosophy should present in systematic rational form our existing moral beliefs, transmuting but not challenging or adding to them. The other main contention of this work was that the characteristic feature of philosophy was that it worked with concepts which overlapped each other in a way not found in science and that this gave philosophy its special character and methods of argument. In later life, however, Collingwood became more sceptical; in *An Essay on Metaphysics* (1940), ostensibly a continuation of the *Essay on Philosophical Method*, he abandons the view that philosophy has a distinctive character and sees it rather as a part of history – metaphysics now has the purely historical task of bringing to light the absolute presuppositions of human thought at some date in history; to any metaphysical statement in traditional form should be supplied at the beginning the "metaphysical rubric" that "it was an absolute presupposition of thought at such and such a time that . . .". No assessment of the merits of these presuppositions is apparently possible. In identifying philosophy and history he adopted a position, similar to that of **Croce**, which gave an appearance of unity to his historical and philosophical interests. The specimens of the tracing of absolute presuppositions at the end of the *Essay on Metaphysics* and in his *Idea of Nature* are of great independent interest.

Collingwood's views on the nature of history are of great interest though expressed in essays of uneven merit (see his *Autobiography* and the posthumous *Idea of History*). He expresses great contempt for "scissors and paste" history, and takes very seriously the view that history is the history of human thought and that the task of the historian is to relive the thoughts of the people of whom he is treating. He was also a major contributor to aesthetics, especially in his *The Principles of Art* (1938) in which he adopts a position similar to that of Croce but based on arguments of his own. An earlier version of his views on aesthetics is to be found in *Speculum Mentis* (*The Map of Knowledge*), 1924. (J.O.U.)

Plate 28, page 108.

Comte, Isidore-Auguste-Marie-François-Xavier (1798-1857), French philosopher, born in Montpellier in January 1798 of Catholic parents. He gained a place at the École Polytechnique at Paris in 1813 but was too young to go there until 1814. In 1816 he was a leader of a student revolt which resulted in the expulsion of Comte and the rest of the students of his year. In 1817 he became secretary to Saint-Simon, the socialist writer. Saint-Simon influenced him greatly, but because of Comte's greater scientific knowledge and superior powers of exposition it has been held that he was the principal author of much that was published in Saint-Simon's name at that period. In 1822 there appeared under Saint-Simon's auspices Comte's *Plan of the Scientific Works necessary for the Reorganization of Society*, in which most of the ideas of his completed philosophy are contained. In 1824 Comte quarrelled with Saint-Simon and left his service. In 1825 he married Caroline Massin whom he had first met, he says in the *Secret Addition* to his will, while availing himself of her services as a prostitute.

In 1826 Comte began a course of public lectures on his "Positive Philosophy". These were attended by some leading men of science, but Comte had to abandon them owing to mental illness. The next year he tried to drown himself in the Seine. In 1829 he restarted his public lectures, which were published in six volumes from 1830 to 1842 with the title of *Course on the Positive Philosophy*. This is his major work. In it he sets out his theory of knowledge and the sciences and lays the foundations for the new science, which he first called "social physics" and then "sociology". The central thesis of the work is that the attempt to discover extra-mundane causes of the natural world, wheth-

er in theological terms or in terms of metaphysical natures or essences, should be abandoned in favour of the positive method of correlating the facts of observation with one another. The positive sciences, he argued, have been developed progressively, with the earlier ones forming the necessary basis for those that came afterwards. The sequence he sets out, in ascending order of complexity is: mathematics, astronomy, physics and chemistry, and biology (in which he includes psychology). There remains sociology, of which Comte claims to be the founder. As conceived by him, this science consists of the statics and the dynamics of society. As to the former, he held that the various elements are so closely bound together in a "social consensus" that no part can be radically changed without serious effects upon the whole. As to the latter, he held that intellectual development was the prime cause of social change, and that therefore human society passes through the same theological, metaphysical and positive stages as the sciences. There was thus to begin with a theocratic and traditional stage which later was organised between the secular power of kings and the spiritual power of priests. At the metaphysical stage there is a sort of anarchy during which both temporal and spiritual authority are attacked. This transitional stage would be succeeded by the positive era when men of science would form a new and durable spiritual power. An ordered society would then be based on the co-operation that positive knowledge of social facts would bring with it.

Comte had hoped for a professorship at the École Polytechnique, but obtained only minor teaching and examining posts there. These he subsequently lost in the course of bitter quarrels with the administration. In 1842 he and his wife parted, although she continued to attend his lectures. J. S. **Mill** and Littré organized financial support so that Comte could continue with his researches. In 1844 Comte made the acquaintance of Clotilde de Vaux, whose husband was hiding from the police in Belgium. Comte immediately fell in love with her, but was accorded only the privileges of friendship. Comte claimed to have been taught by her the importance of subordinating the intellect to the heart, and after her death in 1846 his writings take on a new emphasis. It is not merely by means of the natural and social sciences and by the spiritual power of scientists that society is to be regenerated, but by means of a secular religion, the Religion of Humanity, of which Comte was to be the High Priest. The details of this new religion are set out in *The General View of Positivism* (1848), *The Catechism of Positive Religion* (1852), and the four volumes of *The System of Positive Polity* (a very early article of his had had this title), which appeared between 1851 and 1854. Having made arrangements for the perpetuation of the cult, Comte died in 1857.

Comte's later writings are a strange mixture of absurdity and insight. On the one hand, there is the Religion of Humanity, with details for the worship of the Great Being (symbolized by the female form) in chapels containing the busts of the benefactors of mankind. There is the Positivist Calendar with months named after Moses, Archimedes and Frederick II, and with days for the celebration of great men (among whom Comte gratefully included friends who had vainly worked on his behalf in the matter of the professorship at the École Polytechnique). On the other hand, Comte had pondered seriously about the ritual and ideology of a society from which religious beliefs and institutions had been eliminated. He saw that in the absence of unifying sentiments a scientific society might degenerate. One of his ideas was that there were moral implications in the scientific activity itself. Thus he held that submission to the facts of nature (what, since Freud, has been called "the reality principle") curbed the exorbitance of egoism, that the acceptance of a scientific argument had a certain kinship with justice, and that understanding was very close to sympathy. Yet his principle of the subordination of the intellect to the heart is an admission that there is more in morality than can be got from science. The intellect, he held, in a phrase that echoes and yet corrects **Hume**, should be not the slave but the servant of the heart. Thus at the beginning of his career Comte had said that in the pursuit of science human wishes and aims should be rigidly excluded, and at the end of it concluded that it is for men to decide in what direction and how far science should be pursued. (H.B.A.)

Plate 29, page 109.

Concept, *see* Ideas, Conceptualism, Universals.

Conceptualism is the view that the objects of thought and the meanings of general terms are concepts, these being mental entities which exist only in minds and are formed or constructed by them. On this view when I think about redness, when, for example, I infer from the fact that something is red the fact that it is coloured, I am scrutinising the concept of red that I possess and discovering that it contains as a part the concept of colour. Again, when I recognize something as red, what I do is see that it falls under or satisfies the concept. Stated in this way the theory has a somewhat uninformative appearance. It seems to repeat, in less familiar words, the state of affairs to be explained. It is more compelling in the form of imagism where the concept is identified with mental imagery of some kind. Imagery is used as a standard of classification. To tell if a thing is red I must compare it with my standard imagery of red. For **Locke** this imagery was abstract. **Berkeley** found abstract and indeterminate images unintelligible and proposed instead a theory of representative images. But a specific representative image will have a multitude of features and so will be ambiguous. **Hume**'s theory of a series of similar images overcomes this difficulty. Conceptualism, like other theories of **universals**, is implicitly regressive. To use a mental standard of classification I must compare the things to be classified with the standard and this comparison is itself a classificatory undertaking, requiring the use of a further mental standard and so on. A difficulty peculiar to imagism, the price, perhaps, of its ready intelligibility, is that it seems psychologically false. The use of images in recognition is the exceptional case. It is often said that images are themselves symbolic in character and thus raise the same problems about meaning as words. (A.Q.)

Condillac, Etienne Bonnot de, (1715–1780), born in Grenoble, France. He took holy orders early in life. In Paris he came into contact with **Diderot** and others of the **Encyclopedists**, by whom he was greatly influenced; he was also for long a friend of **Rousseau**. He began as a disciple of **Locke**, whose philosophy was very popular among advanced thinkers in France at that time and in his first book, *Essai sur l'origine des connaissances humaines*, he is mainly content to follow Locke's views. But in his main work, on which his fame rests, the *Traité des sensations* of 1754, he goes further in an empiricist direction than Locke had ever gone. Not only are all our ideas derived from sensation but all the activities of the mind are mere transformations of the sensations of sense or *sensations transformées*; a memory, for example is a mere after-effect of sensation and attention is the occupation of consciousness by one sensation to the exclusion of others. Condillac expounds this doctrine by the device of imagining a statue being gradually endowed with senses, first smell, then touch, and so on; he can thus consider the contribution of each separately. It is important to his doctrine that he conceives of sensations as arousing pleasure and pain at the promptings of which men's wants, instincts and habits are formed.

This doctrine, which Condillac expounds with grace, simplicity and clarity had a great success in France for a time, where it supplanted Cartesianism in popularity; but his views have had a more abiding influence in Britain, largely because of their influence on James **Mill**, Bain and Herbert **Spencer**. (J.O.U.)

Plate 30, page 110.

Condorcet, Marie-Jean-Antoine-Nicolas Caritat, Marquis de (1743–1794) was one of the prominent circle of **Encyclopedists** in eighteenth-century France. He was early a supporter of the Revolution but was soon proscribed and went into hiding where he wrote his most famous work, the *Esquisse d'un tableau historique des progrès de l'esprit humain* (a historical survey of the progress of human understanding); he was captured and imprisoned and immediately died, possibly from poison. Condorcet was many-sided; he wrote biographies of Voltaire and Turgot and his *Essai sur l'application de l'analyse aux probabilités des décisions prises à la pluralité des voix* (Essay on methods of analysing probability in its relation to majority decisions) (1785) is an important document in the history of the theory of probability. But it is as a philosophical theorist of progress that he is best known. He believed in a permanent human nature and invariant moral principles derived from this nature and independent of custom and religion (of which he was a fierce opponent); progress was therefore a matter of im-

proving institutions and education. He distinguished ten epochs of human society, beginning with the hunter, then the pastoralist, then the agriculturalist; the eighth stage was that of scientific culture inaugurated in the sixteenth century, and the triumph of this culture ensured the possibility and inevitability of indefinite progress in the future. The ninth period began with the French Revolution and the tenth was yet in the future. For his idea of indefinite progress he relied on an analogy with the sciences. Though the human intelligence is essentially limited, there can always be progress in mathematics and the other sciences; similarly an indefinite progress in human affairs does not presuppose perfection in human nature. These views, very influential in their time, were severely attacked by Malthus and others of his school in the nineteenth century. (J.O.U.)

Plate 31, page 111.

Contract, Social, *see* Social Contract, Hobbes, Locke, Rousseau, Hume.

Cook Wilson, *see under* Wilson, Cook.

Correspondence, *see* Truth.

Cosmological Argument, *see* Theism.

Cratylus of Athens was a sophist and was perhaps middle-aged around 410 B.C., though he could have been slightly younger. He developed an extreme form of Heracliteanism and according to **Aristotle** influenced the young **Plato** to think that there could be no knowledge of the unstable physical world. In Plato's *Cratylus* he was shown as defending the natural correctness of names – a development of **Heraclitus'** view that a thing's essence is often revealed in its name. Aristotle asserted that he also went beyond Heraclitus in saying that you could not step even once into the same river, and that he ultimately avoided speech and merely pointed. Cratylus seems to have been an extravagant and somewhat uncritical person, who must have found difficulty in reconciling his exaggerations of Heraclitus' beliefs in the ultimate impermanence of objects and the significance of some names. There are points which suggest that

Plato's interpretation of Heraclitus as having posited constant and universal physical change was derived rather from Cratylus' exaggerated version. See also **Pre-Socratics**. (G.S.K.)

Croce, Benedetto (1866–1952), born in Naples. His first scholarly work was on the history and antiquities of that area. He turned to pure philosophy after a considerable period as an historian and art critic, and to the end of his life he continued to work in those fields. He held no academic post, but was Minister of Education in the Italian government from 1920–21, and again after the Second World War. As a liberal he retired from active politics on the advent of Fascism, with which he never compromised.

Croce's main fame is in the field of **aesthetics**, but his aesthetic theory is essentially part of his general philosophical system which is a form of idealism indebted to, but by no means based on, **Hegel**. His general system he called the philosophy of the spirit; spirit is for him the sole reality, the physical being a construction of the mind; but spirit is not a transcendent something beyond experience, for Croce will not speculate about the transcendent; the spirit is the world and the history of spirit is the history of human experience. Though spirit is one it contains four varieties of experience: first there is cognitive experience of the particular, where the spirit expresses itself in particular embodiments, the sphere of aesthetics; second, there is cognitive experience of the universal, the sphere of logic; third, there is practical experience in particular matters, the sphere of economic interests; fourth, there is practical experience which is concerned with the universal, the sphere of ethics. History is the description of the activity of spirit in these four grades; philosophy can be regarded as being a systematic account of the task and methodology of history and Croce often says that philosophy and history are one; hence the systematic treatise on the spirit also contains a final part on the theory and history of historiography.

Croce stated his aesthetic views not only in the first volume of the *Philosophy of the Spirit* but also in a shorter book a *Breviary of Aesthetics* and an Encyclopedia Britannica article, *Aesthetics*. Art, Croce holds, is vision or intuition; a work of art is an image produced by the artist and reproduced by his audience. The physical artefact, often wrongly accounted the work of art, is produced by the artist as a practical act to perpetuate and aid reproduction of his image which is the true work of art. But we must not distinguish the artists' intuition from its expression – a poetic thought is nothing outside its metre, rhythm and words, and intuition and expression are one; technique is involved in producing the artefact, in the form of mixing the paints, writing down the notes, cutting the stone without breaking it, but expression cannot be separated from imagination; the poem, the sonata and the novel are complete before the mechanical work of writing down is undertaken. Artistic imagination must be distinguished from mere fancy; it is productive imagination which expresses some feeling or emotion, though we must not separate the feeling expressed as content and the image as its form; art is the aesthetic synthesis *a priori* of feeling and image.

Art then simply is the representation of feeling in an image. Though this will normally give pleasure we must not be misled into thinking that art is the practical utilitarian act of producing images as a means to pleasure; nor is art a practical moral activity – the work of art cannot be judged morally though of course the artist as a man has moral responsibilities; nor again must we confuse art with conceptual knowledge.

Since art is an activity of spirit it is a mistake to claim that there can be beauty in nature; but nature, as much as a block of carved marble, can prompt and fix in our memories an aesthetic image – "nature is mute if man does not make her speak". For an image to be successful expression and a work of art is one and the same thing; expression and beauty are a single concept in different words.

Such is Croce's theory of aesthetics in a narrow sense. But we must remember that for Croce aesthetics is the field of the whole of the manifestation of spirit in which it expresses itself in particular embodiments; thus it includes all expression except pure logical thinking. This accounts for the otherwise perplexing claims of Croce that his aesthetics is also a general theory of linguistics, for language is in general the medium of self-expression; hence Croce says that any use of language is identical with poetry. Croce's aesthetic theory has been more influential than any other in recent times. The uncompromising way in which he follows out his basic ideas without regard for paradox has prevented most from following him unreservedly, but few have escaped his influence; his closest follower in the English-speaking world is **Collingwood** in his *Principles of Art*. (J.O.U.)

Plate 33, page 161.

Cudworth, Ralph (1617–1688), English, the most distinguished philosopher among the **Cambridge Platonists**. He published his chief work, *The True Intellectual System of the Universe* in 1678; his *Treatise Concerning Eternal and Immutable Morality* appeared posthumously in 1731. Cudworth took as his task the welding together of the new science of his day and a broadly Platonic tradition of metaphysics and theology. The universe, to him, is not a mechanism, once fashioned and set in motion by God and thereafter self-regulating: nor is it the theatre of God's constant miraculous intervention. Rather, God works by way of a semi-autonomous "Plastic Nature", reminiscent of the Platonic "World-Soul". Cudworth vigorously combated atomistic and materialistic metaphysics, stressing in particular the active, spontaneous and creative powers of the mind.

Right and wrong, to Cudworth, cannot be established by the arbitrary fiat of ruler or deity. Both the Calvinist and Hobbesian concern with will and power as ultimates are criticized in terms of a morality "eternal and immutable". Happiness and freedom are seen as release from self-concern; religion consisting crucially in the choice and pursuit of a way of life. Of philosophers influenced by Cudworth the most significant is Richard **Price,** whose theory of knowledge, though not his moral philosophy, might almost be called a restatement of Cudworth's. (R.W.H.)

Cynicism is the name applied to the philosophical movement or way of life inaugurated in the second half of the fourth century B.C. by **Diogenes** of Sinope, from whose nickname, *Kuōn*, the Dog, it was so called. It continued in phases of varying popularity and purity until the end of the Graeco-Roman world in the sixth century A.D. Since it was never an organised School with official dogmas,

but a succession of individuals emulating the life and practices of Diogenes, considerable variation is found, but a traditional core of precept and behaviour can be extracted.

The end of life is happiness, achieved only by living in accordance with nature, to do which is self-sufficient and constitutes virtue. But this statement is common to both Cynicism and **Stoicism**; they differ in the interpretation placed on it. To the Cynic happiness depends on being self-sufficient. This is a matter of mental attitude, and is natural in being opposed to all convention. His method of becoming self-sufficient was not merely to seek independence from, but actively to dissociate himself from any influence, external or internal, whose ties, responsibilities or distractions might fetter in any way the expression of his individual freedom. For example, his attitude to prosperity was not one of untroubled indifference whether he gained it or lost it, but of uncompromising hostility. Money is the metropolis of all evil, the whip of desire. So the solution does not lie in moderation or temperance, but in the eradication of money and of the lower desires. Property may involve ties; the true Cynic has no property at all. In the same way he has nothing to do with and will attack all ties of family and community, all conventional external values of birth, class, rank, honours, reputation. As the opposite of nature is convention, life according to nature is life stripped of all the accretions of convention, or positively, a life in accordance with the bare minimum necessary for existence. The driving force is the search for the inviolability of the individual under any circumstances. The more one has, the more one wants; the further one is involved, the wider one's needs; the greater one's needs, the more vulnerable one is. But if all needs apart from the absolutely basic are the result of convention and not natural, a man can be free by unshackling himself from them. This is apparent from the conduct of animals who are not bound by convention, and from the ideal of the gods who have no needs at all. Cynicism is thus an extreme philosophy of asserting the freedom of the individual in the face of any circumstances whatsoever with which fortune may face him; the means to this freedom is the renunciation and denial of all external values, relationships and physical emotions and desires and the pleasures therefrom, for the happiness derived from the inviolability, mastery and kingdom of his own will and mind.

But if this asceticism be regarded as a form of escapism, it did not involve the withdrawal of a hermit. The Cynic lived in the full glare of the civilization he condemned, for two reasons. The way of life he led demanded continual practice against his enemies – convention, pleasure, luxury – to keep his body and mind in fighting trim. For example, to form and test *apatheia*, or lack of emotion, he had to face insults. Secondly, Cynicism was a militant evangelism; as the Scout of Mankind, he had to explore human conditions, and having tested them, to report back; as the Doctor, to cure men's minds, to show them the false values of the common currency of convention, deface it, and reveal where happiness lay. But man could not be taught understanding by the verbal pursuit of wisdom, for which conventional education and the learning of the Philosophical Schools were alike reviled. Cynicism as a purely practical ethic offered the short cut to virtue, which could be taught only by the personal example of the Cynic's life, (hence his extreme behaviour and deliberate public contravention of conventional decencies for illustration), and by the precepts distilled from his experience. These precepts often contained illustrations from the uninhibited behaviour of animals and the ideal of Heracles of virtue in endurance. But Cynics were principally characterized by a fearless, shameless freedom of speech in criticism, marked by a mordant wit and repartee which gave birth to numerous apophthegms, and to a new philosophical *genre*, the satirical diatribe. This was misused for its own sake by the less reputable members of the sect, but in the hands of the true Cynic, it was a surgeon's knife, sharpened by his labours, impartially wielded thorough his freedom from fear, to cut the cancer of false values, illusory conventions, pretensions and sham from men's minds.

Cynicism was another (see **stoicism, epicureanism**), and the most drastic, of the philosophies of security which were a common feature of the Hellenistic Age. Arising at a time of great social and economic insecurity, when the old values of the Greek city state, already weakened, were tottering under the impact of Alexander, it offered the individual, whatever his status, freedom from

fear of misfortune, by schooling him to hold valuable only that which could never be taken from him. The embodiment of this self-sufficiency was Diogenes himself. Subsequent Cynics tended to stress one aspect or another of his doctrines. His pupil Crates of Thebes, who gave away his fortune to become a mendicant healer of men's souls, was well-loved as a kind of poor man's consultant. In the third century B.C., when Cynicism flourished, Bion of Borysthenes and Menippus relaxed personal austerity and developed Cynic literary satire; Cercidas of Megalopolis, prominent in politics, applied his beliefs to a doctrine of social reform; Teles was a third-rate mendicant preacher of a type later to become common. After lying dormant in the second and first centuries B.C., Cynicism blazed in the Roman Empire. Apart from prominent adherents like Demetrius, Dio, Demonax, Oenomaus of Gadara, Peregrinus Proteus, Sallustius, we hear of a swarm of riff-raff charlatans imposing on the populace under the Cynic beggar uniform of cloak, knapsack, and stick; they particularly disgusted men like Lucian and Julian who yet admired Cynic ideals. Indeed it was a philosophy peculiarly open to abuse, and when falling short of the highest principles especially repugnant. For the Cynic was something akin to a god, and something akin to a beast.

Perhaps the greatest philosophical importance of Cynicism lay in its influence on Stoicism, strong at the beginning in **Zeno** of Citium and Ariston, and later revived in the first century A.D. by Musonius and **Epictetus**, in one of whose *Discourses* (iii. 22) is found the noblest expression of its ideals. (I.G.K.)

Cyrenaics. A school of **hedonistic** philosophy, founded by **Aristippus** of Cyrene, the friend of **Socrates**, or by his grandson of the same name; flourished at the end of the fourth and first quarter of the third century B.C. when Theodorus, Hegesias and Anniceris led branching sects; thereafter the School disappears before the advance of **epicureanism**.

Ethics was regarded as the only useful branch of philosophy; the end was the enjoyment of the particular pleasure of the moment, which was the sole good to be desired for its own sake. This view is based partly on the observation that the prime natural instinct in all living beings is pursuit of pleasure and avoidance of pain, partly on an epistemology which denied knowledge of external objects and restricted it to the field of sensations: I have a feeling of sweetness; I cannot know that the honey is sweet. Pleasure and pain are motions and as such positive sensations, mere absence of pain is neither. Neither the past nor the future provokes immediate movement; the philosopher will feel no regret for the past nor toil for the future; nor, since only his immediate sensations are knowledge, will he countenance vain opinion, envy, or superstition. Present gratification, accordingly, is the only goal, and all actions, states, social and moral virtues are indifferent in themselves and good only in so far as they produce this end. But the Cyrenaics also maintained that happiness lies not in slavery to pleasure, but in mastery over it. Pleasures differed in degree, and a present pleasure might be followed by a more violent pain, and hence the consequences of an act could not be ignored. Faced with choice, the philosopher's weapon is rational practical intelligence which can be taught and trained; the art of life lay in the intelligent manipulation of circumstances and the prudent adaptation of oneself to them for one's present gratification. Thus the Cyrenaic answer to the problems of a troubled age was not renunciation and dissociation like the **Cynics**, but to accept the vicissitudes of fortune and attempt the intelligent control of them for a personal hedonistic end. The master of a horse or ship, they said, is not one who declines its use, but one who knows how to guide it in the right direction.

But the difficulty of reconciling sensuous end and rational means and external stimulus and the control of reason, troubled the School. Theodorus attempted to free himself from external dependence by redefining the end, although still sensual, as a state of mind, joy, brought about by wisdom. In Cynic fashion he advocated self-sufficiency. Gratification could be gained by any act on the basis of utility to the doer. Hegesias stressed that pleasure and pain depended to a large extent on our attitude to external circumstances; poverty, riches, birth etc., being not in themselves pleasant or painful; but he showed clearly the pessimism likely to result from the original position, by admitting that happiness was not realizable and that

the philospher could only alleviate the preponderance of pain. Anniceris softened the position in another direction, by making some allowance for the pleasures of friendship and patriotism, thus raising the problem of altruistic feelings previously denied by the egoistic hedonism of the School. The School is mainly interesting as a curtain-raiser to the more elaborate and successful philosophy of **Epicurus**. (I.G.K.)

D

Dawes Hicks, George (1862–1941). Professor of Philosophy at University College, London, 1904–1928, he had been educated at Manchester, Oxford, and Leipzig. His work was mainly concerned with the theory of knowledge, in which, though at first strongly influenced by **Kant** and the idealism of **Hegel**, he moved to a position which he called "critical realism". The essence of this view is that objects exist independently of our knowing them, and that what we are immediately aware of is part of the content of the object. Called "critical" in the Kantian sense that it takes the primary question to be, "What are the conditions of knowledge of objects?", it is not connected with American critical realism. Hicks distinguished three "contents", or groups of qualities: the content of the object, and the content immediately apprehended, and the content of the perceiving act; and he maintained that the second does not qualify an entity, such as a sense-datum, separate from the object, but is *part of* the content of the object, and may be erroneous only in being fragmentary. The third content is what persists in our minds, making memory possible. Thus in a perceptual situation the only entities are the object and our act of awareness of it. (R.HALL)

Deduction is one of the technical terms of **logic**. There it is used to denote arguments which are such that if their premises are true the conclusion must also, as a matter of logic, be true. A deductive argument is thus distinguished from an **inductive** argument in which, however convincing it may be, the premises could conceivably be true and the conclusion false. In this use of words the "deductions" of Sherlock Holmes and of all non-technical language are counted as inductions. In the use of logicians the arguments of mathematics are the most notable examples of extended deductive arguments. (J.O.U.)

Deism is the belief that there is a good and wise Supreme Being who created the world but no longer intervenes in it; the God of the deists is essentially the God of Newton's *Scholium*. An eighteenth-century deity in every respect, he is to be known only by the methods of rational argument and more particularly by those arguments which lead to a First Great Cause and to an Intelligent and Benevolent Designer. The importance of deism in the history of ideas is largely due to its use by Voltaire and others as a weapon against Catholic orthodoxy. Its importance in the history of philosophy is perhaps only that it provoked Bishop **Butler** to write *The Analogy of Religion Natural and Revealed*. Butler tries to show that the doctrines of revealed religion and the course of nature are sufficiently alike to argue the same author for both. In particular there are no intellectual difficulties in accepting a theology of revelation which do not arise for the believer in a purely natural and rational theology. But the interest of Butler's arguments on, for instance, immortality is happily independent of their connection with deism. What Butler's arguments do point to in deism is the fact that in its most vulnerable points it is no stronger than revealed religion. While the deist aims his polemics at the Trinity and the Incarnation, he is himself undermined by sceptical attack on the very existence of God. Moreover deism is entirely a religion of the intellect. Whether God exists is for the deist a question of the same order as whether atoms exist. Deism, therefore, even if true, would have little of the type of interest which most religious doctrines possess. The classic deistic statements are John Toland's *Christianity Not Mysterious* (1696), the author of which acknowledged a debt to **Locke**, and Matthew Tindal's *Christianity as Old as the Creation, or the Gospel a Republication of the Religion of Nature* (1730). (A.MACI.)

Democritus lived in the fifth century B.C. He was a native of Abdera, Greece, which was probably also the birth-place of **Leucippus** with whom he is associated as a founder of the **Atomic** theory. It is probable that Leucippus first propounded the

theory and Democritus elaborated it. We have much information about his life, of which a great deal is improbable – he is said to have been educated by the magi and to have blinded himself to free himself from the distractions of sense. It seems, however, that he was the son of wealthy parents and that as a young man he travelled much, including a tour of Egypt and the nearer East, thus reducing himself to poverty. On returning home he won renown by his learned work; he wrote not only on general atomic theory and cosmology but on sense-perception, biology, music and many other subjects; some of his work, such as his attempts to explain colour in terms of the atomic theory, seems to have been based on experiment. He also developed an ethical system which is essentially that held later by **Epicurus**. The goal is happiness, which consists largely in tranquil freedom from fear and anxiety. Mental well-being is more important than the pleasures of sense because the latter are fleeting and frequently lead to pain; though well-being is alone of value wisdom is of great importance since through it alone can we know what pleasures are worthy of pursuit and how to attain them. Considerable fragments, but no complete works, by Democritus survive, and many of these fragments show plainly a mind of great power and subtlety; there are also many informative discussions of his work in later philosophers. But it is for the general atomic theory that he is most important and it is regrettable that on this matter many important points (whether atoms have weight, the original source of motion, necessity) remain conjectural. (J.O.U.)

Plate 34, page 162.

Deontology is the position which regards the fact of duty as fundamental for the understanding of moral thought. In particular deontologists have been contrasted with **Utilitarians**, who regard the obligatoriness of actions as derivative from the goodness of the results that the action will achieve. In recent controversy the most obvious examples of deontologists have been **Prichard**, **Ross** and the Intuitionist school. The word "deontology" is derived from a Greek word "deon" which means approximately "obligatory". (J.O.U.)

Descartes, René (1596–1650). He was born at La Haye, a small town in Touraine, France, and was educated at the Jesuit college of La Flèche; for his teachers he retained a lively admiration, but was dissatisfied with the course of instruction, finding that for the most part it consisted of the transmission of the received opinions of the ancients, and that mathematics alone gave any certain knowledge. In 1618 he departed for Holland to serve as a soldier under Maurice of Nassau. The following year he was in Germany when, on November 10th, he had dreams or visions which apparently revealed to him some fundamental part of his philosophy – most probably, the unity of mathematics and science. He did not at once set himself to write works of philosophy or science, but travelled widely. In 1628 he wrote the *Rules for the Direction of the Understanding*, an unfinished work, not published in his lifetime, which sets out for the first time the rules of his "method", which was to be a method of both science and philosophy.

In the same year he went again to Holland, where with brief interruptions he remained until 1649. In 1634 he had completed and was about to publish his treatise called *Le Monde*, when he heard of the condemnation of Galileo by the Inquisition for teaching, as did the treatise, the Copernican system, and he withdrew it from publication. In 1637, however, he published three short *Discourses* on physical and mathematical subjects, prefaced by the celebrated *Discourse on Method*. Besides being in other respects revolutionary, this was the first great philosophical work to be written in French, and created a style which became a model for the expression of abstract thought in that language. In September 1640 he suffered a grievous blow from the death, at the age of five, of his illegitimate daughter Francine, for whom he cared deeply.

In 1641 he published his *Meditations on the First Philosophy*, together with six sets of *Objections* from various distinguished persons (including **Hobbes and Gassendi**) to whom Descartes had submitted the work, and Descartes' *Replies to the Objections;* altogether these form one of the most important texts of Descartes' philosophy. He followed this in 1644 with the *Principles of Philosophy*, which contains besides other things his views on cosmology, cautiously set forth. This work was dedicated to Princess Elizabeth of Bohemia, a woman of intelligence and sensibility with whom Descartes was in correspondence.

In 1649 Descartes yielded, after much hesitation, to the requests of Queen Christina of Sweden that he should join the distinguished circle she had assembled in Stockholm, and should instruct her in philosophy; in this year he also published the work called *The Passions of the Soul*. The next year, however, as a result of the Swedish climate and the severe régime demanded by the Queen, he caught pneumonia, and died on February 11th, 1650.

Descartes' character has been the subject of much discussion and analysis: his exaggerated secrecy, which led him increasingly to disguise both his interests and his whereabouts, together with his ambiguous relations to the Church, have given rise to many hypotheses, of which perhaps the most fanciful is that he was a Rosicrucian. However, there is no real doubt that his Catholicism was sincere; he believed that his philosophy was in accordance with the faith and constituted the only way of reconciling it with the contemporary advances in natural knowledge. His principal aim was to avoid any prejudiced and hasty judgment of his views that would result in their being misguidedly suppressed. In his attitude to his philosophy, he was self-confident, proud, almost visionary, and did not underestimate his own vocation as a solitary and privileged discoverer of the truth. However, he also enjoyed social life; and had a number of distinguished and devoted friends, with whom he conducted an ample correspondence, which is happily preserved and is of the greatest interest.

Descartes was not only a metaphysician, or a philosopher in the modern sense; like many other "philosophers" of the seventeenth century, he was also a natural scientist, with interests in such subjects as physics and physiology. Above all, he was also a mathematician; the use of the term "Cartesian co-ordinates" in analytical geometry commemorates his invention of such a system (even though in its present form this branch of mathematics owes more to the work, unpublished for many years, of Descartes' contemporary Fermat). Descartes' concern with mathematics, and his own contributions to its powers, above all as an instrument of science, profoundly influenced his philosophical system. In the first place, he believed that the essence of a natural science was the discovery of relationships which could be mathematically expressed; that all natural science must be capable of being unified under mathematics; and that the world, insofar as it can be scientifically explained, must be of such a nature as to admit of mathematical treatment. Second, he thought that mathematics gave in general a paradigm of certain knowledge, and of the methods of acquiring it; hence he set himself to discover in what this certainty consisted, and to test all beliefs by the criterion of such certainty, by methods as clear and effective as those of mathematics.

The criterion of certainty which he was to apply to all received beliefs was expressed by Descartes in the rule – one of the celebrated rules of his "method" – that he would accept only those beliefs that appeared to him "clearly and distinctly" to be true. By "clarity and distinctness" he meant that kind of intrinsic self-evidence which he found to characterise the simplest propositions of mathematics and **logic** – propositions which any man, once he had isolated them in his mind, could see to be true by the "natural light" of reason. Such propositions Descartes also characterised as *indubitable*, in the sense of being not just very hard to doubt, but intrinsically incapable of being doubted; and it is in the form of a search for the indubitable that Descartes' attempt to find certain knowledge takes its most characteristic form. He set himself to doubt anything that admitted of doubt, and to see whether anything was left over that was immune to this process. His application of this procedure of "methodical doubt" is explained principally in the *Discourse on Method* and (in a strikingly dramatic form) in the *Meditations*.

He found that he could doubt many things generally considered very certain: for instance, the existence of physical objects around him. He reasoned that, although he felt very certain at a particular moment that he was seeing and feeling various physical objects, he had on many occasions felt just as certain of such things when later it had turned out that he had been dreaming, and all the things he had supposed to be around him had been illusions. How then could he be certain that the things apparently around him at this moment were not also illusions? He could even doubt that he himself had a body – his body was one physical object among others, and it might be that this, too, was an illusion. What then could be immune to doubt?

At least one thing – that he was doubting; for if he doubted this, it would still certainly be true that he was doubting. From this it followed that he could not doubt that he was thinking, for doubting was only a kind of thinking. Hence he had found at least one indubitable proposition: "I am thinking". From this, however, there followed another, "I exist", for it was self-evident that nothing could think without existing. Thus Descartes could be certain of his own existence because he was thinking – a truth expressed in the famous Cartesian formula "*cogito, ergo sum*", "I am thinking, therefore I exist".

The expression "I am thinking" in this formula is not, however, to be taken only in the narrow sense of "I am doubting". Although, principally in the *Discourse*, Descartes does approach the *cogito*, (as the formula is often called) by way of the impossibility of his doubting that he is doubting, it is quite clear that more is established in the *cogito* than the one proposition "I am doubting". Under the term *cogitationes* (thoughts) Descartes includes a much wider range of what might be called "private experiences", all of which he regards as immediately evident to consciousness and indubitable. For instance, although Descartes can doubt that there are objects around him and that he has a body, he cannot doubt, he holds, that at least he is having experiences as if such objects were there. The certain existence of such cogitationes, regarded merely as subjective experiences, is recognized in the *cogito*; all the experiences of which he is in this way immediately aware are, Descartes reflects, in some sense *his*; and he must exist to have them.

But what is the manner of this existence? He has seen that he can doubt that he has a body, but not that he exists so long as he is thinking; hence, he concludes, the "I" that he has proved to exist is something whose essence is to think. Thus he has proved his existence as a "*res cogitans*" or "thinking being"; or, as he also puts it with dubious justification, as a *substance* whose essential attribute is that of thought.

At this point Descartes turns naturally to the *content* of his thoughts. He finds that he has, among other ideas, the idea of a Perfect Being or God, and reflection on this idea leads him to the conclusion that there must be something outside himself corresponding to this idea – that God must exist in reality, not merely in Descartes' thoughts. Two lines of reflection lead him to this conclusion, both of them derived from scholastic or patristic sources. One is substantially the same as **Anselm**'s ontological proof of the existence of God. The other relies on an application to the realm of ideas of the principle that the less cannot give rise to the greater. An idea of a perfect thing, Descartes argues, could not be brought into being by an imperfect agency. But he himself is imperfect, as is shown by his state of doubt, which is inferior to knowledge. Hence there must really be a Perfect Being, who is the origin of this idea. This argument is derived from **Augustine**; as indeed is the principle behind the *cogito*, that to doubt one's own existence is self-defeating or impossible.

Since he has established that a Perfect Being exists, Descartes has a warrant to reintroduce at least some of the beliefs which he had eliminated in the doubt. For, he reasons, a Perfect Being would not allow him to be deceived to such an extent that he would naturally and systematically believe in such things as external objects if they really did not exist. Hence Descartes feels justified in accepting, though with reserve, some of the most basic beliefs of common sense. In particular, the proof of the existence of God introduces an idea of *permanence* hitherto lacking. The proof of Descartes' own existence in the *cogito* was, strictly speaking, only a proof that he existed so long as he was thinking; even though Descartes seems to have tried, illegitimately, to transcend this limitation already by speaking of himself as a thinking *substance*, that is, an enduring thing. The idea of God as a conserving principle may help to overcome this limitation. Again, Descartes sometimes says that it is only the existence of God that validates memory, and so *deduction*: a process which, unlike the instantaneous steps of *intuition*, presupposes the reliability of memory. Since, however, Descartes has already relied on deduction in his somewhat complex proofs of the existence of God, if not in the *cogito* itself (a much disputed point), there is a strong suspicion of a circular argument here.

Descartes is in further difficulties at this point. He must admit that we are sometimes deceived – this was the starting point of his whole inquiry. How is this fact to be reconciled with the existence, now proved, of a Perfect Being who would not deceive us? Descartes' answer is that the origin of our being deceived is our misuse of our will, of that freedom which also allows men to do moral evil in despite of God. This misuse of the will consists in an overhasty assent to propositions that are not really self-evident, and it can affect even deductive reasonings – thus we make mistakes in mathematics. But if this is so, it may be objected, can we ever be sure that we have taken enough care, that our imperfect nature may not have led us into error? In particular, may not Descartes be mistaken about even the foundations of his philosophical system? Here Descartes merely asserts that God would not allow us to misuse our will to that extent; but this is hardly satisfactory, since the existence of God is itself one of the things proved in the system by reasonings to which these doubts apply. Here again, the argument seems circular. Accusations of circularity were frequently made against Descartes' system in his lifetime, and have been constantly discussed since.

Among the physical objects which he now believes with some firmness to exist, Descartes finds one – what would normally be called his own body – which is in a peculiar relation to the mind, thinking substance, or, as he also calls it, soul, whose existence has been proved in the *cogito*. For one thing, his will can move this body immediately, unlike any other; for another, things that happen to this body affect the mind in peculiar ways; for instance, when this body is struck, pain is experienced, and when some sorts of desire are experienced, we know (as Descartes puts it, "Nature teaches us") that the body has some need. These latter facts, in particular, mean that the soul is united to the body in a peculiarly intimate way. "My soul is not in my body like a pilot in a ship" said Descartes, echoing Thomas Aquinas; if it were so, the soul would be able only to move the body, not also to feel "through" it.

Ultimately, Descartes holds, the peculiar nature of this union cannot be explained. In this connection, he wrote to the Princess Elizabeth, there are three basic and unanalysable notions – the body, the soul, and the union between them. Nevertheless, elsewhere Descartes attempts to explain at least some features of the union. In particular, he holds against much ancient and traditional opinion that the soul is not the principle of life of the body. The body, as a body, is just a machine with its own internal economy and sources of energy, and "it is not that the body dies because the soul leaves it, but that the soul leaves it because the body has died". While the body is alive, however, a soul is joined to it in such a way that some of the movements of the body are produced by the soul, and some experiences of the soul are produced by changes in the body. In the *Passions of the Soul* Descartes suggests that there is in the body a physical place of this interaction, and that this is the pineal gland at the base of the brain. This gland, he supposed, could be moved directly by the soul, and thus agitate the "animal spirits" which, in common with many seventeenth century theorists, he believed to flow and to transmit movement to all parts of the body; in the opposite direction, changes in the animal spirits induced by stimuli to the body could move the gland and thus affect the soul.

This naive causal account of the relations of soul and body was thought unsatisfactory even by many Cartesians. The **occasionalism** of **Malebranche**, and, in one of its many applications, the "pre-established harmony" of **Leibniz** were other seventeenth century attempts to solve the problem.

Descartes held that this problem arose only in the case of human beings. In the case of animals, he seems to have thought that all their movements **were** produced by purely mechanical causes in a system of stimulus and response, and that they were accordingly merely machines, having in the proper sense no souls. However, Descartes is not always consistent on this issue, which raises important problems about his concept of consciousness.

The problem of the union of soul and body is, in a very real sense, central to Descartes' metaphysics. In his view, which is the classical expression of **dualism**, there are in the realm of created beings two and only two fundamentally different sorts of substances or existing things: "thinking" and "extended" substances, souls and matter. This dualistic view was the heart of Descartes' attempt to reconcile the Catholic faith and the advances of seventeenth century science. Although there was some causal interaction between souls and bodies, he thought that he had sufficiently isolated souls from the realm of extension, which alone was subject to the mechanical laws which science was developing.

Natural science, he believed, could ultimately complete a deductive theory of all mechanical changes in extended nature, and so of all physical events, since every physical event must be only a change of motion in extension: these would include all movements of human bodies which were not the product of **free-will**, but free-will and the soul itself would remain essentially outside the reach of the scientific laws.

Apart from the difficulties already mentioned concerning the relations of soul and body, one notable problem about Descartes' dualism is the question of the number of each type of substance. It is clear that on Descartes' view there can be an infinite number of thinking substances or souls. The case is different, however, with extended substance: Descartes seems to have held, in effect, that there could be only *one* extended substance, which constituted all of mechanical nature. This substance could be more or less dense, but not discontinuous: Descartes holds that the notion of absolutely empty space is unintelligible, and that a vacuum cannot exist. Influenced by a purely geometrical concept of extension, he in fact equates extended matter and space and is faced in consequence with many difficulties, particularly in his theory of motion. These views were effectively attacked by Leibniz as was Descartes' related belief that the quantity of motion in the universe remains always constant.

The only essential property of matter, on the Cartesian view, is extension. The idea of extension is, like the idea of God and the fundamental ideas of mathematics, innate; by "innate" ideas Descartes means **a priori** notions which the mind can find in itself alone and which it does not derive from experience. Moreover, we can form clear and distinct ideas of other qualities which can belong to physical objects, viz. size, shape, motion, position, duration and number: all these are "modes" of extension. Since we can clearly and distinctly conceive these qualities, we know *a priori* that it is possible that there should be in reality physical objects possessing them. However, we in fact have more than the mere innate idea of these qualities as possible attributes of physical objects; we also have what Descartes calls "adventitious ideas" – that is, ideas formed in our minds without our willing them, and apparently caused by some outside source – of objects around us actually possessing these qualities. Since God is no deceiver, we have good reason to think that such objects actually exist.

The objects around us appear to have other qualities besides these, as we also have sensations of such things as colours, sounds, odours, tastes, degrees of hardness etc. About these qualities (often called in the seventeenth century "secondary" qualities, as opposed to the former group of "primary" qualities) Descartes holds that we can have little certainty. The ideas of them are confused and unclear, and while he thinks that the goodness of God makes it probable that there are in the physical objects real differences corresponding to the differences of these various sensations, he finds unintelligible the notion that these various qualities as given to sensation actually exist in the objects. Thus Descartes, although he does not commit himself firmly on the point, leans towards the view found in **Locke** and others, that primary qualities exist in objects, but secondary qualities, as we perceive them, do not. He shares with Locke the representative theory of perception that goes with such a view. He differs from Locke, however, both in the exact list he gives of primary qualities, and in holding that, although we have ideas of sensation, none of our knowledge of physical objects really comes from sensation. Sensation can give us only unclear and confused ideas, and we understand physical reality only by an act of the intellect, through the ideas of extension and its modes, which can be made clear and distinct.

Descartes's conception of a complete natural science, consonant with his other views, is of an entirely deductive system derived from self-evident *a priori* premises. These premises were ultimately of a philosophical or metaphysical character. Metaphysics and science are for him fundamentally one, and in his *Principles* he indeed attempts to derive the first principles of his science from reflection on the nature of God. Every physical event, including changes in the human body, was governed by the same physical laws – thus medicine, ultimately, must be part of the one physical science. All the sciences were one with physics, and physics one with philosophy, a state of affairs which Descartes pictured in his description of the Tree of Knowledge, of which the roots were metaphysics, the trunk physics, and the branches the other sciences.

This science Descartes expected to be of not merely theoretical interest. In common with his older contemporary, Francis **Bacon,** he frequently emphasises the practical benefits to be expected from the scientific study of nature; in particular he hoped that the study of physiology might enable man to discover the causes of senescence and thus to prolong life.

Despite the entirely *a priori* character of the science which he imagined, Descartes admitted, from the beginning, and increasingly after discouraging experience, that experiments were necessary to the discovery of physical truths, and he himself engaged in many experiments, for example in physiology and optics. The need for these experiments and their function are not entirely clear granted the nature of his system and its *a priori* claims, and his interpreters have found many problems in his various and not entirely consistent accounts of this matter.

The influence of Descartes on the history of philosophy has probably been greater than that of any other thinker, with the exception of **Aristotle**. It extended far beyond the Cartesians, such as Malebranche who adopted many of his views, or even the other **Rationalists**, who agreed with much of his general account of the nature of philosophy and science. In particular, the British **Empiricists**, who rejected almost all his conclusions, were so profoundly affected by his approach that the eighteenth-century Scots philosopher **Reid** stated not so much a paradox as the truth in writing that Malebranche, Locke, **Berkeley** and **Hume** shared a common "system of the human understanding" which "may still be called the Cartesian system". The same influence, in very various forms, has continued to the present day.

What influenced all these philosophers was the most revolutionary element in Descartes' thought, his placing at the centre of philosophy the **epistemological** question "how do I know . . .?" Descartes was effectively the first to try to abandon the impersonal, "God's eye view" of the world common to earlier philosophers, and to ask, not just what the world was like, but how one could know what the world was like. Descartes also transmitted to his successors the view that there could be only one valid method of answering these questions, the method of starting from the immediate data of consciousness, which alone were indubitable, and attempting to "work out" from them to an external world. Descartes himself attempted to do this by appealing to the existence and nature of God. His arguments here represent some of the most traditional elements in his thought; when these were called in question, not just in detail but in principle, other philosophers were left with the task of constructing an external world from the immediate data of consciousness without such transcendental aids.

Thus the philosophy of Descartes, which is itself a transcendental religious metaphysics as well as a philosophy of the New Science, contained the seeds of the empiricism and subjective idealism that came later. It is perhaps only in very recent years that philosophers have determinedly called in question the fundamental Cartesian principle which underlies these systems, that there are immediate data of consciousness, more certain than anything else, from which philosophy must start in its search for knowledge. (B.A.O.W.)

Plate 35, page 163.

Determinism. The thesis of determinism is, roughly, that any event whatsoever is an instance of some law of nature. It is not easy to state this thesis in a precise manner; it is most usually stated in the form: every event has a cause, or nature is uniform; a famous and very graphic formulation by Laplace is that given a knowledge of the state of the universe at some date it is in principle possible to predict all the subsequent history of the universe. The thesis cannot be proved or disproved; we cannot prove it since to do so would require the provision of a deterministic explanation of the totality of events; we cannot disprove it since any failure to find a deterministic explanation of an event can always be regarded, and usually is regarded, as a temporary lacuna in scientific knowledge. The famous problem of the justification of induction can be stated in the form: science presupposes the principle of determinism, and if this principle is unprovable then science rests on unprovable presuppositions. **Hume** was responsible for the classical statement of this problem, to which philosophers have never found an agreed solution. It appears, however, that the deterministic hypothesis has been abandoned in some fundamental physical

enquiries in which statistical laws are sought regarding events for which, taken singly, no deterministic explanation is sought. For this, and other reasons it is commonly suggested that the principle of determinism should not be regarded as a true or false statement but as a methodological principle which may or may not be used in a scientific investigation.

Frequently, however, the thesis of determinism is understood to involve the thesis that the will is not free, that choice is illusory and that how we act is determined. To speak of a determinist is usually understood to involve reference to this special position; there are philosophers who accept the principle of determinism but regard it as compatible with the **freedom of the will**, but it would be misleading to speak of these philosophers as being determinists. The principle of indeterminacy in physics can be thought to provide a solution to the problem of the freedom of the will only at the expense of confused thinking, for there is no way of basing human responsibility on the impossibility of simultaneously determining the position and momentum of elementary particles. (J.O.U.)

Dewey, John (1859–1952), American philosopher. Few philosophers have exerted a more widespread influence in the world of practical affairs. Nor is it accidental that this should be so, for in all his writings Dewey is guided by the idea that philosophy is a thoroughly human undertaking which must be judged in terms of its social or cultural impact.

During the nineteenth century philosophy had for one reason or another become largely an academic subject engaged in by professors and little heeded by men of practical affairs. All of Dewey's work was designed to reverse this trend. He was an uncompromising naturalist with a vigorous distrust of anything that smacked of the esoteric. The key to healthy philosophy would be first of all the philosopher's recognition that he was a human being like any other, and that his own thoughts and reasonings like any others had natural origins and natural purposes. Philosophizing is a mode of human behaviour; it arises in certain contexts rather than others; and it should be judged in terms of its capacity to meet the challenge of the very conditions which give rise to it. To state the matter otherwise, philosophy is tied to culture both at its inception and at its termination. For, on the one hand, it arises from the natural tendency to reflect upon the problems generated by the culture of its time; and, on the other hand, it needs to be judged in terms of its tendency to resolve those problems, its completeness as an evaluational spur to the culture of the future.

There is a sense in which one can say that Dewey replaced the problem of truth with the problem of value. As we shall see, any attempt to summarise Dewey's views on the concept of truth is difficult and hazardous. But, whatever the outcome, it is quite clear that his primary concern is the question of value. The demands of truth can become, as the record of academic philosophy demonstrates, esoteric in the extreme; and when a demand becomes esoteric Dewey is inclined to be impatient of it. His tendency is to replace the question "what conclusion is true?" with the question "what conclusion, considering the conditions of the problem which gives rise to our thinking at all, is the one which we *ought* to come out with?" Theory of value is his central concern in everything that he writes. And it is not surprising that his philosophy led him to revolutionary ideas concerning the educational process. Dewey's programme of progressive education was a natural off-shoot of his philosophy as a whole.

Let us look more closely at Dewey's naturalistic account of human thinking, always remembering that the account is meant to apply to philosophical thought as well as to any other kind. He was strongly influenced by C. S. **Peirce**'s contention that all thought is a movement from a doubtful to a settled situation of belief. Indeed, most of Dewey's description is derived either from Peirce or from William **James**; but he stated it in a way peculiarly his own. Thinking (or intellection) is a form of activity engaged in by a human biological organism whenever habitual patterns of action are disrupted. The function of thought is to solve the problems which give rise to it. It will be judged by the relative degree of permanence of the settled belief or action to which it leads. More specifically, its function is described by Dewey in five stages. (1) Given the breakdown of habit, the organism nonetheless presses on to further action. Overt action being thwarted, this tendency amounts to what Dewey calls "suggestions" (2) "Intellectualiza-

tion" takes place as the problem is formulated as one to be solved, as one meets the situation from the standpoint of a question to which an answer is sought. (3) The next step is the imaginative construction of "hypotheses" which might serve as guides in the actual search for an answer. An hypothesis is a guide to observation and the collection of evidence. (4) "Reasoning" in the narrow sense of the term consists in deducing from any hypothesis one pleases the actual differences it would make in the course of experience. Deduction thus serves as a device for setting up the conditions of experiment. (5) Experiment itself, or "testing", is simply the action (overt or imaginative) which is required to check the hypothesis against those differences of fact entailed.

Notice that when you view the matter in this way your ultimate question may be worded somewhat as follows: Given the problem with which you start, and given a complete run-through of the five stages enumerated, is the end result with which you come out one which you *ought* or *ought not* to have reached? The problem is one of judging an activity in a context. It is a valuational problem, and is to be differentiated from any esoteric question about final and absolute "truth".

Dewey's evasive style of writing, and his tendency to rephrase his major contentions in the face of rigorous attacks, caused some difficulty at this point. In his earlier writings he tended, following James, to state his position as a view concerning the meaning of truth. Thus, he tended at first to say that what we *mean* by "true" is contained in a description of the criteria to be satisfied by any "proper" end result of the process just described. Such a description would provide the full import of the remark that "the true is that which works" – a remark too often thrown back at Dewey without full consideration of its detailed meaning for him. Nonetheless, under vigorous attack, especially by **Russell**, Dewey's way of talking significantly changed. The purport of Russell's attack rested on the claim that one must carefully distinguish the *meaning* of truth from the *criteria* we apply in establishing its presence. Thus, in order to establish that "Caesar crossed the Rubicon" is true, I must no doubt engage in future research and establish that, when adopted as an hypothesis, it "works". But what I *mean* in calling the proposition true is that it "corresponds" in some sense with what actually took place a good many years ago.

The controversy between Dewey and Russell fills many pages, but the upshot can be expressed as follows. Dewey tends in his later writings to discard the words "truth" and "true" altogether. It is as though he were to say: "Perhaps in its traditional use this word has had a tendency to signify correspondence. If so, I can only say that it signifies something wholly unmanageable. Pray, on what metaphysical cloud can one sit in order to observe this mysterious relation of correspondence between a proposition uttered now and an event which transpired so many years ago? I give you your word; and say merely that I am uninterested in it. My concern is with the conditions under which the hypotheses we adopt are or are not *warrantedly assertible*. It is those conditions which must be our guide in judging discourse, not the esoteric notions of professors about truth by correspondence."

Russell's further claim that, difficult as it is, the notion of truth by correspondence cannot be avoided – his claim that Dewey, while ostentatiously ushering it out of the front door, surreptitiously introduces it through all the back windows – cannot here be adequately treated.

It is, however, easy to see how Dewey applies his general thesis in the more restricted area of **ethics** and morals. The subject matter of ethics is the conduct of men, and its purpose is to formulate in general terms the basis of the distinction between good conduct and bad conduct. It follows for Dewey that the first task of ethics is to understand the nature of these biological organisms whose conjoint behaviour constitutes the social context. The second task is to understand the kinds of problem situation which give rise to our effort to distinguish good conduct from bad conduct. Once we have performed these two tasks, and not before, we may be in a position to formulate the difference between "good" and "bad". Dewey states the main outlines of his moral theory in a book significantly entitled *Human Nature and Conduct*. Human nature is analysed in terms of three key concepts: impulse, habit and intelligence. The dynamic character of the human organism is expressed in the concept of impulse. Habits in turn are conceived as those relatively stable patterns of activity which result

from the constant interplay of impulse from within and social pressures from without. Intelligence is described in functional terms as the form of activity whereby, when habits are frustrated or upset, the organism seeks to reinstate action. Thus, degree of intelligence will be judged in terms of the degree of permanence with which action is reinstated relative to the problem which thwarted action in the first place.

This will be recognized as part of Dewey's general description of the thought process; but it is now introduced as a clue to the moral philosopher's search for the good for man. He proposes the following definition of "good":

"Good consists in the meaning that is experienced to belong to an activity when conflict and entanglement of various incompatible impulses and habits terminate in a unified orderly release in action." (p. 210)

In short, we *ask* the question "what is good?" only relatively to a general type of problem situation. A general definition of "good" must therefore be provided in such a way as to cover the essential features which would be required of any acceptable solution of just such problems. Those who read Dewey are sometimes puzzled by his persistence in insisting that what he calls "mere enjoyment" is not evaluational. If, however, one attends to his general line of argument the insistence is clearly seen as an essential part of his view. "Merely" to enjoy or like something is not to solve any problem. Dewey wishes to preserve the force of the word "good" as a commitment of choice between one course of action and another. This defines for him the fundamental moral or ethical problem.

From such a basis it is easy to see how the general outlines of Dewey's social philosophy emerge. Societies can be described in terms remarkably similar to the terms "impulse" and "habit". Societies, like individuals, are dynamic and active. Like individuals they develop relatively stable patterns of action. Once again, the stable patterns are the result of interplay between forces from within and forces from without. And societies, like individuals, develop habits which break down under unexpected pressures and strains. Thus the role of intelligence at the social level is comparable to the role of intelligence at the level of individual action. Societies must seek to establish patterns of activity stable enough to resist shock; a course of action must always be judged according to its degree of success in removing the conditions of breakdown.

If one combines this thesis with Dewey's general naturalistic claims, one is prepared to understand his tremendously influential role in setting social science on its feet. Always sceptical of the esoteric, Dewey had no respect for those who seemed to him to approach problems "from the top down". It seemed to him that political philosophy had for too long sought the justification of courses of action in elaborate metaphysical doctrines. The only intelligent approach to human problems was for him an approach "from the bottom up". That is to say, the experimental methods of inductive science must be applied without preconceptions as to where one *must* come out. Social science should tackle concrete problems by running through precisely those five stages of intelligent activity which we earlier listed. Above all, it should run the risk of bold hypothesis and tackle the task of checking every hypothesis against the evidence.

Dewey's philosophy of education is an integral part of his general social philosophy. Education should be based upon the premise that all genuine thought grows out of real problem situations. To educate a child by subjecting him to a rigid and standardized training in "the three R's" is once again to work "from the top down". If education is to proceed "from the bottom up" it will adjust itself to real problems felt by the child, and will educate him by training him to invent hypotheses, think out their consequences, and test them in actual practice. The emphasis on what the child feels as a real problem in contrast to what the teacher preconceives as gospel – this is the clue to Dewey's educational theories.

The dangers are evident; and before his death Dewey watched "progressive education" have its day in America until its excesses produced a strong reaction in favour of a return to "the three R's". Dewey was aware of the excesses, and repeatedly deplored them; but there is no evidence that he ever changed his mind concerning his general theory.

As a naturalist, wary of the esoteric, implacable foe of working from the top down, and scornful of metaphysics, Dewey was bound to attack religion and its hold upon the mind of the West. Metaphysics at large is the object of his attack, and one finds in his writings two rather different grounds for attack. Religion suffers heavy punishment on either ground. The first is that metaphysical thinking really makes no difference at all so far as the progress of man's intelligent control of nature is concerned. It is froth which adds nothing in the onrush of man's increasing understanding through the experimental method of science. The second ground of attack is that metaphysical thinking makes a very great deal of difference – for the worse. It is said to block inquiry, to make philosophy dogmatic and stagnant, to close men's minds to possibilities inherent in natural science.

Dewey attacked religion on both these grounds, and they may very well be compatible. For the contingent fact that men entertain a theory may have very bad effects even though from the standpoint of logic the theory is entirely barren of predictive consequences. But Dewey never wished to pose as an iconoclast, and he coupled his attacks upon religion with a positive claim that his way alone would lead to a release of the religious energies of mankind. His professed goal is to divorce the meaning of the adjective "religious" from the traditional sense of the noun "religion". The intent of this divorce will be seen at once in the following quotations. First, the definition of "religious":

"Any activity pursued on behalf of an ideal and against obstacles and in spite of threats of personal loss because of conviction of its general and enduring value is religious in quality."

What then of "religion"?

"If I have said anything about religions and religion that seems harsh, I have said those things because of a firm belief that the claim on the part of religions to possess a monopoly of ideals and of the supernatural means by which alone, it is alleged, they can be furthered, stands in the way of the realisation of distinctively religious values inherent in natural experience. For that reason if for no other, I should be sorry if any were misled by the frequency with which I have employed the adjective "religious" to conceive of what I have said as a disguised apology for what have passed as religions. The opposition between religious values as I conceive them and religions is not to be bridged. Just because the release of

[continued on p. 113

PLATE 17. BERKELEY, George (1685–1753), portrait painted in 1725 by J. Smibert (1688–1751).
(*National Portrait Gallery, London*)

Photo: Anderson

PLATE 18. BOETHIUS, Anicius Manlius Severinus (c. 480–c. 524), painting by Justus van Ghent (fl. 1446–1480/5). (Barberini Palace, Rome)

98

PLATE 19. BONAVENTURA (John of Fidanza) (1221–1274), painting by Francisco Zurbarán (1598–after 1664). (*Louvre, Paris*)

PLATE 20. BOOLE, George (1815–1864), engraving.
(*University College, Cork*)

PLATE 21. BOSANQUET, Bernard (1848–1923), photographed in 1917.

PLATE 22. BRADLEY, Francis Herbert (1846–1924), portrait by R. G. Eves (1876–1941).
(*Merton College, Oxford*)

Photo: *Radio Times Hulton Picture Library*

PLATE 23. BRAITHWAITE, Richard Bevan (1900–), photographed at the Joint Session of the Aristotelian Society and the Mind Association at Birmingham University, August 16 1952.

PLATE 24. BROAD, Charlie Dunbar (1887–), pencil portrait drawn in 1948 by Ruskin Spear (1911–). (*Trinity College, Cambridge*)

PLATE 25. BUTLER, Joseph (1692–1752), portrait.
(*Magdalen College, Oxford*)

PLATE 26. CAMBRIDGE, the Library of Trinity College. Trinity has been a centre of philosophical thought from its foundation in 1546 to the nineteenth century and the present day.

PLATE 27. CICERO, Marcus Tullius (106–43 B.C.), bust in the Vatican Museum, thought to be a copy made at the end of the first century A.D. of a bronze bust made in the time of Cicero.

PLATE 28. COLLINGWOOD, Robin George (1889–1943), photograph.
(*Pembroke College, Oxford*)

PLATE 29. COMTE, Isidore-Auguste-Marie-François-Xavier (1798–1857), engraving.

Photo: from „Littérature française" by Bédier and Hazard, Larousse, Paris

PLATE 30. CONDILLAC, Etienne Bonnet de (1715–1780),
engraving by Volpato after Baldrighi.

PLATE 31. CONDORCET, Marie-Jean-Antoine-Nicolas Caritat, Marquis de (1743–1794), lithograph by Delpech after Maurin.

PLATE 32. CORDOVA: The Great Chapel of the Cathedral. Averroes and Maimonides were born at Cordova which was capital of a Spanish province and an important town.

these values is so important, their identification with the creeds and cults of religions must be dissolved." (J.W.S.)

Plate 36, page 164.

Dialectic derives its name from the Greek verb meaning "to converse", and originally meant "the art of conversation, discussion or debate". Aristotle, in saying dialectic was invented by **Zeno** of Elea, was presumably referring to Zeno's paradoxes, which refuted some hypotheses of opponents by drawing unacceptable consequences from them. But it was first applied generally by Socrates, who, as presented in the earlier dialogues of Plato, constantly practised two techniques, both hypothetical in form: refuting an opponent's statement by getting him in the course of questioning to accept as an ultimate consequence of it a statement contradicting it (*elenchus*), and leading him on to a generalisation by getting him to accept its truth in a series of instances (*epagoge*, translated "induction").

Plato himself regarded dialectic as the supreme philosophical method, "the coping-stone of the sciences", and it was to be the final stage in the formal education of his philosopher-kings. But his references to dialectic, though always laudatory, are often vague, and he may have had various conceptions at different times. It seems always to have involved the search for unchanging essences, for example, above all for the idea of the Good, but almost any form of non-specialised abstract reasoning could fall under it. Sometimes it was certainly the method of refuting hypotheses, and at a later stage it included the method of "division" of a genus into species, one of which was then divided, and again as long as repetition was possible.

Aristotle put dialectic on a sound footing for the first time in his *Topics*, which is a handbook, written mainly before his discovery of the syllogism, for finding arguments to establish or demolish given positions, or *theses*, such as "Every pleasure is good". Such theses were probably debated in Plato's Academy, to which Aristotle belonged from 368 B.C. until Plato's death in 348, and he wanted to provide general methods for dealing with them. He says that his book is useful for three purposes: training, discussions, and the philosophical sciences. In the process he discovered many basic principles of formal logic, a subject which he developed in his *Analytics* as a theory of demonstration by contrast with dialectic, which is restricted to reasoning from mere opinions. But later, formal logic came to be called dialectic, by the **stoic** logicians.

A descendant of the debates in the Academy was the medieval disputation, in which the contestants continued, mainly by syllogistic reasoning, to maintain theses and antitheses (their opposites). By this means candidates in medieval universities were examined for degrees.

Hegel gave a new turn to dialectic, which he regarded as a process not merely of reasoning, but found in history, and in the universe as a whole, consisting of a necessary movement from thesis to antithesis, and then to a *synthesis* of the two. It is the Hegelian dialectic which was taken over by **Marx** and made part of his philosophy of Dialectical Materialism, substituting "matter" for Hegel's "spirit" as the basis of the dialectical process. (R.HALL)

Dialectical Materialism was originally the philosophical position adopted by **Marx** and **Engels**. It is now the official creed of the Communist party and is interpreted for political ends rather than as a matter of scholarship. Philosophically it is not necessary to look further than Marx and Engels, and perhaps Lenin, in studying dialectical materialism.

Marx and Engels used the term "materialism" rather loosely. For them to be a materialist is to "regard nature as primary", to hold that matter is independently real and that the mental develops out of the material and must be explained in physical terms. This view has to be understood as a negation of the Hegelian idealism of their times; the reality of thought and other mental phenomena is not denied, but only their primacy. Idealism and materialism are treated as being the only possible philosophical positions.

Traditional materialism was however rejected by Marx and Engels; such a view as that of the Greek **atomists**, which treated everything as being some arrangement of material particles in motion according to laws of mechanics, was stigmatized as mechanistic materialism and, while better than idealism, inadequate. A form of materialism which recognized process and development of the novel and more complex was required, and this was dialectical materialism; while "motion in the most general sense" was the essence of all process, a motion more complex than mechanical motion had to be recognized.

The notion of dialectics was derived from **Hegel**; "the dialectic of the concept itself became merely the conscious reflection of the dialectical motion of the real world and the dialectic of Hegel was placed upon its head; or rather, turned off its head on which it was standing before and placed on its feet again" (Engels: *Feuerbach*, ch. 4).

Dialectical materialism, then, sees the world as a process developing and evolving new and more complex phenomena out of the more simple according to dialectical principles, the laws of development. These laws are (1) The law of the transformation of quantitative into qualitative changes; illustration: – if water undergoes the quantitative change of getting hotter there will at a critical point be a qualitative change into steam; (2) The law of the interpenetration of opposites, involving the existence of contradictions within nature; illustration: – motion involves the contradiction of a thing simultaneously being in a place and not being in it; (3) the law of the negation of the negation; illustration: – feudalism is negated by capitalism which is then negated by socialism, so that the new arises by negation of negation. These laws, stated by Engels, do not appear to contain such words as "contradiction" and "negation" in their usual sense and some modern followers have restated the laws in less paradoxical ways and used less paradoxical examples. The essential point that Engels wished to stress is that there is genuine novelty and qualitative difference in the world and that even though everything arises from brute matter we cannot profitably think of everything as merely a matter of complicated mechanical systems.

The importance of this theory in the history of thought is as a general basis for Marx's political and economic doctrines; Marx himself was much more interested in these developments than in an accurate statement of the basis and it is a pity that external factors have spotlighted and fixed what was really of only transitory importance. (J.O.U.)

Diderot, Denis (1713–1784), a cutler's son, born at Langres, France. He received his final schooling at the Jesuit College of Louis-le-Grand in Paris. A man of encyclopaedic learning, he was a natural choice as editor of the *Encyclopédie*, that *summa* of all known knowledge. At first associated with d'Alembert as co-editor, following the latter's withdrawal in 1757 he became sole editor. From 1747 till the appearance of the seventeenth and final volume in 1765, he wrote numerous articles himself on philosophy, religion, political theory and literature, took particular interest in the sections on trade and applied sciences, and edited the articles of the other contributors. This achievement alone would have established his reputation.

The philosophy of Diderot is found in *Pensées Philosophiques* (1746); *Lettre sur les Aveugles* (1749); *Promenade du Sceptique; Pensées sur l'Interprétation de la Nature* (1754); *Lettre sur les sourds et muets* (1759); *L'Entretien d'un Philosophe avec Mme la Duchesse de XXX* (1776).

Following **Locke**, Diderot was a convinced empiricist, accepted scientific "facts" and rejected all metaphysical systems, especially Christian revelation, and the Church's claim to dominate the mind. Atheistic implications exist in *Lettre sur les Aveugles*. No Puritan, he has a secular morality which can be called the religion of humanity. As novelist-dramatist, art-critic and editor-contributor to the *Encyclopédie*, Diderot was a giant among the *philosophes* (intellectuals) of the Enlightenment. (F.A.T.)

Plate 37, page 165.

Diogenes, son of Hicesias, lived in Greece in the fourth century B.C. A prominent citizen of Sinope, he was exiled about the middle of the fourth century, allegedly for defacing the debased currency then appearing in Sinope; thereafter he lived at Athens and Corinth, becoming the prototype of **Cynicism**. It is likely that he was influenced by some aspects of **Antisthenes'** teaching, although Antisthenes was probably dead before Diogenes reached Athens. There is thus a tenuous thread leading back to **Socrates**, and there is some point in the alleged remark of Plato, that Diogenes was a Socrates gone mad.

Virtue, which alone produced happiness, was achieved through the attainment of self-sufficiency, the means to which was freedom from any external family or public restriction or internal disturbance of desires, emotions or fears. By rejecting all property, external goods, conventional values, any associations which could tie or restrict him and disturb his peace of mind, he reduced his needs and vulnerability to the barest natural minimum, retaining mastery of the kingdom which could not be taken from him – his own soul. This was to live in accordance with nature; everything else was convention and of illusory value, against which he carried on uncompromising warfare, seeking in his life and teaching to deface its currency in the eyes of others, as he and his father had defaced the debased currency at Sinope. As a practical ethic this required continual practice and training, both physical and mental. For example, he would embrace a bronze statue in winter to train the body in hardship and eradicate physical desire; he would court insult to test the subjugation of emotion in his mind. Indeed continual endurance of hardship, of which Heracles was the often quoted ideal, was a necessary concomitant of the stark poverty of the Cynic way of life. Diogenes' own life as a stateless beggar of no possessions sleeping where he could in Athens, was a practical demonstration of this, and with precept formed the method of his teaching. Theoretical education and learning were despised. Possessed of a cutting wit and repartee, his attack on convention knew no restraint of fear, authority or decency, either in word or deed, as he deliberately went to extremes to underline his points; hence his nickname, the Dog, from which, in Greek, came the word Cynicism. Diogenes accepted the taunt and many anecdotes of him contain illustrations from animals, which were free from the slavery of human convention. He is credited with some written works, notably a *Republic* and some tragedies illustrating his philosophy, but our tradition is doubtful and obscured by our lack of contemporary evidence, and by the legend that grew up around him. His life clearly is his testament.

Plate 38, page 166.   (I.G.K.)

Dualism is any system of thought which divides everything in some way into two categories or elements, or else derives everything from two principles, or else refuses to admit more or less than two substances or two kinds of substance. Although of course dualistic systems have to be justified by arguments, what leads some philosophers to dualism is the urge to tidy up and sim-

plify our picture of the world, an urge which would drive them on to **monism** if they were not prevented by respect for some radical and irreducible difference which their dualism expresses. The **Pythagoreans** afford an early example of this blockage of the unifying tendency, in their case by a whole series of opposites, which they reduced in turn to two basic principles, the Limit and the Unlimited.

The term, which was introduced by Heyde about 1700 to cover such theological views as Manichaeism, has the same ambiguities as monism, and can likewise be applied to at least three distinguishable and logically independent ontological views. The most outstanding and influential example of dualism, giving precise formulation to what is probably the commonsense view, and going back at least to **Anaxagoras**, is **Descartes'** division of the world into "extended substance" (matter) and "thinking substances" (minds); this kind of dualism might be called *attributive*, as claiming that there are two kinds of attributes and thus that all substances are of just two ultimate kinds. This distinguishes it from *substantial* dualism, the view that there are precisely two substances, which does not *by itself* have the same psychological attractiveness: for once admit that there is more than one substance, and it seems arbitrary not to admit several, unless the two admitted are of fundamentally different kinds. For the same reason, a third possibility, a *partial* dualism, claiming that regardless of the number of ultimate kinds of substance some one kind has just two substances belonging to it, is unattractive. It was in fact rejected by Descartes, who allowed only one substance in the material realm, but in the mental realm a plurality of them.

The term "dualism" can also be applied rather more loosely to philosophical systems which have as their core some important opposition, as in **Plato** between the world perceived by the senses and the world of Forms known by the mind, or in **Kant** the distinction between the phenomenal and the noumenal world.   (R.HALL)

Ducasse, Curt John, (1881–) born in France, and educated in France, England and USA. He is Professor of Philosophy at Brown University. He has worked in many fields of philosophy, but more specially in the field of the methodology of science; in this field his article entitled *Explanation, Mechanism and Teleology* (1925) has been particularly influential. His most important book is his Paul Carus Lectures *Nature, Mind and Death* (1951). This book epitomizes much of his thought: in Part I he discusses the subject matter and method of philosophy, holding that philosophical questions are essentially semantical and about the analysis of value-terms. Part II analyses such fundamental categories as those of substance and causation. Part III defends a view of perception according to which what is sensed is an internal accusative of the sensations and that perception proper always involves interpretation, conscious or unconscious. Part IV contains Ducasse's discussion of the relation of mind to body and of the possibility of survival; after a general discussion of traditional views and their difficulties and of the empirical evidence for survival he tentatively suggests a modified version of metempsychosis as the most plausible hypothesis. (J.O.U.)

E

Edwards, Jonathan (1703–1757), born in South Windsor, Connecticut, is now widely recognized as one of the most brilliant and original philosophical minds produced by America. He stood midway between the Calvinist theological mind of the seventeenth century and the Lockean **empiricist** temper of the eighteenth century. In his own time the significance of his major writings was missed on both sides. For close to two centuries his reputation was confined to the field of specialized theology and distorted by failure to grasp his central philosophical intent. Not until the twentieth century was his role in the drama of eighteenth-century thought reconsidered and gradually understood.

The traditional conception of Edwards was that of a man who in early life showed great promise as a philosopher steeped in the writings and the spirit of Newton and **Locke**; who later as a Calvinist minister sought to revive the fundamental axioms of Calvinism at a time when they were losing their hold on English-speaking minds; who therefore must be considered as an "anachronism" smothering his latent philosophical promise with Hell-fire sermons and esoteric treatises which sought to justify them.

A proper understanding of Edwards will recognize that all of his mature writings are careful and brilliant attempts to defend and reinterpret the fundamental axioms of Calvinism in terms precisely of that deep understanding and profound grasp of the spirit of Newton and Locke which he never for a moment abandoned. He did straddle, as it were, an impossible fence. His subtle revision of the import of Calvinism made him unpopular among the defenders of the orthodoxy he was trying to save; his use of the new philosophical spirit to revive religious orthodoxy at all made him anathema to the run-of-the-mill proponents of the secularized spirit of the "Enlightenment". The fact remains that Edwards' major writings show a deeper understanding of the new philosophical insights of the eighteenth century than do the commonly adulated works of later Americans such as Franklin and Paine.

His major works were three; and each was designed to reinterpret a fundamental Calvinist axiom in the light of Newton and Locke. The axiom of Determinism is defended in the treatise on *Freedom of the Will*. This treatise remains one of the classic defences of determinism, and should be compared with such standard twentieth-century texts as that of *The Freedom of the Will* by the California Associates (1938). The axiom of depravity is defended in the treatise on the *Nature of True Virtue*. The brilliance of Edwards' revision of the concept of depravity is difficult to overestimate. The argument rests throughout upon a thoroughgoing Lockean psychological analysis; its logic is impeccable, and one is struck by the independence of the argument upon any appeal to theological matters such as the story of the Fall of Man. The central theological axiom of Calvinism – the axiom of God's omnipotence and inscrutability – recurs in all of Edwards' writings; but the pivotal document in which he takes his stand on the source of man's knowledge of God is the treatise on the *Religious Affections*. Here too Edwards' argument is based upon a thoroughgoing Lockean empiricist psychology. His defence of the emotive basis of religious experience (designed as a defence of the Great Awakening) is one of the most forward-looking documents of the time. The late eighteenth century committed the great mistake of proclaiming an utterly unempirical "argument from design" as the touchstone of empiricism in religion. Edwards on the contrary saw clearly that the only consistent way to endorse empiricism in religion is to endorse mysticism. The empirical demand is the demand that you have experience of that whereof you speak; and if you speak of God this is a demand for the mystical strain. Edwards' defence of the thesis that such experiences are always essentially emotive in character not only seeks to conform to the demands of empiricist psychology of his time but also results in an astonishing foreshadowing of claims usually associated with William **James'** monumental *Varieties of Religious Experience* published nearly two centuries later.

It should be repeated that Edwards' defence of Calvinism seriously modified it He was a thoroughgoing Antinomian and insofar heretical. But few men anywhere in the eighteenth century more fully grasped or more brilliantly expressed what was new and permanent in the philosophy of the West in the eighteenth century.   (J.W.S.)

Plate 39, page 167.

Eleatics is the name given to the philosopher **Parmenides** and his follower **Zeno**, who lived in Elea (a Greek colony in southern Italy) and argued that reality must be single and unchanging, and by implication that the plural sense-world is therefore illusory. Also counted as an Eleatic, because he accepted these views, was Melissus of Samos, who flourished *c.* 440 B.C.; he amended Parmenides by arguing that Being was infinite, not finite, and incorporeal. He also produced an explicit argument against sensation: we perceive plurality, yet we also perceive that things change, which on Eleatic premises is logically impossible; therefore perception is false, and if there are many they must be of the same kind as the Eleatic One. This conclusion may have aided **Leucippus** in his conception of **atomism**. **Xenophanes**, too, was often regarded in antiquity as an Eleatic, because of the superficial resemblance of his one god with Parmenides' one Being; but Parmenides' logical process of inference is so radically different from Xenophanes' reversal of Homeric anthropomorphism that there were probably no close links between the two thinkers. The Eleatics – their leader, Par-

menides, in particular – had a profound effect on the development of Pre-Socratic thought. The material monism of the Milesians and the structural monism of **Heraclitus** were replaced by systems that envisaged a plurality of essentially immutable elements, and which had now to face the question of the validity of sensation. See also **Pre-Socratics.**   (G.S.K.)

Empedocles of Acragas in Sicily, flourished *c.* 450 B.C. He was a doctor, also a keen democrat; his mystical claims (e.g. that he was a god, having previously been "a boy, a girl, a bush and a bird and a dumb fish in the sea") gave rise to extravagant biographical inventions. To meet **Parmenides'** dilemma he claimed in his physical poem "On Nature" that apparent coming-to-be and perishing were caused by the mixture and separation of eternally-existing "roots" or elements – fire, water, earth, and air (the corporeality of which Empedocles verified by observation). Attraction and repulsion of the roots were caused by specific motive agents, Love and Strife, which also possessed size and bulk. An equivalent to Parmenides' "sphere" of Beings was reproduced when Love permeated the roots and mixed them together; then Strife gradually entered the sphere which was described as a god and caused plurality to assert itself. Thus the senses, if properly used, were *not* necessarily deceptive; in fact sensation was caused by physical effluences from objects entering pores in the sense-organs and meeting with corresponding roots there; thus fire activates fire in the eye, in vision. Empedocles avoided the apparent coming-to-be of traditional cosmogonies by making the entry of Strife into the sphere merely one stage out of four in a never-ending cosmic cycle: domination of Love, entry and gradual increase of Strife, domination of Strife, entry of Love. Our world belongs to the second of these. Corresponding with the transitional stages were two evolutionary stages: when Love is in the ascendant, first disunited limbs, then monsters; when Strife increases, first "whole-natured forms", then our world. In a second poem, "Purifications", Empedocles described a personal cycle of innocence, pollution, fall, purification, and deification. Verbal resemblances with the physical poem suggest that this cycle had some correspondence with the cosmic one. Pollution is caused by bloodshed and strife, and leads to successive incarnations of the type also envisaged by **Pythagoreans** and Orphics. See also **Pre-Socratics**. (G.S.K.)

Empiricism. In its ordinary use, the term "empiricism" (from the Greek "empeiria" = "experience") means the employment of methods based on practical experience, rather than on an accepted body of theory. But in philosophy the word is used only in a quite different, and technical, sense to refer to the philosophical theory that all knowledge is derived from experience. "Radical empiricism" was the name given by William **James** to his own version of this theory.

Empiricism has been developed mainly by a succession of British philosophers, of whom the most important are **Locke, Berkeley, Hume** and John Stuart **Mill**. Although such movements as **Encyclopedism** in France have been inspired by empiricist ideas, empiricism has never taken hold on the Continent, whereas in Britain it has been the dominant tradition in philosophy since the seventeenth century. Moreover, Continental empiricists, like the Frenchman Condillac, have always been directly or indirectly influenced by British philosophy.

The general principles of empiricism are opposed primarily to those of **rationalism**, and it was as a reaction against the systems of **Descartes, Spinoza** and **Leibniz** that modern empiricism originated. There are two central questions at issue between rationalists and empiricists. The first concerns **a priori** concepts (or "innate ideas" as they were misleadingly called in the seventeenth century), that is, ideas which, it is claimed, are not derived from sense-experience but independently produced by reason or intellect. Rationalists allow that some concepts are empirical (for example, that we derive our idea of redness from our experience of seeing red objects), but they maintain that our knowledge of the world also involves *a priori* concepts like those of cause and substance. It is fundamental to empiricism to deny the existence of such ideas. Empiricists therefore argue either that allegedly *a priori* concepts can be analysed or broken down into a combination of simpler concepts derived from experience, or sometimes, and more radically, that they are not genuine concepts at all (for example, that "substance", as a metaphysical term, is simply a word to which no meaning can be assigned). The second dispute between rationalists and empiricists concerns *a priori* propositions or statements. It is generally agreed that all necessary truths are *a priori*, since we can only learn from experience what has been and is likely to be the case, not what *must* be so. Empiricists, who believe that we have no means of acquiring knowledge except through observation of what actually happens, contend that necessary truths are true by definition, or **analytic**. Rationalists, on the other hand, hold that some *a priori* statements are synthetic; that is, that they tell us something about the nature of the world. The assertion "every event must have a cause", for example, has been said to be a self-evident principle of this kind: *a priori* because it states a necessary connection, and synthetic because it is not simply true by definition (as "every *effect* has a cause" is). It is characteristic of empiricism to deny that reason can assure us of the truth of a genuinely synthetic statement and therefore that any proposition can be both *a priori* and synthetic.

As a result of their disagreement over these matters of principle, rationalists and empiricists have very different attitudes towards natural science and towards metaphysics. Rationalists have been inclined, broadly speaking, to think of beliefs based on experience as infected with error. For them, an understanding of the world is not to be gained through sense-perception, which is confused, but through metaphysical speculation. But precisely because metaphysics claims to give knowledge of a reality transcending experience, metaphysical inquiry depends upon our having *a priori* concepts. The empiricist tradition has therefore been antagonistic to metaphysics, and has set a high value on science as a means of acquiring knowledge. It is no accident that Hume described Newton as "the greatest and rarest genius that ever arose for the ornament and instruction of the species".

The solutions that empiricists offer to particular philosophical problems are essentially applications of the general principles that have been described. Hume's account of causation is a classical example of this. Hume is well aware that the relation of cause and effect presents crucial difficulties for empiricism and that he has to show that the idea of a cause originates in experience. He maintains, and in this he has been generally followed by later empiricists, that the causal connection between two events *is*, in effect, their regular succession, which is a matter of observation. He allows that the idea of a cause involves the idea of necessity, but this he also traces to its origin in experience. The repeated observation of B following upon A produces in us the habit of thinking of B when we perceive A. It is the experience of this habit of thought which is the source of our idea of necessity. "Necessity", Hume writes, "is something that exists in the mind, not in objects". He claims therefore to have refuted the rationalist account of causation as a necessary connection between objects, and to have shown that the idea of causation is a complex one that can be analysed into simpler elements (for example, the idea of regular sequence) each of which is derived from experience.

Another typical application of empiricist principles is to the theory of mathematics. Mathematics has always been regarded as a stronghold of rationalism, since on the face of it, mathematical propositions are *a priori* and synthetic. $7 + 5 = 12$: it seems both that this *must* be so and that it is a truth about objects that we can know in advance of any experience of them. This challenge has been met by empiricists in two ways, by denying either the *a priori* or the synthetic character of mathematics. The first course is that taken by J. S. Mill, who treats mathematics as a generalisation from experience. $7 + 5 = 12$ is, according to him, a law of nature based on observation. If, however, arithmetic is not necessarily true and is only established by experience, it remains possible that it might also be falsified by experience, difficult though it may be to imagine what that experience would be like. Few empiricists have been prepared to swallow this paradox. They have usually taken the other alternative, of asserting that mathematics is analytic, not synthetic. According to this view, mathematical propositions are true by definition. $7 + 5 = 12$ is a necessary truth, only because we define "7", "+", "5", "=", and "12" in such a way as to make it so. Mathematics therefore does not, as rationalists have thought, give us any information about the nature of the world. (See for example, A. J. Ayer, *Language, Truth and Logic*, Chapter 4). Though there are considerable technical disagreements about the nature of mathematics between present day empiricists they all agree on the essential point that its truths are necessary only because they are in this way uninformative.

Empiricism is primarily a theory of knowledge, but its influence has also been considerable in the field of **ethics**. The reason for this is that empiricists have had to work out an ethical theory that is consistent with their general account of knowledge, rather than that they have always been especially interested in ethics. Moral concepts (like rightness, obligation, duty and so on) must, if they are genuine concepts and if empiricism is correct, be derivable from experience like any others. But according to rationalists this derivation is not possible. We can see that a man is behaving ungratefully, but we cannot similarly see that his ingratitude is wrong. Our idea of wrongdoing, it is said, is not based on experience, and we know that ingratitude is wrong only because reason intuitively grasps the *a priori* connection between these two ideas. The basic principles of morality are self-evident, in the sense that they neither can be, nor need to be, justified by argument or observation. The reply of empiricists in the eighteenth century to this intuitionist theory was, in Hume's words that "morality is more properly felt than judged of". Moral ideas are derived from *inner* experience. We do not, admittedly, observe the wrongness of an action, but we *feel* it, and it is this feeling that we put into words when we say that the action is wrong. (See Hume's *Treatise of Human Nature*, Book 3, Part I). This point of view (often called the moral sense theory) was characteristically combined in eighteenth century empiricism with the theory that our only duty is to produce as much happiness as possible (utilitarianism). Although utilitarianism is not an essential part of empiricist ethics, this combination is an understandable one. For, since they do not believe that moral principles are self-evident, it is natural for empiricists to hold that morality is justified by its tendency to bring about human happiness, which makes an appeal to each person's instinctive feelings of sympathy. Contemporary empiricists have come to realize that it is unsatisfactory to treat moral judgments as statements about feelings, and to regard ethics as a branch of the science of human nature, in the manner of Hume. They have therefore tended to argue that moral principles do not assert *a priori* truths, because they assert nothing, their function being solely the practical one of influencing behaviour. It has been suggested that moral judgments are really commands (for example, "stealing is wrong" = "do not steal") or that they are expressions of feeling (not *statements about* feelings) having no objective validity. This "emotive theory of ethics" rests on a naive view of language, and it has been widely criticized. It seems likely, however, that a thorough investigation of the function of moral judgments may lead to an empiricist ethics that avoids the paradoxes of the emotive theory.

If the empiricism of recent times is compared with that of the eighteenth and nineteenth centuries the most significant advance that can be seen to have been made is the clear separation of logical from psychological issues. The older empiricists were primarily interested in problems, of the kind that have been mentioned, about the analysis of concepts and the logical status of propositions, rather than in psychological problems about the origin of ideas. Nevertheless they were often confused about the questions they were debating and wrote as if their intention was to give a natural history of the mind. Hume and J. S. Mill, for example, felt themselves to be committed to an atomistic psychology, which explained all mental activity in terms of the association of ideas. Modern empiricists, on the other hand, recognise that their philosophy is compatible with any psychological theory that is based on observation, and leave psychology to the psychologists.

The establishment of empiricism purely as a thesis about the logical structure of knowledge has been an important stimulus to the development of mathematical logic. It has also led to the conception of philosophy as the analysis of concepts and propositions, and therefore to an increased hostility to speculative philosophy and to metaphysics in particular. This hostility found its most extreme expression in **logical positivism**, advocated in the twenties and thirties principally by the group of philosophers known as the **Vienna Circle**. The positivists held that apart from the formal or analytic statements of mathematics and logic, no statements were significant except those which could be verified by observation. Metaphysical and theological assertions were consequently rejected, not as

unproved, but as "nonsensical" or "meaningless". At the present time, few empiricists would go so far as this. The tendency is, certainly, not to reinstate metaphysics as a means of knowing a reality transcending experience, but to treat the writings of metaphysicians more sympathetically as attempts to carry out a high-level revision of concepts, a "redrawing of the map of thought" as it has been called. It is a milder empiricism of this type that characterises the contemporary philosophical movements that are sometimes known as "linguistic analysis" or "analytic philosophy".   (E.B.)

Encyclopedists. The first intention of the Paris printer and publisher, Le Breton, was to translate the English *Cyclopaedia* of Ephraim Chambers (1727), but when **Diderot** and d'Alembert became co-editors the scope was enlarged until it became the *Encyclopédie ou Dictionnaire Raisonné des Sciences, des Arts et des Métiers* (1751–1765). This great work in seventeen folio volumes was a monument to the erudition of the French intellectuals or *philosophes*, with the aim of providing information on every branch of knowledge, and giving special attention to the application of science to industry, trade and the arts.

Chief among the contributors was Diderot, who, besides having the general direction of the work, wrote, in addition to the Prospectus, an immense number of articles – on religion, ancient history, political theory, (his article on *Autorité Politique* is the most outspoken pronouncement in the whole work), philosophy, beer; and he also wrote copiously on the applied arts. D'Alembert, who was a member of the *Académie des Sciences* before he was thirty, wrote his celebrated *Discours Préliminaire*, in which he traced the growth of knowledge from the beginning. Although chiefly concerned with geometry, mathematics and the sciences, he wrote the notorious article on *Genève* in 1757 which provoked the ire of the local clergy (identified therein with Socinianism) and also the wrath of **Rousseau**, because d'Alembert had deplored the absence of a theatre in Geneva. This called forth Rousseau's indignant *"Lettre à d'Alembert sur les Spectacles"*. Disgusted with the outcry over this article and for other reasons of prudence and ambition, d'Alembert withdrew his collaboration at the end of 1757, leaving Diderot to carry on alone.

Luckily Diderot's devoted friend, the Chevalier de Jaucourt, who had studied medicine in Geneva, Leyden and Cambridge, then became the general factotum of the work, and wrote articles on the widest variety of topics – philosophy (he had previously published a study of **Leibniz**), politics and literature, war, despotism, government and monarchy etc. Some critics claim that he was as important and as devoted to the enterprise as Diderot himself.

J. J. Rousseau wrote on music, but a more important contribution on *Economie Politique* foreshadowed some of the theories of *Le Contrat Social*. Later, Rousseau came to regard the *Encyclopédie* as the work of the devil; he quarrelled not only with d'Alembert but with Diderot as well, and he fiercely abused all the philosophers and their works.

The fifth volume opened with a notable tribute to Montesquieu, author of the *Esprit des Lois*, whose influence on the *Encyclopédie* was all-pervading. None the less, Montesquieu stood aloof; refusing to write on *Despotisme* and *Démocratie*, he sent an incomplete article on *Goût* which was finished by Voltaire. Nor did the latter, despite interest and encouragement, contribute much. His articles on *Froid, Galant, Garant, Gazette, Genre de Style, Grandeur, Grâce, Hémistiche, Histoire, Idoles, Idolâtrie* are more important for their style than for their content, the article *Histoire* excepted. Voltaire's friend, Marmontel, an indifferent novelist and playwright, contributed articles on literature.

Although the editors claimed that the *Encyclopédie* had attracted the most eminent contributors, two outstanding personalities found its atmosphere too bellicose: Buffon, author of the great *Histoire Naturelle*, who may have contributed one article on *Nature*; and Duclos, a court historian, who wrote only on *Déclamation* and *Etiquette*. The King's physician, Quesnay, contributed two outstanding articles, *Fermiers* and *Grains*, products of physiocratic principles. From the same Physiocratic school of thought came Turgot, to be famous later as Intendant and Minister. He wrote on *Foires et Marchés* condemning barriers to free enterprise; on *Fondations*, showing the disadvantage of unchangeable bequests; a learned article on *Etymologie* and another on *Existence*. As for the German Baron d'Holbach, the Maecenas of the *philosophe* movement, he wrote on mineralogy and chemistry, and

there are grounds for attributing to him the entry on *Représentants* which maintains that a state cannot be prosperous and happy unless the king invites the co-operation of all elements of the population. For the rest, his general philosophy is contained in his notorious *Système de la Nature* (1770) where he insisted that kings are the defenders of the liberty of their subjects. Holbach was an atheist and as such was attacked by Voltaire.

The great majority of the articles are factual and objective, written by specialists without an axe to grind. Their names are mostly forgotten now, but we may mention Daubenton, who wrote on Natural History, Dumarsais on Grammar, Toussaint on Jurisprudence, the illustrious Doctor Tronchin of Geneva on Inoculation, Pichard "*Marchand Fabricant Bonnetier*" on Headgear; the Abbés Yvon and Mallet, two innocents who wrote on Theology.

Other articles, however, were more barbed. Whereas opinions on politics were moderate, for republicanism had no adherents, contributions connected with philosophy (deeply permeated with Lockean empiricism) and religion were double-edged, despite orthodox professions. For instance, under *Capuchon*, the absence from monasteries of *la saine philosophie* is deplored, and under *Encyclopédie* occurs the bland statement that the contribution of the Sorbonne to knowledge will be theology, sacred history, and the history of superstitions. One needs to read between the lines and to follow the cross-references to see how sceptical are these rationalist philosophers to the truths of religion. These latter would not stand up to the laws of evidence demanded in Diderot's article *Agnus Scythicus*. Because of this attitude the *Encyclopédie* was suspect from the beginning, and in the course of its chequered career it came into conflict with the Jesuits, the Jansenists, the Sorbonne, the Pope, the Parlement, the devout party at Court, and private enemies. The first suppression in 1752, thanks to Jesuit intrigue, was repeated in 1759, owing largely to the outcry against the materialism of *De l'Esprit*, a work of Helvetius, a friend but not a contributor. The public prosecutor assumed that this work was the very quintessence of *philosophe* doctrine and it was condemned to be burned. Its fate brought about the second suppression of the *Encyclopédie* but in neither case was the ban enforced for long, and the work went on despite hostility. In 1757 a

Engels

lawyer called Moreau published a pamphlet in which the *philosophes* were called *Cacouacs*, a pejorative definition which caused them intense annoyance. In 1760 Pallissot pilloried the *philosophes*, chiefly Diderot and Rousseau, in the comedy of that name. Other enemies were Boyer, a former bishop, and the poet Le Franc de Pompignan, both of whom were devastatingly ridiculed by Voltaire. But the man who gave most annoyance was Freron, editor of *L'Année Littéraire*, the gadfly or rather hornet journalist (Frelon) whom Voltaire subjected to petulant but ineffective criticism in his play *L'Ecossaise* (1760).

Throughout these vicissitudes, Diderot stood firm, a real *feste Burg*. Thanks to his efforts, the seventeenth and final volume of text appeared in 1765, and the indispensable eleven volumes of plates were complete by 1772. This great manifesto of the *philosophe* movement was, despite omissions and contradictions, the finest tribute to Reason and the power of the human mind which France and the Age of Enlightenment produced. Diderot's avowed aim, which was *"changer la façon commune de penser"* (to change accepted habits of thought) was in large measure realized.   (F.A.T.)

Plate 40, page 168.

Engels, Friedrich (1820–1895), German socialist, was the friend, collaborator and financial supporter of **Marx** during his residence in Britain. To Engels rather than to Marx we owe the exposition of the fundamental tenets of **Dialectical Materialism**. His most important theoretical works are *Ludwig Feuerbach*, in which he treats of materialism and idealism, dialectical and mechanistic materialism and the materialist reorientation of Hegelian dialectics; *Anti-Dühring* in which he restates much of his position in reply to the criticisms of Dühring; and *The Dialectics of Nature* which contains his fullest statement of the laws of development. Engels also shared in Marx's political enterprise, his *Socialism, Utopian and Scientific* being one of the best statements of the position of Marxian socialism; he was also co-author with Marx of the *Manifesto of the Communist Party*.   (J.O.U.)

Plate 41, page 169.

Epictetus (c. 55–c. 135 A.D.,) a **Stoic** of Hierapolis, Phrygia. A freed slave of Nero's secretary, and pupil of the Stoic Musonius, he set up a school in Nicopolis when Domitian banished the philosophers from Rome in 89. His stoicism underlines freedom, providence, practicality, humanity. A man must choose between slavery to externals and freedom in the inviolability of his moral purpose, which alone is completely in his power, unassailable by all external ills. No man can injure or be injured by another, he can only injure himself. For the governing, indeed divine, principle in man is his moral will; hence his sole active duty is to exercise it rightly, and by recognising the rule of divine providence in the universe of which he is an integral part, to accept God's will. Impatient of academic theorising, he concentrated on a practical ethic illustrated by everyday examples; **Socrates** and **Diogenes** were his heroes. His message was not, like that of many Stoics, to an intellectual, social or governing élite, but to the common brotherhood of ordinary men. The humanity and nobility of his teaching shine in the *Manual* and four surviving books of lectures we have from the notes of his pupil Arrian. Failure is human and should not deter one from remaining intent on the ideal; only sham and pretence are denounced. His later influence on both pagan and Christian thought was widespread.   (I.G.K.)

Epicurus (342–270 B.C.), an Athenian citizen. He was brought up in Samos, returned to Athens for a short period of study as a young man, and then spent some years in Asia Minor. He finally returned to Athens in about 306 B.C. where he set up his school in the garden where he taught until his death.

The modern notion of an Epicurean as a man given up to voluptuous high living is based on the slanders of later Greek writers and not on the life or teaching of Epicurus. "Send me some cheese of Cythnos that I may be able to fare sumptuously when I like", runs a fragment of one of his letters indicative of his modest fare; and on his death-bed he wrote movingly to a friend: "On this last, yet blessed, day of my life, I write to you. Pains and tortures of the body I have to the full, but there is set over against these the joy of my heart at the memory of our happy conversations in the past. Do you, if you would be worthy of your devotion to me and philosophy, take care of the children of Metrodorus".

Epicurus is best known for his moral theory of **hedonism** and as a propounder of the atomic theory; yet in neither field was he original. The only original contribution that he made to the theory of atomism, the view that atoms originally fell in a kind of rain in parallel courses but that some few atoms swerved by a free choice, thus setting up collisions, is clearly motivated by moral considerations and is a regression rather than an improvement. This being the case the reader is referred to the general article on **atomism**. On morals, too, he appears to be unoriginal, for the essentials of the ethics of Epicurus can be found in the ethical fragments of **Democritus.** The explicit claims of Epicurus to originality in theoretical matters can be dismissed as false.

But Epicurus was unoriginal in theoretical matters not because he was second-rate but because his interest was essentially practical; he was a secular evangelist who had to preach the secret of true happiness, and as such an evangelist he had a moral earnestness similar to that of the apostles of nineteenth-century **utilitarianism.** Thus Epicurus taught the atomic theory not as a truth to be proclaimed for its own sake but as an antidote to superstition; men were haunted with fear of gods and demons, terrified of death and the torments of the underworld, and thus unhappy; the mechanistic doctrines of atomism, which denied to the gods any control of nature or interest in human affairs and treated the soul as a concourse of atoms which was dissolved at death, were primarily an antidote to these terrors. But a purely mechanistic atomism might suggest that man was a mere machine; the doctrine of the voluntary atomic swerve was an antidote to this danger justifiable only as demanded by ethics but a mere excrescence on atomic theory; "it were better to follow the myths about the gods than to become a slave to the destiny of the natural philosophers".

Epicurus' moral views have been much misunderstood and misrepresented. The theoretical basis is that pleasure alone is good and always good. It consists in the driving out of pain, and when pain is ended pleasure can only be varied but not increased. Pleasure is either bodily, perfect health being its highest form, or mental, when it is freedom from fear and anxiety. But though all pleasure is good in itself some pleasure brings pain with it as an inevitable consequence; therefore not all pleasure is to be chosen. Therefore wisdom is of the greatest importance since it is by wisdom that we are able to make the best choice of pleasures. Epicurus thus introduces the notion of a hedonic calculus.

We have there all the essentials of Epicurus' ethical theory; but he is much more concerned with telling us what the wise choice of pleasures is than with theory. In the letter to Menoecus he says: "When therefore we maintain that pleasure is an end, we do not mean the pleasures of profligates and those that consist in sensuality . . . but freedom from pain in the body and from trouble in the mind. For it is not continuous drinkings, nor the satisfaction of lusts, . . . but sober reasoning, searching out the motives for all choice and avoidance." Pains of the mind are much more important than those of the body, which are either bearable or produce death, which is no evil. Death is neither good nor evil, for only pleasure and pain are good and evil, whereas death "is nothing to us, since so long as we exist death is not with us, but when death comes then we no longer exist." Moreover, though virtue is not in itself a good, no man can live the happy life unless he does live virtuously and the virtuous life is pleasant as such.

Epicurus was not an atheist; but the gods do not control nature nor do they interfere in human life. They live far out in space a life of infinite bliss which would be spoilt if they worried about human affairs; it is impious to believe that the gods have nothing better to do than concern themselves with humanity. Epicurus practised a disinterested worship of the gods conceived as exhibiting the ultimate beatitude.

Epicurus' practical teaching is thus paradoxical. He is a theist who regards ordinary religion as evil; a hedonist who advocates a simple virtuous life of study; a supporter of virtue and the pursuit of truth who holds them to have no value in themselves. The appeal of such a doctrine is to few and the Epicureans were unpopular and traduced already in antiquity. But Epicurus seems to have endeavoured to live the life he preached; he gathered a simple community of disciples round him in his garden; we are told that "he exceeded all others in the bulk of his works", of which some seventy or eighty pages survive; and on his death-bed he spoke contemptuously of his severe pains as weighing nothing against his joy of mind.

Among the surviving writings of Epicurus may be singled out the letter to Herodotus as containing the earliest extant complete account of the general atomic theory and the letter to Menoecus as containing a short account of the ethical position. The philosophical poem by **Lucretius**, *De Rerum Natura*, also well brings out both the doctrines and the practical attitude of Epicurus.   (J.O.U.)

Plate 42, page 170.

Epistemology. There is a wide-ranging, loosely knit set of philosophical problems concerning such notions as those of knowing, perceiving, feeling sure, guessing, being mistaken, remembering, finding out, proving, inferring, establishing, corroborating, wondering, reflecting, imagining, dreaming and so on. This part of philosophy is often called the Theory of Knowledge, or Epistemology – the latter word deriving from the Greek *Episteme* = knowledge or science.

Some of the problems revolve around the notion of a science, in the sense in which we take astronomy to be a science, but astrology not. A fairly typical problem of this kind is the problem why in pure **mathematics** there are conclusive proofs of theorems, when no such demonstrable certainties can be found or even looked for in, for example, history or medicine. It would be absurd for a mathematician to rest content with mere plausible conjectures or even with highly probable hypotheses. Scientists of other sorts seem not to be in a position to aspire higher than high probabilities. We incline to say that a body of truths ranks as a real science only when these are conclusively established; and then we find ourselves forced to say that, judged by this rigorous standard, even physics and chemistry are not really sciences; and this conclusion conflicts badly with our ordinary ideas.

Other problems in the Theory of Knowledge centre not upon the notion of a science, but upon the notions of our personal investigatings, nferrings, perceivings, rememberings, imaginings, and so on. How can I tell for certain whether the stick half immersed in water is bent or not? How can I tell for certain whether I really recollect a past event or am merely imagining it, and whether

I am now awake or dreaming? Might I not be the victim of one continuous illusion?

Whatever sorts of things we may want to find out, our attempt may fail in one of two ways. We may be simply baffled, or we may get something positively wrong. We can be stumped or we can make mistakes in calculating, in counting, in reasoning, in visual estimates of speeds and distances, in recognizing people or places, in recollecting, as well as in more executive things like spelling, aiming and treating the sick. What safeguards have we against mistakes? How, if at all, can we ever know anything? For in knowing, unlike believing, surmising and feeling confident, we cannot be wrong.

When we consider conflicting opinions about what exists and happens in the world around us, e.g. about the relative heights of two church-steeples or about the migration-dates of cuckoos, we think we could decide between the true and the mistaken opinion by, in the one case, simply measuring the heights of the two steeples, and in the other case by observing the arrivals and departures of cuckoos for a number of years in succession. But then we have to face the fact that there are mistakes of measurement and even mishearings of the first cuckoo. How could we decide between conflicting measurements or between conflicting reports of bird-watchers? At this point we are inclined to say that the ultimate decision, if only we could attain it, would be given by sense impressions unadulterated by any assumptions, guesses or expectations – by pure hearings, seeings or tastings in which there is not yet any place for slips or misjudgments. Here perhaps we have the absolutely firm foundation on which we might build knowledge of the world around us. The difference between having knowledge of something in the world around us and merely having a fallible opinion about it would be that the former would be at all points supported by sense-impressions, where the latter, though suggested by them, would be at best only partly supported by them. Where I am or may be mistaken, I have let my imagination jump ahead of the required impressions.

This sort of account of the difference between knowledge and fallible opinion will not be applicable inside the fields of purely abstract truths and falsehoods, like those of pure mathematics; nor yet inside some other fields, like those of ethics. Nor can my knowledge about my present wishes, fears, imaginings and broodings rest on the support of what I see with my eyes or taste with my tongue. It is for our knowledge only of what exists and happens in the world surrounding us, as well as in our own bodies, that sense-impressions, it seems, furnish the granite foundations.

In every case in this field where we would normally claim to be not merely guessing or believing something, but to have discovered or made certain of it, the fact which we claim to know goes beyond any particular momentary visual or auditory impression. If I assert that the cuckoo has arrived, I am asserting more than that at a certain moment I heard a noise of a certain sort. How then can we go beyond our present impressions and still sometimes claim to know? The natural answer to give is that we *infer* from e.g. the sound that we have heard to the ulterior conclusion that the cuckoo has arrived. Our knowledge of the world around us, together with our mere beliefs and conjectures about this world, are all conglomerations of interlocking conclusions inferred, sometimes legitimately, sometimes riskily and sometimes illegitimately from our impressions. Knowledge, unlike belief and conjecture, would be the product solely of legitimate and riskless inferences. But then what, if anything, can guarantee our inferences themselves against being mistaken? Even if the impressions from which we infer are exempt from slips, still the inferences that we draw from them are not so exempt.

If we knew, somehow, from the start some completely exceptionless causal laws, to the effect that whenever such and such a sequence of sense-impressions is had, then such and such other sense-impressions will always follow, then in any particular case we could, without risk of error, infer from the sense-impressions of the present moment to their successors in the next few moments. But we do not start off with any such knowledge. If we get bits of such knowledge, we get them late in the day, after a great deal of observation and experimentation. We discover the ways in which things always or sometimes happen only by finding them happening and collating our findings; and even then the laws and regularities that at any particular time we claim to have ascertained are always subject to subsequent correction. Nature is never without her surprises. The unpredicted sometimes happens and the predicted sometimes fails to happen. So it begins to look as if knowledge about the world around us, going beyond our impressions of the moment, cannot be got at all. For it would have to be knowledge by inference; but we possess, to start with, no warrant to make any such inferences. If we make jumps beyond our present impressions, we can have, to start with, no warrants for making them; and even if they happen to turn out right, this, by itself, cannot justify us in making the same jump on the next similar occasion. One lucky guess may be succeeded by another lucky guess. But we have no reason to expect it, however much we, like gamblers, are irrational enough to trust that our successes will continue.

So far we have been not expounding but rather reconstructing a line of thought that was operative in especially **Locke**, **Berkeley** and **Hume**. We have contrasted our fallible perceptions and inferences with knowledge of what exists and happens in the world around us, with the disappointing upshot that this knowledge seems to be forever out of reach. Those very matters of everyday fact which we are inclined to adduce as obvious instances of things known and not merely guessed or opined – such as that the cuckoo has reached England, or that this church-steeple is taller than that one – seem unable to live up to their promise. The granite foundation of mistake-proof sense-impressions seems unable to carry any mistake-proof superstructure. Perhaps all that I can know from perception is that I am at this moment seeing such and such colours, smelling such and such smells, and hearing such and such noises, and these seen colours and heard noises are untrustworthy clues, if they are clues at all, to what exists or happens in the world around us – if there is such a world.

Considerations like these have led many thinkers to reverse the whole direction of the inquiry. Knowledge, as opposed to guesswork and opinion, is to be found where the sciences at their peak are to be found. What is known to some and is in principle knowable to all is any body of truths conclusively established by the rigorous methods of true science. We can get beyond guesswork and fallible opinion to knowledge by operating as geometricians and arithmeticians operate, namely by pure thought, not vitiated by the deliverances of our senses. Where we can calculate and demonstrate we can know. Where we can only observe and experiment we cannot know. No set of sense-impressions can yield knowledge. Only by exercises of pure thought can we ascertain truths. In the most exacting sense of the word "science" there cannot be empirical sciences, but only purely ratiocinative sciences. Holders of this kind of view are called "**rationalists**". This programme leaves us discontented. We object that even granting that in pure mathematics we can discover uncontradictable truths, still these truths are bound to be completely abstract truths. Pure geometry cannot tell us the positions or dimensions of actual things in the world, but only, for example, that *if* there is something in the world possessing certain dimensions, *then* it has certain other dimensions. Geography could get nowhere without geometry, but geometry by itself cannot establish the position or even the existence of a single hill or island. Truths of reason win the prize of certainty only at the cost of being silent about what, if anything, actually exists or happens. Pure reason can arrive at uncontradictable truths, but none of these truths of reason can ever also be or yield truths of fact. We cannot learn merely from the theorems of Euclidean geometry or from the formulae of algebra whether Ptolemaic or Copernican astronomy is true, or even whether there exist any stars at all.

If these attainable certainties are, by themselves, too factually empty to yield knowledge of the actual world, and if sense-impressions, by themselves, are too anarchic to yield reliable inferences to what exists and happens in the actual world, there seems to remain just one escape-route from the depressing conclusion that we cannot possibly know a single bit of what we most want to know. This escape-route was the one first suggested by **Kant**. Knowledge of what exists and happens must have for its foundation not just the formal and therefore uncontradictable truths of pure reason, nor just the uninterpreted and therefore mistake-proof impressions of the senses, but the truths of reason as the principles organising the sense-impressions, and the sense-impressions as the concrete material to be organised by the truths of reason. It is the application of the formal certainties of the abstract sciences to what we get by sheer seeing, hearing, etc., that enables us first to make anything at all out of

our impressions, and then to sift out what really does exist and happen from what we precariously and often mistakenly suppose to exist and happen. We continue, of course, to be the frequent dupes of illusions and precipitate assumptions. But we know in principle how to check and correct them. We know the methods of making certain; and the principles of our procedures of making certain are the abstract truths of pure reason being put to work as our canons of objectivity in our experimental investigation of the world around us. Pure reason tells us no matters of fact. But it does provide, so to speak, the acid for our acid tests. When we progress beyond the infantile stage of mere sentience to the stage when we try to ascertain things, our investigations begin to be controlled not just by an Utopian ideal of mistake-proof knowledge, but by operative, though initially inarticulate procedures of testing. We begin to look, feel and listen experimentally, methodically and suspiciously. Though we make plenty of mistakes, we begin to take cautionary steps to prevent them and remedial steps to rectify them. We become alive to the contrast between "real" and "apparent" as we master the manifold techniques of deciding between them. We now begin to use our eyes, fingers and ears with some degree of judiciousness, and our seeings and hearings are now exercises not only of our senses but also of our wits. For our still frequent perceptual mistakes, e.g. for our misestimates, misrecognitions and non-discriminations, we properly confess to having been, not deaf or blind, but silly. Perception calls not only for sentience but also for rationality, though not, save in unusual circumstances, for explicit ratiocinations.

The possibility of mistakes always exists; but the possibility of detecting, correcting and forestalling mistakes also always exists. To be judicious is not indeed to be immunised against mistakes, but it is to know how to forestall and correct them. What exists and happens in the world around us is, in principle, ascertainable to creatures who possess both Sentience and Reason, i.e. to creatures who can examine judiciously.

It is important to be on one's guard against a tendency, deep-seated in all of us, to think of people as if they were, like large stores, divided up into departments. We tend to speak as if a person consisted, somehow, of one internal employee or agent called his "Reason", of another called his "Memory", of a third called his "Imagination", of a fourth called, in the plural, his "Senses", or in the singular, his "Sight", his "Hearing", and so on. Now we can indeed properly *distinguish* these and many other human capacities. My memory may be deteriorating with advancing age, while my sight and hearing remain as good as before, and my ability to calculate or argue may even be improving. The lessons, stimulations and exercises which develop the powers of the young musician are not at all like those which develop the powers of the young engineer or geometrician – or, of course, of the young swimmer or skater. The danger is that we may pass from correctly distinguishing, say, the violinist's musical taste from his manual dexterity to personifying his Taste and his Manual Dexterity as separate, internal functionaries; and so puzzle ourselves by questions like, Are his Taste and his Dexterity related as Master to Servant, as Partner to Partner, or even as Rival to Rival?

Questions akin to these have often been raised in epistemology. People have asked whether our knowledge is given to us by our Intellect or by our Senses, and whether our mistakes are the faults of our Senses or of our Imaginations – as if these distinguishable capacities were themselves separate and semi-personal investigators quarrelling with one another inside our minds, and giving to us, their employers, conflicting reports about the world. But it is we ordinary people who try to ascertain things, and while we can certainly differ in eyesight, hearing, memory, judiciousness, inventiveness, and in our capacity to calculate, systematize, experiment, and so on, still these distinguishable abilities are not themselves observers, experimenters, calculators, theorists – or reporters. For the sake of picturesqueness we may say that our Eyes notify us of things; that our Ears or Memories have given us false reports; that our Reason has convinced us; that our Imagination has invented things; and even that our Consciences reproach us. But in serious, theoretical discussions we need to avoid such tempting personifications.

There is another model to which we are tempted to shape our theories of knowledge, what may be called the "Container-model". We are tempted to suppose that because, what is true, a person who at one date had not yet learned what pineapples taste

like, or what "isosceles" means, may at a later date have learned these things, therefore there must by the later date have come to exist inside him something that can be called "the idea of the taste of a pineapple" and "the abstract idea, notion or concept of 'isosceles' "; somewhat as a bird-cage, formerly empty, may now house a canary, or as a picture-gallery may now have hanging on the wall a newly acquired picture. Using this Container-model, we are inclined to assume that in order to find out whether we have yet learned what pineapples taste like, or what "isosceles" means, we can and must, so to speak, peer inside our own minds in order to see whether the required idea or notion is there or not. Yet when we try so to peer inside our own minds, we find the task oddly baffling. What sort of an internal thing can I be looking for when I try to peer into my own mind for the abstract idea of "isosceles"? Certainly most people, though not all, can see in their minds' eyes things like familiar faces, houses and coloured or colourless patterns. But the taste of pineapple can naturally not be visualized at all, nor, by most people, even tasted "on the mind's tongue"; and what we visualize, if anything, when thinking of isosceles triangles, we visualize far too nebulously to meet the very precise requirements of Euclid's definition of an isosceles triangle. Yet very likely we can, without hesitation or error, discriminate the taste of pineapples from that of oranges, bananas, raspberries, etc., and we can decide, without hesitation or error, whether a triangular figure of certain dimensions is or is not isosceles. We have learned and we now know the taste of pineapples and what "isosceles" means, without there existing anything "inside our minds" to be found by inward peering.

To learn is indeed to acquire something or to come into possession of something. But what is acquired is not a thing but an ability, such as the ability to discriminate one taste from others, or the ability to classify geometrical figures, given their dimensions. When the schoolmaster wishes to find out whether a pupil has yet got the ideas of "square number" and "square root", he tests him on some arithmetical problems. The pupil has the ideas if he can tackle the problems; he has not got the ideas if he cannot yet tackle them. This is what it is to have the ideas.

It follows that the question How do we acquire our ideas? has as many different answers as there are different kinds of acquired mental abilities. We become familiar with the taste of pineapples by tasting not only pineapples but also many other kinds of fruit, by comparing these tastes and perhaps also, what is very difficult, by trying to describe in words these different tastes. We get the ideas of "square number" and "square root" only when, having learned to count, add, subtract, multiply and divide, we learn to multiply numbers by themselves and to work out what number, if any, multiplied by itself produces a given number. Correspondingly different kinds of accounts would have to be given of our acquisition of the ideas of "check-mate", "vacuum", "volt", "equator", "joke", "weed", "magneto", "risk", "virus", "dragon", "impossibility", "tomorrow", "debt", and so on. The doctrine that all our ideas come from sense-impressions, though unhelpful, is true enough if it means only that an infant born blind, deaf and without the senses of smell, taste and touch would never learn anything at all. It is false if it means that we get the idea of "square root", say, or "tomorrow" in just the same way as we get the idea of the "taste of pineapples", – and even this latter idea is got not just by having a certain taste-impression two or three times, but by having this impression, noticing it, comparing it with other tastes, and perhaps trying to describe in words the differences and similarities between these tastes. To have learned something, however primitive, from one's sense-impressions, is always more than just to have had those impressions. It is to have become able to cope, in some degree, with some kinds of task or problem, however elementary.

Epistemologists are commonly divided into **empiricists**, like **Locke**, **Berkeley** and **Hume**, and **rationalists**, like **Plato**, **Descartes**, **Spinoza** and **Leibniz**. The Empiricists are said to maintain that all our ideas come from experience; the rationalists that some of our ideas come not from experience but from reason or thought. But what does this apparent tug-of-war amount to? What does "come from" mean? What does "experience" mean? The technical phrase "sense-experience" is used to denote the mere having of sense-impressions. In this use, philosophers sometimes speak of a particular momentary sense-experience.

In contrast with this technical idiom, we commonly use "experience" in another way, to cover continuous or repeated practice in something or accumulating familiarisation with it. Thus a chess-player may have had much or little experience of match-playing in chess; but he would not describe himself as having had, on a particular afternoon, an experience of match-play. Experience, in this use, is what makes a person more expert than he had been. He has learned by having a certain amount of practice. He has tested and developed his abilities by exercising them. An experienced chairman is a man who has been in the chair a lot of times and in a lot of more or less difficult situations.

That all knowledge, e.g. all expertness and all competence, comes from experience, in the second sense, i.e. from training and practice, is an uncontentious truth – at least if safeguarded by the proviso that much of what we learn comes from instruction by others. But this is not at all the same thing as to say that whatever is known is inferred from premises provided, ultimately, by particular sense-experiences, though this is a theory maintained, with reservations, by some empiricist philosophers. The truth that we are not born already knowing anything, i.e. that no ideas are innate, is sometimes erroneously identified with the proposition that whatever we ascertain, when we do come to ascertain things for ourselves, we get by inference from our sense-impressions. But it is obvious that even if, what is questionable, we ascertain some facts by inference from our sense-impressions, when we have learned from training and practice to do this, still this account will not by itself cater for the enormous differences between, for example, ascertaining that the cuckoo has arrived, ascertaining that the king is check-mated, that the ship is now crossing the Equator, that there is a risk of thunder tomorrow, that a certain sentence is ungrammatical or that a certain metal object is a magneto. To ascertain things of these different kinds, we have to have acquired special abilities from special kinds of training and practice. The mere combination of good eyesight with good wits would not enable a Red Indian, say, to tell that the king is checkmated. He must also have studied and practised the game of chess.

Conversely, however, if an ultra-rationalist were

to argue that since we cannot ascertain anything merely from having sense-impressions, therefore our only way of finding out what exists and happens is to do what Euclid did, namely to deduce theorems from axioms, without any recourse to observation or experiment, his position would also be untenable. If, which is rare, he holds that we are born knowing both these axioms and these techniques of deducing consequences, he is saying that we have masteries of things without ever having mastered them, i.e., that we know without having learned, and so are experts, though totally inexperienced. But even if, as is more common, he allows that knowledge of abstract truths and of the techniques of deriving consequences from them itself requires experience, in the sense of training and practice, he still cannot show that this special kind of training and practice can replace the other special kinds of training and practice which make us more or less experienced observers and experimenters – or, for that matter, the other special kinds of training and practice which make us more or less experienced draughtsmen, speakers or dancers. The experience which is omitted from the theories of the empiricists is the experience which is omitted from the theories of the rationalists. Craving for something to avert the possibility of mistakes, the one finds its haven of safety in uncorrupted sense-impressions, the other in uncorrupted ratiocination. But the successful investigator is he who has made sure, not he who has remained in safety. Where mistakes are possible, the avoidance, detection and correction of them is possible. Knowledge comes not by some immunization against the chance of error, but by precautions against possible errors – and we learn what precautions to take by experience i.e. training and practice. It is the expert, not the innocent, who knows.

To take a concrete example. If we ask how anyone can tell for certain whether the king is checkmated, the right answer would be that this can be ascertained by a spectator who has adequate eyesight and uses his eyes; has adequate wits and uses them, i.e. is not absent-minded or distracted, but is attending to the game; and lastly who has become, through training and practice in the game, expert enough to consider possibilities and to eliminate them. But if, instead, we asked whether the check-

mate is ascertained by the spectator's Reason or by his Senses, and whether he was saved from being mistaken by the infallibility of his sense-impressions or by the uncontradictability of his formal principles, we should have debarred ourselves from getting a sensible answer, since these questions, unless taken as merely picturesque, are themselves not sensible questions. The spectator was not saved from making mistakes; he took good care not to make them. He was not notified by reports from his Intellect or by reports from his Senses that the king was checkmated; he found it out by visually studying the chessboard with his wits about him. He knew what to look for, since he had previously learned by training and practice how to play chess and how to follow games played by others.

Similarly, if asked whether the spectator has the abstract idea of "checkmate", we need to construe the question as asking whether he has learned and still remembers what it is for a king to be checkmated, and whether, therefore, he can tell by suitably careful inspection whether at any particular point in any particular game the king is or is not checkmated. To this question the answer is obviously "yes". But if we construe the question as asking whether the spectator has something special in his mind's eye, like a clear or blurred picture of a checkmate, we should answer first that there could be no picture of what is common to all checkmates; and second that it does not matter what, if anything, he visualizes when he hears or uses the word "checkmate". What matters is whether he has learned what it is to checkmate, to be checkmated and decide on inspection that the king is, or is not, checkmated. If he has learned and remembers these things, then he has the idea of checkmate, whether he happens to visualize things or not. If he has not learned them or has forgotten them, then he has not got the idea, whatever he may happen to see in his mind's eye on hearing the word "checkmate". If we forswear the personification of capacities and foreswear the Container-model, we shall not suffer much from dividedness of mind between Rationalism and Empiricism. Their tug-of-war lacks a rope.   (G.R.)

Erigena, John Scotus (*c.* 810–*c.* 877), also known as Eringena ("Irish born"). He left Ireland to live and work at the court of Charles the Bald, King of the West Franks.

In common with other Irish monks of the time Erigena knew some Greek and much of his work consisted in translating and commenting on Greek patristic writings, notably those of Gregory of Nyssa, Denis the Areopagite and Maximus Confessor.

His chief philosophical work is, however, the *De Divisione Naturae*, a sustained speculative treatise on the evolution of the universe in the neoplatonic style of Proclus. For its comprehensiveness and speculative power it stands unique in western thought, from the time of **Boethius** to that of **Anselm**.

Erigena begins from the principle that all that exists is a theophany of divine manifestation which is to be understood by a dialectical penetration of revelation. The dialectic consists in the application of the well known neoplatonic method of division and analysis to the study of *Nature* (understood in the Aristotelian sense of all that which can be generated in place and time).

So elaborated, Nature is subject to four main divisions: nature which creates but is not created, nature which creates and is created, nature which does not create but is created, nature which neither creates nor is created. So all reality consists either of God (the uncreated) or of creatures which go forth from and return to God according to the familiar pattern of Greek emanation theory.

Being a Christian, Erigena tried to avoid the pantheistic conclusions of such a system by distinguishing the divine from the human as that which is not from that which is. It is doubtful however, whether this device is adequate to the goodness of his intention.

Erigena had no immediate followers and his work exerted little historical influence. There is however, considerable systematic affinity between his speculations and those of Nicholas of Cusa and Eckhart later.   (J.G.D.)

Ethics.

I. INTRODUCTORY

Out of the many sorts of inquiry for which the term "ethics" has at one time or another been used, three groups of questions may be selected as the most important to distinguish from one another: (1) *Moral questions*: for example, "Ought I to do that?"; "Is polygamy wrong?"; "Is Jones a good man?". In this sense "ethical" and "moral" mean much the same. (2) *Questions of fact about people's moral opinions*: for example, "What did Mohammed (*or* what does the British Middle Class, or what do I myself) in fact think (or say) about the rightness or wrongness of polygamy?" (3) *Questions about the meanings of moral words (for example, "ought", "right", "good", "duty"); or about the nature of the concepts or the "things" to which these words "refer"*: for example, "When Mohammed said that polygamy is not wrong, what was he saying?" These three sorts of questions being quite distinct, the use of the word "ethics" to embrace attempts to answer all three is confusing, and is avoided by the more careful modern writers. No generally accepted terminology for making the necessary distinctions has yet emerged; but in this article we shall distinguish between (1) morals, (2) descriptive ethics and (3) ethics, corresponding to the three sorts of questions listed above. The case for confining the word "ethics" (used without qualification) to the third sort of question is that ethics has usually been held to be a part of philosophy, and the third group of questions, which are analytical or logical inquiries, or, as older writers might say, metaphysical ones, is much more akin than the first two groups to other inquiries generally included in philosophy. Thus ethics (in the narrow sense) stands to morals in much the same relation as does the philosophy of science to science. The student of ethics will nevertheless have to get used to a variety of terminologies; he will find plain "ethics" used for what we have just called "morals" ("normative ethics" is another term used for this); and he will find, for what we have just called "ethics", the more guarded terms "the logic of ethics", "metaethics", "theoretical ethics", "philosophical ethics" and so on. Works called "ethics" usually contain questions and answers of all three kinds, and the student of ethics must be prepared to find in them ambiguous remarks in which it is not clear *what* sort of question the writer is trying to answer. It is, for example, only too easy to confuse a moral statement with a descriptive ethical one, especially when one is talking about one's own moral views; but it is nevertheless vital to distinguish the moral judgment "It would be wrong to do that" from the descriptive ethical statement "I, as a matter of psychological fact, think that it would be wrong to do that". The first task, therefore, for anybody who takes up the subject, is to learn to distinguish these three types of questions from one another; and for this purpose the following rules may be found helpful. A writer is making a *moral* statement if he is thereby *committing* himself to a moral view or standpoint; if not (that is, if he is merely writing in a detached way about moral views which are or may be held by himself or other people), it is either a *descriptive ethical* or an *ethical* statement; and this is normally indicated by the form of the statement, the moral words being "insulated" by occurring inside a "that"-clause or quotation-marks. Which of the two it is can be decided in the following way: if the truth of the statement depends on what moral opinions are *actually held* by people, it is a *descriptive ethical* statement; but if its truth depends only on what is *meant* by certain words, or on *what people would be saying if* they voiced certain moral opinions, it is an *ethical* statement. Thus, for example, ethics in the narrow sense is concerned directly neither with whether polygamy *is* wrong (a moral question) nor with whether anybody in fact thinks it is wrong (a descriptive ethical question) – though ethics may have a bearing on these two questions, as mathematics has on physics; it is concerned with the question "Precisely what is one saying if one says that polygamy is wrong"?

II. RELATIONS BETWEEN THESE INQUIRIES

Throughout the history of the subject, the chief incentive to the undertaking of all three sorts of inquiry has been the hope of establishing conclusions of the first kind (that is, moral conclusions) by means of a philosophical inquiry. It is from this motive that inquiries of the second and especially the third kinds have mostly been undertaken. Clearly the study of the meaning of the moral words is closely related to the study of what makes arguments containing them cogent or otherwise. One of the best ways of obtaining a clear view of the subject is to consider the mutual relations between these three kinds of inquiry, and the bearing that they can have on one another.

(1) *Descriptive ethics and morals*. Some writers have proceeded directly from descriptive ethical premises to moral (normative ethical) conclusions. For example, the Greek **hedonist** Eudoxus argued that since everyone thought pleasure to be the good, it must *be* the good. In a similar way some modern writers have held that the task of the moral philosopher – the utmost he can do by way of establishing moral conclusions – is to examine carefully the opinions that are accepted by his society or by himself and reduce them to some sort of system. This is to take received opinions as data, and to regard as established a moral system that can be shown to be consistent with them. This type of argumentation will not, however, appear convincing to anyone who considers the fact that a person (for example, in the ancient world) might have said "Everyone thinks that it is legitimate to keep slaves, but may it not be wrong?" Universal assent to a moral principle does not prove the principle; otherwise the moral reformer, who propounds for the first time a new moral principle, could be put out of court all too easily. Still less does it follow, from the fact that some limited set of people hold some moral opinion, that that opinion is right.

(2) *Descriptive ethics and ethics proper*. The commonest way, however, in which it has been sought to bring descriptive ethics to bear on moral questions is not directly but indirectly. It has been thought that a descriptive ethical inquiry might lead to conclusions about the *meanings* of moral terms (conclusions, that is to say, in ethics proper); and that in turn these might be used to prove moral conclusions. Those who have argued in this way have been attracted by a seductive analogy between moral terms and other predicates and adjectives. For example, it might be held possible to prove in the following way, to anyone who disputed it, that post-boxes in England are red: we should first establish by observation that everybody says that things are red when they have a certain recognizable quality, and that they are not red when they do not have this quality; we should conclude from this, that "red" *means* "having this quality". This is the first step. We should then ask our disputant to observe that post-boxes in England have this same quality; and since we have already established that "having this quality" is just what "red" *means*, he can no longer deny that the

post-boxes are red. It might be thought possible to use the same argument in ethics to prove, for example, that certain kinds of action are right. But unfortunately the analogy breaks down at both steps – at the step from descriptive ethics to ethics proper, and at the step from ethics to morals. That conclusions about what people *mean by* "right", for example, cannot be proved by finding out what they *call* right, is evident from the case of the moral reformer just mentioned. If he said that slavery was not right, when slavery was one of the things universally agreed to be right, he would, if the proposed argument were valid, be like a man who said that postboxes were not red when everybody agreed that they were red; we should be able to accuse such a man of misusing the word "red" – for "red" *means* the colour which post-boxes are, so how can he deny that they are red? But the moral reformer can deny that slavery is right while still using the word "right" in the same sense as that in which his contemporaries, who think that slavery is right, are using it. This example shows that there is an important difference between moral words and words like "red" – a difference which invalidates the superficially plausible argument from descriptive-ethical premises to conclusions about the meanings of moral words.

(3) *Ethics and morals.* But the second step in the proposed argument is also invalid, for a very similar reason. We cannot, even if we can establish the meaning of the moral words, pass from this to conclusions of substance about moral questions. This may be shown by the following example: suppose that there are two people who know everything about a certain action (including its circumstances and consequences), and still dispute, as they may, about whether it was wrong. Since they are in dispute, they must be using the word "wrong" with the same meaning; for if this were not so, there would be no real dispute, only a verbal confusion. But since they can continue to dispute, even though they are in agreement about the meaning of the word, it follows that knowledge of the meaning of the word cannot by itself, or even in conjunction with what they both know about the action, determine whether the action is wrong. Some *other* difference must remain between them (a moral difference) which is neither a difference about what the action is (for this they know in the

fullest detail) nor about the meaning of "wrong" (for about this they are agreed). The plausible argument which we have just rejected is a particular application of a type of argument often used in philosophy, and known as "the argument from the paradigm case". Without discussing here whether the argument is cogent in other fields, we can see that it is not in ethics. The assumption that this argument has unrestricted force is linked with the assumption that to discover the use of a word is always to discover to what things it is correctly applied. This is not true of words like "is" and "not"; and it seems not to be true of moral words either. This assumption (to take another example) leaves us with no way of distinguishing between the uses of the two sets of words "Shut the door" and "You are going to shut the door"; for all the words in both sets, in so far as they "apply" to anything, apply to the *same* things.

III.   NATURALISM

The arguments so far considered and rejected all exhibit a common feature. In them, moral conclusions are allegedly derived from premises which are not themselves moral judgments: in the one case the premise was a statement of sociological fact about what people think on a moral question; in the other it was a statement of linguistic fact about how (with what meaning) people use a certain word, together with another premise giving the description of an action whose wrongness is in dispute. This feature is common to a great many arguments which have been used by ethical thinkers; and it has been frequently stated that any argument which derives moral conclusions from non-moral premises must be invalid. A famous statement to this effect was made by **Hume** in *Treatise of Human Nature* (1739–40), III, 1, i. Hume based his rejection of such arguments on the general logical principle that a valid argument cannot proceed from premises to some "new affirmation" not contained, at any rate implicitly, in the premises. The correctness of Hume's view ("no *ought* from an *is*") depends, therefore, on the assumption that moral judgments contain an element in their meaning (the essentially moral element) which is not equivalent, even implicitly, to anything in the conjunction of the premises. It is this assumption which is challenged by those ethical theories known as **naturalist**. The term "naturalist" has been used in a variety of ways, but will be used here as follows: an ethical theory is naturalistic if, and only if, it holds that moral judgments are equivalent in meaning to statements of non-moral fact.

It must be noted that, on this definition, a statement of moral opinion (that is to say a statement in the first of the three classes listed at the beginning of this article) cannot be called naturalistic; for naturalism is a view about the meanings of moral terms, and nobody is committed to any form of it who confines himself to merely *using* moral terms without taking up a view about their meaning, definition or analysis. In general, no view can be naturalistic unless, in the statement of the view, the moral words occur inside quotation marks or a "that"-clause or are *mentioned* (not used) in some other way, and remarks are made about their meaning or their equivalence to other expressions. That is to say, only statements in ethics proper, as contrasted with descriptive ethics and with morals, can be naturalistic. Thus the view that the right action (the action which ought to be done) in a given situation, is that which would produce the greatest balance of pleasure over pain, is not naturalistic, since it does not seek to *define* "right", but only to say what actions *are* right. To be a naturalist, a utilitarian of this sort would have to hold, in addition, that his view was true in virtue of the meaning of "right" – that is to say, that "right" *meant* "producing the greatest balance of pleasure over pain". If he refrains from trying to prove his theory in this way, "refutations of naturalism" pass over his head.

It must also be noticed that, on this definition of naturalism, to call a definition of a moral word "naturalistic" does not imply that the properties in terms of which it is being defined are empirical, that is, perceived by the five senses. As **Moore**, who coined the expression "the naturalistic fallacy", observed, the same "fallacy", as he thought it was, is committed if the properties are "properties of supersensible reality", given only that they are not moral properties. Thus a philosopher who *defines* "right" as meaning "in accordance with the will of God" is, in this sense, a naturalist, unless the word "God" itself is held to be implicitly a moral term. The most important argument by which Moore sought to "refute naturalism" may be restated as

follows, using the example just quoted: if "right" meant the same as "in accordance with the will of God", then, "whatever is in accordance with the will of God is right" would mean the same as "whatever is in accordance with the will of God is in accordance with the will of God"; but according to our actual use of the words it seems to mean more than this mere tautology. (Note that, as before, there is nothing in this argument which forces anybody to abandon the *moral* view that whatever is in accordance with the will of God and only what is in accordance with it is right. It is only the attempt to make this view true by definition which is naturalistic). It has been held, though not by Moore, that what is wrong with naturalistic definitions is that they leave out the commendatory or prescriptive element in the meaning of words such as "right" and "good" (*see below*).

IV. INTUITIONISM

The work of Moore convinced most philosophers that naturalistic definitions of moral terms had to be ruled out. But Moore and his immediate followers showed a great reluctance to abandon what had been the traditional view of the way in which words have meaning. It was taken for granted that the way to explain the meaning of an adjective, for example, was to identify the property which it "stands for" or "is the name of"; all adjectives have the same logical function, that of "standing for" a property, and the differences between them are not differences in logical character, but simply differences between the properties for which they "stand". When, therefore, it became accepted that moral adjectives did not stand for "natural" (that is, non-moral) properties, it was concluded that they must stand for peculiar moral properties, thought to be discerned by "intuition".

There are two main forms of ethical intuitionism. According to the first, we are supposed to intuite the rightness, goodness, etc. of concrete individual acts, people, etc.; general moral principles are arrived at by a process of induction, that is, by generalisation from a large number of these instances. According to the second, what we intuite are the general principles themselves (for example, "promise-breaking is wrong"); by applying these, we ascertain the moral properties of individual acts and people. The second view has the merit of emphasising a very important fact about the logical character of moral words, namely that the moral adjectives, etc. differ from most other adjectives in the following way: we call a thing "red", for example, because of its redness and nothing else; it could be similar in every other way and yet not be red. But when we call a person "good" or an act "right", we call them good or right *because* they have certain other characteristics – for example, an act is called wrong because it is an act of promise-breaking, or good because it is the act of helping a blind man across a road. The intuitionists sometimes express this feature of moral adjectives by saying that they are the "names" of "consequential" or "supervenient" properties. Even if we reject the idea that all adjectives have meaning by being the names of properties, this remains an important discovery. It has sometimes been thought that Hume's "no *ought* from an *is*" was a denial that we can, for example, call an act good *because* it is an act of a certain kind. This is a misunderstanding; what Hume was denying was that it *logically followed*, from an act's being of a certain kind, that it is good. The difference is crucial, but obscure. It has been one of the main problems of recent ethics to give a satisfactory account of the connexion between, for example, goodness and what were called "good-making characteristics". The intuitionists reject the naturalist explanation of this connexion as due to an equivalence in meaning between moral words and words describing the characteristics of things in virtue of which we apply moral words to them. But they give no adequate positive account of the connexion, contenting themselves, for the most part, with saying that it is a "synthetic necessary" connexion discerned by "intuition". The explanatory force of this account is impaired by the failure to say clearly what "intuition" is or what is meant by "synthetic necessary connexion".

But the chief argument brought against ethical intuitionism of all sorts is the following, which is to be compared with that in section II (3). Intuition is supposed to be a way of knowing, or determining definitively and objectively, the truth or falsity of a given moral judgment. But suppose that two people differ on a moral question, and that both, as may well happen, claim to intuite the correctness of their own views. There is then no way left of settling the question, since each can accuse the other of being defective in intuition, and there is nothing about the intuitions themselves to settle which it is. It is often objected further, that what "moral intuitions" people have will depend on their various moral upbringings and other contingent causes. In fact, the intuitionists, who often claim to be "objectivists", belie this claim by appealing to a faculty of intuition which is unavoidably subjective. This illustrates the extreme difficulty, to be referred to below, of stating any clear distinction between "objective" and "subjective" in this field. Intuitionism enjoyed a wide popularity in the early years of this century; but it has now been abandoned even by some of its prominent supporters. Writers on ethics have tended, either to revert to some form of naturalism, open or disguised, or to pass on to one of the kinds of view, to be described below, which recognise that "good", "right", etc. have, logically, a quite different role from that of other adjectives, and that it may be misleading to call them "the names of properties".

V. RELATIVISM AND SUBJECTIVISM

Great confusion has been caused in ethics by lumping together, under the title "subjectivism", theories which are quite different from one another. Before considering subjectivism proper, we must first distinguish from it the *moral* view which is best called *relativism*. A typical relativist holds that we ought to do that, and that only, which we *think* we ought to do; on this theory, the mere having of a certain moral opinion by a man or a society makes that moral opinion correct for that man or society. Since this is a *moral* doctrine and not an *ethical* one (that is, since it says what we ought to do, not what "ought" means) it is not naturalistic (see above); but it is open to the objection that it makes it impossible to say that another man's moral judgment is wrong – indeed, it has the paradoxical consequence that two people who differ about a moral question must both be right. This seems to be at variance with the common use of the moral words; we have here an illustration of a way in which ethics (the study of the uses of the moral words) can have a negative bearing on a moral question – it enables us to *rule out* a moral view as involving logical paradox, but not to *prove* one. It may also be objected to relativism that it does not do what a moral principle is expected to do, viz. guide us in making our decisions on particular moral questions. For if I am wondering what to do, it is no use being told that I ought to do what I think I ought to do; for the trouble is that I do not know what to think. Relativism is mentioned, not for its own value, but because confusion of other views with it has bedevilled nearly all discussion of the views which we are about to consider. These are by contrast all ethical views (that is, views about the meanings of the moral words). They do not commit the holder of them to the acceptance or rejection of any substantive moral opinions.

The first is a form of naturalism, which is not now often avowedly held, but dates from a time when it was thought that a moral sentence must have meaning in the same way as other indicative sentences, viz. by being used to state that a certain object possesses a certain property (see above section IV). It being unplausible, for many reasons (some of which have been given in section III) to hold that the properties in question are "objective" properties of objects, it was suggested that they are "subjective" properties – that is, properties of being related in certain ways to states of mind of the maker of the statement in question. Thus "He is a good man" was held to mean "He, as a matter of psychological fact, arouses in me a certain mental state (for example, a feeling of approval)". This theory makes a moral judgment equivalent to a descriptive ethical statement (see above, section I). If it is taken literally, it is open to the objection that it makes moral disagreement impossible. For if two people say, one that a man is a good man, and the other that he is not, they are, on this view, not disagreeing with each other; for one of them means that he (the speaker) is in a certain mental state, and the other means that *he* (the second speaker) is not in that state; and between these statements there is no contradiction.

Because of this objection, the view has been generally abandoned in favour of others which hold that in a moral judgment we are, not giving information about our mental state, but engaging in a use of language different from the giving of information. This development has been part of the recent realisation by philosophers that it is a mistake to regard all kinds of sentences as having the same logical character and role. For at least two reasons it is best to confine the name "subjectivism" to the view just considered, and not to extend it to those described below. First of all, the terms "objective" and "subjective" have a tolerably clear meaning, and draw a graspable distinction, when they are used to mark the difference between statements of "objective" fact about objects, and statements of "subjective" fact about the speaker (though even here there might be confusion; for in a sense it is an objective fact that the mind of the speaker is in a certain state). But the distinction gets lost when moral judgments are held not to be statements of fact, in the narrow sense, at all. This may be seen by comparing the case of imperatives (though it is not suggested that moral judgments resemble these in all respects). An imperative expresses neither an objective statement nor a subjective statement, since it does not express a statement at all; nor does it express a "subjective command"; for it is hard to understand what this would be. So, if it be asked "Is the command 'Shut the door' *about* the door or *about* the mind of the speaker?", the answer, in so far as the question is meaningful, must be "About the door". And in the same way the moral judgment "He is a good man" may be held to be, in the strongest possible sense, "about" the man in question, and not about the mind of the speaker, even by someone who holds that it is not (in the narrow sense) a *statement of fact* about the man. Thus criticisms of the theories to be described in the next section, on the ground that they turn moral judgments into remarks about the mind of the speaker, are misdirected, and should be reserved for subjectivism as described in the present section. The same applies to the criticism that these theories "make what is right depend on what the speaker thinks is right".

Secondly, the division between those views which hold that moral judgments are used to give some sort of information, and those which hold that they have a quite different function, is the most fundamental in ethics, and should not be concealed by using a term which straddles it. Views of the first sort (for example all the ethical views so far considered) are called "descriptivist"; views of other kinds, including those considered in the rest of this article, are called "non-descriptivist".

VI EMOTIVISM

Though emotivism was, historically, the first kind of non-descriptivism to be canvassed, it is a mistake to think of it as the only kind, or even as commanding general support among non-descriptivists at the present time. It is common even now for non-descriptivists of all kinds to be misleadingly called "emotivists", even though their theories do not depend on any reference to the emotions. Emotivism proper embraces a variety of views, which may be held concurrently. According to the best-known, moral judgments have it as their function to "express" or "evince" the moral emotions (for example, approval) of the speaker. According to another version, their use is to arouse or evoke similar emotions in the person to whom they are addressed, and so stimulate him to actions of the kind approved. A. J. **Ayer** when he wrote *Language, Truth and Logic* (1936), which contains the most famous exposition of emotivism, attributed both these functions to moral judgments; but he has since abandoned emotivism, though remaining a non-descriptivist. C. L. **Stevenson** put forward a kindred view, with the difference that, instead of the word "emotion", he most commonly used the word "attitude". An attitude was usually thought of by him as a disposition to be in certain mental states or to do certain kinds of actions. Stevenson's "attitudes" are much closer to the "moral principles" of the older philosophers (especially **Aristotle**) than is usually noticed by those who use the misleading "objectivist-subjectivist" classification. Stevenson made the important qualification to his view that, besides their "emotive meaning", moral judgments may also have a "descriptive meaning". In one of his several "patterns of analysis" the meaning of a moral judgment is analysed into two components: (1) a non-moral assertion about, for example, an act (explicable naturalistically in terms of empirical properties of the act); and (2) a specifically moral component (the emotive meaning) whose presence prevents a naturalistic account being given of the meaning of the whole judgment. This specifically moral element in the meaning is the function which these judgments have of *expressing* attitudes and *persuading* or *influencing* people to adopt them, towards the act described. Stevenson's views did not, of course, find favour with descriptivists; and even non-descriptivists who have written after him, while recognizing the seminal importance of his work, have for the most part rejected the implied irrationalism of the view that the only specifically moral element in the meaning of moral terms is their emotive force. This, it has been felt, makes moral judgments too like rhetoric or propaganda, and does insufficient justice to the possibility of reasoned argument about moral questions. If moral argument is possible, there must be *some* logical relations between a moral judgment and other moral judgments, even if Hume was right to hold that a moral judgment is not derivable from statements of non-moral fact. Stevenson has some important things to say about moral arguments, but his account of them has been generally held to be inadequate.

VII. OUTSTANDING PROBLEMS

Most of the main problems which occupy ethical thinkers at the present time arise from the complexity of the meaning of moral terms, which combines two very different elements.

(1) *The evaluative or prescriptive meaning* (these more non-committal terms are now often preferred to Stevenson's "emotive meaning"). It is not necessary, and probably false, to attribute to moral judgments, as such, any impulsive or causative force or power to *make* or *induce us to* do what they enjoin; but even descriptivists sometimes admit that moral judgments have the function of *guiding* conduct. It is indeed fairly evident that in many typical cases we ask, for example, "What ought I to do?" because we have to decide what to do, and think that the answer to the "ought" question has a bearing on our decision greater and more intimate than that possessed by answers to questions of non-moral fact. To take another example, it is fairly evident that there is an intimate connexion between thinking A better than B, and preferring A to B, and between the latter and being disposed to choose A rather than B. This intimate connexion is emphasized in the old tag (whose substance goes back to **Socrates**): "Whatever is sought, is sought under the appearance of its being good". It would follow from this that to call a thing good is thereby to offer guidance about choices; and the same might be said of the other moral terms. Descriptivists, however, refuse to

admit that this feature is part of the *meaning* of moral terms.

Their principal opponents, who may be called "prescriptivists", hold that it *is* part of the meaning. Moral judgments, on this view, share with imperatives the characteristic that to utter one is to commit oneself, directly or indirectly, to some sort of precept or prescription about actual or conceivable decisions or choices. In typical cases, disagreement with a moral judgment is displayed by failure to act on it – as when someone has told me that the right thing to do is such and such, and I immediately do the opposite. Such a view does not, like the emotive theory, make moral argument impossible; for according to some prescriptivists logical relations may hold between prescriptions as well as between ordinary statements.

Prescriptivists have to face, like Socrates, the difficulty that in cases of so-called "weakness of will" we may choose to do something which we think bad or wrong. The most promising line for prescriptivists to take in answer to this objection is to point out that in such cases either the chooser is *unable* to resist the temptation (as is indicated by the expression "*weakness* of will"; cf. also St Paul, Romans 7, 23); or else he thinks the thing bad or wrong only in some weaker, conventional sense, having the descriptive meaning of "bad" or "wrong" but lacking their prescriptive force.

(2) *The descriptive meaning.*The second main feature of moral judgments is that which distinguishes them from imperatives: whenever we make a moral judgment about, for example, an act, we must make it because of *something about* the act, and it always makes sense to ask what this something is (though it may be hard to put a reply into words). This (although it has been denied by some recent thinkers) follows from the "consequential" character of moral "properties" (see above, section IV). To every particular moral judgment then, there corresponds a universal judgment to the effect that a certain feature of the thing judged is, so far as it goes, a reason for making a certain moral judgment about it. For instance, if I say that a particular act is good because it is the act of helping a blind man across a road, I seem to be adhering thereby to the universal judgment that it is good to help blind people across roads (and not merely this particular blind man across this particular road). Those who

accept this argument may be called "universalists"; and their opponents, who do not, may be called "particularists". A universalist is not committed to the view that, if it is a good act to help a blind man across a road on this occasion, it would be a good act on all occasions (for example, it would not be a good act if the blind man was known to be hopelessly lost and his destination lay on this side of the road); he is committed only to the view that it would be a good act in the absence of something to make a difference between the two acts – something more than the mere numerical difference between the acts.

The universalist thesis is closely connected with the thesis that moral judgments, besides their function as prescriptions, have also a descriptive meaning (see above, section VI). On this view, in calling an act, for example, good, we are commending it (the prescriptive element in the meaning), but commending it because of something about it. These two elements are well summarized by the *Oxford English Dictionary*'s first definition of "good": "The most general adjective of commendation, implying the existence in a high, or at least satisfactory, degree of characteristic qualities which are either admirable in themselves or useful for some purpose". The word "characteristic" is important; it draws attention to the fact that the word which follows "good" makes a difference to the qualities which a thing has to have in order to be called good (for example, a good strawberry does not have to have the same qualities as a good man). In the case of some words (for example, "knife"), if we know what they mean, we know some of the conditions that have to be fulfilled before we can call a thing of that kind good. Some philosophers (for example **Plato** and Aristotle) have held that the same is true of all words – that, for example, if we could determine "the nature of man" we should therefore be able to say what makes a man a good man. But this type of argument may be based on a false analogy between words like "man" and words like "knife".

A more promising way of bringing the universalist thesis to bear on moral arguments (and thus to some extent satisfying those who insist that ethical studies should be relevant to moral questions) is that exemplified by the "Golden Rule" and worked out in some detail (though obscurely) by **Kant** and his followers. In certain cases it may be a powerful argument, if a man is contemplating some act, to ask what it is about the act which makes him call it right, and whether, if some other act possessed the same features, but his own role in it were different, he would judge it in the same way. This type of argument occurs in two famous passages of Scripture (2 Samuel 12, 7 and Matthew 18, 32). It has been held that a judgment is not a *moral* judgment unless the speaker is prepared to "universalize his maxim". But this raises the vexed question of the criteria for calling judgments "moral judgments" a question which is beyond the scope of this article.

This question, and the whole problem of the relation between the prescriptive and the descriptive elements in the meaning of moral judgments, continues to tax ethical thinkers. It has been impossible in this article to do more than sketch the principal issues and give some account of their origin. (R.M.H.)

Existentialism. The name of a trend or tendency manifested in the history of philosophy of which the following marks may be noted:

(1) there is always present an hostility to abstract theory which obscures the roughnesses and untidinesses of actual life. This may take the shape, as in **Augustine**'s *Confessions* of a profound self-analysis, or as in **Pascal**'s *Pensées*, of an insistence that the claim of the mathematical method of the exact sciences to be a complete and universal method of human knowledge be disputed in the name of a flexible and less restricted concept of the varied and different styles of men's commerce with their natural and human environment. Etienne **Gilson** claims that **Aquinas** in virtue of his insistence on the priority of *esse* over *essentia* be classed as existentialist; whereas the Platonic essentialist tradition be viewed as asserting the priority of essence over existence. This Gilson maintains despite the constantly affirmed apparentation of existentialist tendencies in philosophy to Socrates' preoccupation with ethics as distinct from cosmological speculation.

This brief historical note should indicate that existentialism is the name of a tendency rather than of a determinate set of doctrines.

(2) there is an approximation of the task of the moral philosopher to that of the novelist or dramatist, an element emphasised in recent existentialist thought by the fact that men like **Sartre** and **Marcel** have achieved distinction as writers and dramatists as well as philosophers. In this approximation one may discern a continuity to-day between existentialist philosophizing and **phenomenological** criticism of **Kant**'s formalistic ethics of the kind to be found in the writings of Max Scheler. The existentialist is always, by his bias in favour of the particular and the concrete, alerted against such an essay as Kant's attempt to lay bare the universal principle of all moral action; this even while displaying a certain sympathy with Kant's doctrine of the primacy of the practical over the theoretical reason.

(3) existentialist thought is sometimes profoundly religious (as in **Kierkegaard**), and sometimes overtly atheistic (as in Jean-Paul Sartre). But in existentialist atheism there is discernible an almost obsessionally religious note, very different from that sounded by Anglo-Saxon empiricists in their rejection of religious attitudes, which is more akin to that found in the men of the Enlightenment. Thus Albert Camus' novel *La Peste*, which certainly helped to win its author the Nobel Prize for literature, displays a preoccupation with the problem of an atheistic sanctity, strangely, but unmistakably, religious in its undertones.

(4) Kierkegaard saw himself as offering a *Philosophie und Theologie des Korrektivs*, in the first instance a corrective to the dialectical rationalism of Hegel, and its philosophical interpretation of the Christian religion. One might say that professional philosophers will always find in the writings of existentialist thinkers, resources to correct restricted and confined paradigms of human thought and action. One might mention in this connection, as an illustration and as a parallel, **Wittgenstein**'s regard for Augustine's *Confessions*, and for the stories of Leo Tolstoy. The enlargement of the academic imagination by recollection of the actual poignancy of human life and experience is often achieved through insights to be found in the diffuse, and sometimes unbalanced, writings of the existentialists.

The influence of existentialism in contemporary theology is better sought in the work of Paul Tillich, and of Rudolf Bultmann than of Karl

Barth. The latter's early *Römerbrief* owes much to Plato as well as to Kierkegaard and Dostoevsky; and his massive *Kirkliche Dogmatik* is more in debt to **Anselm** on whose *Proslogion* he published a masterly essay in 1930, than to existentialist thinkers. Indeed members of his school have been known to accuse those who pursue the method of existentialist dialectics in theology, of continuing to this present, the disastrous inheritance of Augustine's self-absorption! (D.M.M.)

F

Fallacy. The term "fallacy" is so used in logic as to refer to an invalid argument or form of argument. Strictly, therefore, only arguments, not statements, can be said to be fallacious; an argument with true premises and conclusion may be a fallacy, while an argument with false premises and conclusion may be exempt from fallacy. If the premises of an argument are true and the conclusion false there must be a fallacy in it; otherwise we can never determine whether an argument involves a fallacy or not by considering the truth or falsity of the statements made in its course.

It should be noted that the term "fallacy" applies properly only to a deductive step in an argument (see **Deduction**); what would be a fallacy regarded as a deduction might well be perfectly sound in a merely probable argument. Thus there is a fallacy known as the fallacy of affirming the consequent which is of the form "If p then q; but q; therefore p". An example would be "If it has been raining the roads will be wet; but the roads are wet; therefore it has been raining". Here the conclusion does not follow, for there may in fact have been no rain but only a burst main; but clearly wet roads are a good ground for suspecting that it has been raining.

The ways in which arguments can be bad are numberless; many of the traditionally named fallacies are of little interest and may be found in any traditional logic book. But some of the more interesting named fallacies will be briefly explained.

(1) *Denying the antecedent.* Of the form "If p then q; but not p; therefore not q"; e.g. "If it has been raining the roads will be wet; but it has not been raining; therefore the roads will not be wet".

(2) *Petitio principii (begging the question).* This is the assumption of a premise which cannot be known to be true unless the conclusion is known to be true. Sometimes it is said that to take as a premise a proposition which cannot be true unless the conclusion is true involves begging the question; in which case, as some have not shirked saying, every valid argument would be a case of begging the question.

(3) *Simple conversion.* This is to conclude from "All A is B" to "All B is A"; it is of course valid to conclude from "No A is B" to No B is A".

(4) *Undistributed middle.* This fallacy consists in arguing syllogistically with premises in which the term occurring in both (the middle term) is in neither premise used to refer to everything to which it can refer (to its whole extension) Thus in "All liars are rogues and all thieves are rogues, therefore some thieves are liars", the middle term "rogues" is undistributed in both premises; in neither is anything said about the whole class of rogues.

(5) *Ignoratio elenchi.* This is to produce a proof which does validly prove something, but not what it was required to prove.

(6) *Equivocation.* An argument in which a term is used in different senses at different stages of the argument.

(7) *Post hoc ergo propter hoc.* An argument from the fact that something followed on something else it must have been caused by it. Many superstitions are supported by this argument; bad luck after walking under a ladder or breaking a mirror or spilling salt is held to be because of doing so. But regular sequence is clearly a valid ground for an inductive argument to a causal relationship. (J.O.U.)

Fatalism, *see* Freedom of the Will, Determinism.

Fichte, Johann Gottlieb (1762–1814), German philosopher, was of Saxon peasant stock. Aided by a local landed proprietor he studied theology, philology and philosophy at Jena and Leipzig. He met **Kant** in 1791 and became his close student and disciple. In 1794 he became professor at Jena but was dismissed in 1799 on a charge of teaching atheism. An ardent patriot, he delivered his *Addresses to the German Nation* in Berlin in 1807–1808 and was largely instrumental in the rebirth of Prussia after her defeats at the hands of Napoleon.

He became professor at the new University of Berlin in 1810.

Fichte held that there were two possible methods in philosophy, dogmatism which deduces the idea from the thing or **idealism** which deduces the thing from the idea. Which method one follows depends on one's mental make-up, but idealism is preferable since we cannot explain consciousness satisfactorily in terms of being, as dogmatism would do, but can construct experience, though not the thing-in-itself, from consciousness as a datum. Thus Fichte discarded the thing-in-itself and instead of deriving the nature of the thinking self from the manifold of experience, like Kant, he set out to deduce the manifold from the activity of the ego. The clearest statement of this not very easy doctrine is perhaps to be found in his *Introduction to the Theory of Knowledge* (1797).

Fichte's ethical views were developed in his *Theory of Morals* (1798). We may act so as to cause ourselves self-contempt or esteem, the latter being conscience. Moral action must spring from conscience not from obedience to authority. The basic ethical demand is that we should act according to our conception of duty, our conception of the action which we would acknowledge as ours without reservation through all time. Thus the moral life is a series of actions leading to the complete spiritual freedom of the ego. Moral evil arises from our lazy incapacity to think out our actions to the full. Certain individuals have the power to act morally in a pre-eminent way and these people through their example are an inspiration to others; in this fact lies the basis of religion and a church is a union of individuals associated for the purpose of stimulating and strengthening moral conviction.

The state, according to Fichte, has the task of ensuring that all men limit their freedom by regard for the freedom of others; but it can only do this if it also attempts to secure the same rights for all, which it can do only if it ensures that all men have property and economic self-dependence. In the light of this view Fichte was led to some socialistic doctrines about economic matters, including the transference of all foreign trade to the state. But, contrary to received legend, he did not share the organic view of the state typical of many German idealists. (J.O.U.)

Plate 43, page 171.

Freedom of the Will. The cluster of problems about the freedom of the will arises from an incompatibility, real or apparent, between sets of beliefs none of which we are ready to abandon. On the one hand we believe that we can sometimes choose whether to act in a certain way or not; we believe that we are responsible for so acting or refraining from action; we believe that for those parts of our history which do not lie within our choice we cannot be held responsible. On the other hand we believe that nature is uniform, that whatever happens results from and can be explained by a set of causes and conditions, and in particular that our actions result from our inherited character as modified by environment. But if all that happens is determined by its context then it would seem that our actions are determined by their context and our choices are determined by their context; in particular, if our actions arise from an inherited character as modified by our environment, then it would seem that we are no more responsible for our actions than we are for our inherited character and environment.

Moreoever a mere denial of the principle of **determinism**, unplausible in itself, does not obviously eliminate the problem; for if our actions do not arise out of our character as modified by environment it is hard to find any other account of their genesis which will make us responsible for them; certainly we are hardly to be held responsible for what occurs purely fortuitously.

No solution to these problems has been found which commands anything approaching general consent. Those philosophers who regard determinism as incompatible with freedom and therefore deny or weaken the deterministic thesis are usually called **libertarians**; they have had no conspicuous success in finding an account of human action which makes responsible choice intelligible. Those philosophers who retain the doctrine of determinism and accept that we have not in a full sense freedom to choose are known as determinists. Many philosophers are, however, unwilling to accept either of these paradoxical positions and try instead to show that the opposition between determinism and freedom is only apparent. Thus it is frequently said that the true antithesis to acting freely is acting under compulsion; but, it is said, laws of nature are descriptive, not prescriptive and do not constrain; even the laws of motion describe how things do in fact move and do not compel them so to move. Consequently they maintain that we do in fact often act freely (not under constraint) even though our actions can always in theory be subsumed under (descriptive) natural laws. It is not however clear that in these contexts compulsion is the antithesis of freedom; and though I do not digest my food under compulsion it would be odd to say that I do it of my own free will.

It is, however, true that the determinist at least need not think of laws as prescriptive. Those who think that human actions are in some way prescribed are called fatalists or predestinationists. According to the doctrines of fatalism and predestination some powerful entity (Fate or God) has a plan according to which things happen in a prearranged fashion; the laws of nature can, but need not, be thought of as prescribed by fate or God as a method of executing the plan. Thus the fatalist and predestinationist accept, as the philosophical determinist does not, that human action is purposively determined or compelled; notoriously doctrines of creation and divine foreknowledge raise problems about human responsibility for the theologian.

(J.O.U.)

Frege, Gottlob (1848–1925), German philosopher. Frege's historical importance is twofold: as the founder of modern mathematical logic, and as a philosopher of **logic** and of **mathematics**. He invented the notion of a *formal system* with the intention of attaining the ideal of mathematical rigour, and in *Begriffsschrift* (1879) gave what was at once the first example of a formal system and the first formulation of the sentential and predicate calculi. He drew for the first time the distinction between axioms and rules of inference and introduced the device which distinguishes modern logic from its predecessors and makes it superior to them, the use of variables and (nested) quantifiers.

Frege then turned to the application of his formal system to arithmetic. In doing so, he discovered the possibility of formalizing arithmetic without introducing any non-logical concepts or axioms, at least if the notion of a class or set is admitted as a logical one. This possibility rested on the famous definition of a cardinal number, later rediscovered by **Russell**, as the class of all classes which can be mapped one-to-one on to a given class, together with the definition of the ancestral of a relation (that is, the transformation of a recursive into an explicit definition) which had already been given in *Begriffsschrift*. The definition of cardinal number follows naturally from the discovery that the fundamental numerical notion is that of "just as many as". An unreflective person, asked what it meant to say that there were just as many things of one kind as of another, might reply that it meant that if one counted up the first set and then counted up the second, one would arrive at the same number. But Frege observes that it is possible to say that a set has just as many members as another set without being able to say how many each has; thus if a waiter checks that there is just one knife to the right of each plate, then he knows that there are just as many knives as plates on the table. He has mapped the set of plates one-to-one on to the set of knives by means of the function "object to the immediate right of". Moreover, counting itself is a particular case of setting up a one-to-one mapping; for what I in effect do when I count a set of objects and find that there are n of them is to define a function on the set whose values are the numbers from 1 to n. Finally to explain "just as many as" in terms of one-to-one mapping gives a sense to saying of some infinite set that it has just as many members as another set, whereas of course an infinite set cannot in the ordinary sense be counted.

In order to prepare the way for the symbolic work Frege wrote a book, *Die Grundlagen der Arithmetik* (*The Foundations of Arithmetic*) (1884), expounding his theory without symbolism. This is a classic of philosophical exposition, and contains an entirely effective annihilation of then prevalent philosophical accounts of numbers and of arithmetic. It also contains some profound philosophical insights. In order to answer such a question as "What is the number 1?", Frege says, we have to give an account of the sense of sentences in which the symbol "1" occurs. We must not make the mistake of asking for the meaning of a word in isolation: only in the context of a sentence does a word have meaning. If we ask for the meaning of a word in isolation, we shall be inclined to answer by describing the mental images which are called up in us by hearing the word. But these mental images are entirely irrelevant to the sense of the word. The same word may call up different images

141

in the minds of different people; different words may call up the same image in the mind of one individual. In any case the image cannot determine the sense of sentences containing the word. Elsewhere, Frege distinguishes two features of the meaning of a word: the images and associations which the word calls up, which Frege calls the "colouring" of the word; and the sense properly so called. Colouring is subjective, and can vary from person to person. The sense of the word is objective; it is that feature of the meaning which alone is relevant to the determination of the truth-value of a sentence containing the word. When we know how to determine the truth-value of sentences containing the word, then we know all there is to know about the sense of the word; nothing further can be demanded. Among the most important sentences in which a singular term can occur are those expressing judgments of identity: Frege points out that stipulating the criterion of identity for Xs is a necessary part of determining the sense of the word "X". It is evident that the first part of **Wittgenstein**'s *Investigations* is deeply indebted to these ideas of Frege.

In a famous article published in 1892, Frege introduced a distinction which had not occurred in *Grundlagen*, that between the sense and the reference of a word. The reference of a singular term is the object about which we are speaking when we use a sentence containing it. But we must not think with J. S. **Mill** that the meaning even of a proper name consists just in its having the reference that it has; its sense is not uniquely determined by its reference. Thus, to use an example given by Frege elsewhere, one explorer might discover a mountain to the south and give it a name, while another explorer gave a different name to the same mountain seen to the north, and it might be many years before it was realised that it was the same mountain they had seen; the two names would then have different senses but the same reference. The sense of the whole sentence is a *thought* (somewhat analogous to the "proposition" of Russell); the thought is what is primarily said to be true or false, and is something immaterial though objective. Hence the reference cannot be a constituent of the thought; if I am talking about Everest, the mountain itself cannot be part of the thought I express. All the same, I do succeed in talking about the mountain itself, and not some shadowy correlate of it; the reference is in general something non-linguistic, something "in the world".

Whether an expression is a proper name or not is for Frege a question only of its logical behaviour. Thus "red" and "5" (used as nouns) can count as proper names since "red is a primary colour" and "5 is a prime number" are logically of exactly the same form as "Krushchev is a clever man". If an expression functions like a proper name, and possesses a definite sense, then it *is* a proper name; and it has a definite sense if we have assigned a sense to all the sentences in which it can occur. Whether an expression has a reference or not depends upon whether we should ordinarily say that there was something answering to that designation; for example, "the perfect number between 10 and 30" has a reference in virtue of the fact that, as we should ordinarily say, there is a number which is perfect and between 10 and 30. The idea that there is a further philosophical question as to whether there *really* exists an object for which the expression stands arises from the fallacy of "asking after the reference of a term in isolation". Frege calls an "object" anything which is the reference of a singular term; for him it is as legitimate to speak of numbers (and other "abstract entities") as objects as of men or cities as objects. Hence arithmetic is a collection of truths about objects just as much as any other science, and it is the task of the mathematician to *discover* these truths, which hold good independently of whether we discover them or not.

Frege distinguishes two fundamentally different types of expression, which he calls "saturated" and "unsaturated". Singular terms are saturated, as are complete sentences. Unsaturated expressions are predicates like " . . . is tall", relational expressions like " . . . bores . . ." and functional expressions like "the capital of . . .", in short expressions containing gaps which become saturated when the gaps are filled by saturated expressions. Unsaturated expressions are not merely sequences of words which could be written down on their own, for it is required that we can indicate where the gaps occur and which gaps must be filled with the same term and which may be filled by distinct terms (variables are a device for indicating this). Thus an unsaturated expression is rather a *feature* in common to several sentences than an isolable *part* of those sentences.

An unsaturated expression has a reference as well as a saturated one; but its reference is an unsaturated kind of thing, something which can no more be thought of as standing on its own than can the expression which denotes it, and which is therefore totally unlike an object. The reference of a predicate Frege calls a "concept" ("property" would be a happier term in English), that of relational and functional expressions "relations" and "functions." The reference of an unsaturated expression is to be distinguished from its sense just as sharply as the reference of a proper name from *its* sense; concepts, relations and functions are just as much "in the world" as are objects. If we say that Jupiter is larger than Mars, the relation holds between the *references* of the words "Jupiter" and "Mars", and not between their senses, and hence must be a feature of the world (the "realm of reference") as are the planets themselves. It is nevertheless an entity of a quite different kind; if an expression stands for a concept or a relation, it cannot stand for an object, and indeed it cannot even be sense to try to say about a concept what it makes sense to say about an object, or conversely. We do talk about concepts, however: if I say, "God exists", I am not ascribing a property to a particular object, I am talking about a certain *kind* of thing, about a property or concept, and saying about it something that it makes sense to say only about a property, viz. that there is something which has it, that there is something of that kind. Number-statements are to be understood in the same way; "There are three trees in the garden" says something about the concept *trees in the garden*, and cannot be understood as an assertion about an object.

If we want to understand the nature of concepts and relations, we must consider functions in mathematics. The number 4 is a certain function of the number 2, namely its square, but it is not itself that function. In fact we cannot as it were isolate the function, but only particular numbers which are that function *of* certain other numbers. Indeed, Frege is able to regard concepts and relations as special cases of functions, since he holds that a sentence as a whole has a reference, namely its truth-value; concepts and relations are thus functions whose value is always truth or falsity. This doctrine cuts clean through the old controversy between nominalists and realists. For Frege the

colour red for example, is a genuine object, and the reference of the *noun* "red"; but it cannot be the reference of the *adjective* "red" and is not alluded to in the sentence "Tulips are red".

The doctrine leads in Frege's formal system to a rigorous distinction of type between predicates; classes are, however, treated as *objects* (entities of lowest type). This is an illustration of the interdependence between Frege's philosophy of logic and his formal system. A formal system is to be constructed not merely with an eye to convenience, but ought to mirror the essential features of language (this was in essence Frege's retort to Peano's objection that his assertion sign was formally redundant). This does not mean that a formal system has to copy natural language: the use of variables and quantifiers, for instance, solves the problem of generality not by giving a coherent account of the devices used to indicate generality in natural languages, but by inventing a totally new device (the theory of quantification seems a better claimant for the title "paradigm of philosophy" than Russell's theory of descriptions). Natural language may actually be incoherent and can be criticised as such; thus Frege regards it as a defect of natural language that in it singular terms may be formed which have a sense but no reference. The quest for an ideal language was initiated by Frege.

In 1893 and 1903 Frege published two volumes of his *magnum opus, Die Grundgesetze der Arithmetik*, which sets out his construction of arithmetic out of logic in his logical symbolism. The theory contains "naive set theory", that is, the assumption that for every property there exists a class having as members precisely those objects which have that property. Shortly before the publication of volume II Russell wrote to Frege explaining the contradiction he had found in naive set theory. Frege hastily added an appendix stating how the contradiction could, as he thought, have been avoided by weakening one of his axioms. Lesniewski later proved that a further contradiction would arise, but it is doubtful if Frege discovered this; but in any case many of the proofs would have broken down under the revised axiom, and Frege lost heart for rewriting and completing the book. At the end of his life he came to consider the whole theory of classes, and the project of deriving arithmetic from logic, an error. Frege produced little work of interest after 1903, and probably did not follow the work that was being done in the subject he had founded. Nor did he receive much credit in his lifetime. The work he had done was transmitted to other logicians through the writings of Peano, Russell and **Whitehead**; only Dedekind, Zermelo and Russell gave him the credit that was his due. He was little known among philosophers, although three of great importance were profoundly influenced by him – **Husserl**, Russell and Wittgenstein. In recent times there has been a great awakening of interest in him; logicians are fully aware of his work, and some, such as Church, **Carnap** and **Quine**, have been directly influenced by him. Owing chiefly to the fact that many of Wittgenstein's leading ideas can be traced to Frege, philosophers in England and America, though not on the Continent, read and discuss him. Perhaps Frege's greatest achievement in philosophy, in which he was followed by Wittgenstein though not by Russell, was to reject the Cartesian tradition that **epistemology** is the starting-point of philosophy, and reinstate philosophical logic as the foundation of the subject. (M.A.E.D.)

G

Gassendi, Pierre (1592–1655), French. Gassendi was not a man of great originality, yet his indirect influence on the course of philosophic and scientific speculation was important and profound. Both **Hobbes** and **Descartes** knew him well and derived from him, not so much specific doctrines or solutions of philosophic problems but rather certain habits of thought. Gassendi set himself the task of providing an explanation for the doctrines of the current orthodoxy that would be based upon the scientific theories of the ancient **atomists** and the moral views of **Epicurus**. For example, he regarded mental activities as fully explicable in terms of physical distortions of the material of the brain and he elaborated a most complex theory of "traces" to account for the intelligent behaviour of men and animals. Typically, his solution of the problem of the interaction of imperishable soul and perishable brain was a para-mechanical one. If both Brain and Soul pursued the same goals, they would for that reason act together, a doctrine similar to, but much simpler than **Leibniz**'s pre-established

harmony. Gassendi also exerted a marked influence on moral and political theory, for he reintroduced to Europe the Epicurean doctrine that the highest moral good was to be sought in "tranquillity of soul", a notion which is a likely progenitor of Hobbes' "peace". Men act for the preservation of their soul's tranquillity, which is not always the pursuit of pleasure. (R.HAR.)

Plate 44, page 172.

Gilson, Etienne Henry (1884–), a Frenchman, is one of the outstanding students of **medieval philosophy** of modern times, and the vastly increased knowledge of medieval philosophy we now have is largely due to his work. He started from an interest in **Descartes** and was first led to medieval philosophy in an attempt to understand better the philosophical antecendents of the Cartesian philosophy; medieval philosophy then began to absorb his attention and he came to accept the position of Thomas **Aquinas** on essential points. His most important historical work, *The Spirit of Medieval Philosophy*, was first published in French in 1932. He has also written independent philosophical works in the Thomistic tradition, including *God and Philosophy* (1941). (J.O.U.)

Good, *see* Ethics, Utilitarianism and articles on moral philosophers.

Goodman, Nelson (1906–), born in Massachusetts. Professor of Philosophy at the University of Pennsylvania, he has been chiefly concerned with the theory of knowledge and the philosophy of language; but he has also dealt with problems commonly regarded as metaphysical. In his view, philosophy aims at giving precise structural descriptions of the world, by formulating definitions which exhibit things as patterns of various elementary components of experience. In his first book, *The Structure of Appearance* (1951), he offered such definitions for a number of individual items in phenomenal experience (such as colour spots), using for his primitive building blocks directly presented qualitative characteristics, such as specific shades of coulor and places in the visual field. A prominent feature of Goodman's analyses is the severe restrictions he imposes upon the assumptions he is prepared to employ. He has been a vigorous proponent of **nominalism**, refusing to accept any intellectual tools which allegedly postulate the existence of such abstract "Platonic" entities as classes. Although Goodman has made extensive use of modern logical techniques, he has not hesitated to reject various portions of logic, mathematics and scientific theory that do not satisfy his nominalistic requirements. He has therefore been compelled to invent ingenious means for circumventing the use of logical tools that would commit him to the reality of Platonic universals. He has like **Quine** been highly critical of the widely employed distinction between synthetic and **analytic** statements in large measure because in his judgment the distinction does involve such a commitment.

A problem that has occupied much of Goodman's thought is the clarification of what is to be understood by contrary-to-fact conditionals, such as "If this match had been scratched it would have ignited." He has canvassed various difficulties that he thinks face attempts at explicating precisely the sense of the connective "if-then" in such statements; and he has shown that this problem is intimately related to the problem of formulating the difference between statements expressing laws of nature (e.g., "Water expands on freezing" and those expressing merely accidental universality (e.g., "All the coins in my pocket to-day are made of silver"). In his more recent *Fact, Fiction and Forecast* (1955), Goodman has advanced some ideas toward resolving these questions, and has also suggested in what way he thinks those ideas are relevant to the analysis of inductive inference. (E.N.)

Green, Thomas Hill (1836–1882), English philosopher, educated at Oxford. Green helped to spread into England the influence of **Kant** and **Hegel** against the prevalent trends of empiricism and utilitarianism. The only book of his which appeared in his lifetime was his edition of **Hume**, and his influence was exercised mainly through his lectures at Oxford which were posthumously published.

He maintained that the world was to be thought of as a network of relations, and that mind was required not only to apprehend but also to constitute and sustain these relations. What are the terms related in this network? Any term we may seek to isolate turns out to be itself a network of relations too; and any attempt to find in feeling or sensation the ultimate data of experience must fail. Here Green comes very close to Hegel. The distinction between appearance and reality is not a distinction between a mental world and a world independent of mind, but one between mind as limited and human and mind as universal and absolute – the mind which sustains the universe.

In **ethics** too Green goes a long way with Hegel. Desires are not, as in an animal, isolated forces. In each desire the human self seeks its own satisfaction as a whole. Only thus can a man hold himself responsible and a free agent. Here, however, Green began to diverge from Hegel. The good is personal to the individual whose good it is, even though, being naturally social, he can achieve full satisfaction only if he confers good on others. Green firmly rejected any notion of a corporate self. The divergence dominates his political theory. He noted how **Rousseau**'s conception of a common good led him to that of a general will. But beyond this lay Hegel's view of the State as a unity higher than that of the individual and beyond this again lay extremes of totalitarian authority and nationalistic state-worship. Green's solid English liberalism rejected all such conclusions. He maintained the importance of individual responsibility and of individual rights. But his final position involved serious difficulties. A "common good" means that a man benefits others only "so far as he finds the thought of their being perfect necessary to his own satisfaction". On the other hand, individual rights are not allowed, as in **Locke** or J. S. **Mill**, to serve as a bulwark against social authority; indeed they depend for their existence on social recognition. (J.D.M.)

Plate 45, page 173.

Grotius, Hugo (1583–1645) was a Dutch thinker whose ideas exerted an influence out of proportion to their philosophical acuteness. Their context was political upheaval and assassination, lawlessness at sea, and the Thirty Years War. His belief in toleration and rational ways of settling disputes was based on a profound respect for truth which was in the humanistic tradition of Erasmus. He was not, however, a sceptic; on the contrary he believed that piety based on what was common to different interpretations of the Christian religion, together with reticence about doctrinal disagreements, was a sufficient basis for reconciliation between Catholics and Protestants. His *De Veritate Religionis Christianae* (1627) set forth this code of common Christianity. His *Via et Votum ad Pacem Ecclesiasticam* (1642) suggested a concrete scheme for reconciliation.

His rational outlook was, no doubt, partly the product of his early training by the great scholar Scaliger, who was one of the first to stress grammatical cogency rather than doctrinal convenience in interpreting Scriptural texts. Grotius was an infant prodigy – mastering Latin and Greek by the age of twelve and a Doctor of Law at the University of Leyden at sixteen. In 1603 he was appointed official historiographer to his native province and in 1607 he was made Advocate-general of the Fisc for Holland and Zeeland. As advocate for the Dutch East India Company he became involved in a controversy arising from the seizure of a Portuguese galleon in the Straits of Malacca. Grotius was led to investigate the general grounds of the lawfulness of war. His *De Jure Praedae* (*On the Law of Booty*), written in 1604 and re-discovered and published in 1868, was the result; it led to his abiding interest in International Law and formed the basis of his later masterpiece *De Jure Belli et Pacis* (*On the Law of War and Peace*), 1625. Grotius upheld the general principle that the ocean is free to all nations.

Grotius' work for rational reconciliation nearly cost him his life when he tried to bring together the Remonstrant Republican party led by Oldenbarneveldt and the Anti-Remonstrant Party of Orange led by Maurice of Nassau. In 1618 Maurice effected a coup d'état. Oldenbarneveldt was put to death and Grotius was sentenced to life imprisonment. His wife, however, succeeded in smuggling him out of prison concealed in a case allegedly containing tomes on Arminian theology. He fled to Antwerp and thence to Paris, where he was welcomed by Louis XIII and granted a pension, which was seldom paid. During retirement in France he composed his *De Jure Belli et Pacis*, 1625, which brought him international fame. He later found service under Sweden as ambassador to France, a post in which he enjoyed neither the confidence of the French court nor personal contentment. He died after a shipwreck near Danzig in 1645.

Grotius' contribution to philosophy consisted mainly in his unequivocal defence of natural law as a rationally discernible set of principles binding on citizens, rulers, and God alike. The validity of such a law upholding the security of property, good faith, and fair dealing was a common-place of Christian thought. But the disunity of Christendom after the Reformation and the secular challenge to the authority of the church, which was one of the legacies of the Renaissance, had made its validity difficult to defend on religious grounds. Furthermore the policy of Real-politik pursued by the rulers of the new nation states, as popularized by Machiavelli, made the content of the old law of nature look somewhat artificial. Grotius therefore sketched a foundation for the law of nature which would make it independent of religion and based on a proper understanding of human nature.

Natural law, claimed Grotius, is "a dictate of right reason, which points out that an act, according as it is or is not in conformity with rational nature, has in it a quality of moral baseness or moral necessity; and that, in consequence, such an act is either forbidden or enjoined by the author of nature, God." It was not obligatory because God commanded it; rather God commanded it because it was obligatory. "Just as even God, then, cannot cause that two times two should not make four, so he cannot cause that which is intrinsically evil be not evil." In other words Grotius assimilated moral knowledge to mathematical knowledge and suggested that what **Descartes** and others held to be true of our knowledge of nature was also true of our knowledge of morals. Both were certain and both were accessible to a rational man independently of religious authority.

Grotius held, furthermore, that as men were, as **Aristotle** and the **Stoics** had taught, social by nature, they had a natural interest in the maintenance of a social order. The rules of natural law, therefore, which were almost necessary conditions of any society whatsoever, were self-evident to man as a social animal endowed with reason. They were not simply the products of convention and choice. "For the very nature of man, which even if we had no lack of anything would lead us into the mutual relations of society, is the mother of the law of nature."

Grotius maintained that all other law – Jus Divinum, Jus Civile, and Jus Gentium – were dictates of will subordinate to Jus Naturale. The civil law, for instance, depended for its validity ultimately on the natural obligation of good faith in keeping covenants. Grotius' treatment of the Law of Nations was particularly interesting and important; for he transformed what had been a system of private law establishing relations between subject and subject belonging to different nations into a system of public law establishing relations between state and state. Thus his *De Jure Belli et Pacis* was a monument in the history of International Law.

Grotius' philosophical importance was limited. By elevating natural law and giving it a status independent of custom, law, and religion, he helped considerably in the process of *distinguishing* what we now call moral principles from customary, legal, and religious codes. In stressing the connexion between natural law and man's social nature he made a somewhat oblique and confused contribution to the philosophical controversy about whether moral principles are natural or conventional. By stressing the connexion between man's reason and his acceptance of moral principles Grotius again contributed somewhat obliquely to the understanding of what is meant by *moral* principles – which are, at least, those for which reasons can be given.

Grotius' treatment of these matters was somewhat vitiated by his failure to be clear about the distinction between what we call "laws of nature", which are *descriptions* of what is invariably the case, and "laws" in the legal or moral sense, which are *prescriptions* about what ought to be the case. It was not until the eighteenth century, with **Hume** and **Kant**, that some kind of clarity on this point began to emerge. Hume, roughly speaking developed the connexion postulated by Grotius between moral principles and man's sociality; Kant that between moral principles and man's rationality. Grotius' account of rationality, however, like that of most of his contemporaries, was too much influenced by the model of mathematics. Grotius was therefore one of the forerunners of the Intuitionist school in **ethics** which holds that moral principles are self-evident like mathematical axioms.

In the matter of the validity of law Grotius somewhat confused the issue by suggesting that the validity of law derives from that of a higher law – the law of nature. But his teaching could be ex-

pressed in a less objectionable way if it were suggested that the importance of the theory of natural law was not simply to make a *distinction* between law and moral principles, but also to suggest that law could and should be subjected to moral scrutiny and criticism.   (R.S.P.)

Plate 46, page 174.

H

Hamilton, Sir William (1788–1856) was born at Glasgow and was an undergraduate of both Glasgow and Oxford. He spent some time at the Bar and was then successively Professor of history and then philosophy in Edinburgh. In philosophy his starting point was the common-sense position of **Reid** and the Scottish school; his lectures, later published as his *Lectures on Logic* and *Lectures on Metaphysics* were of great weight in the development of the Scottish philosophical tradition.

Hamilton's main work was the *Philosophy of the Unconditioned*, 1829. In this work he proceeds, by means of a critical examination of the views of **Kant**, Schelling and **Comte** to outline a theory of knowledge of which the main thesis is that to think is to condition; this means that when we think of anything we inevitably determine it by its relation to something else by which it is conditioned; thus every part is a whole of parts and every whole is itself part of some greater whole and the idea of the absolute whole or part is an absurdity. Similarly we cannot think of an unconditioned beginning and can only understand a beginning as conditioned by another phenomenon; the conditioning phenomenon is thus the cause and the concept of cause is made by Hamilton merely a special case of the general principle of conditioning. Hamilton took it that this philosophical view made it impossible to attain absolute truth by philosophy and that we must be satisfied with an enlightened ignorance. But though we cannot know the unconditioned we cannot but have some faith about it; the unconditioned is God who, as unconditioned, is completely incomprehensible.

Hamilton's direct influence, though great in the nineteenth century, has since declined. He is now best remembered as the subject of J. S. **Mill**'s *An Examination of Sir William Hamilton's Philosophy* and as the inventor of a variant of the **logic** of the syllogism in which the predicate as well as the subject is quantified (that is, in which we have not simply the proposition, all S is P and some S is P, but rather all S is all P, all S is some P, some S is all P and some S is some P.)   (J.O.U.)

Hare, Richard Mervyn (1919–), English, Fellow of Balliol College, Oxford. He is best known as a moral philosopher and few recent books on moral philosophy have received more attention than his *The Language of Morals* (1952). Hare holds that the primary task of the moral philosopher is to clarify the nature of moral judgments and terms. Moral judgments, he holds, differ from descriptions of the world not in subject matter but by being more akin to imperatives than to descriptions, their primary function being to guide choice; thus, while to say that something is red is to describe it, to say that something is good is to commend it, to put it forward as a suitable object of choice, though such a commendation requires justification by reference to the description of the object commended and is not a wayward expression of taste or emotion. Notable features of the book are a critical restatement of **Moore**'s arguments against ethical naturalism and an attempt to show that imperatives as well as indicatives are subject to logical rules.   (J.O.U.)

Hartmann, Karl-Robert-Eduard von (1842–1906), German. He is now known chiefly for his *Philosophy of the Unconscious* (1869), a work which was the most widely read of all German philosophical books of its time. Hartmann claimed to produce a synthesis of **Hegel** and **Schopenhauer**; taking from Hegel the notion of the rational Idea and from Schopenhauer that of the Will, Hartmann saw these as elements in a new ultimate – the Unconscious. The rational Idea is properly the guide of the blind Will, but the pessimistic Hartmann regarded them as at variance in sinful man. Hartmann speaks always of Idea, Will and Unconscious as though he conceives of them as things. The book is of no permanent importance in its own right, but is important as part of the background of Freudian psychological theory. Hartmann followed this early work with many others, of which *The Doctrine of the Categories* was most widely read. His reputation has now much declined.   (J.O.U.)

Hartmann, Nicolai (1882–1950), German philosopher, one of the few speculative metaphysicians in the grand style of the present century. He received his philosophical training in the great neo-Kantian school of Marburg, though he himself rejected the Kantian approach to philosophy at an early stage of his thought. He taught in the Universities of Cologne, Berlin and Göttingen. His influence in Germany has been considerable; his *Ethics* (1925) was published in English translation in 1932 and has been widely read in English-speaking countries, but his other work has had comparatively little influence there.

Hartmann considered that the European tradition in philosophy since **Descartes** had been to start with the subject, the thinker, and his thoughts as the indubitable datum on which to build; this, he held, was a fundamental mistake. Knowledge, he said, was the apprehension of an independent reality, an apprehension as immediate as is, according to Descartes, our apprehension of the self. Properly understood all philosophical problems are ontological; they are attempts to understand the kind of being presented to us. The domain of ontology is thus all that can be said of being. In his main works Hartmann sets out an extreme realist ontology; thus he starts with a distinction of real being and ideal being; ideal being includes **mathematical** entities and values which are, as **Plato** held, independent entities though not superior to real entities. On this basis he builds a most elaborate classification of ontological kinds.

Metaphysical problems such as that of **free will** and of the relation of life to the mechanical are, according to Hartmann, essentially insoluble; there will always be, after the best metaphysical work, unresolved mysteries, but we can reduce the unintelligible residue and increase our understanding. Thus there can be no systematic metaphysics outside ontology but only a series of problems raised and partly solved.

Hartmann's ethical work is indebted to **Husserl** and the **phenomenologists** in its method. It is an extraordinarily detailed and subtle description of moral phenomena. There is little argument, for which Hartmann substitutes an appeal to moral consciousness and its immediate deliverances. The deliverances of moral consciousness are, Hartmann holds, of two basic types, answers to questions of what is valuable and answers to problems of conduct (what ought I to do?). He is sufficiently utilitarian to regard the former type of problem as primary. There are two kinds of value, that which is possessed by the things and situations with which agents deal and that which is possessed by agents and their actions. Specifically moral value is to be found in the disposition of the agent, and it is in this connection that Hartmann gives his famous analysis of the virtues, analogous to that of **Aristotle** in the third and fourth books of the *Nicomachean Ethics* but on a far more elaborate scale. For an agent and his actions to have value they must be free; they must therefore be to some extent exempt from determination by natural law and not determined even by values, which command but do not compel. In accordance with his general position on the insolubility of metaphysical problems Hartmann admits that he cannot understand how man can be free in this way; but he is sure that such freedom is presupposed in morality. (J.O.U.)

Plate 47, page 175.

Hedonism is a word derived from the Greek word "hedone" which means pleasure. Three quite different views have been held, all of which are called hedonism, which it is all the more necessary to distinguish because they have been so often confused with each other. First we have ethical hedonism, which is the moral view that the only thing which is good is pleasure; this view does not suggest that we can desire nothing other than pleasure or that it is absurd to speak of anything else being good, but only that it is a mistake of judgment to believe that anything else is good or to desire anything else except as a means to pleasure. **Epicurus** and **Bentham** are famous examples of moralists who have held this view. Secondly there is psychological hedonism, which is the psychological theory that we can desire nothing but pleasure; though this view has often been confused with ethical hedonism it is strictly incompatible with it, for if we can desire nothing else it is as pointless to recommend desires for pleasure as it is pointless to recommend falling when one is released in mid-air. This theory, frequently held by earlier British empiricists was heavily attacked by **Butler**; but it nonetheless appears as a support for ethical hedonism in J. S. **Mill**'s *Utilitarianism*. Thirdly there is

the view that the notion of "good" is to be defined as the same as "pleasant" or at least in terms of "pleasure". Thus **Locke** in his *Essay* (II. xx. 2) says "That we call *good* which is apt to cause or increase pleasure, or diminish pain in us." This view also has been confused with ethical hedonism in spite of the fact that "pleasure alone is good" can have no moral content if it is a mere definition.

(J.O.U.)

Hegel, Georg Wilhelm Friedrich (1770–1831), born in Stuttgart, Germany, was one of the most influential philosophers of all time: indeed, the history of philosophy since his death could be represented as a series of revolts against him and his followers. A little more than a century after his death, few followers were left, but much of his thought had been absorbed by his opponents, and to gain some historical perspective on **Kierkegaard** and **Marx**, on marxism and **existentialism**, on **pragmatism** and analytic philosophy, on neo-orthodoxy and the so-called new criticism, Hegel's influence must be taken into account as one of the key factors.

Although his collected works in German come to about twenty volumes, and in the best critical edition to far over thirty volumes, Hegel himself published only four books: *Phänomenologie des Geistes* (1807), *Logik* (1812–16), *Encyclopaedie der philosophischen Wissenschaften* (1817; thoroughly rewritten edition 1827; revised edition 1830), and *Philosophie des Rechts* (1821). All of these works, as well as his posthumously published lectures on the philosophy of history, the philosophy of art, the philosophy of religion, and the history of philosophy, have been translated into English – for the most part very inadequately. T. M. Knox's version of the *Philosophy of Right* is the most satisfactory English translation.

Hegel's philosophy may be conveniently divided into three phases. The first, largely ignored in the English literature, antedates the publication of his first book in 1807. The second is represented by that book, the *Phenomenology*. The third, which alone has greatly concerned the British Hegelians and anti-Hegelians, is represented by his later works, beginning with his *Logic*. In Germany and France, the first two phases have excited far more interest than the last, at least in the twentieth century. In the first phase we encounter an as yet non-professorial Hegel, who could hardly be more different from the popular image of the man.

Hegel's earliest writings – drafts and essays he wrote in his twenties – were first published in 1907 under the misleading title *Hegels theologische Jugendschriften*. Two of the major pieces – there are four in all – were published in English in 1947 as Hegel's *Early Theological Writings*, translated by Knox. In some of these essays, notably in "The Positivity of the Christian Religion", Hegel's style is brilliant, eloquent, and picturesque, his criticism of the Christian churches, both Catholic and Protestant, and even of Jesus himself, is frequently vitriolic, and his opposition to all dogma and authoritarianism is uncompromising. He does not oppose all religion but finds Christianity incompatible with reason and human dignity. In the oldest fragments, he considers the possibility of a wholly rational religion which would help us to attain a harmonious personality and a high level of morality.

By 1800, Hegel felt that the sort of criticism in which he had earlier engaged was all too easy, obvious, and pointless. It would be a more challenging task to show how Christianity and other beliefs held by eminent men of the past had not been "bare nonsense". Perhaps one could even "deduce this now repudiated dogmatics out of what we now consider the needs of human nature and thus show its naturalness and its necessity". This programme, sketched in 1800 in a preface to a never written work, marks the transition to Hegel's second phase and to his *Phenomenology of the Spirit*. (The English translation renders *Geist* as "Mind" in the title and in large parts of the book; but, especially in the later parts, "Mind" simply makes no sense, and "Spirit" appears more and more often. Actually, "mind", with its primarily epistemological connotation, is misleading throughout and "spirit" is more suggestive).

The use of "necessity" in the last quotation foreshadows one of the central confusions of Hegel's subsequent philosophy. He uses "necessary" as a synonym of "natural" and an antonym of "arbitrary" and "utterly capricious" and he does not distinguish between giving some reasons for a development and demonstrating its "necessity". In this sense he finds reason in history, but he does not claim – as many interpreters suppose – that

historical events or particular entities can be "deduced" in any ordinary sense.

Although Hegel declares in the important preface to his *Phenomenology* that he aims to elevate philosophy to the status of a science, the book – and much of his later philosophy, too – is best understood in the perspective supplied by his *juvenilia*: what he wants is still a substitute for traditional Christianity – a world view that eliminates whatever is incompatible with reason and human dignity while preserving whatever was sound in Christianity and in the thought of all the great philosophers of the past. His prose, though still occasionally picturesque, has on the whole become involved and heavy, and his criticism no longer takes the form of sarcastic denunciation or outright ridicule: rather it consists in relegating all past positions, including various forms of Christianity, to the role of more or less remarkable, though plainly unsatisfactory, anticipations of the philosophic system that Hegel distils out of the cauldron of history.

In spite of the scorn which Hegel's critics have lavished on his allegedly arrogant claims for his own system, the view of the history of philosophy on which these claims are based has been almost universally accepted; and when his claims are understood in terms of this view, as they are meant to be, they prove to be much less presumptuous. Hegel does not pit his own philosophy against rival philosophies, past and present, by way of saying: they are wrong and I am right. He repudiates the common conception of philosophic disagreement which one might call the battlefield view of the history of philosophy. The history of philosophy must be understood, he insists, in terms of development. It was Hegel more than anybody else who established the history of philosophy as a subject of central importance in the modern university, and almost all texts on the subject show, albeit in varying degrees, his influence.

Hegel, then, does not look at his own system as in any sense peculiarly his own philosophy. He is not contemporaneous with his predecessors but able to draw on their cumulative efforts. He can see how the excesses of one are in time pointed out by his successor who, in turn, may well go to the opposite extreme. All along, there is a continual refinement, an increased articulateness, and, as it were, a progressive revelation of the truth.

This raises the question what Hegel expected from the future. Did he admit that his own system was not final? Hegel did not deal with this question explicitly, but he never supposed that history would stop with him. In his lectures on the philosophy of history he referred to the United States as "the land of the future", while insisting that for this very reason the United States must be left out of account at present, seeing that it is the task of philosophy to comprehend "that which is" and not to speculate about the future; and the same course of lectures culminates in the pronouncement: "To this point consciousness has come". If he had foreseen the insights of future philosophers, he would have embodied them in his own system. Since he could not foresee them, he did not talk about them.

For all that, he might have stressed, at least occasionally, that his own system was not final, instead of stressing, as he often did, that it was, if only at the time of speaking, the last word. This is surely a fault, but there are at least two extenuating circumstances. The first is that few great philosophers have not been guilty on the same score: from **Plato** to **Wittgenstein**'s preface to his *Tractatus* it is encountered in classic upon classic. Secondly, there was a peculiarly apocalyptic atmosphere in German philosophy in Hegel's day. We can trace it back at least to **Kant**'s announcement, in the preface to his *Critique of Pure Reason* (1781), that he hoped philosophy would at long last attain the truth by the end of the century. **Fichte** tried to keep Kant's promise in 1794; Schelling, at first enthusiastic about Fichte's effort, soon struck out on his own in an attempt to build on the foundations laid by Kant and Fichte, and published his own *System of Transcendental Idealism* in 1800. Hegel felt that he was completing what Kant, Fichte, and Schelling had begun. In addition, there was a widespread feeling that an era was coming to an end, and Hegel, like the old Goethe, felt that the civilisation he had known was drawing to a close, that he was looking back upon European history and in some sense summing it up. To cite his preface to his *Philosophy of Right*: "When philosophy paints its grey on grey, a form of life has grown old, and with grey on grey it cannot be rejuvenated, but only comprehended. The owl of Minerva begins its flight only at dusk".

In the *Phenomenology* these tendencies are less prominent than in Hegel's later work. It is a work of youthful exuberance, although the preface makes clear that the author's desire to raise philosophy to the level of a science is meant to put an end to romanticism in philosophy. What is wanted is not inspiration and edification, sentiment and intuition, but the exertion of careful and rigorous conceptual thinking – not the enthusiasm of a coterie but the discipline of a science.

Even if one sympathises with these programmatic declarations and with Hegel's sharp and perceptive criticism of romanticism, one may yet conclude that his own brand of rigour was misconceived from the start. The great central idea of the *Phenomenology* is that different outlooks correspond to different states of mind, different stages in the development of the spirit, and are not, taken as a whole, true or false, but rather more or less mature. The book is the *Bildungsroman* of the spirit, the story of the education of the spirit, and this framework allows for many penetrating observations. But it is marred by two pervasive faults: first, the above-mentioned confusion about necessity affects Hegel's attempts to show how one stage necessarily issues in the next; secondly, he assumes not only that *some* outlooks and positions are best understood in terms of a developmental sequence, but – and this assumption is surely untenable – that *all* outlooks and positions can be reasonably arranged in a single development, or even on a scale of rising maturity.

He was probably inspired by the example of Goethe who pushed the Storm and Stress style to its extremes in *Werther* and *Goetz* before seeking respite in the classicism of his *Tasso* and his *Iphigenie*, which in turn led him to *Wilhelm Meister*, from which the original romantics took their cue, and so forth, on and on. But Hegel disregards the actual historic sequence, choosing illustrations for a relatively more mature stage from the Greeks and for a less mature stage from the present. This, though often criticised, is hardly a serious fault, but it has distracted attention from the more serious flaws mentioned previously.

Many of the insights of existentialism are anticipated in the *Phenomenology*, often better formulated than they were by his successors; but one of the worst faults of Kierkegaard, **Heidegger**, and

Sartre – and of Marx and scores of Marxists, too – can also be traced to Hegel: the art of pseudo-demonstration, the apparently rigorous and certainly forbidding train of thought that uses an imposing terminology to show that something follows necessarily which, in fact, does not follow. If one makes a sympathetic effort, one can follow the train of thought; but for all that the conclusion does not follow with any necessity.

One further flaw in the *Phenomenology* is that it is never altogether clear – and this is also true of Hegel's later work, whose "spirit" Hegel is discussing. Often it is clearly the human spirit, and Hegel seems to be writing about the education of humanity. But at other times, "spirit" seems just as plainly an *alias* of God. Hegel clearly did not believe in a transcendent God, omniscient and omnipotent from all eternity; but he did believe that the force which is at work in the development of the material universe and eventually fashions man and finds expression in man's spirit, may legitimately be named after its final and highest manifestation – even as we call an embryo an undeveloped human being instead of calling man the last stage of the human embryo. According to Hegel, it is only in man that the spirit achieves self-consciousness, and it knows only what man knows.

Instead of repudiating traditional conceptions of the Trinity, the Incarnation, or of God, Hegel often uses Christian terms and praises Christianity for realising that God is spirit, that God becomes man, etc. This gives rise to the paradox that "God" finds out about himself only in Hegel's system. The paradox disappears when we say that Hegel did not believe in "God" but, like many philosophers and theologians, did not make a point of this fact, preferring to pour new wine into old skins.

Hegel's *Logic*, the work which inaugurates his third and final phase, is marred to an even greater degree by pseudo-demonstrations and a confused notion of necessity. Again, much remains after allowance has been made for these great faults: above all, perhaps the most sustained attempt since **Aristotle** to articulate the meaning of philosophically interesting and important terms and their relation to each other.

Unfortunately, many readers have never got beyond the first three terms: Being, Nothing and Becoming. Partly as a result of this, partly because it is a commonplace in the literature, they suppose, mistakenly, that all of Hegel is reducible to the three-step of Thesis, Antithesis, and Synthesis. As a matter of fact, he does not speak of theses, antitheses, and syntheses at all, although his immediate predecessors, Fichte and Schelling, did; and neither his analyses in the *Logic* nor his dialectic in general can be reduced to any such three-step. This becomes apparent as soon as one proceeds beyond Becoming to read Hegel's immediately following discussion of *Dasein* (being there), then *Fürsichsein* (being for – or by – oneself), pure quantity, quantum, degree, measure, identity, difference, ground, existence, thing, etc.

The same point is even more obvious in Hegel's philosophy of history. He divides world history into three stages: in the first, in the ancient orient, only one is considered free (the ruler); in the second period, in Greece and Rome some are free; in the modern world all are considered free, at least in principle. Some English translations, however, introduce the word "antithesis" in all kinds of places to render words that literally mean "other" or "opposite"; and secondary sources perpetuate the legend that Hegel construed everything mechanically in terms of three concepts which he actually spurned.

His *Encyclopedia* contains his entire system in outline form. A shorter version of his *Logic*, slightly rearranged, (sometimes cited as his "Lesser Logic") comprises Part One; his philosophy of nature, subdivided into mechanics, physics, and organics, constitutes Part Two; and his philosophy of spirit forms the third and last part. The philosophy of spirit is also divided into three parts, and each of these in turn into three sub-parts; but these tripartite divisions cannot be reduced to theses, antitheses, and syntheses. Subjective spirit comprises sections on anthropology, the phenomenology of the spirit, and psychology. Then comes objective spirit which contains sections on right, morality, and ethical life. Finally, the whole system culminates in a chapter on absolute spirit which is divided into sections on art, revealed religion, and – the pinnacle – philosophy.

The state is discussed in the section on ethical life (*Sittlichkeit*) after family and civil society. It belongs in the sphere of objective spirit – that is, of spirit embodied in institutions. This whole realm is the basis on which art, religion, and philosophy develop. "Although it is true that all great men have formed themselves in solitude, they have done so only by assimilating what had been created by the state".

Hegel's philosophy of objective spirit is developed in more detail in his *Philosophy of Right* and in his lectures on the philosophy of history, from which the last quotation is taken. His philosophy of absolute spirit is elaborated in the eight volumes of his lectures on art, religion, and the history of philosophy.

After Hegel's death, his followers quickly divided into two camps: a right wing that made the most of Hegel's theology and tried to infuse new life into Protestantism, and a left wing of so-called Young Hegelians who included brilliant atheists and revolutionaries – most notably Ludwig Feuerbach and Karl Marx. Marx accepted Hegel's preoccupation with history and development but claimed that Hegel had stood man on his head, as if spirit and ideas were fundamental, while he, Marx, had turned Hegel right side up again by pointing out that material factors are basic. Moreover, "the philosophers have merely interpreted the world differently, but what matters is to change it".

In Denmark, Kierkegaard protested against the Hegelian theologians of his own country. While also heavily borrowing from Hegel, he repudiated any attempt to transcend faith or even to comprehend Christianity, which, he insisted, is absurd but must be believed, or any attempt to hide from the problems of one's own concrete existence in a system.

During the latter half of the nineteenth century, the study of the history of philosophy came to flourish more and more in Germany, displacing creative attempts. But such Hegelians as Zeller, Erdmann, and Fischer made international reputations with their histories. At the same time, Hegelianism came to England and profoundly influenced T. H. **Green**, B. **Bosanquet**, F. H. **Bradley** and J. M. E. **McTaggart** against whom, in turn, G. E. **Moore** and Bertrand **Russell** revolted at the beginning of the twentieth century. In the United States, William **James** rebelled against the Hegelian Idealism of Josiah **Royce** and of dozens of less gifted philosophers. John **Dewey** was a Hegelian when young. In Italy, **Croce** developed the Hegel-

ian tradition. In France Jean-Paul **Sartre**'s *l'Être et le Néant* leans heavily on Hegel. Beyond that, the historical approach to art, religion and literature, no less than philosophy, owes a great deal to Hegel. Perhaps no other thinker since Kant, with the possible exception of **Nietzsche**, has had a comparable influence.   (W.K.)

Plate 48, page 176.

Heidegger, Martin (1889–), German philosopher, is widely considered the chief exponent of **existentialism**, though he has repudiated this label. He was born in 1889, not far from Freiburg where he later studied philosophy under **Husserl**. It was in Husserl's *Jahrbuch* that Heidegger's main work first appeared in 1927, with a dedication to Husserl: *Sein und Zeit (Being and Time)*. In 1933, when Hitler came to power, Heidegger accepted the Rektorat of the University of Freiburg, welcomed Hitler's ascent as the dawn of a new era, praised the abolition of academic freedom (his inaugural address on his concept of the German University was published under the title *Die Selbstbehauptung der deutschen Universität*), and completely dissociated himself from Husserl because he was a Jew.

There has been a good deal of discussion of the question whether Heidegger's philosophy entailed Nazism. It does not, but the pseudo-demonstrations of his rectoral address are of a kind with the mode of argument in his more philosophical writings: with the kind of logic, or lack of logic, that characterizes Heidegger's work, one can "prove" anything at all.

Many of Heidegger's admirers disown the master's later works which are mainly exegeses, particularily of **Pre-Socratic** fragments, marked by a semi-mystical concern with Being. They find his importance in *Being and Time* and in a short lecture, *Was ist Metaphysik?* Heidegger himself denies that there are two phases in his development and claims that his earlier work has merely been misunderstood: he was never an existentialist but always concerned with Being. In *Being and Time* he studies human existence (*Dasein*) as the mode of Being best known to man; but his interest, as he constantly insisted even then, was not anthropological or psychological; he tried to use human existence as a window through which we can look into Being. Although this self-interpretation seems right, it is far from clear how such phenomena as care and conscience, guilt and dread, and death and resolution, which are discussed in *Being and Time*, can be understood non-anthropologically. Throughout *Being and Time* one waits in vain for adequate illumination on this point, and when the book, subtitled "First Half", ends one is led to expect a resolution of this problem from Part Two, which never appeared. Heidegger's enormous influence, especially in Germany and France and Belgium, has been based on an interpretation of his early work which, even in *Being and Time*, he repudiated – but apart from which it is difficult to see how the book makes sense. Understood psychologically, or anthropologically, his observations in *Being and Time* are, moreover, of very doubtful accuracy. What has made the work so influential in spite of all this is probably a combination of at least four factors: Heidegger dealt with phenomena of almost universal human interest; in the post-war world this interest was especially intense; he managed to discuss these matters with a seeming rigour and an elaborate terminology which gave academicians a good conscience; and he is a master at generating excitement and maintaining suspense. There are probably few philosophers to whose vogue Andersen's fairy tale, *The Emperor's Clothes* is more applicable. (W.K.)

Plate 49, page 209.

Heraclitus of Ephesus, Greek city of Asia Minor, flourished *c.* 500 B.C. Of aristocratic family, he withdrew from society and in notoriously obscure terms attacked the Ephesians, and men in general, for their stupidity. Men failed to apprehend the *Logos*, the formular constituent of all natural objects – a kind of common structural characteristic in part identifiable with fire. Things in the world were divided into opposites - an analysis of differentiation applied also by **Anaximander** - and change could be expressed as between opposites. These, apparently plural and discrete, were actually "one and the same", being connected in a "joining that stretches in both directions" by the Logos, which ensured the ultimate balance and continuity of changes between opposites. Thus Heraclitus saw the unity of the world in its structure and behaviour rather than in its material. Fire, nevertheless, is the primary material, and controls the "turnings" into

each other of the three great cosmic components, fire, sea and earth. Change, or "strife" as Heraclitus called it, was necessary for the continued unification of opposites: not perhaps continuous change in everything (as **Plato**, thinking rather of the exaggerated Heracliteanism of **Cratylus**, maintained) but the certainty of ultimate change between opposites. Wisdom consists in understanding the Logos, how the world works; for man is a part of the world, himself governed by the Logos, which exists in his soul as its active and fiery part. This fiery part, which must be preserved from the moisture produced by sleep, stupidity, and vice, makes contact with the Logos-element in outside objects, and in some form can survive even death. Thus Heraclitus produced a surprisingly coherent system, one which gave a real motive for philosophy, and which for the first time gave some account of epistemology. Its obscure presentation, and **Parmenides'** re-alignment of thought, prevented it from being as influential (until the **Stoics**) as it deserved to be. (G.S.K.)

See also **Pre-Socratics.**

Hobbes, Thomas (1588–1679), English philosopher educated at Magdalen Hall, Oxford. In 1608 he became tutor to the young son of William Cavendish, Earl of Devonshire. He spent the rest of his long life in similar employment, mainly with the Cavendish family. He was tutor to Charles II during his exile in Paris in 1646 after the battle of Naseby.

Hobbes was a thorough-going academic whose intellectual history can be conveniently related to his three visits to the continent. His first visit in 1610 inspired him with a desire to master the thought of the ancient world. His dissatisfaction with the Aristotelian tradition of the Schools was probably also encouraged by his talks with Francis **Bacon**, whom he used to visit during the latter's retirement. In 1628 he published a translation of Thucydides, partly to warn his fellow-countrymen of the dangers of democracy.

In 1628, during his second journey to the continent, he developed both better health and a passionate interest in geometry whose method he thought he might use to present his conclusions about democracy as irrefragable demonstrations. He thought, like Bacon, that knowledge meant power, and hoped to cure the ills of a society on the verge of civil war by sketching a rational reconstruction of society like a geometer's figure.

Hobbes' third journey to the continent provided the final ingredient for his natural and civil philosophy; for he visited Galileo in 1636 and conceived the imaginative idea which permeated his whole philosophy – the generalisation of the science of mechanics and the geometrical deduction of the behaviour of men from the abstract principles of the new science of motion.

Hobbes claimed originality for two main parts of his philosophy – his optics and his civil philosophy – and his first contributions to philosophy were in these fields. His *Little Treatise* (1630–1637) was an attack on the Aristotelian theory of sense and a sketch for a new mechanical theory. On returning to England his thoughts were turned again to politics, owing to the turbulent state of the country. In 1640 he published his *Elements of Law*, while Parliament was sitting. This demonstrated the need for undivided sovereignty. (It was published later in 1650 in two parts – *Human Nature* and *De Corpore Politico*). When Parliament impeached Strafford Hobbes feared for his life and fled to the continent, priding himself in later times on being "the first of all that fled". His *De Cive* followed soon after in 1642 (published in English in 1651 under the title *Philosophical Rudiments Concerning Government and Society*), in which he tried to demonstrate conclusively the proper purpose and extent of the civil power, and the relationship between church and state.

Hobbes' originality consisted not simply in his views about optics and politics but also in the links which he forged between them. For he thought that an all-inclusive theory could be constructed starting with simple movements studied in geometry and culminating in the movements of men towards and away from each other in political life. He envisaged a deductive trilogy comprising works on Body, Man, and Citizen, but the march of events constantly interrupted his project. He started on his *De Corpore* soon after the publication of *De Cive*, but it was not completed till after his final return to England; for after the advent of Charles II to Paris Hobbes turned aside from his physical speculations and started work on his masterpiece, *Leviathan*, which stated in a pungent form his views

on Man and Citizen. It was published in 1651 and soon afterwards Hobbes was permitted by Cromwell to return to England. For Hobbes, while conceding popular representation used the **Social Contract** theory to demonstrate the necessity of an absolute sovereign – by consent, not by Divine Right. So his doctrine was one which could be used to justify any *de facto* government, provided that it governed – first of all that of Cromwell and later that of Charles II.

After his return to England Hobbes soon became involved in a dispute with Bishop Bramhall on the subject of **free will**. His *Questions Concerning Liberty, Necessity, and Chance* was the result (1656). Hobbes was then led into a most humiliating controversy; for in chapter 20 of *De Corpore*, which he published in 1655, he had inserted an attempt to square the circle. This was seized on by John Wallis, professor of geometry at Oxford, and Seth Ward, the professor of astronomy, both of them Puritans and foundation members of the Royal Society. They were irritated by Hobbes' criticisms of the universities and ruthlessly exposed his mathematical ineptitude. The wrangle lasted for about twenty years.

Hobbes' energy, however, which was remarkable for one so advanced in years (he played tennis up till the age of seventy), was not completely absorbed in this abortive controversy. In 1657 he published the second part of his trilogy, the *De Homine*. After the Restoration Hobbes was received at Court, where his wit was appreciated. But at the time of the Plague and Great Fire some reason was sought for God's displeasure, and a bill being brought before Parliament for the suppression of atheism, a committee was set up to look into *Leviathan*. The matter was however dropped, probably through the intervention of the King; but Hobbes was forbidden to publish his opinions. He turned to history and in 1668 completed his *Behemoth* – a history of the Civil War, interpreted in the light of his opinions about man and society. It was published posthumously in 1682. He was also sent Bacon's *Elements of Common Law* by his friend John Aubrey and, at the age of seventy-six produced his *Dialogues between a Philosopher and a Student of the Common Laws of England*. (Published posthumously in 1681). At eighty-four he wrote his own autobiography in Latin verse and at eighty-six published a translation of the *Iliad* and *Odyssey* for want of something better to do. He died at the age of ninety-one.

CONTRIBUTION TO PHILOSOPHY

(1) *Philosophical method.* Hobbes, like his contemporaries **Bacon** and **Descartes**, believed that method was the key to the attainment of knowledge. Man's natural reason was in decay for want of a proper method and clouded over and corrupted by the vaporous doctrines of the Schools, who, true to their Aristotelian tradition, spoke of "essences", "spirits", and other such superstitious nonsense which strengthened the hold of the Catholic Church and encouraged sedition.

Hobbes, therefore, saw philosophy not simply as an aid to clear thinking but as a necessary preliminary to rational government and the avoidance of civil war – the worst of all evils from which cometh "slaughter, solitude, and the want of all things." But he understood philosophy in a very wide sense " . . . such knowledge of effects or appearances as we acquire by true ratiocination from the knowledge we have first of their causes or generation. And again, of such causes or generations as may be from knowing first their effects." He had in mind the method of geometry and the resoluto–compositive method of Galileo by means of which phenomena were analysed into their simplest components and rationally reconstructed in an intelligible pattern. And, like all his rationalist contemporaries, he believed that the reality beneath the deceptive appeareances of sense was geometrical in character. So the use of reason in philosophy, which Hobbes regarded literally as a kind of adding or subtracting "of the consequences of general names agreed upon for the marking and signifying of our thoughts" resulted, in his case, both in what is now called analytic philosophy, or the attempt to elucidate the meaning of concepts, and in what is called metaphysics – the generalisation of a set of concepts (in Hobbes's case mechanical ones) to fields which are not usually their proper home. This was meant to reveal the ground–plan of all that is.

(2) *The metaphysics of motion.* Hobbes' analysis was, as a matter of fact, usually subservient to his wider speculations. For his dream of a trilogy covering Body, Man, and Citizen coloured all his work. He conceived of the actions of men as particular cases of bodies in motion, explicable in terms of all-pervasive mechanical laws. This was made plausible by the introduction of the concept of "endeavour" to postulate infinitely small motions of various sorts – especially those in the medium between man and external objects, in the sense-organs, and within the body. The phenomena of sense, imagination and dreams were regarded as appearances of minute bodies conforming to the law of inertia, and the phenomena of motivation were explained as reactions prompted by external and internal stimulation – a commonplace of modern psychology. Hobbes became famous, however, (and notorious), for his suggestion that all human motivation is a particular case of one of two basic bodily movements – appetite, or movements towards objects, and aversion, or movements away from them.

(3) *Politics.* In his political writings these basic responses appeared as the desire for power and the fear of death, which were the reality beneath all the appearances of political behaviour. He thought that a multitude of men became a commonwealth by the device of authority in which men gave up unlimited self-assertion against each other – their "rights of nature" – and authorised a man or a body of men to act on their behalf. This "social contract", which was presupposed by sovereignty was a consequence of the overwhelming fear of death which haunted men in a state of nature. Hobbes also deduced from this "ideal experiment", or Galilean resolution of civil society into its simplest components, that such a sovereign *must* be absolute, the sole reason for the institution of government being the safety of the people.

(4) *Ethics.* This deductive scheme determined the general pattern of Hobbes' thinking about morals, law, and religion. But in all these spheres his analytical acumen suggested lines of thought that were of lasting value. In moral philosophy he held that the rules of civilized behaviour (then called "natural law" or "the laws of nature") were deducible from rules of prudence which any reasonable man must accept who is afraid of death.

Civilization, he contended, is based on fear, not on natural sociability. By "good" we mean what is an object of desire, by "evil" what is an object of aversion. He believed, too, in **determinism** and made important contributions to the **free will** controversy by maintaining that "free" is a term properly applied to man and to his actions, not to his will, which is but "the last appetite in deliberating". A man is free if there is no constraint on his actions; but his actions are necessitated, as they have causes, even though they may be free. For "contingent", not "free" is the opposite of "necessitated". Hobbes was also singularly clear-sighted on the subject of punishment. He held that punishment is by its nature retributive; for this is part of the meaning of "punishment". But its *justification* must be sought along **utilitarian** lines.

(5) *Law.* In his theory of law Hobbes is famous for his view that law is the command of the sovereign. This was, historically speaking, a very important thesis in that it attempted to make clear the procedural difference between statute law (which was then in its infancy) and the Common Law. It also insisted on distinguishing the questions which are so apt to get confused: "What is the law?" and "Is the law just?" In many respects Hobbes anticipated the Austinian school of analytic jurisprudence of the nineteenth century.

(6) *Religion.* Hobbes' views on religion were, to a large extent, directed to showing that there were general grounds as well as scriptural authority for the belief that the sovereign was the best interpreter of God's will. Religion was a system of law, not a system of truth. To establish this Hobbes made some illuminating remarks on the distinction between knowledge and faith. He suggested that we could *know* nothing of the attributes of God. The adjectives which we used to describe him were expressions of our adoration, not products of reason. He was particularly vehement in defending what he called the "true religion" against the twin threats of Catholicism, with its extra-mundane authority, and the Puritans who took seriously the priesthood of all believers. In the course of this onslaught he dealt mercilessly, from the point of view of mechanical metaphysics, with the concepts of Scripture, such as "spirit", "inspiration", "miracles", and "the kingdom of God". On the problem of evil he pointed out very acutely that the only solution was to stress God's power. Did not God reply to Job "Where wast thou when I laid the foundations of the earth?"

(7) *Philosophy of language.* Many modern philosophers hold that Hobbes' outstanding contribution to philosophy was his theory of speech. He tried to combine a mechanical view about the causes of speech with a nominalist account of the meaning of general terms. He was particularly vitriolic about the doctrine of essences adhered to by the Schools, and showed that this and many other of their more bizarre doctrines derived from muddling up the use of different types of terms. Names could be either names of bodies, of properties, or of names. If one of these classes of names was used as if it belonged to another class, an absurdity would be generated. "**Universal**", for instance, was a name for a class of names, not for essences designated by names; such names are "universal" because of their use, not because they refer to a special type of entity. Similarly redness (which is a property) is not in blood in the same way as blood (which is a body) is in a bloody cloth (which is another body). In this sphere Hobbes used crude distinctions; but he anticipated modern techniques of logical analysis by supplementing the demand for concreteness and clarity of speech by a theory of how absurdities are generated by insensitivity to the logical behaviour of different classes of terms. But of much more general importance was his insistence that speech was essential to reasoning and that it was reasoning, in the sense of laying down definitions and drawing out the implications of general names, that distinguished men from animals.

(8) *Assessments of Hobbes.* Though Hobbes has been criticized at almost every point of his scheme, different ages have tended to concentrate on different aspects. Some major criticisms have been directed against a whole trend of thought rather than at Hobbes' particular expression of it. Examples of such major criticisms would be that directed against the general failure of rationalists to distinguish geometry from empirical science, the former dealing only with relations between ideas which may have no application to phenomena; another would be the exposure of the fallacy in ethics whereby a transition is made from statements of fact (for example, about human nature) to rules laying down what ought to be done. **Hume** was the first to make a systematic attack on the rationalistic and naturalistic trends in Hobbes' thought. A similar general criticism would be that directed against mechanical theories of

man which confuse the reasons for actions with their causes and give descriptions of human actions in logically inappropriate terms.

Hobbes' particular version of these various trends of thought has, however, awakened a surprising variety of different reactions in different ages. His contemporaries were alarmed at his denial of any sort of extra-human authority, at his thorough-going doctrine of human selfishness, and at his suggestion that we can know none of God's attributes. **Spinoza**, who owed a lot to Hobbes, purged his political doctrines of their inconsistencies and converted political philosophy into a theory of power. **Locke** criticized Hobbes mainly for his doctrine of human selfishness and for his willingness to substitute the terror of an arbitrary sovereign for that of a state of nature. **Leibniz** was full of admiration for Hobbes – especially for his nominalism – but aghast at his determinism and agnosticism about God's attributes. During the eighteenth century criticism was focussed on Hobbes' account of the passions – especially his attempt to show that benevolence is a special case of self-love. The **Utilitarians** regarded Hobbes as their intellectual ancestor and were impressed by his individualism, his mechanical psychology, his nominalism, and his theory of law and punishment. And **Marx** viewed Hobbes as a pioneer of materialism and approved of his determination to use knowledge for practical purposes rather than merely to understand. Modern philosophers have tended to criticize Hobbes for his naturalism in ethics and for his mechanical account of man. They have, however, dwelt on the startling similarity between Hobbes' account of a state of nature and international affairs. They have praised Hobbes for his interest in language, for his analytic techniques, and for his clarity in handling political concepts. And even if they disagree with most of the details of his scheme, they accord Hobbes the doubtful honour of being the father of modern psychology and one of the first systematic social scientists.

Plate 50, page 210.   (R.S.P.)

Hocking, William Ernest (1873–), born at Cleveland, Ohio. He was a disciple of Josiah **Royce**; and, in a period during which most professional philosophers in America abandoned the kind of philosophical **idealism** advocated by Royce,

Hocking has defended it with an eloquence which has made him a significant factor in American intellectual history. His influence has been especially strong in religious and theological circles. His most important books have been *The Meaning of God in Human Experience* (1912), and *Human Nature and Its Remaking* (1923).

He is a professional philosopher who has devoted much energy, and exerted considerable influence, outside of academic circles. His *Rethinking Missions* (1932) is perhaps the best example of this; but he has also published extensively on such problems as freedom of the press, morale in wartime, and international political affairs.   (J.W.S.)

Hook, Sidney (1902–), born in New York. "**Naturalism**" is the most appropriate label for Hook's position. He has written extensively on the philosophy of Karl **Marx** (*Towards the Understanding of Karl Marx*, 1933; *The Meaning of Marx*, 1934, with others; *Christianity and Marxism*, 1934; *From Hegel to Marx*, 1936). He was an advocate of Marxism as he understood it; but with the passage of time he decided that what he approved therein was certainly not what the usual "Marxists" advocated (*Marx and the Marxists, the Ambiguous Legacy*, 1955).

He was profoundly influenced by the philosophy of John **Dewey**, but it would be a mistake to consider him an orthodox **Pragmatist**. See, for example, *The Metaphysics of Pragmatism*, 1927.

He has been active in expressing himself on practical issues in American life. See, for example, *Heresy, Yes, Conspiracy, No*, 1953, *Education for Modern Man*, 1946, and *Common Sense and the Fifth Amendment*, 1957. One of his better known works is *Reason, Social Myths and Democracy*, 1940.
                                                          (J.W.S.)

Hume, David (1711–1776), was born in Scotland. He was not what we should now call a professional philosopher. He never held any academic post, though he once (1745) stood unsuccessfully for the Chair of "Ethics and Pneumatic Philosophy" at the University of Edinburgh. He was a man of letters, a man of society, and to a lesser extent a man of affairs. His ruling passion, he himself tells us, was a love of literary fame, and this he achieved in his lifetime mainly by his essays on moral, political, and economic subjects, and by his historical works. The only post of any importance which he held was that of secretary to the British Embassy in Paris (1763–1769), where he was for a short time Chargé d'Affaires, and where he cut a considerable figure in French society. Though never by his own profession an atheist, and not without friends among moderate churchmen, he was certainly a sceptic and an opponent of all established religions, and enjoyed notoriety as an "Infidel". He was popular with women and distinctly susceptible to their charms, but he never married. His character was lovable, mild, sociable, unsuspicious and virtuous. These qualities earned him a curious kind of lay canonization in his later years, when his newly built house in a yet unnamed street off St Andrew Square, Edinburgh, was labelled by his friend Miss Nancy Orde "St David Street", and this became the recognised name of the street.

But it is as a philosopher that Hume has remained famous, and this fame was not won without the exercise of the sterner virtues. His first philosophical work, *A Treatise of Human Nature* was completed by 1737, when he was twenty-six years of age. It was the product of ten years of unremitting and exhausting intellectual effort, "projected", he tells us, before he left college, probably 1726, planned before he was twenty-one and composed before he was twenty-five, i.e. 1736. His letters tell us of his alternating moods of optimism and despair, sickness and recovery, during this period.

The aim of the *Treatise* was ambitious; to remedy the defects of all previous philosophies, which seemed to Hume to be founded on uncertain hypotheses and "depend more upon invention than experience", by establishing the foundations of a genuinely empirical science of human nature. The first step was to investigate the understanding and the passions, on which all human judgments and actions depend, including scientific discoveries as well as moral convictions, political institutions, art, literature and trade. "There is no question of importance, whose decision is not comprised in the science of man" (*Treatise*, Introduction).

The *Treatise*, divided into three books, "Of the Understanding", "Of the Passions" and "Of Morals", was intended to lay the foundations of the science of man.

The mind, Hume said, consists of nothing but perceptions, and these are of two kinds, impres-

sions and ideas. Roughly speaking, impressions are what we call sensations, feelings, emotions. Ideas are what we call thoughts. The former are forceful and vivacious, the latter are nothing but fainter copies of the former, and Hume does in fact sometimes speak of them as "images".

Impressions are of two kinds, primary impressions of sense, which arise in the soul "from unknown causes", and secondary impressions of reflection, which arise as the result of our ideas. Aversion, for instance, is caused by the idea of pain, itself a copy of the primary impression of pain.

Ideas are of two kinds, simple and complex. The simple ideas are copies of simple impressions and always resemble and are derived from impressions we have actually had. Complex ideas are combinations of simple ideas and need not mirror any actual combination of impressions (if they do, and do so vividly, they are memories). Thus we are able to think of dragons and other things which we have never perceived. We never have a simple idea which is not derived from a corresponding impression; and all our complex ideas are constructed out of simpler ideas derived from impressions. This, Hume says, is the same as to say we have no "Innate Ideas"; all our ideas are derived from experience. The objects of our thoughts are confined to such as we have experienced, or conceivably might experience, by the senses or inner feeling.

All these propositions, Hume thinks, are evident from experience, known from observation of our own minds. Empiricism is an empirical fact.

Though the fancy may join ideas as it pleases, it tends usually to join those whose corresponding impressions have been either alike, contiguous in time or place, or related as cause and effect. Hume attached the very greatest importance to these principles of association. "Here is a kind of *attraction*, which in the mental world will be found to have as extraordinary effects as in the natural, and show itself in as many and as various forms." (*Treatise*, I, 1, IV). "These are the only ties of our thoughts, they are really *to us* the cement of the universe." (*Abstract*, p. 32).

The meaning of a word, according to Hume, is the range of ideas associated with one another by resemblance, with which the word is associated by contiguity; in plain English, all objects sufficiently like those in whose presence we have heard the word used. Understanding a word is the activation of these associations.

Space and Time present difficulties. They are neither impressions nor associated groups of impressions. Each is a "manner" in which impressions appear to us, and which is mirrored in the manner of appearance of the resulting ideas. Time is the "manner" in which all perceptions occur, i.e. successively or simultaneously. Space is the manner in which coloured and tangible points are disposed, i.e. alongside one another. Since size and duration are defined in terms of the manner in which unitary perceptions are disposed, these latter cannot themselves have size or duration, and are consequently simple and indivisible. Since no ideas are infinitely divisible, we have no idea of infinite divisibility, and it is therefore inconceivable, whatever the mathematicians may say.

Hume then discusses the use we make of ideas in reasoning. (*Treatise*, Book I, Part III).

Reasoning, according to Hume, consists in the discovery of relations. These may be either "relations of ideas", which yield demonstrative reasoning, showing what is conceivable and what is inconceivable (i.e. absurd or self-contradictory), or relations in which objects happen as a matter of fact to stand one to another. That three is half six, and the internal angles of a triangle equal to two right angles, are relations of ideas, so depending on the nature of the ideas related, that the latter cannot be conceived as otherwise related. That mercury is heavier than lead, that Caesar was murdered in the Forum, that the number of the planets is nine, are matters of fact, which could conceivably have been otherwise. A matter of fact, since the opposite of it is conceivable without absurdity or contradiction, cannot be demonstrated. Its truth or falsehood can only be learned from experience. The only important field of demonstrative reasoning, Hume said, was mathematics. Consequently any books, such as most works on Metaphysics and Theology, that contain neither mathematical demonstrations nor empirical reasoning concerning matters of fact, can contain "nothing but sophistry and illusion", and should be "committed to the flames".

Though matters of fact cannot be demonstrated,

they can be inferred with probability, and the completest probable evidence Hume is willing to call a "proof". The relation on which such inferences depend is always that of cause and effect. There is no other relation, according to Hume, which enables us to infer the existence of an object which we have not observed from the existence of one which we have. This relationship is therefore of "prodigious consequence", and the account Hume gives of it is the most notable and fundamental feature of his philosophy.

Hume insists that neither the proposition that everything has a cause, nor any proposition assigning a particular cause to a particular occurrence is demonstrable. *A priori*, it is perfectly conceivable that some events should be fortuitous, and that anything should cause anything. Nothing but experience teaches us of the orderliness of nature, and what in particular causes what.

But how does experience teach us that one thing A is the cause of another thing B? The cause, we all suppose, immediately precedes the effect and is contiguous to it in space. These features we can verify by our impressions of sense. But there is a third feature which we cannot so verify. The effect *necessarily* follows the cause. It is this *necessary connexion* that enables us to infer the one from the other. And it is not a *logical* connexion, demonstrable or self-evident like the proportions of numbers. What is it then?

Hume's answer is as follows. The necessary connexion we seek is the foundation of the inference from cause to effect. Let us then see what is in common life the foundation of the inference; if we can find it, *that* must be the necessary connexion. It is not far to seek. If, for instance, flame has always been attended by heat, and has never occurred without it, then when we see a flame we infer the presence of heat, and "without further ceremony we call the one cause and the other effect." The necessary connexion we refer to when we say flame causes heat, consists in nothing but the fact that heat has regularly followed flame in the past, and that we cannot help expecting it to do so again. The "must" of causal necessity expresses our readiness to infer, and this readiness is due to experienced regularity.

This account of causal inference Hume subsumed under the general principle of association

[*continued on p. 177*]

PLATE 33. CROCE, Benedetto (1866–1952), photograph.

PLATE 34. DEMOCRITUS (fifth century B.C), bronze bust found at the villa Papiri at Herculaneum. The bust is a Roman copy of a Greek original. (*National Museum, Naples*)

PLATE 35. DESCARTES, René (1596–1650), portrait ascribed to Pierre Mignard (1612–1695).
(*National Gallery, London*)

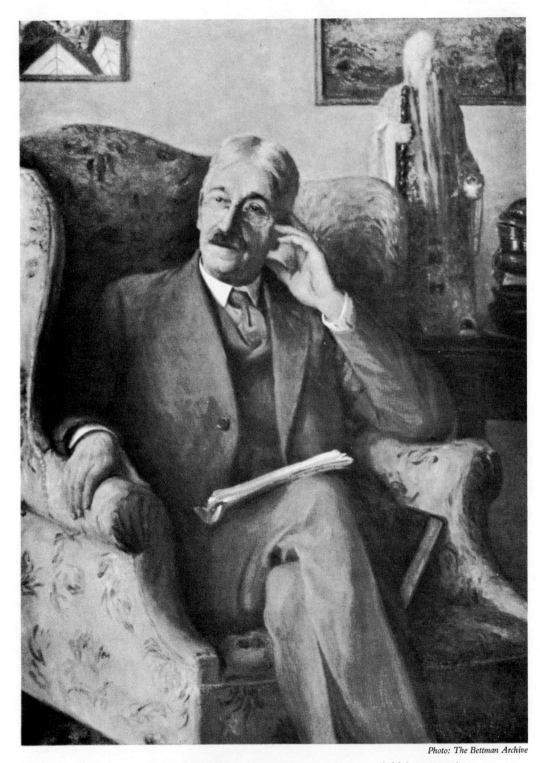

PLATE 36. DEWEY, John (1859–1952): portrait by Edwin B. Child (1868–1937).
(*Philosophy Hall, Columbia University, New York*)

PLATE 37. DIDEROT, Denis (1713–1784), bust made in 1777 by Jean Baptiste Pigalle (1714–1785). (*Louvre, Paris*)

PLATE 38. DIOGENES (fourth century B.C.), statue.
(Villa Albani, Rome)

PLATE 39. EDWARDS, Jonathan (1703–1757), engraving.

PLATE 40. ENCYCLOPEDISTS: frontispiece designed for the *Encyclopédie* by Cochin fils in 1764 and engraved by Prévost.

PLATE 41. ENGELS, Friedrich (1820–1895), portrait.

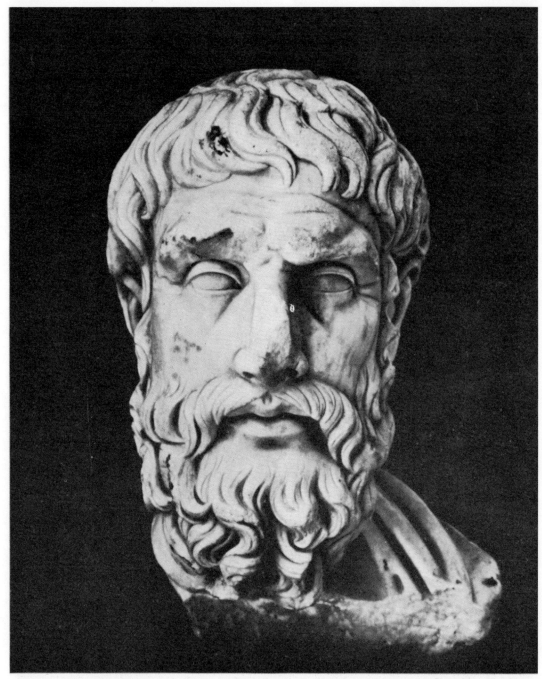

PLATE 42. EPICURUS (342–270 B.C.), stone head of the Hellenistic period.
(*Metropolitan Museum of Art, New York; Rogers Fund* 1911)

PLATE 43. FICHTE, Johann Gottlieb (1762–1814), pencil drawing by Henschel.
(*Schiller National-Museum, Marbach*)

PLATE 44. GASSENDI, Pierre (1592–1655), engraving.

PLATE 45. GREEN, Thomas Hill (1836–1882), etching by W. Sherborn.

PLATE 46. GROTIUS, Hugo (1583–1645), engraving.

PLATE 47. HARTMANN, Nicolai (1882–1950), photograph.

PLATE 48. HEGEL, Georg Wilhelm Friedrich (1770–1831), engraving by Bollinger after Zeßer.

of ideas. Seeing the flame is an impression, associated by resemblance with the ideas of flames seen in the past, each of which is associated by contiguity with the idea of heat. So the impression of flame readily evokes the idea of heat. The vivacity of the impression transfers itself in part to the associated idea, and the frequent repetition of the transition from impression to associated idea gives it a customary facility, a kind of felt unavoidability. These two features, the vivacity of the idea, and the steadying click of custom, make it what we call a *belief.* Where the regularity in past cases is unbroken, and the custom consequently full and perfect, we have *certainty* and *empirical proof.* Where either the regularity or the resemblance of the present case to the past cases is imperfect, the inference is uncertain, and we speak of *probability.*

So far Hume has attempted to present a constructive theory of knowledge, sceptical only in so far as it undermines the pretensions of Metaphysicians and Theologians to demonstrate matters of fact *a priori* (e.g. the existence of God, or how the world began), and the pretensions of natural scientists to prove exact and final truths, or provide rational explanations *a posteriori.* It opens the way for a tentative and descriptive science of man, in every way as respectable as the physical sciences.

But in *Treatise* Book I, Part IV, where Hume discusses the fallibility of both reason and the senses, and the nature of the mind, he reaches conclusions so sceptical, that no science could possibly be founded on them.

Hume's argument against the efficacy of reason is designed to support his preceding contention that belief is a psychological state due to instinct and habituation, not the completion of a logical exercise. If the exercise of reasoning were ever carried to its logical conclusion it would destroy all assurance of anything. Belief therefore, since it undoubtedly occurs, is due to something else; it is natural, not logical. The sceptic's arguments fail to carry conviction because they are "remote and strained", carrying us far beyond the experiences of common life, not because they are invalid.

But now the baby of science has been thrown out with the bath water of metaphysics, as Hume realizes in his last despairing chapter of *Treatise* Book I. "Shall we then establish it for a general maxim that no refined or elaborate reasoning is ever to be received? By this means you cut off all science and philosophy."

Hume need not have despaired. His arguments for the self-destructiveness of reason are fallacious. We make, say, a calculation according to sure mathematical principles. But we may have made a mistake. Our conclusion has then only that degree of probability which is the probability of our not having made a mistake. But in estimating this probability we may again have made a mistake and the probability of our original conclusion sinks to the probability of our not having made this second mistake. And so on *ad infinitum.* This process would, according to Hume, ultimately reduce the probability to zero. The answer is that there is no reason why these probabilities should decrease. The probability of a firm's profits for the year being what the accounts show is equal to the probability of there being no error in the books. But the probability of the auditors being right in thinking that there is no error may well be greater than the original probability of the accounts being correct.

Hume's account of sense-perception is equally unsatisfactory. All the perceptions of the mind are impressions or ideas. How do these give rise to knowledge of physical objects? The impressions of sense are interrupted, and part of, and dependent on ourselves. Physical objects are relatively permanent, distinct from, and independent of us. They are not therefore known by sense alone. Nor can they be inferred by an argument from effect to cause. For to know that a given sensation is due to a certain material thing, we must have been able to observe the two separately and notice the constant conjunction between them. And how we can observe the material thing as something distinct from the sensation is precisely the question at issue.

Neither sense nor reason then produces our belief in material things. Hume concludes it must arise from the imagination. By certain weird "propensities" of the imagination, quite different from the orthodox principles of association of ideas, we are impelled to construct a picture of a relatively permanent and regular world in which the gaps in those interrupted series of impressions we call mountains and fires are filled with fictitious unperceived impressions. This "world" provides the material for the causal investigations of natural science, which soon convince us that impressions and their sensible qualities, such as colour and warmth, are wholly dependent on our perception of them and cannot have an independent existence. Science consequently bids us accept an unimaginable world of atoms with no qualities at all, and sense and imagination bid us accept a world which is scientifically impossible. "Carelessness and inattention" are the only remedies for this, as for all other sceptical quandaries.

Hume's account of the mind is similar. There is nothing discoverable but impressions and ideas. These are just so many distinct occurrences, like the successive pictures in a cinema display. But there is no screen and no audience. The perceptions stand in relations of succession, similarity and causation. There is no other real bond between them. The self is a mere figment, an imaginary string on which the beads are strung. "I am nothing but a bundle of perceptions." But who or what imagines the string? How is the series conscious of its own serial existence? Hume cannot answer, "pleads the privilege of a sceptic" and says the question is too hard for him (*Treatise*, appendix).

The absurdities of Hume's accounts of sensory perception and of the mind arise from the starting point of his philosophy – the doctrine of impressions and **ideas**. These, supposed by Hume to be the undeniable elements of which experience is composed, are in fact but the ghostly fragments of a metaphysical ghost exploded by Hume himself. That ghost was the "simple indivisible incorporeal substance", conscious only of its own ideas, and performing on them sundry ghostly acts, perception, volition, judgment, doubting, etc., which **Descartes** had foisted on philosophers as the human mind. Hume rejected the ghostly substance and its ghostly acts (*Treatise* I, IV. 5), but retained the "ideas", or "perceptions" as he preferred to call them, and attempted to reconstruct the world of common sense out of their spontaneous antics. He appears to succeed in his account of causality by the simple trick of substituting the word "object" for the word "impression", wherever the latter would yield nonsense.

Experience, we may admit, provides us with all the content of our thoughts and all the evidence for our beliefs. But experience does not consist of sensations and images succeeding and mimicking one another in the void. It consists of flesh-and-blood human beings learning to perceive, remember, understand, to manage one another and their material environment, and to take some notice of their sensations and emotions and make use of the power of seeing things in "the mind's eye". These processes are difficult enough to understand, both from the philosophical and the psychological standpoint; but we must start by taking them as we find them, and not by assuming that we find nothing but coloured points disposed in a certain manner and dancing to an accompaniment of sounds, smell, tastes and sentiments. Such an assumption can lead only to scepticism.

Fortunately for Hume's fame, the main contentions of *Treatise* Book I, Part III, are independent of the doctrine of impressions and ideas. The distinction between relations of ideas and matters of fact, the undemonstrability of causal connexions, the inductive character of all factual reasoning, and the analysis of natural necessity in terms of our disposition to expect what we have learned from past experience to expect, all these stand on their own feet and still seem to contain important truths.

Hume's contribution to Moral Philosophy is closely parallel to his contribution to the Theory of Knowledge. As he distinguished matters of fact from relations of ideas, so he now distinguishes ethical judgments from both of them. An ethical judgment states neither that something could not conceivably be otherwise, nor that something is as a matter of fact the case. And just as matters of fact cannot be inferred from relations of ideas, so ethical statements cannot be inferred from either. Just as the discovery of matters of fact depend on relations of necessary connexion, which seem to be objective, but are really dispositions of the mind, so ethical judgments depend on rightness and wrongness, goodness and badness, which seem to be objective qualities of persons and acts, but are really the approvals and disapprovals of the judger's mind. Just as our dispositions to expect depend on our experience of regular conjunctions, so our approvals and disapprovals depend on our past experience of pleasant and unpleasant consequences. Just as the task of the natural scientist is to regulate our expectations by the most general and well substantiated regularities, so the task of the moralist is to regulate our approvals and disapprovals by the most general and well substantiated tendencies of actions and character, to promote human happiness. Just as the task of the epistemologist is to describe the psychological mechanisms of belief, so the task of the moral philosopher is to describe the psychological mechanisms of approval and disapproval. And the psychological mechanisms which Hume describes are equally fantastic in either field, and equally irrelevant to his main contentions.

The main psychological principle which Hume seeks to apply in all his descriptions both of human behaviour and human approval and disapproval, is **hedonism**. Nothing but pleasure and pain influence voluntary action. The influence may be direct, as when I let go of a hot plate because it hurts my hand, or indirect, as when the fear of pain prevents me from touching a plate I believe to be hot. And this occurs because fear is a "disagreeable" (i.e. painful) sentiment. If heat were not painful, the belief that the plate is hot could not affect my actions. Reason by itself cannot influence conduct. It only does so "obliquely" either by discovering the means to gratify some "passion" (i.e. pleasant or unpleasant secondary impressions), or by discovering the existence of some object which arouses such a passion.

Hume is thus provided with two arguments against the widely held view that reason alone distinguishes moral good and evil. The first is that reason alone cannot influence conduct, but moral judgments sometimes do. This argument is based on his psychological theory. The second argument is that reason is the discovery of truth and falsehood, which belong only to statements about matters of fact and statements about relations of ideas. Since moral judgments are different from either of these, and cannot be deduced from them, reason cannot decide moral questions. This second argument is independent of Hume's psychological theories, and based on what is widely regarded as Hume's major contribution to Ethics, the contention that there is no logical argument from "is" to "ought", from description to evaluation.

The obligations of justice, i.e. keeping promises, respecting property, and allegiance to the state, present difficulties to Hume. For it is certain that the individual acts they require do not always increase the happiness of the agent, or even that of all concerned. Hume's answer is that these obligations rest on artificial conventions, without which society could not hold together, and which could not perform their function if each man supported them or not as it suited himself in the particular circumstances. Our sympathetic concern for the long-term happiness of our fellows creates a *moral* obligation to be just (which is not of much effect by itself), and our concern for our own and our friends' happiness leads us to set up a system of laws and penalties, which create a *natural* obligation to be just. And by "obligation" Hume means only a sort of motive.

This account enables Hume to argue forcibly against the **Social Contract** theory of political obligation, and to make a valuable suggestion about the nature of promises. Since contracts (i.e. exchanges of promises) and governments are both only useful artifices, and owe their obligatory power solely to their utility, it is pointless to try and base one upon the other, quite apart from the fact that the social contract is in fact a myth. Promising is neither uttering a verbal spell, nor performing a mental act by which a metaphysical entity called an "obligation" is created out of the void. It is simply operating the machinery of a convention, according to which, by general custom, if, after saying "I promise to do it", I do not do it, I am not trusted again. We have here the germs of the important modern theory of the "performatory" use of language.

It will be seen that the impartiality of genuine moral approval is for Hume founded on "sympathy", which alone gives us a concern for the happiness of our fellows in general. Sympathy, he admits, is a pretty feeble motive, and moral principles control selfish passions mainly by means of the system of sanctions which self-interest leads us to set up. It may be asked then why virtue and vice seem to us so very important, independently of the rewards and punishments they sometimes receive.

Hume's answer is interesting but not convincing. If we approve and disapprove according to our personal interests and situation, our judgments will be variable and opposed to those of other people. Finding this *inconvenient* and looking for an invariable and common coin, as it were, for valuing human beings, we find none so suitable as sympathy, that mild preference we have for anybody's happiness, other things being equal. So we ask of any human characteristic or institution, is it in general likely to promote the long-run happiness of all whom it affects? The feelings of approval or disapproval which we experience through sympathy after asking this question are that which it is the proper office of ethical terms to express.

Conclusion. Hume can hardly be said to have succeeded in laying the foundations of an empirical science of human nature. None of his important contentions are based on field work or experiment, they rest not on discoveries of new facts, but on appeals to what we all already know. We have all learned how to distinguish causal connexions from coincidences, estimate likelihood, make and follow demonstrations, and make moral judgments on general and impartial considerations. No one in common life looks for empirical exceptions to mathematical truths, or attempts wholly to anticipate by abstract reasoning the verdict of experience on questions of fact. It is perhaps not so clear that no one in common life approves what increases misery or disapproves what decreases it. But it can be said that many things have come to be recognized as certainly bad because of the misery they produce, and that no moral judgment has ever been justified in any other way except by appeal to some moral principle which itself either lacks justification or is controversial.

Hume's achievement is that he has shown us how at least to try to describe clearly how we do certain things which we very well know how to do in familiar contexts, and so make it clear that in unfamiliar contexts we are sometimes not really doing these things, though we think we are. The metaphysician who pretends to reason concerning the origin of the universe or the immortality of the soul seems to be doing the same sort of thing as the man who reasons about the origin of Stonehenge or the evaporation of water. He is not really doing so. In fact he is doing things we have all learned *not* to do in the familiar contexts.

Since Hume, it has never been possible for anyone who understood him to do Metaphysics in the old way. Among the more important philosophers influenced by Hume were Jeremy **Bentham** and Immanuel **Kant**. Bentham, first of the English utilitarian school, said that scales fell from his eyes when he read Hume. Kant confessed that Hume first woke him from his dogmatic slumber. Many

of Kant's important tenets, especially his accounts of Space and Time, causality and substance, necessary truths, personal identity and practical reason are either explicitly or implicitly answers to problems raised by Hume.

As to the science of human nature, though Hume made no contributions to it, he did make clear that reasoning and moral judging are describable activities, just as much as walking and the behaviour of animals, and as such are equally open to scientific investigation. The pity is that, seeing as he did that man is a part of nature, he yet tried to subsume his philosophy under the principle of impressions and ideas, which belongs to a wholly opposite conception of man, and that his perverse love of sceptical paradox made him revel in the absurdities that resulted, instead of honestly trying to solve them.

Plate 51, page 211. (D.G.C.MACN.)

Husserl, Edmund, (1859–1938), German philosopher, founder of the movement known as **Phenomenology**. The main influence on Husserl's thought was the intentional psychology of **Brentano** under whom he studied in Vienna in 1884–6. Husserl taught at Halle, and held philosophical chairs at Göttingen and Freiburg. His principal works are: *The Philosophy of Arithmetic* (1891) much criticized by **Frege**; *Logical Investigations*, (1900–1901, revised edition 1913–21) somewhat unreadably summarized in English by Farber: *The Foundation of Phenomenology*); *Ideas for a Pure Phenomenology* (Book I, *General Introduction*, 1913, English translation 1931; Books II and III posthumously published, 1952); *Phenomenology of the inner Time-consciousness* (1905–10, published 1928); *Formal and Transcendental Logic* (1929); *Cartesian Meditations* (1931); *Experience and Judgment* (1948).

Husserl's Phenomenology represents a vast extension and transformation of Brentano's "psychognosy", which was an attempt to work out a logical geography of mental concepts as a necessary preliminary to any empirical psychology. Husserl accepts Brentano's main thesis that states of mind are to be basically characterised in terms of "intentionality" or directedness-to-objects, all states of mind being *of* objects (whether real or unreal), and different states of mind being *of* their objects in varying manners. He also *starts* by building on Brentano's classification of mental states into Presentations, Judgments, and Affective-Desiderative attitudes. But he carries this psychognosy very much further, and develops it into such a ramifying tangle of fine distinctions, that it becomes an independent discipline rather than the mere prolegomena to an empirical psychology. Husserl is, for example, deeply interested in the distinction between those conscious states in which something is merely "meant" and those in which it is concretely "present", the latter being said to "fulfil" the former; he is interested in the distinction, analogous to Frege's distinction between "sense" and "meaning", between the object as such and the object *as* it is meant – the victor of Jena is in a sense different from the vanquished of Waterloo; he is interested in the way in which successive thoughts or intuitions are "synthetized" in the developing consciousness of the "same" object, he is interested in the way in which we pass from a problematic assertion to an assertion of probability, he is above all interested in the processes involved in the understanding and meaningful use of words.

Husserl also stresses, as Brentano does not, that the sort of investigation he is pursuing is conceptual or "eidetic" rather than empirical, that he is trying to see what factors are involved in, and what possibilities flow from, the mere *notions* of perceiving, believing, predication etc., rather than to find out what empirically obtains when we perceive, believe or predicate. A wholly imaginary instance may therefore be as decisive in a phenomenological investigation as one that is actual. Husserl further widens the scope of Brentano's psychognosy by making it include any and every *object* of a mental intention, not, however, in a naturalistic or regalistic, but in a "bracketed" or phenomenological form. We can, that is, discuss the ideal objects of mathematics, sense-given natural objects or sociological groups, in so far as these latter are possible *cogitata* of mental references in which, to use Husserl's terminology, they are "constituted". As "constituted" in consciousness, the choir of heaven and the furniture of earth enter into the subject-matter of Phenomenology. The name "phenomenology" in fact derives its significance from this "bracketed" treatment of anything whatever. For its use connotes that we propose to study things as they *appear* in consciousness, and that, from the point of view of our study, we do not care whether what thus

appears is ever *more* than an appearance. The things postulated by physics, theology or normative ethics remain phenomenologically interesting whether or not they are metaphysically real. Husserl's Phenomenology in its full development is in fact not unlike the philosophy of **Kant**, an affinity of which Husserl himself was fully conscious. Husserl, like Kant, wished to discover *a priori* principles governing mind, phenomenal nature, law, society, ethics, religion etc., which should never go beyond what *appears* to consciousness, and which should derive their warrant from the nature of such conscious appearances.

In the actual carrying out of his phenomenological venture there are, however, some singularities. Great use is made of the terms "intuition", "experience", "description" in contexts where the subject-matter is notional, and where such terms can only be misleading. The notion of "acts" is scrupulously explained, but their description reads like an account of ghostly performances. In the *Logical Investigations* there is even said to be a "categorical intuition" of the meanings of the logical connectives "and" and "or", and though this use, too, is innocuously defined, it leaves a legacy of misunderstanding. After 1907 Husserl also became addicted to a quasi-Cartesian approach; the phenomenological philosopher was represented as having to "put out of action" any sort of realistic conviction so that the "structures" of his own consciousness might become reflectively evident. Great use was made of the notion of an *Epoche* or transcendental suspension of belief: the abstraction necessary for a conceptual investigation became a mystical exercise for which the natural world dissolved, while phenomenological structures made their appearance. But Husserl, like other saints, fell a victim to his own ecstasy: he was unable to come out of this transcendental suspension. The harmless "bracketing" of commonsense realities became the metaphysical thesis that they can have none but an "intentional" existence in and for consciousness. Husserl does not see that we cannot suspend a belief if the belief suspended is meaningless. After 1907, therefore, Phenomenology passes over into a form of traditional German **idealism.**

The works of Husserl form a slowly declining series: as the fruitful analyses diminish, the metaphysical generalities increase. *The Logical Inves-*

tigations, with its fine studies of Meaning, Intentionality and Knowledge, is undoubtedly one of the greatest of philosophical masterpieces: in the later works there is much, but not so much, to admire. But the influence of Husserl's thought increased as its philosophical importance declined: hence the strange drop from Phenomenology to **Existentialism**. (J.N.F.)

Plate 52, page 212.

Hutcheson, Francis (1694–1747), born in the north of Ireland. He ran a private academy for a time in Dublin, and occupied the Chair of Moral Philosophy at Glasgow from 1729 to his death. His biggest work, *A System of Moral Philosophy*, was published posthumously by his son. Hutcheson opposed himself to any "rationalist" and *a priori* account of value-judgment in the manner of **Clarke**. To Hutcheson, the discernment of value was not an activity of reason but of certain "internal senses" specially furnished by God for that purpose. The "moral sense", for instance, inclines us by "strong affections" to seek the greatest happiness of the greatest number. Hutcheson's doctrine looks back to **Locke**, with his distinction between the external and internal senses, and to Shaftesbury, whose somewhat untidy "moral sense" theory Hutcheson developed and systematized; and forward to **Hume** and the **Benthamites**. For it was through Hutcheson that Hume learned that moral judgments cannot be ultimately justified by reason alone – a view he was to extend far beyond ethics into his general philosophy. And here too is the first clear statement of the **utilitarian** "greatest happiness" principle. Seen in the light of both Hume and the utilitarian group, however, Hutcheson's philosophy–shored up by theology and proliferating in special *ad hoc* senses (sense of decency, of honour, of religion etc.) – shows up as a rather unwieldy and unstable structure. (R.W.H.)

Plate 53, page 213.

I

Idealism, in its philosophical sense is quite distinct from "idealism" as ordinarily used, when it generally refers to high moral aims. While the term has sometimes been employed by philosophers to cover all views according to which the basis of the Universe is ultimately spiritual, it has most commonly stood (in opposition to **realism**) for a theory according to which physical objects can have no existence apart from a mind which is conscious of them, thus not covering those who, while they believe in God, also ascribe a substantial existence to matter as quite conceivable independently of being experienced, although ultimately created by God.

Idealism in this narrower sense originated in the eighteenth century with **Berkeley**. He argued that the *esse* (existence) of physical objects was *percipi* (to be perceived) or that they were only "ideas" (hence the term "idealism"), mainly on the ground that we could not conceive as existing in abstraction from our sense-experience any of the qualities we ascribe to them. He also used the negative argument that we could not possibly know unexperienced physical objects. These two arguments in some form are common to most idealist thinkers. He then argued that ideas, being passive, cannot cause anything and in the absence of unconscious matter those which cannot be explained by human action must be due to the direct action of a non-human spirit, spirits being the only possible causal agents since they alone are "active", i.e. possess volition. The difficulty that physical things seem to exist when no man is perceiving them he met by saying that they exist in God's mind, thus providing a new argument for God.

Berkeley made practically no converts in his lifetime, and the "idealist" school only began to gain ground with **Kant**. The latter however approached the subject in a very different way from Berkeley. He based his idealism on an argument, founded largely on his theory of knowledge, that everything spatial or temporal is only appearance. He contended that we can account for our *a priori* knowledge of things only by supposing that our mind has imposed on them a structure to which they must conform. The human mind could not impose a structure on reality but only on appearances, so for this very reason he held our knowledge to be limited to appearances. The latter only exist as objects of actual or possible experience and so must obey the conditions which our mind imposes, since otherwise they could not appear to us. This was the reason, he thought, why we are able to apply categories such as substance and cause to the physical world, but this very reason debars us from proceeding to metaphysics, as Berkeley did, and applying them beyond the realm of human experience. This, Kant insisted, does not cast any doubt on science, on the contrary it is the only way of saving science from the sceptic. Science tells us the truth, but only the truth about appearances (phenomena). If we claimed that its function was to tell us the truth about reality, we should have to admit that it was wholly illusory. Kant consequently called himself an "empirical realist" but a "transcendental idealist". By this he meant approximately what recent thinkers have expressed by saying that physical object propositions are true but have to be analysed in terms of our sense-data. He also argued that, if we hold that reality is in space and time, we are involved in certain self-contradictions ("antinomies"). We have in that case to hold either that the world in space and time is infinite or that it is finite, and either alternative he maintained leads to self-contradictory conclusions, so that the only solution is to say that reality is not in space or time at all. The physical world can still be said to be infinite in the potential sense that, however far we go, we can always find new phenomena. Kant did not, like Berkeley, use idealism as the basis of an argument for God but repudiated all theoretical arguments for theism and maintained an agnostic view as to the nature of reality, which he expressed by saying we can have no knowledge of "things-in-themselves". He did however think there was an ethical argument which could establish the existence of God, not indeed with theoretical certainty or clarity, but sufficiently to justify belief. He was convinced of the objectivity of the moral law and he argued that the moral law commanded us to strive for ideals which could only be realised if we were immortal and if the world was ordered in the interests of the moral law, which we could only conceive by thinking of it as created and governed by an omnipotent and perfectly good being. His denial of the reality of time led to the paradoxical consequence that our own real self is timeless and therefore unknowable, a conclusion which he, however, welcomed because it enabled him to solve the problem of freedom by saying that the real self is free, whereas our appearance self is completely determined by past appearances at least in the sense of being predictable from them, thus reconciling freedom with universal causality, which he thought necessary for science.

The chief idealists in the first half of the nineteenth century, **Fichte**, Schelling and **Hegel**, were all Germans and all much influenced by Kant, but they completely transformed his philosophy. The first element in Kant's philosophy to be rejected was the concept of unknowable things-in-themselves. It was argued that there could be no ground for asserting something quite unknowable and no meaning in doing so, and that Kant's attempt to exclude metaphysics involved inconsistencies since he himself only excluded it by making metaphysical assumptions of his own. Now, if we reject things-in-themselves, we have left only minds and objects of experience, so we have what Kant called dogmatic idealism again. The resultant philosophy which gradually developed ("absolute idealism" or "absolutism") held that reality can be known to be ultimately spiritual, but that spirit can only realise itself in relation to an objective material element and this is the reason for the existence of the latter. Object implies subject, but subject also implies object, though subject was viewed as ultimately prior. Reality as a whole was conceived not as dependent on a mind distinct from finite minds (God) but as itself a single all-embracing experience of which the finite minds are differentiations (the Absolute). Such a view stressed the unity and rationality of the cosmos and even described it as perfect despite the evil in its parts, which was conceived as arising from the fact that they were only parts.

It is reasonable to class Hegel as an idealist, as is usually done, but he is a very obscure writer, and it is disputable in precisely what sense he was one. He undoubtedly thought that matter was the manifestation of spirit, but it is quite unclear what he supposed to be the status of unperceived physical objects (perhaps because he was not much interested in this problem). His philosophy centred on a "dialectic" by which he sought to show that, starting with the most abstract and empty of all concepts, mere being, we could pass by an *a priori* process of thought to the highest logical categories of the spiritual life. A leading characteristic of this mode of argument, which he also regarded as characteristic of the nature of reality itself, is that it proceeded in triads. An inadequate concept was taken first, its inconsistencies led to its being replaced by the opposite extreme, but the latter displayed fundamentally the same defects, and the only cure was to combine the good points of the two in a third concept. This, though solving the previous problems and taking us a stage nearer the truth, displayed inconsistencies in its turn so that a new thesis and antithesis arose, the antinomy between which was solved by a new synthesis, and so on till we reached the fundamental category of the "absolute idea" and proved the whole of reality to be the expression of spirit. Such a process of thought Hegel worked out both in logic and the more concrete subjects of ethical and political thought. The dialectic was regarded not merely as an argument but as an account of the development of thought and civilization. Thus e.g. in politics men seek liberty at the expense of order, and order at the expense of liberty, but both when carried to the extreme turn into the same evil, the rule of the strongest regardless of others, and the story of political development is largely the story of the attempt to effect successive syntheses of the two which preserve more and more of what is of value in order and liberty. But unfortunately Hegel gave the impression that the final synthesis had already been achieved in the Prussian state of his day, so that his philosophy was used to bolster up stubborn conservatism, and still worse, the impression that the state is the representative of the Absolute on earth, and so can do no wrong. He was thus cited (probably unfairly) in favour of German imperialism. On the other hand the "Hegelian left" developed the almost equally one-sided doctrine of marxism, which however repudiated idealism altogether and made the ultimate reality of matter and the dependence on it of the human mind a fundamental part of its creed. Though passages can be cited in which Hegel denies that the universe is completely rational, his philosophy went very far in this direction. It may be doubted whether he believed in a personal God in any ordinary sense, but he called himself a Christian and attached to the Christian dogmas great importance as at least symbolic representations of the spiritual nature of reality. He however classed philosophy as superior to religion.

Other very distinguished German idealists were **Schopenhauer**, the pessimist, and Lotze.

Idealism spread from Germany to Britain in the latter half of the nineteenth century and became dominant in Oxford and Scotland. Of the British school of idealists the following most deserve mention. T. H. **Green** (1836–1882), who exercised a great influence at Oxford, was specially concerned to bring idealism into connection with Christianity and with liberal political ideas. He used a more subtle form of Berkeley's argument to show that physical objects cannot be conceived except as in relation to mind and therefore should be thought as dependent on a divine mind, but he discarded Berkeley's empiricist tradition in theory of knowledge and insisted like Kant and Hegel on the place of thought in perception. His argument for God was based mainly on the view that relations imply mind and yet are independent of human minds.

F. H. **Bradley** (1846–1924), also of Oxford, in his leading work *Appearance and Reality* began with an attempt to show that all our ordinary concepts and especially the concept of relation are self-contradictory. This argument however led him not to scepticism but to the conclusion that we must suppose the existence of a perfect thought-transcending Absolute in which all these contradictions are reconciled. Everything is conceived as "appearance" because as taken by itself it is self-contradictory, since it cannot be rendered intelligible except in relation to the Whole, but it still really exists as an element in the Whole. Bradley developed the coherence theory of truth, according to which the definition and criterion of truth are both to be found in coherence in a system. Truth is for him a matter of degree, all our judgments being both partly false since they are all corrigible in the light of a wider system and partly true since they all embrace some elements in the real. He did not mean to deny that in a limited system for ordinary purposes judgments could be taken as absolutely true or false. A coherence theory is expounded by B. **Blanshard** among contemporary Americans.

J. M. E. **McTaggart** (1866–1925), who taught at Cambridge, developed a form of idealism according to which there is no supreme divine mind or Absolute but reality consists of a number of spirits united in a supersensuous harmony, of which spirits every human being is one. He claimed by an elaborate argument, mainly *a priori* and not in any way dependent on the acceptance of religious authority or religious intuition, to have shown that matter, time and also almost all the unsatisfactory features of human experience are only appearance, that there is nothing in reality but spirits loving each other, and that we are immortal and will eventually all cease to experience things in time and come to realise our timeless nature, this involving the enjoyment of a bliss greater than anything we can now conceive. Especially in the twenties of the present century, a great influence was exercised by the Italian idealists **Croce** (1866–1952) and Gentile (1875–1944). Croce has probably been the most influential philosophical writer of the present century on aesthetics.

It will be seen from the above that acceptance of the idealist case against independent matter still leaves room for a number of different views. It may be combined with theism, as by Berkeley, or it may take the form of absolutism, or of some kind of pluralism. It may even be maintained that physical objects are merely abstractions from human experience. Other idealists have taken the view that what we call inanimate matter is the appearance of very inferior minds, or at any rate psychic entities of some sort, if they are too inferior to be called minds (*panpsychism*). This view has been supported by the argument that the problem of the relation between the human body and mind can only be solved if we regard our body (or brain) as the appearance of our minds, which naturally led to the theory that everything else physical also is the appearance of something mental.

While the idealist school still flourishes in some countries, it would be hard to-day to find British philosophers who would call themselves idealists. There are indeed many who reject the view that physical objects should be regarded as entities existing independently of experience except in the hypothetical sense in which this statement simply means that under suitable conditions they would appear in experience, and some trends in modern science are widely regarded as supporting this conclusion, but it is not usual to-day to call such thinkers idealists because in other respects they are usually so different from traditional members of the school. In particular they usually found their conclusion on an empiricist theory of knowledge and

reject metaphysics. A term more commonly used of such thinkers is "phenomenalist". (A.C.E.)

Ideas. The term "idea" has a double history in philosophy in English. In neither case has its philosophical use been at all closely related to the current employment of the word in ordinary speech. In the first place, the word "idea" is one of the accepted translations of the Greek ἰδέα, and hence occurs commonly in translations or discussions of **Plato**; examination of its use in this context belongs, however, more properly to the study of Plato than to the present article. Secondly, the term "idea" was very extensively employed by **Locke** in the late seventeenth century, and it remained in current philosophical use for at least the ensuing hundred years. The expression "idée" had already been much employed by French writers, notably by **Descartes** and **Malebranche**, and Locke's use of "idea" no doubt derived from that source.

The word was in fact the cause of a very great deal of unclarity and confusion in the philosophy of the eighteenth century. An early critic of that philosophy, Thomas **Reid**, went so far as to suggest that all the major errors of Locke, **Berkeley** and **Hume** could be traced to this source – particularly of Berkeley – and that, but for unclarity at this key point, some of their tenets could scarcely have been stated. This contention, though somewhat extreme, was by no means baseless.

The root of the trouble was that the meaning of "idea", throughout that period, was either made undesirably wide, or – more frequently – left highly indeterminate. Locke, in introducing the expression, writes of it thus: "It being that term which, I think, serves best to stand for whatsoever is the object of the understanding when a man thinks, I have used it to express whatever is meant by *phantasm*, *notion*, *species*, or whatever it is which the mind can be employed about in thinking." This remark is conspicuously unclear. In actual fact Locke uses the word "idea" in at least four ways. 1) He often uses it in the sense – itself not perspicuous – of the modern expression "sense-datum", to refer to the "immediate objects" of sense-experience. 2) He uses it also, occasionally, in the sense of an *image*, notably in his discussions of imagination and memory. 3) *Concepts* are often spoken of by Locke as ideas: for instance, to have the "idea" of whiteness is to know what "white" means, to have the concept of that colour. Alternatively, one might say that, for Locke, the term "idea" sometimes designates the *meaning of a word* (4) Less clearly, Locke sometimes seems to mean by "ideas" what a man has in his mind when he *thinks* or *understands* (whatever that may be).

Now the greatest danger in such an excessively liberal use of a single term is that it makes it possible for the writer to discuss very different things in identical language, and hence constantly tempts him to forget how different they are. In the present case perhaps the most seriously harmful result was that, from Locke to Hume, no adequate distinctions were ever drawn between *perceiving, thinking, understanding, imagining*, and even *believing*. More accurately, there was a constant tendency to assimilate all the latter to *perceiving*, and thus to render malformed from the outset any attempted analysis of them. Hume, indeed, sought to improve the position to some extent by distinguishing ideas from "impressions" – the latter term being intended for separate reference to actual sense-data or sensations. Since, however, Hume now held ideas to be *like* impressions except for a lower degree of "force and vivacity", his subsequent analyses of belief, imagination, and thinking in general still retained the inappropriate underlying model of perception.

Berkeley's case is somewhat different, however. He accepted the term "idea" as so familiar in philosophical writing that he offers no account of its meaning whatever; he proceeds, with entirely unjustified confidence, as if it were already quite clear and well-understood. He employs the word from time to time in all of Locke's diverse senses, and is apt to fall into the resultant misconstructions particularly of thinking and understanding. But more important in his own case is the additional unclarity of one of these senses in particular, that, namely, listed as (1) above. Berkeley wished to combine the ontological thesis that there exist only "spirits" and "ideas", that *esse* is *percipi* or *percipere*, (that to exist is to perceive or to be perceived) with the contention that this theory was really nothing more than an elucidation of common-sense beliefs. Though he wished to present a metaphysical doctrine, he wished also to maintain that it was *already* generally believed. He appears

to succeed in this partly – as Reid contended — in virtue of his double, or at any rate fluid, use of the principle that we "perceive nothing but ideas". For in view of the indeterminate meaning of "idea", he is able at times to represent this principle as a truism – ideas just *are* "the things that we perceive": but at other times he stresses that ideas are mental entities, that "they have not any existence without a mind"; and then combining these, he can appear to have shown that the things that we perceive exist only "in a mind". It would be unjust to the subtlety of Berkeley's argument to suggest that it rests wholly on so simple a manoeuvre. However, this concealed unclarity does probably account for Berkeley's strange conviction that his startling doctrines were *obviously* correct, and were scarcely in need of supporting argument; and it is, perhaps, in his writings above all that the employment of the term "idea" calls for critical scrutiny.　　　　(G.J.W.)

Induction is one of the technical terms of **logic**; but it has not unfortunately a very clear meaning since it is used in at least two ways. In one way it is used to stand for any procedure which is not **deduction** by which one attempts to justify the acceptance of some conclusion. Thus the procedures of mathematics and pure logic are deductive, but the arguments of the scientist and the detective are inductive. But the term is also used, principally by **Popper** and those who agree with him, to stand for one particular view about how scientists and detectives do try to justify their conclusions, the view to be found in **Bacon** and J. S. **Mill** that the laws and theories of science are arrived at by a special sort of argument in which the premises are singular statements of observation and experiment; to this view is opposed the view that scientists arrive at their laws and theories by a process of testing hypotheses – but on the wider acceptation of the term this too would be a view as to the nature of induction.　　　　(J.O.U.)

J

James, William (1842–1910), psychologist, born in New York. It is usually said of James that he was an original, a prolific, and a highly sensitive thinker rather than a rigorously consistent one. There is some truth in this; but it must not be overworked. The development of James' thought passed through three major stages: the early stage of his work in psychology, the middle stage of his defence of **pragmatism**, and the late stage of his more esoteric papers on a version of realism known as "neutral monism". We may agree that James was always more interested in the specific problems in which at any given time he was immersed, than he was in constructing a system which would demonstrate that all of his work would fit into a consistent pattern. But we must not overlook the fact that there is a very close affinity between his three "periods". There is nothing random about them. Each may be looked upon as a logical outgrowth of its predecessor; and all three can be read as the products of a mind with a uniform temperament and a single philosophical intent.

Few men were as influential as James in the transformation of psychology into a science. His two volume work on *The Principles of Psychology* remains a classic in the field, and is considered by many to be his major work.

The key to James' work in psychology is his method of approach – a method generally called "functionalism". At the outset of the *Principles* James stipulates that "the pursuance of future ends and the choice of means for their attainment are thus the mark and criterion of the presence of mentality in a phenomenon." (Vol. I, p. 8.) This in effect is James' working definition of "mind"; and his intent throughout is to base the transformation of psychology into a science upon rigorous empirical demands. Our conception of mentality must be rooted in careful and painstaking inspection of what mentality *does* – i.e. in the difference which its presence makes. Functionalism in psychology is a version of the general demand that anything whatsoever be understood as *being* no more and no less than precisely that which makes the differences in experience which its presence makes.

James was at the same time a thoroughgoing introspectionist. His chapters on *The Stream of Thought* and *The Consciousness of Self* are unexcelled in the literature of introspectionist psychology. A rigorous empiricist effort to determine experimentally how mind functions in experience can only for him be done by looking inward. Few things indeed make James the man more lovable than his prodigious energy as an introspectionist. One pictures him as *straining* to look inward as uncompromisingly and as accurately as possible; and often the attempt to follow him can be positively exhausting.

But paradoxically enough James the great introspectionist was to set in motion a tendency which later culminated in Behaviorism and the revolt from introspection. It was not enough for James to reach by introspection his now classic conclusion that the essence of the mental life is experienced as a "*flow*" in which each succeeding moment grasps back upon and "owns" its predecessor. He was driven to look still more and more closely until at last he came up with a startling conviction:

"Whenever my introspective glance succeeds in turning around quickly enough to catch one of these manifestations of spontaneity in the act, all it can ever feel distinctly is some bodily process, for the most part taking place within the head." (Vol. I. p. 300.)

In later life, the essay with which James ushers in his final stage of neutral monism is entitled "Does Consciousness Exist?" His answer is: no, not as a stuff. In so saying he remarks that the "I think" of traditional philosophy seems to him (so far as he can rigorously introspect) no different from the omnipresent but vaguely sensed "I breathe" of every normal waking moment of experience. There is surely very little difference between this remarkable claim and the purport of the passage just quoted. The denial that consciousness is in any sense a unique kind of "stuff" was latent from the beginning in James' functional approach to psychology.

The scope of James's work in experimental physiology as recorded in the *Principles* should also be mentioned. And perhaps his most famous thesis so far as subsequent developments in the science of psychology are concerned, is the thesis identified as the "James-Lange" theory of the emotions. The thesis is that emotion is no more than the *feeling* of bodily state and hence must follow rather than precede bodily state. Crudely and inaccurately stated: I do not strike a man by whom I am insulted because first I am angry; my anger is simply the feeling I experience as a result of being in the total bodily state part of which is striking the man. The reader may find it obvious that this theory won fame (or infamy, as you choose) as a forerunner of the later excesses of Behaviorism.

In philosophical circles James is most often identified as the defender of Pragmatism as a theory of truth. He acknowledged C. S. **Peirce** as the source of his pragmatism; but it must be remarked that the word carries a very different meaning for James than for Peirce. Peirce formulated his "pragmatic maxim" as one among several rules or principles governing intelligent inquiry. For him it was a rule for achieving *clarity of meaning*. It demanded of any concept or hypothesis that its meaning be expressed by careful specification of the "sensible difference" its being true would make. Peirce combined this demand with a strict correspondence view of truth and with a rock-bottom principle of fallibilism which refused to allow the identification of *any* clarified hypothesis with final truth.

In James, many of Peirce's rigorous distinctions are lost, and the "pragmatic rule" assumes a far more over-arching status than the "pragmatic maxim" had for Peirce. James' view can be fairly expressed without too gross oversimplification in the following compact way: that if a concept literally *means* no more nor less than what you do with it, then its *truth* must consist in no more nor less than a successful doing. With this claim Peirce would certainly not agree.

It is clear, however, that James' pragmatism expands into a general philosophical principle the functional approach of his psychology. Ideas, like minds, are to be treated in terms of their *function*. To judge of an idea that it is true is to claim that it successfully leads one through the labyrinth of experience. An idea is not a mystery but a tool; its essence lies in its predictive capacity.

James alternatively labels his view "Pragmatism" and "Radical Empiricism". The labels carry roughly the same meaning. According to James the errors of traditional **empiricism** were mainly two: first, that too much attention had been paid to the origins of our ideas out of past experience and not enough to their function as pointers to future experience; secondly, that concentration on the discrete elements of experience had generated inattention to the equally real relatedness of those elements. For James the essence of pragmatism lay

in its stress upon the *relatedness* of ideas as elements in experience to *future* experiences which fulfill their meaning. Thus pragmatism is the only genuinely radical empiricism.

James, of course, did not completely transform the empiricist tradition. For all his demand that **Hume**'s "bricks" of experience are not the entire picture, that the "mortar" which holds the bricks together is equally a part of experience, it remains the case that he accepts Hume's bricks. His philosophy falls in the tradition of what is generally labelled "sense-datum analysis". The later claim that sense-datum analysis is precisely *not* empirical description did not for a moment occur to him.

A further peculiarity of James' pragmatic theory of knowledge involves his use of the word "concept". According to many philosophers a concept can never be anything less than a complete proposition. Not so for James. He discusses often and at length the distinction between concepts and percepts; and he repeatedly defines the mental life as a continuous "substitution of concepts for percepts". But in the last analysis James always defines a concept as a *percept functioning in a certain way*. This is wholly in accord with his functionalist bent. A concept for James is either a word (which is a percept) or an image (which is a percept) which *functions* in human experience in a predictive manner. Many have been confused by his examples of conceptual thinking ("my image of Memorial Hall as I sit in my study"), for his examples invariably involve the *use* of *images*. If James' psychology rests upon suspicion of any difference of kind between minds and bodies, so his theory of knowledge rests upon suspicion of any difference of kind between percepts and concepts.

James always claimed to be a "realist". But he was not overly technical in his use of words, and by this he meant many things. He sometimes meant that he was "hard-headed", sometimes that he was practical, sometimes that he was in tune with common sense. In later life, however, in a period often described as esoteric, he defended a technical version of **realism** in philosophy under the label "Neutral Monism".

In one way or another both of James' earlier stages presupposed realism even in the technical philosophical sense. The psychology presupposed that neural reflex arcs, the pancreas and the fluids of the spinal column are what they are and lead a life of their own independently of human investigation and human awareness of them. Similarly the whole of his pragmatist philosophy presupposed that "working" or "leading successfully to future experience" is something that ideas do or do not do whether we will or no. James' realism in later life is merely an attempt to make these continuous suppositions of the earlier periods explicit.

At the same time, latent in his psychology is the refusal to distinguish mental and material "stuff". If James as a realist was to commit himself to a "stuff" of the world which is independent of human investigation, he could not remain consistent with the functionalism of the psychology and at the same time label it either "mental" or "material". He therefore took the bull by the horns and called the stuff of the world "neutral". Minds must be this stuff organized in one way; material objects the same stuff organized in a different way. This is the thesis of his late articles.

Now, his theory of knowledge had, as we have said, accepted rather than rejected the "bricks" of Hume's version of the analysis of experience; and James persisted in his claims to radical empiricism. It is therefore not surprising that his label for the "stuff" of which the world is composed is the label: "bits of pure experience". Thus James the neutral *monist* is not inconsistent with James the perpetual proclaimer of *pluralism*. His monism consists in the thesis that there is only one *kind* of stuff in the world and that it is neither mental nor material. His pluralism persists to the end in the claim that the actual stuff of the world is "bits of pure experience". And indeed his claim that the differences between mind and matter consist in differences of organization is the final version of his insistence that the relations between experiences are as important as the items related.

There is no denying the fact that James' prolific and often piecemeal writings are not always consistent. But the degree of inconsistency must not blind one to the fact that there are general and uniform themes throughout. Under careful scrutiny James' thought turns out to be more of one piece than is usually conceded. Behind the scattered surface there is a marked uniformity of pattern.

Amongst his more famous works two should be mentioned which have been ignored in the fore-going analysis. The first of these is his remarkable essay *The Will to Believe* (1897). Few philosophical essays are more clearly the product of a man's personal experience. James here incorporates in his philosophy a decision which enabled him to surmount a period of acute melancholy and depression tantamount to a nervous breakdown. His argument is threefold: (1) There are "forced options" in a man's intellectual life. By this he means that there are certain questions on which one *must* make up one's mind either for or against an urgent and important idea. There is no middle course. Thus, one *must* either believe that one is free or believe that one is not free; one *must* either believe that there is a God or believe that there is not a God. In either case, according to James, the attempt to straddle the fence and *not* commit oneself, is pragmatically the equivalent of the negative option. (2) In such cases, when decision transcends the evidence – that is to say, where in the nature of things evidence cannot settle the matter one way or the other – the only truly *empirical* approach is to recognize the need for transcending the evidence. To maintain a consistent empirical attitude one must look as it were for evidence at second remove; and this one does by examining the effects upon the integrity and power of one's life which follow upon selection of one option rather than the other. (3) But more than this, James makes the startling claim that in cases of this sort the very act of believing tends to make what is believed more true. Thus if I seriously believe that I am free I will in fact *act* as a free agent; whereas if I seriously believe that I am completely determined in all that I do I will *act* accordingly.

The other work which should be mentioned is his monumental study *The Varieties of Religious Experience* (1902), perhaps the first and surely a perennial classic in the psychology of religion. The theme springs from the claim of *The Will to Believe* that where belief transcends evidence the only empirical approach is to examine the effects of belief upon the integration of men's lives. James claims that religious belief can be "justified" by its tendency to organize and energize men's lives. By "religious belief" James meant in general a more or less orthodox commitment to the divine or supernatural element in reality. He failed to anticipate that later and less orthodox pragmatists might claim that excessively naturalistic beliefs like communism and scientism can "integrate" one's life and actions more efficiently than the orthodox "over-beliefs" with which he was concerned. He did not foresee the expansion of the sense of the word "religion" to include *any* integrating belief; but his psychological approach to the justification of religious belief paved the way for that expansion.

Whatever one may say about James' doctrines, whether one applauds or deplores them, one thing is almost universally admitted. It is impossible to read him without learning to love and admire the man. Even where you feel that he is entirely wrong you are forced to respect him. Every line he wrote breathes a spirit of uncompromising intellectual honesty. (J.W.S.)

Plate 54, page 214.

Jaspers, Karl (1883–). He is generally considered the chief exponent of German **Existentialism**, next to **Heidegger**, although he has repudiated both this label and the philosophy of Heidegger. He was born in Oldenburg, Germany, in 1883, and his professional career invites comparison with that of William **James**: he took his doctorate in medicine, published a *General Psychopathology* in 1913 (completely rewritten sixth edition, 1953), became a university lecturer in psychology in 1913, published a *Psychology of Weltanschauungen* in 1919, and then became a professor of philosophy at Heidelberg. In 1932 he published what he himself considers his philosophic *magnum opus*, *Philosophy*, in three volumes, of which the second bears the title *Existenzerhellung (Illumination of Existence)*.

His wife is Jewish, and he had no traffic with the Nazis. Under the Hitler regime he published books on **Nietzsche** and **Descartes**, then was forbidden to lecture. Since the Second World War he has averaged more than a book a year, notably including *Von der Wahrheit* (Of Truth), a tome of over 1100 pages, published as volume one of a *Philosophical Logic*, a book on Schelling, and a tome of just under 1,000 pages, the first of three volumes on *Die Grossen Philosophen* (The Great Philosophers). None of the works mentioned so far have been translated into English, but a spate of his minor works have been; for example *Reason and Existence, The Perennial Scope of Philosophy* (German title, *Der philosophische Glaube*), and *The Way to*

Wisdom (German title, *Einführung in die Philosophie*). Jasper's influence on professional philosophers in Germany has been slight and on professional philosophers in the English-speaking world, nil. But he has a wide audience, and some theologians are interested in his work.

Jaspers represents a sustained protest against the "professors' philosophy" of the later nineteenth century. The two giants of the period after **Hegel** are, to his mind, **Kierkegaard** and Nietzsche, but their specific claims and theories are immaterial. Kierkegaard's "forced Christianity" and Nietzsche's "forced anti-Christianity" are dismissed: what matters is their concern with human existence and the unexampled fluidity and elusiveness of their thought: "Out of every position one may have adopted out of every finitude, – that is – we are expelled: we are set *whirling*." It is only after reason has suffered shipwreck in its quest for certainty that true philosophizing can begin.

The conception of shipwreck (*Scheitern*) is central: the experiences of failure, of death, of guilt – Jaspers speaks of extreme situations or border situations (*Grenzsituationen*) – confront us with the inadequacy of all philosophies and become, to cite Jaspers's characterisation of his own *Nietzsche*, "an introduction to that shaking up of thought from which *Existenzphilosophie* must spring".

Jaspers' consistent disparagement of all content poses a problem about the contents of his own voluminous writings. They are very largely filled with highly subjective paraphrases of the alleged positions of other writers, followed again and again by an appeal to the reader (*appellieren* is one of Jaspers' key concepts) to be seriously concerned with his own existence instead of seeking refuge in finished positions. (W.K.)

Plate 55, page 215.

Jevons, William Stanley (1835–1882), was born in Liverpool and educated at University College, London. His early studies were in chemistry and after working for some years as a metallurgist in Australia, he went back to University College to study economics and philosophy, henceforward his main interests. In 1863 he was appointed to teach logic and economics at Owens College, Manchester. He returned to London in 1875 as professor in his old college. His chief works on logic were *Pure Logic* (1864), *Elementary Lessons in Logic* (1870), *Principles of Science* (1874) and *Studies and Exercises in Deductive Logic* (1880).

Pure Logic is a study of **Boole**'s work in which Jevons introduced some notational improvements and amended the meaning of the plus sign for the logical sum to the now generally accepted *inclusive* sense of "or", i.e. if "*x*" stands for the class of red things and "*y*" for the class of square things then "*x* + *y*" represents the class of those things which are red or square or both red and square. An appendix to the book contains some theoretical objections to Boole's system which are not, however, well founded. Jevons' later work on Boolean algebra included the construction of a logical calculating machine, the so-called *logical piano*.

Principles of Science is a comprehensive work on the logic of induction. Written in conscious opposition to J. S. **Mill**'s account of induction as depending on a process of elimination, this book contains an elaborated account of inductive reasoning in which hypotheses framed by the informed insight of the scientist are subsequently confirmed by evaluating the evidence in their favour in accordance with the calculus of probability. He makes an important point against Mill by insisting on the essential uncertainty of all inductive conclusions. Though less attractively written than Mill's *System of Logic*, *Principles of Science* is a book that keeps much closer to the facts of scientific practice. Jevons' general view of induction has received a powerful and original formulation in the work of a present-day philosopher, Professor K. R. **Popper.** (D.J.O'C.)

John of Paris or Jean Quidort (*c.* 1269–1306), Dominican friar and Paris Master. A brave thinker and an able political philosopher, he defended civil prerogatives against the Augustinian Giles of Rome, who taught that all dominion was subject to the spiritual power, and James of Viterbo, who taught that the Church was the paramount realm. His *De Potestate Regia et Papali*, based on **Aristotle** and Thomas **Aquinas** defined and balanced two sets of divinely instituted rights, and anticipated the later doctrine of indirect control. He also defended Thomas Aquinas against the "Corrective" of the English Franciscan, William de la Mare. His *Correc-*

torium Corruptorii and *Quodlibet* indicate the philosophical dispute of the period. He denied that matter can exist without form, that matter exists within soul, and that a single organic substance needs a plurality of forms. He maintained the real distinction between essence and existence in finite things, but in his own way, for he seems to have made existence an entity apart from essence and not to have appreciated how far Thomas had advanced from **Avicenna.** (T.G.)

Jurisprudence is now the English name for a loosely related group of studies concerned to investigate certain general questions about law which knowledge of particular legal systems does not suffice to answer. Among the general questions of Jurisprudence are: What is law? Can there be law without coercion? Is international law really law? How does law differ from and how is it related to morality and justice? How do Judges reason in deciding particular cases? How do social and economic conditions affect the law and how are they affected by it? Are there any fixed principles by which laws may be appraised as good or bad?

Jurisprudence may thus be distinguished from ordinary legal study as a discipline concerned to further the understanding and reasoned criticism of law as distinct from knowledge of its details. In pursuit of these general aims it has drawn heavily on other disciplines, especially philosophy. Distinctions are sometimes made between Jurisprudence, Philosophy of Law, and Legal Theory, but these mean little; it is more important to distinguish between different types of inquiry as follows:

I. ANALYTICAL INQUIRIES

The elucidation of the expression "law" and of terms embodying fundamental legal concepts (e.g. rights and duties, legal personality, ownership, sources of law) is now regarded especially in England as an independent and important study. The systematic analysis of legal concepts was begun by **Bentham** in *The Fragment on Government* (1776), *The Principles of Morals and Legislation* (1789), and the *Limits of Jurisprudence Defined* (1782), and developed by his disciple John Austin in *The Province of Jurisprudence Determined* (1832) and in *Lectures on the Philosophy of Positive Law* (1863). Modern forms of analytical study of law have been developed in the "pure theory" of law of Hans Kelsen, described in *General Theory of Law and State* (English translation, 1947) and by jurists influenced by linguistic philosophy. Analytical jurisprudence is usually associated with (though logically independent of) "legal positivism" i.e. the doctrine that there is no necessary but only a historical connection between law and morality.

II. CRITICAL AND EVALUATIVE INQUIRIES

The doctrines of Natural Law developed by the scholastics (especially by Thomas **Aquinas**) from Aristotelian metaphysics and Christian theology founded a lasting tradition in the criticism of law. Its distinguishing feature is the insistence (1) that there are fixed principles for the guidance of human conduct not made by man but discernible by reason; (2) that these principles constitute a *natural* law by which all man-made law is to be judged. Some theorists hold that failure to conform to natural law renders human law invalid; others look upon natural law not as a test of legal validity but only as a standard of criticism.

Criticism of law (on **utilitarian** grounds) was a major concern of Bentham and Austin in spite of their insistence on analytical studies and their objection to Natural Law doctrines. Most modern critical jurisprudence is based on a variety of social policies and is independent of natural law theory, though since the last war its essentials have been reasserted in Germany and by neo-Thomists elsewhere.

Study of the judicial process especially in America stimulated two forms of jurisprudence, one constructive, the other sceptical. Both emphasized the fact that since all legal rules have only a central core of settled meaning, when Courts apply general rules to the many borderline cases, the reasoning involved is not (despite appearances) deductive but represents a choice between social values. One movement, led by Roscoe Pound (often termed "functional" jurisprudence) is concerned to determine the social interests which should guide Courts in the area left open by legal rules. The sceptical movement originating with O. W. Holmes (*The Path of the Law*, 1897) and J. C. Gray (*The Nature and Sources of Law*, 1902) stressed the diversity of non-legal influences on judicial decisions latent beneath the legal forms. Later "Realist"

writers challenged the conventional conception of law as consisting of rules as distinct from more or less predictable operations of the Courts (see for example Jerome Frank's *Law and The Modern Mind*, 1930). These developments were anticipated by the advocacy of unfettered judicial discretion by Continental jurists of the "Free law" school (e.g. Ehrlich, *Freie Rechtsfindung*, 1903) and also by Scandinavian writers (especially Axel Hägeström 1868-1939).

III. SOCIOLOGICAL INQUIRIES

Various general theories concerning the interplay of law with economic and social forces fall under this head. The **Marxist** doctrine that law is determined by economic conditions and destined to "wither away" has been developed by Russian writers, for example E. B. Pashukanis, in his *General theory of Law and Marxism* (1924). Official Soviet legal theory has suppressed the anarchical side of this doctrine. Non-Marxist theories e.g. E. Ehrlich's *Fundamental Principles of Sociology of Law* (1913 tr. 1936) insist that the "formal" law to be found in statutes is a less important social influence than moral and other non-legal norms ("the living law"). Though general programmes for "sociological jurisprudence" have often been announced the best work done consists of studies of the relation of special legal institutions to specific economic or social conditions, for example Berle's and Means' *The Modern Corporation and Private Property* (1932).

IV. HISTORICAL INQUIRIES

The work of Savigny, *The Vocation of Our Age for Legislation and Jurisprudence* (English translation, 1831) and Sir Henry Maine's two works, *Ancient Law* (1881) and *Early History of Institutions* (1875) are usually described as historical jurisprudence but no single form of inquiry is distinguishable under this name. Savigny thought that the naturally developing law of a society should be interfered with only in accordance with its natural genius which could best be grasped in the earliest of its legal forms. Maine wished to free the understanding of early law from modern preconceptions concerning the nature of law, and to exhibit characteristic stages of legal development followed by "progressive" societies. (H.L.A.H.)

K

Kant, Immanuel (1724–1804), the son of a saddler, born in Königsberg. He was educated at a grammar school of the city, and at its University, where he later taught first as a *Dozent* (lecturer) and afterwards, for many years, as professor. As a student he had, apart from philosophy, studied mathematics and physics; and, throughout life, he kept an interest in these subjects. What is known as the Kant-Laplace theory of the origin of the solar system is partly based on an early cosmological essay of his. Externally, his life was the quiet and uneventful life of an unmarried scholar, devoted to his work and his few friends. He had no particular taste for music and the fine arts but he was well acquainted with ancient and modern literature. His interest in the political events of his time was intense. He sympathized both with the American and the French revolutions. Kant is now widely acknowledged to have been one of the greatest of all philosophers.

Two main streams of European philosophy influenced his thought – **rationalism**, which reached him through his own teachers, in the form given to it by **Leibniz** and Wolff; and **empiricism**, the impact of which he felt most strongly when he came across some of **Hume**'s writings in a German translation. His own mature philosophy begins with the *Critique of Pure Reason* (1781), and is best known under the name of the Critical Philosophy. It is a synthesis – as distinct from a mere combination – of rationalism and empiricism, each of which, in his view, gave a one-sided and distorted account of the structure and content of human knowledge.

Perhaps the best approach, though not the only one, to the core of Kant's philosophical system is through his twofold classification of judgments. According to him every judgment is (i) either analytic or synthetic and (ii) either *a priori* or *a posteriori*. A judgment is analytic if its negation results in a logical absurdity. For example "A father is male", "A green thing is coloured" are analytic judgments, since their negation, namely "A father is *not* male", "A green thing is *not* coloured" is in each case logically absurd. Their truth is clear from a mere analysis of the terms in which they are made. A judgment which is *not* analytic is synthetic. Synthetic are all judgments about empir-ical matters of fact, in particular those stating empirical laws of nature such as "Copper conducts electricity". These judgments, whether true or false, certainly can be denied without contradiction. A judgment is *a priori* if it is "independent of all experience and even of all impressions of the senses". Thus "Man has an immortal soul", which can be neither confirmed nor falsified by experience, is – if it is meaningful – *a priori*. Again all analytic judgments are *a priori*. Their truth, and indeed their logical necessity, can be made evident without resort to experiment or observation by a mere analysis of their terms.

If we combine these two classifications, and notice that all analytic judgments must be also *a priori*, we see that there are three classes of judgments, mutually exclusive and jointly exhaustive, namely: (i) analytic (and *a priori*) (ii) synthetic *a posteriori* and (iii) synthetic *a priori*. It is worth remarking here that Leibniz considers all judgments to be analytic. That is, even empirical judgments according to him could in theory have their terms analysed till their connection was seen to be logically necessary. According to Hume and his modern followers all judgments are either analytic (and so *a priori*) or synthetic *a posteriori*; none are synthetic *a priori*.

Kant is convinced to the contrary. He finds synthetic *a priori* judgments (i) in the mathematics and science of his day and (ii) in morality. An example would be the judgment "Every event has a cause". This can be denied without logical absurdity and yet, in its complete generality, is something neither confirmable nor falsifiable by sense-experience. (If no cause of an event is known, we can always go on looking for it. On the other hand even if we hold that all known events have causes, there may be others which have none. The dominant form of Quantum Mechanics at the present day does in fact successfully reject the principle of causality.)

The occurrence, then, of synthetic *a priori* judgments gives rise to two philosophical tasks, first to exhibit them clearly and, if possible, completely; and secondly to demonstrate not only that these judgments are made, both in the course of any theoretical inquiry and whenever moral duties are ascribed to a person, but further that one is justified in making them. This problem Kant formulates by asking "How are synthetic *a priori* judgments possible?" It is the central question of the Critical Philosophy. Its answer required a critique of all theoretical and moral knowledge as well as an examination of the claim of metaphysics to yield transcendent knowledge, i.e. knowledge of what transcends every possible experience.

1 *The Critique of Pure Reason.* The task of this first critique is (i) to exhibit what synthetic *a priori* judgments enter into pure mathematics and natural science, and show "how they are possible"; and (ii) to examine the claims of **metaphysics**. It is important, if we would distinguish in Kant's philosophy between what is of more purely historical interest and what is still relevant to contemporary issues, to note that Kant was convinced that the mathematics of his day, Newtonian physics, and Aristotelian logic were complete to the extent that their analysis by the methods of the critical philosophy would yield all those fundamental synthetic *a priori* propositions from which any others could more or less easily be deduced by ordinary reasoning. Experts are divided on the question how far the development of non-Euclidean geometry, relativity and quantum theory and of the new mathematical logic forces one to admit that Kant cannot possibly have succeeded in producing the complete outline of *a priori* knowledge.

One of the fundamental assumptions of the Kantian philosophy is that perceiving and thinking are different. Following the psychology of his day, he attributes them to two distinct faculties of the mind, the one to sense and the other to understanding. Apart from analytical judgments – which merely elucidate the meaning of their terms – every judgment consists, or appears to consist, in applying a concept to some particular. Apprehension of particulars belongs to the faculty of sense; apprehension of concepts, and the rules according to which they are applied, belongs to the understanding. In order to grasp the function and the legitimacy of a synthetic *a priori* judgment it is necessary to inquire into its constituents – the type of concept and of particular which make it what it is.

To begin with concepts, these are of three types. First, the *a posteriori* which are concepts abstracted from sense-perception and applicable to it (thus "green" is so abstracted from perceptual data and applied to them when we judge that something is

green); secondly, the *a priori* concepts which, though not abstracted from sense-perception, are nevertheless applicable to it; and thirdly, the Ideas. These last are neither abstracted from sense-perception nor applicable to it. While Kant's account of *a posteriori* concepts contains nothing not familiar to the traditional empiricism, his account of *a priori* concepts and of Ideas is all his own, and distinctive of the Critical Philosophy. We shall as we proceed see how essential this account is (i) to an understanding of the nature of those synthetic *a priori* propositions which are contained in mathematics, natural science, metaphysics, morality, aesthetic judgment and teleological explanation; (ii) to an understanding of their claim to be true; and (iii) to the decision whether and how far the claim is to be held justified in each of these cases.

(1) *Kant's Philosophy of Mathematics.* In discussing the mathematics of his time – arithmetic, classical analysis and Euclidean geometry – Kant is first of all trying to show that the propositions embodying their axioms and theorems are synthetic *a priori*. He is not concerned with analytic statements to the effect that the axioms of a mathematical theory logically imply its theorems. It is fairly generally agreed – since the discovery of non-Euclidean geometries and their successful use in physics – that the postulates of Euclidean geometry can be denied without logical absurdity, and that they are independent of sense-perception – which amounts to what Kant meant by saying that they are synthetic and *a priori*. The synthetic *a priori* character of arithmetical propositions is disputed by many experts (see, however, section IV), although some arithmetical propositions concerning "the totality of all integers" have been denied without contradiction and are independent of sense in that they do not describe sense-perceptions of any kind. Kant holds that even such judgments as "$7 + 5 = 12$" are synthetic because the notion of "12" is not "contained" in the notion of adding 7 and 5.

Assuming now that the axioms and theorems of every system of pure mathematics are synthetic *a priori* judgments, Kant has to ask: How are they possible? Are there, perhaps, particular objects other than sense-perceptions which the concepts of arithmetic and geometry characterise? Kant's answer is, that indeed there are such.

According to Kant space and time – as opposed to the sense-perceptions which are located in them – are (i) *a priori* and (ii) particulars rather than general notions. In one argument aimed at showing the *a priori* character of space and time he appeals to the possibility of varying in imagination all features of a perceptual object except its being in space and time. (The colour, shape or the like of a perceptual object is indeed quite different from its spatial and temporal situation.) One of his arguments showing space and time as particulars and not general notions consists in emphasizing the point that "division" is a quite different process in the two cases. Space divides into sub-spaces and time into temporal intervals. Division of a general notion on the other hand is into its various species (as e.g. "animal" divided into "vertebrate" and "non-vertebrate").

Now if space and time are *a priori* particulars, Kant can explain the legitimacy of the synthetic *a priori* judgments of arithmetic and geometry. Those of arithmetic describe the structure of time with its repetition of units; those of geometry describe the structure of space with its extended patterns. Mathematical synthetic *a priori* judgments are thus shown "possible" by the fact that in making them one applies *a priori* concepts (concepts which though not abstracted from sense-perception are applicable to it) to *a priori* particulars – namely space and time. Kant holds that we become aware of the structure of space and time by constructions which, though analogous to the drawing of diagrams on black-boards, do not consist in the production of chalk marks or other physical objects.

Kant characterizes an explanation of the legitimacy of synthetic *a priori* judgments, such as the one just described, as "transcendental" and he calls his whole philosophy on this account not only "Critical" but also "Transcendental" Its concern is "not so much with objects as with the manner of our cognition of objects, in so far as it is possible *a priori*".

(2) *Kant's philosophy of science.* By an analysis of science and of commonsense knowledge of fact Kant proceeds to show that in these fields too, just as in pure mathematics, synthetic *a priori* judgments are employed, which it is the task of the Critical or Transcendental Philosophy to exhibit, and to examine for their legitimacy. Here also, he urges, we must recognize our synthetic *a priori* possessions and prove our right to what we possess.

We all make judgments to the effect that this or that particular event *caused* something else to happen. Moreover, before the advent of quantum mechanics the general principle of causality – that every event has a cause – was generally accepted. The judgment expressing this principle is, according to Kant, a synthetic *a priori* one. Moreover, the concept "x causes y", which is involved in the general principle, and applied whenever we make a particular causal judgment, is an *a priori* concept. It is certainly not abstracted from any *perceived* necessary connection, since all that we ever perceive is succession of occurrences. That we do not abstract the relation of causal necessity *from* perception had already been shown by Hume, whose views in this respect Kant substantially adopts. Yet we do apply this concept *to* perception. The name which Kant adopts for concepts which are not, as are the mathematical ones, characteristic of space and time, but yet are applicable to perception, is *Categories*. The fact that they are constituents in synthetic *a priori* judgments makes it necessary to list them systematically.

There are certain clues by the help of which Kant believes that this can be done. First, we have the difference between subjective perceptual judgments and judgments which are objective and empirical. Compare, for example, the two judgments, "What now appears to me is green" and "This is a green object". The first judgment does not claim to be about any public thing, anything independent of my perception, anything perceivable by others as well as by me, anything which might still be there even if I ceased to exist. The second claims to be objective, to be about a substance which exists independently of my perception. Yet both the subjective perceptual judgment and the objective, empirical one have the same perceptual content. Hence, Kant argues, in making the subjective perceptual judgment the concept, or more precisely the Category, "substance" is not being applied. In making the objective empirical judgment it is applied. This leads to the conclusion that if we compare objective empirical judgments with subjective perceptual ones having the same perceptual content, and if we as it were subtract the latter from the former, what will remain is one or more Categories.

A *second* clue concerns not only the discovery of the Categories but also the criterion for when we have discovered them all. This clue is the difference between the matter of objective, empirical judgments and their form. The matter of such a judgment is always expressed by its *a posteriori* concepts. The form can be expressed by the fact that the judgment has a certain structure. Thus the judgment "If the sun shines, the stone will get warmer" has the *if – then* form, it has the structure of a hypothetical judgment: and this, according to Kant, expresses the fact that in making the judgment we are applying the Category "x causes y". In considering on the one hand the difference between subjective perceptual and objective empirical judgments of the same perceptual content, and on the other hand the difference between the matter and the form of the objective empirical ones, Kant thinks we can see that the form or structure of objective empirical judgments embodies the Categories.

If, then, every form of judgment – all the varieties of the logical structure to be found in judgments – is completely listed, we should thereby arrive at a complete list of the Categories. Now Kant held that the traditional logic (slightly modified by himself) did contain a list of all the possible logical forms of judgment; and so it contained, implicitly, all the Categories. Most experts agree that Kant over-estimated the completeness of the traditional logic in this respect. We shall not attempt more here then merely to set out the Categories, as Kant listed them. They are (i) The Categories of quantity viz Unity, Plurality, Totality (ii) the Categories of quality viz Reality, Negation, Limitation (iii) the Categories of relation viz Substance–and–accident, Causality–and–dependence, Community or Interaction (iv) the Categories of modality viz Possibility – Impossibility, Existence – Non-existence, Necessity – Contingency. It would not be profitable to go farther into detail about the derivation of these Categories. The principle is the same as illustrated above in the case of "causality". First the perceptual content common to an objective empirical judgment and the corresponding perceptual judgment is separated from their differing logical structure or form. The logical

form of the objective empirical judgment is then, in a more or less obvious way, identified with a Category.

Synthetic *a priori* judgments consist in applying the Categories to the data given to the senses in space and time, i.e. to the perceptual manifold. Since the Categories are *not* abstracted from the manifold so given, their application to it is not the mere declaration of what is found in perception. (How could we declare that we have found e.g. causal necessity in perception, when all we have perceived is regularity of sequence between events?) Kant's real, or alleged, insight into the nature of applying the Categories to the manifold of perception is one of the central points of his Critical Philosophy. He himself compared it with the revolutionary idea of Copernicus who "made the observer turn round (the sun) and kept the stars still". Application of the Categories to the manifold of perception and indeed their bare applicability, is what constitutes the subjective manifold of otherwise disconnected appearances in space and time into the objective (or inter-subjective) reality, in which we discern physical objects as the source of systematically connected perception, as substances capable of causal relations and of interaction with other substances.

To be an object – as opposed to a mere subjective impression – is thus, for Kant, to be the bearer of Categories. The Categories are not abstracted from the manifold of perception but are, as it were, imposed by the subject on it. The reality of inter-subjective objects is due to the thinking subject – thinking being the connecting of the manifold by means of the Categories. Such phrases Kant himself uses in trying to give a preliminary indication of the function of the Categories. We must content ourselves here with the indication without pursuing him into the extensive details of his complete account.

One point, however, must be made. Kant distinguishes sharply between the *pure* Self which imposes the Categories and the empirical Self. All empirical self-awareness does itself already presuppose the application of the Categories. The empirical subject which apprehends its own states, and is thus aware of itself, is not the same subject which "imposes" the Categories. There is no self-awareness of the pure self.

Once we understand that the Categories, in being applied to the perceptual manifold, constitute objects we are on the way towards understanding those synthetic *a priori* judgments which are not mathematical. Kant conceives them as the principles according to which the Categories are applied to the manifold of perception. They express the conditions under which objective experience – as opposed to the being aware of disconnected appearances – is possible. They are the presuppositions of our apprehending objects of common-sense and science. The conditions for applying the Categories, expressed by the non-mathematical synthetic *a priori* judgments, are according to Kant connected with the fact that objects and perceptions are all located in time. They are temporal conditions. This is more obvious in the case of some synthetic *a priori* principles than others. Again we cannot go into detail about how the allegedly complete list of these principles is got and must be content with an enumeration; (i) To the Categories of quantity there corresponds the principle "all perceptions are extensive magnitudes" (ii) To the Categories of quality, there corresponds the principle "in all appearances the real which is an object of sensation has intensive magnitude, that is degree"; (iii) The principle corresponding to the Categories of relation, is that "objective experience is possible only by means of the presentation of a necessary connection of perceptions." (This last principle is more concretely expressed in three synthetic *a priori* propositions which are presupposed in Newtonian physics; the principle of the conservation of substance: "All change (succession) of appearances is only alteration of substance"; the principle of causality: "All alterations occur in accordance with the law of connection of cause and effect" and the principle of interaction: "All substances in so far as they are apprehended as coexistent in space are in thorough-going interaction"). (iv) To the Categories of modality there correspond three principles which are held to explain possibility, reality, and necessity as characterizing our judgments about the objective world.

Having found the synthetic *a priori* principles in their alleged completeness, Kant can enter upon the question of their justification – this in what is perhaps the most difficult part of the Transcendental Philosophy, the so-called "Transcendental Deduction of the Categories". Its central point is this: application of the Categories to objects – in accordance with the principles – is legitimate because to be an object is nothing else than to be capable of being characterised by the Categories. – That in our thinking about matters of fact we employ Categories and that their application constitutes objective reality is, it seems, Kant's most important contribution to the theory of knowledge and the philosophy of science – whatever one may think about his claim to have discovered the presuppositions of *all* objective and scientific knowledge completely.

(3) *Kant's metaphysical views.* The analysis of mathematics and theoretical knowledge results in the thesis that all theoretical knowledge consists in "categorizing" – ordering by means of the Categories – perceptual material located in space and time. Knowledge is thus both perceptual and conceptual – the joint product of perceiving and thinking. We can only think what cannot be perceived; we cannot know it. We can think, indeed must think, that there exists something apart from space, time and the Categories, a "thing in itself". Kant's doctrine of the existence of a merely thinkable but not perceivable thing in itself (an "intelligible" or "*noumenon*") he calls "transcendental" idealism as opposed to "transcendent" idealism which would claim knowledge of it. Any attempt to apply the Categories to things in themselves results in illusion and confusion.

Another source of such illusion is the improper use of the Ideas of Reason. Just as Kant derived the Categories – concepts not abstracted from experience but applicable to it – from the possible forms of judgment so he derives the Ideas – concepts neither abstracted from nor applicable to experience – from the possible forms of logical inference. In doing so he again accepts the traditional logic as, on the whole, complete. The guiding principle is this: We can always go on asking to have the premises of our inferences deduced from higher premises without limit. (We can always go on asking for the "conditions of the conditions, of the conditions . . . of the truth of any statement".) An Idea is formed when we assume that this *potentially* infinite eries is *actually* given in its totality. Kant recognizes three types of deductive inference, each giving rise to a potentially infinite sequence of premises; and hence to three Ideas, namely (*a*) of the absolute unity of the thinking subject,(*b*) of the absolute unity of the sequence of the conditions of appearance,(*c*) of the absolute unity of the conditions of objects of thought in general. Each of these Ideas of Reason provides the spurious subject matter of a spurious metaphysical discipline; the first the subject matter of speculative psychology (containing alleged *a priori* knowledge about the soul); the second that of speculative cosmology (containing alleged *a priori* knowledge of the world); the third that of speculative theology (containing alleged *a priori* knowledge of God).

According to Kant all metaphysical knowledge of matters of fact is expressed in or deducible from the synthetic *a priori* principles. If either (i) the Categories are taken as characterising things in themselves; or if (ii) the Ideas are taken as characterizing something that is given in experience, metaphysics becomes spurious. The mistaken employment of the Categories and Ideas leads, so Kant tries to show, to obstinate fallacies. These can be recognised and resolved only when the nature and function of the Ideas and of the Categories is understood. Among these fallacies a special interest attaches to alleged proofs of the existence of God, in particular to the ontological argument. According to this we can deduce God's existence from the fact that we can conceive (think) the notion of a perfect being: A perfect being must exist since lack of existence would be imperfection. Kant's reply is that existence is not a predicate.

Other fallacies are so-called antinomies. Of these the most important for Kant's system as a whole is the antinomy between (i) the freedom of the will (where the will is considered as causing those actions of a morally responsible subject for which it is responsible) and (ii) the principle of natural causality which applies to all phenomena (and is among the conditions of objective reality). Here Kant distinguishes between the Idea of moral freedom which has no application to phenomena and the Category of causality which has such application. Our experience of moral obligation logically implies the Idea of moral freedom. It is a notion we can and must think; but we cannot know. We cannot think *and* perceptually apprehend it. The Idea of non-phenomenal freedom which we must assume if man is a moral being is quite compatible with the Category of causality, the application of

which to phenomena is a condition of the knowledge of matters of fact. We return to this in Section II.

Whereas the application of the Categories to phenomena has a constitutive function – constituting them objects – the Ideas have, as we have seen, no function of that kind. They have, however, a "regulative" function. They "direct the understanding to a certain goal . . . which serves the purpose of giving the greatest unity and the greatest breadth at the same time." The Ideas, we have seen, have their root on the one hand in the demand that we should search for the conditions of any true judgment; on the other hand in the assumption that the totality of these conditions, which form a potentially infinite sequence, is *actually* given. This assumption, unlike the demand, is the source of a pretended knowledge. But the demand does indeed confer greater unity on our judgment; since in following it we connect them systematically by deductive relations.

II *The Critique of Practical Reason*. This part of the critical philosophy is concerned with the synthetic *a priori* principles which underlie our knowledge of what *ought* to be the case, in particular our knowledge of what we ought to do. It aims at exhibiting these principles and at demonstrating their legitimacy.

The moral law – by which we are enabled to decide whether an action is or is not obligatory – is found by analysis of man's moral experience and of the language in which he formulates it. The morality or otherwise of an agent's action, Kant tries to show, is not a quality of his behaviour; nor is it a quality of any desire he has to bring about some state of affairs. These qualities do not imply that the person is doing his duty for the sake of duty. To know this we must know what Kant calls his maxim. An agent's maxim is the general rule which he would formulate in justifying his action (I did what I did because whenever conditions obtain which then and there obtained one should do this type of action).

Now Kant argues that a person's maxim is moral if it conforms to the moral law – provided that there is a moral law. The law which he derives from the analysis of moral experience is purely formal. It is the famous categorical imperative: the maxim of my action – and therefore the action performed in accordance with it – is moral if and only if I can will that it should become a universal law. By this formal test the maxims are divided into moral and non-moral, precisely as by purely formal tests syllogisms are divided into valid and invalid. The maxims are the material which is tested by the formal test. We cannot go into Kant's exposition of how the moral law functions in thought and action. Nor can we consider his demonstrations that the moral law can be expressed in alternative, but equivalent, ways. The most striking of his alternative formulations of the categorical imperative is this: "Act in such a way that you treat humanity both in your own person and in the person of all others, never as a means only but always equally as an end." No one who lives in the European tradition will find anything obscure or too technical in this formulation.

By our experience of the conflict between duty and desire we are committed to the categorical imperative. Is this commitment, then, objective – not only in the sense of being true to our moral experience, but in the sense of being possible in a world which stands under the law of causality? Kant answers that the commitment is in the full sense objective. The Idea of freedom, which can be thought but not known, is not only demanded by our sense of duty. It is, as we have noted earlier, compatible with the rule of the principle of causality in the phenomenal world. Man *qua* phenomenal being is causally determined, but *qua* non-phenomenal or noumenal being he is free. He cannot know *what* his freedom is. He knows none the less *that* he is free. The consistency of moral freedom with the causal order of nature can be proved. But the nature of moral freedom must remain a mystery.

From the above account it is clear that according to Kant morality "needs neither the idea of another being above man, for man to recognize his duty, nor does it need another motive apart from the law that he should fulfil his duty . . ." Unavoidably, however, morality gives rise to the assumption that virtue has some connexion with happiness, that the two are adequately correlated, and it thus suggests the Idea of a power which would secure this correlation. But the connection between religion and morality is not logical. It is based on an act of faith which explains the – otherwise mysterious – consistency between moral freedom and causally determined nature. To have made room for this act of faith in the existence of God is, according to Kant, a greater achievement than to have provided fallacious proofs of it.

III *The Critique of Judgment.* In the first two *Critiques* Kant has tried to discover and justify the principles which are presupposed in our *objective* judgments as to what is the case, and as to what ought to be the case. In the Critique of Judgment he is concerned with discovering *subjective* principles which are at the root (i) of our search for system in our explanations of natural phenomena and (ii) of our apprehension of beauty. The key notions into which this third Critique inquires are purpose and purposiveness (the latter in the sense of a harmony which we might apprehend without recognizing any *specific* purpose.)

The notion of purpose is involved in *any* scientific explanation. Always, such explanation is based on the implicit assumption that the special empirical laws which we discover are something more than merely an unconnected conjunction, a heap of unrelated generalizations. We look for a certain systematic unity. This implies that they can be considered "*as if* an understanding (though not our own) had given them to our cognitive faculties, in order to make possible a *system* of experience in accordance with the laws of nature". This assumption, as is emphasized by the words *as if*, is not a statement of fact. It is a subjective, methodological principle.

Apart from the general assumption of a harmony between our understanding and the nature which we try to understand, Kant considers particular fields of inquiry, and the teleological explanations sometimes used in them. They have their use as preparing the way for causal explanations, or as filling temporary – perhaps even permanent – causal gaps. The notion of purposes in Nature is a methodologically useful and indispensable Idea; but as an Idea it has unlike the Categories no objective application.

Of teleological explanations Kant argues that they foster the assumption that "the universe has its source in an intelligent being . . . existing outside the world." But not even the most complete teleology amounts to a proof of God's existence, since teleological principles are merely subjective expressions of "our cognitive faculties being what they are".

Kant, we have seen, admits purposiveness without purpose. Indeed he defines beauty as "the form of purposiveness in so far as it is perceived *apart from the presentation of a purpose*." The unity of aesthetic experience is due to an *indefinite* interplay of the faculties of perception and imagination on the one hand and the understanding on the other. An aesthetic experience, as it were, calls for the application of concepts by the understanding, but overflows every conceptual characterization.

Any aesthetic judgment, apart from ascribing purposiveness to what is judged beautiful, claims further that the beautiful object is necessarily connected with pleasurable feeling, that *qua* beautiful it is not an object of interest and that it pleases universally. This universality claimed for aesthetic judgments is quite different from the (objective) universality of synthetic *a priori* judgments. It has a merely subjective foundation in our cognitive faculties. In this respect aesthetic judgments are on an equal footing with teleological explanation.

Kant's Critique of Judgment was in no way meant to supersede the two other Critiques. Only by maintaining that he treated "purpose" and "purposiveness" as Categories constitutive of an objective reality could such an interpretation be supported. But he clearly treated these notions as Ideas.

IV *Kant's influence*. As regards mathematics, Kant's view that it consists of synthetic *a priori* propositions describing the structure of space and time and constructions in them has been to a large extent adopted on the one hand by Hilbert and the formalist school and on the other by Brouwer and the Intuitionists. In addition Hilbert treats the actual infinite as a Kantian idea. As regards his philosophy of science, this has been kept alive by antiphenomenalists, and it has been substantially adopted by Einstein (see the *Einstein* volume in the *Library of Living Philosophers*, Chicago 1949). His view of the function of Ideas influenced C. S. **Peirce** and other pragmatists such as Vaihinger. Kant's demonstrations of the antinomies which arise when Ideas are taken to characterize objective reality is one of the sources of the Hegelian doctrine that reality is self-contradictory and that the contradictions are resolved by a dialectical reconstruction of "the Idea".

The influence of Kant's anti-naturalistic views has been very strong among later ethical intuitionists; and his distinction between pure and practical reason is widely accepted by moral philosophers of most schools.

The critical philosophy, especially the Critique of Judgment, had considerable influence on the rise of the German idealistic philosophy, particularly of **Fichte** and his followers, who unlike Kant regarded the self as not only apprehending but as somehow creating the world. (S.K.)

Plate 56, page 216.

Kierkegaard, Sören Aabye (1813–55), Danish philosopher, man of letters, and theologian. Some would dispute his right to the title "philosopher", but his main philosophical work – *Concluding Unscientific Postscript*, written in 1846, when its author was thirty-three, remains a contribution to the theory of knowledge of great importance. If it requires to be read against the background of its author's hostility to the degenerate **Hegelian** scholasticism of the Danish philosophy of his day, it also invites a fascinating comparison, in its practice of the method of indirection, in its attempt to say the unsayable, with **Wittgenstein**'s *Philosophical Investigations*.

Although Kierkegaard died at the age of forty-one, his output was voluminous; and the fields on which he touched are as wide in extent as those explored by Hegel, with whose *Phenomenology of Spirit*, and indeed earlier theological *Jugendschriften* his early works invite comparison. If his religiously defined hostility to Hegel's indentification of the real with the rational marks him historically as a critic of the supreme philosophical synthesis of romanticism, his early explorations of e.g. the aesthetic as contrasted with the ethical mode of life, reveals him the heir of the German thinker whose followers he criticized so sharply.

No one more demands to be read rather than read about, or expounded. There is no doubt that his personality repels many; its pathological quality is manifested in his controversial behaviour as well as in his treatment of his fiancée, Regine Olsen. Moreover his continually changing methods of writing, with their shift from pseudonymity to controversial or homiletic directness, set further obstacles in the way of a more than passing familiarity with his *oeuvre*. But the reader of his early writing will at least have his sense of the field with which the moral philosopher is concerned enlarged; the student of his *Postscript* and the *Philosophical Fragments*, which precede it will encounter work in the theory of knowledge of an evocative subtlety to bear comparison with that of Wittgenstein and **Wisdom**; and in such essays as that on *The Difference between a Genius and an Apostle*, and such discourses as those on *Training in Christianity*, the philosopher of religion will find a contribution to the phenomenological exposition of the character of distinctively Christian faith of lasting importance and insight. (D.M.M.)

Plate 57, page 217.

Knowledge, *see* Epistemology, *A priori*, Empiricism, Rationalism.

L

Law, *see* Jurisprudence, Freedom of the Will, Induction, Logic.

Leibniz, Gottfried Wilhelm, (1646–1716) German philosopher, the son of the Professor of Moral Philosophy at the University of Leipzig. When Leibniz was six years old his father died. At the age of fifteen, Leibniz entered the University, graduating in 1663 with a thesis entitled *Disputatio Metaphysica de Principio Individui*. This work contained many of the ideas of his later writings in embryo. From 1663 to 1666 he studied Jurisprudence at Jena and published a paper on legal education. This paper recommended him to the notice of the Archbishop of Mainz who thereupon took him into his service. Leibniz entered wholeheartedly into the Archbishop's plans for preserving peace within the Empire and between Germany and her neighbours. This led Leibniz to a search for a rational foundation for the Christian religion, acceptable to Protestants and Catholics alike, which would provide a sound basis for active religious toleration. Sent to Paris on a mission to Louis XIV, Leibniz did not succeed in seeing the king, but in a stay of four years, he made the acquaintance of **Malebranche**, Arnauld, Huygens and Tschirnhausen. He also invented a calculating machine which was an improvement upon **Pascal**'s machine

in that it could extract roots, multiply and divide as well as add and subtract. In 1673, he visited London, met Boyle and Oldenburg and demonstrated his calculating machine to the Royal Society, which thereupon elected him to membership. In 1676, the Archbishop of Mainz died, and in default of work more suited to his tastes and ability, Leibniz became Librarian to the Duke of Brunswick at Hanover. On his way to Hanover, Leibniz spent a month at Amsterdam, reading everything of Spinoza's which **Spinoza** could be persuaded to let out of his hands. Finally he was allowed to meet Spinoza and discussed with him those parts of his writings which he had been permitted to read. This was his last personal contact with fellow philosophers. From this time till his death he was at Hanover, travelling abroad only in connexion with his work on a history of the House of Brunswick. He had to be content with the exchange of letters and articles on philosophical problems with fellow philosophers and mathematicians. In his correspondence with Clarke, he attacked the absolute space and time of the Newtonian system, opposing to it his own system of monads and relative space and time which he set out in more detail in the *Discourse on Metaphysics* and the *Monadology*. In his correspondence with Arnauld, he defended his view of individuality and human and divine freedom to which Arnauld had objected on reading a summary of the Discourse. In his later years, Leibniz was involved in a controversy with the friends of Newton as to the authorship of the Infinitesimal Calculus. There is no doubt that both Leibniz and Newton were working on the Calculus during the same period. It also seems clear that there was nothing unlikely in its simultaneous and independent discovery. Many other mathematicians were working upon related ideas at that time. Further, there is no doubt that Leibniz's notation was more convenient than that of Newton; in fact it is still in use. Leibniz was similarly unfortunate in obtaining recognition for his original work in logic. In our day, he is largely valued for his original work on symbolic logic, but it was not until this century that it was known. His discoveries had to be made over again while his work lay buried in masses of manuscripts in the royal library at Hanover. Leibniz ended his life in a similar state of neglect. George I had refused to allow him to come to England, telling him to attend to his duties as Librarian, and when Leibniz died in 1716, not a single member of the court of Hanover followed his body to the grave. The Academy of Berlin, of which Leibniz was founder and first President, ignored his death as did the Royal Society of London. The studied neglect of 1716 has given place to the admiration of the twentieth century for a man of originality and insight, with great capacity for the detailed working out of large and new ideas.

Leibniz was a first class mathematician and scientist, sharing with Newton the honour of having discovered the infinitesimal calculus and contributing the concept of kinetic energy to mechanics. He was also an excellent philosopher whose metaphysical system is peculiarly interesting to our generation in that it can also be interpreted as a system of logical doctrines. Leibniz established his basic positions with arguments drawn from science, logic and metaphysics and believed that his "new principle, pre-established harmony", was "proved" in all these disciplines, as well as in religious and moral theory.

Leibniz's account of substance as essentially active, arose out of his dissatisfaction with the extended substance of the "new philosophy" and his equal dissatisfaction with atoms and the void, and with the absolute space, time and matter of Newtonian mechanics. His objections to all these concepts were both scientific and metaphysical. He showed that **Descartes's** formulation of the laws of motion was scientifically unsound, and the view of the spatio-temporal world connected with it, with its view of motion as miraculously imparted to essentially inert matter, metaphysically unsatisfactory. He described "atoms of matter" as contrary to reason, since the "smallest particle of matter" is an absurdity. If it is extended, then it is further divisible; if not, it is not "smallest", in fact, not a particle of matter. Moreover, the laws of motion demand that the elements involved should be bearers of energy. No extended being can be active, nor can it be a true unity. The only possible element must be a "simple substance, without parts". This simple substance Leibniz called a monad.

Since the monad has no parts, it is indestructible except by annihilation and can come into existence only by creation. It can produce no effect on another monad, so there is no causal interaction. ("The monad has no windows"). Since it is non-extended it is neither in space nor in time, and it is not material. Furthermore, since the only essential of a monad is that it should be active, all monads are of the same kind. However, there is no doubt that the observed world which is the starting point for speculation about substance, appears to be spatio-temporal, and to have bodies moving about in it in causal relations with one another. It also appears that there are entities of different kinds, stones, plants, animals and men. These appearances are in Leibniz's phrase, "well-founded", in that they can be systematically connected with real properties of the system of monads, and it is suitable to use spatio-temporal descriptions in some contexts, to speak of change and causal connexion and of different kinds of beings.

The proper description connected with the appearance of different kinds of things is of monads as varying in their degree of activity. There is an infinite series of monads ranging from the completely active to the almost inert. No created monad is completely inactive, and none is completely active, but those at the lower end of the scale would be mere matter, if there were any such thing. God is the only completely active monad, but it is not quite clear whether He is to be looked on as the chief monad, or whether His role as creator makes this an unsuitable description. The proper activity of monads is perception, representation or "mirroring", to use Leibniz's metaphor. "Perception" is applicable to stones and plants as to men and animals. (This was a current usage of "perception" in the seventeenth century. The lodestone was said to perceive the iron and the sunflower the sun, since they "changed in the neighbourhood of" the perceived body). All monads then, perceive in their varying degrees of clearness all other monads, so that though the monads are simple substances, they have a multiplicity of aspects, and the perceptions are true perceptions in that the monads were so created that their states would be in pre-established harmony with one another. Pre-established harmony is "proved" by the joint facts, the impossibility of interaction and the actuality of perception. The less active monads present the well-founded appearance of materiality though all monads are inactive to a certain extent, and so possess "prime matter". High and low grade monads mutually mirror one another, and every "body" is a colony of monads of varying degrees of activity in pre-established harmony. A human being is such a colony and the relation between mind and body is no longer the Cartesian miracle but part of the natural order, one case of the universal mirroring. The history of each monad is the unfolding of its states in accordance with its own principle so that continued interaction is the appearance of the unfolding of the states of each monad in harmony with the unfolding of the states of every other monad. Leibniz used the figures of two synchronised clocks and of two choirs singing from the same score to explain how there could be the appearance of interaction without the reality. He described the unfolding of the states as "appetition", applicable equally to purposive human activity and to the moving of the iron towards the lodestone and the sunflower towards the sun.

Space is the well-founded appearance of the "order of possible co-existences" and time of the "order of possibilities which are inconsistent". Space and time as conceived by mathematicians are abstractions, *entia rationis*, their continuity the appearance of true continuity which belongs to the series of monads and to the series of their successive states. The monads form an infinite series according to the principle of degree of activity, in which series, each term differs by an infinitely little from the terms next to it. Similarly, successive states of a monad form a continuous series each according to its own principle. Leibniz described the "*plenum*" of the universe with its two ordered series of compossibles and incompatibles as the "actual infinite". His space and time are not only infinitely divisible, but infinitely divided, not into the mathematician's abstractions of atom, point and instant but into the "real beings", the monads.

In describing the series of monads, Leibniz invokes his famous principle of the Identity of Indiscernibles. If two beings have exactly the same set of properties then they are "indiscernible", i.e. identical with one another. This is not open to the objection that two beings might have all the same properties but be in different places, because for Leibniz, the "place" of a monad is in the series. Its properties are a function of its place, so that to have the same properties, the two beings would have

to be in the same place, i.e. be one and not two. Leibniz also invokes the principle in exhibiting absolute space and time as absurdities. These absolutes have meaning only as the place of material bodies. To place a body here rather than there in absolute space, earlier rather than later would present no true alternatives. The two states of affairs in each case would be indiscernible, so that God in creating the world, could not make a rational choice. This objection is made in a letter to Clarke, who defended the Newtonian system. Clarke replied that no reason is needed for God's choice other than His will, but Leibniz maintained that the principle of Sufficient Reason was valid not only in relation to the various parts of the world, but also in relation to the acts of God. For every matter of fact, there must be a sufficient reason why it is so and not otherwise.

The doctrine of the monads is developed in the *Monadology*, but in the *Discourse on Metaphysics*, Leibniz presented arguments drawn from the nature of propositions and their truth and falsity which lead him to the same conclusions. The Discourse is an elaboration of a letter to Arnauld, presenting the outline of his logico-metaphysical system. In it, Leibniz assumed a close relationship between matters of fact and the propositions which stated them. He wrote that for philosophers, logical reasons would be convincing, but that they would not be suitable for ordinary men. The logical counterpart of the arguments for simple substances was that every proposition is of the subject-predicate form and that every true proposition has its predicate contained in its subject. Just as there is no interaction between monads, there are no relational propositions, and as a monad contains its states enfolded in it, so every true proposition contains its predicate in its subject. Leibniz's logical calculus presupposes that in its most satisfactory formulation, a true proposition would have as its subject a name showing the analytic constitution of the subject and a name for one or more of these constituents as its predicate. Any true proposition is expressible in the form ABC is A (or AB or B or AC or C or ABC). This view is closely connected with Leibniz's life-long search for a "universal characteristic", a language which could express truths established in any field, even in morals and aesthetics. False propositions in this language would appear as manifest absurdities, ABC is not A, or not B and so on. Disagreement would then disappear, for calculation has taken the place of inference.

The logical arguments aroused Arnauld's complete dissatisfaction on metaphysical, religious and moral grounds. If every true proposition is analytic and the state of every monad contained in its concept, then human freedom is a myth and God constrained. Leibniz's reply was that every actual state of affairs has hypothetical but not absolute necessity. When God chose to create the actual Adam, everything that goes with him was created too, but God freely chose to create the actual Adam. Moreover, in creating the actual Adam, God had regard to all the free acts that would ever be performed by men, and adapted the whole state of affairs to them. Free and spontaneous activity is allowed for in the pre-established harmony of all monads and their states. All monads choose the best and their capacity to discern the best varies with the degree of clearness with which they mirror the world. God, with perfect knowledge and goodness, freely chose to create this, the best of all possible worlds.

This is one of the points at which Leibniz's system shows a fundamental inconsistency. Leibniz wanted both true contingency of matters of fact and yet such a complete system that the concept of every individual contained all that it was ever to become. He wanted to maintain a real distinction between mathematical and empirical propositions, the former true according to the principle of contradiction, and their opposites impossible, the latter true according to the principle of sufficient reason, but nevertheless, their opposites a manifest absurdity. Men's reasons for their acts "incline without necessitating" yet Leibniz maintained also, that the proposition "Julius Caesar did not cross the Rubicon", properly formulated by someone with complete knowledge of Julius Caesar and possessing an adequate language would appear as a self-contradiction. God who alone possesses complete concepts of each individual can "read off" any state of any monad from any other state of that or any other monad. The distinction that Leibniz certainly wished to maintain between the truths of logic and mathematics on the one hand and contingent truths on the other, was that the former are true of all

possible worlds, the latter of this world only. The former depend on God's intellect but not on His will, but He wills that the latter shall be true in choosing to create this world. The true statements about this world form a system such that it is not possible that some of them should be true and the others false. Correspondingly, while it is abstractly possible that any part of the universe should be other than it is, no part can be other than it is and the other parts remain the same. A state of affairs must be not only possible, but also compossible with all other states of affairs. Leibniz provided a formal system by which possibilities as combinations of simples might be derived. He called this the "Combinatory Art", and it may be compared with a table of elements in chemistry. A formula for a possible combination of simples might guide discovery of a hitherto unknown entity. Used with a well chosen system of "names", the combinatory art could provide an encyclopaedia of all knowledge and a method of communication with people of all languages. (One would think that Leibniz's ideal might have at least been reached in modern mathematics and logic, but the fact remains that in order to follow the work of German mathematicians and Polish logicians, Anglo-Saxons have to learn a new set of formulae.)

Leibniz's metaphysical system is completed by his proofs of the existence of God. The system of created monads is, in a sense, complete in itself, that is, it is necessarily as it is granted that any part of it exists. But no one part of it contains the reason for its own existence, so that the reason for its existence must lie in a being which does contain its own reason for existence, that is, in a necessary being, which we call God. This argument, the "cosmological argument", appears in the Monadology and there is nothing in it which is peculiar to Leibniz. The **rationalists**, generally, take the existence of God as the necessary creating and sustaining cause of the universe. Leibniz's formulation of the "ontological argument" is peculiar to him in two ways: he couples it with a new argument, from the existence of necessary truths, and he completes it by a proof that the concept "God" is a possible concept. Hitherto, according to Leibniz, philosophers have succeeded in proving only, that *if* God's existence is possible, then it is necessary. The argument from the existence of necessary truths presupposes that all truths are "made true by" facts of some sort. There is no difficulty with contingent truths – they are made true by empirical facts. What makes the truths of logic and mathematics true? What do we know when we are said to know them? Leibniz's answer is that we are knowing the truths as they are present to the mind of God. God's intellect is the "place" of the eternal truths. For contemporary philosophers, this is the solution of a pseudo-problem. Necessary truths are not true *of* anything; they are either analytic or self-contradictory and we do not need to look beyond our own concepts for their validation.

The ontological argument is preceded by a proof that the concept "perfect being" is possible. Leibniz first distinguished properties which were perfections from properties in the ordinary sense. A property is a perfection if it may be possessed in a superlative degree, and if its possession does not imply the ruling out of other properties. Spatial and temporal properties are not perfections, since all superlatives involving them are self-contradictions, e.g. "greatest size", "last event", etc. Sensibly perceived properties are not perfections since their ascription to an object carries with it the denial of other properties; to ascribe "red" to an object implies that it is not blue, not green, etc. "Good", "wise", "knowledgeable" are all adjectives whose superlatives do not involve self-contradiction, so that they may be ascribed to the perfect being, who must possess all perfections *in* perfection. The concept "perfect being" is therefore a possible concept, and since existence is itself a perfection (assumed by Leibniz), "perfect being" is not only a possible concept, but actualized. At this point, Leibniz's manner of thinking is exhibited as most alien to our own, but this difference may be detected in all stages of his system. Not only do contemporary philosophers deny that existence is a predicate, they deny also that an analysis of concepts can yield knowledge of the actual world. The identity of indiscernibles is treated as a logical statement, having no bearing on the constitution of the actual world, and Leibniz's logical doctrine of propositions remains a logical doctrine with no bearing on the nature of what there is in the world. This position may be summed up in the words of C. W. **Morris**, who says: "Leibniz's rationalistic metaphysics, which came from the simple conversion of formal logic into a metaphysics through the neglect of the criterion of the empirically meaningful, is, in terms of the present conception of the relation of logic to empiricism, no longer the necessary cosmological corollary of his logical doctrines." This is a fair statement of what, in Leibniz, modern philosophers find interesting. It is a distortion if taken as the keynote of Leibnizian commentary. We might notice the words, "neglect of". We cannot be said to neglect a criterion which we should reject if explicitly offered to us. We might agree that if Leibniz had lived through philosophical developments up to the present day he would now accept the criterion of the empirically meaningful, but this is to speculate.   (R.L.S.)

Plate 58, page 218.

Leucippus, probably a native of Abdera, Greece, who lived about the middle of the fifth century B.C. Though of the greatest importance as the first to formulate the **atomic** theory he is a shadowy figure about whom we have no detailed personal information and from whose work only one doubtfully authentic sentence survives. Our earliest authorities usually refer to Leucippus in conjunction with **Democritus**; it is quite impossible therefore to determine what was the original contribution of each. It is however reasonable to believe that Leucippus is in the tradition of the **pre-Socratic** Milesian philosopher-scientists, but his theory was designed to take notice of the criticisms of the **Eleatic** philosophers, with whom he was probably personally aquainted; in particular, the doctrine of the void was intended to answer the Eleatic difficulties about the notion of not-being, so that that which was not (the void) could be said to be (there was a void). The decisive importance of Leucippus in the history of thought is that he first proposed a completely mechanistic account of the world without reference to purpose or other teleological principles, and that he singled out as fundamental those properties of matter which can be the subject of quantitative science.   (J.O.U.)

Lewis, Clarence I. (1883–), born at Stoneham, Massachusetts; Professor of Philosophy at Harvard University until his retirement in 1953. He has made fundamental contributions to mathematical **logic** and the theory of knowledge. His major achievement in logic is the calculus of "strict implication", one of the first successful symbolic systems of "modal" logic. It is called a modal logic because it employs the modal term "impossible" in defining "*p* implies *q*" as "It is impossible for both *p* and not-*q* to be true". Lewis developed his system as an alternative to **Russell**'s system of "material implication" because the latter yields such "paradoxical" theorems as "A false proposition implies every proposition", and does not capture the sense in which one proposition is commonly said to imply another. However, Lewis recognized that his and Russell's systems are but two out of a large number of distinct but self-consistent calculi which can be constructed, none of which is intrinsically superior to the others. He therefore held that the sole ground of choice between them is the pragmatic one of greater convenience in organizing our intellectual experience which may result from adopting one system rather than another.

Lewis generalized this claim in his pragmatic theory of the *a priori*. According to him, just as the map-maker must provide the principles of map-making in consonance with which he represents some territory on a map, so it is the mind which supplies the categories or principles of interpretation in terms of which it interprets the sensuous content of direct experience. The categories and the relations of entailment between them are thus *a priori*, but place no limitation upon the content of the sensuously given. On the other hand, there are alternative systems of categories, just as there are alternative logics and alternative principles of map-making. But a choice between these alternatives can be made only on the pragmatic ground that some categorial schema may be more convenient than are others for organizing experience with a view to achieving the practical objectives of human beings.

However, so Lewis has argued, every claim to knowledge of objective reality involves an interpretation of what is sensuously presented, and therefore makes a prediction concerning some future consequence of what is presented. To claim, for example, that the round rosy thing in my visual field is an apple, is to assert among many other items that if I were to bite into that thing I would experience a characteristic taste. But since such predictive judgments may be erroneous, Lewis concludes that all empirical knowledge is only probable. He then outlines a conception of probability (it turns out to be akin to **Carnap**'s notion of logical probability) which he believes is relevant to this context of discussion. Lewis also applies the main principles emerging from his general account of knowledge to some outstanding issues in ethics, and claims that judgments about moral values can be as objective as are judgments about matters of fact. (E.N.)

Libertarianism is the thesis which attempts to vindicate the **freedom of the will** and responsibility for action by denying the principle of **determinism** at least in the case of some spheres of human activity. It is not easy to state this thesis in a positive way. If it be said that human actions are uncaused it might seem that they are attributed to pure chance, in which case it would be absurd to attribute responsibility to the agent. If we are to be held responsible for actions it would seem that in some way they must arise out of our character; indeed it is often easy to predict the actions of people whom we know well on the basis of their character, and this is not naturally taken to diminish their responsibility. But if we say that action is determined by character we are not responsible for our inherited character or for the environment by which that character is modified. Thus the libertarian is faced with a double problem; he has to justify rejection of the deterministic thesis and yet when he has rejected it he has no obvious alternative explanation of action which would preserve responsibility. It is in fact customary for libertarians to use such language as "a creative act of will" but it is not clear that such expressions can be used to do more than affirm choice without explaining it. (J.O.U.)

Locke, John (1632-1704), born at Wrington, in Somerset, England, the son of a lawyer of no great distinction. He was sent to Westminster School at the age of fourteen, and after staying there a rather unusually long time he secured a place at Christ Church, Oxford, in 1652. There he was trained in, was influenced by, but heartily disliked, the lifeless and obsolete philosophical orthodoxy of the day. He took the degree of B.A. in 1656, of M.A. in

1658, and in 1659 he was elected to a Senior Studentship in his college – an office supposed to be tenable for life, though Locke was actually dispossessed, on political grounds, in 1684.

In the early years after his election, Locke's main interests appear to have been scientific. Through his friendship with Sir Robert Boyle, who was in Oxford from 1654 to 1668, he was brought into close and practical contact with current work in physics and chemistry, and on his own account he had taken to the study of medicine. In fact he obtained, though with some difficulty, a medical degree from his University, and, in 1674, a faculty to practise medicine. His interest in philosophy, however, was eventually re-awakened by the study of **Descartes**; and Descartes' influence is clearly discernible, among many others, in the vocabulary and the pre-occupations, if not often in the conclusions, of Locke's own philosophical work.

His connection with Lord Ashley, afterwards Earl of Shaftesbury, began in 1666. They first met by chance in Oxford, but by the middle of the following year Locke had become one of Ashley's most esteemed friends and advisers, partly as his physician, but also generally on public affairs. In 1671 Locke composed two short drafts of what was to grow, over the next twenty years, into his *Essay concerning Human Understanding;* but for the present he was deeply engaged in the private and political affairs of his patron, who became Lord Chancellor in 1672. In 1680, after many vicissitudes in the scheming Shaftesbury's fortunes, and several journeys abroad for the sake of his own health, Locke was back in Oxford; but in 1683, after his patron's death in extreme political disfavour, Locke judged it prudent to retire to Holland, in the comparatively calm and liberal atmosphere of which he passed, to the great profit of his writings, the next five years. Henceforward, after the Whig revolution of 1688, he rapidly became a celebrated national figure. His *Essay* and his *Two Treatises of Government* both appeared in 1690; and until 1700, when his health became precarious, he both wrote much on current issues of controversy and held various active political appointments. In that year he brought out a fourth edition of his *Essay*.

Locke's *Essay*, by far his most important work, is a vast, untidy composition, bearing all too clearly in its wanderings and repetitions the signs of having been written piecemeal over a period of many years. Its style is sober and, usually, clear; but Locke was not careful over points of detail, not always consistent with himself, and by no means rigorous in working out the full consequences of his position. Nevertheless, there are many philosophical problems on which his remarks continue to provide at least a valuable starting-point; and the great and immediate celebrity of his work is a sign of, at least, the historical appositeness of its appearance, and perhaps also of the general acceptability of its point of view.

Locke's official concern is with **epistemology**, the theory of knowledge; his purpose is, as he puts it, "to inquire into the origin, certainty, and extent of human knowledge, together with the grounds and degrees of Belief, Opinion, and Assent". However, underlying this official "analytic", clarificatory programme, and greatly influencing its course, is the unsystematic and indeed almost unconscious statement of what can justly be regarded as a metaphysical doctrine. Locke very properly believed that philosophers ought not to proceed in total disregard of the natural sciences; he believed that they ought to take account of the impact of scientific discoveries upon their own beliefs, and on the ordinary opinions of "common sense". But, half unwittingly, he went in fact much further than this. He evidently believed, or even assumed, that the world is really and fundamentally what the physicist says it is, no more and no less – that *the* answer to questions about the nature of the world, is the answer a physicist would provide. He even adapts to this conviction a fragment of the medieval apparatus which he had reluctantly acquired in his student days: the "nominal essence" of a substance, he says, consists merely in those observable qualities which determine the ordinary application of its name; its "*real* essence", on the other hand, consists in the physical structure of its "insensible parts". In this and in many other passages, Locke in effect erects the current physicists' atomic, or "corpuscular", theory of matter into the ultimate metaphysical truth. It was, incidentally, this aspect of Locke's position which was regarded by **Berkeley** as most odious, dangerous, and mistaken; on the other hand, it of course fitted in with, and no doubt also contributed to, that

207

half-unconscious acceptance of the scientific "world-outlook" which has been, since the seventeenth century, so marked a feature of European civilization.

The general picture of the world which Locke thus took for granted may be summarised as follows: the physical universe really consists of indefinitely many material bodies, which are composed of corpuscles, or "insensible particles" – these particles in turn being conceived of as very small bodies. This whole system operates mechanically; Locke sometimes actually refers to ordinary objects as "machines", and he says also that impact, or "impulse", is "the only way which we can conceive bodies operate in". Now besides this system of mechanically interacting material bodies there exist also, Locke believes, *im*material substances, some at least of which are associated, in a manner not clearly understood, with particular material things, namely human bodies. These bodies have certain physical features known as sense-organs; and it is a fact, and in Locke's view a fact not further explicable, that when these sense-organs are stimulated – mechanically of course – the resultant motion "produces in us those different sensations which we have", or "produces in our minds . . . particular *ideas*". In addition to such "ideas of sensation", we acquire further "ideas of reflection" from "the perception of the operations of our minds within us, as it is employed about the ideas it has got". These **ideas** together, Locke holds, supply the whole of the material of consciousness, experience, perception, and thought; all are derived "from experience" (the vague but fundamental tenet of **empiricism**); and "we can have knowledge no farther than we have ideas".

Thus the mind, Locke says, "in all its thoughts and reasonings, hath no other immediate object but its own ideas, which it alone does or can contemplate". This conviction leads – though Locke does not follow it – to serious difficulties both as to perception and as to knowledge. As to perception, it is of course possible, on Locke's principles, to ask whether the "ideas" of which we are said to be aware in our minds do in fact faithfully represent to us the character of their causes, "external" material things. Locke's own answer to this question is that, in part, they do: our ideas of "primary qualities" – "solidity, extension, figure, motion or rest,

and number" – do represent to us qualities that bodies do really possess. Ideas of "secondary" qualities, on the other hand – "as colours, sounds, tastes, etc." – are merely modes in which bodies happen to appear to organisms constituted as we are; there is "in truth nothing in the objects themselves, but powers to produce various sensations in us by their primary qualities, that is, by the bulk, figure, texture, and motion of their insensible parts". In making this distinction Locke gives striking expression to his conviction that the world *really is* nothing but a physical mechanism; it will be observed that the qualities he asserts to be really "in" bodies are precisely those relevant to their mechanical behaviour. However, he seems not to notice the difficulty that, if we can "contemplate" *only* our own ideas, it is at least not apparent how we could ever decide what relations hold between these and "external" bodies; how could we tell that our ideas were faithful representatives in *any* respect, if we can never contemplate that which they represent to us? It was indeed urged by Berkeley that, on Locke's view, we should have no solid ground even for the conviction that any "external" bodies exist; still less, then, is Locke in a position to assert so confidently that those bodies really do have certain qualities, but only appear to have others.

Locke's difficulties as to knowledge are somewhat similar. Defining knowledge as "the perception of the connexion and agreement, or disagreement and repugnancy, of any of our ideas", he is first obliged to add the inconsistent rider that our ideas must be perceived also to "agree with the reality of things", and then to evade the resulting question as to how, on his principles, this latter perception can occur. He sometimes appears to hold that knowledge, *strictly speaking*, can be *only* of the relations between ideas; but even if so, it is not clear how he could consistently admit that even so much as a well-grounded opinion could be achieved as to the relation between ideas and "the reality of things".

It will be observed that these major difficulties in Locke's position derive alike from his basic principle, that we can be actually – "immediately" – aware only of the contents of our own minds. It is in this way that ideas, in his system, become what has been described as an "iron curtain" between

[continued on p. 225

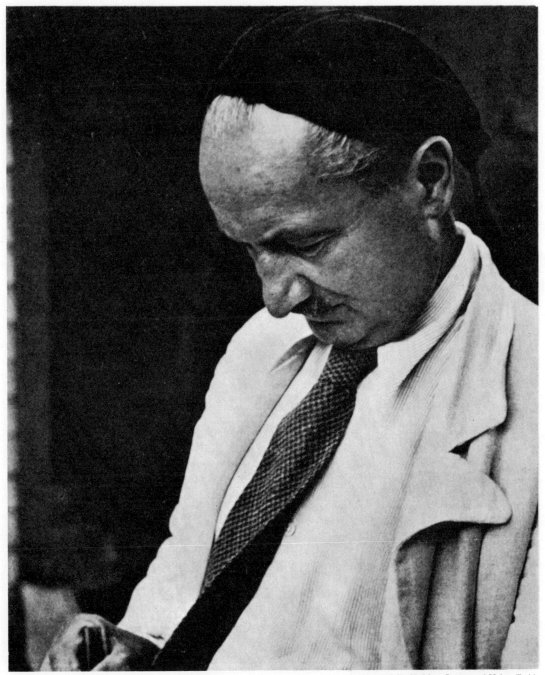

Photo: Felix H. Man, Conzett and Huber, Zurich

PLATE 49. HEIDEGGER, Martin (1889–), photograph.

Tho: Hobbes
Malmesburiensis
Philosophus
Scepticus.
obijt anno

PLATE 50. HOBBES, Thomas (1588–1679), portrait by an unknown artist.
(*National Portrait Gallery, London*)

PLATE 51. HUME, David (1711–1776): portrait by Allan Ramsay (1714–1784).
(*Scottish National Portrait Gallery, Edinburgh*)

PLATE 52. HUSSERL, Edmund (1859–1938), photograph.

PLATE 53. HUTCHESON, Francis (1694–1747), portrait by Allan Ramsay (1714–1784).
(*The University, Glasgow*)

PLATE 54. JAMES, William (1842–1910), self-portrait.

PLATE 55. JASPERS, Karl (1883–), photograph.

PLATE 56. KANT. Immanuel (1724–1804): portrait painted in 1768 by J. W. Becker (1744–1782). The portrait was commissioned by the bookseller Kanter in Königsberg.

PLATE 57. KIERKEGAARD, Sören Aabye (1813–1855), drawing made in about 1840 by his cousin Christian Kierkegaard.

Photo: Exclusive News Agency

PLATE 58. LEIBNIZ, Gottfried Wilhelm (1646–1716), engraving.

Photo: R. L. Jarmain

PLATE 59. LOCKE, John (1632–1704): portrait by Sir Godfrey Kneller (1646–1723). (*Christ Church, Oxford*)

PLATE 60. LUCRETIUS, Titus Lucretius Carus (98–55 B.C.): page from an illuminated manuscript of Book Five of *De Rerum Natura* written on vellum in the fifteenth century. (*British Museum, London*)

Photo: Steam and Sons

PLATE 61. McTAGGART, John Ellis (1866–1925), portrait by Sir William Rothenstein (1872–1945).

PLATE 62.   MARITAIN, Jacques (1882–), photograph taken in 1945.

PLATE 63. MARX, Karl (1818–1883), drawing by N. Zhukov.

Photo: National Portrait Gallery

PLATE 64. MILL, John Stuart (1806–1873), portrait by George Frederick Watts (1817 1904).
(*National Portrait Gallery, London*)

the observer and the world. And it is important to notice that this principle was not, as Locke seems to have supposed, forced on him by his adherence to scientific theory. For the scientific account of perception addresses itself to the question, how perception occurs – the orthodox answer being, in Locke's day, that it occurs by means of the mechanical operation of "insensible particles" upon the sense-organs. Now this is not an answer to the question, what it is that is really perceived. It may be that some occurrence "in the mind" is the last item in the causal transaction between the observer and his environment; but it does not follow that what occurs in his mind is all that he really observes. To suppose that this does follow is to fall into one of the classic misunderstandings of scientific theory – one which, to some extent by the force of Locke's example, has constantly recurred in the history of philosophy.

Locke's political writings were for the most part avowedly directed towards supplying a theoretical justification for the political views of those who wished to overthrow the arbitrary government of the Stuarts, and to replace it by a monarchy of strictly limited powers. Of his *Two Treatises of Government*, the first is a successful refutation of a view that scarcely deserved such extended notice. Locke's target here is the absolutist theory, not, unfortunately, of the powerful **Hobbes**, but of the zealous Royalist Sir Robert Filmer. Filmer had argued that the authority of a king is identical with that of a father over his children, and is derived directly from God's grant of such authority to Adam. Locke gravely points out, first, that a father's authority over his children is not absolute, at least when they become adult; second, that the relation between a king and his subjects is not genuinely analogous with that between a father and his children; and third, that it would in any case be a matter of some difficulty to trace the direct descent of patriarchal authority from Adam to Charles II. It is in the second *Treatise* that Locke states his own case.

In the exposition of his political principles Locke adopted the pseudo-historical convention of the period. He describes, purporting to trace an actual process, societies as emerging from a pristine "state of nature", as a result of a "contract" made among individuals jointly to submit themselves, for the sake of certain advantages, to a ruler or rulers. Now Hobbes had argued that, in such a case, the designated ruler could only be absolute; if any members of society were to be effectively restrained, the ruler must have absolute power over all. Locke argues against this, first, that the ruler's rights are limited, as are those of everyone, by the "law of nature"; and second, that in any case his powers are assigned to him as a trust for the good of the members of society, and hence can properly be taken away again if that trust is broken. Though thus opposed to authoritarianism, Locke was of course in no sense a democrat. He had no uncritical faith in elected assemblies, still less in the populace at large; he did not envisage universal suffrage. He believed that monarchy was certainly the best political arrangement possible, provided that some assembly could hold the monarch to the terms of his trust, and itself be in some degree answerable to the people. Unlike Hobbes, he did not think it essential that any person or persons in society should be a centre of final sovereignty, and able in the last resort to settle all disputes. This, no doubt, was because, unlike Hobbes, he believed in the rational basis of the principles of conduct, and believed also that human beings were rational enough to be trusted, with certain safeguards, to follow those principles. This made it possible for him to rely upon some measure of enlightened co-operation in political affairs.

It may perhaps be said, in summary of the above, that Locke's real achievement was to bring together most of the threads of the "advanced" thinking of his time. In his philosophy he seemed to have escaped from the mazes of minute and insignificant subtlety into which the scholastic tradition had degenerated; to have taken account of the new stirrings of Cartesianism; and above all to have brought philosophy firmly into line with the latest and best in scientific theory. The general picture of the world, against the background of which Locke pursued his epistemological inquiries, was, as has been said, exactly that of the seventeenth – and eighteenth-century physicist; and there is little doubt that Locke's views owed much of their prestige to their declared alliance with the flourishing physical sciences. The fact that those views embodied serious misunderstandings was soon observed by philosophical critics, notably by Berkeley and **Leibniz**; they expressed so exactly, however, the spirit of the age, that they easily survived such criticism. Moreover, there is of course merit enough in Locke's many discussions of particular problems to ensure that he should still be read with close attention, as being at least in the historical mainstream of modern philosophy in the English language.

In his political theory also, unadventurous as it may seem, and artificially presented as it undoubtedly is, Locke was giving clear expression to the enlightened opinion of his day. It is true that his theory is presented as stating the conditions to be satisfied by any good society at any time; but in fact – not surprisingly – its real contribution was to the political thought of his own society and age. The seventeenth century in English politics was a period in which the character and role of kingship, or more generally the character and relations of ruler and subject, were topics of incessant uncertainty, conflict, and debate; that age was, even more than most, an age of transition. It can hardly be said that Locke contributed directly to the comparatively enduring settlement of 1688, but he did express the thought of those who worked for that settlement. In this also he was the embodiment of his age, and in his good sense, sobriety and devotion to reason, he remains a justly admired representative of it.   (G.J.W.)

Plate 59, page 219.

Logic. (1) Logic may be defined as the theory of the conditions of valid inference or, more shortly, as the theory of proof. Some remarks are necessary about this rough definition if it is not to be misleading. Inference is a process by which we pass from a belief in one or more statements (the *premises*) to a belief in a further statement (the *conclusion*) whose truth, if the inference is a good one, is either guaranteed or at least made probable by the truth of the premises. Inference is therefore a mental process and it might be thought that this means that logic is concerned with the processes of thought and so connected in some way with psychology. This is not so. The study of the *conditions* of valid inference does not involve studying any processes of thought. At least in the case of strict deductive proof with which we are chiefly concerned, it is the formal or structural properties of arguments in

which we are interested. What this involves will be made clear below.

In its early stages, logic may be considered as a natural history of arguments. Just as the biologist studies the structure and working of plants and animals and tries to see how different species are related to each other, so the logician studies the structure and working of different types of argument and tries to relate them together systematically. But the logician is interested only in those features of arguments in virtue of which they are admitted to be *valid*. It is clear that we all rely on inference to provide much of our knowledge and that our inferences may be more or less reliable. At any rate, we all distinguish, at a common sense level, between good inferences and bad ones though we may not find it easy to say what we mean by a satisfactory inference, still less to codify the rules which distinguish good inferences from bad. It is one of the tasks of logic to provide a systematic way of making these distinctions.

This is however only one of its tasks. In Greek and medieval times, logicians were interested mainly in the classification and working of arguments. And part of the interest of modern symbolic logicians has been to give a more detailed and complete account than their precedessors had provided of the various kinds of valid arguments and their connexions. An equally important task of logic, at least since the work of **Frege** has been the critical examination of mathematical concepts and methods. As mathematical proofs are a particularly striking and successful kind of proof, their study falls under the general heading of the theory of proof. But this aspect of logic, important as it is, is highly technical and difficult. No further reference will be made to it here where we shall be concerned only with elementary and practical aspects of logic. But it is necessary to remember that modern developments in logic (which now constitute the main body of the science) are almost entirely due to the work of mathematicians. This fact will explain the highly formal character of its methods.

Two main types of inference have interested logicians, *deductive* and *inductive*. Well known examples of deductive inference are the geometry of Euclid or syllogisms such as: (1) If all mammals are warm blooded and all mammals suckle their young, then some warm blooded creatures suckle their young.

That a deductive argument is valid is a guarantee that the conclusion cannot be false if the premises are true. The conclusion follows rigorously from the premises so that it is impossible, without self-contradiction, for anyone to affirm the premises together with the negation of the conclusion. It is part of the task of logic (and a matter of some difficulty) to give a complete and satisfactory account of the conditions under which a statement can be said to be inferable from, deducible from or entailed by others. Many logicians would say that the concepts of proof and valid inference are best restricted to cover only those cases that conform to the rules of deductive logic. However that may be, the process of inductive inference has received a good deal of attention from logicians. A brief account of some of its problems will be given in Section VI below. Sections II to V relate to deductive or formal logic.

II

It has been a common practice of logicians since the time of **Aristotle**, who founded the science, to use symbolic devices for the expression and study of arguments. This is because logicians are not interested in particular arguments or the ordinary linguistic expressions into which they are cast or in the subject matter of arguments. They are interested rather in the *general rules* governing the validity of arguments and therefore in those features of arguments which are relevant to their validity. These features are structural ones, the form or skeleton of an argument which is often blurred or concealed by the way it is expressed in ordinary language. By the study of argument structure, the enormous diversity of reasonings on all sorts of topics and in all sorts of languages can be reduced to standard patterns which can be systematically related together. That the validity of a deductive argument depends upon its structure (or *logical form*) and not upon its subject matter can be seen intuitively in the following examples. (2) and (3) below can be seen on inspection to be valid although they are concerned with different matters:

(2) If no metals are soluble in water and some crystalline substances are metals, then some crystalline substances are not soluble in water.

3) If no Christians are pantheists and some mystics are Christians, then some mystics are not pantheists.

The logical form common to both can be represented thus:

(4) If no A's are B's and some C's are A's, then some C's are not B's.

Here the terms relating to the subject matter of these syllogisms have been replaced by *variables*, that is symbols that do not themselves name or refer to things or properties but can, like pronouns, stand for (and may be replaced by) words or phrases referring to things or properties. They can be looked on as just a convenient way of marking blank spaces in the form of the argument, to be filled in at will with suitable terms. We could (rather less conveniently) write (4) as:

(5) If no · · · are - - - and some * * * are · · · then some * * * are not - - -.

the different ways of filling in the blanks being merely devices for labelling the positions of possible terms. Such labelling is obviously required if the logical form is to be preserved. The use of variables is familiar to most people in the use of x, y and so on in school algebra.

Aristotle introduced the use of variables into logic in his treatment of the syllogism, partly, as it seems, to be able to formulate rules of logic that were universally true. Modern logic uses symbols other than variables, just as mathematics does, and some of these uses will be explained below. Meanwhile, it is worth noting that the use of symbols in formulating logical expressions has important advantages besides the exhibition of logical form and the statement of general rules. Their use brings a clarity and conciseness into logic without which little progress could be made. This can be appreciated if we consider how clumsy and inconvenient it would be to paraphrase in ordinary language even a simple algebraic expression like:

$$(x + y)^2 = (x^2 + 2xy + y^2)$$

The development of logic, like that of mathematics, depends on having available a concise and apt symbolism for its concepts and operations.

III

The basic branch of logic is the logic of propositions or, as it is often called, the propositional calculus. This was not the first part of logic to be developed. Aristotle paid little attention to it. And though Stoic logicians in ancient times and some of the medievals made contributions to this part of logic, its systematic development is the work of G. **Frege**, C. S. **Peirce** and modern logicians. The propositional calculus treats arguments whose basic constituents are propositions. The word "proposition" may be taken here to be synonymous with the phrase "indicative sentence". The defining property of a proposition for this purpose is that it must be either true or false and cannot be both. Thus questions or commands do not qualify as propositions. A typical example of a simple propositional argument is:

(6) If smoking is not a cause of cancer, then statistical correlations are not a reliable sign of causal connexion. But statistical correlations are a reliable sign of causal connexion. Therefore, smoking is a cause of cancer.

Its logical form may be shown by replacing the proposition "smoking is a cause of cancer" by "p" and "statistical correlations are a reliable sign of causal connexion" by "q" and rewriting as follows:

(7) If, if not-p then not-q, and q, then p.

(7) which exhibits the logical form of (6) is an *argument-form* which becomes a concrete argument if the variables "p" and "q" are replaced by particular propositions. And since this form is a valid one, whatever propositions we put for "p" and "q" will yield a valid argument.

In general, propositional arguments can all be conveniently symbolised by putting variables, p, q, r, . . . for the constituent propositions and finding further symbols for the words and phrases that bind the propositions together into their logical form. In (7), these words are "if . . . then . . .", "and" and "not". They are called in logic *propositional connectives* or *logical constants* and their symbolic equivalents in the commonly used notation of Russell and Whitehead's *Principia Mathematica* are:

> not $\sim$
> and .
> if . . . then . . $\supset$

A further commonly occurring constant is:

> or $\mathbf{v}$

(here to be read in the *inclusive* sense of "or", that is, "$p\ \mathbf{v}\ q$" means "either p or q and possibly both are true").

Thus (7) becomes under further translation:

(8) $((\sim p \supset\ \sim q).\ q) \supset p$

Brackets are used here to show the *scope* of the logical constants. For example, (8) read without brackets would be ambiguous and could be understood in a number of different ways. Brackets or other similar devices are necessary to show the binding force of the constants.

All the argument forms of propositional logic can be expressed in symbolic form with the aid of this set of signs.

IV

Two problems arise once we have a method of formalizing propositional arguments:

(i) How do we distinguish the valid argument forms from the invalid?

(ii) How can we prove new valid formulas on the basis of those we already know to be valid?

(i) raises what is called the *decision problem*. At this level of logic, it can be solved easily enough. One simple decision procedure is the method of truth tables. By this method, we first list all the possible combinations of truth and falsity for the constituent propositions of the argument form in question. There will be 2^n of these where n is the number of different propositions. For (8), there are 2^2 or 4 such combinations; p and q both true, p true and q false, p false and q true and p and q both false. We then find the truth value of the whole expression for each of these four cases. This is done by applying the definitions of the logical connectives in terms of truth values. These definitions may be set out in a tabular form as follows:

p	q	$\sim p$	$\sim q$	$p \cdot q$	$p\ \mathbf{v}\ q$	$p \supset q$
T	T	F	F	T	T	T
T	F	F	T	F	T	F
F	T	T	F	F	T	T
F	F	T	T	F	F	T

Applying these rules to (8), we complete the truth-table in four stages, as follows:

Stage 1. We set out the truth-values of the negated and unnegated variables in columns according to the rules:

```
((~ p ⊃ ~ q) . q) ⊃ p
  F     F    T   T
  F     T    F   T
  T     F    T   F
  T     T    F   F
  1     2    3   4
```

Stage 2. We complete the column under the logical constant of narrowest scope according to the rules for "⊃" above:

```
((~ p ⊃ ~ q . q) ⊃ p
  F T F   T   T
  F T T   F   T
  T F F   T   F
  T T T   F   F
  1 5 2   3   4
```

Stage 3. We complete the column under the logical constant of next widest scope, i.e., we join columns 5 and 3 according to the rule for "." :

```
[(~ p ⊃ ~ q) . q)] ⊃ p
  F  T F   TT    T
  F  T T   FF    T
  T  F F   FT    F
  T  T T   FF    F
  1  5 2   6 3   4
```

Stage 4. Lastly, we complete the final column under the logical constant of widest scope joining columns 6 and 4 according to the rules for "⊃":

```
[(~ p ⊃ ~ q) . q] ⊃ q
  F  T F   TT TT
  F  T T   FF TT
  T  F F   FT TF
  T  T T   FF TF
  1  5 2   6 3 7 4
```

It will be seen that the argument form comes out true for all its truth-possibilities. This is the characteristic of a valid formula of the calculus of propositions, an invalid one reducing to F for at least one of its combinations of truth values.

But a decision procedure merely tells us of any argument form taken at random whether or not it is valid. It provides no means of proving new formulas or of relating valid formulas together into a system. A standard method for this is to construct an axiom system in which all the valid formulas of the calculus can be deduced from a small number of formulas (the *axioms*) taken as a starting point. (A very imperfect but well known example of an axiom system is the geometry of Euclid). Deduction consists in operating on the axioms and on the formulas derived from them in accordance with the rules of the system. These rules must specify what symbols may be used and how they may be combined (Rules of Formation) and what manipulation of the axioms and derived formulas is permitted (Rules of Transformation). Axioms may be chosen in any convenient way provided that the set we select is consistent, that is to say, yields only valid formulas. It should also, if possible, be "complete" or be capable of yielding *all* the valid formulas of the system. Proofs must be found that these conditions of consistency and completeness are satisfied. For the calculus of propositions, this can be done without much difficulty.

v

The logic of propositions is only the first level of logic and most arguments cannot be expressed in its symbolism or tested by its methods. For example, even so elementary an argument as (2) above cannot be adequately formalised as an argument form of the propositional calculus. (Most syllogisms can be expressed in a calculus of properties which is an alternative interpretation of the calculus of propositions, presence or absence of a property being treated as analogous to truth or falsity of a proposition. But this cannot be developed into a general logic of predicates.) And a slightly more complex but still elementary example:

(9) If A is larger than B and B is larger than C, then A is larger than C,

introduces still further complications.

An argument in the form of (2), that is (4), is clearly valid but it is not valid in virtue of its *propositional* form. For it is clear that:

(10) (p . q) ⊃ r

is not a valid form of the calculus of propositions. (2) is valid in virtue of the *internal structure* of its constituent propositions. More particularly, it is valid because of the way in which the words "all", "some" and "not" and the descriptive phrases (or *predicates*) "metals", "soluble in water" and "crystalline substances" link the premises with each other and with the conclusion. To formalize such arguments we need, in addition to the symbolic apparatus of the logic of propositions, the following further signs:

(i) variables x, y, z, . . . standing for *individuals*

(ii) signs for *predicates*, F, G, H, . . . These may stand for *monadic* predicates, like "blue", "square", *dyadic* predicates like "larger than", "loves" which need two individuals to complete their occurrence, *triadic* predicates like "between", "lends" and so on.

(iii) quantifiers: (a) the universal quantifier, "(x)", read "for all xs"

(b) the existential quantifier, "(Ex)", read "There is an x such that . . ."

With this additional apparatus, (2) can then be formalised:

(11) $((x) (Fx \supset \sim Gx) . (Ex) (Hx . Fx)) \supset (Ex) (Hx . \sim Gx)$

and (9) can be formalized:

(12) $(x) (y) (z) (Fxy . Fyz) \supset (Fxz)$

We are faced again in the *predicate calculus* with the same two problems that we met in the logic of propositions, the problems of finding a decision procedure and of constructing a satisfactory axiom system. There are axiom systems for the predicate calculus for which proofs of consistency and completeness can be given. But it has been proved (by Professor A. Church) that no general decision procedure is possible for this part of logic although decision methods can be devised for important fragments of it.

These are still comparatively elementary levels of logic and it is easy to find sentences which cannot be formalized by this apparatus. (For example: "There is only one god" or "$2 + 2 = 4$"). These must be taken care of by still further developments of logical technique which we can only mention here.

VI

Reference was made in section I to the study of inductive arguments. The basic importance of such arguments both in common sense reasoning and in natural science makes it necessary for logic to take account of them. Broadly speaking a proof by inductive methods is one which seeks to establish a general statement by considering a sample of the particular cases falling under it. This type of reasoning in which inference proceeds "from the known to the unknown" is called *ampliative* or

problematic induction. (It is much the most important of the various types of induction distinguished by logicians and the only one which will be considered here.) We may conclude, for example, that all green plants form starch in the presence of light on the basis of observations made on a limited number of specimens of a limited number of species. Since we go beyond our evidence in reaching the conclusion, the conclusion may turn out to be false. At any rate, it appears that such conclusions never follow rigorously from their premises. Whereas a deductive argument is either valid or invalid, the conclusion being either completely guaranteed by the premises or not at all, in an inductive argument the evidence will give more or less support for the conclusion but cannot guarantee it completely. Earlier logicians, in particular, J. S. **Mill**, thought that induction could be made to yield certain conclusions with the help of suitable ancillary premises to be provided by philosophical argument. But since the work of W. S. **Jevons** (1874) it has been generally accepted that inductive arguments cannot guarantee certain conclusions.

The mere fact that we tend to make generalizations on the basis of our past experience does not of itself present a problem for logicians. All animals capable of learning show in their behaviour an expectation that future events will resemble past ones and that unobserved instances will resemble those which have been observed. The tendency to generalize is merely a fact of biology. It turns out however that some of our expectations about the future course of nature are justified by events and some are not. And it is clearly a matter of great importance to have procedures for distinguishing in advance expectations and generalizations that are well-founded from those that are not. The main task of inductive logic is therefore the study of the critical checks which are necessary to discipline our proneness to generalize.

Natural science provides us with a large body of well established and closely knit generalizations of various kinds and so offers us a model of inductive reasoning. The influence of this model has been such that the phrase "inductive logic" has come to be synonymous with "the logic of science". And it is interesting to note that the earliest important study of inductive reasoning was made by Francis **Bacon** at a time when the experimental study of nature was beginning to play a significant role in the intellectual life of Europe. There is no doubt that the study of scientific methods and techniques is the surest guide to a correct view of inductive reasoning.

The example of natural science shows that to arrive at justified generalizations about nature is not the only aim of inductive reasoning. A major function of scientific reasoning is *explanation*. And an important part of inductive logic is the analysis of the notion of the explanation of natural phenomena. Indeed the existence of regularities or uniformities in nature has often been established in the course of seeking an explanation of some apparently exceptional observed event. It was in this way, for example, that attempts to explain Galvani's observation of a mysterious contraction in the muscle of a dead frog led to the formulation of laws about the behaviour of electric currents.

The logic of induction has had two main lines of development, the study of devices for *eliminating* irrelevancies and the study of methods for *confirming* hypotheses. The example of natural science shows that both elimination and confirmation are essential to scientific procedure. J. S. Mill's "methods of experimental inquiry", variously criticized and improved by later writers, consist essentially in a technique for eliminating irrelevant factors in phenomena under observation. They are embodied in a practical way in some of the various experimental techniques used in natural science. Indeed, this part of inductive logic may be said to consist in the logical analysis of experimental procedures. Recent developments in the study of experimental design link these matters closely with technical developments in mathematical statistics. So far, however, little work on these lines has been done by logicians. In the same way, study of the logic of confirmation which has in the past been associated with the theory of probability and its applications has now to take account of advances in statistical techniques. It has sometimes been said by logicians even in recent years that there are no precise rules for assessing inductive evidence. This was true only before the development of mathematical statistics which now provides very precise rules for just this purpose. The results of such assessments cannot indeed often be exact but the extent of their inexactness can usually be measured.

VII

Having considered both deductive and inductive methods of inference, we have made a very brief review of the elementary parts of logic. But the question naturally arises: Are all arguments either of the deductive or the inductive sort? If we use the word "argument" in its ordinary sense, the answer is clearly: No. Obviously, there are many fields of dispute such as literary criticism, theology, political theory, much of traditional philosophy and many parts of law where the issue cannot be decided by formalized deductive methods nor yet rendered more or less probable by inductive procedures. And it is clear that many of these arguments, though indecisive, look like rational procedures and are intended to be such, inconclusive as they are. It would seem therefore that logic ought to concern itself with them. Many contemporary philosophers would wish to support this view.

It would certainly be unwise to try to prescribe in advance what the science of logic can or cannot be expected to achieve. Conservative logicians at the end of the eighteenth century thought that logic was a completed science and would no doubt be astounded could they be shown its present state. But it must be emphasized that logic in its present state cannot take account of any argument which is not reducible to the standard forms of deductive logic or exhibited as a confirmable hypothesis. The example of inductive reasoning shows that not all legitimate types of reasoning need be demonstrative in character. But the types of reasoning in question here are those which not only fail to demonstrate but fail even to *support* their conclusions since they have no established and publicly agreed canons of propriety.

Such arguments are therefore "arguments" only in a vague and metaphorically extended sense of the word and cannot even qualify to be considered evidence in favour of their purported conclusions. Whether future developments will extend the province of logic to include the "arguments" of the literary critic, the theologian or the metaphysician, no one can say. But it is clear in the light of the history of logic that the prospects for making such arguments respectable are not promising.

(D.J.O'C.)

Logical Positivism is a name given (by Blumberg and Feigl, 1931) to the philosophical movement emanating from the "**Vienna Circle**". Often applied, in a vaguely opprobrious sense, to analytic philosophy in general, it is best confined to its original purpose, in which usage it is largely synonymous with so-called "logical", "scientific" or "consistent" empiricism.

The Vienna Circle originated in the early nineteen-twenties as an informal discussion group at the University of Vienna, presided over by Moritz **Schlick**. The more prominent members included Rudolf **Carnap**, Otto Neurath, Friedrich **Waismann**, Philipp Frank, Hans Hahn, Herbert Feigl, Victor Kraft, Felix Kaufmann and Kurt Gödel. Other associates, more or less remote in distance, time or opinion, were Hans Reichenbach, Carl Hempel, Karl Menger, Richard von **Mises**, Karl **Popper**, Joergen Joergensen, Charles W. **Morris** and A. J. **Ayer**. A fair number of the original circle were not philosophers by training, but mathematicians, physicists or social scientists, sharing a common interest in the philosophy of science and a common distaste for the academic metaphysics then prevailing in Germany and Central Europe. Historically, their logic was the logic of **Frege** and **Russell**, while their "positivism" owed less to **Comte** than to the "neo-positivism" of **Mach** and Poincaré, Einstein's general relativity, and by way of these, to Karl Pearson, John Stuart **Mill**, the writers of the Enlightenment and the earlier British empiricists (most notably **Hume**). The strongest immediate influence, however, was that of **Wittgenstein**, who though not a member of the circle was acquainted with some of its members, and whose *Tractatus Logico-Philosophicus* (1921) supplied the background to many of its discussions, as also did Schlick's *Allgemeine Erkenntnislehre* (1918–1925), and Carnap's *Logische Aufbau der Welt* (1928).

After some years of comparatively private and unselfconscious existence, the group was formally constituted in 1929 as the Vienna Circle, the name – due to Neurath – being chosen for its agreeable associations with woods, waltzes and other local amenities. A manifesto-cum-bibliography (*Wissenschaftliche Weltauffassung: Der Wiener Kreis*) was issued under the auspices of a cognate body, the "Verein Ernst Mach"; a conference was held at Prague; and the journal *Annalen der Philosophie*, purchased in 1930, rechristened *Erkenntnis*, and edited by Carnap and Reichenbach, enabled the circle to establish and maintain contact with an increasing body of sympathizers in Britain, the United States and Northern Europe. Further conferences, in the name of the "unity of science", were held at Königsberg (1930), Prague (1934), Paris (1935 and 1937), Copenhagen (1936), Cambridge, England (1938) and Cambridge, Mass. (1939). Other enterprises included the publication of several series of books and monographs, the most ambitious of these being Neurath's still uncompleted project for an "International Encyclopaedia of Unified Science".

This enlargement of activities was accompanied by some loss of identity, and by the mid-nineteen-thirties logical positivism was already diffusing into the wider and vaguer movement of logical empiricism. The meetings of the Vienna Circle proper were abruptly terminated, in 1936, by the murder of Schlick; its dissolution soon completed by the pressure of events in Europe, whereby the majority of its members were driven into exile in Britain or the United States. Many have remained, and some have died there; the survivors include active and distinguished figures, such as Carnap and Feigl, but they no longer form a definite group. The residual influence of the movement is probably strongest in the United States, where an Institute for the Unity of Science continues in being. Elsewhere its explicit contentions have ceased to excite much controversy, though many of its ideals are still operative in present-day analytic philosophy.

The logical positivists preached a quasi-scientific agreement among philosophers, and at first were surprisingly close to practising it, at least among themselves. Some technical differences apart, it is therefore possible, if hazardous, to credit them with a collective point of view. The main features of this have already been briefly indicated: a thorough-going empiricism, backed by the resources of modern logic and tempered only by a possibly exaggerated respect for the achievements and capabilities of modern science; an equally thorough-going rejection of metaphysics, on logical grounds, as not merely false or futile, but meaningless; a restriction of philosophy, therefore, to the task of eliminating its own problems, by clarifying the language employed in framing them; and the more constructive aim of analysing and unifying the terminology of the sciences, by reduction to a common denominator in the language of physics.

Empiricism is the doctrine that all knowledge is ultimately derived from experience. As stated by Hume, it involves the psychological claim that all ideas are direct or indirect copies of sense-impressions, from which the conclusion is drawn that knowledge is either of internal relations between ideas (as in mathematics), or else has reference, in the last resort, to the content of sense-impressions ("matter of fact and existence"); all else being committed to the flames as "sophistry and illusion". Following Wittgenstein, logical positivism began by adopting a more logically orientated version of the same view. Experience (it was held) can be resolved into its ultimate constituents, namely the immediate and incorrigible sensory observations of which the observer's world consists. The structure so presented is reflected in language; more precisely, it can be shown by logical analysis that the propositions in which knowledge is expressed are similarly reducible to elementary proportions, corresponding one-to-one with actual or possible items of sense-experience. The relation between complex and elementary propositions is "truth-functional", inasmuch as the truth of a complex proposition depends solely on the truth or falsity of its simple components. It is not a matter of adding anything more, but simply of a greater degree of logical complexity. Nothing is added, because the propositions of logic and mathematics are concerned only to regulate the formal relationships between symbols. In themselves, they say nothing about the world, and have no content; their function is to state equivalences and relations of derivation between other propositions, and although, if true at all, they are necessarily true, this is only because they are "tautological", true by definition, or, in an older terminology, "analytic". From this it follows directly, as Hume saw, that there can be no hope of a deductive metaphysics; for if logic is empty, the manipulation of empirical data cannot be expected to lead beyond experience. It remains to be shown that the propositions of metaphysics are literally without meaning.

Truth, on the above view, is either formal or factual, and consists, in the latter case, either in direct correspondence between elementary proposition and sensory datum, or else, at a more complex level, in an (implicit) correspondence of structure, plus the occurrence of appropriate sense-experiences. A proposition has meaning only if it can, in principle, be true or false. Hence the class of meaningful propositions ; exhaustively divisible into those whose truth-or-falsity can be established on formal grounds (i.e., logic and mathematics), and those in which it is, or could be, factually confirmed by verification (or falsification) through sense-experience. The principle involved is crudely stated in the slogan that "the meaning of a proposition is the method of its verification". A more judicious, if less incisive, formulation would be that a proposition *has* meaning if sense-experience would be sufficient to decide its truth.

The "propositions" of metaphysics and theology are plainly not formal, since they claim to report on matters transcending ordinary experience. Yet metaphysicians have no dispute with ordinary facts, and from this it appears that no empirical evidence could serve to confirm or discredit their conclusions. Since their statements cannot be tested by experience, they are no more factual than formal, and must therefore be reckoned (in this somewhat technical sense) "nonsensical" or "meaningless". Strictly speaking, indeed, they are not propositions at all. The same applies to the "pseudo-propositions" of **epistemology** and **ethics**, so far, that is, as they refer to "things-in-themselves" or "subsistent values", and are not reducible, on the one hand, to factual statements about the psychology, etc., of perceptual or moral judgment, or, on the other, to logical analysis of the language in which these judgments are formulated. One result of such analysis has been the claim that ethical judgments do not state ethical facts, but express the emotions of the speaker, and perhaps incite others to share them. Metaphysical utterances may also be said to do this, and so to convey poetical emotion, or a possible "attitude to life". The objection to them is that they do so under a misleading appearance of imparting information about supersensible fact.

If all formal propositions belong to logic, and all factual propositions, in a broad sense, to the empirical sciences, it is not easy to find a haven for the propositions of philosophy, including, of course, the verification principle itself. Wittgenstein, faced with this difficulty, had been ready to denounce even his own arguments to this end as "nonsense", albeit of an important and elucidatory character. Unwilling to accept such a paradox, logical positivism was prepared to grant the legitimacy of analysis, which thus becomes the whole duty of philosophers. Philosophy is not a theory, but an activity – the logical clarification of the concepts, propositions and theories proper to empirical science. The verification principle was similarly interpreted as a definition, recipe or criterion of meaning, not as an assertion which could be either true or false.

The simple identification of meaning and method of verification has many curious and improbable consequences. The literature of logical positivism is much preoccupied with this problem, and attempts to deal with it have been largely responsible for later divergencies within the school. Briefly, the difficulties are that the principle appears to distort or deny the meaning of many propositions acceptable in science and everyday life; and that its conception of meaning is in any case private, incommunicable and variable from one observer to another.

Historical propositions, for example, are not directly verifiable in terms of events, and have to be interpreted as predictions about what *would* be found on a future inspection of records, etc. The content of such propositions is thus identified with the indirect evidence for their truth. Nor is there any means of distinguishing a future statement of observation from a present one, since their method of verification is the same. General propositions, such as natural laws, etc., are again in principle unverifiable, since no finite series of observations would be sufficient to guarantee them true. Similar difficulties attach to statements about material objects, whose verification in terms of immediate sensory observations would likewise require an infinite series of such experiences to complete it. Sooner than discard them as meaningless, it was declared that propositions of this type were not really propositions at all, but directions for making observations. Alternatively, they were hypotheses, capable of confirmation (or, as some said, falsification) by experience, and to that extent legitimate for the purpose of science. (Generalizations can, of course, be conclusively *falsified* by a single observation, and by that test would rank as genuine pro-

positions; but the refutation of a particular claim, that at least *one* X was Y, would then require an exhaustive enumeration, as before).

In order to avoid these complications, some writers (notably Ayer) proposed to distinguish "strong" and "weak" forms of the verification principle. On the latter view, a proposition does not have to be conclusively verifiable, its meaningfulness being sufficiently warranted if there are sensory observations which would be "relevant" to its truth or falsity. The intention of this formula was to deny meaning to metaphysical propositions, while conceding it to empirical assertions of the kind mentioned above. As has since been recognized, however, it is altogether too lenient in this respect, since no metaphysician need scruple to declare that sense-observations are in some degree relevant to his speculations. Later formulations of the principle have sought to remedy this defect, only to run into other and more technical difficulties; with increasing complexity it has increasingly taken on the appearance of an *ad hoc* device for the exclusion of an already proscribed class of statements, rather than being in itself a reason for excluding them.

Further problems arise from the all-important role allotted to sense-experience in the process of verification. Since such experience is necessarily private to the observer, it would appear that propositions can only have meaning for him if they can be rendered in terms of what would, in principle, be accessible to his immediate experience. Carnap's *Logische Aufbau der Welt* is an elaborate attempt to perform this reconstruction of scientific and empirical discourse from within the confines of an "egocentric" terminology. The **solipsism** involved is "methodological" only, since the aim is to effect a theoretical reduction of concepts and propositions merely, and not of facts. But the doubt remains as to how, on these assumptions, communication is possible, or the data of the sciences intersubjectively verifiable. Logical positivism was much divided on this question. The more orthodox opinion, expounded chiefly by Schlick, was that the "structure" of individual experience *could* be communicated and compared with that of others, though its "content" must remain ineffable, even to the observer himself. The more radical party, headed by Neurath and Carnap, would have none of this lapse into "metaphysics", and preferred to secure the objectivity of science even at the cost of abandoning its supposed sensory basis. Scientific hypotheses, they argued, are tested by referring them, not to private and unverifiable sensations in the observer, but to publicly observable facts. The mental life of the observer is of no interest to science, and allusions thereto are, indeed, strictly without meaning. His acts of *reportage*, bodily states and general behaviour are another matter, however, since they can be publicly checked and recorded; and it is these, or rather the records thereof, that form the "protocols" or elementary data of scientific theory. This thesis, of "physicalism", has a close resemblance to behaviourism, but differs in that it does not explicitly deny the facts of mental life or reduce them to facts of bodily behaviour. Its contention, rather, is that statements in the language of introspective psychology are formally replaceable by statements in the language of physics; and that only in the latter format are they of any use to science. As such, the thesis is certainly questionable, but is not refuted by the traditional arguments for dualism.

A more far-reaching claim of this sort, chiefly associated with Neurath, is that all the sciences depend ultimately on protocols couched in terms of physical objects and processes, and hence that all empirical statements can be expressed in the language of physics. Particular sciences may well have laws of their own – that is an empirical question; but the concepts employed can all be defined in physical terms, which thereby form a *lingua franca* of science. This was the theoretical foundation of Neurath's energetic campaigning for the "unity of science".

The physicalist retreat from empiricism was carried still further, for a time, by Carnap and Neurath, in proposing to dispense with the correspondence theory of **truth**. The parallel between language and fact is an essential, yet suspiciously metaphysical feature of Wittgenstein's theory of meaning, since, on his own showing, the extra-linguistic relationship involved is inexpressible within the resources of language. Schlick's pursuit of "incorrigible", immediately-verifiable protocols equally ends in the unutterable. Yet the problem is easily disposed of. Statements, it was insisted, are comparable only with other statements, not with external fact; and knowledge must accordingly be depicted as a system of mutually supporting statements, to which newcomers are admitted as true if found to be consistent with those already accepted. The belief in a set of "basic" propositions underlying knowledge thereby becomes otiose; the "protocols" required are simply a relevant selection of propositions drawn from the established system; and coherence becomes the test of truth. The difficulty, of course, is to know which system is the right one; for many are possible, and some, at least, must be false, since their internal consistency does not prevent them from being inconsistent one with another. Carnap's declaration of trust in the system underwritten by the protocols of accredited scientists was understandably viewed as an anticlimax, if not a confession of defeat – an impression soon confirmed by his abandonment of this theory and return to a qualified admission that sentences could be "confronted" with facts.

These changes of front are less radical than they seem, particularly when account is taken of Carnap's other views. Much of his energy as a logician has been devoted to "formalizing" the internal structure (or "syntax") of language, very much as Hilbert and his followers have formalized mathematics, by treating its propositions as meaningless marks on paper and discussing the rules for their combination (in a "metalanguage"). Carnap's "logical syntax" embraces the grammatical, or formation rules of language, whereby sentences are formed from its vocabulary, and the logical, or transformation rules, whereby sentences are formally derived from one another. Much importance is attached to a threefold classification of these sentences: syntactical sentences, which make reference to words or other sentences, are said to be in the "formal mode of speech"; empirical or object-sentences are those dealing with things and states of affairs; but there is also a third class, of "pseudo-object sentences", which *seem* to be about things (as when a table is said to *be* a thing), when in fact they really are, or can be translated into, statements about words (namely, that "table" is a thing-word). These are said to be in the "material mode of speech". The main point of these distinctions, in the present context, is to enable it to be argued that most, if not all, of the not hopelessly metaphysical propositions of philosophy, which appear to be alluding, e.g., to the existence or status of abstract entities, such as universals, are actually syntactical assertions about words, misleadingly cast in the material mode of speech. Philosophy is thereby identified with logical syntax, the higher-level discussion of language, and long-standing philosophical controversies, such as that between **idealism** and **materialism**, turn out, when translated into the formal mode, to be disputing a conventional choice between alternative "languages", rather than issues of a transcendental character or importance.

Hence the ready and even nonchalant passage of logical positivism from the phraseology of a quasi-idealist sensationalism to that of a quasi-materialist physicalism; the decision between them being a matter of methodological convenience, not a substantial change of belief. Hence also the urge to eliminate the "semantic" element, of reference to external fact, from the notions of truth and meaning, and to bring the whole compass of language under one syntactical roof. The collapse of this position has since led Carnap to turn his attention to the semantic field itself, but his contributions to that subject scarcely belong to the literature of logical positivism.

If logical positivism has ceased to rank as a fashionable philosophy, the reason is largely that its approach to language now seems unnecessarily rigid and doctrinaire. Its assumptions have turned out too simple, its methods too elaborate, to deal successfully with the informality of "natural" languages, and restriction to the analysis of artificial model-languages has also restricted the interest of the results. Apart from some notable contributions in the relatively technical fields of **induction**, **probability** and the methodology of science, the main legacy of the school has been to concentrate attention on the problem of meaning, and to establish standards of logical rigour and clear, unrhetorical expression, that have since been generally emulated. The attack on metaphysics, if not wholly conclusive, may be said to have damped the ardour, chastened the style and improved the understanding of its remaining devotees. Nor is the influence of the controversy by any means exhausted; ethics and epistemology have both had something to learn from it; and its repercussions are still plainly audible in recent philosophical theology.　(P.L.H.)

Lucretius – Titus Lucretius Carus (98–55 B.C.), Roman poet. The only personal information we have about him is that he was driven insane by a love potion, wrote some books (which are presumably the six books of the philosophical poem *De Rerum Natura*) in sane intervals and committed suicide at the age of forty-four. There is no reason to doubt that this is true. The poem, as well as being one of the greatest literary works in the Latin tongue, is a complete and accurate account of the Epicurean theory of the soul, of sense-perception, of astronomy, of heredity, of thunder, earthquakes, magnetism and indeed all that was most likely to seem to the credulous to be supernaturally caused and therefore a source of religious terror. There is not a systematic treatment of the Epicurean ethical theory, but the orthodox Epicurean view that pleasure is the sole good, that the most worthwhile form of pleasure is the freedom from fear of the mind and that the main reason for the study of nature is the practical one that it will help us to liberate ourselves from superstitious fears of the gods and life in the underworld is presupposed throughout. There is no reason to suppose that there is anything original in Lucretius; he himself makes no such claim; but his poem is an accurate and passionate statement of the Epicurean position. It is also one of the greatest masterpieces of Latin literature.　(J.O.U.)

Plate 60, page 220.

M

Mach, Ernst (1838–1916), Austrian philosopher and physicist, who, after a short period as Professor of Mathematics at Graz became Professor of Physics at Prague (1867–95) and then at Vienna (1895–1901).

Mach's lasting importance is as a philosopher and methodologist of science. His general philosophical position was an extreme positivism; **Kant,** he held, had in his *Critique of Pure Reason* "banished into the realm of shadows the sham ideas of the old metaphysics", but metaphysical notions were still prevalent in the philosophy of science and even within science itself. His main aim was therefore to give an account of the nature of science which should exhibit it free from all metaphysical and non-empirical elements and to reconstruct the basis science of mechanics in accordance with these philosophical requirements. "We know", he said, "only one source which directly reveals scientific facts – our senses"; therefore science must be reconstructed so as to be manifestly an account of sense-given facts. But the objects of our sense are colours, warmths, smells, sounds and the like, not bodies and still less atoms, absolute space, absolute time, absolute motion and other conceptions of Newtonian mechanics; therefore science must in the final analysis be an account of sensations. No other statements can have any scientific significance.

Experience, claimed Mach, provides us only with a manifold of constantly changing and unrelated sensations; we cannot claim to find objectively in the world any basis for our concepts of bodies in motion in space or of laws of nature. "According to our conception, natural laws are a product of our psychological need to feel at home with nature; all concepts transcending sensation are to be justified as helping us to understand, control and predict our environment, and different conceptual systems may be used to this end in different cultures and at different times with equal propriety. "If we wished to ascribe to nature the character of producing like consequences in like circumstances, we would not know how to discover these like circumstances. The natural occurs only once. It is only our schematic ways whose sole and sufficient justification is that they enable us to control and predict our environment. To claim that there are in nature the objective counterparts of this conceptual apparatus is an unjustifiable piece of metaphysics; we may find the concept of a body, for example, useful, but we must not allow ourselves to think that there are bodies in the natural world; we experience only sensations."

But though a set of scientific concepts has but a temporary, pragmatic justification and though scientific laws are tools and not objective statements. Mach does not consider that there is nothing to choose between any two conceptual schemes. A conceptual system is better if it is simple, comprehensive and free from internal contradictions; such a system is more useful to us and more fruitful. But we must not be misled into saying that nature itself is simple, economical and the like; the difference between economical and cumbersome conceptual

systems is one of utility not of truth, for we impose the system and nature is neither a simple nor a complex system itself. We must not however go to the other extreme and regard our choice of scientific laws as purely conventional; the system of concepts must be suited to the facts which it is used to describe and laws of nature are descriptions of the world, even if schematic, and so must be judged true and false by reference to experience. Critics have frequently insisted on the difficulty of reconciling Mach's empiricism with the more *a priori* elements in his view.

In accordance with the view of the nature of science described above, Mach claimed that it was misleading to talk of proof in science. If scientific laws are conceptual tools they cannot be inductively proved from the facts, and the deduction of laws from other laws is of no ultimate significance and may easily give a misleading appearance of rigour to science. The only justification that can be given or need be given for accepting a scientific law is, according to Mach, that it survives testing in use.

Mach was not satisfied with giving this general picture of the nature of science; he considered that contemporary science was to some extent vitiated by not conforming to this picture. In particular he held that science constantly hypostatized the elements in its conceptual system, ascribing to them counterparts in nature for which experience could give no warrant and which were therefore metaphysical. In *The Science of Mechanics* Mach therefore applied his general position to a criticism of the form given to Mechanics by Newton and his successors and attempted to show how the scientific content of mechanics could be retained without appeal to absolute space and time, force and other non-empirical notions. Though largely philosophical in purpose some of the arguments, such as those directed against Newton's alleged proof of absolute motion, have scientific importance – Einstein acknowledged a debt to them.

Mach's influence on the development of **empiricism** on the continent of Europe was very great; the **Vienna Circle** of logical positivists acknowledged him as their basic guide. His pure sensationalism was abandoned quite early in favour of "physicalism", but most of the leading ideas of logical positivism can be traced to him. Though his main works were translated into English at an early date and much read his influence on Anglo-Saxon philosophy has been less noticeable there against the background of a more developed empiricist tradition. (J.O.U.)

McTaggart, John Ellis (1866–1925), Fellow of Trinity College, Cambridge. He was a student and admirer of **Hegel**, an idealist and a systematic metaphysician. In his great work the *Nature of Existence* he sets out, with the aid of two empirical premises to the effect that something exists, to show by rigorous *a priori* argument the general nature of the universe as a whole and of its constituent parts. The conclusion that the universe is a society of minds in close relation to each other is arrived at by a process of argument of great ingenuity and clarity; in the course of this argument occurs the celebrated proof of the unreality of time. In the second part of the work McTaggart attempts to draw by less rigorous methods various conclusions from the results of the first part. The unusual formal simplicity, rigour, lack of rhetoric and candour of this work, combined with unusual audacity of thought and ingenuity, make it of value even to those who are out of sympathy with idealistic metaphysics in general. Among his many uncommon views should be mentioned his belief in the immortality of the soul combined with atheism. *An Examination of McTaggart's Philosophy* by C. D. **Broad** contains a very elaborate critical statement and discussion of McTaggart's position. (J.O.U.)

Plate 61, page 221.

Maimonides or Moses ben Maimon (1135–1204), a Spanish Jew, the most eminent of the medieval Jewish thinkers who attempted to find a synthesis of Greek, especially Aristotelian, philosophy and Jewish monotheistic religion. His writings greatly influenced not only his orthodox co-religionists but such unorthodox philosophers as **Spinoza** and such orthodox Christian philosophers as Thomas **Aquinas**. His most celebrated work is *The Guide of the Perplexed* in which he attempts to reconcile Aristotelian philosophy and the Greek sciences with the literal truth of the Old Testament; in this task he relies greatly on the Arab philosophers **Avicenna**, to whom he is much endebted for his doctrine of immortality, and **Averroes**, from whom

he took the notion of the identity of essence and existence in God. Philosophy and revealed theology are treated by Maimonides as quite different in nature but as complementary. It is the task of philosophy to confirm rationally the truths of religion and to disprove doctrines which seem to contradict revelation. (J.O.U.)

Malebranche, Nicolas (1638–1715), French philosopher. The heterodoxy of **Descartes** divided the professional philosophers of his time into distinct and bitterly opposed factions, who, in the manner of the day, began a busy search for authorities. Those who followed Descartes found their authority in **Augustine** and those who opposed him took Thomas **Aquinas** as master. The most celebrated of the Augustinians was Nicolas Malebranche. Individual things he believed to be limitations of the one material substance and individual minds limitations of an immaterial substance, against which was contrasted the perfect freedom of God, a characteristic doctrine of Augustine. Malebranche provided an **occasionalistic** solution of the problem of the causal interaction of the two substances for he held that there was no capacity for action whatever in finite things – minds or bodies; a doctrine he claimed to be the mark of a Christian philosophy. These considerations, coupled with the problem of how an immaterial mind-substance could perceive material bodies led him to a kind of neo-Platonic metaphysics. We perceive nothing directly, but God implants in our minds the idea of a corporeal world. This world does in fact exist and corresponds to our ideas of it because the ideas of God which are the source of our perceptions are also the archetypes of the world of material things. (R.HAR.)

Marcel, Gabriel (1889–) is a French philosopher and playwright. Marcel's philosophical work has been principally communicated to the world through his diaries, which have appeared in three parts. *Journal Métaphysique*, 1927, *Etre et Avoir*, 1935, and *Présence et Immortalité*, 1959. The Gifford Lectures, which he delivered in Aberdeen in 1949 and 1950 on *The Mystery of Being* represent the nearest he has come to a sustained exposition of his views. While his use of the diary-form makes him an impossible writer to summarize, it gives to his philosophical work a suggestive and exploratory quality which is peculiarly valuable to those patient enough to read it.

Marcel is often characterized as a "Christian Existentialist", and as such contrasted with **Sartre**; but this is a serious misdescription (although Marcel has written a valuable, critical essay on Sartre). The author of a doctoral thesis on Coleridge's philosophical conceptions in their relations with Schelling's philosophy, Marcel's work, as revealed in his diaries, shows him initially a student of the English-speaking idealists, of F. H. **Bradley**, and in particular, of the American, Josiah **Royce**, on whom he wrote in 1917, an interesting book first published in 1945, and of **Bergson**. With Royce he has continued to share a profound sense of the depth of men's attachment to the community to which they belong, and the notion of loyalty as well as that of fidelity is one to which he has repeatedly returned. From Bradley he acquired something of that author's elusive presence to the subjective; and the reader of R. G. **Collingwood**'s pamphlet on *Faith and Reason*, 1929, and his later *Essay on Metaphysics*, 1949, will perhaps learn more from Marcel's diaries than from any other source, of the precise sense and ramifications of Collingwood's distinction between "proposition" and "presupposition". Marcel's diaries also reveal his characteristically French preoccupation with the Cartesian problem of the relation of mind and matter. In his later years he has given serious attention to the implications of parapsychological phenomena, especially telepathy, interpreted as a mode of human communion.

Received into the Catholic Church in 1929, Marcel remained always aloof from the neo-Thomist enthusiasms of **Maritain**. For him Maritain's ontological intuition was chimerical and altogether inadequate as a point of departure for metaphysics. Rather for Marcel metaphysics was the name of a kind of exploration or analysis whereby the process, in which men drew near the secret of their existence, was separated off from all that might masquerade as itself, and was taken hold of in its uniqueness for what it is, and not something else. Thus for all its looseness of texture and diffuseness of exposition, Marcel's thought has a critical and analytical quality, evidenced, for example, in his discussion of the notion of an *argument* for the existence of God, in his laying bare of the precise content of men's hope of immortality, in his contribution to the pervasive debate concerning the nature and possibility of metaphysics, and through his distinction between "problem" and "mystery".

A playwright as well as a philosopher, his plays are of unequal merit, while often helping to give his philosophy that concreteness which he has always craved. But one of the best of them – *Homme de Dieu* – focuses a number of emphases of its author's thought. In it, a French Protestant pastor, who has achieved a real measure of success in his vocation, issuing from his forgiving his wife an infidelity, finds his whole conceit of himself, including his apparent generosity towards his wife, called in question. He becomes utterly suspicious of his every motive, and is plunged into an abyss of self-distrust, and self-accusation. Marcel realizes there an experience of self-knowledge which recalls at once the Socratic injunction to know oneself, and the agonizing anagnorisis achieved by Sophocles' Oedipus. In the end, on the brink of suicide, the pastor is pulled back by the necessity of fulfilling some humdrum, routine duty of his office for a parishioner. Thus Marcel indicates that, on his view, it is only within a community that men can find the courage required to endure the reality of their situation. For all his stress on the dimension of subjectivity, he remains profoundly hostile to any sort of radical individualism, which he would judge false to the subtle actualities of the human situation.

(D.M.M.)

Marcus Aurelius Antoninus (121–180), Roman Emperor, and Stoic. In his latter years he wrote the *Meditations* as a personal spur and refreshment amid the burdens of his lonely office. His Stoicism is rooted in **Epictetus** but he felt with a deeper religious fervour than other Stoics the natural communion of man in the organic unity of the universe. An all-beneficent providence has placed in men a divine control, reason; it is thus in their power, by the sole fulfilment of this moral essence untouched by externals, to make themselves one with the rational purpose of the universe. This is man's active duty to himself as a citizen of God's State. But Marcus, as Emperor of Rome, saw equally important duties to his fellow men, his natural kin. Yet his love of humanity did not blind him to their depravity, and convinced of the transitory nature of temporal affairs, he found no incentive in his Stoic principles to fashion an ideal state, only a sense of urgency to do what he could in the post assigned him by God. The philosopher king remained a moral not a political ideal; Marcus is fundamentally concerned with his own moral character functioning in relation to others; his thoughts turn readily from Rome to the City of God. (I.G.K.)

Maritain, Jacques (1882–), a Frenchman; late in life he was called to Princeton University as a Professor. Originally a follower of **Bergson** he later became one of the best-known modern exponents of **Thomism**; his *Introduction to Philosophy*, 1920, (translated into English, 1933) is orthodox scholasticism in traditional scholastic terms. His best known philosophical work has been *The Degrees of Knowledge* (1932; translation 1938), in which he distinguishes natural scientific knowledge, metaphysical knowledge and mystical knowledge, which he regards as all valid forms of knowledge, complementary to each other. (J.O.U.)

Plate 62, page 222.

Marx, Karl (1818–1883), born at Trier, Germany, died in London. Marx was not primarily a philosopher. His fame rests on a prodigious effort to discover and formulate the laws that govern the behaviour of men in society, and on the creation of a movement designed to transform the lives of men in conformity with these laws. He was a sociologist, economist and active revolutionary into whose purview philosophy entered not as a separate study but as an element in his general theory of man. Nevertheless, he began as a philosopher and his philosophical position, despite considerable gaps and incoherences, can be pieced together from his early writings which were, for the most part, not published in his lifetime. The Marxist philosophy of our own day is an amalgam compounded out of published and unpublished sketches by Marx himself, out of the metaphysical works of his collaborator **Engels**, (who spoke of "the dialectics of materialism") and of the subsequent glosses upon these and the development of them by later commentators. The term, "dialectical materialism", by which the philosophical doctrines at present binding on orthodox communists are known, was invented by the Russian Socialist Georgi Plekhanov.

One of the principal reasons for Marx's lack of interest in philosophy as a specific field of study was doubtless his belief, derived, like much else in his system, from **Hegel**, that ideas could not be profitably studied in isolation, since they were an inseparable part of the activity of individuals and groups, and were literally unintelligible unless seen as an aspect of the total activity of men. Theory must not be viewed as something distinct from practice. The real opinions, motives and concepts of men are embodied in their acts and in their unreflective behaviour as well as their explicit beliefs. Moreover to insulate any one activity, even for the purpose of scientific inspection, and consider it without regard to its place in the historical evolution of the total human activity to which it belongs, is to misunderstand and misinterpret it. Such a tendency to "abstraction" is itself a symptom of a particular delusion, socially and historically conditioned, which Marx undertook to explain and dispel. To understand Marx's philosophical theory it is therefore necessary to grasp his view of what men are and how they come to act as they do.

Like the leading French materialist radicals of the eighteenth century to whom he owed much, Marx believed, in the first place, that man was an object in nature, a three-dimensional lump of flesh, blood, bone etc., to whom the laws of nature discovered by the sciences applied no less fully than to other material objects. Like these materialists, he denied the existence of an immaterial soul, of spiritual substances of any type and therefore of God, and regarded theology and metaphysics as tissues of falsehood, usurping the place of the natural sciences which alone could provide true solutions to all questions of fact, among them the laws governing the evolution of individuals and societies.

For Marx men differed from objects in nature principally because they were able to invent tools. Man was endowed with a unique capacity not only for using but for creating instruments to provide for his basic needs – for food, shelter, clothing, procreation, security and the like. These inventions then altered man's relations to external nature and transformed him and his societies, thereby stimulating him to make further inventions to satisfy the new needs and tastes brought about by the changes which, alone among the animals, he brought about in his own nature and world. For Marx technological capacities are man's fundamental nature: they are responsible for that awareness of the processes of living and conscious direction of them which is called history. Men are made what they are, and differ from each other, not owing to some fixed inner principles of their natures – for there are none such – but by means of the work that they cannot avoid doing if they are to satisfy their needs. Their social organization is determined by the ways in which they labour and create in order to preserve or improve their lives. For the eighteenth century **materialists** the history of mankind was to a large degree the story of avoidable human error, of the follies and illusions which clouded men's minds before scientific method, founded on empirical observation and accurate reasoning, revealed both the right questions to ask and the right ways of seeking for the answers – a long night of ignorance and superstition illuminated by the occasional flashes of genius, which the leaders of men, kings or priests or soldiers, largely exploited for the purpose of keeping mankind in subjection to themselves.

For Marx the story is less simple. Like the fathers of sociology, Hegel and Saint-Simon, he did not believe in timeless truths about individuals or societies, holding universally, any one of which was in principle capable of being discovered by anyone at any time and in any circumstances. He held that any technological advance in human development carried with it its own intellectual and moral horizons. Men's ideas were not born in isolation from the rest of their activities: ideas were – and could not but be – weapons in the pursuit of the goals of men or social groups, exactly as other tools or inventions or ways of behaviour, such as armies, or gunpowder, or agriculture, or slavery, or the feudal system. Man-made technology determines ideas and forms of life, and not the other way about: needs determine ideas, not ideas needs. The windmill created the feudal regime and the spinning wheel the industrial one: this epigram is a characteristically Marxist formulation of the basic factors of human history. The windmill, for Marx, creates a certain type of social organization,

and this in its turn gives rise to opinions and attitudes and ways of life likely to promote, maintain and resist attack upon that particular society – that is to say that particular type of distribution of power and authority among men – whether the men in question realize it or not. For Marx the mental life of men which takes concrete form in moral, philosophical, political, juridical, religious, artistic works and institutions, can be understood only as part of the whole life of society, the goals of which are determined primarily by the techniques which it employs to satisfy its needs. Inventions and discoveries transform the needs – and the forms of life – which gave rise to them, and create new desires, new inventions, new orders of society. But the key to the understanding of social life will always consist in determining the forms taken by the struggle for survival or for the satisfaction of basic wants or for the power which can satisfy these wants in a given time and place. This is the dominant factor in any society; to grasp its character is to be able to explain – and predict – the particular development of ideas, attitudes, moral and social rules, ways of filling hours of leisure, and most important of all, the structure of power and authority in a given society to which the outlook of men necessarily adapts itself. This is a technological theory of the development of social life; it is historical through and through, in that it claims to be able to account for the entire physical and mental life of men by determining their specific place on the single evolutionary path along which all life necessarily moves, which, whether men know this or not, determines all their ideas, wishes, hopes, fears and forms of self-expression at a given stage. Consequently to call anything a timeless truth about men or society must be in principle absurd. For there is nothing timeless in the lives of man: all truths consist in some relationship between men's thoughts and the objects about which they think, and since both objects and thoughts do not stand still but alter with changing historical conditions, things will look different to those who are hemmed in by a given society and press against its walls – in whose interest it is to alter or destroy it – from the way in which it will look and feel to those who are in a high degree of harmony with it, and therefore, either instinctively or consciously, opposed to change. There is, for example, no social or moral truth which will be equally valid for both classes; thoughts, beliefs, moral feelings are for Marx forms of action, and their validity – or truth – will, like that of propaganda, depend upon the interests of the group to which the beholder belongs. All that can be judged objectively is their relative effectiveness. Those elements in a given culture survive which contribute to, and are therefore transmuted and absorbed by its successor – the next stage in the struggle for material progress. Like the **rationalist** philosophers of the seventeenth and eighteenth centuries, Marx believed that human liberty consists in the systematic mastery of whatever resists human needs, whether in external nature or in his own wild and self-destructive passions. Freedom is planned control of available resources; the more rational the method of control, the ampler the resources, the larger the number of persons exercising such control, the greater the freedom.

This vision has obvious affinities with the philosophy of Hegel, which influenced Marx decisively. Like Hegel, Marx believed that history was the key to understanding man and his attributes: for there was a discernible pattern and intelligible goal in the development of human capacities. Certain types of activity, whether intellectual or practical, could not occur until and unless the appropriate faculties had become sufficiently developed; this itself stimulated into existence new faculties and activities, neither possible nor conceivable at an earlier stage. Hence, for Marx, as for Hegel, the tendency to scrutinize theories, philosophies, creeds, in isolation, in order to determine their truth or falsehood, was to be guilty of "vicious abstraction": to leave out the contexts in which alone these thoughts could have occurred or made sense, was to make it impossible to give adequate answers to the questions. Truth and falsehood, depth and shallowness, for Marx necessarily relate to the social worlds to which the ideas in question organically belong. Thus the notion, for example, of individual freedom, or of private property and the ideas connected with them, such as economic justice, individual rights etc. can literally have no meaning in, let us say, certain types of primitive societies where the idea of ownership does not exist; and the doctrines embodying these historically evolving notions cannot, therefore, express timeless truths or eternal values, the very idea of which turns out to be a chimaera. This applies to all concepts save perhaps that of the historical process itself. For Hegel this objective order in human development was part of the growing self-awareness of the Universal Spirit. Marx who rejected the notion of an impalpable reality, translated it into terms of concrete social development. For him reality was the story of the growth of self-mastery and the mastery of nature by human society through technological progress; and, as part of the story, of the development of successive beliefs, outlooks, cultures, attitudes, which, even if at times they acquire a momentum and decisive influence of their own, are but the "reflections" of this material advance in "men's heads", each leaving to its successor only what was effective in it, that is, only that which helped in the creation by men of a life – necessarily social – which would respond effectively to their material needs.

What form did this development take? Hegel had taught that human progress took place in the form of a discontinuous "dialectical" spiral, characterised by sudden leaps from one stage to another. For Hegel every stage in the path historically traversed by human beings, takes the form of a tension between some dominant attitude – embodied in appropriate actions and institutions – and its opposite – something that struggles against it from within; leading to a conflict between opposed principles or forces, into which the human consciousness and human activity inexorably splits itself. It is this continuous duel between conflicting trends at every level of human thought and feeling and behaviour, that is responsible for change and progress. Whenever the mounting tension reaches a critical point, there is a collision, an explosion, humanity (or some section of it – a church or nation, or culture) takes a leap on to a new shelf. The contending forces mutually destroy each other, but generate something new – a novel state of consciousness or form of life, which in its turn struggles with its own inner contradiction towards a new crisis, and so on in an upward spiral, indefinitely. The notion that conflict and crisis are the sole cause of progress is as old as **Heraclitus**, but Marx translated the Hegelian categories of the spirit and his logical apparatus (sometimes with logically absurd consequences) into sociological ones. For him historical development consists of conflict generated in the first place by material needs and technological inventions, and it occurs not in men's minds but in society – between groups of men at war with one another. For Marx a class is a body of persons unified by some objective social interest: an objective interest being the need to achieve or acquire that which renders those who have it more free, that is better able to master their own lives in order to achieve the rational satisfaction of their own needs. For Marx the history of mankind is a history of the struggles of classes. His philosophy of history is the source of all his philosophical beliefs.

Ever since according to him primitive communism, with which (if not in his, then in his collaborator Engels' view) the life of man began on earth, was ended by those technological inventions which placed those who controlled them in a position to extort labour and other forms of service from those who did not, the life of men has been dominated by the efforts of those who have cornered the means of production to preserve their power and exploit other men in their own interests. This takes the form of treating the exploited as cattle – that is, of appropriating the difference of what it costs to keep them active and capable of production, and the value of their products. This Marx calls "Surplus value" out of which all capital is formed, and to secure which the class struggle is waged. In the course of this great coercive hold over one section of society by another, the masters become, willy-nilly, engaged in a social and economic activity aimed at the perpetuation and increase of their power. This very activity cannot but breed technical methods which alter the social structure, and add – however little the masters may have intended this – to the skills and powers of the exploited. These last, trained in their own arts by their masters, in their turn overthrow them, only to be threatened with the same fate themselves when their own exploitation of the class below them duly reaches the (technologically conditioned) stage of crisis, explosion and the "dialectical" leap on to a new level. Ideas are weapons which the master class generates and uses in the course of its struggle for power. The function of such ideas, in virtue of their very origin, must always begin by militating in favour of the dominant class. Those among the exploited who accept these ideas – and the institutions in which they are embodied – uncritically accept something which militates against their own interests and in favour of that of their masters. They may be unaware of this, and accept these ideas and institutions as if they were eternally valid – guaranteed by religion, or metaphysics, or order of nature, which is regarded as eternal, unalterable and just; and so they treat what in fact are products of changing human interests, human skills, human struggle for power, as if they were something ordained by an eternal divinity or some objective standard of truth or goodness or beauty, which is the same for all men, at all times, in all places. Such standards do not exist for Marx. Everything is valid only in its own place and time, and intelligible only in terms of the social structure which requires it. As for the illusion that there exist universal human values, or that institutions created by the masters may be right for, or beneficial to, the oppressed – that is to him a form of "alienation" (another Hegelian category), an inevitable concomitant of the painful progress of mankind.

"Alienation" is a phenomenon which occurs when something created to minister to human needs, acquires an institutional life of its own, an independent existence, and presents itself to men not as an artificial weapon forged by them in pursuit of some need which may, indeed, have vanished long ago, but as an objective entity with power and authority, like some inexorable law of nature or of an all-powerful God. For Marx the moral and religious values of what he calls the capitalist system of his own time, which dominate the whole of society, from the powerful and rich to the humblest and poorest, are precisely such forms of alienation: values and institutions whose sole purpose (although this may have been forgotten) is to prop up the power of a given economically dominant class, have come to be regarded by the whole of a society as being independently valid for all men; with the result that institutions designed to forward the interest of the masters, in their ossified and canonized form destroy the lives not only of the oppressed, but to some degree of the oppressors too. This is no less true of moral and political systems; indeed of everything which, designed as it inevitably must be, to forward the interests of one passing class, unconsciously twists the lives of it victims, so that men are exposed no longer merely to the ravages of uncontrolled nature, but become Frankensteins at the mercy of monsters of their own making – institutions, habits, beliefs, whose origins are forgotten and whose functions are no longer understood. Men treat commodities as if they possessed a life and value of their own; the producer is cut off from the product he creates, and from the tools themselves, which acquire a delusive independent status of their own, often against the interest of their creators.

At the same time merely to grasp and see through this predicament will not conjure it away. The ideas which are to destroy these survivals must themselves, to be effective, like all influential ideas, be part and parcel of a self-liberating and therefore practical revolutionary activity, which cannot occur until the victims have reached a certain stage of social, and, only by this means, intellectual and moral organization. "Alienation", that is, the destruction of human solidarity by the existence of institutions originally designed to promote them, is, according to Marx, inevitable so long as the lives of men are dominated by class war – the inescapable form of the human struggle towards the mastery of nature and of their own irrational passions. Only when the last class in the ladder of classes – the proletariat – the men who possess nothing and are therefore bought and sold as a commodity, triumphs over its oppressors, as in the pattern of history it inevitably will – only then will the historical dialectic reach its final resolution: the class war will cease; and the ideas and institutions which have been used by one set of men against the freedom of another will be replaced by institutions and ideas useful to all mankind.

If everything that matters in human life is conditioned by the class to which a man belongs, and by the position of that class in the class war, then it follows that a man's ideas, however powerful their influence, must be determined by his social and economic status, and not the other way about. Marx therefore calls ideas an element in the superstructure, which is determined by the basic "structure", that is, the economic constitution of a given human group, itself determined by what instruments of production are in use, and who controls them. Such superstructures Marx calls ideologies.

Sometimes he speaks of them as if they were networks of fictions, designed to rationalize – give false but comforting explanation of – facts from which a given class or sub-class recoils instinctively, because they point to its own inevitable destruction at the hands of its opponents – the class which they exploit. Thus he speaks of the ideas of bourgeois society as a conscious or unconscious rationalization of its interests – what it wants the world to be if it is to survive in it – disguised as universal ideals. Since it will, in fact, not survive, these rationalisations are fallacious and delusive. Yet Marx does not, (as Engels does), assert that chemistry, for instance, or mathematics, are invalid because they are bred in, and used by, members of the governing class of their own time. He is prepared to say that social conditions may be unpropitious to the appearance of this or that physical or mathematical discovery or invention, which must wait for the historically appropriate moment (for example, the discovery of the steam engine in ancient Alexandria or the submarine of Leonardo da Vinci); that the progress of science is intimately bound up with the progress of technology and its accompanying social institutions, but not that a given chemical formula or mathematical theorem actually distorts the lives of men who belong to a class opposed to that of its inventors, as historical or ethical or legal ideas certainly appear to him to do. His followers attempted to expose specific scientific theories, as well as certain logical and philosophical doctrines, as class conditioned delusions, or deliberate deceptions, But Marx stopped short of this conclusion. Moreover, he seemed to believe that even though the objective conditions making for their effective application to society had conspicuously not yet been realised, his own doctrines were, nevertheless, relatively free from the inescapable distortion and bias which he denounced so bitterly in the ideas of his opponents.

This ambivalence also characterizes his moral and political ideas. Sometimes he speaks as if moral judgments, and indeed all value judgments, whether explicit, or implicit in behaviour and ways of life, are never anything but open or disguised weapons in the struggle for power or survival. If this is the case, then the ethics of a given class – say the "bourgeoisie" – needs no examination, for it is merely a form of camouflage which will vanish with the inevitable destruction of that which it protects. It follows that no attempt at reaching rational agreement by discussion between self-conscious members of different classes about moral (or for that matter any) issues, can ever be of use, since the members of a class condemned by history have, in principle, been rendered incapable of understanding the world in which they live by a kind of defensive mechanism which creates for them a fool's paradise, and prevents them from perceiving the ruin to which they are inexorably condemned by history.

At other times, however, Marx speaks of values as if they were not distinguishable from facts at all. Mankind is marching in a single direction, class conquers class, until there are no classes left to vanquish, and men are free from the distortion to which the class struggle had condemned them, and can at last take up the task of organising their lives together in a rational manner. No rational being wishes to be frustrated or destroyed. A rational man is one who understands the laws and factors at work in his society. To ask for the impossible is irrational; to believe in it is to be deluded by a Utopia. To say of a course of conduct, therefore, that it is good, or right, is identical with saying that it promotes, rather than hampers, the advance of humanity towards the classless society, which is nothing but reason in action. To say that, although X should, Y will, happen, is ultimately meaningless, for "should" means "justified by reason", and therefore bound to be realized if history is indeed the march of reason in the form of the class war, as Marx supposed. Hence "good", "realistic", "successful", "free", "scientific", "effective", "objective", "socially determined," all coincide in meaning and evil, folly, failure, subjectivism, efforts to swim against the stream of history, are also equivalent expressions. Don Quixote is not merely ridiculous, but wicked: to be finally defeated and to be vicious are identical. Justice, mercy, freedom, universal human values to which non-Marxist socialists appealed, are for him lying figments. The only true appeal is to the movement of history—to that which is in tune with the needs of the class which embodies the most advanced section of mankind. If a given act promotes the interests of this class, it is good and, which is to say the same thing, will succeed; if it hampers it, it is bad, an illusion, likely to lead to failure and the "alienation" of the actor from the marching army whose interests determine all true values.

The view of ideals as mere rationalizing illusions ("ideologies") and the view of ideals as determined by this kind of cosmic utilitarianism, is never fully reconciled, either in the writings of Marx or of his successors. So, too, his political concepts are never wholly clear: thus, he defines the state sometimes as the committee of the ruling class for the purpose of coercing those below, sometimes as leading a distinct life of its own by aiming at something which it cannot, given the logic of history, ever be – namely an impartial arbiter between the classes. In either case the state must disappear: for, with the victory of the proletariat, there will be no one left to coerce. Rational men will not disagree about ends: disagreements will only be technological – about means, capable of being settled by argument between experts without the employment of force. Hence the instrument of coercion – the state – will wither away. Similarly Marx sometimes speaks as if the revolution is as inevitable as the class war – it is an objective, automatic certainty; at other times the overthrow of the social system depends on conscious and timely efforts by the workers and their leaders, which depend on deliberate human choice. Again there are times when Marx speaks as if each stage of the class struggle represents an advance on its predecessor, and is therefore a "better" condition, since it is nearer the ultimate goal – the only sense of "good" he can consistently recognize. Yet he seems to accord independent value to cultural achievements of whatever stage of progress; thus he accords a higher worth to the works of Aeschylus, Dante and Shakespeare than to the art of the bourgeoisie. At other times he speaks as if no value could be attached to any of the stages in the evolutionary ladder until the final cataclysm, when classes and their despotism disappear for ever. Nor have later thinkers succeeded in dispelling these and other obscurities in his moral and political doctrines. (I.B.)

Plate 63, page 223.

Materialism, in its philosophical sense, is the view that all that exists is material or is wholly dependent upon matter for its existence. This view comprises (*a*) the general metaphysical thesis that there is only one fundamental kind of reality and that this is material, and (*b*) the more specific thesis that human beings and other living creatures are not dual beings composed of a material body and an immaterial soul, but are fundamentally bodily in nature.

The best known form of materialism is the speculative **atomism** of **Democritus** and **Epicurus**. This view arises as an attempt to give an account of change in terms of the ultimate elements of the world. According to this theory, the ultimate elements are indivisible and indestructible particles moving about in empty space. The things, animals and people of the natural world are formed by the coalescence of these particles and decay as they disintegrate and form new and different combinations. On this view, thought is a form of sensation and sensation is explained in physical terms as the changes brought about in the atoms composing the soul by atoms radiated from things outside the body and received through the organs of sense. When the body decays or is destroyed, sensation is no longer possible and the soul itself disintegrates into its ultimate atoms. Thus the distinction between soul and body is not a distinction between the immaterial and the material, but between different sorts of material wholes. Materialistic atomism was revived in the seventeenth century and became the creed of such eighteenth century atheists as the Baron d'Holbach. This author's *System of Nature* (1770) is regarded as a classic of materialism, but is not altogether consistent since in it such mental characteristics as sympathies and antipathies are attributed to the ultimate material atoms. Nevertheless d'Holbach defines feeling in physical terms as a way of being moved and of receiving impulses through the body, and he rejects immaterial souls on the ground that they are described only in negative terms and hence remain inaccessible to genuine description and explanation.

With the growth of the physical sciences speculative atomism was adopted as an explanatory principle of physics and chemistry and thus gave rise to scientific materialism. This outlook gained support from the evidences of geology and the theory of organic evolution, from which it appeared that life and mind had developed from inanimate matter. Advances in physiology reinforced this view, since it was claimed that the existence

and scope of mental life depended upon the size and configuration of the brain. The German physiologist Karl Vogt (1817-1895) became notorious for his statement that thought was related to the brain much as bile is related to the liver and urine to the kidneys. (In fact Vogt's utterance was an echo of some phrases from Cabanis' *Relations of the Physical and the Moral in Man* (1802) where it is suggested that the brain may be regarded as digesting impressions or secreting thoughts). But neither Vogt nor his better known contemporary Ludwig Büchner (1824-1899) provided any clearly expressed account of the nature of mind. Thus, although Büchner recognised that thought is not something that could be "secreted", he has little positive to say about it except that it is "caused" by physical processes.

In the twentieth century there have been two main forms of materialism, **dialectical materialism** and physicalism. The former is the official philosophy of the Communist world and is largely based on writings by **Engels** and Lenin. Dialectical materialists describe Vogt and Büchner as "vulgar materialists", but their own view, while it is clear as regards the dependence of mind upon matter, is vague as regards the nature of mind itself. It would seem that dialectical materialists hold that although mind is distinct from matter and irreducible to it, it is nevertheless a secondary form of existence. This view that mind is a new and distinct type of being that has emerged from matter is known as Emergent Materialism.

Physicalism was formulated by some members of the Logical Positivist movement. It rests upon the view that whatever can be meaningfully said must state what is verifiable. The Physicalists argue, however, that there can be no genuine verification of a statement purporting to state the private experiences of one individual. A man may say that he feels a pain, but no one else can test this. What others can do is hear his utterances or see his movements. Nothing can be verified publicly by more than one observer except physical occurrences. From this the Physicalists concluded that the only meaningful statements about minds must refer to bodily behaviour of some sort. It was therefore their view that psychology was, in a broad sense, a part of physics. Whereas some psychologists had advocated Behaviourism as a policy of only admitting those data that could be observed by more than one observer, the Physicalists advocated it on the ground that any other policy would have no meaning.

It is important to notice that materialists do not deny the existence of mind or consciousness, for to do so would itself be an exercise of the very thing it purported to deny. What they deny is that mind or consciousness are characteristics of immaterial souls. The strength of the case for materialism is a result of the obscurities in the notion of a wholly incorporeal existence. This is held to be non-spatial and hence incapable of movement. But then its mode of operation on and with material bodies seems inexplicable. On the other hand to describe sensation in terms of physical movements or chemical changes is obviously to omit what is most characteristic of it. The most acceptable form of materialism appears to be the view that mind is not a thing, whether material or immaterial, but the powers, capacities and functioning of certain sorts of bodies. Yet the critic of materialism is on strong ground in insisting on the gulf between experience on the one hand and physical processes on the other.

(H.B.A.)

Mathematics has always been a subject of great interest to philosophers not only in its own right but also as of crucial importance for the problem of the nature and extent of the knowledge that the human mind can gain through pure reasoning and without recourse to observation or experiment. No doubt we come to grasp such truths as that $2 + 2 = 4$ only in the course of experience, but this is not an experimental truth as it is an experimental truth that if two drops of water are put with two drops of water one small puddle results; if mathematical knowledge is occasioned by experience it is not based on experience; we do not need to send expeditions to Africa to see if $2 + 2 = 4$ holds there also. Thus mathematical knowledge seems to be a case of pure rational knowledge, gained by thinking alone and independent of empirical verification; it is what is technically called **a priori** knowledge. Consequently mathematics appears to be a refutation of the empiricist thesis that all knowledge is based on sense-experience, a counter-example so indisputable that among empiricists only J. S. **Mill** has been so bold as to try to deny it by claiming that mathematical truths are really but well-established empirical generalizations.

But mathematics is a challenge to philosophy in yet another way, for it is a hard problem to discover what mathematics is about; what is the number two, and what is it to add two to two, for two is surely not any physical thing and adding is not putting with as two eggs can be put with two eggs? The problem arises also with regard to geometry, for if the theorem that the internal angles of a triangle are equal to two right angles be understood to refer to triangles drawn on paper it is almost certainly false; what then are the triangles, rectangles, lines and points of which the geometer speaks?

When we consider these difficulties it is not surprising to find that **Plato**, the first great philosopher of mathematics, regarded mathematics as the supreme example of knowledge of a suprasensible world of intelligible entities accessible to the reason alone and that **Russell**, at the beginning of his career, accepted an essentially similar position. Yet such a view is not one which can appeal to a robust common-sense; certainly the empiricist must find an alternative to it. The most famous attempt to find an alternative in the history of philosophy prior to the end of the nineteenth century is that of Kant. For him the problem of mathematics was central; the reader must be referred to the article on **Kant** for an exposition of his views, for they cannot be stated except in the context of his whole position.

At the end of the nineteenth and beginning of the twentieth centuries first **Frege** in Germany and then, independently, Russell in England developed the most famous of modern theories of mathematics which is usually called the Logistic theory. Briefly, their view was that mathematical terms – number, addition and the like – could be defined in purely logical terms and that mathematical theorems could be deduced from purely logical axioms; mathematics was therefore an extension of **logic**. This theory will now be briefly sketched.

In the late nineteenth century the Italian mathematician Peano had succeeded in showing that the arithmetic of finite cardinal numbers could be derived from five primitive propositions or axioms and three undefined terms – *Zero, number* and *successor of*. Now it is clear that mathematics cannot be regarded as continuous with logic unless all the terms of mathematics can be defined in terms of logic; this meant that Russell and Frege, basing their work on that of Peano, had to define *zero, number* and *successor of* in logical terms. This task they claimed to have successfully performed, Frege in *The Foundations of Arithmetic* (1884), a masterpiece of philosophical writing that is neither very long nor very difficult, and Russell in *The Principles of Mathematics* (1903). The key terms Russell used in his definition are *class, belonging to a class* and *similarity*; thus he defined number in general as "the class of classes similar to a given class". We cannot usefully now go into technical detail; the essential point to grasp is that definitions of the basic terms of mathematics were given so that any mathematical proposition could be rewritten so that all reference to numbers vanished and was replaced by reference to classes, membership of classes and relations between classes. No one could deny that the concept of a class belonged to logic.

But if mathematics is to be identified with logic we must not merely be able to reduce the vocabulary of mathematics to that of logic; we must also be able to deduce the five axioms of Peano, or whatever else we take as a set of axioms for mathematics, from purely logical axioms. This gigantic task was undertaken by Frege in his *Grundgesetze der Arithmetik* and by **Whitehead** and Russell in *Principia Mathematica*, the most famous logical work since the *Analytics* of **Aristotle**. Many philosophers would claim that Whitehead and Russel essentially succeeded in this project, and regard the logistical theory of mathematics as established. The whole of mathematics, it is claimed, has been shown to be but an elaboration of a set of trivial logical axioms.

Opponents of the logistical thesis would urge that not all the axioms required are so trivial. Difficulties concerning the axiom of choice and the axiom of reducibility are too technical for short explanation; but we may shortly consider the *axiom of infinity*. Russell's definition of number is such that in effect to speak of the number three is to speak of the class composed of all classes having three members and to speak of the number nine is to speak of the class of classes with nine members and so on; but if there were only eight objects in the universe then the class of classes with nine

members would be empty – it would be a null class – and similarly for all numbers greater than eight; so that all numbers greater than eight would be equal to each other and equal also to zero, which is absurd. To avoid ever getting to a stage in the sequence of finite integers when they would all become equal to zero Russell and Whitehead introduced the axiom of infinity which in effect says that there are an infinite number of objects in the universe; but this is not obviously true and if true is not obviously a logical truth. Whether such difficulties can be surmounted without abandoning the logistic thesis is still an open question.

Of alternative theories, the best known is formalism; as stated by its best known exponent, Hilbert, this is the view that mathematics is to be regarded as an abstract calculus of which the terms, numbers, are given no interpretation beyond being things which satisfy the axioms; the essential of mathematics is self-consistency, which is a purely formal property. Critics of this view claim that mathematical terms must be given more than this purely formal meaning if mathematics is to be applied – as it obviously can be; even within mathematics we need to say such things as that four has two square roots, and here "two" must be given more than a formal meaning.

There is no agreed answer to the central problems of the nature of mathematics; but in spite of disagreement it becomes more and more probable as work progresses that an account of mathematics can be given which while admitting its *a priori* character will not require us to accept a Platonic view involving some rational insight into a world of eternal essences which are the subject of mathematical investigation. (J.O.U.)

Meaning, see Ideas, Logical Positivism, Meinong, Wittgenstein.

Medieval Philosophy. The Middle Ages are significant in the history of thought as the period in which living religious traditions came into full contact with Greek philosophy. This experience was common to Muslims, Jews and Christians, and in each case the chief philosophical factor was the text of **Aristotle**, accompanied by a vague current of **neoplatonism** which affected the interpretation of Aristotle and occasionally showed itself independently. All three religions were faced with a choice between the primacy of theology, the primacy of philosophy, and the possibility of a harmonious synthesis of both. The efforts at synthesis provided the most interesting thinking of the period.

The Muslims came into contact with Greek philosophy as they extended their conquests over Asia Minor towards the gates of Constantinople. **Avicenna** (Ibn Sina, 980–1037) succeeded to his own satisfaction in harmonizing the Koran with a neo-platonic type of doctrine of the emanation of all things from God, worked out in Aristotelian terms. **Averroes** (Ibn Rushd, 1126–1198) was throughout the Middle Ages regarded as the Commentator of Aristotle *par excellence*, but his adherence to the theory of the eternity of matter and his denial of personal immortality were incompatible with orthodox Islam. After his death a theological reaction, already preluded by the notable mystical thinking of Algazel (Al Gazali 1058–1111), put an end to the creative period of Arabic philosophy.

Jewish thinkers living in Muslim countries, especially Spain, underwent similar philosophical influences. Avencebrol (Solomon ibn Gabirol, 1021–1058), the author of *The Source of Life*, was thoroughly neoplatonic in spirit. **Maimonides** (Moses ben Maimon, 1135–1204) wrote *The Guide of the Perplexed*, which is the most remarkable development of Aristotelian philosophy in harmony with Jewish monotheism and had considerable influence on **Aquinas**. A theological reaction also stifled medieval Jewish philosophical speculation.

The earliest period of Christian philosophy in the Middle Ages, from the end of the eighth to the end of the eleventh century, saw a gradual but by no means uninterrupted recovery from the barbarism of the Dark Ages. Philosophy had no independent existence, but philosophical notions persisted through the study of the Fathers, especially of **Augustine**, and through the reading of **Boethius**. The more elementary parts of Aristotelian logic were taught under the name of dialectic among the seven liberal arts, and the remarks of Porphyry in his *Isagoge* directed attention to the question of the relation of universal concepts to fact. The neo-platonic system of **Erigena** in the ninth century was an isolated product of individual genius.

The twelfth century was the period of the recovery of the text of Aristotle, but already the need of more material for study was evident in the new speculative urge of **Anselm** (1033–1109), the originator of the ontological argument. The brilliant speculative mind of **Abelard** (1079–1142) was partly stultified by the lack of material for reflection and criticism. In the course of this century however, and in the earlier part of the next, the writings of Aristotle were made available in Latin translation and came to be understood. It should be borne in mind that for the Middle Ages Aristotle was the leading source of what we should now call science as well as what we should now distinguish as philosophy. The rise of universities, as at Paris and at Oxford, was also a stimulus to systematic study.

The thirteenth century was the most important in medieval philosophy because it was the period of the critical assimilation of Aristotle. The more conservative theologians, who are sometimes described as Augustinian because their leading authority remained Augustine, made use of the new Aristotelian knowledge and method while keeping them in strict subordination to the tradition of Christian theology. Such was **Bonaventura** (1221–1274). **Albert the Great** (1206–1280) gave himself wholeheartedly to the new learning, and his disciple Thomas **Aquinas** (1225–1274) provided the classical medieval synthesis of Aristotelian philosophy and Christian theology. His pacific manner sometimes obscures the fact that he was ready to suggest modifications on either side whenever he thought them desirable. The nearest comparable synthesis is that of John Duns **Scotus** (1266–1308) in the next generation. Meanwhile the more radical Aristotelians, sometimes called Averroists on account of their rather uncritical attachment to the interpretations of the Commentator, arrived at philosophical conclusions which they could not square with theology. **Siger** of Brabant (*c.* 1235–1284) seems simply to have honestly expounded his difficulties, but others come under theological suspicion of substituting philosophical conclusions for doctrines of faith.

While **Aquinas** remains important as having tried to erect a metaphysical philosophy on an empirical basis, that empirical basis needed further analysis. In the fourteenth century the criticism of **William of Ockham** (*c.* 1290–1349) brought philosophy to a more completely empirical starting point. This might have been an invitation to a more critical metaphysic, but there was no great mind to take up the challenge. Medieval philosophy tended to decline into that sterile logic-chopping which a later age, typified by **Hobbes**, was to consider characteristic of the schoolmen. The neo-platonic system of Nicholas of Cusa (1401–1464) was again an individual achievement.

The revival of scholastic philosophy after the Renaissance, associated above all with the name of Francisco Suarez (1548–1617), falls outside the Middle Ages, but it was a revival which failed to last because it did not come to terms with the rise of modern science. For the more recent revival see **Neo-Thomism**. The spirit of medieval philosophy is sometimes summed up in the phrase which speaks of philosophy as the handmaid of theology, but this was a phrase of a conservative theologian, Peter Damiani (1007–1072), who was anxious to curb the pretensions of rational speculation. It is better summarized by **Anselm** when he speaks of faith seeking understanding. The great medieval philosophers, while presupposing the truth of Christianity, sought with candour and persistence for whatever new light could be thrown on their view of the world by what they could recover of Greek philosophy.   (D.J.B.H.)

Meinong, Alexius, (1853–1920), Austrian philosopher, who developed **Brentano**'s intentional psychology, and whose realism greatly influenced **Russell**, **Moore** and other British and American Realists. Meinong spent most of his life as a professor at the University of Graz. His principal works are: *Hume Studies* (1877, 1882); *Psychological-ethical Investigations towards Value-theory* (1894); *On Assumptions* (1902); *On Possibility and Probability* (1915); *On Emotional Presentation* (1917); *Groundwork of the General Theory of Value* (1923). Findlay's *Meinong's Theory of Objects* covers much of the above material for the English reader.

Meinong's Psychology is rooted in that of Brentano: he assumes that directedness-to-objects is the distinguishing property of the mental. The analysis of mental states is, however, complicated by distinguishing two "elements" in them: (a) an "act-element" (which carries no connotation of activity), which represents the *manner* in which a state of mind is directed to its object, and (b) a "content-element" which is defined as that which gives a state of mind its direction to one object rather than another. The difference between thinking of dragons and believing in dragons is a difference in "act", whereas the difference between believing in dragons and believing in ghosts is a difference in content. By the "content-element" Meinong does not mean any mental image or representation, much less the object itself: the use of the term practically only expresses the fact that its being *of* a certain object is intrinsic to, and not adventitious to, a state of mind. Meinong builds on Brentano's threefold classification of states of mind into Presentations, Judgments and Affective-Desiderative attitudes. But he divides Presentations into those involving Passive Perception and those involving *Active Production*, for example, ideas of relations. He also places beside Judgments certain judgment-like attitudes which lack *conviction*, that is, *Assumptions (Annahmen)* and shows how important these are in art, play, pretence, fantasy, hypothesis etc. And he separates the affective and desiderative attitudes which Brentano confounded.

The main interest of Meinong's doctrine does not, however, lie in his Psychology but in his *Gegenstandstheorie* or Object-theory. According to Meinong, if we ask ourselves exactly what our various mental states bring to mind, we shall see that different types of mental state correspond to typically different objects. Thus our various "productive presentations" introduce us to various "objects of higher order" which are founded on the objects of passive perception, for example, a particular grouping or pattern is "objective" and yet is not something that we passively see. Such founded objects are said to Meinong to *subsist (bestehen)* or have subsistence (*Bestand*), and not to *exist*, a use of terms taken over by Moore and Russell. Meinong further held that *what* we judge and *what* we assume is a peculiar complex object called by him an "objective", which involves other objects as its material, and which cannot be said to exist, but which may either be or not be *a fact (tatsächlich)*. "Objectives" are the Russell-Moore "propositions". They are expressed by a complete sentence or a that-clause, for example "that Caesar conquered Gaul", but their status *as* objectives does not depend on their being expressed or thought.

The most famous (or notorious) of Meinong's doctrines is concerned with objects which do not exist or with objectives which are not facts. According to Meinong such objects or objectives are *genuine* objects or objectives, with a make-up which is independent of thought or expression. Their very non-existence or not-being-the-case entails this objective status, for the non-existence of a golden mountain is quite *different* from the non-existence of a round square, and the not-being-the-case of the former existence differs from the not-being-the-case of the latter. But Meinong does *not* hold as Russell for a time did, that non-existent objects *subsist*, or have any sort of being (*Sein*). He only maintains that they have a describable *nature* or *Sosein*, which is unaffected by the circumstance of their existence or non-existence. We may say, for example, that a round square is round and square, but not that there *is* a round square. For Meinong, therefore, "Something is F" is *not* equipollent to "There is an F", as it is for Russell. There are serious difficulties in this position, but it is much subtler and more arguable than the view usually attributed to Meinong. Meinong holds further that objects that cannot be said to exist play an extremely important role in knowledge. Objects *incompletely determined*, for example, a man living next door, and which violate the law of excluded middle, are none the less the means through which the mind refers to objects which exist and are completely determinate. In his theory of Knowledge Meinong makes use of Brentano's concept of self-evidence (*Evidenz*), but he adds to absolute self-evidence the important notion of a surmise-evidence (*Vermutungsevidenz*), with which he justifies sense-perception, memory and induction.

In his theory of Value Meinong holds that feelings may fuse either with the act or content element of our presentations or judgments, yielding *four* types of feeling: (*a*) presentation-act-feelings in which we *sensually* like or dislike something, without caring about its reality or its character; (*b*) presentation-content-feelings (aesthetic feelings), in which we do not care about the reality of something but do care about its character; (*c*) judgment-act-feelings, in which we do care about the reality of something but not about its character (scientific feelings), and (*d*) judgment-content-feelings, or *valuations* proper, in which we care about both the reality and character of something. In Meinong's earlier work no absolute or impersonal values are admitted: so-called absolute values are merely values for an impartial spectator. But in his later work he argues that feelings and desires may be the mental index or "content" corresponding to peculiar objective determinations. Feelings introduce our mind to "dignitatives", for example, beauty, goodness, while desires introduce them to "desideratives", that is to various objective "oughts", that a picture, for instance, *ought* to be rehung. The objects thus introduced *sometimes* really subsist and there can be considerable surmise-evidence that they do so. (J.N.F.)

Metaphysics is that part of philosophy which has the greatest pretensions and is exposed to the greatest suspicions. Having the avowed aim of arriving at profound truths about everything, it is sometimes held to result only in obscure nonsense about nothing. This equivocal status is not the least of those features of metaphysics which require explanation.

It will be well, first, to set out a number of descriptions of the subject given by some who are themselves metaphysicians or critics of metaphysics or both. From these descriptions we may gather a list of characteristics each of which we may expect to find in some examples of metaphysics and some of which we may find in all. The task will then be to explain how these characteristics are related; to decide, if possible, which of them are central; and perhaps to distinguish different kinds of metaphysics.

The name of the subject is the name given by scholars to a treatise of **Aristotle**. Aristotle described the subject of his treatise in a number of different ways which he regarded as equivalent. He called it the study of the first principles of things. He said it was the science of existence in general, or of "being as such", contrasting it in this respect with the various special sciences which each studied only one part or aspect of being. He described it also as the study of "substance", a term which occupies a central position in the work of most of the great metaphysicians who came after him. Substance he declared to be what primarily existed, and was prior to all other things in respect not only of existence, but of explanation and of knowledge as well; that is to say, the explanation of anything else involved the idea of substance; knowledge of anything else involved knowledge of substance; and the existence of everything else depended on the existence of substance. Metaphysics, then, is regarded by Aristotle as a single, comprehensive study of what is fundamental to all existence, all knowledge and all explanation. It will at once be evident that different identifications of substance, i.e. of what has this fundamental character, will yield different systems of metaphysics.

If we set beside Aristotle's account of his subject the words of the English metaphysician, F. H. **Bradley**, we notice a different element in the definition. Bradley says: "We may agree, perhaps, to understand by metaphysics an attempt to know reality as against mere appearance, or the study of first principles or ultimate truths, or again the effort to comprehend the universe, not simply piecemeal or by fragments, but somehow as a whole". The mention of first principles, the contrast with "piecemeal" studies, are Aristotelian. But the emphasis on knowledge of reality *as against mere appearance* is an additional element.

There is a more striking shift of emphasis when we turn to the great critical metaphysicians, **Hume** and **Kant**. Kant emphasized above all the non-empirical character both of the subject-matter and of the method of traditional metaphysics. Its method was **a priori**, the employment of pure reason alone; its subject matter was transcendent. Neither its results nor its methods could be checked by experience. For it argued to conclusions about things which transcended experience, in accordance with principles which experience did not establish. The resulting controversies were endless; and "the battlefield of these endless controversies is called metaphysics". Kant concluded that we should turn the light of reason on reason itself, that we should undertake the critical examination of pure reason in order to determine what it is, and what it is not, capable of. The first, and perhaps the only, task of metaphysics is to determine its own limits. Kant here echoes, in a more specific form, the suggestion of Hume that we should "inquire seriously into the nature of human understanding and show, from an exact analysis of its powers and capacity, that it is by no means fitted for such remote and abstruse subjects". This inquiry Hume describes as "cultivating true metaphysics with some care in order to destroy the false and adulterate".

There is a certain modern account of metaphysics which does not seem at all obviously related to what has gone before. **Wisdom** describes a metaphysical proposition as, characteristically, a sort of illuminating falsehood, a pointed paradox which uses language in a novel way in order to make us aware of differences and similarities which are concealed by our ordinary ways of talking. Again, **Wittgenstein**, compares a metaphysical suggestion to the invention of a new kind of song. The thought common to both is, perhaps, that it is characteristic of the metaphysician to propose for use, or to offer for contemplation, a shift in our ideas, a revision of our concepts, a new way of looking at the world.

The composite picture which these descriptions yield is not a very clear one. (1) Metaphysics is a comprehensive study of what is fundamental in the order of knowledge, explanation and existence; (2) it is the study of reality as opposed to mere appearance; (3) its subject is, or has been, what transcends experience; (4) it is, or ought to be, a study of the intellectual equipment and limitations of human beings; (5) its method is, or has been, *a priori* rather than empirical; (6) it proposes a revision of the set of ideas in terms of which we think about the world, a change in our conceptual scheme, a new way of talking. The list of characteristics is heterogeneous, and may seem scarcely coherent. Before we relate the list to actual examples of metaphysics, perhaps we can trace some general connections between some of its items. For instance, while it might be possible to interpret a metaphysical system as (6) a proposal for conceptual revision, an invitation to look at the world in a new way, the system will not generally be presented by the metaphysician as such a proposal, but rather as (2) a picture of things as they really are instead of as they delusively seem, a description of reality as opposed to appearance. Again, starting with a concern with (1) what is fundamental to existence, the metaphysician may reach the same antithesis (2); for he may express his sense of the importance of what he regards as fundamental by saying that it alone really exists and all else is appearance. If this revised picture of reality is a radical enough revision, the distinction between appearance and reality may have to be drawn between what falls within and what lies outside experience (3); and evidently, if the concern is with what transcends experience, the method must be non-empirical (5). It is obviously less easy to connect (4) the recommendations of Hume and Kant with many of these characteristics; but at least there is an easy connection between the examination of the intellectual equipment of human beings and part of (1), viz. the determination of what is fundamental in the order of knowledge and explanation.

Now to compare this list of characteristics with actual systems of metaphysics. It is certainly true that most of the great metaphysicians have proposed radically revised pictures of the world, bold, comprehensive and often startling; and that most of them have accorded a central place in the picture to some few key concepts, or to some specially favoured type of entities given the title of "substance". It is also true that the choice of key concepts and entities, and the resultant picture of the world, have varied greatly from one metaphysician to another. Sometimes even "substance" has been dethroned, e.g. in favour of "process"; and among candidates for the role of substance the choice has been wide. Besides God, the divine substance, who has a place in most systems, **Descartes** recognized two types of substance, matter and minds; **Berkeley** one only, minds or spirits; **Leibniz** a class of entities (monads) each of which, though non-spatial and non-temporal, was somehow a model of the entire universe. **Spinoza** recognized only one comprehensive substance, God or Nature, infinite and eternal, of which mind and matter were merely two aspects. Kant regarded substance as belonging to the world of our ordinary experience, yet set Reality itself, as totally unknowable, outside that world. Hume, though inclined to deride the whole notion of substance, thought that if anything deserved the title, as being capable of independent existence and fundamental in the order of knowledge, it was particular sense-impressions and the imagination's copies of these. It is inevitable that we should inquire into the reasons for this diversity; and it is impossible not to decide that in part it reflects historical changes in the general intellectual situation as human thought

advances or develops in different particular spheres, and in part individual variations in the interests, attitudes and preferences of different metaphysicians. These interests and preferences, those advances and developments, are dramatised into cosmic *tableaux*, expressed in the form of highly abstract myth, uncontrolled, as Hume and Kant remarked, by a critical examination of the kind of reasoning employed. The point may be illustrated from the case of Descartes. His main interest was in the development of science, and he had very clear ideas about the proper direction for this development. Mathematics, and in particular geometry, seemed to him to provide the model for scientific procedure. He thought that the fundamental method in science was the deductive method of geometry, which he conceived of as rigorous reasoning from self-evident axioms; and he thought that the subject-matter of all the physical sciences must be fundamentally the same as the subject-matter of geometry, and hence that, from the point of view of science in general, the only important characteristics of things in the physical world were the spatial characteristics which geometry studies. It is not the holding of these beliefs which makes Descartes a metaphysician. It is rather the dramatic expression they receive in his doctrines about the essential nature of knowledge and existence. He offers a picture of a world in which the only realities, apart from God, are purely material substance with none but spatial characteristics, and pure thinking substances whose being essentially consists in the ability to grasp self-evident axioms and their deductive consequences. Knowledge is nothing but the results of exercising this ability. Whatever else ordinarily passes for reality or knowledge is downgraded, given an inferior status. Such a drastic revision of our ordinary scheme of things naturally creates problems, calls for further explanations and adjustments. Thus Descartes teaches, on the one hand, that it is only through confidence in God's veracity that we can have reason to believe in the existence of material things; and on the other that it is only through our wilfulness that we ever believe what is false.

Again and again in the history of the subject such a preoccupation with some advance, achieved or hoped for, in a particular branch of thought, has found expression in some similarly bold new vision of the nature of the world . Not only mathematics and the physical sciences, but history, biology and formal logic as well, have all inspired metaphysics. Developments in the study of history underlay the Hegelian system; and the late metaphysics of Logical Atomism can be seen, in part, as the expression of a profound satisfaction with advances in formal logic at the end of the nineteenth and the beginning of the twentieth centuries. Nor is it only a concern with theoretical disciplines that supplies the drive to metaphysical revision. Religions and moralities too may seek and find metaphysical support. Elements of diverse kinds may be fused in a single system, such as that of Spinoza, which expresses an attitude at once thoroughly scientific and profoundly moral.

The critical metaphysicians, Hume and Kant, demand separate and special attention. Kant pointed out that the metaphysician necessarily employed concepts which have an application in our ordinary experience or at least are derived from concepts so employed; but that the metaphysician's own use of these concepts characteristically ignored or went beyond the empirical conditions of their employment. Any such extension of the use of these concepts, so far from extending our knowledge beyond the limits of experience, was quite illegitimate, and the results were empty or senseless. Kant maintained that the positive task of metaphysics was to show how the most general and fundamental concepts we employed were interrelated to form an organizing framework of ideas and principles, a framework which supplied the necessary conditions of the kinds of knowledge and experience which we in fact possessed. The negative task was to show both how inevitable was the metaphysical temptation to use these general concepts in ways which disregarded the empirical conditions of their employment, and how inevitably empty were the results of succumbing to this temptation. At this point we find in Kant a residue of that very kind of metaphysics which he declared to be impossible. For the framework of ideas which it was the positive task of metaphysics to elucidate was thought of by Kant as the framework of things only as they appeared to beings with our cognitive constitution, not of things as they were in themselves. What was ultimately real was in principle unknowable; and this unknowable reality acquired a more positive

role when Kant was concerned to secure metaphysical foundations for morality: it appeared as the authoritative source of morality's commands. Hume, Kant's predecessor in time, shared with Kant the conviction that significant discourse was limited by the conditions of actual experience, and that much traditional metaphysics trespassed beyond those limits. But Hume inherited from **Locke** and Berkeley a curiously limited conception of what experience actually supplied us with. The real elements of experience, he held, were separate and fleeting impressions of sense and feeling. Our ordinary picture of a world of continuously existing and interacting material things and persons could not be rationally justified on this basis; but it could be explained, as the product of the associative mechanism of the imagination set in motion by the ultimate elements of feeling and sense.

It will be obvious that both Hume and Kant, while criticizing in principle the revisionary schemes of other metaphysicians, were to some extent metaphysically revisionary themselves. Kant's doctrine that only what is unknowable is ultimately real, and Hume's doctrine that it is imagination which makes us believe in the existence of material bodies, are alike in doing violence to the concepts of imagination, reality and knowledge which we actually employ. Nevertheless, in virtue both of the positive and of the critical aspects of their work, these two great philosophers exercised an influence on metaphysics which may well appear decisive. This is particularly true of Kant. Both philosophers concerned themselves with the general structure of our thought about the world. Both wrote, much of the time, in an idiom more suggestive of empirical psychology than of an investigation into concepts and the conditions of their use. But behind the psychological idiom of Kant we can find the outline of a far more coherent account of the general structure of our conceptual scheme than we can find either in Hume or in those later empiricists who wrote in the spirit of Hume while discarding much of his psychology. The criticisms made by both Hume and Kant of the metaphysical employment of concepts without regard to the conditions of their empirical use still stand. But on the critical as on the positive side Kant's contribution is ultimately more effective than Hume's. For though these criticisms were later expressed most vociferously and in their most extreme form by the school of Logical Positivists who were heirs of Hume rather than of Kant, the effectiveness of this expression suffered from the weaknesses and limitations of the associated empiricist metaphysics.

Over much of the philosophical world in this century the doctrine of the impossibility of metaphysics became almost an orthodoxy, and the adjective "metaphysical" a pejorative word. Some of the reasons for this devaluation should now be clear. The conceptual distortions and final incoherence of systems, the abstract myths parading as Reality, the grandiose claims and the conflicting results – these seemed to many the essence of the metaphysical enterprise and sufficient reason for condemning it; and the extravagances of metaphysics were by some of them contrasted with the sobrieties of a method of philosophical analysis which aims to make clear the actual functioning of our concepts in use. But though the repudiation of metaphysics was natural, it does not follow that it was justified. Metaphysical excess might be no more essential to metaphysics than tyranny to government. To show that the repudiation was not justified calls for some reordering of the facts which we have already before us.

When Aristotle described the subject of his treatise, he distinguished it sharply from the special or departmental disciplines. But the distinction was not drawn in a wholly clear way. It was implied that the "science of being as such" was more general and comprehensive than the special sciences. Clearly this most general science was not to be merely a *compendium* of the others; yet when the special sciences are put on one side, what subject for study is left? It is difficult to avoid the impression that the projected science of being, if such a study exists at all, must have some curiously elusive yet very fundamental subject-matter of its own, somehow lying behind those aspects of reality which are studied in departmental disciplines. Behind these aspects of reality is Reality itself, "being as such", the subject-matter of metaphysics. Already the tendency of metaphysics towards the transcendent becomes intelligible. In default of a further clarification of the nature of the enterprise, it will inevitably appear as the gropings of pure reason in a mysterious realm to which ordinary access is impossible. Another

consequence may appear equally inevitable. For in order to describe this realm, the only materials that we have, or can make, available must be taken, or fashioned, from the conceptual equipment which we use for the less rarefied purposes of daily discourse or departmental studies. If we are to put such concepts to work to describe the transcendental realm, we must cut them off from the conditions of their ordinary employment and deprive them of their ordinary force; yet they must *seem* to retain something of their ordinary force, or we shall not even seem to be saying anything significant. So transcendental metaphysics proceeds by way of conceptual distortion to a termination in uncashable metaphor.

This is a kind of caricature of the rake's progress of metaphysics. Its purpose is to enable us to see more clearly the significance of the Kantian revolution. When Kant denied that knowledge of reality was possible, he was in effect denying that metaphysics had, or could have, any such peculiar subject-matter of its own. But he did not thereby deprive the metaphysician of employment. The positive task of the metaphysician was not to think about a special world, but to think about the structure of our thinking about the ordinary world; not to acquire knowledge of objects beyond our experience, but to clarify the nature and conditions of knowledge of objects within our experience. So metaphysics is indeed a more general and comprehensive study than any special science; for it aims to make clear the fundamental general structure of all our ordinary and scientific thinking. Its method is indeed non-empirical; for it inquires into the conceptual structure which is presupposed by all our empirical inquiries.

This conception of metaphysics may appear to differ from the Aristotelian conception. There is no mention of "being as such", of what is prior in the order of existence. But this difference is apparent only. If we investigate the fundamental categories of human thought, the connections between them, and the dependencies of one on another, we are thereby committed to inquiring into the relations between the various types of entity, or being, which we admit into our conceptual scheme. The idea of ontological priority is not discarded, but simply given a clearer meaning. It is the idea of a transcendent reality as a possible subject of inquiry which is abandoned. The Aristotelian conception is not rejected, but rescued from perversion.

It might be said that the aims of metaphysics, so understood, are no different from those of philosophical **analysis** in general, which also proposes to investigate the actual functioning of our concepts; or that, at most, the difference will simply be one of scope and generality. But this is an important difference, which entails another: a difference in method. When the analytical philosopher proposes to investigate some particular concept – say, that of memory, or cause, or truth – he finds his surest method of procedure to lie in a careful examination of the actual use of the verbs, adjectives and nouns by means of which we introduce this concept into our discourse. Such an examination has great power to reveal the complexities of his concept, the multifariousness of the phenomena which it covers, and, up to a point, its connections with other concepts. The results arrived at in this way may be perfectly adequate for the purposes of a regional analysis, which legitimately takes much for granted; and they provide an indispensable corrective to the conceptual distortions to which metaphysics is prone. But this method of illuminating the workings of a particular part of our conceptual apparatus is apt to assume, rather than to reveal, the fundamental structure of the apparatus as a whole; and it is precisely this general structure which the metaphysician wishes to understand. The connections and dependencies which he has to make explicit lie below the surface of the linguistic phenomena. They do not lie so far below the surface that they cannot be detected and recognized. But their detection and recognition require a wider-ranging vision than is compatible with attention to the surface phenomena alone.

We have seen that many traditional metaphysicians have not been content to describe the actual structure of our thought about the world in its most general and fundamental aspects. Rather they have wished to substitute a revised structure, which somehow symbolized their own intellectual preoccupations and attitudes. It is almost as if, in order to record their sense of the importance of a certain change of direction in thought, they had to exaggerate the extent and implications of the change; as if our *whole* view of the world had to be at least temporarily altered, in order to accommodate a new vision of one of its aspects. Perhaps indeed there was a certain historical necessity about this; and it is not surprising that to some historically-minded critics this side of metaphysics has seemed to be the only side. We have seen reason to think that this is a mistake. The most fundamental concepts and categories of human thinking are not those which undergo drastic changes with advances in the sciences or alterations in social living; and the investigation of this central core of thought provides metaphysics with a constant subject-matter. But it would be a mistake on the opposite side to suppose that the central tasks of metaphysics can be performed once for all, and the subject regarded as closed. For even though its central subject-matter does not significantly change, the idiom, the needs, and the emphases of metaphysical elucidation vary from age to age and even from one philosopher to another. Old truths have to be restated in a new idiom; different parts of the picture call, from time to time, for more or less emphatic illumination. Metaphysical elucidation can reach no final and complete form. But that does not mean it is impossible. Some projections of the picture involve less distortion than others; and even those projections which involve the grossest distortions of the picture as a whole may nevertheless represent a part of it with a peculiar clarity. (P.F.S.)

Mill, James (1773–1836). Born in Aberdeenshire, Scotland, Mill studied for the ministry at Edinburgh University but religious doubts led him to give up this career and at twenty-nine he went to London. In 1808 Mill met **Bentham**, converted him to Radicalism and became his chief lieutenant. In 1819 he entered the East India Company and lived to become its chief administrator. A remarkable account of his character and opinions is given in the *Autobiography* of his eldest son, John Stuart **Mill**.

Metaphysics. In his *Analysis of the Phenomena of the Human Mind* (1829) Mill tries to show that all knowledge is reducible to feelings (sensations, ideas, pleasures, pains) occurring in certain orders – some successive, some simultaneous. Feelings tend to become associated in regular patterns if they occur *together*. To explain a notion is always to analyse it into ideas that have become associated. The doctrine is reductionist, atomistic, and did not succeed in the author's intention which was to make the human mind as plain as the road from Charing Cross to St Paul's.

Morality. The doctrine of association encouraged Mill to think that almost anything could be accomplished by education; and that men (who necessarily seek only their own happiness) could be so constituted by education as to find their own happiness in devotion to the common good (*Encyclopedia Britannica*, 1820, "Education"). The test of right actions lies in their consequences: it is a universalistic test – the right is that which promotes general happiness, not the happiness of the agent. Moral praise and blame, reward and punishment constitute a social device for the artificial encouragement of actions useful to society and discouragement of those that are harmful to society.

Politics. Mill rejects all notions of "natural rights" and makes an attempt (perhaps the first ever made) to defend representative institutions on purely utilitarian lines (*Encyclopedia Britannica*, 1820: "Government"). Men need government in order to defend their lives and interests from other men: but any government is made up of *men* – who will have a private interest in plundering and enslaving their subjects. A power is therefore needed to act as a check upon the "sinister interests" of government: and the only effective way of setting up such a power is by choosing representatives. But how can we ensure an identity of interest between community and representatives? By frequent elections. Mill advocates not a representative government but a representative anti-government. Who is to choose the representatives? Mill excludes women and children and younger men on the ground that they have a *natural* identity of interest with their husbands and fathers. Mill contemplates other exclusions and finally advocates votes for the middle class since they are the real leaders of society and have been throughout the whole history of the world. Mill had unbounded confidence in representative institutions accompanied by complete freedom of discussion.

Certain critics, for example Halévy, are inclined to rank James Mill, as a thinker, above John Stuart Mill. However it can hardly be denied that James Mill is the perfect doctrinaire in all that he attempted. This weakness shows most in his treatment of government. The argument proceeds from assumptions without historical backing: only one reason is given for each step taken – one is supposed to be decisive and one is therefore enough. Macaulay's attack (*Edinburgh Review*, 1829) fastens upon this deductive method.   (K.B.)

Mill, John Stuart (1806–1873), born in London. J. S. Mill was educated at home by his father James **Mill**. At eighteen he entered the East India Company's service, where his father was also employed, and remained with the Company until its extinction in 1858, at which time he had become its chief London administrator. At the age of twenty, Mill suffered a "mental crisis" followed by a long period of depression and disillusion, during which he found consolation in reading Wordsworth's poetry. On his recovery he reacted for a time against the intellectual and moral opinions of his father and his circle, and came under the influence of Coleridge, Carlyle and John Sterling. In 1831 he met Harriet Taylor and the two formed a passionate attachment which gradually came to be tolerated by her husband but not by most of their friends. It seems that on the whole Mrs Taylor's influence helped to free Mill from his Coleridgean inclinations.

Mill's first original work consisted of essays on economic questions (written 1830–34, published 1844). At about the same time he began work on the philosophy of logic and devoted to it the "spare time" of his most fruitful years. *A System of Logic, Ratiocinative and Inductive* was published in 1843 and made Mill a famous man. The *Political Economy* appeared only two years later. In 1851 John Taylor died, and thereafter the two friends married and began work together on a number of essays and on the *Autobiography*. They both worked in the shadow of death, and were attempting to complete a bare outline of their views – "a sort of mental pemmican, which thinkers, when there are any after us, may nourish themselves with, and then dilute for other people". The partnership came to an end in 1858, when Harriet died at Avignon; *The Essay on Liberty* (a "joint work") was published in the following year. Mill now retired, living partly at Blackheath and partly at Avignon and carried out many of the projects he had discussed with his wife. He became a well-known public figure, a champion of women's rights, of the working-classes and of electoral reform. In 1865 he was elected M. P. for Westminster and was then able to propose votes for women as an amendment to Disraeli's Franchise Bill. He died at Avignon at the age of sixty-seven, the outstanding English radical of his day and a main link between liberal thought in England and the rest of the world.

At the age of fifteen, Mill gave his enthusiastic assent to the ethical system of **Bentham**: admiring, even at that age, Bentham's total rejection of intuitive modes of reasoning in morals. Bentham introduced scientific methods into the discussion of moral questions. This position Mill never consciously abandoned: and in his logical inquiries, and in his later reflexions on Justice and Liberty, he attempted to show that the ultimate test must be an experimental and **utilitarian** one. Mill also agreed. with Bentham in holding that all our conduct is determined: and that all our deliberate acts are motivated by the belief that a certain line of conduct will lead to our own greatest good. Our decisions rest upon our characters and beliefs, as well as on our situations. Mill held that we can to a degree correct our beliefs and improve our characters – if we *want* to do so. The desire to have or to know may be efficacious: and so also may the desire *to be*. This (Mill says) embodies what is really inspiriting and ennobling in the (incorrect) doctrine of **free will**. Mill at least makes clear that moral discussion has point: it may help to decide a man what sort of person he would like to be.

The fundamental principles of Mill's ethics are (1) That pleasure alone is good or desirable in itself; (2) That actions are right in proportion as they tend to promote the happiness of all concerned, wrong as they tend to promote unhappiness; and happiness means pleasure and the absence of pain (*Utilitarianism* Ch. 1).

(1) "Happiness is desirable, and the only thing desirable, as an end; all other things being desirable as means to that end." Mill demurs about giving a proof of this thesis but tries to connect pleasure or happiness with being the object of a desire; and being good in itself. We can see that each man desires his own happiness; that, of course, does not imply that happiness is desirable or good. But Mill was neither the first nor the last to hold that there must be some intimate connexion between being

good and being desired. Perhaps his view is that we learn to call things *good* and *bad*, *desirable* or *undesirable*, through our experience of desiring and getting or not getting what we desire. Some of the things we have desired turn out to be worth while: others not. Is happiness one of the things men desire – and one which turns out to be *good*? Mill says that to desire a thing is to think of it as pleasant – to hold that it brings or would bring pleasure. This evidently widens the meaning of "pleasure": the word becomes a technical term for whatever anyone desires for its own sake: and certainly not all these things can be called "desirable" or "good". In fact Mill is not at all prepared to treat all objects of desire alike: he makes many distinctions and conveys his own definite preferences. Some desires are primitive: others the result of experience, training, self-discipline and special associations. A hungry man (whatever his character) desires food: a miser desires to have money and a spendthrift to spend it. The pleasures of the miser, the spendthrift and the virtuous man are educated pleasures. Mill points to the qualitative differences: the *kinds* of pleasure. These are readily recognizable: while quantitative differences (Bentham's "circumstances") are often difficult or impossible to assess. Mill may have supposed that qualitative differences are ultimately reducible to quantitative ones: but he is at no pains to say so. In effect he says that we ought in all our decisions to give preference to the "higher" pleasures, which include the social and generous pleasures and those of the cultivated feelings and intellect.

(2) "Actions are right in proportion as they tend to promote happiness." The happiness to be considered is not that of the agent, but that of all concerned in the action. Mill is not often critisized for holding this universalist view; but for having pretended to prove that the general happiness must be something which "the aggregate of all persons" in fact regard as desirable or good. There are two points to be distinguished: (*a*) What is the nature of a right action? (*b*) Who will be moved to do it? On the first question, Mill may be taken either as offering an analysis of the accepted definition of "right action" or as putting forward a point of view. Mill like Bentham, was not always very clear which he was doing, but in the main he seems to be doing the second – and seems to recognize clearly that

other views are meaningful though mistaken. On the second question Mill argues that men have natural social impulses which lead them to consider the good of all concerned in an action: these may be strengthened by training and experience:

Some actions will in fact bring happiness in the long run, others will not. In effect Mill argues that we ought to choose the action which (at the time of decision) *looks most likely* to produce most happiness: it is the only possible practical version of Utilitarianism. But even this seems to ask more than is reasonable: how can one always stop to calculate? Mill answers very definitely that one should usually be guided by those *general rules* which have been formulated as a result of the long experience of men in society: "the beliefs that have come down are the rules of morality for the multitude, and for the philosopher, until he has succeeded in finding better". The philosopher is entitled to test traditional rules; to ask whether the general observance of a rule makes for greater happiness than the general observance of any alternative rule would do, or than leaving the matter outside the scope of rules. And in applying such a test, preference must be given to the "higher" kinds of pleasure. The place assigned to rules is a marked departure from the view of Bentham: Mill actually defines morality as "the rules and precepts for human conduct". Only where there is a clash of duties (where one and the same action is required by one rule and forbidden by another) should one choose simply by reference to the probable consequence of the action individually considered. Mill seems to commit himself to the view that in all other cases the right act is the one which is in accordance with a valid rule. A rule is valid only because it passes the utilitarian test: and it is difficult to believe that Mill meant us to follow such a rule where it is *known* that on this occasion it will bring more harm than good. (Perhaps this is meant to be covered by his remarks on conflicting duties.) The rules of justice – which forbid us to harm, trespass upon, or interfere with the liberty of, another – are to be observed, no matter what advantage might *seem* to come from setting them aside: for a strict and reliable adherence to these rules is itself of the greatest utility to everyone.

However, Mill is prepared to restrict the sphere of duty. Duty is something which a man may be compelled to do: and should not be widened beyond

necessity. These are many good, noble and generous deeds which a man is rightly praised for doing, but which should not be required of him by any rule. The sphere of virtue includes that of duty but extends beyond it. Mill also denies that we have any duty to ourselves: if a man fails to take proper care of his own interests this is not itself a case of wrong-doing.

Mill's somewhat negative view of duty leaves to the individual a wide choice to do or become what he wishes. In the *Essay on Liberty*, he argues that this freedom is being endangered by the interfering powers of public opinion. Society has a right to make laws for that part of a man's conduct which may affect prejudicially the interests of others; in this sphere the question whether a particular rule is justified or not is a proper question. "But there is no room for entertaining any such question where a person's conduct affects the interests of no person besides himself, or need not affect them unless they like." In the private sphere, the question whether to regulate or not is an improper question. The argument begins to look like a rehabilitation of Natural Rights. Mill argues, for example, that censorship *could not be* expedient in any civilized society. Utilitarian language hardly suffices to convey the moral importance which Mill attaches to proper pride, love of liberty, and sense of dignity. "It is the privilege and proper condition of a human being, arrived at the maturity of his faculties, to use and interpret experience in his own way." It may now seem odd that Mill should have worked to bring about a government based on the working classes and committed to Socialism. But he believed the workers could be educated in time and hoped for constitutional safeguards of the rights of minorities: the State was to pay for education but not to undertake it: and a social ownership did not for him imply ownership by an omnicompetent State.

Mill's thinking on politics began when he read Macaulay's attack on the essay on Government by James Mill. Macaulay denied the possibility of making deductions from principles: the only study of politics must be the direct study of history. Mill came to disagree both with his father and with Macaulay. In Book VI of the *Logic*, he distinguishes two quite different types of sociological inquiry. The first is both specialized and hypothetical: e.g., What would be the effect of repealing the corn laws in the present condition of society and civilization in England? We suppose that "the state of society generally" remains constant: and use the deductive method as employed in physics. The causal factors to be changed must be analysed and their laws known (e.g. the psychological laws governing trade): the predicative answer holds good only in the present state of society. But societies pass through different general states and we must suppose that the total causes of any such state are to be sought in its immediate predecessor. Mill believed (with **Comte**) that economic, social, and cultural conditions mutually affect each other, the state of knowledge being the most important factor. History does, when judiciously examined, afford empirical laws of society: e.g. an age of Faith leads to an age of Reason; and an age of Reason to a scientific or "positive" age. We could not have predicted such changes but we can do something to understand the law which governs them. This *general* science of society does not begin with a hypothesis and go on to verify it. It begins with generalizations from history and tries to show how a given type of transition can be explained by reference to laws discovered in the special sciences (geology, botany, economics, psychology, genetics). This "inverse deductive method" was taken from Comte – whose "friendship" with Mill shows some analogies with **Rousseau**'s for **Hume**. Mill's modest-seeming account of a general science of society has been totally rejected by K. R. **Popper**, who argues that the whole notion of a "law" of the successive total states of society is a misuse of the concept of law.

In his philosophy of politics Mill fights on two fronts: against *a priori* and intuitive philosophy and against simple empiricism. The same situation is seen in his logic. Mill insists that his logic is "a logic of experience" but goes on to show that science must be systematic, analytic and (at some vital points) deductive. In the *System of Logic*, Mill attempts to show (1) that "necessary propositions" are merely verbal; (2) that the traditional immediate inferences are "merely apparent" and not real inferences; (3) that the syllogism, considered as an argument from the premises to the conclusions, is also "merely apparent" inference; (4) that the syllogism is important on account of the assertion of the major or universal premise; (5) that the

assertion of a universal proposition on the basis of particular evidence is a genuine inference; hence pure deduction is not, but induction is, genuine inference; (6) that the principles of mathematics are inductive and rest upon observation; (7) that in some cases we can properly claim to know universal propositions based on induction.

Mill has not much interest in formal logic for its own sake; his main theme is *generalization* and the grounds on which it rests; and the methods appropriate to the sciences. It should be admitted at once that Mill's account of mathematical knowledge has satisfied nobody. Mill never properly distinguished between pure and applied mathematics, and confused the errors of counting and measurement with those of calculation. It was left to others to show that Mill's own highly original account of deductive reasoning as a system of tautologies, can be extended to cover mathematical reasoning also.

The logical doctrine rests on an account of meaning which introduces the notion that not all words are simply names for things. Mill uses "names" for all terms in a proposition: John, George, Mary are "singular names" and so is "the King who succeeded William I" – a many-worded name. Predicates are "general names" (e.g. man, old, white) which are "capable of being truly affirmed, in the same sense, of an indefinite number of things". But Mill picks out proper names from all other terms; they are arbitrary in the sense that they merely denote a person or place: they are not bestowed in virtue of any property supposed to belong to it. Mill says they merely "denote"; but descriptive words and phrases say something which may be true or false. "The King who succeeded William I" denotes Rufus for anyone who understands what the phrase *means*, and sees its truth. This other sense of meaning, Mill calls "connotation". "Man" connotes certain properties: and Mill says "it denotes whatever individuals have those properties" e.g. John, George, Mary. So that general names both connote and denote. Here Mill is mistaken: a definite description may denote an individual (Rufus) but a predicate term does not denote: I can state that J. S. Mill was not a great scientist without referring to any great scientist – which one would it be? General terms are not names: and Mill at all events makes clear that they have a meaning which does not involve naming at all. He also says that such words as "and", "of", "in", "truly", while they contribute to the formation of names, "have no title whatsoever to be considered as names". Naming, then, is not the only kind of meaning: a truth not fully assimilated by philosophers for several generations.

A proposition which merely asserts part of what its subject-term *means* (connotes) is "merely verbal" or tautological. The immediate inferences of traditional logic are also tautological, depending for their truth (although Mill does not state this very clearly) on the *meaning* of the logical words employed. (If all men are mortals then some men are mortal: the transition depends on the meaning of "all", "some", "If . . . then . . .") But what of the syllogism? It is notorious that the conclusion of a syllogism must be "contained in" the premises – otherwise it is invalid. All the same I can know that all men are mortal without knowing that the Duke of Wellington is so: I might never have heard of the Duke of Wellington. Mill sees that the "novelty" of the conclusion of a syllogism arises from the fact that we can know a universal proposition without knowing all its particular instances: when I discover a new instance I make a new *application* of the universal proposition and so reach a new conclusion. But Mill is more concerned with the question. How can we know factual universal propositions? We come to know them by inference from a set of instances. This inference is inductive. The whole importance of syllogistic argument in science depends on our having universal premises. And this comes from induction: it is the only "genuine" inference.

In *Logic* Book III, Mill examines the nature of induction. It depends on the "assumption" that the course of nature is uniform, that what happens once in certain circumstances, will always happen again if like circumstances occur. And we know by an examination of nature "that the assumption is warranted." The simplest induction proceeds on the basis of simple enumeration of like instances: "The swans we have seen are all white – therefore all swans are white". It is by this very method that we learn that nature is uniform. Mill distinguishes between uniformities of co-existence and uniformities of sequence. The former include the "togetherness" of the properties of natural kinds, and of spatial and numerical properties. These can be known only by observation (including counting and measurement): in many cases the evidence for them is superabundant. Uniformities of sequence may be characterised loosely as *causal*: one sort of event leading always to a certain sequel. We learn then in the first place by simple enumeration: but Mill holds that in *causal* inductions something more like a deductive proof is possible by the help of his celebrated "Methods of (Causal) Induction".

By "cause" Mill means a sufficient cause – or rather that factor which added to the ordinary course of events in the universe, is sufficient to produce a given effect. We know (according to Mill) a most important truth about such causes: that every event has one. This we learn by simple observation, but having learned it we can use it to discover and prove particular causal laws. For the sufficient cause of X must lie in its immediate antecedent events and circumstances. This limits the search for the cause of X: we find it preceded by the circumstances A, B, C etc., and one or other of these, or some combination of them, must have caused X. The Methods (Agreement, Difference, Agreement and Difference, Concomitant Variation) may do two things: (1) enable us to eliminate the circumstances that are not always found preceding X; (2) provide us with more and more cases where a certain other factor is found in X's antecedent environment. Of course the second part is enumeration; what Mill emphasises is that an elimination is itself a kind of proof. If we can find an instance of A not followed by X, then A cannot itself be the sufficient cause of X. And this, he holds, must strengthen the case for the remaining candidates, B, C etc. Mill writes of his Methods as constituting "a scientific test": but this claims too much. For, first, the picking out (from X's antecedents) of likely factors must depend on a knowledge of the field got without the help of these Methods: and second, this "knowledge" is itself subject to revision. (What we thought could not possibly be relevant may turn out to be the vital factor.) Methods of elimination cannot lead to a *decisive* verdict in favour of the candidates that remain, unless the set of possible candidates is decisively limited. Which strictly speaking it cannot be in such inquiries. That repeated experiment does, at least by elimination, increase the *probability* in favour of remaining factors, is hard to doubt:

but a decisive test is of course quite another matter.

The Methods are common to all *causal* inquiries at the basic experimental level: at higher level different sciences employ methods or strategies or experiment. In Book VI of the *Logic* Mill distinguishes four methods: The Geometrical Method, applicable where different laws do not modify each other's action (Mill's example suggests that this method hardly belongs to observational and experimental science at all); The Chemical Method, of direct experiment, which has to be applied where the causes combine in a way that has defied analysis; The Physical Method, which can be used when the laws of different causal factors are already fairly well known. It is then possible to suggest that a certain change was the result of a certain combination of forces: and continued experiment will provide a test. Finally Mill recognized the Historical Method, which is applicable where phenomena are complicated and beyond the scope of experiment, as in the social sciences.

Mill refers to his own views as "the experience philosophy". The point of this description comes out in his constant appeal to facts (which can be known by experience) and – at a metaphysical level – in his **phenomenalistic** account of our knowledge of things and of minds (see *Examination of Hamilton's Philosophy*.) Mill's approach is near to Hume's: he adopts an account of bodies in terms of our perceptions of them. He distinguishes clearly (as **Berkeley** did not) between two kinds of order in experience: (1) the uniform causal order which connects together bodies or physical changes of certain kinds; (2) the order which connects different ideas or impressions in our minds and leads us to form the notion that they are all perceptions of the same individual thing. The second kind of order (as Hume saw) is not a uniformity in the succession of our ideas: the *uniformities* we look for are between bodies and not between sensations. Mill attempts an analysis of this order and goes on to define a body as a "permanent possibility of sensation": i.e. to talk of a table is to talk of an order of this type in actual or possible sensations. No attempt is made to found this possibility upon an actual external substance, nor upon God. But Mill recognises that there are "other successions of feeling besides those of which I am conscious". How are

we to describe the order of experiences which constitutes an individual mind? Mill here comes upon "a final inexplicability" – the fact that a mind which is a series of feelings should be aware of itself as past and future.

In his essays on natural theology Mill defends the possibility of a mind existing without a body, hence the possibility of immortality. He also examines, in a scientific spirit, the question whether the world as we know it is largely the work of a divine intelligence; and if so, whether that divine intelligence has communicated with man by a miraculous revelation. The argument from design carries some weight: it suggests that there is a God who desires the good of his creatures (i.e. those of his creatures known to us) but that he has many other tasks in hand. At this point Mill switches the question from the region of belief to the region of simple hope. Without actual belief, a man may contemplate the notion of divine perfection, meditate upon the gospels, hope for immortality. This has a practical value. These reflections are found in Mill's letters and connect with his early serious Wordsworthian concern for the cultivation of the best that is to be found in human feeling and imagination. But his *Essays on Religion*, which appeared after his death, surprised his more downright agnostic and atheistic friends. "There are hints in Stuart Mill of an original nature which was sentimental and almost religious, and which was not made for the purely intellectual and abstract system imposed on it since childhood" (Halévy).   (K.B.)

Plate 64, page 224.

Miracles, *see* Theism.

Mises, Richard von (1883–1953), a prominent associate of the **Logical Positivists** of the **Vienna Circle** until he sought refuge from Hitlerism in the USA. He wrote a general account of positivism in 1939 (in English as *Positivism*, 1951), but it is as a theorist of probability that he is best known. His main work in the field of probability was *Wahrscheinlichkeit Statistik und Wahrheit* (1928) which was published as *Probability Statistics and Truth* in 1939. Von Mises claimed to set up a scientific definition of probability to replace our vague notions in everyday thought; he made no claim to analyse our ordinary notion of probability. He defined probability as being the limiting value of the frequency of an event within a collective; a collective is an indefinitely large reference class whose members occur in a random order, that is, a class in predicting the character of whose members no gambling system will be of avail. Thus to say that the probability of heads is one half is to say that the limiting value of the fraction given by dividing the number of heads by the number of tosses is one half. The series of tosses constitutes the collective. Von Mises was able to show that the axioms of mathematical probability followed tautologically from this definition, which has however been attacked, especially for its use of the notion of limiting frequency outside pure mathematics; others have objected to von Mises allowing no meaning to probability statements which were not of the form "The probability of event *e* within the collective *K* is P".   (J.O.U.)

Monads, *see* Leibniz.

Monism is any doctrine that there is only one substance, or one "world", or that reality is in some sense *one*, that is, unchanging or indivisible or undifferentiated. For instance, the alternative claims that "everything is mental" or "everything is material" are crudely expressed forms of monism, each opposed to the common sense **dualism** of mind and matter. The term was invented by C. Wolff (1679–1754), who used it only of these two theories, which have the best right to the labels **"idealism"** and **"materialism"** respectively. It later came to be used also of the theory of absolute identity held by Schelling and **Hegel**, namely, that mind and matter are not reducible one to the other, but both to one common substance of which they are phenomenal modifications. (Compare the later "neutral monism" of William **James** and, at one time, **Russell**). Subsequently the term was more widely applied, to any theory attempting to explain phenomena by, or reduce them to, a single principle; and opposed not merely to dualism but often also to pluralism, of which an example is Russell's Logical Atomism, which he also called "absolute pluralism". As a result of these extended uses, the term is systematically ambiguous, and one should distinguish between *substantial* and *attributive* monism, the former being the

view (1) that the apparent plurality of substances is due to different states or appearances of a single substance, which was God-or-Nature to **Spinoza**, for example, and the Absolute to **Bradley**. Attributive monism, on the other hand, is the view (2) that whatever the number of substances, they are of a single ultimate kind, that is, there is only one realm of being. One could also distinguish from these absolute views a *partial* monism, namely (3) that within a given realm of being (however many there may be) there is only one substance. These varieties of monism need not all stand or fall together; and have, for reasons requiring lengthy argument, been held selectively: for example, Spinoza held (1) and hence trivially (3), but rejected (2) in favour of an infinity of ultimate kinds, whereas **Descartes** rejected (1) and (2), but accepted (3) within the material realm, and **Leibniz** rejected (1) and (3), but accepted (2), all monads being souls; thus each of these thinkers accepted monism in at least one sense but not in others. The appropriate sense of "monism" always needs to be made clear from the context. But in each of its forms it is the supreme expression of metaphysical tidiness.

                    (R.HALL)

Moore, George Edward (1873–1958). From 1898–1904 and 1911–1939 Moore, an Englishman, was Fellow of Trinity College and lecturer and, subsequently, Professor in the University of Cambridge. He held the Order of Merit and was Fellow of the British Academy. His direct personal influence on British philosophers of his time has been immense.

The three main topics dealt with in Moore's writings are philosophical method, ethics, and perception. He wrote little about his method because his energies were given to practising it, but probably it is as a contribution to the right method of doing philosophy that his work will be of lasting importance.

This method clearly appears in an article in 1900 on *Necessity*, is proclaimed in his programmatic essay of 1925, *A Défence of Common Sense*, and is reaffirmed in his autobiographical remarks of 1942 in *The Philosophy of G. E. Moore*. What interests him about the things we say in ordinary life is neither their meaning nor their truth, since he believes them to have a well-known meaning and to be in many cases certainly true, but something about them which he calls an analysis of their meaning. With philosophical views, on the other hand, he is anxious to discover what they could mean and whether they are true, because they are often attempted analyses whose results deny the commonly accepted meaning and truth of what they analyse.

In these investigations Moore makes two appeals, which have often been confused by critics, namely an appeal to the truth of what we hold in common sense and an appeal to the propriety of what we say in ordinary language.

His attitude to common sense, like that of Thomas **Reid** in the eighteenth century, is that many of its beliefs are such that, though, like the laws of **logic**, they are neither *provable* nor *disprovable* there are far better reasons for accepting them than for accepting any of the philosophical doctrines which contradict them. Unlike any philosophical belief, we all do hold and cannot help holding them, and various kinds of inconsistency issue from our attempts to deny them.

Since the expressions, like "good", "know", "see", "real", whose meaning Moore analyses are in common everyday use, he has felt justified in assuming that we all understand them very well, and, therefore, justified in using them to interpret some of the strange things that philosophers say and in accusing any philosopher who goes against them of "an abuse of language".

In common with many philosophers from **Plato** until quite recently, Moore holds that the meaning of an expression is a kind of entity, often called a concept, notion, or proposition, which the expression stands for, conveys, represents, or names, and which is called up before the mind of anyone who understands the expression. Hence his contrast between knowing the meaning of an expression and knowing the analysis of the meaning, which a contemporary analyst would express as that between knowing how to use an expression and being able to say how it is used, is put by Moore himself as a contrast between having the concept expressed by a given expression before the mind and being able to say or do something in regard to that concept. As to what exactly an analyst has to do in regard to the concept before his mind, Moore seems to have had three separate views, often held in the same work. In general the analyst has to *inspect* the

concept and try to describe it; in particular he has *either* to say how it can be *divided* into a set of constituent concepts and how these constituents are interrelated *or* to say how the concept is to be *distinguished*, by way of similarity and difference, from other concepts which are brought before the mind by the given expression and by other related expressions. The division method, with its dependence on the concept theory of meaning, has a very ancient history and predominates in the work of Russell and the early Wittgenstein, while the distinction method, in a form uncommitted to the concept theory, is favoured by Wittgenstein's later work and by contemporary analysts.

Again, Moore has often thought that in order to give an analysis of a concept one must find a concept or set of concepts identical with the concept to be analysed and, therefore, also find an expression synonymous with the expression used to express the concept to be analysed. This "translation approach" to analysis is now generally abandoned.

Taking "what is good?" as the central question of ethics, Moore distinguished the sense in which the question demands an inquiry into the analysis of the notion of *good* from the senses in which it seeks to know either what things are good or what kinds of things are good. Although he did in his first ethical writings, *Principia Ethica*, attempt a brief answer to the question "What kinds of things are good?", according to which there is an "immense variety" of such kinds of things, including "the pleasures of human intercourse and the enjoyment of beautiful objects", most of his work here and elsewhere is devoted to an analysis of the notion of *good*. In accordance with his method of inspection, he advises the analyst of *good* to "attentively consider what is actually before his mind" in the hope that "if he will try this experiment with each suggested definition (i.e. analysis) in succession, he may become expert enough to recognise that in every case he has before his mind a unique object". Under the influence of the method of division, he has said that a definition "states what are the parts which invariably compose a certain whole; and in this sense the notion 'good' has no definition because it is simple and has no parts". This simple concept for which he thought the expression "good" stood he called a "non-natural" quality, and any attempt to identify it with another concept he called a commission of the "naturalistic fallacy". When, however, he used the "distinction" method of analysis, he counted it as an analysis of *good* if he could "distinguish this from other" concepts. In his later writings he has inclined to hold that the word "good" is not after all the "name of a characteristic" but that its use *may* be to express an attitude or approval. The notion of *right* is made dependent on the notion of *good* in that, agreeing with the **Utilitarians**, Moore analyses it as the cause of things which are good in themselves.

In discussing the notion of perception, Moore assumes that there is no doubt about the meaning of such expressions as "I see a book" and "This, which I see, is a book" and usually no doubt about the truth of what they say. He then argues that whenever we see an opaque material object, such as a book, we *ipso facto* see, in a second sense, a particular part of it, such as the surface turned towards us, and also see, in a third sense, what he calls a sense-datum, such as a particular patch of colour. His task then is to distinguish and relate the three concepts expressed by the one word "see" and the three concepts expressed by their respective grammatical objects, namely "material object", "part of the surface of a material object" and "sense-datum". To the question how these various concepts are related to each other, he has provided many answers but never one which satisfied either himself or other philosophers. The reason for this failure is mainly due, it seems, to two assumptions which he has constantly made, namely, that the word "sense-datum" is the name of a peculiar kind of *entity*, which is present in every perceptual experience, and that when I say "This, which I see, is a book", I must be trying to *identify* the *sense-datum with* something.　　　　(A.R.W.)

Plate 65, page 289.

Morris, Charles (1901–), born at Denver, Colorado. For many years Professor of Philosophy at the University of Chicago, he has been at the University of Florida since 1958. His main philosophical contributions have been to the philosophy of language. He has sought to fuse the behaviouristic pragmatism of his teacher, George H. Mead, with the logical empiricism of the **Vienna Circle**, and to develop systematically the fertile but sketchily worked out ideas of Charles **Peirce** on signs with-

in this conceptual framework. However, Morris has gone far beyond Peirce in taking into account non-linguistic as well as linguistic signs. His division of semiotics (or the general theory of signs) into three major branches, has been widely adopted. The first is syntactics, which studies the relations signs have to one another in virtue of their purely formal or structural properties. The second is semantics, which analyses the relations of signs to what they designate. The third is pragmatics, which examines the modes of response that users of signs make to them. In recent years, Morris has been concerned with effecting a synthesis of the chief traditional ideals of life, so as to make them adequate to modern conditions; and he has also carried on extensive empirical studies on the relations between types of philosophical belief and forms of human physique and culture.　　　　(E.N.)

N

Nagel, Ernest (1901–), born at Novemesto, Czechoslovakia, now Professor of Philosophy at Columbia University. He emigrated to the USA in 1911 and was naturalized in 1919. He is best known for his work in the philosophy of science. In this field his text-book, written with M. R. **Cohen** *An Introduction to Logic and Scientific Method*, is generally considered the best of its kind; his *Principles of the Theory of Probability* in the *International Encyclopedia of Unified Science* is also well-known, as are many other articles in the same field. In metaphysics Nagel counts himself as a **naturalist**, holding that the world must be understood in terms of efficient causation and as involving no ultimate ingredients beyond matter.　　　　(J.O.U.)

Plate 66, page 290.

Naturalism. Like most of the words ending in "ism" and used to name a type of philosophical position, "naturalism" has only a vague and imprecise sense, or set of senses. More widely, a philosopher is a naturalist if he considers that the totality of things which we call "nature" and which are studied in the natural sciences is the totality of all things whatever, and if he denies the need of any explanations of the natural in terms of the supernatural; such a philosopher will normally hold that any reference to a deity or to a realm of values, or to mind thought of as something more than a natural phenomenon is illegitimate. With regard to such nineteenth century thinkers as T. H. Huxley, naturalism especially connoted a belief that life and thought could be completely explained, in principle, as arising by evolution from matter. In **ethics** naturalism is the view that statements about the rightness, wrongness, goodness and badness of things are statements about the natural world and not about special values beyond the ken of science; thus a naturalist might maintain that to say that something is good is to say that it is likely to satisfy desire, which is a scientifically testable statement. But, unfortunately, G. E. **Moore**, in his *Principia Ethica*, widened the notion of naturalism for his special purposes so that everyone was guilty of the "naturalistic fallacy" who attempted to define ethical concepts in terms of concepts which were not specifically ethical; thus even those who defined "good" as meaning "willed by God", a view clearly utterly opposed to naturalism as ordinarily understood, were said by Moore to have committed the naturalistic fallacy. Unfortunately this usage of Moore's has become so widely known that the term "naturalism" has probably now lost whatever utility it ever had.   (J.O.U.)

Natural Law, *see* Jurisprudence, Grotius and Hobbes.

Neoplatonism is a term usually designating the last creative effort of pagan antiquity (*c.* 250 to 550 A.D.) to produce a comprehensive philosophic system which could satisfy all spiritual (intellectual, religious, moral) aspirations of man by presenting an all-inclusive, logically coherent image of the universe and of man's place in it and by explaining how man can achieve salvation, i.e. be restored to his lost original condition. It should be stressed that "Neoplatonism" is a modern term. The men to whom we apply it claimed to be simply Platonists. Whether this claim was legitimate or whether Neoplatonism radically differs from original Platonism is controversial. In any case Neoplatonism succeeded in synthesizing most of earlier philosophic thought (particularly that of **Aristotle**, the **Stoics**, and Pythagorism; only **Epicureanism** was excluded) with Platonism. But it also assimilated many religious beliefs, myths, rites, and cults of Greek and of Oriental polytheism, including alchemy, magic practices (often based on affinities between planets and metals, etc.) and in its universe could find a place for all traditional deities and semi-deities of popular religions.

Neoplatonism teaches a deity (or a supreme principle; it would be inappropriate to think of it as a person) elevated above or transcending the universe, so that it can be called beyond being or even non-being in the sense of "higher than being". At the same time this transcendent deity is the source out of which everything flows (or proceeds, or progresses), without ever becoming separated from it, so that it is also immanent in everything. The aforementioned "flow" is not a temporal process; it is, if we may say so, timeless history. What starts it is not an intentional, creative act; it is rather like a timeless, involuntary, permanent effulgence or emanation. But this emanation does not consume its source, which, on the contrary remains forever undiminished and full. Some scholars describe the relation between the supreme principle and all its emanations as that of "dynamic pantheism".

As the supreme principle is above being, no predicates can really be applied to it, as all predicates are predicates of beings. The best we can do is to speak of it as "One" to express that it is undifferentiated and in this sense of the word lacking any determinateness, simple and therefore without quality. It is "One" not in the way in which we speak of something as being "one this" or "one that", but "one" as a substance. If we think of it as the source of all being, we can also refer to it as "goodness" in the sense that it is the ultimate "Why" of everything.

The timeless process of effulgence is best described as gradual "dispersion" of the original unity, by which it passes into ever-increasing multiplicity. Along a descending scale of being, the realm of the supra-sensible reality (first: mind, or thought thinking itself, or spirit; next: the soul) emanates, then comes sensible reality (in time and space). One more step and the dispersion becomes annihilation (as light, emanating from its source in a cone, gradually fills progressively larger parts of space, becoming progressively dimmer, until it fades out into complete darkness). This annihilation (or, as it is sometimes expressed, this annihilating factor) is in Neoplatonism referred to as the result of matter (or matter). In some way, exceedingly difficult to comprehend, this matter, although sheer nothingness (void, absence, lack) is, at the same time, the "Why" of nothingness. The supreme principle as the source of all being was called "goodness", accordingly matter as nothingness or its reason can be called "evil", though some Neoplatonists insist on describing it as simple "not-goodness".

The successive steps or, as they are often called, hypostases are, as observed, the results of some kind of necessity (just as everything that is full must overflow). From this point of view, the universe is flawless. Everything is as it ought to be. This seems to leave no place for any ethics. But Neoplatonism is keenly aware of man's imperfect condition. This imperfection stems precisely from man's (or rather his soul's) "remoteness" from the deity. Thus the effulgence, though necessary, engenders the longing to "revert" (to "regress", to "return") and so to undo the "progress" which may now be interpreted as some kind of flaw or (intentional) fall. This longing man shares with all other beings. The way to its satisfaction is taught in ethics. Thus, whereas in its theoretical aspects Neoplatonism is monistic, its practical aspects are dualistic.

The concept of a deity which is inaccessible to reflective thought demands as its correlate some kind of knowledge above rational, reflective thinking. To acquire this higher kind of knowledge man must suppress all determinateness of thought, to call himself back from his "dispersion". Having himself finally become one, in rare moments he is able to "face" the One, a condition described by some Neoplatonists as rapt contemplation of the One, by others as being absorbed into or united with the One. It is the condition of ecstasy, for which to prepare us is the main purpose of moral life. The "virtues" of steadfastness, self-control, fairness, and prudence serve this purpose. Depending on how far man has progressed on his return journey, they appear on the different levels of his spiritual life in appropriately different forms, for example, as civic, purificatory, exemplary virtues. In the moment of ecstasy all intellectual and moral aspirations of man are satisfied.

One of the most striking aspects of Neoplatonism (and one which makes it totally unacceptable to an empiricist) consists in its "derivation" of all

sensible reality from a supra-sensible one (the latter being more real than the former), this "derivation" representing a type of causation radically different from causality in space and time. It should be obvious how greatly that which today is called scientific explanation of the universe differs from what a Neoplatonist would consider to be such. He is likely to think of scientific explanations as shallow and perceiving only the surface of reality. The empirically-minded scientist, on the other hand, is likely to consider Neoplatonism as utterly fantastic. But should we not expect causation which produces beings, to differ radically from causation obtaining between beings produced?

It is customary to see in **Plotinus** the founder of Neoplatonism (though much has recently been done to do justice to his forerunners and particularly to consider Platonism from the time of **Cicero** on – the so-called Middle Platonism – as the fertile soil out of which Neoplatonism developed). It is furthermore customary to consider the year 529, in which the Emperor Justinian ordered the school of Plato (the Academy) in Athens closed, to be the end of pagan philosophy in general and of Neoplatonism in particular. In these three hundred years different neoplatonic schools developed. We particularly distinguish the school of Plotinus, the school of Pergamum, and the school of Alexandria.

Two outstanding representatives of the early phase of the school of Plotinus are Porphyry (234–c. 305) and Iamblichus (died c. 330). The former edited the writings of Plotinus; this is the edition (which he prefaced by a biography of his master) which we now possess. A radical enemy of Christianity, he attacked it in *Against the Christians* with great acumen and erudition. Some of his arguments particularly in matters of chronology and authorship of parts of the Scriptures have not yet been superseded. His *On the Cave of the Nymphs* is a good example of the allegorizing interpretation of poetry (in this case of Homer), practiced by many neoplatonists. His aphoristic *Starting Points* are an excellent introduction to the main neoplatonic doctrines. Very readable is his consolatory *Letter to Marcella*, his wife. Particularly influential was his *Introduction to Aristotle's Categories*, a commentary on five fundamental concepts (genus, species, difference, property, accident, later called predictables). A passage in which he poses (but does not answer) the question whether **universals** have an existence (independent of both minds and particular things) gave impetus to the medieval controversy between **nominalism**, **realism** and **conceptualism**. He, much more than Plotinus, stresses will as the factor responsible for the "fall" of the soul.

Iamblichus in a series of treatises (*Exhortation to Philosophy, Life of Pythagoras, General Mathematics* etc.) expounded what he considered to be Pythagorean doctrines. His *Egyptian Mysteries* are a philosophico-allegorical interpretation of Egypt's rites and religious doctrines. Perhaps he himself instituted something like neoplatonic mysteries, a blend of Greek and Oriental mystery religions. He is inclined to subdivide the entities of the suprasensible realm (for example, he has two Ones, two Minds) and later Neoplatonists carried such subdivisions and distinctions further and further. As a magician he appears in Byron's *Manfred*.

The school of Pergamum, founded by a disciple of Iamblichus, Aidesios, was particularly interested in the practice of magic. Its best known representative is the Emperor Julian the Apostate (born 332 A.D.). In his attempts to stem the growth of Christianity he as the Emperor Gallienus probably did before him, tried to revive polytheism with the help of Neoplatonism; perhaps a writing by Sallustius, *On Gods and the Universe* was intended to serve this purpose. Neoplatonism was to provide polytheism with allegorico-philosophical interpretations, thus making it attractive again to the educated, while permitting the uneducated to practice it according to tradition, justifiably so, as it contained wisdom in a form accessible to them.

The main representatives of the school of Plotinus in its later phase of the so called School of Athens which is simply Plato's Academy turned Plotinian, were Proclus (410–485 A.D.) and Damascius. The former, sometimes called Neoplatonism's schoolman, gave a particularly comprehensive and systematic presentation of Neoplatonism in two works, *Elements of Theology* and *The Theology of Plato*. In his writings some tensions inherent in Neoplatonism come to light. Though he derives everything from the One alone and is second to none in characterizing it by absolute simplicity (and therefore ineffability), he at the same time derives all reality from two (instead of one) principles (which

are ultimately either Pythagorean or Platonic), viz. the Limit and the Unlimited, these being in some way present also in the One (he reminds us of Pythagoreans who said of the number One that it alone is both odd and even). In addition to the One he assumes the existence of Ones, immediately following the One (whether as a particular hypostasis is unclear) and identifies them with gods. And he explicitly derives matter from the One. Of great importance is for him the "triadic" principle according to which everything as it emanates, in one aspect remains in that from which it emanated, in another is turned away from it, in a third turns back to it. A number of his hymns are remarkable documents of neoplatonic religiousness.

An author not yet identified, but pretending (and for centuries believed) to be Dionysius the Areopagite, St Paul's disciple, and therefore enjoying great authority, compiled a series of writings, for example *Divine Names* and *Mystical Theology*, which combine Proclus with Christianity (on this problem see below). They are particularly well known as representing the so-called negative theology.

Damascius was the head of the Academy at the time of its closing (see above). In a way, he presents the consummation of a tendency latent in all Neoplatonism in that he declares *all* rational knowledge to be merely parabolic so that no aspect of reality is accessible to it.

The school of Alexandria occupies a particular position. Its Neoplatonism is comparatively simple (in some respect closer to Middle Platonism than to Plotinus) and a number of its members accepted Christianity, whereas the school of Athens to the very last remained one of the strongholds of polytheism. Hypatia (murdered by Christian fanatics) and her pupil, Bishop(!) Synesius belong among its representatives.

Despite the anti-Christian attitude of many Neoplatonists (inherited by men like Macrobius or Symmachus) Neoplatonism had always had great attraction for philosophers within the orbit of Christianity and, after the Arabs discovered and assimilated Greek philosophy, also within the orbit of Islam and Judaism. On one hand this is natural, considering Neoplatonism's sympathy for religion in general, the loftiness of its concept of the divine, its assumption that the supra-sensible is more real than the sensible, its asceticism. On the other hand, there is something paradoxical about it. Christianity is a strictly historical religion (as are Judaism and Islam). Incarnation, central for Christianity and considered to have absolute and unique importance, is an event in time with all the contigency of an historical event. Neither it nor the moment at which it occurred can be logically deduced. But Neoplatonism, true to its Hellenic heritage, always remained a rational system, in the sense that it presented the universe as a kind of giant syllogism, with one event following from another in the same timeless manner in which conclusions follow from premises. What happens in time is contingent and can therefore have no essential, ultimate significance for the universe at large or for man. But in spite of this fundamental difference, Christian thinkers time and again tried to express Christian doctrines in terms of Neoplatonism. Even in our times we find such attempts. Perhaps some of them are simply the result of the fact that its author never, albeit unwittingly, became entirely reconciled to the contingent, historical character of Christianity.

In this context **Augustine** deserves special mention. Though influenced by Neoplatonic ideas (which he partly found in neoplatonic writings, partly in the sermons of St Ambrosius), he in a famous passage of his *Confessions* (Book VII) stated the fundamental similarities and differences between Christianity and Neoplatonism.

Excerpts from some of Plotinus' writings, falsely attributed to Aristotle under the title *Aristotelian Theology*, were important for the transmission of Neoplatonism to the Middle Ages.

Of men strongly influenced by neoplatonism, **Erigena**, Master Eckhart, Nicolaus of Cusa, Marsilio Ficino, and R. **Cudworth** (together with other so-called **Cambridge Platonists**) should be mentioned.   (P.M.)

Neo-Thomism. The scholastic philosophy which had its origin in the Middle Ages gradually faded out in the course of the seventeenth and eighteenth centuries on account of its failure to maintain contact with the development of the experimental sciences and the new approach to the theory of knowledge. Since the later scholastics had failed, it was assumed that their medieval predecessors were equally unworthy of attention. But the incapacity of modern philosophy to evolve a realistic metaphysic eventually aroused the suspicion that it might be useful to re-examine the thinkers of the creative period of medieval philosophy, especially Thomas **Aquinas**.

The pioneer of this Thomistic revival was an obscure seminary lecturer at Piacenza, Vincenzo Buzzetti (1777–1824). Among his students were the brothers Domenico Sordi (1790–1880) and Serafino Sordi (1793–1865). Both became Jesuits and tried, at first with little success, to influence the fellow-members of their order in the direction of **Aquinas**. In the end, however, they gained over a few thinkers of some prominence in Italy, Luigi Taparelli d'Azeglio (1793–1862), Matteo Liberatore (1810–1892) and Giovanni Maria Cornoldi (1822–1892), together with the German Joseph Kleutgen (1811–1883). These, along with Gaetano Sanseverino (1811–1865) at Naples and the Dominican Tommaso Zigliara (1833–1893), made the movement known. Another supporter was Giuseppe Pecci (1807–1890), whose brother Giocchino became Pope under the name of Leo XIII and lent his official support to the revival of Thomism and its application to modern intellectual needs.

What was required to make the revival effective was both an intensive study of the history of medieval thought and a practical demonstration that it was still relevant to contemporary philosophical problems. Here the leadership of the movement passed to France, Belgium and Germany. In Italy and Spain Neo-Thomism has tended to remain in isolation as a clerical preserve. But the Institut Supérieur de Philosophie at Louvain, founded in 1889 under Désiré Mercier (1851–1926), has been the most powerful centre of a progressive Thomism. Thanks to scholars like Martin Grabmann in Germany and **Gilson** in France the history of medieval philosophy has gradually been revealed. **Maritain** is the Neo-Thomist whose name is most familiar to the general public.

The movement has had little effect in England except among a few Anglican writers, of whom the most prominent is Dr. E. L. Mascall. Only in the United States have some welcomed it as a pure philosophy apart from Christian theology, like Professor Mortimer Adler at the University of Chicago. But it would be of no value to the Christian theologian unless it could be shown to have independent validity as a philosophy.

The Neo-Thomist claims that the central tradition of Greek thought was continued and developed legitimately in a theistic direction by the medieval Aristotelians. He holds that this tradition has not been made out of date by modern philosophy. He has, therefore, to produce a theory of knowledge which will satisfy the questions and difficulties which have arisen from **Descartes** onwards and to show that this theory of knowledge justifies the main outline of Aristotelian and Thomistic metaphysics. He has to show also that this philosophical view of the world harmonizes with the approach of the modern scientist. He must be as ready to shed what time has really destroyed of the medieval outlook as to assimilate the positive contributions of later philosophy. And he has to talk a language which his contemporaries can understand. Among books which make a notable effort to fulfil these requirements may be mentioned Pierre Rousselot's *Intellectualism of St Thomas*, Joseph Maréchal's *Le Point de Départ de la Métaphysique*, with Gilson's *Being and Some Philosophers* and *The Unity of Philosophical Experience*. That Neo-Thomism has not has not yet attained the results for which its originators hoped is evident, but it can be judged fairly only as a movement which is in progress and is capable of further development. Of late is has begun to come into fruitful contact with the **Phenomenologists**, the followers of **Husserl**, and with the recent evolution of formal logic. (D.J.B.H.)

Nietzsche, Friedrich (1844–1900), born at Röcken, Prussia, profoundly influenced continental European philosophy and literature, especially in Germany and France. In the English-speaking world, especially among philosophers, he has won relatively few admirers. Amateur psychologists have often tried to "explain" his ideas, but Sigmund Freud, according to Ernest Jones' biography, "several times said of Nietzsche that he had a more penetrating knowledge of himself than any other man who ever lived or was ever likely to live". Freud also remarked that Nietzsche's "premonitions and insights often agree in the most amazing manner with the laborious results of psychoanalysis".

Nietzsche was the son of a Protestant minister and the grandson of two. He studied classical philology and was appointed to a professorship at Basel, Switzerland, before he had completed a doctoral dissertation. The degree, a prerequisite for such a position, was conferred hurriedly, and Nietzsche went to Basel in 1869 and became a Swiss subject.

In the Franco-Prussian War of 1870–71 he served briefly as a medical orderly on the Prussian side and returned to Basel with shattered health. He formed a friendship with Richard Wagner, but the composer, born like Nietzsche's father in 1813, appreciated Nietzsche mainly as a brilliant apostle and errand boy. Whenever Nietzsche showed an independent mind, Wagner showed no interest. A break was thus inevitable, and it came about when Wagner made his peace with the young German Empire, which Nietzsche loathed, and settled in Bayreuth where his anti-Semitism became as influential as his music. Nietzsche had no sympathy for the idealization of "the pure fool" in Wagner's *Parsifal*, which he considered an insincere obeisance to Christianity, and Wagner, a Francophobe, was so displeased by Nietzsche's enlightened, anti-romantic *Human, All-too-Human*, also published in 1878, with a dedication to Voltaire, that he refused to read it.

The following year, Nietzsche retired from his professorship for reasons of health, and during the next ten years he devoted himself entirely to writing. He lived very modestly and in utter solitude in Switzerland and Italy, and every book represented a hard-won triumph over half-blind eyes, intense migraine headaches, and manifold physical agonies. His writings were ignored until Georg Brandes (né Cohen) began to lecture on them in Copenhagen in 1888. During the following decade Nietzsche attained world-wide fame, without knowing it. For he suffered a mental and physical breakdown in January 1889, and remained insane until his death.

His first book, *The Birth of Tragedy* (1872) was ill-received by German scholars; but by 1912 F. M. Cornford, the great British classicist, hailed it as "a work of profound imaginative insight which left the scholarship of a generation toiling in the rear" – an estimate shared more or less by Jane Harrison and by most German classicists today.

The book broke with the "sweetness and light" conception of Greek culture and called attention to the "Dionysian" element and the tragic outlook.

He published four more, equally unacademic essays, collected as "Untimely Meditations" (the English title, *Thoughts out of Season* misses the intended allusion to Descartes), before he changed his style to write books of aphorisms, studded with psychological observations: *Human, All-too-Human* (1878, with two sequels, 1879 and 1880), *Dawn* (1881), and *The Gay Science* (1882; second edition with substantial additions, 1887). In the English version, the last title was rendered "The Joyful Wisdom"; but "Science" is more appropriate, for Nietzsche thought that his aphorisms, though lacking the gravity of the German academic style, were closer to the true scientific spirit and to the experimental method in particular. After attempting all kinds of psychological explanations of diverse phenomena, he was struck, for example, by the apparent importance of the striving for power and of fear, and in *Dawn* tried to see how far he might get in an attempt to explain all kinds of behaviour in terms of these two concepts.

Eventually he came to the conclusion that Greek culture had been based on an unsentimentally competitive spirit and that "the will to power" is the most basic human drive. What man – and, according to Nietzsche's next book, *Thus Spoke Zarathustra*, every living being – wants above everything else is a higher, more powerful state of being in which the manifold frustrations of his present state are overcome. It is only when man fails in his endeavour to perfect himself, to recreate himself, to become a creator rather than a mere creature, that, *faute de mieux*, he often settles for the hunt after crude, physical power over others. Of many of his critics Nietzsche might well have said, substituting "powers" for "pleasures" in one of J. S. **Mill**'s remarks that *they*, and not he, represented "human nature in a degrading light, since the accusation supposes human beings to be capable of no powers except those of which swine are capable".

Nietzsche's conception of "the will to power" cannot be understood apart from "sublimation" – a word which he was the first to use in its modern sense. His anti-Christian polemics, which became more and more central in his later works, depend in part on Nietzsche's claim that Christianity "demands not the control but the extirpation of the passions". Christianity, he says, failed to realize that the sex impulse, for example, is "capable of great refinement" and it "made something unclean out of sexuality".

Still, Christianity itself is an expression of the will to power – but the will to power of the weak and frustrated whose resentment gave rise, he argues, to a pervasive antagonism against all physical and intellectual excellence, a predisposition in favour of everything low, a levelling tendency, a hatred of sex, and the depreciation of body and intellect in favour of the soul and of this whole world in favour of another, fictitious world. In one of his last works, *The Antichrist*, in which his style has become shrill, and no attempt is made to offer judicious qualifications, he cites 1 Corinthians 1 to illustrate his claims: "God has chosen the weak things of the world to ruin what is strong, and base things of the world ... and what is nothing, to bring to naught what is something". Here he finds an outlook "born of resentment and impotent vengefulness". And he also cites Chapter 6, "the saints shall judge the world" and "we shall judge angels". Here he finds a will to power that has run amuck.

His critics feel that it is Nietzsche who has run amuck; but they have generally misunderstood him because they overlooked that he did not find in Christianity what they have found in it. Few indeed are aware of the fact that Nietzsche says, also in *The Antichrist*: "When the exceptional human being treats the mediocre more tenderly than himself and his peers, this is not mere politeness of the heart – it is simply his *duty*". Christianity he associated with resentment and the hope for boundless power in another world from which, according to some of the greatest Christians, the blessed will behold the torments of those who got the best of things in this world.

Nietzsche was not only a moralist but also a moral philosopher. His view of traditional **ethics** might be summed up in the words which F. H. **Bradley** used to characterize metaphysics: "the finding of bad reasons for what we believe on instinct". But Nietzsche did not believe that moral idiosyncrasies were literally instinctive. On the contrary, he was struck by the great variety of moral views in different times and places; and he derided the philosophers' "conceit that they have long known what is good and evil for man".

His views on this subject are best cited from *Beyond Good and Evil* (1886), especially from sections 186 and 260: "With a stiff seriousness that inspires laughter, all our philosophers ... wanted to supply a *rational foundation* for morals; and every philosopher so far has believed that he had provided such a foundation. Morality itself, however, was accepted as 'given'." "Because our moral philosophers" were parochial and myopic, "poorly informed, and not even very curious about different peoples, ages, and the past, they never laid eyes on the real problems of morality; for these emerge only when we compare *many* moralities".

Nietzsche poses two questions: how does our prevalent morality compare with other moralities? and what can be said about morality in general?

In answer to the first question we must try to construct as a first step "a typology of morals"; and Nietzsche finds "two basic types": "There is *master morality* and *slave morality*". Our prevalent morality, for which different moral philosophers have sought different "rational foundations" is one of the many mixed types and profoundly inconsistent. For it originated historically out of two different traditions.

Nietzsche does not believe that every man is by nature either a master or a slave. What he claims is rather that moral codes have originated "either among a ruling group whose consciousness of their difference from the ruled group was accompanied by delight – or among the ruled group, the slaves". The first type of morality is rooted in self-affirmation. The noble type calls itself "good" and those who are not noble "bad" – and Nietzsche adds: "The opposition of "good" and "evil" has a different origin". He does not glorify brutality. "The noble man, too, helps the unfortunate, but not, or almost not, out of pity, but more prompted by an urge which is begotten by the excess of power".

In Aristotle's words, Nietzsche's "masters" feel that "it is vulgar to lord it over humble people." Indeed, Nietzsche's "masters" closely resemble Aristotle's portrait of "the great-souled man". This parallel is not accidental: Aristotle's ethics greatly influenced Nietzsche's and helped to convince him that modern bourgeois morality is not morality par excellence; also that Christianity represented, to

cite *Beyond Good and Evil* (sec. 46) the "revaluation of all the values of antiquity".

The first of the three essays that comprise Nietzsche's next book, *Toward a Genealogy of Morals* (1887), bears the title: "Good and Evil versus Good and Bad". It deals at length with slave morality which contrasts good and *evil*. According to Nietzsche, it is rooted "in the resentment of those who are denied the real reaction, that of the deed, and who compensate with an imaginary revenge". Not self-affirmation but resentment is primary here: evil is the slave's primary concept "from which he then derives, as an afterimage and counterinstance, a 'good one' – himself".

The strong and noble man is above resentment. "Here alone it is also possible ... that there be real '*love* of one's enemies'. How much respect has a noble person for his enemies! And such respect is already a bridge to love". "Beyond good and evil" does not mean beyond good and *bad*. What it does mean is stated repeatedly in *Zarathustra*: "you are too *pure* for the filth of the words: revenge, punishment, reward, retribution"; "*that man be delivered from revenge, that is for me the bridge to the highest hope*".

In one of his last works, *Twilight of the Idols*, Nietzsche leaves no doubt that, although he far prefers master morality to slave morality, he does not by any means accept master morality. On the contrary, he calls attention to its inhuman aspects; and in the final analysis he finds both types of morality "entirely worthy of each other".

This brings us to the second question Nietzsche pressed: what can be said about morality in general? Nietzsche makes two points in reply. First, "every morality is, as opposed to *laisser aller*, a bit of tyranny against 'nature'; also against 'reason'; but this in itself is no objection". Some discipline and constraint, although arbitrary in a sense, is the prerequisite of all achievements "for whose sake life on earth is worthwhile; for example, virtue, art, music, dance, reason, spirituality". (*Beyond*, 188). Point two: a morality is a prescription for living with one's passions. Nietzsche tries to show this in the case of **Stoicism**, **Spinoza**, **Aristotle**, and Goethe, and claims that moralities are "baroque and unreasonable in form – because they are addressed to 'all' and generalize where generalizations are impermissible". It would be folly for

St Francis to try to live like Goethe, or vice versa.

Nietzsche finds the greatest power in those who can sublimate and control their passions, employing them creatively. The libertine, who lacks self-control, has less power; and the ascetic, who cannot master his passions short of extirpating them, strikes Nietzsche as weaker than such men as Socrates or Goethe.

Although religion and ethics constituted Nietzsche's primary interests, he also ventured into epistemology and metaphysics. In epistemology he made many interesting suggestions without ever working out any theory. His importance for metaphysics is twofold. First, he offered a psychological analysis of belief in *another* world and argued that *this* world is the only one. And he criticised, especially in *Twilight of the Idols*, metaphysical conceptions of mind, consciousness, ego and will. He even derided "the will" as a phantom which "does not explain anything". Secondly, he offered a metaphysic of his own when he suggested earlier, especially in *Zarathustra*, that "the will to power" is the ultimate reality. His psychological explanations can probably be reconciled with his critique of metaphysical conceptions, but his reification and cosmic projection of the will to power seems clearly inconsistent with his own central intentions. It appears as a misguided attempt to outdo **Schopenhauer**, whom the young Nietzsche had admired. Nietzsche's doctrine of the eternal recurrence of the same events at gigantic intervals, finally, has struck practically all his readers as merely bizarre. But this was not intended as a metaphysical theory: Nietzsche was under the demonstrably mistaken impression that modern science, if it refrains from inconsistently postulating a Creator, entails such a view. And he thought that for almost all men nothing could be more depressing than this prospect, while the overman (*Übermensch*) the human being who has overcome himself and given his life meaning by becoming a creator, might actually say, unlike Goethe's Faust: abide, moment – and if you cannot abide, at least return.

Nietzsche's influence on the existentialists and psychoanalysts, on N. **Hartmann**, Scheler, Spengler, Rilke, Buber, Thomas Mann, Malraux, and Gide has been very pronounced. The literature about him is vast, and includes poems and novels.

Richard Strauss wrote a tone poem, *Thus Spoke Zarathustra*. (w.к.)

Plate 68, page 292.

Nominalism is the theory which holds that the objects of thought are simply words and that there is no more to the meaning of a general term than the set of things to which it applies. At its most modest nominalism holds that there is no independently accessible thing, **universal** or concept, which constitutes the meaning of a word. The only way to find out the meaning of a word is to see what things it is applied to. To say that the meaning *is* this class of things, the word's extension, is to go further and seems to entail that we never really know the meaning of any general word since many words with the same extension differ in meaning (e.g. *man* and *featherless biped*). A more traditional version of nominalism contends that there is nothing more in common to the things a general term applies to than the fact that it applies to them. But to say this, it is argued, makes classification arbitrary and cannot explain why it is that men have made the classifications they have or how it is that they all make the same classifications. In practice, therefore, most nominalists follow Hobbes in holding that the things a general term applies to are related by resemblance. But this similarity theory, it is often claimed, is only a disguised form of **realism**, since resemblance is itself a universal. Nominalism was one of the possibilities envisaged in Porphyry's celebrated comment on the *Categories* of **Aristotle** which posed the problem of universals for medieval philosophy. Roscellinus believed that only individual sensible things were real and took the doctrine of the Trinity to be an assertion of the existence of three gods and, on similar grounds, Berengar of Tours rejected transubstantiation. Many contemporary analytic philosophers follow Hobbes in upholding the similarity theory but **Russell** has remained faithful to realism.

(A.Q.)

Number, *see* Frege, Russell, Mathematics.

O

Occasionalism. For **Descartes** a human being was the point of union of material substance and immaterial substance. Descartes's followers were unable to accept his own curious doctrine of the mechanism by which one of these disparate substances could act upon the other. It was to provide a solution to the problems raised by the undoubted action of one substance on another that the theory of Occasionalism was developed. In each substance, mind and body, the chains of cause and effect were supposed to be complete and independent, since it was clear that modifications of an immaterial substance could be neither the causes nor the effects of modifications of material substance. The correlation between the run of events in the one substance and the run of events in the other was explained by the intervention of God. Geulincx (1625–1669) gave the doctrine its characteristic form. Since doing something involves knowing how to do it, material bodies, knowing nothing, cannot act; their apparent action upon each other is the act of God. Since God is the sole cause, apparent psycho-physical causation need present no problem for the occurrence of an event in the one substance, mind, provides the Occasion for a Divine Act, in the other substance, body.   (R.HAR.)

Ontological Argument *see* Theism, Anselm.

P

Pantheism is the doctrine that everything is divine, that God and Nature are identical. Pantheism is more often discovered as an instrument of poetic expression than as a conclusion of philosophical argument. The great exception here is **Spinoza**. Spinoza's initial definition of substance inexorably leads on to the conclusion that there can only be one substance, truly so-called, and that it must be infinite. For there could be nothing other than itself to limit it and so constitute it finite. Spinoza's definition of God which follows the traditional definitions, makes God the possessor of infinite attributes. But the only being of infinite attributes is the one substance, which is Nature. Hence God and Nature must be identical. The history of Spinoza's reputation illustrates the knife-edge along which the pantheist walks. From the stand-point of the theist, a pantheist appears one who reduces God to Nature, and is thus essentially an atheist. From the stand-point of the sceptic, the pantheist takes an unwarrantedly religious view of Nature, and ap-

pears as a covert theist. All metaphysical doctrines, such as the **Idealist**, which assert that the Universe is a Unity tend towards pantheism. For the Universe is then something more than any of its finite parts; and there can be no deity distinct from it. It may be surmised that the collapse of such metaphysical doctrines deprives intellectual pantheism of its only support.   (A.MACI.)

Parmenides, Greek philosopher of Elea in Southern Italy, born about 515 B.C. He wrote a philosophical poem consisting of a prologue and two parts, of which considerable fragments have survived. The prologue describes Parmenides' meeting with a goddess who reveals the truth outlined in the first part of the poem; of the two possible paths of inquiry, *It is* and *It is not*, only the first is tenable – "for you could not know what *is not* (for this is impossible), nor could you give expression to it". Thus Parmenides recognized the existential "is not" as an artificial concept, but was misled by his inability to distinguish the existential and predicative "is" into denying that negative predication was possible. This seemed to entail that there could be no differentiation in the real world (since if A can be distinguished from B then A *is not* B, which was, by Parmenides' logic, impossible). Thus reality, "that which is", must be single, homogeneous, indivisible, everlasting, and motionless. Since Being still necessarily implied concrete bulk at this period it was spatially finite, "like the mass of a well-rounded sphere". Some of Parmenides' arguments against not-being were perhaps directed particularly against **Pythagorean** dualism. But he himself, in the fragmentary second part of his poem, which professedly gave "the opinions of mortals" and was "deceitful", outlined a cosmology in which the world was composed of two opposed substances or "forms", fire and night. What was evidently quite an elaborate account included explanations of thought and knowledge (produced by the excess of one opposite, the hot or the cold, in the limbs), and astronomy, which had points in common with **Anaximander**'s. The purpose of this "Way of Seeming" is obscure. Perhaps Parmenides felt that his true conception of Being was too austere for practical life and ordinary people, and intended to show that the apparent world could be accounted for on the basis of a single pair of apparent sensible opposites, without introducing so-called reality-principles like the Limit and Unlimited of the Pythagoreans.   (G.S.K.)

Pascal, Blaise, (1623–1662), a Frenchman, rightly famous as a mathematician, scientist, theologian and one of the earliest great French prose writers rather than as a philosopher in the narrower sense. His earlier years were devoted to mathematics and the physical sciences; his experiments with the barometer are famous, the ascent of the Puy de Dôme by his brother at his direction being a decisive confirmation of the theory of air pressure but recently advanced; the barometer carried by Pascal's brother fell steadily as he climbed. In 1654 Pascal underwent a profound experience of religious conversion; he became a strong adherent of the Jansenists and much of his energy was henceforth devoted to theological and religious propaganda and controversy. He continued however to work occasionally at mathematics, doing work on the theory of the cycloid preparatory to the theory of the calculus and with Fermat laying the basis of the mathematical theory of **probability**. Pascal's posthumously published *Pensées* constitute the part of his work most interesting to a philosopher; most notably he argues for the reasonableness of faith on the ground that there are no rational grounds either for belief or disbelief and so belief is not less reasonable than disbelief; but this being so it is wiser to gamble on the truth of religion since this policy involves success if religion is true and no significant loss if it is false. The section containing reflections on geometry also has some wise and clear remarks on definition and the nature of deductive systems. (J.O.U.)

Plates 70 and 71, pages 294 and 295.

Peirce, Charles Sanders, (1839–1914), born at Cambridge, Massachusetts, son of Benjamin Peirce who was America's leading mathematician of that time. Much of Charles' early formation was scientific. He took his A.M. in mathematics, and in 1861 was the first ever to take the Sc.B. in chemistry at Harvard. He came to philosophy through reading Schiller and was later enthralled by **Kant**. He associated with most of the leading American thinkers of his day – among them **James**, Wright and Holmes. But he obtained little academic recognition and was never appointed to a permanent university post. He spent most of the latter part of his life almost as a recluse and died in comparative poverty in 1914. He published a number of philosophical articles during his career but no book on philosophy. Much of his best work remained unpublished until it was edited in the *Collected Papers of C. S. Peirce* (8 volumes: 1931–58).

Epistemology: The central problem in modern **epistemology** has been to reconcile the subjective nature of thought with our claim to know what is distinct from thought. This had not been a problem for **Aristotle**. He considered that the mind simply discovered an order that pre-existed in reality. But Kant inverted Aristotle's position and claimed that the order in our knowledge came from the mind alone. Peirce accepted the modern problem and offered his own solution.

Peirce began by holding that we are conscious that we experience the real directly. The real consists of the things that exist whether we think about them or not. Moreover, if we are to avoid unpleasant surprises, we must endeavour to adapt our conduct to these things. So far he agrees with Aristotle. But it is clear that we deal with things according to the ideas we have of them. Our ideas however are selective constructions, based on a partial experience of things; this experience is coloured by our history, circumstances and purpose. The selective nature of knowledge led Peirce to agree with Kant that the mind constructs to some extent the order in knowledge. He next set about showing that if we examine what an idea or concept is we should be able to reconcile what is true in the differing explanations of Aristotle and Kant.

In reply to the question: What is a concept?: Peirce formulated in 1878 his famous **pragmatic** maxim: "Consider what effects, which might have conceivably practical bearings, we conceive the object of our conception to have. Then, our conception of these effects is the whole of our conception of the object." He illustrates the maxim by saying that our idea of "wine" means nothing "but what has certain effects, direct or indirect, upon our senses". So too, if we call a thing "hard", we mean that "it will not be scratched by many other substances". He summed up: "Our idea of anything is our idea of its sensible effects." Peirce offers his maxim as an instrument for distinguishing true knowledge from false. True knowledge – a correct idea of an object – enables us to predict what will happen when we come to deal with that object. He is making use of the notion of verification of hypotheses. He had learned the importance of this notion from modern science. In fact for Peirce all our ideas are analogous to scientific hypotheses.

Peirce's 1878 formulation of the maxim contained in germ his later views. But it was formulated too exclusively in view of explaining our ideas of material things; it gave the impression of leaving no place for an idea such as moral goodness; a *regulative* idea such as the latter does not lead to direct sensory verification but controls our conduct in our dealings with persons and things. Furthermore, William James and the popular pragmatists took the maxim in a phenomenalist sense. Peirce developed his views in later years and set about avoiding all suspicion of phenomenalism. He did this essentially by insisting that pragmatism (or "pragmaticism" as he eventually called his teaching to distinguish it from that of James and others) teaches that an idea has meaning through any possible practical conduct that it can lead to or regulate. An idea does not necessarily have to lead to immediate sensory verification. It is enough if it gives meaning to our conduct. For example, the notion of truth as an ideal-limit, though it has itself no direct sensory content, inspires us to keep on adding to our knowledge. Lastly, Peirce completed his theory by saying that each idea gives rise to a possibility of regular conduct in regard to what the idea expresses. Hence each idea is finally interpreted in a "habit". These habits, interpretants of our ideas, are "guides to action". Our ideas find living and consistent expression in our habitual modes of conduct.

We can sum up briefly this part of Peirce's solution to the problem of knowledge. The meaning of a concept or hypothesis lies in the conduct that it gives rise to. An hypothesis that can be verified is a true one. When our concepts lead us to conduct that is neither surprised nor found wanting, the essential subjectivity of knowing is seen to be overcome. Our constructed concepts lead to actions that respect things as they exist in themselves independently of thought.

But since the knowledge of an object or situation that an inquirer possesses is always inadequate, it is not enough that any single individual should apply the maxim. The researches of fellow-inquirers correct and fill in the knowledge gained in individual inquiry. The community of research (this includes all men with scientific inquirers as its *élite*) gathers more knowledge than any single individual and works to overcome mistakes in individual verification. In this way knowledge is pooled and correction is a cooperative affair. But since even the community existing at any given moment may be wrong about something – and in any case will not know everything about it – every inquirer has to envisage his research within the indefinitely continuing research of a constantly growing company of inquirers. Hence the community seeks truth as an ideal-limit. Searchers after truth make their way all the time towards a state of perfect knowledge; but they will never arrive at this state. That does not however rule out absolutely certain knowledge. We can be sure, for example, that Napoleon lived. But we can go on indefinitely acquiring knowledge about his life.

The need for honesty in scrutinizing one's data, for integrity in cooperating with others and for a genuine love of truth led Peirce to understand that truth is not only to be seen intellectually but has to be won morally. Not only does the serious beginning of inquiry demand self-discipline but the partial and selective nature of our knowing exacts self-control as we weigh what we know of an object against what future experience may reveal of it. In other words, the work which we carry on of forming concepts, drawing consequences from them and verifying these consequences must be carried out in a self-disciplined and cooperative way within the community of seekers and against the background of the social ideal-limit of truth.

To round off this section we may remark: (1) The influence of modern science on Peirce's epistemology is clear: (*a*) in his considering all concepts to be analogous to constructed hypotheses that can be verified; (*b*) in his theory of cooperative research. (2) As a solution to the subject-object dilemma of modern philosophy he offered a dynamic theory of truth that makes room for empirical research, moral effort and an ideal-limit view of knowledge. This is a valuable contribution. (3) But it must be admitted that Peirce left many logical problems untouched and never coordinated his own findings to any adequate extent.

Categories: Like Aristotle Peirce wanted to classify the main aspects of reality through a doctrine of **Categories**. Aristotle's categories however had been objectivist; they were concepts inserted between the direct experience of the subject and the objects of experience. For our times Peirce believed that we need categories that express aspects of the world in terms of our direct perceptive experience. He formulated three such categories: Firstness, Secondness, and Thirdness.

Firstness is the spontaneous aspect of things: it is exemplified especially in the free surge of the mind in the formation of hypotheses; it indicates life, growth and variety in the universe. In any single instance of Firstness, such as an act of immediate consciousness before it is reflected on, there is undifferentiated unity. But otherness and the struggle resulting from it are also an inescapable fact of experience. Hence comes the next category.

Secondness points to the element of duality in experience; resistance presupposes another being, a second. Through this category Peirce emphasises existence, "that mode of being which lies in opposition to another … A thing without oppositions *ipso facto* does not exist". In this sense existence is not a predicate but something that is experienced in willing and, perceiving as we come up against the "brute fact" aspect of the world and the sheer individuality and limitation of each individual thing over and against every other thing. But spontaneity and opposition do not exhaust our experience of reality; there is continuity or regularity.

Thirdness caters for continuity, especially continuity in thought since the latter reveals what continuity is to be found elsewhere. Peirce calls Thirdness "law". He means that we can reflect on an idea like "wine" or "hard" and see that it applies to many things; that shows that there is regularity in the real, and this regularity is the foundation of law. He speaks of "law" or "general principles" as being "active" in things. What he is saying is that the uniformities we discover in the real order have meaning for us only in so far as we ourselves can act regularly in their regard. So we can conceive the laws of the universe as analogous to our own habits of action. One may note that Thirdness links up directly with his epistemology.

Peirce meant his categories simply to draw attention to the most important features of our experience, features too that metaphysical thinking would be concerned with. He declared that each of the three aspects is to be found in all lived experience. However we shall see in the next section that Peirce thought that in one instance the first category could be found in a pure state without the other two.

God, the Self and Immortality: (1) *God*: Peirce accepted as a philosophical hypothesis the idea of a personal and omnipotent God. He then outlined several different ways of arguing the reality of such a Being. We shall refer briefly to three of these: (*a*) The living variety of the universe and the spontaneity that finds its highest expression in human personality enables us to *perceive* (he uses the term in a wide sense) an infinite Spontaneity or Firstness at the source of limited instances of Firstness. (*b*) It is clear that an order of dynamic finality exists in the world. The manner in which the human mind is adapted to interpreting and predicting the course of nature through the hypotheses of science brings out such purposiveness most clearly. The only full explanation of this adaptation of parts of the world to one another and of the mind and the world is that an absolute Mind has presided over the creation and development of things. Peirce adds that the evolutionary hypothesis supports this for there has not been time enough to allow for haphazard and unguided development from chaos to the present order. (*c*) When we reflect on the hypothesis of God as the creative Source of the universe, we are gradually impelled to accept this hypothesis as the only possible explanation of existence. An instinctive belief in God fits every movement of our nature. Our inclination to pray and our awe before the totality of things go to confirm the truth of the hypothesis.

Pierce concluded that God is unlimited in knowledge and power. Nothing is opposed to his Being (no Secondness in him) and he is above all conceptual order (no Thirdness). But we are forced to conceive him to some extent in the image of a man. Such anthropomorphism is not false: rather it is figurative. It is justified in its intention provided that we do not seek to make our representation of God too precise. One might remark here that Peirce found language extremely inadequate for describing the infinite Being. But he succeeded in avoiding the trap of a geometrically immutable Deity and he presented a God with whom men could enter into living relationship.

(2) *The Self:* Peirce rejected the Cartesian atomistic and thought-transparent self. Indeed he stressed to such an extent the connections that each *ego* has with other men and the universe that to read some passages alone one might think that he rejected a unitary self. He also insisted that we have to interpret our own thoughts. They are as much signs to us as are the words of other people and the things of the universe. But if he rejected the Cartesian self, he had no time either for the view current among the other pragmatists that reduced human personality to a "bundle of habits". He pointed out instead that moral self-control imparts to a man's actions that unitary form which we call character. Moreover, "unity must be given as a centre for habits". Lastly, Firstness presupposes some minimum unity; Secondness is based on the self as distinct from everything else; and Thirdness of its nature points to unified continuity in human thought. In a word, Peirce admitted a unitary self. But it was a self of a much more complex unity than Cartesian philosophy had thought of.

(3) *Immortality:* Peirce never made up his mind about immortality. Early in his career he admitted that in its favour was the failure of **materialism** to explain much of the universe. But against it was the dependence of the working of the mind on the body. As the years went on he laid more and more stress on the spiritual aspects of the universe as evidence for personal immortality. But he stopped short of saying that such evidence was apodictic.

Peirce exercised little real influence during his life. William James popularised a form or pragmatism that derived largely from a misunderstanding of Peirce's pragmatic principle and his insistence on moral effort in the search for truth. **Royce**'s theory of the social infinite owes a lot to Peirce's teaching on the community of inquirers but Peirce dismissed Royce's logic as execrable. **Dewey** took over some of the empirical emphases in Peirce's methodology. But by and large Peirce's general philosophy made no impact until recent years with the publication of the *Collected Papers*. At present he is at least being commented on quite frequently, especially in the United States. But it is too soon to say in what direction his influence will be felt most. (J.O'C.)

Peter of Spain, also known as Petrus Hispanus, lived in the thirteenth century. He is believed by some to be Petrus Alphonsi O.P., but is now generally identified with Petrus Juliani who was born *c.* 1210–1220 at Lisbon. Juliani studied at Paris, was doctor of medicine to Pope Gregory X at Viterbo in 1272, Archbishop of Braga and Cardinal of Tusculum in 1273, was elected to the Papacy as John XXI 13 September, 1276, and died 20 May, 1277 owing to the collapse of a study which he had had built.

The opinion of K. Prantl that his *Summulae Logicales,* which remained a fundamental logical text till the seventeenth century, was a translation from a Greek text of the eleventh century Michael Psellus was soon refuted, and the supposed original is now known to be a much later derivative.

Of the twelve tractates in the *Summulae*, 1–5 and 7 correspond in their own admirably concise and formal way to the books of **Aristotle**'s *Organon*, with the exception of the *Posterior Analytics*, those on the *Predicables* and *Predicaments* (2 and 3) being, however, placed after that corresponding to the *Peri Hermeneias*. This order had already been adopted by William of Shyreswood, a master under whom Peter may have studied in Paris, in his *Introductiones in Logicam*. The remaining tractates, 6 and 8–12, forming the *logica moderna*, are concerned with the "properties of terms", supposition, amplification etc. being interrupted by the last tractate of the *logica antiqua*, on fallacies. It is noteworthy that the best evidence points to this dovetailing of the old and new as authentic, and Shyreswood had already given a precedent in this respect.

A notable innovation in the *Summulae*, destined for enormous influence, is the method of describing the syllogistic. The major premise is by definition that which is first stated, and the major extreme is by definition that extreme which appears in the major premise. Here Peter was extending to the first figure the definitions which Shyreswood, following Boethius, had adopted only for the second and third. Exclusion of all reference to the conclusion is fully explained by his definition of a syllogism as consisting not of three but of two propositions (the premises). This metalogical apparatus is of course quite distinct from the much later decree that the major premise, defined as that containing the major extreme, itself defined as the predicate of the conclusion, must stand first. But there is some reason to think that in the sixteenth and seventeenth centuries the Petrine method was mistakenly taken as asserting this, and that it was failure to distinguish the two sets of definitions which occasioned the rise and spread of this curious tenet.

Peter also wrote a *Syncategoremata*, in which is to be found the principle that "when an entire copulative (conjunctive) proposition is negated, no determinate part of it is negated, but each of its parts under disjunction". This is one of the two equivalences relating negation, conjunction and disjunction formerly ascribed to De Morgan, now often named after **William of Ockham**.   (I.T.)

Phenomenalism is the doctrine that human knowledge is confined to the appearances (phenomena) presented to the senses or, less restrictively, that appearances are the ultimate foundation of all our knowledge. It takes two main forms: first that of a general theory of knowledge and secondly, more usual at the present time, that of a theory of perception. (1) As a general theory of knowledge phenomenalism is the view that we can know nothing that is not given to us in sense-experience and it denies, with more or less thoroughness, the validity of inferences made from things that fall within our sense-experience to things lying outside it. One version, sometimes called agnosticism, asserts that, although we cannot infer the character of what lies outside our sense-experience, we can at least infer that there is something outside it. **Kant**'s Thing-in-itself, **Hamilton**'s Unconditioned and **Spencer**'s Unknowable are outcomes of this line of thought. Some philosophers, understandably reluctant to suppose that we can know that there is something that lies beyond the bounds of possible knowledge, maintain that nothing at all exists beyond the appearances presented to our senses. This view, sometimes called sensationalism, is roughly exemplified by the doctrines of **Hume**, J. S. **Mill** and **Russell**, although both Hume and Mill were dissatisfied with their attempts to explain the observing mind that is the subject of sense-experience in terms of the appearances presented to it. To describe phenomenalism, as is often done, as the view that we do not know things as they really are but only as they appear to us, is misleading. By implying that there are things over and above the appearances presented to us, it begs the question in favour of agnosticism.

(2) In its usual modern form, as a theory of perception, phenomenalism was first clearly expounded by J. S. Mill in 1865 and his compact formula – a material thing is a permanent possibility of sensation – is as good as any. Much the same point is conveyed by Russell's remark: the thing is the class of its appearances. More recent phenomenalists have preferred to state their doctrine in a linguistic, instead of an ontological, idiom. Material-object statements, they say, are reducible to or translatable into statements about sense-data. The whole content of our beliefs about material things can be expressed in terms of what is immediately given in sense-experience. The usual argument for this conclusion starts from the straight-forward consideration that everything we know by perception must be either inferred or uninferred. Now unless some of it is uninferred we are landed with an infinite regress. This inescapably uninferred perceptual knowledge, it is widely, though not universally, agreed, is knowledge of appearances, that is of sense-data. So much is common ground to many theories of perception. The characteristic phenomenalist contention at this point is that there can be no valid inference from appearances which purports to conclude to the existence of transcendental things, to things, in other words, that do not appear to us and so of which we have no direct knowledge. What reason could we have for believing that there now exists something unobserved that stands in a certain relation, that of being its cause for example, to what we are now observing? Only that we have in the past actually observed such things regularly standing in that relation to sense-data like our present ones. It is, of course, logically impossible that we should have such evidence for things transcending sense-experience since these are unobservable by definition.

Phenomenalists are not, however, solipsists. They do not believe that there is nothing we can know to exist apart from our own sense-experiences. But, while not rejecting all inference from sense-data, they will only countenance inference to things that could in principle be experienced. The permitted variety of inference is simple extrapolation to what are variously called possible sensations (Mill), sensibilia (Russell) and hypothetical sense-data. Our actual experience displays enough regularity for us to establish laws of correlation between experiences of different kinds. When some part of one of these regular patterns is presented to us we can reasonably understand that the rest of the pattern is available if we modify the conditions of observation appropriately (for example, by stretching out our hands or opening our eyes). Our experience, though fragmentary, is orderly enough to enable us to construct from it a material world that is, in Hume's phrase "continuous and distinct". There is some disagreement about the way in which this conclusion should be expressed. Russell speaks of "sensibilia", actual entities just like sense-data except in the respect that no observer is aware of them. Others, feeling that there is still a faint whiff of the transcendent, even of the self-contradictory, about this, prefer to say that what we infer is the truth of hypothetical propositions.

There are three main lines of objection to this theory. First, it is argued that the phenomenalist translation could never, even in principle, be carried out, either because we lack the verbal means to effect it or because the appearances associated with a given material object are infinitely numerous and complex. Secondly, it is said that the translation is spurious since the antecedent clauses of the hypothetical statements making up the translation must themselves mention material objects, for example the bodies and especially the sense-organs of observers and the physical conditions of observation. Thirdly, a lot of discomfort has been felt, even by philosophers well-disposed to phenomenalism such as H. H. **Price**, about the fact that unobserved material things, which are only clusters of possibilities according to the theory, exert a causal influence. How can the collection of possible sense-data, which is all the water at the bottom of a well consists of, manage to emit an actual noise when an unobserved, and so equally hypothetical, stone strikes it? A more fundamental line of objection starts further back by attacking the presumption shared by phenomenalists with many other theorists of knowledge, that the only immediate objects of perception are sense-data.

Phenomenalism has close affinities with the theory of perception put forward by **Berkeley**, who

at one point, indeed, explicitly propounds phenomenalism but fails to follow it up. What we infer, in his view, is not possible experiences of our own but actual, and pretty transcendent-looking, experiences of God's. Mill could be said to have derived his phenomenalism from Hume's account of perception by making one crucial change: what Hume regarded as an imaginative fiction Mill saw as a legitimate piece of intellectual construction. Russell with his theory of sensibilia, has never been a complete phenomenalist and Price was led by the argument about the causal efficacy of clusters of mere possibilities to augment his families of sense-data with ghostly relics of Lockean substance called Physical Occupants. The most thorough and unwavering phenomenalist of recent times is **Ayer**.

Phenomenalist theories of mind have been advanced with more or less conviction and enthusiasm by Hume, Mill, Russell and Ayer, theories which see the mind as simply a related cluster of actual experiences. **Mach** and Pearson expounded a phenomenalist philosophy of science which gives an attractively hard-headed account of the theoretical entities of natural science (electrons, viruses etc.). In **Carnap**'s *Logische Aufbau der Welt* a completely generalised phenomenalism is worked out in impressive formal detail in which our entire conceptual apparatus is decomposed into its ultimate phenomenal constituents. (A.Q.)

Phenomenology. In its broadest meaning, the term phenomenology signifies a descriptive philosophy of experience. The name of **Husserl** is most closely associated with this term in twentieth century thought. C. S. **Peirce** defined the descriptive discipline of "phaneroscopy" or "phenomenology", but no relationship between him and Husserl has been established. Husserl's version of phenomenology is unrelated historically to **Hegel**'s conception of "phenomenology of the spirit". Although there can be no doubt about Husserl's gradual tendency, in his later years, to evolve a "philosophy of the spirit", he felt hostility toward speculative philosophy in his formative period. The indebtedness of phenomenology, in Husserl's sense, is nevertheless many-sided. The influence of **Brentano**, **James**, the British empiricists, **Descartes**, **Leibniz** and **Kant** is to be noted particularly.

The Husserlian version of phenomenology was

developed slowly and painstakingly. The aim to reconcile the *a priori* validity of formal reasoning and psychical processes, and to extend the scope of the "*a priori*" to the entire field of experience, was a primary motive leading to a science of "pure" phenomenology. Phenomenology was first defined as "descriptive psychology". The inadequacy of that definition soon became apparent, and Husserl managed to clarify his conception of it in the elaboration of a "transcendental" phenomenology. From the beginning, phenomenology was committed to the ideal of the greatest possible freedom from presuppositions. Accordingly, speculative constructions are ruled out, and there can be no talk of an inaccessible realm beyond the reach of possible experience. The slogan "Back to the things themselves!" expresses this principle very well.

The term "transcendental" is a name for a purely reflective point of view. Kant indicated its general nature when he spoke of "transcendental" as meaning the attending to the experiencing of an object, rather than to the object itself. The aim is to make the reflection as "radical" as possible, proceeding to the sources of evidence in immediate experience, and "questioning" everything for its evidence. Toward that end, a procedure of "reduction" is instituted, requiring the suspension of all beliefs, and of all scientific knowledge as well. Descartes' procedure of doubt serves as a convenient means of introducing the method of phenomenology. One could be mistaken in his judgments about the world, or anything "transcendent" of experience. But the "immanent" experiences concerning the world, or concerning any alleged or imagined objects, cannot be doubted. This is to go along with Descartes' "beginning", the purpose being to make something systematic and fruitful out of it, rather than to let it go as kind of rhetorical flourish in a philosophical meditation.

The aim is, then, to delimit the entire, endless realm of experiences, in all their types – perception, phantasy, etc. That can in any case be defined as a self-contained field for inquiry. If all beliefs in existence, or in truths of any kind, are suspended, we are left with the experiences themselves, and with the objectivities as meant by the experiences. The two sides – the meaning side and the meant side, as such – are called the *noetic* and *noematic* sides of experience. This "correlative" mode of viewing experience is essential to the procedure of phenomenology. With all beliefs placed in abeyance as a matter of method, one can speak of "pure subjectivity", or of "pure experience". It is a "radical" procedure because all natural and traditional assumptions whether metaphysical or theoretical, have been suspended. It would be a misunderstanding, however, to infer that the world has been "discarded" or denied. The "thesis" of existence has simply been "put out of play", and the "world" must now be placed in quotation-marks: it is the correlate of my meaningful experience, but it is no longer regarded as independently real. It is a "bracketed" world.

The "reduction" to the stream of inner experiences which has been described must be performed by an individual thinker, who will carry the procedure as far as possible. Because one must begin with his own experiences, "transcendental egology" is the first stage. The "exhibiting" or evidence of other minds must be provided for if solipsism is to be avoided. In the language of phenomenology, that is made possible by "empathy", "appresentation", and "apperception by analogy", based upon the resemblance of other bodies to one's own body. The phenomenologist then speaks of "transcendental intersubjectivity", and of the "constitution" of the objective world.

The term "constitution" is unfortunately used in more than one sense in the literature of phenomenology. It really names the *constructive* programme of descriptive analysis, which is called for once the "purification" of the "reduction", or, as it turns out, a series of "reductions", is completed. "Creation" is not what is meant by a descriptive phenomenology. To speak of the "constitution" of the world of nature within the frame of pure consciousness should not suggest that the world is made out of consciousness. If all things are to be viewed as objects of and for experience, it is appropriate to speak of the synthetic and "idealising" processes by which complex structures and meanings are "constituted" out of the stream of experiences. The meaningful (noetic) experiences and the meant (noematic) objects are both included in the scope of the endless descriptive inquiry.

The value from a critical point of view is evident. The programme of reflecting upon all knowledge and experience, with the ideal of evidence in mind, as meaning the "self-givenness" in experience of what is meant, may well have an emancipating effect upon thinkers.

The transcendental or purely reflective "reduction" to one's stream of experiences is united with another type of "reduction", called "eidetic reduction". In plain words, "eidetic" means "essential", and "reduction" is used in the sense of "restriction". One is not concerned with natural events in phenomenology. There are no causal methods; they belong to the special sciences. The interest is restricted to the descriptive analysis of essential structures and relations, in all types of experience, such as perception, remembrance, etc., and in all the "intentional" or meant objects of experience.

The procedure of phenomenology is regarded as having the advantage of avoiding the doubts and errors of ordinary natural experience. The investigator of the "immanent" realm of experience allegedly has the advantage of not being "at the mercy of the facts". He may indeed make mistakes in his descriptions. But he is incomparably more secure than the natural investigator. At least, that is the argument. On the other hand, it must be admitted that the defender of natural experience as having a very high degree of probability may submit a formidable case. It is unfortunate that the attempt to justify the pure "inner" realm of inquiry against severe opposition led to the demeaning of natural experience and its methods.

But that is not the only reason. The historical role of phenomenology is seen in its alignment with the foes of naturalism. It became a means of outflanking and disposing of **naturalism** as a philosophy; and, positively, of serving as a well-defined idealistic philosophy. In its opposition to naturalism it was in the company of the dominant academic philosophers of the time, who were concerned with circumscribing the methods of the sciences, and with defending the traditional preserve of a spiritual philosophy of values. Although phenomenology is a highly distinctive philosophy, with much novelty in its methods and in its descriptive results, it has little that is new to offer in its basic arguments for **idealism**. If mind or spirit were removed, Husserl argues, there would be no nature; for spirit is what gives meaning to being.

The chief justification of phenomenology lies in the value of its descriptive findings. Its studies of time-consciousness, "origin-analyses" of the basic concepts of **logic**, and analysis of perception and other modes of experience have greatly extended the range of our vision for descriptive purposes. It is on "seeing" that the greatest emphasis is placed. "Seeing" is a finality; it cannot be based upon anything more fundamental. The field of description encompasses the whole network of psychical relations, and particular attention is devoted to the process of "idealisation", without which scientific experience and thinking would not be possible.

The subjective method of phenomenology should not be presumed to displace the objective empirical methods of the sciences. Apart from the motive of overcoming opposition, it is characteristic of the enthusiasm with which a new point of view is promoted, to make excessive claims for its potentialities. Like so many other innovators, Husserl did not know when to stop, in his relentless drive toward a universal philosophy. At times, he revealed awareness of the limits of his achievements, as when he mused that he would never set foot on the "promised land". The pure eidetic science of transcendental phenomenology, which would enable philosophy to provide scientists with thoroughly clarified concepts and basic principles, remained an ideal for him, just as it had been an unfulfilled promise for the great rationalists.

The charge has been made that phenomenology has no access to the "problem of being". As a "pure" subjectivistic procedure, it excludes all judgments of existence. From its point of view, all the special sciences are "dogmatic", because they make assumptions concerning being, and their concepts and principles have not been rendered "evident" in immediate experience. How, then, can a phenomenologist speak of "being"? Does it not avoid what should be considered a vitally important problem? The answer can only be given by emphasizing the specialized service which phenomenology can render. It is not equipped to deliver a universal philosophy, which requires active cooperation with the sciences. It can, however, make important contributions within the limits of its area of activity, as determined by its carefully defined conditions for inquiry. The "clarification" of the basic concepts and principles of the sciences and of the "ontologies", of which we still have so few (geometry, for example), in terms of immediate experience, is in itself a programme sufficiently important to make it an indispensable discipline. The descriptive analysis of experience from the radically reflective point of view undertakes to make clear the contributions of the knower to experience. That has already been carried to a point hitherto scarcely approached in the history of philosophy. The service to logic and psychology offers no doubt the most promising prospects of this descriptive work.

The impact of phenomenological findings on psychology has been impeded by sharp critical exchanges, caused by misunderstanding on the part of some psychologists, and righteous indignation on the part of Husserl – not unmixed, however, with something of the acrimonious spirit of the "schools" in Germany. The critique of the "natural science of psychology" was intended by Husserl to show the need for a "rational psychology", which would do for naturalistic psychology what geometry has done for physical science. This is characteristic of the hopes for phenomenology. Husserl portrayed it as furnishing the "mother-ground" for all the basic concepts and principles of the sciences. The "First Philosophy" which he envisaged was to be truly the "foundation" for all knowledge which could pretend or hope to be scientific.

The influence of phenomenology has been extensive, and to some extent it has borne fruit of a type quite uncongenial to Husserl. He regarded the so-called "realistic" phenomenologists as dogmatic metaphysicians. The broader phenomenological movement includes a prominent religious wing, with some evidence of mysticism. The "intuition of essences" of phenomenology has not only been misused to include the non-rational, but has also at times deteriorated to the level of banal descriptions of familiar objects of experience. Attempts have been made, with varying degrees of success, to develop a phenomenological approach to social science, history, art, mathematics, psychology, and psychiatry, as well as logic and the philosophy of values. Ill-fated in Husserl's own view was the rapidly growing "existentialistic" movement, admittedly owing something to phenomenology, while disavowing the severe limits of its subjectivism in the name of a "philosophy of existence". The "correlative point of view" of phenomenology is superseded in that movement by talk of "trans-

cendence", "paratranscendence", and "mystery".

It is possible to formulate a strictly methodological version of phenomenology, with no ulterior commitments to idealism or any other dogma. The phenomenological procedure is then subsumed under the general class of methods of inquiry, along with all the "objective" methods – inductive, causal, and explanatory. Although its findings may well be valuable for all other disciplines, it is also true that it could have no subject-matter without the factual "mother-ground", which is primarily represented by the natural and cultural sciences.

Phenomenology is regarded as a "reactionary" philosophy in Soviet Russia, and by **dialectical materialists** generally. Naturalists have not been reserved in their misgivings concerning a subjectivistic philosophy of "pure reflection". A strict phenomenology, freed from all pretence to metaphysics, and from excessive claims to "absoluteness", would, however, be as defensible in its way as symbolic logic has always been in its own universe of discourse. (M.F.)

Plato (*c.* 427–347 B.C.), son of Ariston and Perictione, was born in Athens and lived there for most of his eighty years. Though at first marked out for politics, both by his lineage and by his interests, he in fact devoted himself almost wholly to study, to theory, and to teaching. One cause of this was the disgust he came to feel at the low level of politics in his time; he found that bad faith and injustice and cynical selfishness were widespread, and that ingenuous good faith could not stand against them. The only hope for politics, it seemed to him, was to found a school and create therein a new kind of political character.

The main cause of his renouncing political practice was probably **Socrates**. He fell deeply under the spell of Socrates' magnetic and searching thought, and was profoundly shocked when, at the age of about 27, he saw Socrates condemned to death on the absurd charge of corrupting the young men and not believing in the city's gods. He has left us unhistorical but magnificent pictures of Socrates' defence, imprisonment, and execution, in his *Apology*, *Crito*, and *Phaedo*.

After this disaster, most of the friends of Socrates left Athens for a time; and Plato now had a period of travel, in the course of which he visited the Greek cities of Sicily and southern Italy, made political and scholarly friends there, and widened his conceptions of man and study. By about 385, at the latest, he was back in Athens, and was founding, near the grove of the hero Academus, what has come to be called the "Academy", and what may loosely but usefully be called the first university. He gathered about him a number of pupils and fellow students, who united themselves in a "museum", or friendly society dedicating itself to those patrons of letters and music, the Muses. The members, who must have been very few and very rich compared with the undergraduates of today, might stay there for twenty years or even for life, taking part in the common studies, religious exercises, and meals. The ultimate practical purpose of the society was held to be the restoration of decent government to the Greek cities. Some of the members left after a time and went into practical politics. Some, including Plato himself, wrote political advice to their friends elsewhere. But the studies pursued were far from wholly practical. Plato held the restoration of decent government to require a complete foundation of theoretical knowledge; and he sought to lay such a foundation, as deep and as firm as possible. The studies which he encouraged hence came to appear to the man in the street as obscure, fine-drawn, and impractical; and there is a story that, when he advertised a lecture on "The Good", people came hoping to learn how to be happy, but heard only what seemed to them to be higher mathematics. Mathematics certainly became, after philosophy, the study most pursued by the society.

Since Plato never married (his writings suggest that he had no sexual interest in women), he was able to devote himself to his school; and he appears to have done so for most of the remaining forty years of his long life. He had, however, two very important relations with the outside world; his interventions in the politics of Syracuse and his published writings.

During his travels Plato had made a friend of Dion at the court of Syracuse. In 367 Dion urged Plato to come to Syracuse and instruct the new ruler, Dionysius II, who being young and well-intentioned might be made into the new kind of statesman desired by Plato. Plato saw that he must go and went; but he had little hope of realising his

ideal in Dionysius, and had probably lost by this time most of his original eagerness for political practice. The matter turned out very badly. This was not because the royal pupil had no relish for Plato or philosophy. On the contrary, he became very attached to his teacher and to the subject. It was because he came to suspect his teacher's friend Dion of aiming at too much political power. No doubt this suspicion of Dion was fostered by Dion's rivals among the courtiers. Plato had not been at Syracuse six months before Dionysius expelled Dion on the ground that he was plotting against him. Loyalty then compelled Plato to support Dion and demand his recall, while jealousy and suspicion drove Dionysius to try to separate Plato from Dion. Dionysius never let Dion return, and for some time he did not let Plato leave.

Six years later, in 361, Dionysius sent for Plato again, and ensured Plato's compliance by making it a condition of the restoration of Dion. Once he had Plato, however, he did not recall Dion but on the contrary finally confiscated Dion's property in Syracuse. Plato had to use the influence of a neighbouring ruler in order to be allowed to return to Athens.

Jealousy begins with false beliefs; but by acting on them it makes them true. Dion now became in fact the irreconcilable enemy of Dionysius. He invaded Syracuse and drove Dionysius from it in 357, ruled it himself for four years, and then was assassinated. The assassin apparently had had relations with Plato and was considered a member of the Academy. This was a terrible blow to Plato.

Plato's publications are all preserved, and make five modern octavo volumes. They constitute not merely the greatest philosophical work there is, but also one of the greatest pieces of literature in the world. They are philosophy *par excellence*; and, if anyone asks what philosophy is, the best answer is: "read Plato". For it was Plato who brought the word "philosophy" into use; and it was he who mainly invented and first practised the sort of study for which "philosophy" is the name. To say that there is little philosophy in a major work by Plato is self-contradictory; or it expresses an arbitrary and improper change in the meaning of the word. The socalled **Pre-Socratic** philosophers, and even Socrates, were not philosophers in the full sense of the word, though they were certainly Plato's in-spirers.

Plato's works, though not dated, can now for the most part be confidently assigned to one of three periods, the early, the middle, and the late. The early works constitute an extremely striking presentation of the figure of Socrates.

All but one of these works are dialogues; and this is part of Plato's conception of philosophy as well as part of his literary originality. Philosophy is essentially a kind of *logos*; and Plato's notion of *logos* may be analysed in modern terms as "the reasonable use of words in thinking". The reason-able use of words involves submitting them to crit-icism by others and testing them by their implica-tions; and this involves dialogue. The typical early Platonic dialogue draws out the implications of a statement, in order to test it for consistency with itself and with other statements being considered at the same time. The question whether to adopt a statement must not be answered until we have answered the question, what are its implications and connections. Since more implications may be-come visible to us in the future, it is usually better to adopt a view provisionally and until someone persuades us otherwise with a better argument.

In his middle dialogues Plato shows some dis-satisfaction with the hypothetical and negative pro-cedure of his Socrates in the early dialogues, and some hope of finding an unhypothetical starting-point on which to base intuitive certainty and good politics. He thinks that such a starting-point can be found, if at all, only in the region suggested by the following statements.

Through all the multiplicity and variety of just and unjust acts, persons, and situations, in this world, there evidently is in some way only *one* Justice and only *one* Injustice. And so with every other collection of things to which we apply the same name, as "beautiful" or "couch". Various and divergent as beautiful things are, there is somehow only *one* Beauty. We can distinguish from each and all of the many beautiful things the *one* Beauty it-self, what Beauty itself *is*, which must be there because otherwise there would be no sense in call-ing anything beautiful.

The one Beauty itself is not merely distinct from each and all of the beautiful things. It is also sep-arate from them. For it must be completely beau-tiful, purely beautiful, unchangingly beautiful; and no beautiful thing is such. This comes out very clearly when we consider the one Equality itself; for probably no two sticks in this world ever are exactly equal; and if they were our measurements would never be able to tell us that they were. Thus we arrive at an astounding and thrilling con-clusion: there is a second world, other than our world of visible things, consisting of the Ones Themselves, each of which is perfectly, purely, and eternally, what it is, visible only to the mind itself, that is to say, properly speaking not visible but intelligible, grasped only by the pure intellect using bare words.

Can this be right? Let us go back and approach by a slightly different way. Socrates has made us familiar with the enterprise of asking what a thing *is*. He has asked what courage *is*, what virtue *is*, what knowledge *is*. And he has rejected all such answers as: "Well, look at Laches if you want to know what courage is; he is a courageous man". Socrates has replied that he wants, not this or that courageous man or act, but the *one* courage itself. And surely he was right. The question "What is courage?" expresses a possible enterprise which is not the enterprise of collecting examples. The Socratic search for "Definitions" was in fact the search for one or other of these elusive but necessary Ones in Themselves. They must be there, to make sense of our world and our speech; but their forms are to be discerned only by the eye of the mind. There is an intelligible world of "Forms" or "Ideas".

The word "idea" meant to Plato first visible form and then form in general. Thus it meant some-thing objective. It never carried the subjective meaning it has today. In any case it is hardly more than a label to him, a label for "that one thing itself which (something) in itself is, complete, pure, and eternal"; and this phrase in turn is Plato's distilla-tion from Socrates' search for definitions and from the fact of common names.

These Forms, then, so unexpectedly but so sim-ply discovered, are the required starting-point, both for good practice and for good theory and indeed for a kind of religion (for Plato called them divine). To believe in them and to pursue them is to be a philosopher; that is the deeper definition of what philosophy or the pursuit of wisdom *is*. To be ignorant of them, or to disbelieve in them when they are pointed out (which unfortunately is the usual human state), is to be essentially not a philosopher. Knowledge of them is the first possible kind of knowledge. Indeed it is strictly speaking the only kind of knowledge; for strictly speaking only the unchangeable can be known, and only the Forms are unchangeable. If you say that the moon is full, and then the moon wanes, you cannot strictly speaking have known that the moon was full. Only what completely is can be completely known. There is a difference of kind between knowledge, which has for its object the Forms, and opinion, which has for its object this transitory and confused world.

The Forms are, however, the explanation of the visible world, so far as it has one. This cosmos is the mixed result of Mind and Necessity, and hence our account of it cannot be better than a likely story. But certainly whatever reality there is in visible things comes to them from the Forms after which they are called. A visible couch shares in, or perhaps rather imitates, or stands in some other relation to, couch itself, and derives its half-reality therefrom. We may also suppose that, besides the Forms and the visibles, there is a Third Thing, a receptacle of all becoming, which like gold takes any shape, and is to the Forms as mother is to father, a sort of room or seat of becoming, to be grasped imperceptibly by a kind of bastard reasoning.

All opinion is defective; but it is not all equally defective. On the contrary, those who know the Forms will have far better opinions about this world than those who do not. And that is the key fact for good politics, since it implies that kings should be philosophers. The only good government is government by those who know, and this means government by those who know the Forms. The ideal city would be a philosophocracy.

Whether such a city could ever come into existence is very doubtful; but how it would maintain itself if it did come into existence is clear. The ruling philosophers would take care to see that their rule was absolute and not limited by unchangeable laws or by popular votes, that they handed it over only to other equally adept and right-minded philosophers, and that the supply of suitable successors was assured by appropriate education of the best persons. Education would be in fact by far the most important part of practice. Those chosen to receive it would be primarily the children of the rulers; but impartial selection would reject some of these as inferior, and add some superior children from the common people. The same kind of impartial search for the best, overriding all useless customs however dear, would give us women as well as men rulers, would make these women exercise naked as well as the men, and would abolish family life among the rulers in favour of a conventional system of common parents and common children, which, together with communion of property, would fuse the whole ruling class into a united and selfless whole whose ascendency would never be in doubt.

The primary education of these rulers would not be very different from what Plato had himself received. It would, however, be publicly organized and more intense; and the physical or gymnastic part would be more military in character. The two greatest differences would be, first, the ever present risk of failure in the next examination and consequent relegation to the masses, and, second, the complete absence from their music and poetry of all corrupting or degrading suggestions, such as frenzied music and Homer's assertion that the gods could not restrain their laughter on a certain occasion. For whatever is read in literature in early years goes deep into the soul, especially any suggestion of self-control or self-abandonment.

Those who passed all tests up to the age of twenty would be sure of some sort of place in the ruling class for life; but whether this place was ever to be higher than that of a private in the army would depend on their success in the studies and exercises and examinations in the following fifteen years. Here Plato is strange indeed; for what he proposes as a suitable training, for the higher ranks of the army and for the administrators and rulers, is the advanced study of mathematics followed by the abstract study of the Forms and finally of the Form of the Good. Nothing is said about history or politics or economics. His reason is that those who are to keep a city as good as possible must above all know what pure and absolute Goodness Itself is, to which end they must previously know about the other pure and absolute Forms Themselves, to which end in turn they must first know mathematics. Mathematics provides a bridge from the sensible to the intelligible world. For in mathematics we draw sensible squares and triangles, and yet are interested in intelligible triangles and squares. We use the visible as a suggestion of the intelligible, and thus are gradually brought to the desire and power to study the intelligible itself, by mere words without accompanying visible images, as the adept philosopher does.

Only those who can and will persevere the whole way up this path will be governors of our ideal city. They will by then be at least fifty years old. One curious consequence of this education will be that the rulers will dislike ruling. They will have a passion for the Forms and wish to be left alone with them. But this is no disadvantage. On the contrary, the love of power makes bad rulers; and our reluctant rulers will nevertheless rule willingly enough, because they are just men and recognize the justice of recompensing their city for the supreme education she has given them. Besides, they will have plenty of leisure to devote to their abstract philosophizing.

This ideal city of Callipolis, the first surviving Utopia and by far the most interesting one, is constructed in Plato's splendid dialogue *Republic*, which is one of the ten best books there are. It is a work of his maturity, and the high point of his powers. Later in life he published two more dialogues on politics, and they show a change of interest. Here he still affirms that knowledge is the only right basis for government, that knowledge may and should dispense with laws, and that communal living is the best. But he seems to think now that knowledge and communal living are hardly ever practical possibilities, and therefore we had better spend our efforts in finding what is best to do in their absence. He has no doubt that in their absence we should have recourse to the reign of law. Law, while much inferior to the man who knows the Good, is much the best ruler for us ignorant and ill-tempered persons; and should be sacred among us. So when in his old age he plans another ideal city, which he calls Magnesia, his account consists mainly in a mass of legal details, and the dialogue describing Magnesia is named *Laws*.

Philosophy in the narrow sense is the analysis of conceptions; and this is mainly the invention of Plato's later dialogues. We find here in abundance that minute concentration on our conceptions themselves, that reflection, which is also characteristic of English philosophy in the middle of the twentieth century. It is fair to write this; and it is also true that the later dialogues of Plato are stimulating reflection at the present day; but we must qualify in two ways. First, Plato himself never became well aware of reflection as such; he continued to think of his theoretical philosophy as a study of the world rather than of man, as metaphysics rather than as logic and epistemology. Second, the results achieved are often not of great value; there are weary wastes of logical and metaphysical oddities, tiresome enough in Plato himself, intolerable when expounded by devoted interpreters. Yet it is never to be forgotten that these late dialogues, or rather that activity in the Academy of which these dialogues are an expression, formed the most successful analytical mind there has yet been, the mind of **Aristotle**.

The best of the late dialogues are the first two, *Parmenides* and *Theaetetus*. The conflict of opposed views natural to a good dialogue is at its greatest in the *Parmenides*, which consists of two parts. The first appears to destroy Plato's own theory of Forms with well-founded and unanswerable arguments. The second appears to be a formidably long and boring kind of metaphysical nonsense; it is described by the main speaker as "a laborious game", and ends with the following words: "Let this be said, then; and also that, as it seems, whether one is or not, both itself and the others, both to themselves and to each other, all in every way both are and are not and appear and do not appear. – Very true." Whatever this be, a joke, or ultimate truth, or something between, it is a remarkable achievement and has a queer value of its own. The discussion of the Ideas in the first part does in fact amount to a pretty clear revelation of the reasons that make the theory impossible, and is therefore a fine example of candid self-criticism. It is very strange that the *Parmenides* thus contains both an extreme example of frankness and an extreme example of mystification.

The *Theaetetus* is Plato's most successful work in purely analytical philosophy. The conceptions analysed are perception, knowledge, subjectivity, truth, change, error, *logos*, simplicity, and (by implication) definition. Plato introduces there the classical comparisons of the mind to a waxen tablet and to a dovecote, and the classical comparison of Socrates' conversation to midwifery. The conclusions of the dialogue are mostly negative and valueless by themselves: "Knowledge is not perception: it is not true opinion; it is not even true opinion with *logos*. Error is not thinking one thing instead of another, or misrelating what I see to what I know, or misusing the knowledge that I have; it is hard to see how it can occur at all." Nevertheless, anyone who studies and absorbs this dialogue will be greatly enlightened.

After the *Theaetetus* and the *Parmenides*, the *Sophist* is the greatest of Plato's late works. In outline it is a series of attempts to define the sophist by successive divisions of a genus, as if we defined the angler by dividing the genus craft, to which he belongs, into acquisitive and constructive craft, and placed the angler in acquisitive craft. We could then subdivide acquisitive craft into acquisition by consent and acquisition by subjugation, and again place the angler in the half to which he belongs. If we continued long enough, we should come to a class that was co-extensive with the angler and constituted a definition of him. This process of definition by division is prominent in the late dialogues. Plato appears to have hoped for a long time that it would supply a sure way of constructing definitions, as opposed to merely destroying definitions as Socrates' technique had done. Aristotle, however, showed that there is nothing sure about the procedure; every step in it is merely an unsupported assertion. And its prominence in the late dialogues is a large cause of their relative unfruitfulness.

The *Sophist* fortunately contains, besides six long divisions, a long passage of much more value. Here Plato resumes from the *Theaetetus* the puzzles in the notions of not-being, error, and falsehood. He then discovers as many puzzles in the notion of being. He finds difficulties both in the notion of being as many and in the notion of it as one only. He finds that in the battle of giants between materialists and idealists neither side can defend itself. If we say that the real is what we can grasp with our hands, we deny the obvious facts of justice and wisdom and soul. On the other side, if we say that only the Ideas are real, we deny that the real can live or move or think.

Plato believes that he now has a solution of these difficulties. It consists in analysing the way in which we apply many names to the same thing (whereas the theory of Ideas was reached by considering that we apply one name to many things). From the fact that we may call the same man both white and squat and short and brave he develops the doctrine that some pairs of things communicate with each other and others do not, and that some things communicate with everything but most do not. Among the things that communicate with everything are Same and Other; for everything is the same as itself and other than every other thing. But to be other than another thing is *not to be* that other thing. Thus otherness is a kind of not-being; and this kind of not-being is omnipresent, since everything is other than every other thing. Now this is a perfectly respectable kind of not-being, unlike the not-being that has puzzled us; for there is nothing queer about being other than something else. This kind of not-being is not opposite to being but merely other than being. Not-being therefore firmly exists and has its own nature, although father **Parmenides** forbade us to say so.

Not merely does not-being exist; it is also shared in by thought and statement, which therefore admit of being false. That appears as follows. A simple statement consists of a name followed by a verb, as "man learns"; and cannot consist of anything less complicated. It necessarily has a subject and is either true or false. It is false if what it says about its subject is *other* than what is about its subject. As it really can say, about a really existing subject, something really other and not so as if it were so, it really can be false. False statement is possible. But then false thought is possible; for thought is the same as silent internal statement.

Once in his old age Plato returned to the ethical topics of Socrates and made Socrates his main speaker again. This was his *Philebus*, an ugly and disappointing but acute and still useful dialogue. It begins with a last statement of his method of division, the most puzzling and least rewarding of them all. It then devotes itself to what appears to be a solution of the problem left open many years ago in the *Republic*, namely, what is the Good? The Good must be perfect, adequate, and desired by all who know it. The main contenders for the place are pleasure and knowledge. No one would choose either alone if he could have both; but which is the better? Socrates develops a strange classification of things into the definite, the indefinite, the mixture

[continued on p. 30]

PLATE 65. MOORE, George Edward (1873–1958), pencil portrait drawn in 1947 by Percy Horton (1897–).
(*Trinity College, Cambridge*)

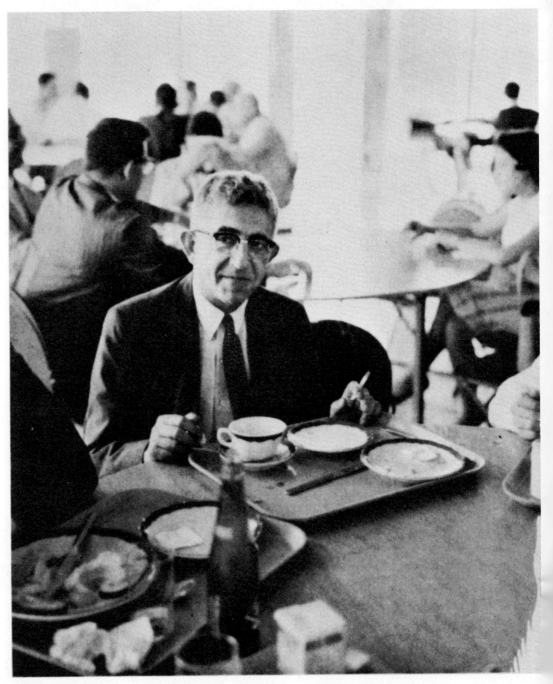

PLATE 66. NAGEL, Ernest (1901–), photographed in 1959.

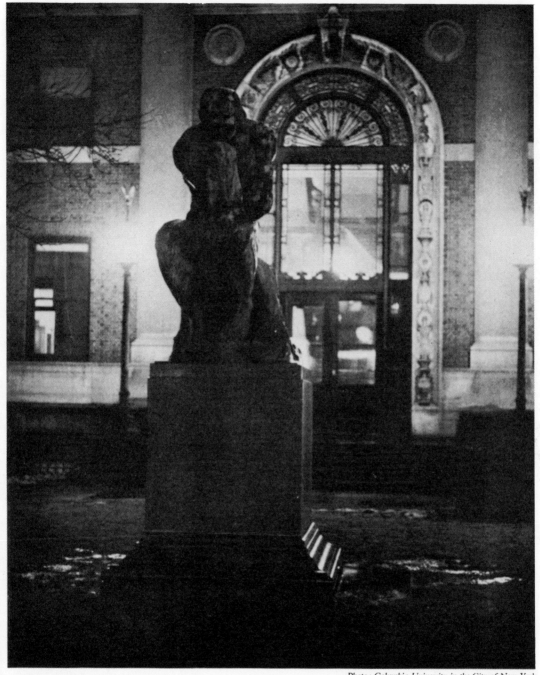

Photo: Columbia University in the City of New York

PLATE 67. NEW YORK, Columbia University: Philosophy Hall, a centre of academic philosophy teaching in the United States, with a copy of "The Thinker" by Rodin (1840–1917) in the foreground.

PLATE 68. NIETZSCHE, Friedrich (1844–1900), head by Otto Dix, 1913.

Photo : Barnaby's Picture Library

PLATE 69. PARIS UNIVERSITY, The Sorbonne. The University of Paris, founded in 1180, has always been a centre of philosophical study and thought and in the twentieth century it has been a centre of existentialism. The College of the Sorbonne was founded in 1258, rebuilt in 1885, and is the home of the Faculty of Arts.

Blaise Pascal

PLATE 70. PASCAL, Blaise (1623–1662), engraving by Edelinck.

PLATE 71. PASCAL, Blaise (1623–1662): the Abbey of Port-Royal des Champs which Pascal visited frequently. (*Bibliothèque Nationale, Paris*)

Photo: *University Press*

PLATE 72. PLATO (*c.* 427–347 B.C.): manuscript page from one of the earliest whole manuscripts of Plato's works, written in 895 A.D. This page shows the end of the *Protagoras* and the beginning of the *Gorgias*. (*Bodleian Library, Oxford. Ms. E. D. Clarke* 39, *f.* 368*v*)

Photo: Radio Times Hulton Picture Library

PLATE 73. PRICE, Henry Habberley (1899–), photographed at the Joint Session of the Aristotelian Society and the Mind Association at Birmingham University, August 16 1952.

PLATE 74. PRICE, Richard (1723–1791), engraving by Thomas Holloway after Benjamin West.

Proff^r Thomas Reid D.D.

Photo : A. J. B. Strachan

PLATE 75.   REID, Thomas (1710–1796). portrait by Sir Henry Raeburn (1756–1823).
(Fyvie Castle, Aberdeen)

299

PLATE 76. ROME, the Forum Romanum, which must have been a well-known meeting place for the Roman philosophers. Indeed, Cicero delivered many of his speeches here.

PLATE 77. ROSS, Sir W. David (1877–), photographed at a reception at Christ Church, Oxford.

PLATE 78. ROUSSEAU, Jean-Jacques (1712–1778), portrait by Allan Ramsay (1714–1784).
(*National Gallery of Scotland, Edinburgh*)

302

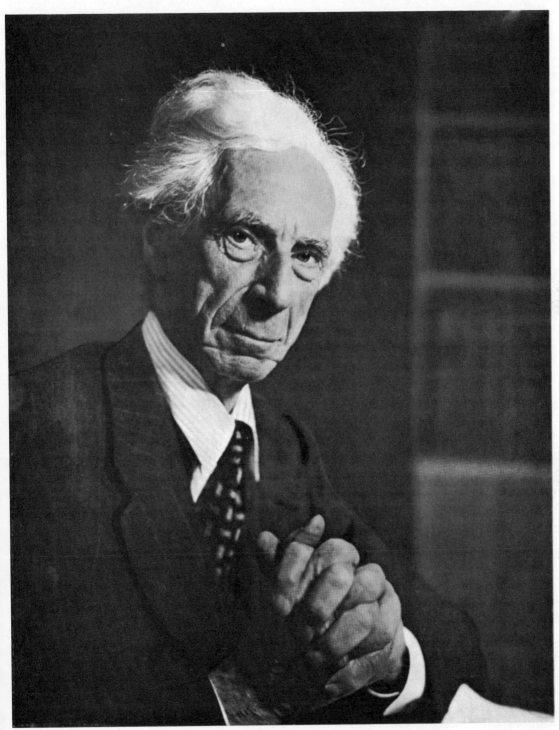

PLATE 79. RUSSELL, Bertrand (1872–   ): photograph.

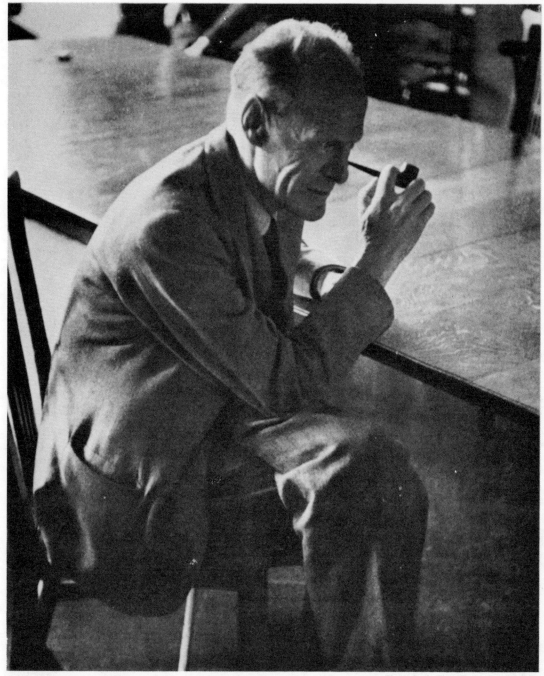

PLATE 80. RYLE, Gilbert (1900–), photographed at the Joint Session of the Aristotelian Society and the Mind
Association at Birmingham University, August 16 1952.

of these two, and the cause of their mixture; and decides that pleasure falls into the indefinite class but mind falls into the cause. He then goes into a long and close analysis of pleasure. It is caused by the restoration of living substance. But there are also mental pleasures of expectation. Pleasures are often accompanied by false opinions, and can themselves be false. There is a neutral state of neither pain nor pleasure; and pleasure itself is not the mere absence of pain. The greatest pleasures and pains occur in bad states of the body or soul, not in good states of them. States of pleasure mixed with pain can occur in several ways. But there are also true and absolute pleasures. Pleasure cannot be the Good, because it is a genesis, and therefore exists for the sake of something other than itself. In the course of this long psychological analysis of pleasure, Plato has some useful remarks on perception, memory, desire, imagination, envy, comedy and laughter.

He then gives a much shorter analysis of knowledge. He observes that some arts are more exact and mathematical than others. He distinguishes between popular and philosophical arithmetic. Dialectic is the most accurate of all the arts, though perhaps not the most useful. Finally the dialogue returns to the Good. This cannot be either knowledge or pleasure alone, for neither of them is perfect. It must be a mixture of the best of each of them, including all the sciences, and those pleasures that are pure and necessary. In this mixture the most valuable part is beauty and symmetry and truth, and that is the cause of its goodness. Each of these three is more akin to knowledge than to pleasure. Knowledge therefore stands nearer than pleasure to the Good. And we may finally announce the following order of value: measure, beauty, mind, science, pure pleasure.

Another dialogue of Plato's old age, the *Timaeus*, is devoted to the physical world, and offers an elaborate cosmogony, cosmology, physics, chemistry, and human physiology, pathology, and medicine, while at the same time declaring in the manner of the middle dialogues that there can be no science of such matters. For a long time the western world read only this dialogue of Plato's, thus obtaining a very inaccurate impression of him. At all times, however, most of Plato's readers have tended to take his second-best and leave two thirds of his best.

They have tended to take his authoritarian politics and his mystical religion of the Ideas with its inclination to unreason. But of his best they have taken only his literary beauty. They have ignored his great lead in the analysis of conceptions, that is, his invention of philosophy in the narrow sense; and they have ignored his magnificent ideal of reasonable thinking and acting. This ideal is presented to us in the person of Socrates; but it is presented only by the writings of Plato. (R.R.)

Plate 72, page 296.

Plotinus (205–270 A.D.), the originator of the philosophy known in modern times as **neoplatonism**. He himself and his successors thought of themselves simply as Platonists, and believed that their in some ways profoundly original philosophy was no more than an exposition of the real thought of **Plato**. We know nothing of the race or family of Plotinus, though the not very reliable fourth-century writer, Eunapius, says that he came from Upper Egypt. His education and cultural background were certainly completely Greek. Our first fixed date in his life is 232, when he came to Alexandria to study philosophy. He could find no teacher to satisfy him until he was introduced to Ammonius Saccas, with whom he remained for eleven years. Ammonius was a self-taught, non-writing philosopher and we know next to nothing of his teaching, but his influence on Plotinus and his other pupils (who probably included the Christian Origen) was clearly very considerable. In 243 Plotinus started for the East with the Emperor Gordian's expedition, in the hope of learning something about Persian and Indian philosophy. But he never made any contact with any Eastern sages who may have been available, for Gordian was murdered in Mesopotamia in 244 and Plotinus escaped with some difficulty to Antioch, and went from there to Rome. There is no evidence that at this or any other period in his life he acquired any knowledge of Indian thought. His philosophical background is entirely Greek.

Plotinus spent the rest of his life at Rome teaching philosophy, and after ten years there began to write the treatises which were collected by his disciple and editor, Porphyry, into the edition which we know as the *Enneads* (composed of six sets of nine treatises each). Porphyry also wrote his master's life (which is printed in all editions of the Enneads), which is our main source of information about Plotinus. It gives a vivid and detailed picture of the man and his method of work at Rome. He seems to have been a person of great charm and nobility and character, and of an extensive and businesslike practical kindness of the sort which is not perhaps very common among philosophers. His method of teaching was informal, based on the reading of Plato and **Aristotle** and their commentators, and including a great deal of free and vigorous discussion of difficulties raised by members of his audience; traces of these discussions are to be found in the published treatises.

Plotinus died at the age of sixty-six after a long and painful illness (probably a form of leprosy), which he bore with courage and dignity.

The philosophy of Plotinus, though professing to be an exposition of the real thought of Plato and owing a great deal, not only to the reading of Plato's *Dialogues*, but to the close and critical study of Aristotle and of the philosophical writers, Platonists, Pythagoreans and Aristotelians, of the century or so before his own time, is in many ways thoroughly original. The primary purpose of his teaching was to lead men (those few who were capable of it) back to awareness of and eventual union with the source from which they and all things came, the One or Good, which in giving them being gave also the impulse to return. Attainment of this required perfect moral purity and the utmost intellectual effort. Mystical union for Plotinus required a very solid ethical basis and a prolonged exercise of the intelligence before it could be attained, though in its attainment the wise and good man to whom alone it is possible passes beyond even the highest intellectual activity. Those who think that mysticism has nothing to do with virtue or intelligence are not recommended to read the *Enneads*.

It is, then, to show men the way back to their ultimate goal, the Good, that Plotinus expounds his view of the nature and structure of reality, which is in broad outline, as follows. The One or Good himself (though the terms One and Good are neuter in Greek Plotinus always tends to pass over to the masculine pronoun in speaking of his First Principle) the source or first principle of being, is beyond all determination or limitation and so

beyond all description or definition. Language can only point the way towards him without reaching him. Even the names of One or Good are not adequate descriptions of him. But though he is beyond the reach of language he is by no means for Plotinus a mere negation or abstraction. It is because he is more, not less, than any conception we can form of him that he is beyond thought and language. Nor is he really remote. He is present to all according to their capacity to receive him, though few, in Plotinus' view, are capable of the tremendous intellectual and moral discipline necessary for that adequate reception.

From the One or Good reality proceeds in a series of stages of steadily increasing multiplicity, limitation and separation. Its generation from the One is both free, in the sense of being perfectly spontaneous and unconstrained, and necessary in the sense that it is not conceivable that it should not happen. The Good cannot but be self-diffusive or self-communicative. This is the significance of the metaphor of emanation or radiation (as of light from the sun) which Plotinus often uses, with full consciousness that it 'is a metaphor. The whole process of production or generation is timeless, and all the stages of reality are eternal. Even the last and lowest, the physical universe, is eternal as a whole, though in the sublunary world its individual parts are continually perishing and being replaced by others. But in the timeless process of generation, at each stage, two elements can be distinguished in thought, one in which the product proceeds from the producer as an unformed potentiality, the other in which it returns upon its source in contemplation and so is formed and actualised by it and gains in its turn (except at the last and lowest stage) the power to produce. This double rhythm of outgoing and return runs through the whole of Plotinus' universe.

The One is not being, but beyond being, and the source of being. In the Platonic language of Plotinus "being" cannot be used by itself except to denote the sum or totality of beings, and there is no such thing as indeterminate or unlimited being. True being for Plotinus is the first level of reality which proceeds from the One, the Divine Intellect which is also the totality of Platonic Forms or Ideas. In this Divine Intellect thought and its content are one, and the Ideas are themselves living intelligences, so that it can be regarded as either a unity-in-diversity of Forms or a unity-in-diversity of minds, each of which thinks and so is the whole. In terms of our consciousness Intellect is the level of intuitive thought which is identical with its object and does not see it as in some sense external to it. The Forms of Intellect are, as in Plato, the archetypes of the quasi-realities of the world of the senses. They are finite in number, though infinite in productive power. Plotinus, in those of his writings where he considers the question most carefully, makes an important departure from Plato in admitting individual as well as universal Forms, a Form of Socrates as well as a Form of Man, an admission which he reconciles with the traditional doctrine that the Forms are finite in number by adopting the **Stoic** idea of cyclic world periods, repeating themselves endlessly in every detail.

From Intellect proceeds Soul, the active principle which forms and orders the visible universe. Its characteristic intellectual activity is discursive thought, which does not simply possess its content in itself but has to reason to it. Time is the life of the soul in this discursive motion. But Soul in Plotinus has a very wide range. At its highest it is fully illuminated and formed by Intellect and raised to its level: and it has a lower phase (which Plotinus often calls Nature) which is the immanent animating principle of the material universe and all animal and plant life within it (and indeed of the life which Plotinus recognises in things we should regard as inorganic). From Nature come the forms of bodies, the lowest and weakest of realities, so weak that they have no power of further production. All levels of soul from the lowest to the highest are permanently present in ourselves, and we have to choose on which level we will live, whether we will remain on the level of the lower soul, immersed in the concerns of body, or whether we wake to the consciousness of the higher realities present in us and under the impulse and illumination of the Good and Intellect purify ourselves morally and intellectually and so live on the level of Intellect and at last attain to the union with the Good which is only possible there.

The material universe for Plotinus is a living organic whole, bound together by that universal sympathy in which his contemporaries, philosophers and magicians alike, believed. Plotinus himself believed in the reality of magic, though, as it could not affect the higher life of the soul, it was of no importance to him. Matter itself, though it proceeds like all else from the Good, is the principle of evil because it is the absolute limit, the utter negation and deficiency of being that marks the end of the descent from the Good through the successive levels of reality. But the material universe for Plotinus, though affected (at least in the regions below the moon; celestial matter is not evil for Plotinus) by the evil of its materiality, is good and beautiful as a living structure of forms and the best possible work of soul, and Plotinus' attitude to it is by no means merely negative or pessimistic, as was that of the Gnostics whom he detested and vigorously attacked.

The direct and indirect influence of the thought of Plotinus on the Christian theologians of the fourth and following centuries was considerable, as was its influence later on the philosophy of Islam. The indirect influence on Christian thought continued throughout the Middle Ages in the West; and the publication of Ficino's Latin translation of the *Enneads* in 1492, and of the *editio princeps* of the Greek text in 1580 made Plotinian Neoplatonism an important influence on the thought of the Renaissance. The philosophical changes of the seventeenth century led to a decrease in the influence of Plotinus; the last group of English philosophers who were deeply influenced by his thought were the **Cambridge Platonists**. Since then the philosophical influence of Plotinus has been confined to the comparatively few individuals who have made the considerable effort required to study him seriously. (A.H.A.)

Political philosophy has traditionally been a wide and amorphous subject, including within itself widely different questions. Thus it is clear that political philosophy must in some way include a consideration of the state; but widely different questions can be raised about it. There is the logical and analytical question about the meaning of the word "state", which may or may not be identical with the metaphysical question about what sort of an entity the state may be; there is the question of the classification of types of states, as democracies, aristocracies, etc.; there is the question of the relative merits of different types of states; there is the question of what allegiance the individual owes to the state, and why. There is no doubt that all these questions, and others, have been thought of as part of political philosophy in the past and, unfortunately, not even distinguished from each other often enough; in particular the theoretical task of analysis and classification have rarely been separated or even satisfactorily distinguished from the evaluation questions, from the time when **Plato** in his *Republic* defined oligarchy and democracy as progressive perversions of aristocracy. There is no doubt that a great deal of political propaganda at a very general level masquerades as theoretical analysis; thus **Rousseau** in his *Social Contract* purports to show that there can be no duty of obedience to law except in a very radical form of democracy, a view that it is unlikely that he would have held if he had not thought democracy to be the best form of political organization. It is for these reasons impossible to give a short account of what is studied under the heading of political philosophy or to give a unified picture of its methods and aims.

Probably, however, it would be agreed that the most central and frequently raised problems of political philosophy have been two, to which some attention may be given here. First, there is the problem of the ground for the duty of obedience to civil authority, the question why we ought to obey the law and the government. This question must be sharply distinguished from the question why people do in fact obey the law and the government and from the question why it is wise to obey them; the question why people do obey the law is one belonging to sociology and psychology and the answer is that people obey the law for all kinds of queer reasons as well as on more rational grounds; the question why it is wise to obey the law is one of prudence to which part of the answer is that it pays since otherwise we are liable to penalties at the hands of those who wield force superior to ours; but when faced with superior force we have no duty to obey for that reason – prudence, as Rousseau pointed out, will tell us to obey when we must and to disobey when we can. Political philosophy is not concerned with either the sociological or the prudential question but with the grounds of our duty of obedience.

If we ask how we could ever come to have a duty to obey some individual the most obvious answer is that we might do so by promising to do so; it can seem plausible to say that that is the only way in which we can acquire a duty of obedience to a private person. This is the sort of consideration which leads to the doctrine of the **Social Contract** as an answer to the problem of the duty of obedience. The theory of social contract has many forms having little more in common than that whoever has a duty of civil obedience has this duty because of a contract made to obey in consideration of some benefits expected to arise from membership of society. In **Hobbes** the contract is between all future subjects to obey some sovereign who is no party to any contract so long as the sovereign successfully protects them; in **Locke** there is a subsidiary political contract between government and subjects which delimits the rights and duties of both; in Rousseau the contract is between men who will constitute themselves into a sovereign assembly – the same men will be both sovereign and subject. The essential point which gives the social contract its attraction is that a duty of obedience in politics is explained by the simple and intelligible notion of a promise.

The social contract theory quickly comes under fire on the grounds that it is contrary to historical fact to maintain that states are founded upon contract and that, even if the original members of a state had owed their duty to obey to a contract, their descendants are not parties to and are not bound by such a contract. In the face of this objection the contract theorist has usually fallen back on the notion of a tacit, implied or virtual contract; it is often held, for example that by staying in the country and making use of the civil and social benefits it confers we imply a promise to obey the laws. To this **Hume** replied in his famous essay on the *Original Contract* that this is rather like saying that one shanghaied on board a ship implies a promise to obey the captain if he does not jump overboard.

But the most serious objection to the contract theory is one which leads straight to the utilitarian theory of obedience. If it be asked why we should promise to obey the civil authority, Hume argued, the most plausible answer is that by so doing we help to ensure the general well-being, since civil order is necessary to human happiness; but in that case, Hume went on, the promise is superflous since we might just as well regard the general well being as the direct ground for civil obedience. This is the utilitarian answer to which Hume subscribed: it is our duty to obey because obedience to law and existing authority is necessary if we are not to fall into anarchy, to which almost any settled society is preferable; there is no special political duty of obedience, but obedience is a necessary means for the achievement of our moral duty to our fellow-men. This view is in essentials shared even by idealistic thinkers like T. H. **Green**.

Both the social contract theory and the utilitarian theory of the grounds of obedience go naturally with one particular answer to our second main question, that of the nature of the state. On both these views the state is a contrivance having as its justification the well-being of the individuals who compose it; on the social contract theory it is a mere machine invented for that purpose; on either view the state is nothing over and above the individuals who compose it. But there is an alternative view of the nature of the state, often called the organic theory, with which a different view of the duty of obedience naturally goes. On this view the state is a natural organic unity and man is a political animal in the sense that a man is essentially a part of a community and not an individual who may or not may combine with his fellow men; the state is more like a family in which father, mother and children have their natural roles to play, or we might even compare the position of the individual man in relation to the state to the position of the hand relative to the body. We cannot distinguish the welfare and rights of the hand from the welfare and rights of the body, for a hand is only a hand in so far as it is functioning as an element in the unity of the body; nor should we try to distinguish the rights and welfare of the individual from the welfare of the state, for the ultimate welfare of the individual is the welfare of the political organism within which alone he can fully develop. Given this view of the state it becomes an absurd to ask why the citizen should obey the civil power as to ask why the hand should obey the will of the body; indeed it is only when functioning within the state that the individual is truly himself, truly free. Some such view as this is occasionally hinted at, though never affirmed by **Plato** and **Aristotle**; it became most popular in Germany in the early nineteenth century when patriotism arising from the war with France, the romantic movement and the general monistic tendency of idealism led such thinkers as **Hegel** and **Fichte** to accept views of this type, which in their turn can easily lead to totalitarian politics in practice.

It would be quite wrong, as was pointed out earlier, to think that this sketch gives a complete picture, or even outline, of the field of political philosophy; but it may serve the purpose of indicating the central positions from which political theories start and their grounds. (J.O.U.)

Popper, Karl R. (1902–), born and educated in Vienna, Senior Lecturer in Philosophy at the University of New Zealand from 1937 to 1945, and since then Professor of Logic and Scientific Method at the London School of Economics. His major contributions have been to the logic of science. Although he has never subscribed to the early phenomenalist tendencies of the **Vienna Circle** or to the instrumentalist interpretation of scientific theory professed by some adherents of logical empiricism, the general orientation of his thought is similar to that associated with this philosophical movement.

In his first book (*Die Logik der Forschung*, 1934, translated in 1959 as *The Logic of Discovery*) Popper defined scientific statements to be those which deny that something logically conceivable is actually realized. Accordingly, it is not sufficient for a statement to be counted as scientific that there may be confirmatory observational evidence for it; it is essential for such a statement to be capable of being disproved by some conceivable spatio-temporally located event which, were it to occur, would exemplify a possibility that the statement excludes. It is this feature of its statements that Popper thinks demarcates science from metaphysics. He therefore proposes an amended version of the relative frequency notion of **probability**, in order to make such probability statements refutable and so scientific; but he also outlines a conception of logical probability which, unlike the frequency notion, he believes to be relevant for the task of assessing evidence for a hypothesis. (See **Carnap**). In addition, the book contains a vigorous critique of the Baconian view of scientific procedure (which he calls "inductionism"), and argues that it is the use of the hypothetico-deductive method which is distinctive of modern science.

Popper is perhaps better known as the author of *The Open Society and Its Enemies* (1944, second edition 1950). Although it contains many reflections on the logic of science, the book is primarily a thorough-going criticism of social philosophies (in particular, those of **Plato**, **Hegel** and **Marx**) which minimize the efficacy of individual human effort and subscribe to a belief in laws of inevitable historical development. In opposition to such philosophies, Popper advocates piece-meal social engineering as the sound scientific approach to social problems.   (E.N.)

Positivism is the name given (*a*) to the doctrine and movement founded in the nineteenth century by the French philosopher Auguste **Comte** (1798–1857), and (*b*) to the general philosophical view of which Comte's Positivism is only one instance. Positivism in the broader sense (henceforth to be referred to in this article with a small p) is the view that since all genuine knowledge is based on sense experience and can only be advanced by means of observation and experiment, metaphysical or speculative attempts to gain knowledge by reason unchecked by experience should be abandoned in favour of the methods of the special sciences. All positivists hold that the task of philosophy is to understand the methods by which the sciences are advanced but not to seek for any independent knowledge of the world. They often argue that as soon as means have been found for advancing knowledge of a subject, it ceases to belong to philosophy and becomes a separate science or a part of one.

Francis **Bacon**, who considered himself the "trumpeter" of the new sciences which were becoming detached from philosophy in the sixteenth and seventeenth centuries, may be regarded as the source both of positivism and of the name that was given to it in the nineteenth century. In his *On Principles and Origins* (1623–24) he refers to an ancient legend according to which Cupid was the oldest of the gods and existed at the beginning of things alone with Chaos. Cupid, according to this myth, had no parents, and Chaos no beginning. Bacon interprets the absence of parents to mean the absence of any cause, and surmised that by "Chaos"

was meant the ultimate matter from which all material things are formed. This ultimate matter, he writes "is a thing positive and inexplicable and must be taken absolutely as it is found, and not to be judged by any previous conception". It is improper, he says, "to require or imagine a cause when we come to the ultimate force and positive law of nature . . . For nothing has corrupted philosophy so much as this seeking after the parents of Cupid; that is, that philosophers have not taken the principles of things as they are found in nature, and accepted them as a positive doctrine resting on the faith of experiences; but they have rather deduced them from the laws of disputation, the petty conclusions of logic and mathematics, common notions, and such wanderings of the mind beyond the limits of nature".

Bacon here gives expression to a number of important items of the positivist doctrine. He rejects the idea of "deducing" the ultimate facts of nature. He believes that philosophers should not attempt to wander beyond "the limits of nature". He thinks that there are ultimate facts that should be approached without any "previous conception". He warns against a too enthusiastic search for causes. He says that there are ultimate facts that should be accepted "on the faith of experience". When he applies the adjective "positive" to these "inexplicable" facts and to the doctrines based on them, he is not using the word in the sense in which it is opposed to "negative", but in the sense in which positive religion (consisting of revealed doctrines, accepted by faith, and not provable by reason) is opposed to natural religion (the doctrines of which are established by rational proof), or in which positive law (laid down by specific authorities for particular populations) is opposed to natural law (held to be rationally apprehended and independent of the will of legislators). Probably as a result of Bacon's usage – Bacon was much admired by the eighteenth-century empiricist philosophers both in England and in France – the adjective "positive" came to be applied to the methods of the natural sciences in respect of their reliance on observation and use of experiment. Saint-Simon, whom Comte later served as secretary, in his *Essay on the Sciences of Man* (1813) applies the word "positive" to the sciences which are based on "facts which have been observed and analysed". The sciences which are not so based Saint-Simon calls "conjectural". Comte himself uses the word in this sense in an article entitled *Plan of the Scientific Works necessary for Reorganisation of Society* which was published under Saint-Simon's auspices in 1822. He later brought it to full prominence in the title of his major work, *Course on the Positive Philosophy* (1830–42). Comte here explains that he used the word "positive" to emphasize his view that the function of theories is to co-ordinate observed facts rather than to explain in terms of causes. It is Comte's "Positive Philosophy" which later came to be called "Positivism", a name which Comte welcomed but did not himself invent.

Comte's Positivism can best be understood in terms of his famous Law of the Three States according to which the human mind advances from a theological stage through a metaphysical stage to the final positive stage. At the theological stage the attempt is made to penetrate to the inner nature of things and to explain their behaviour in terms of supernatural beings. At the metaphysical stage, which is really only a sophisticated modification of the earlier one, explanations are given in terms of abstractions, essences or forces, which, on Comte's view, are nothing but depersonalised deities. As examples of this mode of thought Comte cites the physical doctrine of the ether, the chemical doctrine of affinities, and the biological doctrine of vital spirits. At the final, positive stage the attempt to penetrate to the inner nature of things and to discover the origin and destination of the universe is abandoned. Instead, the positive thinker tries to establish, by means of reasonings based on observations, the invariable co-existences and sequences of phenomena. It was Comte's view that all the sciences pass through these stages, as for example, astronomy in its development from sun-worship and astrology, and chemistry in its development from alchemy. Like Bacon, Comte emphasised the enhanced power over nature that the advance of science brings with it.

Comte's Positivism, however, was much more than a philosophy of science and an account of intellectual development. Comte held that the time must come when human society itself is studied by the positive methods. He called this positive science "sociology" and sought to lay its foundations in the

Course on Positive Philosophy and later writings. It was his view that to each of the three stages of intellectual development, the theological, metaphysical and positive, there corresponded forms of society and social outlook. There is the theological social outlook in which there is respect for tradition and authority upheld by priestly learning. Metaphysical criticisms of the traditional doctrines bring with them an era of social criticism when such unverifiable doctrines prevail as belief in natural rights and the sovereignty of the people. In Europe this was the era of the Reformation and the French Revolution. With the advance of positive social science the negative and sterile disputation of the revolutionary era would be replaced by a stable society where agreement is established on the basis of incontrovertible social knowledge. A new form of authority would then reside in a new spiritual power consisting of men of science whose knowledge would enable humanity to achieve a peaceful unity of thought and action. In his later years Comte elaborated this part of his doctrine into a Religion of Humanity, of which some account is given in the article on Comte. Some of the most eminent of his early supporters such as Littré in France and George Eliot and J. S. **Mill** in England refused to follow him in this. Nevertheless, Positivist Societies were established in various parts of the world on the model of that which Comte himself had founded in 1848. In these Humanity was the object of ceremonial worship, and sociology was taken as the warrant for sociolatry. The movement was particularly strong in Latin America, but flourished for many years in England, mainly in London and Liverpool. Leaders of the movement here were Richard Congreve, who resigned his fellowship at Wadham College, Oxford in 1855 in order to devote himself to its promotion, and Frederick Harrison, another fellow of that college. *The Positivist Review*, later called *Humanity*, was published from 1893 until 1925. An attempt was made to revive Positivism in England, just after the Second World War. The altars are still tended, though infrequently, in Paris and Rio.

Both the theoretical side of Comte's Positivism and positivism in the more general sense are natural growths in the age of scientific advance. We have already suggested that Bacon may be regarded as the first positivist. He can even be regarded as

311

the forerunner of Comte's ceremonial Positivism, since in *The New Atlantis* he writes in some detail of a cult of great men. Positivism has formed a part of the empiricist tradition in philosophy. There are traces of it in **Locke**, who held that the "real essence" or "internal constitution" of things (what Comte called the "inner nature") was unknowable. When Locke said that no "science" of nature was possible, he was drawing a limit to the sphere of rational explanation in the manner of Bacon before him and Comte after him. It was **Hume**, however, who gave this view its most cogent expression. All genuine human knowledge, he argued, is concerned either with matters of fact or with logic and mathematics – called by Hume "relations of ideas". The latter kind of knowledge is certain. It has that character of not being otherwise thinkable which philosophers call "necessity". But no amount of mathematical or logical reasoning, can, on its own, tell us anything about the nature of the world. Its conclusions are, in that regard, as Bacon said, "petty". Knowledge of matters of fact, on the other hand, is knowledge about what is in the world. To that extent it is not "petty". But such knowledge can never have the certainty and necessity of logic and mathematics. We can always conceive of the facts of the world as different from what they actually are, and there is no means of proving that the world must have been as it is. But this is just what metaphysical philosophers have tried to prove. They have claimed to provide knowledge of the world which has all the necessity of mathematics. But this is where there is confusion. On the one hand there is knowledge of matters of fact – of how things are and which things accompany which others. And on the other hand there is logic and mathematics which are not about the world at all. All the books which fall into neither of these categories can contain nothing but "sophistry and illusion".

This view was very widely held in the nineteenth century, especially by men of science. It was not, however, strongly represented in the universities, where various forms of Idealist metaphysics prevailed. But in the twenties of the twentieth century Hume's positivist arguments were revived and strengthened. It was now argued that a form of words that expressed neither a verifiable matter of fact nor a truth of logic or mathematics was meaningless. The field of what is meaningful contains only what is in principle verifiable or what is a mere matter of logic. This criterion excludes most of the things said in books on metaphysics which are therefore not false but without sense. This view is known as **Logical Positivism**.

Positivism gets much of its strength from the contrast between the continuous and agreed progress which has been achieved in the natural sciences since the time of Galileo, and the situation of deadlock and disagreement that has at all times obtained in metaphysical philosophy. This seems to suggest that in the special sciences a fruitful method has been employed, whereas metaphysical philosophers have got lost in an intellectual impasse. Comte and the earlier positivists argued that metaphysical problems are beyond the power of man to solve. The Logical Positivists of our own day have argued that when verifiability is taken as a criterion of meaning, the problems of metaphysics are seen to be mere pseudo-problems which remain unsolved not because they are difficult but because they have no sense. The weakness of all types of positivism is the assumption that there are facts, each distinct from every other, which observation and experiment can reveal and correlate. When they attempt to explain what these facts are, positivists give as widely different answers as the metaphysicians. Bacon's "simple natures", Hume's "impressions", and the "atomic facts" of twentieth-century positivists raise theoretical problems which are as elusive as those of self-confessed metaphysicians.   (H.B.A.)

Pragmatism. The word "pragmatism" was very little used in the English language, and not at all in philosophical contexts, until it was introduced by the American philosopher C. S. **Peirce** in 1878 as the name of a logical maxim for determining the meaning of words which he had formulated. In his own words, Peirce offered the rule: "Consider what effects, which might conceivably have practical bearings, we conceive the object of our conception to have. Then our conception of these effects is the whole of our conception of the object"; alternatively Peirce said that pragmatism was "the theory that a conception, that is, the rational purport of a word or other expression, lies exclusively in its conceivable bearing upon the conduct of life; so that, since obviously nothing that might not result from experiment can have any direct bearing upon conduct, if one can define accurately all the conceivable experimental phenomena which the affirmation or denial of a concept could imply, one will have therein a complete definition of the concept, and there is absolutely nothing more in it". Thus if we wish to determine the meaning of the word "hard" we should consider the experimental phenomena which would be implied by saying of something that it was hard, such as that it would scratch most things and few would scratch it – which is therefore part of the meaning of "hard". Undoubtedly this doctrine has, and was intended by Peirce to have, important consequences, such as that "almost every proposition of ontological metaphysics is either meaningless gibberish . . . or else downright absurd". But it is important to realize that Peirce took "pragmatism" as a name for a special maxim for getting clear about the meanings of words and not for a complete philosophical position; being a confirmed coiner of technical terms he would have been quite as willing to subscribe to "synechism" and "fallibilism" as to "pragmatism". Above all, Peirce certainly did not regard his pragmatic maxim as being in any way a theory of truth but of meaning; to him it seemed evident that truth consisted in correspondence between statement and fact.

But very early the word "pragmatism" was borrowed by other philosophers who gave it new and vaguer meanings; so much was this so that Peirce wrote that "to serve the precise purpose of expressing the original definition, he begs to announce the birth of the word 'pragmaticism', which is ugly enough to be safe from kidnappers". The earliest philosophers thus to borrow and distort the concept of pragmatism were William **James**, F.C.S. **Schiller** and John **Dewey**; what they have in common with each other is first and foremost a theory about truth which has since been regarded as the essence of pragmatism. In his *Pragmatism* James said that "ideas become true just so far as they help us to get into satisfactory relations with other parts of our experience" and that "the true is the name of whatever proves itself to be good in the way of belief". If we wish to find the connexion of this view with that of Peirce it perhaps comes out in the following quotation: "Pragmatism . . . asks its usual question. Grant an idea or belief to be true", it says, "what concrete difference will its being true make in one's actual life? How will the truth be realised? What experiences will be different from those which would obtain if the belief were false? What, in short, is the truth's cash-value in experiential terms?'". The superficial similarity here to the words of Peirce is obvious but the position utterly different; the doctrine that the meaning of an hypothesis can be determined by considering its experimental consequences is conflated with the doctrine that the true is the good in the way of belief to yield the conclusion that the true is what has good experimental consequences.

The notion of pragmatism has become particularly connected with this doctrine about truth, partly owing to the controversies between James, Dewey and Schiller on the one side and **Russell** on the other. The gravamen of Russell's attack is that the pragmatists have confused the meaning of "true" with the criteria that we may use for deciding whether a belief is true and have thereby surrendered to an irrationalist position; two of his most important articles are "Pragmatism" and "James's Conception of Truth" which are printed in *Philosophical Essays*. Largely as a result of Russell's attacks Dewey simply abandoned the use of the word "true" and claimed that it could be adequately replaced by a notion of "Warranted assertibility".

Lying behind this view about truth is the conviction of James and Schiller that everything must be understood in the light of human purpose, including thought; thoughts are but tools by which human beings try to achieve ends and they must be judged by their efficiency in subserving these ends; thus beliefs are tools for dealing with experience and must be judged as such. From this "pragmatism" has come to be a name for any position which lays emphasis on results as a test of satisfactoriness. Though there are many philosophers still who would acknowledge a great debt to Peirce, James and Dewey, few would regard "pragmatism" as being longer the name of a living philosophical position. Certainly the sense which Peirce, its inventor, gave to the word "pragmatism" is now obsolete except in historical discussion of Peirce.

(J.O.U.)

Predestination, *see* Freedom of the Will, Determinism.

Pre-Socratics. The term "Pre-Socratics" is used of a dozen or so of the earliest Greek thinkers, down to the time of **Socrates**, who attempted to define the constitution of the world and the nature of reality. They range from **Thales**, active in the early sixth century B.C., to **Democritus** in the latter part of the fifth. The earliest Pre-Socratics came from Ionia, the Greek colonization area in the centre of the west coast of Asia minor. City-states like Miletus were materially prosperous in the first half of the sixth century B.C. and in close contact through trade with the foreign cultures of Egypt and Lydia (and so with Babylonia) as well as with the Greek colonies of the Black Sea and the west. In addition, Ionia was itself heir to an old literary culture going back beyond Homer. These were conditions which encouraged, though they do not altogether explain, the surge of speculative thought in Miletus, Ephesus, Colophon and Samos. The interest in philosophy soon spread overseas: **Pythagoras** migrated from Samos to one of the Greek colonies of Southern Italy, while **Xenophanes** wandered all over the Greek world. **Parmenides** and **Zeno** were natives of Elea in south-west Italy: **Empedocles** belonged to Acragas in Sicily. Thus most of the Pre-Socratics belonged either in the east or the west of the Greek world, and Athens became involved only when **Anaxagoras** moved there from Ionia in the seventies of the fifth century B.C.

In spite of their differences from each other the Pre-Socratics form a logical, not merely a chronological, category. Socrates turned Greek speculative thought in a totally new direction by rejecting physics and concentrating on ethical questions. Except for the **Sophists**, in whose tradition Socrates in this respect belonged, earlier *philosophoi* or "lovers of wisdom" had subordinated human problems to the assessment of external physical reality. Thus those whom we term Pre-Socratics were called by **Aristotle** "investigators of nature", *physiologoi*: for they studied the *physis*, the nature or constitution, of things as a whole. Many of them had more specialized physical interests too; indeed some of the earlier ones, like the Milesians Thales and **Anaximander**, were men of many-sided intelligence who won fame with their contemporaries not for their theoretical accounts of reality, which in some cases may have been of only incidental

importance even to their authors, but for their ability to solve practical problems like the measurement of the distance of a ship at sea, the transport of an army over a river, or the accurate delimitation of the seasons. All the Pre-Socratics tried to describe the nature of the heavenly bodies; some, Thales and Pythagoras most conspicuously, had special mathematical interests apart from astronomy; Empedocles, Anaxagoras and Diogenes of Apollonia were concerned with medicine and embryology; and most of them seem to have attacked notorious natural problems like the causes of earthquakes, of rainbows, of magnetism, or of the flooding of the Nile. It is important not to overlook this strong practical interest, combined as it surprisingly was with a quite unempirical dogmatism when it came to dealing with larger problems of the nature of the world. What gave these men the right to be considered as philosophers, unlike the other astronomers, geographers and doctors who were active especially in the latter half of the period, was their common assumption that the world possessed some kind of integral unity and determinability which could be understood and explained to others in rational terms.

The first part of this assumption can be seen in earlier quasi-mythological cosmogonies and theogonies; but it was the treatment of these problems in straight forward descriptive terms and the rejection of personification that gave Thales and his successors, for later Greeks as for us, the title of "philosopher".

Although they abandoned much of the mythological language, the Pre-Socratics continued to be affected at certain points by inherited pre-philosophical assumptions. Thales, in declaring that all things came from water, was probably giving rationalistic expression to a partly mythopoeic Egyptian idea, paralleled also in Babylonia, that the world had arisen from Nun the goddess of primeval waters; though this was itself a reflexion of the annual re-appearance of the earth as the Nile recedes. A more important debt to myth appears in the central presupposition that the world is coherent and intelligible, is somehow a unity in spite of the diversity of its appearances. This presupposition formulated itself in the anthropomorphic *genetical* tendencies of traditional mythology. Thus in the Hesiodic *Theogony*, a poem put together perhaps in the early seventh century B.C., the family of gods is traced back to the very beginning of the world, when Gaia, mother earth, together with the different parts of the underworld, appears as the first distinct cosmological entity out of an originative gulf called *Chaos* (which means, not confusion, but simply "gap"). At the same time Eros or sexual love, the anthropomorphic motive for further differentiation, comes on the scene. Gaia gives birth to the male sky-god, Ouranos, also to mountains and the inner seas; then sky-god and earth-goddess mate together to produce the encircling river that connects them, Okeanos. Further generation takes place from these same parents; according to other accounts rain is the seed of sky which fertilizes earth so as to produce plants and crops. This quasi-mythological cosmogony is complicated by confusions produced by the synthesis in the *Theogony* of several different versions. A cruder and more completely mythopoeic story which occurs later in the poem, according to which Ouranos lies continuously with Gaia and refuses to allow her to bring forth offspring until he is mutilated by Kronos, probably represents a more primitive version by which the original *chaos* or gap was that produced by the initial separation of earth and sky. At all events the mythological idea that different components of the world are connected with deities who have a traceable ancestry, as human beings have, led on to the view that the world as a whole can be derived from a single ancestor or pair of ancestors – for example earth, or earth and sky. This assumption of a genetical unity in the world, determinable by the description of a possible lineal descent of plural world-constituents from a single cosmogonical agent, deeply affected the earlier Pre-Socratics, who for the Gaia or *Chaos* of Hesiod substituted a single originative material like the water of Thales or the air or mist of **Anaximenes**. Even where cosmogony was rejected – as for example by **Heraclitus**, who declared that this world-order was made by neither gods nor men, but had existed always – the assumption of an essential unity and determinability in the world was retained. This important general presupposition, the reasons for which were not discussed by the Greeks themselves, was presumably also due in part to the observation of natural regularities, of the sun, the seasons and so on, which encouraged the

comfortable belief that the world worked in accordance with laws not completely unlike those which ordered human societies. The narrower view of the main natural constituents as divine people with a single remote ancestor was a more specialized manifestation of this anthropomorphic approach.

The survival of anthropomorphism can also be seen in the devices used by some Pre-Socratics to account for the ultimate source of physical change. The Eros or sexual love of Hesiod found its counterpart in the idea of legal retribution in Anaximander, of war or strife in Heraclitus, or of love and strife in Empedocles. Indeed, less primitive thinkers have had to fall back on metaphor here; for example Aristotle used Eros to explain how the Prime Mover can move without being moved. Two other points at which the Pre-Socratics were influenced by inherited pre-philosophical assumptions were in their conceptions of divinity and of the soul. To a large extent they had abandoned the traditional Olympian pantheon. Yet they all retained the idea that what was all-powerful and indestructible was divine; thus the Milesians seem to have applied this description to their primary kinds of matter. As for soul, its constitution was largely ignored by the earliest Pre-Socratics; but for the Pythagoreans, Heraclitus and Empedocles it served as a physical link between man and the outside world. These thinkers were here reinterpreting the popular idea that the soul is related to *aither*, the material of the pure upper air and of the stars. At the same time confusion was caused in Pre-Socratic psychology by the failure to distinguish perception and intelligence or mind; here the effects are evident of the influential but inconsistent treatment of soul in Homer, where *psyche* meant sometimes life-stuff, sometimes consciousness-stuff, and sometimes intelligence.

Before summarising the main developments of Pre-Socratic thought it must be emphasized that our knowledge of these thinkers is very incomplete. We do not possess anything like the intact works of any Pre-Socratic. What we have is in the form of short isolated fragments, varying in length from one word to a few sentences, which have survived through being quoted by later authors of antiquity. Of the Milesians there is almost nothing – a phrase or a sentence of each; of Pythagoras nothing; of Heraclitus just over a hundred genuine sayings, mostly very short (the longest consists of fifty-five words). There remain about one hundred and fifty hexameter lines of Parmenides, about three hundred and forty of Empedocles; this, little as it is, may have formed something over a third of the original works, which were probably quite brief. Of Anaxagoras we possess about a score of fragments amounting to approximately a thousand words in all; these form probably not less than an eighth and not more than a half of his original book. Of Democritus, known to have been an extremely prolific writer, only between two and three hundred fragments survive, nearly all of an ethical character and largely irrelevant to his more unusual physical theories. Extracts from original works are, of course, only one source of information about the ideas of a dead thinker, and we rely heavily for our knowledge of the Pre-Socratics upon summaries and commentaries made by historians of thought in ancient times. Thus **Plato** himself made brief incidental judgments, many of them of a humorous or ironical kind, upon some of his predecessors – Heraclitus, Parmenides and Anaxagoras in particular. Plato seems to have taken Pythagoreanism seriously, but used most of the other Pre-Socratics as symbols for various kinds of wrong-headedness. Aristotle, on the other hand, believed in the systematic assessment of his predecessors. The Pre-Socratic physicists were of special interest because, in spite of grave misunderstandings of causation, they seemed to him to have been making what he called "lisping" but not valueless attempts to express the truths which he revealed. There has been dispute between twentieth-century critics about the value of Aristotle's detailed opinions on his early predecessors. It has certainly been demonstrated that he was capable on many occasions of seriously distorting their views, not intentionally but through a lack of historical objectivity and because he was looking at the Pre-Socratics from the avowed standpoint of his own philosophy. At the same time Aristotle's information and judgments are always valuable and often indubitably correct; and they can only be safely rejected in those cases where we possess reliable contrary evidence, which for the most part can be provided only by relevant original fragments, and where in addition his motives for distortion can be detected.

The correct assessment of Aristotle's judgments is particularly important because virtually all subsequent ancient accounts of the Pre-Socratics were strongly influenced by him. The chief source of information for later writers was *The Opinions of the Physicists*, a history compiled by Aristotle's colleague Theophrastus as part of the great Peripatetic encyclopaedia of knowledge. But Theophrastus himself, although on many points he seems to have checked original sources, was also heavily influenced by Aristotle's opinions, which are sometimes reproduced in words seen to be borrowed from Aristotle's *Physics* and *Metaphysics*. In many cases he seems to have been unable to ascertain disputed points, no doubt partly because not all the Pre-Socratics were still readily available in their own words. Indeed, although the Greeks themselves assumed that each Pre-Socratic (though not Pythagoras) wrote at least one book, to which they usually assigned the stock title "On Nature", it is doubtful whether some of the earlier ones produced writings that achieved wide currency even in their own time. They perhaps relied more on oral propagation, and the extracts from Heraclitus, notably, are primarily framed as oral apophthegms. Even when Pre-Socratic books were available their often metaphorical and poetical language did not always meet with sympathetic interpretation from the scientist Theophrastus. Thus his history, even if it had survived entire, would itself require much interpretation and modification, and even then would often not take us back beyond Aristotle; but except for a section on sensation it too exists only in fragments. Fortunately an unknown Stoic in the second century B.C. made a summary of it; this was recopied and expanded by one Aetius three or four hundred years later, and his work has been reconstructed from extracts in two slightly later extant writers. One more source must be mentioned: the Neoplatonist Simplicius is of great importance because, although he lived a thousand years after the Pre-Socratics, he found it desirable for the purposes of his commentaries on two treatises of Aristotle to set out the views of some of Aristotle's predecessors in their own words; for by his time many of the Pre-Socratic writings, and even the later summaries of them, had become extremely rare. To him, then, we owe in particular a great proportion of what we possess of the original words of Parmenides, Empedocles, Anaxagoras, and Diogenes of Apollonia.

Of the chronology and biography of the Pre-Socratics we are also imperfectly informed. For a crucial hundred years between the rise of the Sophistic movement and the foundation of the Lyceum they did not greatly interest most Greeks. Aristotle was interested in their ideas, not in their personal lives; so it was left to the mendacious Alexandrian biographers, from the third to the first century B.C. to produce such dubious stories as that Heraclitus buried himself in dung or that Empedocles cast himself into Mount Etna. A few plainer facts have survived, which depend upon more reputable sources. Most of the chronological information, too, goes back to a more respectable but still largely speculative side of Alexandrian learning. Sotion classified the Pre-Socratics into eastern and western schools and, following Theophrastus, related them to each other as master and pupil. Then the chronographer Apollodorus left a standard account, in verse, of the dates and opinions of philosophers and others; he assumed that each thinker's period of greatest activity came at the age of forty, which he made to coincide with the nearest of a series of epochs or dated historical events. Further, a pupil was regularly made forty years younger than his putative master. Fortunately we know a few objective dates by which to check Apollodorus: for example the eclipse predicted by Thales must have been that of 585 B.C., and Melissus, the follower of Parmenides, was Samian admiral against Athens in 441 B.C. In general the Apollodoran dating, though over-schematic, seems to be roughly reliable.

The ancient distinction between East-Greek and West-Greek schools is useful up to a point. The westerners were less purely materialistic in their search for unity, indeed the Eleatics rejected the sense-world altogether. In Pythagoras and Empedocles there was a mystical or religious trend that would not have been tolerated in the more matter-of-fact, if no less dogmatic, atmosphere of eastern, Ionian thought. But there are many exceptions: Pythagoras was an Ionian by upbringing, though he moved to southern Italy; the Ionian Heraclitus discovered unity in structure rather than material; Melissus, though a follower of Parmenides, was an Ionian from Samos. Apart from the Sicilian Empedocles, the post-Eleatic pluralists mostly came from the eastern end of the Greek world (for example, Anaxagoras, and the Atomists Leucippus and Democritus) and tended to revert to traditional Ionian explanations of detailed cosmological phenomena.

Thales and his two successors, Anaximander and Anaximenes, are sometimes grouped together as "the Milesians". They considered that the unity which they assumed to exist in the world was to be found in the material of which the world was made or from which it had originated. Thales thought this material to be water. Aristotle, unfortunately vague here, wrote as follows: "Thales . . . says that it [namely the element and first principle of existing things] is water – and therefore declared that the earth is *on* water – perhaps taking his supposition from seeing the nurture of all things to be moist . . .". Now Thales may have been affected by this and similar observations, but his primary stimulus for the choice of water was probably the Near-eastern story that the world arose from a great surrounding flood. He was undoubtedly interested in Egypt and also had opportunities, through Sardis, for contact with the Babylonian records on which his most famous exploit, the prediction of an eclipse during a particular year, must have depended. Unfortunately it is hard to tell how far Thales carried the theories that he founded on Near-eastern empiricism. Was the unity of the world simply based, in the old genetical manner, on a distant origin from a single parent, namely water? Or is the world still somehow made of water? Aristotle naturally assumes the latter, since it fits his own idea of a persistent material substrate. Probably Thales did not distinguish very clearly between the alternatives; if things came from water, they must still be watery in a way – after all they are still supported and surrounded by an indefinite watery mass. Nor, probably, did he specify precisely how the world assumes its present diversity. According to Aristotle he declared that all things are full of gods, and that magnetic stone must possess soul because it can move iron. If, then, apparently inanimate things like stone possess soul and therefore life, then the world as a whole might seem to be interpenetrated with soul or life, which because of its immense power and scope must be divine and so could cause the development of the present plurality.

Anaximander was somewhat younger than

Thales, whom he must have known. He seems to have felt that if the originative stuff were identical with a present world-component like Thales' water, then the other components, for example fire, which is in many ways opposed to water, could not have asserted their identity. Anaximander accepted the idea of the single originative material, divine and all-encircling, but called it "the Indefinite" – implying that it was both boundless in extent and not identical with any nameable constituent of our world. Cosmogony took place when a nucleus that produced fire and dark mist separated off from the Indefinite. The mist solidified at its centre into earth, and was surrounded by a ball of flame which burst to form the heavenly bodies. These were wheels of flame encased in mist, each shining out through a single aperture. The earth, a broad flat-topped cylinder, stays in its place because it is equidistant from everything else – a brilliant advance on the idea of Thales or Anaximenes that the earth floats on water or air. Within the world things are divided into mutually opposed substances like heat and cold, winter and summer, day and night, the interactions of which are both motivated and regulated by a sociological metaphor: first they encroach on and then they "pay penalty and retribution to each other for their injustice according to the assessment of Time". (The anthropomorphism here may lie partly in the language; but the use of traditional poetical language and the absence of an abstract vocabulary was a constant brake on philosophical development at this period.) The cosmological regularity was derived from the divine Indefinite substance itself, which thus transmitted its unity to the developed world.

In the next generation Anaximenes reverted to the concept of a specific cosmogonical substance: air/mist (*aer* in Greek) or breath. The objection probably felt by Anaximander was overcome by the important idea that the originative stuff can take on other forms, and so turn into the other materials of our world, by condensation and rarefaction – by variation of its amount in any one place. This explanation of physical change, which was confirmed, though wrongly, by the observation that the temperature of exhaled breath varies with the compression of the mouth, succeeded in making material monism logically feasible for the first time. The consequent cosmogony and cosmo-

logy were not too implausible; for mist, as Thales may have observed of water, seems to permeate many changes in Nature – rarefied, it turns into fire (for lightning bursts out of cloud), condensed, it becomes earth by way of water, which seems to turn into earth, for example when the sea recedes. But Anaximenes' choice of basic substance was not entirely scientific; for the cosmic material, also called "breath", was likened by him to the human soul, often associated with breath, and so had a vital, kinetic, directive power in the world. Thus the motive of change was still largely anthropomorphic.

In Anaximenes' maturity, around 535 B.C., Pythagoras migrated from Samos to Italy and established there an exclusive semi-religious, semi-philosophical society. He wrote nothing himself, and assessment of him is particularly precarious. He taught that the soul migrates from one body and species to another; consequently all living things are akin, and abstinence from meat, as well as other taboos, had to be observed. In common with those known as Orphics he believed that the soul must be kept pure. An important means of purification was music. Here the mystical and scientific trends link up; for Pythagoras discovered by the experiment of stopping a single string that the musical scale is numerical – that the major harmonic intervals can be expressed in ratios of whole numbers. If music, which is related to soul, is numerical, then the whole world must somehow be numerical too; Pythagoras' followers, developing this typically over-bold induction, seem to have assigned concrete bulk (still assumed to be the mark of existence) to the points which, as units, both made up numbers and delimited lines, planes, and volumes; so that physical objects, composed as they were of determinable geometrical shapes, could be resolved into sums of concrete unit-points. Further, the world could be analysed into ten pairs of opposites, of which the archetype was limit and the unlimited. These were the elements of number, too: odd numbers are limited, even numbers (because they can be halved *ad infinitum*) unlimited. The world came into being when the unit as limit drew in the unlimited and subjected it to various determinations. Most of these ideas were probably later than Pythagoras; but the master himself had ascribed special importance to the decade, and there is no reason to remove from him the famous theorem associated with his name. It may have been a follower, though, who drew the full damaging implication from the consequent irrationality of the diagonal: that some natural lengths, all of which should be composed of unit-points, could not be expressed in terms of whole numbers at all.

Pythagoras' longer-lived coeval Xenophanes, likewise an emigrant from Ionia, devoted much of his poetry to attacking the traditional Homeric description of the gods – both their immortality and the very basis of their anthropomorphism: for each species should on this view envisage gods in their own shape, which seemed absurd. Xenophanes put in their place a single, motionless god who "shakes all things by the thought of his mind". This idea of a divine, intellectual source of change may have affected Empedocles and Anaxagoras; his destructive rationalism was probably more generally influential. Apart from attacking anthropomorphism he appears to have parodied the exaggeration and dogmatism of Ionian physical theories by such suggestions as that the sun continues each day in a straight line. Although not primarily interested in physics, and a professed sceptic over the acquisition of certain knowledge, Xenophanes is not without scientific importance, since he used the testimony of marine fossils found inland to show that the earth must once have been mud – a rare use at this period of rational inference from a well-testified and correctly assessed observation.

Further modifications of the Milesian approach were made by Heraclitus, active in Ephesus probably around 510–480 B.C. Philosophically as well as socially an extreme individualist, he undermined the genetical conception by abandoning cosmogony and stating that the unity of things was to be found in their essential structure or arrangement rather than their material. This common structure or *Logos*, which was not superficially apparent, was chiefly embodied in a single kinetic material, fire. It was responsible both for the regularity of natural changes and for the essential connexion of opposites – for Heraclitus adopted this traditional analysis of differentiation – through balanced interaction. The regularity underlying change was for Heraclitus the significant thing, but like the Greek poets he also emphasized the ubiquity of change

(and was consequently subjected to exaggerated interpretation, *see* **Cratylus**), which he termed strife or war; for without reaction between opposites and world-masses the *Logos* and the unified cosmos would cease to exist. Philosophy was not a game: knowledge of physics was ethically essential, for man is part of his environment; his soul, which in its unadulterated state is a kind of fire, is connected through sensation and breathing with the fiery *Logos*-constituents of the outside world. This enabled understanding to be distinguished from mere perception.

Development of these fruitful ideas was interrupted by a philosophical explosion on the other side of the Greek world. Parmenides wrote a poem claiming that we can only meaningfully say of anything that "it is". The predicate "is not" is literally nonsense: not-being is impossible, inexpressible, and inconceivable. Since not-being was equated at this time with empty space, there could be no movement; but Parmenides rejected change on metaphysical rather than physical grounds, since any change involved its subject in *not-being* what it was before. This confusion between existential and predicative "is" was not cleared up until Plato. From the single premise "it is" Parmenides proceeded to the conclusion that reality or "being" is homogeneous, motionless, solid, and indivisible. "Since there is a furthest limit, it [namely Being] is bounded from every side, like the mass of a well-rounded sphere"; he was still obliged to use materialistic language, and would no doubt, if pressed, have said that his reality was concrete. From now on, however, there was a gradual development of more abstract language which could attribute to the new and odd kinds of philosophical reality a status different from that of phenomena. Parmenides, ignoring Heraclitus here, seems to have started from the old problem of how an initial unity can turn into a plural world. His emphasis on "limit" suggests that he was deliberately rejecting the "unlimited" component of Pythagorean **dualism**. His follower **Zeno** of Elea, too, is thought by many to have directed his paradoxes (which show that space is continuous, not composed of discrete points) against the Pythagorean view of matter. A curious and professedly "deceitful" appendix, in which Parmenides outlines a cosmology based not on one but on two substances, probably reflects, as well as some reaction against Pythagoreanism, his doubts over rejecting the world of manifest experience. Certainly it gives a hint that pluralism is a possible escape from his dilemma.

To meet this dilemma Empedocles posited no less than four "roots" or permanent kinds of matter: fire, water, earth (Heraclitus' world-masses), together with air, the concrete existence of which Empedocles had now confirmed by special observations. To these were added two kinetic agents, Love and Strife – motives of attraction and repulsion which, anthropomorphic as they obviously are, were described concretely as "equal in length and breadth" to the four roots. The different substances in Nature, apart from unmixed earth, water, and so on, were compounds of roots welded together by the admixture of Love. Empedocles felt obliged to propose a uniform stage of existence – not a true cosmogonical origin, which might imply illegitimate "becoming", but a recurrent period in a cycle – in which all things are mixed by Love in a homogeneous mass equivalent to Parmenides' "sphere" of Being. Only Strife, by coming somewhat obscurely to "the lowest depths of the vortex", is excluded. Then, by the gradual intrusion of Strife, the roots begin to separate into different combinations, until eventually Love is excluded in turn and Strife has separated the roots into isolated masses. A world could only be formed in one of the two intermediate stages between the total domination of Love or Strife: our world belongs to the stage when Strife is increasing. Each intermediate cosmological stage produces different stages of animal evolution, causing monsters and bisexual creatures as well as the more efficient species of our present world Sensation can be valid, since it is caused by material effluences from objects entering pores in the sense-organs: earth is perceived by earthy components in the body, fire by fire, as in vision, and so on. Empedocles also wrote a more mystical poem called "Purifications", according to which the soul, originally divine, is polluted by Strife and cast into the world of opposites; after successive incarnations it may purify itself and regain the realms of Love.

Anaxagoras, like Empedocles active around the middle of the fifth century B.C., similarly maintained that physical change, being merely the aggregation and dispersion of different kinds of per-

manently-existing matter, did not imply that "what is" must turn into the vicious "what is not". But for him these kinds of matter were not four or six, but as many as there were different natural substances. Originally these were all mixed together in a sort of Parmenidean One; then the motive substance, now described as Mind, and as "subtlest of all objects and purest", started a rotation and so, by separation and re-aggregation, a cosmogony. Objects in the world are compounded of lumps or particles called "seeds". There is "a portion of everything in everything" – a portion, probably, of every natural substance (except Mind, which only exists in some things) in every seed. Each seed possesses the apparent character of the portion that predominates. Thus the original unity is preserved in the developed world, and yet evident alterations can be explained by exchanges in the ratio of the portions between different seeds. Anaxagoras argued against both the Pythagoreans and the Eleatic Zeno that matter is infinitely divisible, but evidently did not notice the incompatibility of this principle with "a portion of everything in everything". At all events his theory, though complicated and in places self-refuting, preserved appearances without contradicting the Eleatic premise; it further avoided the difficulties of Empedocles' cyclical scheme, and the objection that the formation of natural substances out of Empedoclean "roots" *did* seem to involve coming-to-be of a kind.

It was at about this time that the Sophists, professional teachers of wisdom, made themselves felt. They believed that the current physical systems and the Eleatic rejection of the phenomenal world were either over-complicated or absurd or both, and were in any case irrelevant to practical life and quite unconfirmed by evidence. **Protagoras** and Gorgias, the most important of them, taught that knowledge of the constitution of the world lay outside human reach, that man should assess things on the basis of his own individual experience. Yet there now appeared a much simpler physical explanation of the world and its changes: Atomism, a system originated perhaps around 440–430 B.C. by **Leucippus**, of whom we know very little, and elaborated by **Democritus**. (It was also, of course, later adopted by **Epicurus** and expounded by **Lucretius**.) The Atomists began by denying the Eleatic implication that empty space, the void, cannot exist. There *is* not-being, in this sense. In addition there is homogeneous, solid matter, which is not continuous (as was Parmenides' Being) but is contained in an infinite number of indivisible, and also invisible, atoms. Reality consists, then, in atoms and the void. The atoms are constantly in motion, because of their collisions with and rebounds from each other; no metaphorical cause of motion was needed. They differ only in position and shape; sometimes atoms of different shapes get caught up with each other to form complexes. A world arises when collisions and rebounds in an isolated group of atoms happen to start a vortex, which causes heavy complexes of atoms to go to the centre, light ones to the circumference. Man himself is a complex of atoms and his soul is made of mobile spherical ones. Leucippus adapted the Empedoclean theory of sensation: objects emit effluences, "membranes" of atoms which, sometimes distorted in passage, make physical contact with the atoms of the sense-organ and then of the soul. It follows that there are no real qualities: appearances are secondary (but not therefore negligible; Democritus had a developed ethic, aimed at moral well-being), and in reality there are only atoms and void. Thus Atomism simultaneously fulfilled the conditions of Eleatic logic and the aims of Milesian material monism. Entirely an *a priori* construction, it has almost nothing in common with contemporary atomic theory, though this itself has grown out of Gassendi's direct revival of Democritean atomism.

Various other theories of an eclectic nature were propounded from the mid-fifth-century B.C. onwards: by Hippon, for example, and Archelaus. Cratylus exaggerated Heracliteanism by holding that everything is in flux all the time, while Diogenes of Apollonia produced an unusually coherent old-style monistic system in which air is basic substance, with warm air as divine and intelligent, directing all things for the best. This was the kind of teleology that Socrates wanted; but Socrates rejected physics and concentrated on ethics and the soul – soul or mind being the obvious teleological agent in his still anthropomorphic view. In many ways the Socratic reaction, aided by the Sophists and by current anthropological, medical and social ideas, brought physical speculation to a depressingly sudden halt; but by his interest in definitions Socrates initiated a deeper study of logic, without which philosophy could make no further real progress.

The Pre-Socratics, who for the most part made little appeal to their lay contemporaries, plainly had great influence on their philosophical successors: negatively, in the main, on **Plato**, but positively on **Aristotle** in his revival of physics. **Atomism**, furthermore, survived for centuries through **Epicurus**, while Stoicism was deeply indebted to Heraclitus. Great historical importance in the development of thought the Pre-Socratics certainly had; but it may legitimately be asked whether their fragmentary science and philosophy have any value other than as a necessary primitive stage on the way to serious speculation. The inevitable deficiencies of these lively thinkers are striking but instructive: their love of inference unconfirmed, for the most part, by observation, let alone experiment; their retention of mythical and metaphorical explanations of change; their inadequate linguistic resources, which delayed or distorted the formation of abstract concepts; their reluctance to examine what was implied by knowledge, and their rudimentary logic. Yet they also had great virtues; and apart from the admirable quality of the rapid and systematic intellectual progress from Thales to Democritus, or the comprehensiveness of systems like that of Heraclitus, the Pre-Socratics illustrate in a particularly clear form certain problems of materialistic philosophy and the limitations of some of their classical solutions: problems, for example, of presupposed unity and observed plurality; of unseen or structural types of unity; of the physical source of change; of the evaluation of sense-perception, and the interrelation of ethics and physics. It is perhaps in this respect that Pre-Socratic thought may be said to have philosophical as well as historical value. (G.S.K.)

Price, Henry Habberley (1899–), English philosopher, Wykeham Professor of Logic and Fellow of New College, Oxford, 1935–59. He has written mainly on perception and the philosophy of mind, though also on philosophical problems in psychical research.

In his first book, *Perception*, he rejected previous theories about the relation between **sense-data** and material objects, especially the theory that the latter *cause* the former and so are known solely by their effects. In his own view, the sense-data not only belong directly to the physical object, but are related intimately among themselves, forming a "family", that is a set of series each converging on a standard member; these standard members compose the Standard Solid, which has the shape ordinarily called "the real shape of the thing". The Standard Solid is not identical with the physical object, hence Price is not a phenomenalist. For Price a "thing" is a family of sense-data *together with* the coincident physical object, but he can say so little about the object that he runs close to **phenomenalism**.

His later *Thinking and Experience* rejects theories which make thinking consist entirely of the use of symbols or of images or of concepts treated as subsistent objects, and contends that recognition is basic, concepts being "recognitional capacities".

Plate 73, page 297. (R.HALL)

Price, Richard (1723–1791), English theologian, a Minister at Newington Green, London and a D.D. of Glasgow. He wrote his most notable philosophical work in the sphere of ethics. His *Review of the Principal Questions in Morals*, first published in 1758, is the earliest clear and cogently developed **deontological** theory – that is, an account of morality which makes "right" and "obligation" the fundamental concepts. Price sees these as indefinable, *a priori* and objective, and thus is at loggerheads with the school of **Hutcheson** and **Hume**. He attacks not simply the detail of their arguments in support of an ethic of "sentiment", but the basis of their **empiricism** itself. Universal notions and concepts such as substance, duration, infinity, cannot, he thinks, be explained from a radical empiricist standpoint. No more can the basic notions of morals.

Price followed **Butler** in his rejection of psychological **hedonism**, but did not fully share Butler's confidence that duty and interest for the most part coincide in this life. He argued that a hereafter must be postulated in order to make sense of our moral experience; but, unlike many who have used similar arguments, he saw that an *infinitely* long after-life cannot be demonstrated in this way.

Particularly valuable throughout Price's moral philosophy are his serious acknowledgement of the facts of moral conflict and his tough-minded refusal to accept over-simplifying "supreme principles", such as those of the egoists and utilitarians of his day. (R.W.H.)

Plate 74, page 298.

Prichard, Harold Arthur (1871–1947), White's Professor of Moral Philosophy in the University of Oxford. He was probably the outstanding member of the realist movement at Oxford of which Cook **Wilson** was the officially acknowledged leader. His only largescale publication on theory of knowledge was *Kant's Theory of Knowledge* (1909), a polemical work in which he opposes his realism to **Kant**. In later years he rather modified these views, holding that we perceived only coloured patches and not bodies, of which we could have only inferential knowledge. In moral philosophy his paper *Does Moral Philosophy Rest on a Mistake?* (1912) was largely influential in the revival of intuitionist ethics; Prichard claimed that we could know simply by attending to the matter that certain acts were duties and that any attempt to produce a general theory of why such acts were duties was a mistake. In ethics, however, as in epistemology, he grew sceptical in later years; in *Duty and Ignorance of Fact* (1932) he admitted a considerable element of subjectivism into our assessment of our duties. His influence through personal contact was immense; some idea of it can be gained from the memoir by H. H. **Price** in *Proceedings of the British Academy* Vol. XXXIII. His stringent arguments on the meaning of words undoubtedly still influence Oxford philosophy. (J.O.U.)

Probability is an important concept for the philosopher to study for many reasons. There is the problem of how, when and why the mathematical theory of probability is applicable to reality; there is the problem of the relation of statistical data to probability; most important of all, probability is a key concept in the understanding of scientific method, of the relation of evidence to law and theory, of the rationality of belief. Philosophers have always given some attention to probability; but in the past half century it has gained more and more interest and there have been many books, some of them very technical, published in this period which have been devoted entirely to this topic.

If we concentrate on such statements as "The probability of heads when a penny is tossed is ½" the Frequency Theory of probability may well seem most plausible as an interpretation of the statement. According to the frequency theory the above statement means, roughly, that in the long run the frequency with which a tossed coin will fall heads upwards when tossed will be one time in two. Special attractions of this theory are that, in a well-known version of it, it follows from the definition of probability that the axioms of the mathematical theory must be applicable and that it manifestly ties up probability very closely with statistical data. On the other hand it is very difficult indeed to give a satisfactory version of this theory when, as is necessary, more accurate expressions are introduced than "in the long run" to indicate what frequency is relevant. The frequency theory was first stated in detail by **Venn** in his Logic of Chance; other wellknown exponents are **Mises** and Reichenbach.

But if we turn our attention to such statements as "Probably there is life on Mars" the frequency theory becomes specially unplausible; when dealing with the probability of theories, hypotheses and special events it is hard to see how we could be referring to any sequence of events or any frequency within such a series, though some philosophers have attempted to sustain such a view. When dealing with such examples it is much more plausible to regard the word "probable" as indicating that the statement "There is life on Mars" should be accepted with some reserve; that it is made in a condition of evidential satisfactoriness midway between those that we might indicate by such expressions as "We know that there is life on Mars" and "There is no ground for supposing life on Mars".

Very many philosophers are nowadays agreed that the notion of probability is used in both the frequency way and in the evidence-assessing way and that we must understand it according to context. Though they disagree on many points of comparative detail this is the view of **Carnap**, **Braithwaite**, and **Russell**. When a numerical statement is in principle possible in the form "The

probability of an X being Y is p", some explanation of a frequency type is given; but where a statement is of the form "Probably it is the case that so and so", where no numerical valuation seems plausible, the word "probably" is taken to be indicative of caution and reserve in making the statement.

It should be added that the classical definition of probability, found in the great French mathematical writers on probability, was that the probability of an event was the ratio of favourable to total possibilities; for the purposes of philosophy this is quite inadequate, since it seems that the "possibilities" referred to are hardly distinguishable from probabilities and it is hard to see how to add up favourable possibilities without falling into severe logical difficulties. (J.O.U.)

Protagoras of Abdera, the Greek Sophist, flourished *c.* 450–440 B.C. He was famous as a teacher of *arete*, practical excellence or political and rhetorical skill; he worked in different cities and took fees for his teaching. He was credited with several books, on logic, cultural origins, and human behaviour. Protagoras attacked the dogmatism both of contemporary religion and of contemporary philosophy. Of the gods he said: "I am unable to know about the gods either that they exist or that they do not, and what form they have; for there are many things that prevent knowledge – both the obscurity of the subject and the shortness of human life". Contradictory statements could be made on any subject, and each could be true according to circumstances; there was no single absolute truth to be discovered by man, since a man's own nature was intimately involved in any judgment. This is probably the reference of Protagoras' famous dictum "Man is the measure of all things, of the existence of the things that are and the non-existence of the things that are not". This seems to be directed particularly against the extremism of **Eleatic** ontology, which was subjected to critical examination by Protagoras' contemporary, Gorgias, also. See also **Pre-Socratics**. (G.S.K.)

Pythagoras of Samos, Greek philosopher, flourished *c* 530 B.C. He left Samos to escape the tyranny of Polycrates and settled in Croton in South Italy, where for a time he had great political influence.

He established there a community of disciples, partly religious and partly scientific. The master himself wrote nothing and since his followers attributed their own developments to him out of piety it is especially hard to assess his ideas. Some lines of Xenophanes prove that Pythagoras believed in the transmigration of the soul – even between different species, since all living things were akin. He was also renowned for his scientific and mathematical knowledge, and there is no reason to disconnect from him the theorem that bears his name. He also probably made the important discovery that the musical scale has a numerical basis, that is, that its main harmonic intervals can be expressed in ratios of the first four integers. These integers together formed the Decad, to which sacred significance was attached in the community; but whether Pythagoras himself maintained like his successors that not only music, but the whole world, was somehow numerical and was made up out of "limit" and "the unlimited", is uncertain. See also **Pythagoreans** and **Pre-Socratics**. (G.S.K.)

Pythagoreans. The community founded by **Pythagoras** in Croton in S. Italy split into a mathematical and a religious side. The latter lived according to taboos based on Pythagoras' idea of the kinship of living things and the necessity for purification of body and soul. The "mathematicians", while probably not rejecting these ideas, associated them with developments of Pythagoras' discovery that the musical scale is numerical. Since music was held to have special power over soul, which permeated the cosmos, the whole world must be somehow made out of number. The elements of number, and thus of the world, were the even, representing the unlimited, and the odd, representing limit. A table of ten pairs of basic opposites within the world was drawn up, in which odd, male, straight, good, at rest, etc., came under "limit", their contraries under "unlimited". Unfortunately there is little evidence here apart from Aristotle's rather vague account, which did not distinguish early from later Pythagoreanism. Most of these ideas were probably formed by the time of **Parmenides**, who seems to attack Pythagorean dualism. By this time, too (though one piece of ancient evidence may suggest that the development was later), the units which formed

number were probably conceived as possessing spatial magnitude; so that lines, surfaces and solids could be expressed as sums of units, and objects were literally made out of number. The Pythagorean cosmogony may in part have developed a little later: an initial unit "drew in" the unlimited, in the form of the void, and somehow divided into other units separated by the unlimited. These unit-point-atoms then grew into lines, planes and solids. At the centre of the universe lies fire; the stars, of which the earth is one, each produce a sound according to the speed of their revolution, and these make up a "harmony of the spheres" inaudible by men. See also **Pre-Socratics** and **Zeno**. (G.S.K.)

Q

Qualities, Primary and Secondary, *see* Atomism, Descartes, Locke.

Quine, Willard V.O. (1908–), born at Akron, Ohio, Professor of Philosophy at Harvard University, a distinguished mathematical logician, actively concerned as well with the general philosophy of logic and the theory of knowledge. His purely formal work in logic deals with a large variety of highly technical problems. Probably his best known and most influential contribution to this area of research is his improved version of the reduction of mathematics to logic that had been given by **Whitehead** and **Russell** in their *Principia Mathematica*. The improved version was obtained by Quine through the introduction of important novel devices in order to avoid, among other things, various debatable assumptions in *Principia*.

However, many of Quine's technical contributions to mathematical logic are motivated by broad philosophical considerations. Unlike many students of the subject, he does not believe that formal logic is "ontologically" neutral, since according to him system of logic commits us to accepting the existence of some distinctive sorts of entities (e.g., concrete individuals such as physical objects, or abstract entities such as classes or attributes). He has therefore proposed a criterion for determining just what ontology is presupposed in any given statement. Contrary to traditional views, he has argued that the ontology (i.e., the kinds of entities whose existence is presupposed) is not determined by the proper names which may occur in a statement, but rather by the types of variables in it for which substitutions may be made. Quine has compressed this criterion into the formula: to be is to be the value of a variable. On this criterion, for example, anyone accepting the statement "some dogs are white" (or in standard logical locution, "There is an x such that x is a dog and is white") is committed to believing in the existence of things that are dogs; but he is not thereby committed to a belief in the existence of platonic **universals**, such as doghood. Quine's philosophical predelictions make him reluctant to accept the existence of universals. However, though he has tried to reconstruct mathematics in conformity with his **nominalistic** preferences, he has been admittedly unsuccessful. But he has not refused to employ platonistic logical assumptions when he found them indispensible for his formal constructions.

Quine has also challenged the familiar distinction between synthetic (roughly, contingent or empirical) and **analytic** (or necessary) statements, on the ground that none of the proposed criteria for analyticity make that distinction clear. According to him, therefore, arithmetical laws do not differ sharply in respect to their "necessary" character from physical laws; and both types of statements might be abandoned in the eventuality of apparently disconfirming evidence, though the former with doubtless greater reluctance than the latter. Moreover, Quine maintains it is only the total system of assumptions (including those of logic) in which a given statement is an element that can be subjected to experimental test. He has therefore criticized proponents of the verifiability theory of meaning as misguided in their attempts to fix the meaning of isolated statements in terms of their alleged sensory significance.   (E.N.)

R

Rationalism, in the usage of philosophers, is the characteristic of a philosophical theory which claims that by pure reasoning, without appeal to any empirical premises, we can arrive at substantial knowledge about the nature of the world. There is also a well-known use of the word in which it refers to the view that faith in the supernatural is inadmissable and that religious claims must be tested by rational criteria, but, in the absence of clear evidence to the contrary, the former sense of the word should be presumed in modern philosophical literature. It is in that sense that **Descartes**, **Leibniz** and **Spinoza** are quoted as classical examples of rationalism.

Rationalism is opposed to **empiricism**, the doctrine that experience is a necessary basis to all our knowledge; but neither of these terms has a precise meaning. Thus we might expect that a pure empiricist would claim that all knowledge requires empirical premises, and J. S. **Mill** did at times make this claim; for him even mathematical truths are empirical generalizations. But most empiricists have admitted that mathematical truths are *a priori*; they are still considered to be empiricists if they claim that mathematical truths are analytic, formal truths which give no information about the nature of the world. Thus there is a tendency to consider that a rationalist is one who claims to have synthetic *a priori* knowledge, who claims to know, wholly or in part, what the world is like by pure reason. But Leibniz is usually considered to be the most extreme of the rationalists because he claimed that in principle all truths could be known by pure reasoning, experience being but an inferior substitute for reason; yet Leibniz held that all truths of reason were guaranteed by the principle of contradiction and therefore, in modern terminology, analytic. However, Leibniz's claim that the contradictory of every true proposition is self-contradictory, is very paradoxical, and we may say that the rationalist is one who claims knowledge which is not based on sense-experience and which cannot be regarded without paradox as being purely formal. But this is still not precise; **Kant** claimed synthetic *a priori* knowledge, but claimed that he was not a rationalist because it was not dogmatic knowledge about things themselves but only about phenomena; he thought that it was one of the main virtues of his critical system that it avoided being either rationalist or empiricist. We must not seek for unobtainable precision; by rationalism philosophers mean positions like, or sufficiently like, that of Descartes, who proved the existence of God and the physical world from one premise, considered rationally indubitable, "I think, so I am". There is no criterion of what is sufficiently like this.

The vast majority of philosophers today deny the possibility of rationally deducing any truths not implicit in the premises; it is very uncharacteristic of modern philosophy to proceed by alleged proof of theorems by strict argument. The main task of the non-empiricist philosophers now is therefore to find a procedure to substitute for rationalistic proof as a method of justifying their beliefs.

(J.O.U.)

Real, *see* especially Metaphysics, Realism, Universals, Bradley.

Realism was a term first used to stand for the view that **Universals** have a real being independently of being thought, either *transcending* particulars, as held by **Plato**, or at least *in* particulars, as held by **Aristotle**. But to-day the term is most commonly used to signify the belief that physical objects exist independently of experience, when this doctrine is expounded philosophically. The view has of course always been held very widely, but it was developed and defended in detail mainly after the beginning of the present century in reaction against "idealism". The specifically "realist" school which engaged on this enterprise was primarily British and American. Its most important members were **Russell**, G. E. **Moore** and C. D. **Broad**. The school has had numerous ramifications under the influence of its logical researches and of **Wittgenstein**'s thought, but we can only speak of it here in so far as it concerned itself with the specific problems of realism and remained realist.

Idealism had rested on two main types of argument. The first claimed to show that the existence of independent physical objects was inconceivable because we could not separate the concept of a physical object from the concept of a consciousness relatively to which it existed. This contention was itself based on the belief that any quality commonly ascribed to physical objects involves a reference to sensation, and on general arguments to the effect that we can only know what is relative to mind. Moore traced the former belief to a confusion between "sensation" as meaning the act of sensing and "sensation" as meaning what is sensed; in the one sense it must be mental, in the other it need not be so. Against the latter it was urged by realists that knowing, so far from implying that the object known is essentially relative to the know-

ing of it, implies on the contrary that it is independent of being known. An attack was also made on the "internal" theory of relations, from which it had been deduced that no two related things could have existed as they were apart from the relation, and it was insisted that some relations and in particular the knowing relation need make no internal difference to their terms. The rather facile tendency of idealists to dismiss certain aspects of experience as unreal was also criticized and much attention was devoted to the problems of infinity on the ground of which time and space had been pronounced mere appearances. Here Russell's logical work in *Principia Mathematica*, where he showed how the concept of infinity can be handled self-consistently and intelligibly in mathematics, could be utilized. The coherence theory of truth was also attacked in favour of a view which found the definition of truth in correspondence to an independent reality and which in discussing criteria of truth attached more weight to experience than to coherence in a system. The rationalist view of knowledge and of reality taken by most idealists was rejected, and later the school on the whole moved towards the doctrine that there are no logical connections in the real world and that all *a priori* reasoning is essentially linguistic. It must be emphasized however that these views are not necessarily connected with realism about physical objects any more than with idealism.

The second type of argument for idealism was the negative one that we cannot justify the belief in independent physical things even granted that the belief is not self-contradictory. This contention was found harder to meet, and two quite different lines of reply were adopted. Some realists argued that idealism is inevitable if we start with the "representative" theory of perception, according to which we never perceive physical objects directly but always only something mental or at least dependent on mind ("sense-data"). Consequently they, diverging from almost all previous philosophers, tried to maintain a direct theory of perception. The chief difficulty about this lies in the occurrence of "illusion". In order to meet it the usual assumption of the representative theory that, if we perceive something directly, we must perceive it as it is, was abandoned, and a number of ingenious expedients utilized. A few realists adopted more paradoxical views and contended that it was not absurd to regard as included in the real external world many of the phenomena ordinarily stigmatized as illusions. Russell, for example, suggested in *Our Knowledge of the External World* that physical things have not, as ordinarily supposed, one single shape each but comprise all the different shapes that could be seen from all points of view, all existing objectively. He did not long retain this hypothesis, but it remains a possibility to be considered that spatial properties might be quite objective and yet somehow relative to the point from which they are viewed (compare "left" and "right"), and also, as he suggested too, that even if not directly perceived themselves, they may consist of groups of entities like the sense-data we perceive directly. The concept of sense-data has however been very widely attacked in recent times on the ground that we do not normally experience, for example, mere coloured patches but from the beginning physical objects, a criticism which had indeed been anticipated by many idealists. A popular theory to-day is that the distinction between the direct and the representative theory of perception is merely one of language. Both sides, it is said, agree on the empirical facts when we for example perceive a round object as elliptical, and these we can express by saying either that we perceive elliptical sense-data produced by a round object or simply that the object is round but looks elliptical. In that case the word "sense-data" would not stand for existent entities, as it did with earlier thinkers.

Other realists retained the representative theory but tried to justify the belief in independent physical things as providing the best causal explanation of our experience and capable of adequate verification by the constant fulfilment of the predictions made on the assumption that it is true.

A distinction which might serve as a double-edged weapon was however drawn by Moore in 1925 and very widely adopted in his country. He maintained that we can know with certainty that our common-sense propositions about physical objects are true but that it is a difficult philosophical question how they can be analysed, and he mentioned among the possible modes of analysis that according to which statements about physical objects are reduced to statements about the sense-data we perceive under certain conditions. This analysis was very widely adopted by philosophers under the influence of the Russell-Moore tradition, but such a view can no longer be regarded as realism. On the other hand, because they eschewed metaphysics, these philosophers would not usually be called idealists. Still more recently, however, there has been a marked reaction against such views. In addition to objections against the possibility of carrying out the proposed analysis in any given case without still presupposing some independent physical object propositions, it is condemned as based on the supposedly discredited concept of sense-data as ultimate entities. This goes with a tendency to insist that we must accept it as a fact that we have certain knowledge of physical things even if we cannot say much about the question how we have the knowledge. It is commonly no longer believed to be the business of the philosopher to criticize those beliefs which we cannot help holding in practical life but rather to treat this fact as itself a guarantee of their truth. Such an outlook is supported by the argument that the words themselves which the idealist or sceptic uses in criticizing the notion of matter are derived from experience of the very things criticized and by a tendency to treat mind rather than matter as the concept requiring further analysis and justification. The business of philosophy is held to be to interpret common-sense language and not to reform or replace it.

Realism as such, however, is compatible with an immense variety of doctrines. There is, for example, nothing in it that excludes theism, and the great majority of theists have in fact also been realists, though the specifically realist school of the first half of the twentieth century which has busied itself specially with the problem of physical objects is not sympathetic at any rate to any metaphysical arguments for theism. The theory of knowledge which naturally goes with realism, because it insists on the independence of the object known, suggests an objective theory of ethics, of which indeed Moore was one of the strongest defenders, but the empiricist tendency of this school has on the whole told against such views, and still more against a Platonic theory of Universals as independent subsistents, to which for example Russell was inclined in his earlier period. The atmosphere of realism has been hostile to the formation of general philosophical theories of the Cosmos. Unless we regard

Whitehead *qua* metaphysician as a realist, the propriety of which is doubtful, **Alexander** (1859–1938) provides the only very important exception.

(A.C.E.)

Reid, Thomas (1710–1796), the originator of the distinctive Scottish philosophy of common-sense. He was himself a Scot, educated at Aberdeen and a professor first at Aberdeen and then at Glasgow, where he succeeded Adam Smith. Reid, like **Kant,** was prompted to his original philosophical position by reading the works of **Hume,** his contemporary and personal acquaintance. To Reid it seemed that the sceptical conclusions that he found in Hume were the correct conclusions to accept given the premises from which Hume started; this starting point was the theory of **ideas,** the theory that the immediate objects of the human mind in thought and in perception are peculiar mental entities called ideas. This starting-point, Reid considered, was common to all the modern philosophers – **Descartes, Locke, Berkeley** and Hume, for example, – though only Hume had drawn from these premises the sceptical conclusion to which they properly led; only Hume had taken the thoroughgoing position that if we have access only to discrete and unconnected ideas we cannot have connected knowledge transcending ideas. But Hume's conclusions, so extreme in scepticism, were untenable; no one could consistently maintain them. Therefore the basic premises, the theory of ideas, must be abandoned, for what leads by correct inference to falsehood must be false. In his *Inquiry into the Human Mind* Reid therefore attacked the theory of ideas as neither intuitively evident nor a hypothesis successfully helping to explain what it was introduced to explain.

Reid set out his own theory of knowledge in his *Essays on the Intellectual Powers of Man,* his most famous work. Here he set out a realist, but by no means rationalistic or speculative, account of perception, memory and conception to take the place of the way of ideas. Common sense is, he says, "that degree of judgment which is common to men with whom we can converse and transact business". But, Reid held, "all knowledge and all science must be built upon principles that are self-evident, and of such principles every man who has common sense is a competent judge when he conceives them distinctly". First principles may be nec-

essary, as in mathematics, or contingent. Reid gives a list of principles of common sense in the contingent sphere which are very similar to the list which G. E. **Moore** gave in his "Defence of Common Sense"; they include (1) "the existence of everything of which I am conscious" (2) "that the thoughts of which I am conscious are the thoughts of a being which I call myself, my mind, my person", (3) "that those things did really happen which I distinctly remember" (4) "our own personal identity and continued existence", (5) "that those things do really exist which we distinctly perceive by our senses, and are what we perceive them to be". Anyone who doubts these principles will be so far incapable of rational intercourse and those philosophers, such as Hume, who profess to doubt them do not do so sincerely and consistently. Reid conducts his attack on scepticism in a way very similar to that used by defenders of common sense in recent times; his critical work is at all times clear and acute, though his own positive views do not emerge so clearly from his writings as do the inconsistencies and unplausibilities of Locke and Berkeley.

Plate 75, page 299. (J.O.U.)

Ross, Sir W. David (1877–), born at Thurso, Caithness, Scotland, a former Provost of Oriel College, Oxford. He has two distinct international reputations. First, he is an Aristotelian scholar of the first rank; his editions of Aristotle's *Metaphysics, Physics* and *Analytics* with elaborate commentary and textual apparatus, are among the most important work on Aristotle in the twentieth century. He is more responsible than anyone else for the restatement of intuitionist **ethics** in the modern period. **Prichard** was the moving spirit in the revival of intuitionism – the doctrine that we apprehend our various duties as such directly and do not derive them from any such ulterior principle as that of utility – but Ross, first in *The Right and the Good* and later in his Gifford Lectures *The Foundation of Ethics,* gave Oxford intuitionism of the early part of the century its fullest and most systematic statement. Most of the characteristic doctrines derive from Prichard, such as that our duty is to set ourselves to act rather than to achieve any actual performance and that it is our duty to set ourselves to do the act which subjectively seems to us to be the act which is objectively our duty; but Ross's statement of the position is a model of precision, clarity and moderation. (J.O.U.)

Plate 77, page 301.

Right, *see* Ethics and articles on moral philosophers.

Rights, *see* Ethics and Locke.

Rousseau, Jean-Jacques (1712–1778), French writer. Rousseau spent his life wandering from country to country, from faith to faith, from job to job, and from mistress to mistress, often in bad health and always the victim of his over-sensitive and emotional temperament.

His early essays portray the natural man as a creature of good instincts and simple tastes who has been corrupted and deprived of happiness by civilization, and particularly by urban life, class distinctions, and governmental tyranny. His novel *La Nouvelle Héloïse* glorified sentiment and emotion against the contemporary claims of reason and self-restraint. Its popularity and influence were immediate and immense. His next tale *Emile*, the greatest of all writings on education, had an even wider and more lasting effect. It held that education should not curb or discipline the natural tendencies of the child but encourage them to grow and blossom. Teaching should come not from books and verbal instruction, but by example and direct experience of people and things. The family not the school is its proper field; and love and sympathy, not rules and punishments, the tools for the task. Religion should not be an affair of creeds and dogmas, of texts and formalities, but the infusion of the heart with feelings of awe and worship, feelings revelatory of a God who is beyond our reason. In his posthumously published *Confessions* Rousseau gave the world the first completely uninhibited picture, in all its colours bright and dark alike, of a human soul.

Rousseau's work was of great historical importance as the first attack of the romantic movement against the eighteenth century stronghold of classical rationalism. But the works noted above are not in the narrow sense philosophical, and his claims as a philosopher must rest on his theories of government. These are found (apart from his early essays) in his greatest work, the *Contrat Social* (So-cial Contract) and in the *Considerations on the Government of Poland*. Rousseau was not a systematic nor even a coherent and orderly thinker. His writing is passionate and rhetorical; he saw society as Carlyle saw history – by flashes of lightning.

In the *Social Contract* Rousseau urges that government is justified only if sovereignty remains with the people. Every law must be passed by the direct votes of all the citizens. Representative democracy is rejected. He saw that this system gives absolute power to the majority and he makes various unconvincing attempts to explain why minorities must acquiesce. He rejects any limitation on the majority and any notion of individual rights. He realised that such a system would work only in very small states (and he was much influenced here by the examples of the Greek city-state and the Swiss canton). To remedy the weakness of such states he looked to federation but he never worked out this solution.

The application of laws to particular cases was assigned to a body which Rousseau called "the Government" whose constitution would vary according to the size of the state and other local conditions. All associations within the state should be eliminated so that the individual should feel no rival loyalties to his citizenship.

Here Rousseau's influence on European history and especially on the French Revolution was profound. His book remains the classic defence of democracy.

Rousseau, however, was well aware of the objections to direct democracy, and tried to meet them. It is incapable of continuous legislative activity, and he appears to have met this by the belief that laws could be few and general and that much of what we should call legislation could be left to "the Government". The people may also be ill-informed, short-sighted, and irrational. The remedy here is a "Legislator" a semi-divine individual who should draft legislation and persuade the assembly to enact it.

In the course of formulating these problems he was led to his key conception of the "General Will" and the "Will of All". The former is the will of a body of men directed to their own common interests, the latter a mere aggregate of private individual selfish wills. This conception had two separate aspects each of which had a more subtle and long-term influence than the obvious revolutionary implications of the theory of direct popular sovereignty.

First there is the suggestion that a state is a person and has a will of its own distinct from the individual wills of its citizens and entitled to override them. This foreshadows much difficult and debated work on corporate personality and group psychology and could obviously lead to a mystic nationalism with unlimited claims on individual loyalty.

Second there is the suggestion that the General Will is infallible. We cannot call any law an expression of it unless that law is genuinely in the public interest. Thus the General Will becomes an ideal conception to which actual laws may only approximate. Direct democracy is justified by the argument that if the people themselves make the laws under which they live they lose no freedom. But obedience to the General Will is justified by the argument that it is directed to the common good which is my good (or at least the good at which I am morally obliged to aim). Law is not an external command with the sanction of force, but the voice of my own moral or higher or true self. So political obligation can be (like the service of God) "perfect freedom".

But now it was not obvious why democracy was needed. As **Spinoza** has said "Provided the laws are good, it does not matter who makes them". This tendency foreshadowed the theories of **Kant** and **Hegel** which identified duty with freedom, the State with the moral ideal, and laws with right and justice. This led to the glorification of the State as the supreme expression of morality.

Rousseau never clearly distinguished nor successfully reconciled these different strands. His work is therefore important as a source of ideas not as a system of arguments. (J.D.M.)

Plate 78, page 302.

Royce, Josiah (1855–1916), born in California, the most important spokesman for **idealism** in America during the period between the Civil War and the First World War. His writings were copious, and in a style which caused **Santayana** to describe them as a "swollen stream"; but even Santayana conceded that "Some clear principles and ultimate possibilities turned up . . . now presenting one face and now another, like chips carried down a swollen

stream." We will confine ourselves to a description of two of these "chips".

The first may be called the Principle of Universalizability. Royce constantly required of any philosophy that it be self-applicable; that is to say, that the view of the world it expresses be such as to account consistently for the very fact of its being expressed. By means of this weapon he sought to discredit virtually all philosophies alternative to his own version of **idealism** – most vigorously in the case of evolutionism and of **pragmatism**. One of his most persistent arguments in favour of his idealism is that it alone satisfies this principle of self-applicability.

The second "chip" is the Principle of Idealism itself. Royce insisted that everything – literally *every thing* – has both a "that" and a "what". In short, of anything whatsoever we may say either *that* it is or *what* it is. And Royce's thesis is that no philosophy is satisfactory which is forced to assert "that" in the face of inability to specify "what". Now, the "what" of anything is simply its "meaning"; and it therefore follows for Royce that the core of a sound philosophy is a clear account of meaning. There are, he maintains, two types of meaning: external and internal. The external meaning of anything consists in the relations in which it stands to all other things. Royce espoused what is known as the theory of the internality of relations; but this must not be confused with his claim that the relations in which a thing stands constitute *its* external meaning. His thesis comes more clearly in view when he claims that the external meaning of a thing depends entirely upon its internal meaning; that is, that the relation in which anything stands to other things depends upon what it itself is. What then is the internal meaning of anything? Royce's answer is that it consists in its peculiar "embodiment of purpose". Given all this apparatus, Royce then argues at length that "embodiment of purpose" is precisely the mark and criterion of "mentality", and that, therefore, the internal essence of anything is mental. This is his version of idealism.

Now, if everything (including the false and the fictitious) embodies purpose, what is the criterion of truth or reality? His answer is: the test of reality is whether any given purpose fits in with the "ideal community" of the purposes of all of humanity – past, present and future. Thus Royce's "Absolute", his "ultimate Real", is the ideal community of all human purposes. Aware that absolutism in German hands had led to political anti-individualism, Royce devoted much labour to a defence of American democratic individualism. The defence requires, he maintains, the proof of the reality of three things: Time, Evil and Freedom. The fact that Royce had an extremely acute logical mind (his contributions to mathematical logic were not insignificant) is especially evident in his handling of these "proofs".

It should be added that Royce's efforts to interpret the teachings of the Christian religion in terms of his philosophy, and in terms of his own understanding of the significance of natural science had considerable influence upon the theologians of the time.   (J.W.S.)

Russell, Bertrand Arthur William, third Earl Russell, (1872–), English philosopher. His father, Viscount Amberley, was the eldest son of Lord John Russell, the Liberal statesman, who became the first Earl Russell, and his mother was a daughter of the second Lord Stanley of Alderley. He was their second son and third child. His god-father was John Stuart **Mill**. Both his parents died before he was four years old and he was brought up by his grandmother, Lady Russell. After being privately educated, he won a mathematical scholarship to Trinity College, Cambridge, in 1890. In 1893 he was placed Seventh Wrangler and he then turned from mathematics to philosophy, obtaining first class honours in the second part of the Moral Sciences Tripos in 1894. Two years later, he published a work on German Social Democracy, the first of his many books. He was a Fellow of Trinity College, Cambridge, from 1895 to 1901 and a Lecturer in Philosophy from 1910 to 1916. During this period he was mainly occupied with his work on mathematical logic, but he retained his interest in politics and in 1907 unsuccessfully fought a by-election at Wimbledon as candidate of the National Union of Women's Suffrage Societies. He was a militant pacifist in the first world war and was dismissed by Trinity College in 1916 after he had been prosecuted and fined for writing a leaflet about the case of a conscientious objector. In 1918 he was again prosecuted for writing an article in which he was held to have libelled the British Government and the American Army and he was sent to prison for six months. While in prison, he wrote his *Introduction to Mathematical Philosophy* and began work on the *Analysis of Mind*.

In the years following the war Russell paid visits to Russia and China. He was disillusioned by the results of the Russian revolution, of which he had at first approved, but very favourably impressed by the old civilization of China. Though reinstated by Trinity in 1919, he resigned before taking up his duties there. He stood unsuccessfully as a Labour Candidate for Chelsea in the General Elections of 1922 and 1923 and in 1924 went on the first of many lecture tours to the United States. In 1927, in collaboration with his second wife, he founded a progressive school at Beacon Hill near Petersfield and there put into practice his theories on education. In the following decade he engaged extensively in political and social journalism. He continued to uphold pacifism but renounced it on the outbreak of the Second World War, the greater part of which he spent in the United States. After holding professorships at the Universities of Chicago and California, he was in 1940 as the result of social and religious prejudice judicially pronounced unworthy to be a professor at the College of the City of New York. He was then employed to lecture at the Barnes Foundation in Philadelphia, from which he was ejected in 1943, in circumstances which led him to bring a successful legal action for wrongful dismissal. In 1944 he returned to England having been re-elected to a fellowship at Trinity. Since the war he has continued to write, lecture and broadcast on a variety of subjects, his numerous books including two volumes of short stories. For a time he was in favour of the atomic bomb as a deterrent to the Russians, but he has recently been a protagonist in the campaign for nuclear disarmament.

Russell succeeded his elder brother in the earldom in 1931. He has been four times married and has three children. He was elected a Fellow of the Royal Society in 1908, an Honorary Fellow of the British Academy in 1949 and in 1949 also was awarded the Order of Merit.

We have seen that Russell started his career as a mathematician and he has stated that he was induced to take an interest in philosophy by his desire to find some reason for believing in the truth of mathematics. Under the influence of the works of F. H. **Bradley** he became a convert to **Hegelian** Idealism, but was soon re-converted by G. E. **Moore** to an extreme form of **realism**. Among other things, he was impressed by the argument that the fundamental idealist doctrine, that what is known is conditioned by the knowing of it, denies to the properties of mathematics any objective validity. Further, it seemed to him clear that mathematical propositions are irreducibly relational, and this led him to reject both the idealist thesis that relational judgments are vicious abstractions and the view, ascribed to **Aristotle** and **Leibniz**, that all propositions are of the subject-predicate form. In his early book on Leibniz, Russell argued that it was Leibniz's acceptance of this view that provided the key to his metaphysics. On the other hand, while admiring John Stuart Mill, Russell was not satisfied with his theory that the propositions of pure mathematics are empirical generalizations. For this did not seem to him to afford a sufficient guarantee of their truth.

His own solution was to reduce mathematics to logic. This involved, first, the analysis of the fundamental terms of mathematics into purely logical concepts, and secondly the elaboration of a system of logic which was adequate to furnish the premises from which the propositions of mathematics could be deduced. The first part of the undertaking was carried out in the *Principles of Mathematics* and the second in *Principia Mathematica*. His definition of number, in which he had been anticipated by the German mathematician **Frege**, made use of the concept of a one-one relation; that is, a relation such that if x is so related to y, no other term is so related to y and x has the relation to no other term. Two classes are said to be similar if their members can be correlated by a one-one relation. Then the number of a class is defined as the class of all those classes that are similar to it, and a cardinal number is defined as anything which is the number of some class. At that time Russell believed in the existence of classes. Later, he came to think that they were logical fictions, and thereby put the status of numbers again in question. But this was a difficulty which he did not resolve.

Principia Mathematica occupies an architectonic position in the development of symbolic logic. The breach with Aristotelian logic consisted not so much in the use of a special notation as in the greater generality of Russell and **Whitehead**'s system, and above all in their attempt to make it rigorously formal. How far they succeeded in this, or in their programme of deriving mathematics from logic, is a technical question about which there is still dispute. Other systems of logic have since been developed which lay claim to a greater rigour, but to a large extent they are constructed on the basis of Russell and Whitehead's work.

Perhaps Russell's most original contribution to this field was his introduction of the theory of types. This arose out of his discovery of a contradiction which made **Frege** say, when the news was communicated to him, that the whole foundation of mathematics had been undermined. It can be fairly easily set out. Most classes appear not to be members of themselves: for example it is not true that the class of men is itself a man. But some classes do appear to be members of themselves. For instance, the class of all the things that can be counted would itself appear capable of being counted. Now consider the class of all classes which are not members of themselves. Is it or is it not a member of itself? If it is, it is not, and if it is not, it is. Similar contradictions can be found in other fields. A notorious example is the paradox of Epimenides the Cretan who said that all Cretans were liars. Another starts from the point that some words are predicable of themselves and others not. Thus the word "short" is short but the word "long" is not long. Let us call those that are so predicable "autological" and those that are not "heterological". Then is the word "heterological" predicable of itself? If it is, it is not, and if it is not, it is.

Russell's solution of the paradoxes was to arrange objects into a hierarchy of types, so that what can be true or false of objects of one type cannot significantly be said about those of another. In particular, if a given class is the extension of a given predicate, it is nonsensical to apply that predicate to that class. Thus it is not false but nonsensical to say that the class of men is human: the question whether the word "heterological" is itself autological or heterological is a meaningless question. Even when a predicate does appear to characterize objects of different types, it does not have the same meaning in each case. Thus a predicate like "being countable" becomes, as Russell puts it, systematically ambiguous.

The theory of types, of which only the outline has been given here, has a certain *ad hoc* air about it. Not all forms of self-reference are logically vicious: and we seem to have no adequate rules for picking out the cases in which it is to be prohibited. But the theory has had a strong historical influence. By calling attention to the fact that a sentence might be grammatically well-formed and yet succeed in saying nothing, it prepared the way for the logical positivists' rejection of metaphysics, their declaration that the statements typically made by metaphysicians were not even false but literally meaningless.

Russell has always tried to integrate his logic with his theory of knowledge, and he accordingly identified his statements of lowest type, the statements that formed the basis of his semantic hierarchy, with those that were epistemologically primitive. In his *Problems of Philosophy* he drew a distinction between what he called knowledge by description and knowledge by acquaintance and he took as his basic propositions, as those which supply the foundation for all our empirical knowledge, propositions which refer only to things with which one is directly acquainted. The meaning which he here gave to "acquaintance" was such that if one was acquainted with an object it followed that the object really existed and really had the properties that it was apprehended as having. The existence and properties of things that were known only by description he regarded on the other hand as being problematic.

At that time Russell held that the things with which one could be acquainted were one's own private sense-data, images, thoughts and feelings, both present and past since he allowed memory to be a form of direct knowledge, one's own self and **universals**. Subsequently he dropped one's self from the list, for he came to hold that selves did not exist as separate entities, that is as distinct from the experiences which were attributed to them, but he has continued to hold that we are acquainted both with our own sense-data and with universals. Contemporary criticisms of the notion of sense-data have not disturbed him but there is reason to think that he would have liked to dispense with universals. The recognition of such abstract entities runs counter to the "robust feeling for reality" which he has always claimed for his philosophizing. He does not, however, see how it is possible to dispense with them. He allows, it may be wrongly, that one can successfully take the nominalist step of reducing them all to the single relation of resemblance, that one can, for example, substitute for the quality "whiteness" the relation of resemblance in being white: but he does not think that much is to be gained by this as resemblance, in his view, is itself a universal.

When he wrote *The Problems of Philosophy* Russell believed that physical objects were known only by description. They were postulated as the causes of sense-data. But following his principle "Wherever possible substitute constructions out of known entities for inferences to unknown entities", a principle which he has called the supreme maxim in scientific philosophy, he abandoned this view in favour of the theory that physical objects are logical constructions out of actual and possible sense-data. This amounts to claiming that statements about physical objects can be faithfully translated into statements about sense-data. This theory was developed by Russell in *Our Knowledge of the External World* and in two of the essays reprinted in *Mysticism and Logic*. Roughly speaking, his view was that at any given moment each observer perceives a private three-dimensional world with its own private space, or spaces, since he distinguishes the space of sight from the space of touch. He calls such private worlds "perspectives". In addition to these perceived perspectives, there exists also an infinite number of unperceived perspectives, namely all those that would be perceived if an observer were in the appropriate state and position. These contain not sense-data but what Russell called "sensibilia", entities which are generically similar to sense-data but are not actually sensed. He does not fully work out this theory, which encounters obvious difficulties even if one is willing to assume that sensibilia and unperceived perspectives literally exist.

In more recent years, Russell has reverted to a causal theory of perception. He has come to think that it alone can do justice to the evidence which is furnished by science. A curious feature of his causal theory is that he locates sense-data in the percipient's brain. He does not mean by this that when we think that we are perceiving the world around us; we are, in any literal sense, really observing only our own brains. His argument is rather that an event's position in space-time is determined by its causal relations and that "the causal and temporal connections of percepts with events in afferent and efferent nerves gives percepts a position in the brain of the observer". It might be thought that if percepts are to be admitted as entities one would do better to maintain that they are not the sort of things that can be located in physical space at all.

Russell's reductionism was carried to its furthest point in the *Analysis of Mind*, where he adopts a theory which is akin to the neutral monism of William **James**. He there holds that both mind and matter are logical constructions out of elements, primarily sense-data, which are themselves neither mental nor physical. They are distinguished by the fact that certain elements, such as images and feelings, enter only into the constitution of minds, and by the operation of different causal laws. Thus the same sense-data when correlated according to the laws of physics constitute physical objects and when correlated according to the laws of psychology help to constitute minds. In their mental aspect they engage, among other things, in what Russell called *mnemic causation*, a kind of action at a distance by which experiences produce subsequent memory images. Though Russell has given up the reductionist view of the nature of physical objects, he has retained it with respect to minds, in the sense that he rejects the notion of consciousness or the self as a substantial entity. On the other hand, while he has dallied with behaviourism, he has never denied the existence of states of consciousness which are not definable in physical terms.

Russell's predilection for William of Ockham's razor is not merely due to a love of intellectual economy for its own sake, though this may have played its part. His main reason for using it has been epistemological; his belief that the more entities you allow yourself to postulate, the greater is the risk of your being wrong. There are also semantic considerations which are displayed in his famous theory of definite descriptions, a theory which he himself regards as one of his most important contributions to philosophy. This theory was sketched by him in a paper on Denoting, which was written in 1906 and republished in *Logic and Knowledge*, more rigorously formulated in the first volume of *Principia Mathematica*, and further ex-

plained in the *Introduction to Mathematical Philosophy*. The philosophical problem which gave rise to it was that of showing how it was possible to speak meaningfully of non-existent objects, such as the present King of France, or even of objects which could not possibly exist such as the round square, as in the statement "The round square is a contradiction". His solution was to show that expressions of the form "the so and so", at least in this usage, never function as names. It does not follow from the fact that they are meaningful that there is any object which they mean. His method of showing this was to give a rule for translating the sentence in which the definite descriptive phrase occurs, in such a way that the phrase no longer looks as if it were a name. Thus, to take his own best known example, the statement "The author of Waverley was Scott" becomes in his translation a conjunction of the three statements "At least one person wrote Waverley"; "At most one person wrote Waverley"; and "It is not the case that anyone both wrote Waverley and was not identical with Scott". To put it symbolically, as Russell would prefer, he holds that to say that the thing which has φ has ψ, when φ is the property concealed in the definite description and ψ the property attributed to what it describes, is to say that there is an x, such that x has φ, and, for all y, if y has φ y is identical with x, and x has ψ. Thus, any description of the subject goes into the predicate, and what Russell calls a "bare particular" is left to be the value of the variable x.

This theory, which has been called "a paradigm of philosophy" has recently come in for criticism on the ground that it makes definite descriptive statements false when they fail in their reference, whereas it would be more in accordance with ordinary usage to say in that case that they were neither true or false. A more serious objection, which does not directly impugn the truth of the theory but does diminish its importance, is that Russell throughout assumes a defective view of meaning, in that he identifies the meaning of substantives with their denotation. The main reason why definite descriptions, and even ordinary proper names, like "Homer" and "Napoleon", are turned by him into predicates is that they do not guarantee the success of their reference. It is always logically possible that they should denote nothing.

But if the statements in which they occur are to be meaningful Russell thinks that their analysis must terminate in statements containing substantival words whose denotation is guaranteed. The ultimate values of his existential variables are denoted by what he calls logically proper names.

This is the basis of the doctrine of Logical Atomism which Russell, under the influence of his pupil **Wittgenstein**, put forward in the years following the first World War. The view is that, in the last analysis, the world consists of atomic facts and these facts are characterized by their directly, as it were photographically, corresponding to elementary propositions. The elementary propositions are those which are expressed by conjoining a lowest level predicate with one or more logically proper names. And once more tying up his logic with his theory of knowledge, Russell tends to assume that these logically proper names stand for sense-data: for it is plausible to argue that only demonstrative expressions which stand for sense-data are bound to succeed in their reference. It may be thought, however, that the whole enterprise is misconceived, since there seems no good reason to suppose that for a referential statement to be meaningful it is necessary that its reference should be logically guaranteed.

In the *Inquiry into Meaning and Truth*, Russell gave this theory a new aspect by identifying particulars with qualities. His motive was to eliminate what he regarded as the metaphysical notion of substance. He therefore followed **Berkeley** in treating the things of common-sense as collections of qualities, united by what he called the relation of compresence. This view is retained in Russell's last important philosophical work, *Human Knowledge: Its Scope and Limits*, which is otherwise of interest chiefly for his attempt to deal with the problem of induction. He takes the view that inductive reasoning stands in need of justification and he elaborates a set of principles which he thinks would be sufficient for the purpose. He does not, however claim that any of these principles can be known to be true.

From the purely philosophical point of view, Russell's work in the field of ethics and of social and political philosophy is not of comparable interest with his work on logic and the theory of knowledge. He has been persuaded that ethical statements have no objective validity, a conclusion which he confesses to disliking on emotional grounds; and he is therefore inclined to hold that the main questions in ethics are psychological and social; the question of what people desire and how they may attain it. In the sphere of education and of politics he is above all an advocate of liberty. Though he is more keenly aware of the irrational features in human conduct, his political position is in many ways strongly reminiscent of that of John Stuart Mill.

It has been shown that Russell has often changed his philosophical views, but his approach to philosophy has been highly consistent. His aim has always been to try to find reasons for accepted beliefs, whether in the field of mathematics, natural science, or common sense. He has been a consistent sceptic, not in the sense that he denies our claims to knowledge, but that he questions them. He has adhered also to a single method: the method of starting with propositions which are the least susceptible to doubt, and trying to reconstruct the edifice of knowledge on this basis, with as few assumptions as possible. The result of this is that his justifications have usually taken the form of analyses: even so he has not been interested in analysis for its own sake, but only as a method of proof. In this way, as in the power and elegance of his literary style, he remains in the high tradition of British Empiricism, the tradition of Hobbes, Locke, Berkeley, Hume and Mill. He is its outstanding representative in the twentieth century.   (A.J.A.)

Plate 79, page 303.

Ryle, Gilbert (1900–), born in Brighton, England, now Waynflete Professor of Metaphysical Philosophy in the University of Oxford; he is probably the most widely influential British philosopher of his generation.

He was at one time much influenced by the earlier writings of **Husserl**, but already in the early nineteen-thirties he was adumbrating one of the characteristic doctrines of modern linguistic analysis when he suggested that the task of philosophy was "the detection of the sources in linguistic idioms of recurrent misconceptions and absurd theories" (Proceedings of the Aristotelian Society 1931–2). In his Tarner Lectures *Dilemmas* he developed this position, suggesting that philosophical problems arose from apparent conflicts between general truths none of which we could sincerely abandon; the task of philosophy was therefore to resolve these apparent conflicts by an elucidation of the concepts which were used in stating these truths; philosophy was then essentially the dissolution of dilemmas arising from our imperfect understanding of our own conceptual apparatus. This position is akin to, but not identical with, that of the later **Wittgenstein**.

Ryle's best known work *The Concept of Mind* exemplifies this theory of the nature of philosophy. Ryle considers that the problems of the nature of mind and of the relation of the mind to the body arise from a misunderstanding of the concept of mind and the concepts of such mental "states" and "activities" as those of willing, thinking, imagining. We are inclined to construe the concept of mind as of an extra object situated in the body and controlling it by a set of unwitnessable activities; this is what he calls the dogma of the ghost (the mind) in the machine (the body.) Ryle regards this picture as totally misleading and in a series of brilliant studies he attempts to disabuse us of it by showing that mental concepts refer not to ghostly acts but to dispositions to behave in certain ways in appropriate circumstances, to the style of actual witnessable performances and similar unproblematic matters. He protests vigorously that he is not putting forward a doctrine of behaviourism, not denying in any way the reality of the mental life, but only attempting to clarify the nature of the mental. But the work has often been attacked as behaviouristic and it has been suggested that Ryle at this stage had not wholly freed himself of the "reductive" tendencies of the analytic methods of **Russell**. In any case few would dispute that the book is one of the most important to have appeared in the last twenty or thirty years.

In his treatment of mind and elsewhere Ryle has made much use of the notion of a "category mistake"; we make a category mistake when we misunderstand what kind of concept we are using or considering, as if we were to think that the University of Oxford were something that we could visit in addition to the Colleges. To think of the mind as a hidden substance is such a category mistake.

Apart from his studies in the nature of philo-sophy and the concept of mind Ryle's main work has been on the nature of meaning and the philosophy of logic; he has also contributed to Platonic scholarship.   (J.O.U.)

Plate 80, page 304.

S

Santayana, George, (1863–1952), born in Spain. He went to the USA in 1872 and was educated in Boston and at Harvard. Though a contributor to the co-operative volume, *Essays in Critical Realism*, Santayana's philosophy resists assimilation to a single school.

He was a thoroughgoing **sceptic**, and yet the basis of his philosophy is an extreme version of a Platonic doctrine of Essence. As a sceptic, he insists that the existence of anything can never be proved, and that all beliefs as to existence are based upon irrational "animal faith". As a Platonic realist, however, he insists that we have certain, indubitable, and positive knowledge of a realm of real **universals** which he calls "essences." The proposed bridge between these two sides of his thought is the claim that essences (which both are and are not real) do not *exist*.

The above paragraph has used the word "real" in **Plato**'s sense; and it must be added that Santayana does not generally so use it. "To be real" means for him to exist in space and in time; and he insists that all reality in this sense is material. In his metaphysical scheme the "Realm of Matter" is the basic real. Essences, according to this way of talking, are ideal only. Thus, in an unorthodox way, Santayana seeks to combine **realism** and **idealism**.

Another strange union in his philosophy is that of hard-boiled naturalism with a deeply sensitive aesthetic romanticism. Though he is generally classified as an American philosopher, his temperament was Spanish and Mediterranean and he never became an American citizen. As an intellect he sought to be "hard"; but emotionally he was extremely "soft". His fundamental thesis in aesthetics, that beauty is feeling objectified, enabled him to express both tendencies. He could combine the harshest naturalistic description of what exists in space and time (the stone of sculpture, the canvas of painting, the sound waves of music) with the most sensitive appreciation of the ideal content of the work of art.

His metaphysical distinction between the "reality" of matter and the "ideality" of essence assists him in this. He was himself a poet of considerable talent; and the literary quality of his prose is generally very high.

In religion Santayana repeatedly proclaimed his naturalism and his materialism, insisting that the essence of religion is myth and poetry. Emotionally, however, he was unquestionably Roman Catholic. He never concealed his utter disdain for Protestantism, and in his later works (for example, in *The Idea of Christ in the Gospels*) he shows that his Catholicism is more than skin deep. The last years of his life he spent in a Catholic retreat in Rome.

Plate 81, page 369. (J.W.S.)

Sartre, Jean Paul (1905–), French novelist, playwright and philosopher, born in Paris on 21st June, 1905; founder of the periodical *Les Temps Modernes.*

Sartre's principal philosophical work, *L'Être et le Néant*, was published in 1943. Although it is a very long book, its scope was definitely limited by the author. A second major work, *L'Homme*, containing in effect its author's ethics, has been announced as forthcoming since 1955, but has not yet appeared. Similarly the fourth and concluding volume of his most elaborately conceived novel, *Les Chemins de la Liberté*, is only represented by substantial fragments which have appeared in *Les Temps Modernes*. His published works also include studies of the imagination, and of the nature of literature, as well as plays, and stories.

As a philosopher, Sartre is notoriously labelled "existentialist"; and commentators tend to find his intellectual ancestry in **Hegel** and **Kierkegaard**. It is arguable, however, that he is nearer in spirit to **Fichte** than to either of the others, treating the idea of human freedom in ways sometimes strikingly akin to those in which Fichte radicalized and released from every sort of limitation **Kant**'s insistence on the unique dignity and status of free action. For Sartre, who is an atheist, men give to the world what semblance of meaning and order it may be judged to possess. In places he seems fired by an image of man as Prometheus in a universe where there is no Zeus to chain him to the rock, except at the half-admitted level of his own fantasies. From the confusing and distracting effect of such illusions it is the task of the philosopher, (here working in a manner very closely akin to that of the true novelist), to help men by reflection set themselves free. Here a certain kinship in ethos with psycho-analytic practice can be discerned. But there are other places where Sartre seems to regard this freedom as something almost terrifying in the burden it lays on men, of decision that can find no vindication from without.

In the intellectual patterns Sartre weaves with the notion of freedom, he can hardly be said to follow a consistent design. Sometimes "freedom" is the name of a state of stability and transparency of life which always eludes, but ever beckons, the moral agent; at other times it is, in fact, the essential ingredient of characteristically human existence, and is virtually identifiable with the "freedom of open possibilities", whose reality and importance has been recently defended by such British metaphysically-minded moralists as A. E. **Taylor**, and C. A. Campbell. In other places it is near the name of a quality of life manifested necessarily in any society in which great literature is written and enjoyed. Elsewhere (as implied above) the notion advertises the metaphysical openness of the world, which has no creator, and therefore can only find what design it may assume, from human effort; in the language of traditional metaphysics, men are primary, not secondary causes.

If Sartre's work belongs in one sense to the tradition of those who have found in the confused and confusing, but also intoxicating, notion of "freedom", the point of departure for speculative construction, it is marked out by the persuasive subtlety of the author's introspective analyses of human situations. If he never discusses in the manner of a critical philosopher "our knowledge of other minds", his work manifests an extraordinary sensitivity to the labyrinthine weavings of that kind of human awareness. His bias is always solipsistic; he finds in the forms of human communion, highly esteemed by **Marcel**, sources of menace to personal integrity, opportunities for self-deception and masquerade. A vein of pessimism pervades his discussions of human relations, both in novels and in treatises. But the minuteness of his analyses at their best, will illustrate the manner in which on occasion, critical philosophical problems, like that of "our knowledge of other minds", are, in fact, re-

Scepticism

solved by exhaustive and sustained description and re-description of the field of the problem concerned.

Again where the subject-matter of the "philosophy of mind" is concerned, his studies of imagination and literature help the contemporary British reader to appreciate the real contribution made to its problems, by independently minded writers in the idealist tradition, like R. G. **Collingwood**; the range of examples Sartre is able to adduce, enlarges the reader's sense of what that "mind" is about which he is philosophizing. For those for whom the work of "philosophers of mind" is primarily critical, Sartre provides a valuable corrective against a tendency to diminish the stature of the person whose intellectual dispositions and operations, whose choices, reflections and regrets they are trying to clarify, to that of a dwarf of straw. The often undisciplined efforts of men to come to terms with their existence, which his work expresses and to which it so bears witness, is an element in the human scene that cannot simply be disregarded by the analytic philosopher. The publication, therefore, of his work, *L'Homme*, must be eagerly awaited.

As a novelist Sartre altogether lacks the achieved distinction of, for example, Albert Camus' *La Peste* (although nothing that he has written has plumbed the depths of boredom reached by Simone de Beauvoir in her *Les Mandarins*, 1954!). *Les Chemins de la Liberté* bears witness to his deep involvement in political matters, particularly the Communist question as it has been raised for French intellectuals. Existentialist styles of thought have been sharply criticised by Marxist thinkers; yet Sartre himself, at the outset of the present decade, espoused the stand-point of the Party, remaining loyal until the 20th Party Congress, and the Hungarian tragedy of 1956. To this period belongs his breach with Camus, and the latter's interesting study of revolt as a human phenomenon, (*L'Homme Revolté*, 1951). His attitude was also sharply criticized by a former associate and an accomplished student of Marxism, M. Maurice Merleau Ponty, who followed his excellent anatomization of Stalinist ethics, *Humanisme et Terreur*, 1948, with an essay on the dialectic, *Les Aventures de la Dialectique*, 1955, which although aimed at Sartre explicitly, had more than ephemeral value as a contribution to the

understanding of the sense and role of dialectic in Marxist theory and practice.

For an understanding of Sartre's thought, the ambivalence of his attitude to the Communist Party is significant. In endorsing its causes, he thought to free himself from the self-deception, the *mauvaise foi*, he believed endemic in traditional moral judgments. Moreover, although Marxist-Leninism is deterministic, Lenin, who had shown himself in controversy, for example over the tenability of a positivistic philosophy of science, an unbending champion of Marxist orthodoxy, had also on the plane of revolutionary action in the second decade of the century, revealed something of the tremendous possibilities of free action, decisively and resolutely planned and executed. The image of *Prometheus Victor* joins its attractive force to that exercised by the other image of the suffering and estranged proletarian.

A proper evaluation of Sartre's speculations, with that curious fusion of the radically introspective with the overtly utilitarian, of emphasis on the inward life of the subject with a nearly philistine confidence in the world-transforming possibilities of human initiative, must wait the publation of his work on ethics.   (D.M.M.)

Plate 82, page 370.

Scepticism is a doctrine which holds the possibilities of knowledge to be limited. In one form it contends that there are things which cannot, in principle, be known at all; in another that knowledge of some things can only be attained with difficulty and given certain precautions. In this second form it supports a methodological policy of reserve and circumspection in the formation of beliefs. Its opposite is dogmatism. Different species of scepticism are distinguished in two principal ways: by reference either to the methods of inquiry whose reliability is questioned or to the kind of objects whose knowability is doubted. Doubt of methods may be general, on the ground that there is no infallible way of getting knowledge and that all methods have failed at some time or other. But more usually scepticism of methods is partial and depreciates the trustworthiness of one recognised source of knowledge in the interests of another. Reason and sense-experience have been set against one another and again jointly defended against the

338

pretensions of authority, revelation and intuition. On the other hand, defenders of faith like **Pascal**, have expressed a radical scepticism about the ability of reason to arrive at religious truth. Thus **Averroism**, which distinguishes the natural truth accessible to reason from the supernatural truth that is beyond its reach, is ambiguous. It may be a sincere belief that the unaided human intelligence cannot acquire religious knowledge, but it may also be ironical and imply that since reason is unable to acquire such knowledge it cannot be acquired at all.

It is more usual for particular and limited varieties of scepticism to be defined by means of the objects held to be unknowable. Sceptical arguments have been used to deny that we can get knowledge of any matters of empirical fact, of the external world of material objects, of the minds of others, of the past, of the future, of nature as a whole, of values and of any objects of religious or metaphysical speculation which lie beyond sense-experience. Scepticism about objects has three levels or degrees. The sceptic may admit that the objects in question exist but deny that we can ever know any more than this about them. **Kant**'s position on things-in-themselves is sceptical in this sense as is that of the inductive sceptic about laws of nature. Secondly, he may assert that the objects in question do not in fact exist: the standpoint of the ordinary religious sceptic about God, of the ethical sceptic about an order of values and of many philosophers about a substantive and immortal soul. Finally, he may assert that the objects in question could not possibly exist and therefore that knowledge of the sort he is doubting is logically ruled out. **Berkeley**'s attitude to material substance and **Hume**'s to real or intrinsic connections between events are instances of this type.

General or total scepticism has always been rare, most sceptics being the partisans of one method or one type of object. There are good reasons for taking general scepticism to be a kind of dialectical extravagance. To start with there is an obvious air of paradox about it. It seems self-refuting to say that nothing at all can be known, for to assert it is to claim at least one piece of knowledge, the truth of the sceptical principle itself. This was clear to Pyrrho, the first sceptical philosopher who concluded that the principle could only be held ten-

tatively, a rather enfeebling manoeuvre. According to **Russell**'s theory of types general scepticism, since it refers to itself, is not capable of significant formulation. In general, it can be argued, that if one is to have any reasonable ground for scepticism there must be something of which one is not sceptical. The usual reason for sceptical doubt is the experience or possibility of failure in claims to knowledge. Failure reveals itself through inconsistency and to recognise this we must be aware that contradictory statements have been made and that the law of contradiction is true. Furthermore past experience of failure in a given type of thinking is only relevant to one's future confidence in it if the rationality of inductive argument is assumed. A man could conceivably exhibit complete scepticism by refusing to claim any knowledge at all. What he could not do is offer a rational defence for his procedure.

Scepticism as a philosophy began with Pyrrho (c. 300 B.C.) in the same way as it has from time to time recurred, as the expression of discontent with the intellectual chaos produced by the conflict of dogmatic systems. For Pyrrho philosophy was a practical art whose aim was detachment and peace of mind (*ataraxia*). This goal could not be attained unless the inevitably frustrating search for truth were abandoned. Most of the conceivable arguments for scepticism are to be found in the thought of the Greek sceptics as reported by Sextus Empiricus. Aenesidemus put forward ten "tropes" which set out in detail the reasons for doubting the reliability of perception. Agrippa's five "tropes" are more compact and more far-reaching. As well as the relative or subjective nature of perception, he lists the infinite regress of proof propounded by Carneades, the conflict of opinions between men, the inevitably hypothetical character of all ultimate premises and the logical circularity of the syllogism, later emphasised by J. S. **Mill**. Some sceptics, Arcesilaus for example, concluded that since certainty was not to be had men must make do with probability and Carneades suggested that coherence of beliefs was a measure of reliability, that the more systematic one's body of beliefs the more reason there was for confidence in it. Since the period of the Greek **Sceptics** (of the fourth to second centuries B.C.) scepticism has reappeared from time to time in the history of thought. **Abelard**'s *Sic et Non*,

(Yes and No) a collection of contradictory opinions by the Fathers on points of doctrine, introduced a sceptical technique that was used by **Kant** in setting out the antinomies with which he sought to prove the impossibility of constructive metaphysics. The anti-Aristotelian and anti-Scholastic logicians of the Renaissance prepared the way for the more thorough-going sceptics of the sixteenth century whose most distinguished representative was Montaigne. **Hume** is the most penetrating and comprehensive of modern sceptics. He argued that our belief in bodies, minds and causes rested not on reason or the senses but on the workings of the imagination which was naturally constituted so as to make a coherent structure out of the disorderly flux of sense-impressions that was all we really knew. Hume's intentions are ambiguous and insecure enough for it to have been plausibly argued that he was not really a sceptic at all but rather a defender of "natural belief" against irrelevantly rigorous criteria of knowledge.

This interpretation is in sympathy with a doctrine deriving from G. E. **Moore**, and ultimately from **Reid**, which argues that common-sense beliefs are more deserving of our confidence than the arguments of sceptical philosophers and that philosophical scepticism is insincere, or, at best, "methodological", a technique for bringing to light principles and criteria of knowledge ordinarily taken for granted. To the followers of **Wittgenstein** philosophical scepticism is a symptom of conceptual confusion and disorder, an indication that language is being misunderstood and put to an improper use. It is argued that we can only learn what "knowledge" and "certainty" mean by hearing them used in connection with material objects, past events, other people's feelings and so on, and that it is senseless to inquire whether these paradigm cases are genuine instances of knowledge and certainty.

Wisdom and **Ayer** have suggested that problems in the theory of knowledge have a characteristic pattern and commonly arise in a sceptical form. In each case there is an apparent conflict between (1) our evidence, what is given or known directly (sense-impressions, present events, other people's words and deeds, particular occurrences), (2) what we claim to know (material things, past events, other people's feelings, laws of nature) and (3) the

fact that what we claim to know goes logically beyond the evidence for it. Sceptical theories say that we must abandon the claims to knowledge (2). But there are less catastrophic ways out of the difficulty. Causal and analogical theories resolve the inconsistency by appealing to principles that validate inference from the evidence to logically distinct conclusions. Reductive theories like **phenomenalism** deny (3); intuitionist theories like naïve **realism** deny that we are confined to the evidence specified in (1). To many philosophers scepticism is of no serious importance as a philosophical theory. Its point is to make us aware of what is involved in our claims to knowledge and perhaps, by doing so, to render them more secure.   (A.Q.)

Sceptics, name given to certain groups of philosophers in the Hellenistic-Roman period who, doubting the adequacy of senses and reason to furnish knowledge of the nature of things, advocated the withholding of assent and suspension of judgment. There are three phases: (1) Pyrrhonism (late fourth and third century B.C.), inaugurated by Pyrrho, expounded by his pupil Timon; (2) the Middle and New Academy (third to first century B.C.), Arcesilaus, Carneades, Clitomachus, Philo of Larissa; (3) from the first century B.C. the new Pyrrhonism of Aenesidemus and Agrippa.

The common ground of this movement was an epistemological attack on all philosophies which were dogmatic, that is, claimed to have discovered truth, There seems no way, said the Sceptics, of penetrating beyond the awareness of phenomena or "appearances" to a knowledge of external objects. Sense perception can be shown to give differing and contradictory reports and there is no criterion in sensation itself to distinguish true from false impressions. Nor can this be supplied by reason or judgment, for there is no criterion of correct judgment, and an attempt to find one can merely lead to an infinite regress. Thus there seems to be no criterion of knowledge; phenomena give no certain evidence of anything beyond themselves; we must withhold our assent from their truth and falsity and live in a state of suspended judgment. Naturally difficulties and disagreements arose in the department of **ethics**.

Yet to Pyrrho of Elis (*c.* 360–*c.* 270 B.C.) the ethical end of imperturbability was the mainspring of his philosophy. This was a typical goal of his troubled age; the novelty of Pyrrho lay in the method by which he sought to attain it. With no means of arriving at knowledge, no single thing could be said to be in itself any more this than that; no argument judged more certain than its opposite; the external stimulus of belief, desire, emotion thus severed, produced indifference, on which followed tranquillity. But now a man is left with no better guide for action than custom and convention.

Pyrrhonism faded out before the dialectical scepticism of the Middle and New academy, a logical attack directed principally against the **Stoic** theory of knowledge, which held that special sense-perceptions caused by real objects, corresponding exactly to them and of such a type that they could not have been caused otherwise, irresistibly demanded the assent of the wise man. Arcesilaus of Pitane (315–241/0 B.C.) argued that this must depend on judgment, of which there is no criterion; that there is no distinguishable mark between true and false perceptions; that the latter may be as irresistible as the former. He went on to deny that anything was apprehensible, and thus also the possibility of knowledge. He seems to have been less interested in ethics, but maintained that certainty was unnecessary for action, an adequate criterion being a reasonable defence for one's action. In teaching he adopted the basic sceptic practice of arguing impartially on both sides of any question. While his scepticism may have found roots in **Socrates** as well as Pyrrho, it is not easy to see how his teaching of Plato was integrated with his views. Carneades of Cyrene (214/213–129/8 B.C.), the most formidable of the Sceptics, developed and systematized the whole attack against dogmatism. With a wealth of brilliant argument against the possibility that true and false sense-impressions are distinguishable in themselves, and against the capacity of any rational process, which being based on sensation loses any certitude with it, to do more than test formal validity, he swept the irresistible perception of the Stoa from the field. With a criticism that the attribution of human qualities to God involved contradiction, he severely damaged their anthropocentric theology; insisting on the necessity of freedom of will for moral action, and distinguishing between causality and succession, he attacked the theories of divination, providence and fatalism. In a systematic review of all ethical ends be brought the Stoic moral goal into logical difficulties, and he himself, on a famous embassy to Rome in 166/5, argued the relativity of moral terms. In practical life he proposed a theory of probability as a guide for action; there were three grades of probability: the probable: the probable and undisputed; the probable, undisputed and tested; the latter being the highest state of belief that is reached when a whole system of connected ideas is formed agreeing logically with each other. A man thinks he sees a snake in a dark room; after investigation he believes it to be a coiled rope, from the consistency of the evidence for that view. Carneades left no writings, but was fully reported by his voluminous successor, Clitomachus of Carthage. Philo of Larissa was still maintaining scepticism in the first century B.C. but his successor, Antiochus of Ascalon, turned the Academy to an eclecticism in which Stoic views were incorporated.

It was outside the Academy that the sceptical movement flowed strongly for the next two or three centuries. The new sect professed to look beyond the Academy to the more complete scepticism of Pyrrhonism. Academic sceptics had no right to deny dogmatically the possibility of knowledge; assent should be witheld even from this; the word sceptic in Greek implied a persistence in inquiry. On the other hand there seemed no basis even for opinion; a man could but take things as he found them and live by custom, convention, tradition. But they accepted gladly the Academic tradition of dialectical argument, and combining with this the **empiricism** of the Empiric Medical School, drew up a complete systematisation of sceptic argument classified under formulae, each abundantly illustrated. Aenesidemus of Cnossus, probably an earlier contemporary of Cicero, dealt with the relative nature of sense-perception in his Ten Tropes (or Modes) of Withholding Assent. No perception is "pure", but so far relative to the percipient, object and concomitant external and internal circumstances, as to render the object itself inapprehensible. Later Agrippa in his Five Modes of Attack used relativity like Aenesidemus, and found four types of fallacies in their arguments: discrepancy of theories, infinite regress, hypothetical assumption, circular reasoning. We finally hear

341

of two ultimate Modes: nothing is apprehended intuitively, because of the disagreement of philosophers of which there is no criterion; nor can anything be apprehended through something else, or one is involved in circular reasoning or infinite regress. The attack on causation, fundamental to any dogmatic philosophy, is likewise classified by Aenesidemus in Eight Modes, directed against the inadmissibility of a dogmatic jump to the non-apparent, unconfirmed by any evidence from appearances. There is no certain connection between reality and phenomena; a reason is arbitrarily chosen to suit the theory of the moment. There is also an interesting argument on the relativity of cause and effect: if cause is productive of effect it must exist before it (which will lead to an infinite regress); but since cause is relative to effect it cannot be prior in existence (and their relativity makes any argument concerning them circular). The whole edifice of scepticism may be explored in the works of Sextus Empiricus (late second century A.D.) all the more valuable for their lack of originality.

The gadfly of Scepticism was clearly of immense importance in an age dominated by the dogmatic philosophies of Stoicism and Epicureanism; indeed a persistent movement of doubt and inquiry which insists on keeping open for examination any assertion seems fundamental for all philosophy. In particular the examination of sense-perception, causality and probability is of great interest for much recent philosophy. (I.G.K.)

Schiller, Ferdinand Canning Scott (1864–1937), British philosopher, Fellow of Corpus Christi College, Oxford, and, in later life, Professor of Philosophy in the University of Southern California. He was a personal friend of William **James**, with whose pragmatic philosophy he was in close sympathy, though he claimed to have arrived at the basic principles of **pragmatism** before he had heard of the name or read other pragmatist writings. Unlike James he was a very polemical writer; he was convinced that the fashions in philosophy prevalent at his time in Oxford were obscurantist and quite without worth. As a result a great part of his writings are devoted to attacks, particularly on F. H. **Bradley** and those whom he called the "formal logicians", often couched in an *ad hominem*

form which at a later date is somewhat tedious. But he had a powerful and original mind and his now little-read works contain much that is worth reading.

While subscribing to pragmatism in the form given to it by James, Schiller preferred to call his position humanism, or later, voluntarism. His basic thesis was that all human activities are moulded by and are only intelligible by reference to human purposes. This, he held, was true of thinking as well as action; the conceptual frameworks we employ, the modes of reasoning that we adopt and the beliefs we hold can have their only justification in their utility for human aims. It is mere consistency to apply this doctrine to truth; formally to call a statement true is to evaluate it favourably, as to call an action good is to evaluate it favourably; but the criterion for this evaluation is utility in the cognitive sphere.

Much of Schiller's effort was devoted to the application of his "humanist" thesis to this logic. In his *Formal Logic* (1912) and his *Logic for Use – An Introduction to the Voluntarist Theory of Knowledge* (1929) Schiller maintained that the (then) prevalent view of reasoning as exhibited in logic books was wholly mistaken; his principle charges were that formal logic operated with illegitimate abstractions in speaking of propositions since meaning and truth were dependent on the time, place and circumstances of communication, and secondly that validity as a criterion of success in reasoning was useless since no concrete argument could be formally valid and unquestionably good arguments in all fields made no attempt even to approximate to such an ideal. In place of formal logic he offered an account of reasoning which in its stress of verification, hypothesis and approximation anticipated many features of later accounts of scientific thought.

Schiller's own summary account of his views can be found in his article, *Why Humanism?* in *Contemporary British Philosophy*, Volume I (1924). (J.O.U.)

Schlick, Friedrich Albert Moritz (1882–1936), educated in Berlin, originally as a physicist. After teaching at Rostock and Kiel he was called (1922) to Mach's chair of the Philosophy of the Inductive Sciences in Vienna, where he later founded the **Vienna Circle** (see also **Logical Positivism**). He was a visiting Professor in the United States, in

1929 and 1932. In 1936, Schlick was assassinated in Vienna by a demented student. The impending break-up of the Vienna Circle was hastened by his death.

Despite his scientific training, Schlick's early writings are largely on moral and aesthetic questions, and display a poetic sensibility not often conspicuous in his later work. He subsequently gained notice as an expositor of relativity-theory (1917), and as the author of a treatise on **epistemology** (*Allgemeine Erkenntnislehre* 1918; second edition. 1925), in which many of his more characteristic doctrines occur in preliminary form. Here, in opposition to **Kant**, it is argued, from an **empiricist** standpoint, that the propositions of **logic** and **mathematics** are not synthetic **a priori** but true by definition, **analytic**, and hence empty of content. Scientific theories, on the other hand, are a posteriori systems of concepts, whose truth depends on correspondence, inasmuch as the consequences drawn from them must be capable of verification by observed facts. Nor are these facts sensations merely, as they were for **Mach**; anything answering to a scientific concept may legitimately be taken as real. More typical than this temporary acceptance of realism are Schlick's views on the mind-body problem, which he regards as spurious, in that the supposed dualism involved is merely a duality in our ways of describing the phenomena.

Schlick's later opinions (*Gesammelte Aufsätze 1926–36*, 1938) reflect the influence of **Wittgenstein** and **Carnap**, and consist, in effect, of an extension of the last-mentioned theory to all the traditional problems of philosophy. Such problems arise "only from an inadequate description of the world by means of a faulty language", and the task of philosophy is not to solve them, but merely to clarify the question in dispute. It will then appear that the answer is either ascertainable, in principle, by scientific methods, or else is void from the start, since the question itself is so framed that there could be no evidence relevant to its decision. The metaphysical assertions of **idealism, materialism, realism**, etc. are all in this sense meaningless, that no possible combination of sense-experiences could serve either to verify their claims or even to prove them false.

In basing verification (and meaning) on immediate sense-experience, Schlick, like other empir-

icists, was seeking an incorrigible foundation for knowledge. But the attempt leads to many paradoxes, and even imperils the foundations of communication, since meaning defined in terms of private experience is plainly inaccessible to anyone else. Schlick's explanation, that the "structure" of experience is communicable, but its "content" beyond description, did not give general satisfaction, and the problem of formulating the "basic" or incorrigible propositions required by this theory was a source of much subsequent dissension in the Vienna Circle. (P.L.H.)

Scholasticism, *see* Medieval Philosophy.

Schopenhauer, Arthur (1788–1860), German metaphysician, best known for his main work, *The World as Will and Idea*, and for his acid essays. He was born in Danzig. His father was a businessman, his mother a writer. He spent some time in England in connection with his father's business and read English and French easily. After his father's death he devoted himself entirely to philosophy, being able to live comfortably on his inheritance. He could not get along with his mother and had some other unfortunate experiences with women, and his ridiculously vehement essay *On Women*, which has probably been read more widely than anything else he ever wrote, airs a deeply personal resentment.

His diatribe "On University Philosophy" also has a personal background. He applied to become a lecturer at the University of Berlin, was found acceptable by a committee on which **Hegel** sat among others, and then decided to offer his lectures at the same hours as Hegel. The claim, encountered in the literature, that Schopenhauer ran out of material before the term was up, is utterly implausible; but that he failed to win away students from Hegel, then at the height of his fame, is a fact; and so his university career ended in failure. After that, he outdid himself in vituperating Hegel, Schelling, and **Fichte**, calling them windbags and charlatans, although his own philosophy owed a great deal to Fichte's conception of the will, and he heard Fichte as a student.

The two philosophers he admired most were **Kant** and **Plato**, and he considered himself the rightful heir of Kant, while regarding Fichte, Schelling, and Hegel as usurpers. Like Fichte, he found Kant's doctrine of the unknowable thing-in-itself unacceptable, and thought that he had discovered what the ultimate reality is: will. This will has no purpose or aim and is not reasonable or rational; it is blind striving. At this point, Schopenhauer may have been influenced by the First Part of Goethe's *Faust*. He personally knew and greatly admired Goethe, and, like Hegel, sided with Goethe's *Farbenlehre* (Doctrine of Colours) against Newton.

The details of Schopenhauer's metaphysics and ethics have had little influence. His historical importance is conveniently summed up in terms of three points. First, he was the first major European philosopher to make a point of atheism. **Hobbes** and **Hume** went out of their way to dissociate themselves from atheism, while von Holbach is remembered, if indeed he is remembered, mainly because he was an atheist. Schopenhauer's fame was based on other grounds.

Secondly, he was the first major European philosopher who called attention to, and was profoundly influenced by, the Upanishads and Buddhism. He insisted on the universality of suffering and probably described it in greater detail than any philosopher before him. He is therefore frequently referred to as a pessimist. And he claimed that man can find salvation only by overcoming the blind cosmic will. Outright suicide will do not because it is an assertion of will. (Since Schopenhauer did not accept the Indian doctrine of the transmigration of souls, this point remains unclear). There are mainly three aids to salvation: philosophic knowledge, contemplation of works of art, and sympathy for others, based on the recognition that we are only phenomenally distinct from others while in reality we are one. This ethic of sympathy contrasts very sharply with the ethic by which Schopenhauer himself lived: few philosophers have been more lacking in sympathy for others. In addition to women and other philosophers Schopenhauer loathed Jews.

Finally, Schopenhauer's voluntarism inaugurated an increased emphasis on the will and on the irrational in modern philosophy. Although **Kierkegaard** and **Nietzsche**, Vaihinger and **James**, **Bergson** and Freud clearly did not agree with him, their ideas suggest that Schopenhauer marks an important point of departure in the history of thought. His conception of the intellect as an instrument of the will is especially noteworthy in this connection.

Initially, *The World as Will and Idea* attracted no attention at all, even after Schopenhauer added a second volume by way of elaborating his metaphysic. Of two essays on ethics which he submitted for two prize contests in Scandinavia, one won a prize, the other did not; so he published them together, specifying on the title page "crowned by . . ." and "*not* crowned by . . ." – confident that he would thus immortalize in infamy the academy that had passed him by. Late in life, he witnessed and relished his growing fame. It may be that the widespread disillusionment after the unsuccessful revolutions of 1848 helped to make his pessimism popular, as has often been claimed. Certainly, his clearly written essays, published as *Parerga und Paralipomena*, helped to find him an audience.

Among his declared and devoted admirers were Richard Wagner, whose *Tristan and Isolde* tries to realise in music Schopenhauer's blind will; the young Nietzsche, who later outgrew his earlier infatuation with Schopenhauer; and Thomas Mann. To these one might add uncounted nonphilosophers, especially young people, who have turned to Schopenhauer for inspiration and solace.

Plate 83, page 371. (W.K.)

Scotus, John Duns (*c.* 1266–1308), born in Scotland. Scotus joined the Franciscan order in 1281 and later studied and taught both at Oxford and at Paris. He died prematurely in 1308.

His main works are the two commentaries on the Sentences of Peter Lombard named after the place of their delivery *Opus Oxoniense* and *Reportata Parisiensia*. Understanding of the true character of his thought was for a long time hampered by the false attribution of the later *Theoremata* and *Grammatica Speculativa* to him.

Scotus combines acceptance of the typically Aristotelian theory of knowledge directed to the nature of physical objects and achieved by the abstractive power of the intellect with the more typically Franciscan view of the soul as a substance in its own right, hence with powers of intellection not confined to sensible reality but capable of apprehending the total range of being. The subtle mingling of these two divergent tendencies which earned him his title of *Doctor Subtilis* accounts for his characteristic metaphysical positions.

Scotus argues that the proper object of philosophical speculation is reality or being, without any of the determinations which restrict it to one mode (for example, infinite being or God) rather than to another (for example, sensible being). But the human mind is hampered in its attempt to achieve a metaphysic by having to draw its knowledge from the sensible. So metaphysics is an abstract science of essences bearing upon a univocal field of being which is differentiated in terms of formal distinctions. These fall short of actual differences but are not merely the product of the mind's activity. Actual distinctness or the physical existence with which we are acquainted is finally accounted for by a form of "thisness" or *hacceitas*.

There can be no doubt that Scotus himself was a profound and able thinker but later, in the hands of less able followers, his *Formalism* degenerated into endless verbosity which contributed greatly to the collapse of scholastic thinking.   (J.G.D.)

Plate 84, page 372.

Seneca, Lucius Annaeus (*c.* 5 B.C.–65 A.D.), of Corduba, Spain, a Roman **Stoic**. He switchbacked from a dangerous philosophical and rhetorical eminence under Caligula, to banishment under Claudius; soared as millionaire tutor and confidant of Nero, to sink into prudent retirement and death by enforced suicide. In the main a follower of **Chrysippus,** he was also influenced strongly by Panaetius and Posidonius, but his works have a Latin flavour both in thought and presentation; Cato was his hero, Roman rhetoric his medium. He most notably changed the doctrine of the Stoics by grafting the Roman concept of will on to their intellectualism, and altered its direction by applying their individualistic philosophy to the government of the Roman Empire. His shortcomings as philosopher and politician are due to inherent contradictory tendencies towards worldy ambitions on the one hand and to sincere Stoic idealism on the other; the resulting discrepancy of actions and professions may be mitigated by his honest belief that he was compelled politically to justify means by end, and that his philosophical teaching was the result of self-examination of his own moral struggles. But the weakness of his character formed

his Stoicism, rather than his philosophy his character; thus the question of the capacity of the Stoa as an educative force in politics remained unanswered.   (I.G.K.)

Plate 85, page 373.

Sense-data (singular: sense-datum) is a comparatively new word for an idea that is almost as old as philosophy, namely the immediate object of sense-perception. In the past philosophers have spoken of sensible species, ideas, impressions, representations, sensations and the given. Sense-datum has been preferred to these on the grounds of its comparative neutrality. As a technical term it presupposes as little as possible about the nature and the origins of perception's immediate objects. It is as hard to find a neutral definition for sense-datum as it is to find a neutral term for the idea it expresses. From the time of **Heraclitus**, **Protagoras** and **Democritus** many philosophers have been persuaded that independent, external, material things are not the direct or immediate objects of perception. In any perceptual situation we can always doubt that what we perceive is a real material thing. It might be a hallucination or we might be dreaming. But there is something we cannot doubt, for whatever, if anything, may be going on outside us, we may be sure that our senses are affected in a certain way and this indubitable residue is our current sense-datum. Though we may be in doubt as to how things are, we cannot be in doubt as to how things appear to us to be now. So to say how things appear to us now, with no implication that this is how they really are or how they would appear to anyone else, is to describe our current sense-data. Most of our ordinary perceptual beliefs involve a good deal of inference. In taking what I now see to be a chair, I ascribe to it a back, a texture and a weight, but none of these are at the moment present to my senses. The inferred elements of our perceptual beliefs are the dubitable ones. The sense-datum is what remains when they are suppressed.

It is clear that sense-data are private. My sense-data may resemble yours but this likeness can only be established by a complex and precarious inference and is always a contingent matter. The fact of hallucination shows that it is possible for a man to have a sense-datum to which nobody else's sense-data correspond at all. The privacy of sense-data follows from their being defined in terms of what appears to *me*. There is no very clear or uniform convention about the extent or complexity of sense-data. Are we to call all dreams, hallucinations, memories and images sense-data even when we are not in the least tempted to suppose that we are perceiving some real material thing? Is my current sense-datum the whole of what I am sensibly aware of at this instant or is it what I am aware of by means of any one sense, my current visual field for example; or is it any one discriminable part of a current sense-field? Philosophical usage tends to favour the last of these. A more substantial problem arises about the duration of sense-data. Can I be aware of the same sense-datum twice or do sense-data endure only for one specious present? Some philosophers have held that sense-data can have properties which they do not appear to have. Against them **Ayer** has argued that sense-data are by definition precisely and entirely what they appear to be.

There are two main arguments to prove that sense-data are necessarily distinct from material objects. First, the argument from illusion. My sense-datum, what I immediately perceive, may be just the same in a case where I am really perceiving a friend as it is in a case where I am undergoing the hallucination of seeing him. Since what I immediately perceive is precisely the same in both cases and cannot be a material object in one of them it cannot be a material object in either. Secondly, the causal or time-lag argument. The perception of very remote events, such as the explosion of stars, brings out dramatically something that is always temporally earlier, even if only minutely, than the event of perceiving it. But, it is argued, we can only perceive what is present, since to say that something is present is simply to say that it is contemporary with my current perception.

If sense-data are distinct from material objects, the fundamental and traditional problem of perception presents itself: what is the relation of sense-data to material objects, how can we have any knowledge about material objects if all we immediately perceive is sense-data? Some philosophers, **Hume** for instance, have been sceptical of the validity of any inference from sense-data to material things. More commonly it has been held either, with **Locke**, that we can reasonably infer material

objects as the causes of our sense-data, or, with **Berkeley** and **Phenomenalism**, that material objects are entirely composed of sense-data, actual or possible or both. In opposition to the sense-datum theory two main tendencies can be discerned in contemporary philosophy. One view, that of **Ryle**, is that there are no such things. Another, less radical, view is that though there are sense-data they are not the only things that we immediately perceive, they are the causes rather than the grounds of our perceptual beliefs and for the most part their existence and character is a matter of inference. (A.Q.)

Sensum, *see* sense-data.

Sidgwick Henry, (1828–1900), English philosopher, Knightbridge Professor of Moral Philosophy in the University of Cambridge from 1883 until his death. He was throughout his adult life a Cambridge man and he was a very typical Cambridge product. He wrote on economics as well as on philosophy and was a founder member of the Society for Psychical Research and its first President.

The work for which Sidgwick is remembered is *The Method of Ethics*, published in 1874 but modified and expanded in subsequent editions. He there adopted a hedonistic **utilitarian** position, but with a far clearer recognition of the many-sidedness of moral problems and a far more professional treatment of the problems arising from his viewpoint than is common. Having denied that moral terms can be defined in non-moral terms Sidgwick goes on to contend that morality is founded on one *a priori* moral intuition that "we ought to aim at pleasure", that pleasure is the supreme and only good. Any other basic moral knowledge is concerned with the way pleasure should be distributed; thus we know that similar cases ought to be treated similarly and that "the good of any one individual is of no more importance, from the point of view of the universe, than the like good of any other". From these basic positions Sidgwick deduces the principle of benevolence: "each one is morally bound to regard the good of any other individual as much as his own". Sidgwick acknowledges that in practice people are swayed morally by rules of conduct and not by general principles of universalistic hedonism; he himself is willing to accept these rules of conduct on the ground that they are a means to the utilitarian end. This position is however complicated by the fact that Sidgwick finds himself compelled to acknowledge as self-evident the principle that "it is irrational for me to sacrifice my happiness to any other end" the principle of rational ethical egoism. Sidgwick is well aware of the apparent incompatibility of this principle with the universalistic hedonism which is his other main contention; he regards this incompatibility as the basic problem of ethics, but simply finds himself unable honestly to deny either the principle of egoism or the principle of benevolence. His solution of the dilemma is to suggest that the universe is so arranged that egoism and universal benevolence never come into conflict and that we can follow the principle of benevolence with the assurance that we shall not thereby violate the rational principle of egoism. Thus Sidgwick, in his anxiety to do justice to all the facets of morality, attempts to harmonize a number of positions which are usually regarded as essentially opposed; he is utilitarian and **deontologist**, egoist and universalist. No one has been able to accept this position as Sidgwick stated, it but his acute and candid recognition of the merits of opposed views gives the book much of its worth. (J.O.U.)

Plate 86, page 374.

Siger of Brabant (1235–40 – 1281–84), French philosopher, with Boethius of Dacia and Bernier of Nivelles, a leader of the so-called Latin **Averroists**. These men were members of the Faculty of Arts at the University of Paris and claimed to be pure philosophers, of the school of Aristotle, and in no way theologians. They accepted the distinction of truths of reason and truths of faith which had been made by Averroes and proceeded to work out ruthlessly their philosophy, which was an Aristotelianism coloured by the interpretation of Averroes and **Avicenna**. Some of their doctrines, such as that of the eternity of the world, the unity of intellect in all human beings and determination of human affairs by astral influences, went straight against the Christian dogmas of creation, the individual soul and divine providence; these doctrines and others which they held were condemned in 1270 and again in 1277, but their authors maintained that these philosophical tenets did not conflict with their faith in the truth of revelation. Siger is alleged to have

been murdered by his own secretary who had gone mad. (J.O.U.)

Social Contract theories are theories which attempt to explain the duty of obedience to the laws and civil authority by reference to a contract or compact or promise to obey made for the sake of the benefits gained from the civil society thereby instituted. There are many different versions of the contract theory; a version, not accepted by **Plato**, is given in *Republic* Book II; famous modern versions are those of **Hobbes** in the *Leviathan*, **Locke** in the *Second Treatise of Civil Government* and **Rousseau** in the *Social Contract*. These versions differ from each other as regards both the parties to the contract and its terms; they also differ in the degree to which the historicity of the contract is affirmed, since some authors content themselves with a tacit or implied contract. The theory was destructively criticised by **Hume** in his Essay "Of the original contract" and by **Hegel** in his *Philosophy of Right* from a very different point of view and it must now be regarded as part of history, though it can still be met in popular discussion and writing. See also **Political philosophy**. (J.O.U.)

Socrates (469–399 B.C.), Greek philosopher of Athens. We know nothing for certain about Socrates except that some writers have given us descriptions of him, and that these writers are far from being minutely conscientious historians like Thucydides. He left no writings of his own, and probably never made any. All our information and misinformation about him comes from Aristophanes or Xenophon or **Plato**, whose lives overlapped his, or from **Aristotle**, who was probably born some thirteen years after the year in which, according to Plato, Socrates was tried and put to death for "corrupting the young men and not believing in the gods of the city".

(1) *The Evidence of Aristophanes.* The only statement common to all four of these writers is that there was a philosopher called Socrates. Beyond that, the picture of Socrates in Aristophanes' farce *The Clouds* should be entirely disbelieved, because it contains nothing agreeing with the other three and nothing individual or unusual, but on the contrary appears to be just the popular idea of a sophist at the time, dubbed "Socrates" and given a mask

that resembled the pronounced features of the real Socrates.

(2) *The Evidence of Xenophon.* We have Xenophon's *Memories of Socrates* a work of some 180 pages, consisting mainly of amusing little dialogues between Socrates and various other persons, at some of which Xenophon says he was present; his *Apology of Socrates*, a short report of the trial, which, however, Xenophon does not claim to have attended; his *Oeconomicus*, in which Socrates discusses household management; and his *Symposium*, depicting a party at which Socrates is present. Though in some of his other works Xenophon is a serious historian, it is quite clear that his Socratic writings are fictions embodying scraps of truth, and got up to look like truth by the storyteller's device of saying "I was there". They should be believed only so far as they agree with Plato or Aristotle.

(3) *The Evidence of Aristotle.* Aristotle, who now and then tried to be a historian of philosophy, gives us the most likely account we have of Socrates' thought:

Socrates "occupied" himself with the excellences of character, and in connexion with them became the first to raise the problem of universal definition . . . It was natural that Socrates should be seeking the essence, for he was seeking to syllogize, and "what a thing is" is the starting-point of syllogisms . . . Two things may be fairly ascribed to Socrates, inductive arguments and universal definition, both of which are concerned with the starting-point of science; but Socrates did not make the universal or the definitions exist apart. (Aristotle, *Metaphysics* M. 4. translated by Ross.)

This attributes the following to Socrates:

1. He occupied himself with the excellencies of character.

2. He was the first to raise the problem of definition.

3. He sought the essence, or "what a thing is".

4. He sought to syllogize, that is, to find demonstrative proofs.

5. He also used inductive arguments.

6. He did not make the universals or the definitions exist apart.

The sixth of these, which is contradicted by Plato, will be considered near the end of this article. The other five are well supported by Plato and not contradicted by Xenophon, and had therefore better be accepted by us.

(4) *The Evidence of Plato.* Plato's portrait of Socrates is by far the most copious and impressive. Socrates is the main speaker throughout Plato's early and middle dialogues. His conversation there concerns the nature of virtue and of particular virtues, and tends to the view that virtue is knowledge and vice is ignorance. He takes a particular virtue and asks what it *is*, seeking to find its essence by giving a general definition of it. He produces syllogistic arguments, that is, arguments where two premises when put together necessitate a new proposition, the conclusion. And often he recommends one of the premises by an inductive argument from similar cases. In these ways Plato's account agrees excellently with Aristotle's account.

Plato's account has, however, many more features than the few that Aristotle gives us; and Aristotle does not prepare us for the strange fact that the Platonic Socrates uses his inductions and syllogisms not for but always against proposed definitions of the virtues whose essence he seeks. His conversation takes the form of putting questions to a single respondent; and a well marked pattern appears in these questions. The first question, being a request for a definition, does not admit the answers yes and no and is a matter of doubt. The subsequent questions, however, do demand the answer yes or no; and which of these they demand is usually obvious. Having obtained a number of apparently disconnected answers in this way, Socrates "syllogizes" them, as Aristotle says, and shows that they refute his respondent's answer to the first question. He then asks the respondent to find another answer to the first question, and treats that in the same way. The effect is to show that the answerer is contradicting himself, and does not know what he thought he knew. Socrates does not, however, claim to understand the matter himself. On the contrary, he denies all knowledge of it. He even denies that he intended to convict his answerer of ignorance. "I was never a teacher of anybody." He says that his questions might, for all he knew beforehand, have led to the establishment instead of the refutation of the answer given. This latter denial is, however, impossible to believe. Hence his victims tend to call him "sly", as pretending that he knows less than they do when he knows more. The Greek for slyness is "irony"; and this is the origin of the conception of irony as the conveyance of a statement by words which literally convey the contradictory, and especially the communication of an affirmative statement by the utterance of its literal negation.

There is something repellent about this pattern of talk; and Plato represents it as incurring condemnation from some people. He represents the extraordinary personality of Socrates as including some other questionable traits, namely tendencies to talk homosexually and to maintain paradoxical doctrines in ethics. Yet there is no doubt that he succeeds in making us feel that Socrates' character was wonderful and uniquely valuable. In his *Symposium* he shows us Socrates first as the deep thinker who has got "stuck" in contemplation outside the host's door and pays no attention to the host's servant, then as the pretended lover easily obtaining the seats next the most attractive young men, then as a benign cross-examiner of his host, then as the philosophical sublimator of earthly love into a religion of Beauty Herself, and then as the subject of a daring and successful encomium by Alcibiades. Alcibiades calls him an ugly statue of Silenus that opens to show hidden beauties within. He confesses to having persistently tempted Socrates and thus experienced his unbreakable self-control. He recites Socrates' formidable calmness and endurance on campaign, and affirms his wonderful unlikeness to every other human being alive or dead. All this is to be believed.

Like Xenophon, Plato offers us an *Apology of Socrates*, professing to be the three speeches made by Socrates at his trial. They are certainly not transcripts. They bear at the best only a remote resemblance to what was actually said. Some think that Socrates made no defence at all. But probably the indictment really was that "Socrates corrupts the young men, and does not believe in the city's gods and believes in new divinities". Probably if thirty more jurors had voted the other way he really would have been acquitted. Probably Socrates then really did propose as a penalty that he should be fed at public expense, and really did change this to a fine at the request of Plato and other friends in court. And, if we believe that he was thus intransigent in his choice of a "penalty" after conviction, we should believe that Plato's work is probably true to life in the magnificently proud and unbending tone it makes Socrates take with the court.

Distinct from the question, what Socrates actually said at his trial, is the question, which of the things that Plato makes him say are in fact true, whether Socrates said them at that time or not. It is very probably true that Socrates had, as Plato makes him say he had, firmly opposed at one time the injustice of tyrants and at another time the injustice of the people, both at great risk to himself. It is also very probably true that Socrates did sometimes declare himself to enjoy a mysterious "divine sign", a sort of inner voice which frequently forbade him to do something he was thinking of doing, and whose advice he believed to be always good. It is doubtful, however, whether Socrates really thought that he had been "ordered by the god, both by oracles and by dreams and by every means by which a divine destiny was ever imposed on a man", to convict men of their ignorance by refuting their opinions in cross-examination.

It was easy to escape from the prison at Athens; and probably many of those who voted for his death assumed that Socrates would do so. Plato has an exquisite little dialogue, *Crito*, in which he shows us Socrates' old friend Crito pleading with him to escape, and Socrates refusing. The reason he gives is that, by his choice in pursuing his life in the city of Athens, he has in deed, though not in word, promised to obey the laws of Athens, and he will keep his promise.

Finally in the magnificent *Phaedo* Plato depicts the last conversation and death of Socrates, while letting us know that he himself was not there. We may believe Plato when he tells us that Socrates' wife and children visited him on his last day but were not present at his death; that his friends wept loudly when he drank the poison and were rebuked for it by the unmoved Socrates; that his last words were "Crito, we owe a cock to Asclepius; pay it and do not neglect it"; that Crito answered "That shall be done; think if there is anything else"; and that no answer came to this. The last pages of the *Phaedo* are of extraordinary beauty and grandeur.

We had better not believe, however, that Socrates really defended the doctrines which Plato represents him as defending on his last day. In the *Phaedo* Plato shows Socrates convinced that there is a life after death; he is more likely to be historical on this point in the *Apology*, where he makes Socrates treat it as an open question. In the *Phaedo* Plato makes Socrates say that in his youth he had a period of interest in physical questions; he may have had, but the *Phaedo*-passage is probably only a dramatic way of setting certain points of view in opposition to each other. In the *Phaedo* Plato makes Socrates expound and assume the theory of Ideas, thus coming into conflict with Aristotle's statement that "Socrates did not make the universals or the definitions exist apart". It is very probable that Aristotle is right, as the tradition holds, in saying that the theory of Ideas was the invention of Plato. It was a natural step forward from Socratic definition, but not one that ever occurred to Socrates himself. Plato has introduced it into his *Phaedo* as a way of dedicating to Socrates the fruits of Socrates's teaching, not as a record of that teaching itself.

The greatest value of Plato's Socrates is his superb championship of the ideal of reason, and his high and clear conception of what reason demands. He impresses us, more than any other figure in literature, with the supreme importance of thinking as well as possible and making our actions conform to our thoughts. To this end he preaches the knowledge of one's own starting-points, the hypothetical entertainment of opinions, the exploration of their consequences and connexions, the willingness to follow the argument wherever it leads, the public confession of one's thoughts, the invitation to others to criticize, the readiness to reconsider, and at the same time firm action in accordance with one's present beliefs. Plato's *Apology* has in fact made Socrates the chief martyr of reason as the gospels have made Jesus the chief martyr of faith.

Plate 87, page 375. (R.R.)

Solipsism. Sometimes we idly fancy that the whole world is merely our dream. Solipsism is a theory, rather like this fancy, but based on argument. If asked why I believe in the existence of stars, trees and people, I have to reply "My sight, hearing, touch, in short, my perceptions tell me so. Certainly my perceptions are sorted and supplemented by memory, inference and conjecture, but without perceptions such thinking has nothing to work on. Now perceiving is having sensations.

But you cannot have, for example, my visual or tactual sensations, any more than you can have my toothaches. So you cannot perceive anything that I perceive. The world that my senses acquaint me with is private to me. Even the *you* that I see and hear could no more exist without my existing than my toothaches could. I hanker to believe that independently existing, unperceived things tally with the perceived contents of my private world, but I ought to believe that I alone (*solus ipse*) exist in my own right, all else depending on me as my toothaches do." No important philosophers accept this repellent conclusion. But many, accepting the argument for it, have to postulate non-perceptual reasons for believing in independently existing things and people. We should, instead, reject the step in the argument "perceiving is having sensations". (G.R.)

Sophists. In ancient Greece traditional education had consisted of music (poetry, drama and in general the subjects presided over by the nine muses) and gymnastic. In the more sophisticated social conditions of the fifth century B.C. the need for a further education, equivalent to our higher secondary and university education, became apparent. The sophists were men who offered this higher education; they were itinerant university professors who wandered from city to city giving courses of lectures, mainly on rhetoric and the art of getting on, in return for fees from their audiences. Thus originally the term sophist was not in any way a term of opprobium – it meant something like "professor" – and the sophist was not specially concerned with philosophy; certainly it is quite mistaken to think of the sophists as forming some philosophical school. Some of the sophists, such as **Protagoras**, were indeed very brilliant and influential philosophers, but others confined themselves almost entirely to rhetoric. The establishment of such permanent centres of higher education as the schools of **Plato**, **Aristotle** and Isocrates (all of whom were sophists to the general public) led to the disappearance of the sophists in the middle of the fourth century B.C.

The opprobrium which now attaches to the word "sophist" is due to the skilful propaganda against the sophists, their rivals, by Plato and Aristotle. The basic charge was that the sophists pretended to teach knowledge whereas they taught an art of getting on which neglected the highest values. While there is no doubt some justice in these attacks the spirited defence of the sophists in Grote's *History of Greece* is still worth reading.

Among the sophists the best known names are Protagoras, Gorgias, Prodicus, Hippias, Antiphon, Thrasymachus, Lycaphron and Isocrates. (J.O.U.)

Spencer, Herbert, (1820–1903), an Englishman. He is rarely read now, but achieved an enormous and widespread popular reputation in the later nineteenth century. In his *System of Synthetic Philosophy* he surveyed the biological and social sciences, with a generalized philosophical notion of evolution as a unifying concept; though neither contemporary nor later philosophers and scientists found this survey sufficiently clear and rigorous, it achieved great success and influence with many of those who were impressed by Darwinian biology and ambitious programmes for the development of the social sciences.

In *First Principles* Spencer maintained that we could have knowledge only of phenomena, but that we could nevertheless infer to an Unknowable, an Incomprehensible Power which is the source of phenomena, the most important of which is the Law of Evolution which he obscurely phrased as follows: "an integration of matter and concomitant dissipation of motion, during which the matter passes from an indefinite incoherent homogeneity to a definite coherent heterogeneity". In his essay "Progress, its Law and Cause" he defined progress also as a change from homogeneity; thus he typically identified evolution and progress and could claim that "progress is not an accident, not a thing within human control, but a beneficent necessity." This general conception of evolution antedates the publication of Darwin's work and is based on the work of German biologists who claimed that the feature that distinguished higher forms of organisms was increasing specialization of organs and functions.

Life was defined by Spencer as a continuous adjustment of the internal to the external environment; to live is to be the sort of thing which continually adapts its own nature to be able to deal better with its environment. This is the fundamental viewpoint of the *Principles of Biology* and *Principles of Psy-*

chology which follow the *First Principles* in Synthetic Philosophy. Consistently, he claimed in the *Principles of Ethics* that the principles of ethics "have a natural basis", for moral conclusions follow the general law of evolution. Man is capable of indefinite change by adaptation to circumstances, in particular to the change from wild to settled, civilized life; in this adaptation man represses old selfish traits and develops new ones by virtue of a principle of sympathy. Moral principles are rules which aid the harmonious, readjusted life of civilization. A hedonistic element can be legitimately recognized since "pleasure promotes function" and the law of evolution ensures that those actions we find pleasant will be such as tend to have survival value. Spencer's attempt to draw ethical conclusions from evolutionary principles still finds imitators today. (J.O.U.)

Plate 88, page 376.

Speusippus, an Athenian, born towards the end of the fifth century B.C., died 339. He was **Plato**'s nephew and a member of the Academy, and he was head of the Academy from Plato's death in 347 until his own death. Only fragments of his many works survive and we cannot get a comprehensive view of his philosophy. Four main points may be mentioned. (*a*) Speusippus maintained – against Eudoxus – that pleasure is not good but that pleasure and pain are opposite evils. Plato's *Philebus* is partly concerned with this controversy in the Academy. (*b*) He wrote a number of works of "Classifications". He seems to have held that no one thing can be satisfactorily defined unless all other things are also; to understand a concept is to know how it is related by similarities and differences to all others. (*c*) Speusippus held that the account in Plato's *Timaeus* of the making of the world was simply an expository device (like mathematicians' talk of "constructing" figures or proofs). (*d*) From Aristotle's *Metaphysics* it is clear that Speusippus abandoned Plato's theory of Ideas and also recognised more kinds of entity than Plato, assigning different principles to each kind. (J.L.A.)

Spinoza, Benedict de, (1632–1677) was born in Amsterdam of Jewish parents, who had fled from persecution in Portugal at the end of the sixteenth century, their families having originally come from

Spain. Spinoza was brought up to speak Spanish, Portuguese and Hebrew, but he had a less sure command of Dutch. He attended a Jewish High School in Amsterdam and followed the usual course, including a study of the five books of Moses and the Talmud. One of his teachers was Rabbi Manasseh ben Israel, the man who negotiated with Cromwell the re-entry of the Jews into England. At the age of eighteen, Spinoza went to a Dutch teacher, Van den Ende, to learn Latin and the "new science", studying the works of Copernicus, Galileo, Kepler, Harvey, Huygens and **Descartes**.

Spinoza's father was respected and outstanding among the members of the Jewish community, many of whom were reverts from enforced Catholicism in Spain. Holland was a general refuge for the persecuted and besides the Jewish community, there were Protestant sects of all shades of belief. The leaders of the Jewish community were naturally anxious to present a united front and to cause no scandal to their Dutch neighbours by any hint of free thinking or atheism. Spinoza seems to have wished to lead a quiet life, attending the Synagogue and pursuing his studies. He was becoming critical of orthodox interpretations of the Bible, but he had no wish to disturb the beliefs of others, and until his father's death, was not forced into declaring his unorthodoxy. He was then involved in a law suit with his half-sister about their father's estate. Having won it, Spinoza renounced his inheritance, taking only a "good bed and bed linen". In the course of the dispute, Spinoza's orthodoxy was called in question. The leaders of the Synagogue offered him a pension of 1,000 florins if he would leave Van den Ende and conform. Spinoza refused and was excommunicated, thereupon moving to a suburb of Amsterdam. In conformity with Jewish custom which required all the men to learn a trade, he had mastered the art of grinding and polishing lenses. He now proceeded to earn his living by his art, working at it all day and studying at night. At this time he changed his Hebrew name, Baruch, to its Latin form, Benedict. His *Short Treatise on God, Man and his Wellbeing* was composed at this period. In 1661, he moved to a lodging in a small house at Rhijnsburg, where he wrote his *Tractatus de Emendatione Intellectus*. This house is now the Spinoza Museum. At this period too, Spinoza became acquainted with Henry Ol-

denburg, a German diplomat in London, and one of the Secretaries of the Royal Society. Their correspondence which lasted for fifteen years, throws light on some of the more difficult points in Spinoza's philosophy. In 1663, Spinoza moved to Voorburg, near the Hague. By now his fame was considerable: a society had been formed to study his writings and in response to their insistence, Spinoza allowed to be published his *Renati des Cartes Principia Philosophiae*, with an appendix, *Cogitata Metaphysica*. A Dutch translation immediately appeared. His room in Voorburg became a meeting place for the intellectual leaders of the day, among them, Huygens and Jan de Witt. In 1673, the Elector Palatine offered Spinoza the Chair of Philosophy at the University of Heidelberg, but Spinoza refused it; he wished to be left to pursue his investigations "in accordance with his own mind". By this time, he had almost completed the *Ethics* but he put it on one side and began to write *Tractatus Theologico-Politicus*. The occasion was the outbreak of mob violence against the de Witts after the English defeat of the Dutch navy. It was said that de Witt had brought this disaster upon the Dutch people by his toleration of free thinking and atheism. Spinoza knew the Bible as the source of reasonable living and designed to show that it gave no ground for violence and intolerance. The work was published and immediately condemned by the theologians.

Spinoza now moved into Amsterdam, and completing the *Ethics*, designed to publish it. Information was laid against him to the authorities, and Spinoza withdrew the book. He then began work on a Hebrew grammar and a translation of the Old Testament into Dutch, with the practical object of enabling his fellow citizens to become acquainted with the bible so sadly misinterpreted. These plans were brought to a sudden end by his early death, at the age of forty-five.

In an early work, *Tractatus de Emendatione Intellectus* Spinoza declared the object of his work to be entirely practical, the discovery of "the life of blessedness for man". It entailed a search for that "by whose discovery and acquisition I might be put in possession of a joy continuous and supreme to all eternity". This joy Spinoza called "the intellectual love of God", and it consists in a clear understanding of the nature of men, of their place in the universe and of the nature of the universe, and the rejoicing which is an essential feature of carrying on well, an activity which is essential to men as human beings. Knowledge for Spinoza is a state of clarity of the intellect, to be pursued by the correction of the understanding, freeing it from the vague and confused ideas of sense perception and imagination, and from the hindrance of inappropriate attachment to objects. It is for these reasons that Spinoza's main work, a largely metaphysical treatise, is called the *Ethics*. In it, the system of the universe and man's place in it is shown as intelligible, the free man as finding his blessedness in realising that he is a part of this system which is determined throughout. He rejoices in his true state and this rejoicing is accompanied by the idea of God or the universe: in Spinoza's sense of the word, this is to love God.

When the intellect is working well, making its ideas clear and perceiving their implications, it is in possession of true ideas and of certainty. "He who has a true idea knows at the same time that he has a true idea". (*Ethics* Part II, Prop. XLIII) True ideas are suitably expressed in definitions which may then be deductively developed, the connexion between each proposition and the next being self-evident. We thus reach a system of true propositions. A man who proceeds in this way enjoys knowledge of the second grade, *ratio*; (*Ethics*. Part II, Prop. XL, Schol. 2) knowledge of the highest or third grade, *scientia intuitiva*, belongs to God alone though men may sometimes achieve it in little. It happens when we see the interconnexions between the ideas of a system without the need for a step by step process of inference. The lowest grade of knowledge, *imaginatio*, is knowledge by sense perception and imagination, by vague signs and hearsay. In sense perception, our bodies are acted upon by other bodies, and in imagination, a similar effect in the body is brought about by association, so these two states are experienced as part only of the causal process involved. Sense perception and imagination, though not erroneous in themselves, lead to error if they are not placed in their right contexts, as states of the body, not parts of a system of ideas. Error is always a privation of knowledge, a confusion of ideas not seen as confusion. Vague signs are signs such as "man", "horse", which stand confusedly for a vast number of par-

ticulars, in contrast to "Peter", which stands unequivocally for one body-mind in a determinate place in the spatio-temporal system. "Man" has no place in a system of ideas, but "Peter" may be understood as a body-mind in a system of interacting bodies or body-minds.

The Ethics consists of a system of definitions, axioms and theorems. In Part I, the definitions are basic, not derivable from any more fundamental concepts. They are interconnected and taken together, they form a basis for rational theology, the sciences of the physical world and of the "mental world". Substance is defined as "that which is in itself and is conceived through itself", attribute as "that which the intellect perceives of substance as if constituting its essence". Definition VI equates "God" with "substance consisting of infinite attributes". Taken with axioms III and IV, these definitions yield the concept of God as One, infinite, necessarily existing, containing all being and the sole cause of every existing thing. Axiom III is the axiom of causality and axiom IV gives Spinoza's special meaning of "cause". "The knowledge of an effect depends upon and involves the knowledge of the cause". That is to say, the causal relation for Spinoza is the relation of ground and consequent. Substance, since it is conceived through itself, is its own ground, i.e. it is self-caused and so necessarily existing. There could not be two such beings, for if there were, either one would have to be understood in terms of the other, or both in terms of a third thing which would then itself be substance. Everything but substance is "in something else, through which also it is conceived", so that there is nothing outside substance.

Substance is not only infinite in being all there is but also in being manifested in infinite attributes, each infinitely modified into "modes" which are "in and conceived through" substance under one or other of its attributes. Of the infinite number of attributes we know only two, extension and thought. Although attributes were defined as "that which the intellect perceives of substance", they are not mental, they are *perceived* of substance. They are perceived of substance *as if* constituting its essence. Philosophers have mistakenly supposed that thought and extension were substances, so creating their own problem of making intelligible a connexion between things "which have nothing in common with one another, and so cannot be conceived through one another". (*Ethics*. Part I, Axiom V.) Extension and thought are two attributes of the one substance, not interacting, but each infinitely diversified into modes which occur together. The most interesting case of this "occurring together" is in human beings, where mental events are paralleled by physical events. The mind is "the idea of the body".

The modal system of extension is *facies totius universi* (the aspect of the entire universe). It is studied at different levels in the sciences of geometry, mechanics and biology. In geometry, the concepts of point, line, plane are appropriate, in mechanics, smallest bodies, motion and rest. In biology, the concept of *conatus* is fundamental: it is "the endeavour with which each body perseveres in its own existence". In human bodies, it is sometimes accompanied by awareness, when it is called desire. These sciences are firmly founded in the metaphysical concept of substance under the attribute of extension. There has been no comparable development of the concept under the attribute of thought, but this is what Spinoza hoped to provide. In the Introduction to Part III he says: "I shall consider human actions as if I were considering lines, planes or bodies". Just as a human body is to be described in terms of "smallest bodies" acting on one another, their motions determined by earlier motions, so a human mind is to be described in terms of action, passion, adequate ideas, and a mental event in terms of an earlier event. The essence of an individual is its *conatus*, and the cohesion of physical parts is patterned by the mind's awareness of its own unity and of its union with the body.

The differences among simple bodies are expressible in terms of degrees of motion-rest, and among complex bodies in terms of their own motion-rest and that of their parts. The differences among minds are expressible in terms of the degrees of clearness and adequacy of their ideas. A man whose ideas are clear is said to be free and active in the sense that the causes of his actions lie, as far as is compatible with his finitude, within his own nature. The causes of action of no finite being can lie completely in his own nature; his body is a part of a system of interacting bodies and in all its transactions, its state is the conjoint effect of its own nature and that of the bodies impinging upon it.

The free man has an adequate idea of his own state as such an effect and though it may be painful, the appropriate emotion is joy, in that the pain is seen as occurring in its proper place. If the pain has arisen as the result of the action of another human being, the free man will neither blame nor hate him. Love is "joy accompanied by the idea of an object", "hatred is sorrow accompanied by the idea of an object". The free man, who sees all men as parts of a determined system can only rejoice in his knowledge, so that he cannot hate anyone.

The important concept in explaining human actions, as in explaining any other event, is cause, not purpose. Spinoza's favourite example of error is our belief in free will. A man is aware of his "actions" but ignorant of their causes; he therefore says that he freely chose to act in this way, but this phrase is simply a name for the state of confusion in which the causes of our "actions" are for the most part hidden. "Action" is in inverted commas because in Spinoza's terminology, the doings of men whose ideas are confused and inadequate are to be called "passions". The explanations of the doings of such men is to be sought in their circumstances, not in their own nature. There are three primary emotions, desire which is *conatus*, joy which is the passage of the organism to a higher state of perfection, and sorrow which is the passage to a lower state. All other emotions are compounded from these three, together with the ideas of objects appropriately or inappropriately conjoined. To pass to a higher or lower state of perfection is not to become better or worse in the moral sense, but to become more or less active. The man of inadequate ideas is passive in that what he does depends on what happens to him, not on what he is. He is "less real" than the active man: his personality is shadowy, not manifested in his life.

Spinoza's moral theory is accordingly relativistic and naturalistic. "We call that good which we certainly know to be useful to us". (*Ethics*, Part IV, Ref. I). In itself, it is neither good nor bad, and the man of adequate ideas will attach the term suitably to that which increases his power of action, the passive man to that which he mistakenly sees as ministering to his purposes. He has misplaced emotion, attaching it to objects instead of seeing it in its right place in the causally connected phases of his mental life. Praise and blame are equally inapplicable to human action, though they may be used as causes in affecting the actions of those for whose conduct we feel responsibility. Nothing can be more useful to free men than the society of other free men, so that Spinoza's "good man" will be good in the normal sense. He will naturally try to bring it about that other men are free and wise, understanding that hatred and resentment are as inappropriate towards men as towards rocks and stones. He knows that the only object worth pursuing, knowledge, is better attained in companionship than alone, but he also knows that every other being has his own *conatus*, and no matter how mistaken he may be in his idea of how best to "persevere in his own being", he has an equal right with the wise man so to persevere. The wise man then, will be tolerant of others, interfering with the harmless beliefs of nobody, whether in politics or religion. He will judge that religion to be good which promotes a good life, and that social system which gives security to its citizens and strengthens their "natural right to exist and work without injury to themselves or others". Since there are men of all grades of perfection, some must be led by authority. For this reason, it is of immense importance that theologians and civic leaders should understand the conditions of the good life.

If resentment is inappropriate towards men, it is by a thousand times more inappropriate towards God. God is above good and evil, and though He is equally the cause of perfect and imperfect beings, His power is equally manifest in both. A physical or mental cripple is what he is because of the place he occupies in the system: God has not tried and failed to produce a perfect man. "To Him material was not wanting for the creation of everything, from the highest down to the very lowest grade of perfection: or to speak more properly, because the laws of His nature were so ample that they sufficed for the production of everything which can be conceived by an infinite intellect". (*Ethics*, Part I, Appendix). Such a God can be loved and worshipped by the free man, who sees that it is unsuitable to expect that God should love him in return, be concerned for his needs and allot rewards and punishments. One who loves God does not look to a future life: this life may be one of blessedness, though in thinking adequately, we may be thinking God's thoughts, share in God's rejoicing self-

knowledge, that is to say, in "the love with which God loves Himself", and to this extent, we may be eternal. (R.L.S.)

Plates 89 and 90, pages 377 and 378.

Stevenson, Charles Leslie (1908–), American philosopher, Professor at the University of Michigan. He is best known for his book *Ethics and Language* (1944); in this book Stevenson gives an elaborate statement of the emotivist theory of the significance of ethical terms, a view which had been hinted at by **Hume** and summarily stated by the **Logical Positivists** but had never previously been so carefully treated. Stevenson's principal contention is that to say something is good is to state that one approves of it and to seek to evoke the same attitude in one's hearers. He also maintains that in moral discourse we can attempt to persuade others to agree with us but that the concept of valid argument is not applicable to such discourse. The book is undoubtedly the classical statement of the emotivist position. His paper *Persuasive Definitions* in *Mind*, 1938, has also had great influence; here he seeks to show that a definition is often a disguised attempt to set the thing defined in a favourable or unfavourable light. Stevenson is also the author of a number of papers on aesthetics. Though he writes in the American tradition Stevenson clearly shows the influence of a period of study at Cambridge, England, when **Wittgenstein** was teaching there. (J.O.U.)

Stoicism was one of the dominant philosophies of the Hellenistic-Roman period. It was founded by **Zeno** of Citium at the end of the fourth century B.C., receiving its name from the Painted Stoa (colonnade) where he taught in Athens. To him are attributed all the fundamental doctrines. In the following century **Chrysippus** formulated the definitive system in an extensive series of works. But Stoics did not shrink from change within the framework, and in the second and first centuries B.C., Panaetius and Posidonius made some changes of emphasis and detail. In the Roman Empire it was modified still further by **Seneca**, **Epictetus** and **Marcus Aurelius**, but it always remained in essence the unified comprehensive system of Zeno and Chrysippus. It faded out after the end of the third century A.D.

The Stoics divided their philosophy into logic

(dialectic and rhetoric), ethics, and physics (which included theology); these were intertwined and interdependent, but not of equal importance. Their interest in logic was mainly confined to perfecting their own arguments in defence of their system; it was the wall protecting the garden, the shell safeguarding the egg. Physics, on the other hand, was in a sense at once the starting point and culmination of their ethics; Chrysippus said there could be no other starting point for justice than from physics and their definition of happiness (the end of man) was "to live in harmony with nature"; in other words, like most Greeks, they based their philosophy on their conception of nature. Yet their interest in nature was confined to its relation to and importance for human action; Stoicism was primarily an ethic for which physics provided the foundation.

Their ethics was formulated in response to the needs of the time. At the close of the fourth century, the break up of the Greek city state produced not only physical, economic and political insecurity but also a moral vacuum. The response of the philosophical schools reflects this: the Academy allowed ethics to slip into the background and turned **Sceptic**; the Peripatetics engaged in scientific research, and were content in ethics to make their aim as many human goods as possible; the **Epicureans** offered **Hedonism**, withdrawal. Zeno's reaction was to devise a philosophy of security for the individual without divorcing him from the circumstances in which he found himself.

His starting point was the same as that of the **Cynics**, the belief that insecurity and unhappiness were the result of pursuing, as goods or ends of human action, what was not wholly under the control of the human individual. Health may deteriorate, a fortune be lost, reputation vanish through external causes, which are always liable to destroy them; no physical or external "goods" can therefore be end goods. The only thing completely in our power is the correct moral attitude of mind, which is virtue; even in moral action the result or object of the action is beyond our control. Further, this attitude is based on knowledge (courage was the *knowledge* of what was and was not to be feared); for the Stoic happiness was derived from knowing what was the right thing to do at any given moment, and through this knowledge having the right attitude of mind towards the attainment of the object. The actual attainment of the object was irrelevant to happiness, which depended solely on the moral functioning of the rational element in man. It was argued that the wise man wants only what he can achieve, and so only he can achieve what he wants.

So far the Cynic ingredients. But to understand the Stoic flavour one must turn to the Stoic conception of the universe. All reality was material, mind as well as matter; for, they argued, only matter can move or be moved. But there was an important distinction between active force and passive matter; the active force was *logos*, divine reason, the governor of the universe. Indissolubly permeated throughout passive matter which it qualified, it fashioned the universe into one rational purposeful living whole of which man was an integral part. It was this *logos*, identified with creative fire (or warm air) among the elements, which was the substance of the human soul. Just as reason in the universe is all-important as the ruling active force, so is reason in man, and happiness must depend on it alone; and since human reason is the same as the universal reason, the knowledge of man and his duties cannot be complete until it comprises the universe and man's place in it. For by understanding the working of reason in the universe he can identify himself with its purpose. Man has thus the power to accommodate his own nature to universal Nature, or in the Stoic phrase, to live in harmony with nature.

Physics afforded the justification for the supremacy of moral intelligence, not an account of its field of exercise; for that the Stoics turned to psychology. They observed certain natural impulses and aversions which when developed point to certain ends; the attainment or avoidance of these appear natural for a human being and involve appropriate actions. For example, the principle of all life, the securing of one's own existence, led to physical and external satisfaction, health, comfort, adequate wealth, etc. The instinct to perpetuate the race was the basis of family life and then in general of society, friendship, (and the responsibilities and duties involved). The impulse of the intellect fostered reflection, curiosity, fine arts. As man has been shaped by nature along these lines, the pursuit of all these and avoidance of their opposites are according to his nature and therefore appropriate. But as they are based on the conception of the nature of man alone, and not on the nature of man as a part of the universe, their importance is subordinate to that of the rational. They form a class of intermediate objects with relative value but morally indifferent in having no absolute (i.e. moral) value. Their relative value, fixed from an intelligent survey of human psychology, makes possible the formation of general rules for their attainment or avoidance which is the subject of "appropriate" duties. (The Stoics supplied their own terminology). But the attainment of "intermediates" cannot be good, nor "appropriate" duties perfect acts because sometimes the general rule is wrong; such actions may be done by a good or bad man alike, or for a wrong or insufficient reason; owing to external circumstances it is not completely in our power to fulfil all or any of them. Nevertheless the "intermediates" are involved in virtue because they are also the material (though not the end) of perfect duties; they are the field in which virtue functions; but virtue alone is good, the attainment of the "intermediates", whatever their worth, never so. The "intermediates" are according to human nature, but only the right exercise of moral choice among them can bring man into harmony with universal nature. So Stoicism retained the self-sufficiency of the Cynics, but like the Peripatetics refused to divorce morals from human nature.

It is just this distinctive relationship between virtue and "intermediates" which formed the core of Stoicism and roused most criticism and misunderstanding; this was fostered by certain shifts of emphasis in different Stoics, and not least by their love of paradox. They were fond of stressing the absolute importance of moral intelligence by insisting that there were no half measures. If a man perfected it, all his acts were right, if not, none were; he was either perfectly good and wise, or fool and knave; all mistakes or vices were equal. Although all Stoics accepted this position, some emphasized it more than others, notably Ariston (a pupil of Zeno), whose unorthodox attitude of complete indifference to the "intermediates" largely eliminated the practical side of Stoicism. Chrysippus showed once and for all that the paradox "all sins are equal" meant that all moral mistakes were equally mis-

takes in comparison with perfect virtue, but regarded solely by themselves one could be worse than another. The objects of our natural impulses and the "appropriate" duties involved were not in every case valueless; some had a *prima facie* "worth" and were to be "preferred", others "unworth" and to be "relegated"; others were completely indifferent. The relative value of all this lies only within its class (i.e. the class of "appropriate" duties); health is to be preferred as a general rule without outside considerations, as pain is to be avoided; but circumstances may arise where it is right to reject the preferred or vice versa; for neither health nor pain is good or evil in itself. "Appropriate" duties receive absolute value in each case only from the decision of moral intelligence; nevertheless this decision is concerned with them; one is to incline this way or that. The position is most clearly marked in the educative methods of the Stoa; for while he who was not a wise man was a fool, yet fools could progress towards virtue, (and indeed the Stoics made a serious attempt to trace the growth of moral notions in the human mind). Fools were led along the path by the rules of "appropriate" duties, which acquainted them with the material of ethics. But Stoicism concentrated on concrete acts, and in each case the rules required interpretation. So although fools made progress, they remained fools, being fallible and vulnerable, until they understood that the infallible directing principle of morality came from within, the divine control of reason. They must know in each instance what they should choose and why; for this they must comprehend the logos philosophy. Each individual alone can be the captain of his own soul. Yet it was apparent that most if not all men were still in the progressive stage; consequently Panaetius (c. 185–110 B.C.) and Posidonius (c. 135–50 B.C.) in particular, when faced with a Roman audience demanding a more practical approach than Greek theory, concentrated on the department of "appropriate" duties, with its emphasis on man as a human being and in relation to others in society, on the study of human nature and human psychology. Thus Panaetius derived from the virtues a series of moral and political rules for action. This could not mean that he had abandoned the higher study of man in the universe and the logos philosophy; but it led in the last century B.C. to the criticism that the Stoa was saying nothing different from Peripatetic ethics; which is true if confined to this intermediate stage of Stoic ethics, but nonsense when it is remembered that this stage could not produce happiness, which was completely in man's power to achieve.

It was this essential framework of the end and scope of morality which gave unity and shape to the diverse ramifications of Stoicism. In *ethics*, since the condition for right action was the soundness of moral reason, the greatest danger to it came from the passions, as irrational movements of the mind. Stoics classified the passions under the *genera* pleasure, pain, desire, fear, and regarded them as springing from impulses externally roused and overriding correct judgment. Chrysippus, whose intellectualism brought him to regard all mental forms as modes of reason, went so far as to call them evil reason arising from mistaken judgments; but this embarrassing psychology was criticised by Posidonius, who once more posited an irrational faculty in the mind to explain the moral predicament. But for the Stoics passion involved an assent of judgment which could only be given if reason was in a weak condition. Therefore the passions had to be eradicated. The Stoics in their moral teaching attempted to effect a prophylactic cure for this mental sickness. But they never banished emotion; the sage felt correct emotions derived from his sound state; but emotion from other sources was never permitted to cloud his reason. In politics the Stoics were in a curious position; they had a duty to enter politics since they had duties to their fellow men. But despite the influence of Panaetius, Stoicism remained fundamentally an ethic for the individual. In the last resort duty to the community had to give way to a man's duty to himself; and Stoics tended to think of a community of mankind based on the individual, or of a community of wise men in divine nature. So their politics tended to remain general rather than particular, or to withdraw to a higher plane, as in the cases of Seneca and M. Aurelius. Since the end for a man lay solely in virtue, or the soundness of his moral reason, should extraordinary circumstances arise whereby this was threatened, the wise man was at liberty to commit suicide. Life and death were alike indifferent compared with the end; the door was always open; one would merely be following the summons of the divine purpose in the universe. There were periods in Stoicism when suicide became almost an obsession, although Stoics held no belief in an after-life.

In *physics*, the Stoics, despite their interest in nature, did not engage in scientific research. Even to Posidonius, who had the widest range and most scientific mind of all Stoics, physical phenomena had interest purely as displaying the rational purposive nature of the universe. This the Stoics regarded not with scientific curiosity, but with a religious awe. They argued: the universe is completely material without void; everything is a mode of the original single being combining passive unqualified matter and force; the latter is reason and god. By a theory of mixture whereby a drop of wine would be diffused over a whole ocean, the subsequent complete blend producing a new whole, so divine reason is diffused throughout the universe making of it an organic whole. There is nothing without a tincture of the divine (thus they are both monotheistic and pantheistic); there is nothing which is not subject to the rational law. This position involved firstly a rigid fatalism: all events are part of an unbroken chain of cause and effect; chance is a name given by human ignorance; possibility means that a future event is not excluded by a known law of nature; (compare **Spinoza**, who distinguishes between "contingent" and "possible", but both words merely reflect human ignorance). Secondly, since god is good, providence rules all for the good of the whole. There were gradations here; the logos varied in purity and "tension" in different forms (e.g. man, animal, plant); part contributed to the good of whole, lower forms to the good of higher; e.g. animals which do not possess active reason are created for the use of men who do. While the position of moral reason in man is thus buttressed, critics of the Stoa lost no time in pointing out two consequent difficulties for their ethics. In the first place, the problem of evil became acute. While Stoics maintained that most things regarded as evil are morally indifferent, vice only being evil, yes they did recognise its existence, and the variety and contradictory nature of their answers show that they did not quite know how to meet the problem. There are three main lines of argument: *a)* God could not create evil for its own sake; it is the result of the material in which he has to work, or a secondary result of his provisions for the world.

b) Evil is not the fault of God, but of man's misuse of his bounty, for they have been granted control of their own virtue or vice. *c*) Evil is necessary (i) for there to be good, since opposites only acquire meaning from each other (compare Plato, *Theaetetus*, 176); (ii) as a punishment or an example or to test men; (iii) by some arrangement beyond human comprehension, for the good of the whole. Secondly, Fatalism was involved in Stoic physics, **freedom of will** in their ethics. Chrysippus' defence consisted of a distinction between the initial external cause which immediately preceded the action, and was part of the infinite chain of cause and effect, and the all-important internal cause furnished by the nature of the thing. A stone when moved falls downward by its own nature. The external stimulus to human action binds man to the fatalistic chain, but from his own nature he has the power of decision for his own virtue and vice. Yet even so he can do no more than run willingly between the shafts along the road appointed by fate; otherwise he will be dragged willy-nilly in the same direction. A man's nature is subject to Nature's direction, but it is in his power to work hand in glove with Nature itself. His own happiness alone is in his control, not his part in the functioning of the universe. Their physical theories attracted Stoics to divination and astrology. They were supremely conscious of themselves as members of a divine organism through which extended a sympathy affecting all. There is a deep religious feeling especially marked in Cleanthes (pupil of Zeno), Posidonius, Epictetus, M. Aurelius. Like the microcosm, the living universe was thought to have an eternal cycle of change. There will come a period of "conflagration", when everything is converted to the divine fire, becomes soul only, and evil disappears. Then the fire in turn becomes a wet mass from which the seeds of reason initiate an identical cycle.

Since virtue depended on knowledge, one of the principle tasks of Stoic *logic* was to provide a theory of knowledge. Since all reality was material, knowledge depended on sense-perception, tested by reason. Material images of objects were reproduced directly on the mind. Some images, called "comprehensible" or cognitive, corresponded so exactly to the real object as to demand irresistible assent from reason when in a sound condition; "compre-

hension" (the term meant "grasping", as one grasps an object in the fist) or cognition followed this assent, and became knowledge as an unshakeable certainty in the sage. The extreme weaknesses of this rather mechanical process were rightly attacked by the Sceptics, who pointed out that there is no distinguishable mark between true and false perceptions, that the latter may be as irresistible as the former and that there is no criterion of judgment. This remained the weakest link in Stoicism. In their desire to perfect their arguments, the Stoics made considerable contributions to the study of the syllogism; being empiricists and interested primarily in concrete moral acts they devoted themselves to the hypothetical and disjunctive syllogism, which they classified as **Aristotle** had classified the categorical. Since speech, they believed, was thought in sound, and words arose from the nature of things, they engaged in etymology, and, to far greater effect, in the study of grammar, the development of which owed much to Stoicism. The sage, perfect in all spheres, was also the perfect orator, concentrating on truth and preciseness, and eschewing emotional devices.

Most of the components of Stoicism are not original, but in the attempt to unify much previous philosophical thinking, including apparently incompatible theories, into a comprehensive system, something new was produced. It is true that the two impulses towards comprehensiveness and towards internal unity and consistency produced a magnificent crop of paradoxes. While the Stoics emphasized them in the Socratic tradition for teaching purposes, they remained inherent in the system. Not least paradoxical was their emphasis on the power of all men to achieve their happiness in an all-beneficent universe, combined with the admission that the world was full of human depravity. In the history of the School, the sage tended to become more and more of an ideal, but he always remained a practical ideal; man was not born perfect, but it was in his power to become so. In fact in the later Stoa, during the Empire, most emphasis was laid on practical ethics. This combination of practicality and noble ideals made the Stoa perhaps the most popular and dominant School of philosophy for some five or six hundred years; it survived both the devastating attack of the New Academy, and the acquisitive eclecticism of later

Academics and Peripatetics. Although its natural basis and intellectual framework was Greek, and completely alien to Christianity, there were many points of contact between the two in ethics; Seneca was later represented as a secret Christian in correspondence with St Paul; and Epictetus appeared in the Christian curriculum. Any influence of Stoicism on later philosophy is not easy to trace, but there are some remarkable similarities to the Stoa in the philosophy of Spinoza.   (I.G.K.)

Strawson, Peter Frederick (1919–) is a Fellow of University College, Oxford. His most notable work is on the philosophy of logic. In his *Introduction to Logical Theory* (1952) he examined the general nature of formal **logic**, concerning himself especially with the relation of formal systems to discourse in ordinary "informal" language; in general this examination tended to show that the gulf between formal and informal discourse is wider than orthodox accounts of the nature of logic tend to suggest. In two important papers on "Truth" he criticised the semantic and correspondence theories of **truth** and put forward the view that the phrase "is true" has no assertive or descriptive function but is used to perform the act of confirming or endorsing a statement. In a paper called "On Referring" he criticized **Russell**'s celebrated theory of descriptions, holding that such a statement as "The present King of France is bald" presupposes rather than states the existence of a King of France. His most recent work is *Individuals: An Esssay in Descriptive Metaphysics*, 1959; in this he studies the ways in which we actually distinguish individual things of all kinds, and concludes that the space-time location of bodies is fundamental to all our ways of locating all kinds of things. This study he calls descriptive metaphysics in contrast with speculative metaphysics which, in Strawson's opinion, is largely concerned to set up new conceptual systems.   (J.O.U.)

Subjectivism. Like most terms ending in "ism", the term "subjectivism" is used very vaguely and loosely in philosophy; roughly a view is said to be subjectivist if it maintains that the truth of some class of statements depends on the mental state or reactions of the person making the statement. Thus in **ethics** and **aesthetics** a subjectivist will hold

that to say that something is good or beautiful is to say something about one's reaction to something, perhaps that it gives one a special feeling of pleasure, and not to say anything about the "objective" characteristics of the thing; it is necessary to distinguish such a subjectivist view from the expressive theory (found for example in **Ayer**'s *Language Truth and Logic*) which holds that when we say something is good we do not make a statement about our reactions to the thing but rather are thereby reacting to the thing in words in a way analogous logically to cheering or throwing one's hat in the air. The view that what is perceived exists only when and because it is perceived, expressed by **Berkeley** in the words *"esse est percipi"*, is also termed subjectivism or subjective **idealism**; such subjectivists believe, usually on the basis of the fact of perceptual illusion and the physical and physiological theories of science, that colours, sounds, smells, etc. exist only "in the mind" and not in the natural world. Not all uses of the term "subjective" are specifically philosophical; thus in medicine a pain may be called subjective if it has no physical basis but is induced in the patient imaginatively by himself.   (J.O.U.)

Substance, *see* Aristotle, Descartes, Spinoza, Leibniz, Locke, Dualism, Monism.

Synthetic, the opposite of **Analytic**. For "synthetic *a priori*", *see* A priori.

T

Taylor, Alfred Edward (1869–1945), British philosopher. He began his philosophical career at Oxford, where he accepted a position similar to that of F. H. **Bradley** who was a Fellow of the same College, Merton. His earliest philosophical writings, *The Problem of Conduct* and *Elements of Metaphysics*, are thus idealist in character. He left Oxford quite early in his career and his main productive years were spent as Professor of Moral Philosophy, first at St Andrews and then at Edinburgh. Away from Oxford, he abandoned his Bradleyan position and adopted one based on **Plato** and Christian theism. In his Gifford Lectures, *The Faith of a Moralist* (1930) he argued that our moral knowledge is such that it presupposes necessarily the existence of a

God who controls the universe with a moral purpose and the immortality of the human soul. But Taylor is better known as a Platonic scholar of extraordinary learning than as an original philosopher. While at St Andrews he produced the famous "Burnet-Taylor heresy" in collaboration with Burnet, the Professor of Greek in that University. Burnet and Taylor argued that the Platonic dialogues must not be treated as dramatic representations of Plato's own views but as essentially accurate historical documents, containing reports of the positions of **Socrates** and the **Pythagoreans** of the fifth century B.C. Though this position never won general acceptance it nevertheless powerfully affected all subsequent Platonic scholarship. Taylor's *Plato, the Man and his Work* remains the most important synoptic view of Plato's work yet published. (J.O.U.)

Teleological Argument, *see* Theism, Deism.

Thales of Miletus, a Greek seaport in Asia Minor, predicted an eclipse which occurred in 585–4 B.C. He was a *sophos* or sage of many interests: among other things he organized the diversion of a river, and urged federation on the Ionians. His mathematical and astronomical discoveries, later somewhat exaggerated, included methods of mensuration, for example of the height of pyramids, and the compilation of a star-catalogue for nautical use. He probably visited Egypt, and for his estimation of the eclipse must also have had access to Babylonian celestial records. How prominent and how precisely formulated was his more theoretical cosmology we do not know. He certainly believed that the flat earth floated on water, from which it had originated. Here he was probably adapting a common motif of Near-Eastern, and especially Egyptian, mythology. He may also have thought, as **Aristotle** asserts, that the world and its parts were still essentially watery. He seems to have said that "all things are full of gods", meaning that they are permeated by soul, or movement- and life-principle, which because of its extent and power must be divine. Even the magnet-stone, apparently inanimate, causes motion and is therefore alive. At least it is clear that by abandoning personification and attempting to explain the whole world rationally

Thales deserves his traditional title of the originator of Greek philosophy. See also **Pre-Socratics**.
(G.S.K.)

Theism is the belief that there is a God and more specifically the belief that God is omnipotent, omniscient and benevolent, distinct from the universe which he has created and in the affairs of which he intervenes. To be a theist is not in itself to hold a philosophical theory, but it is to be committed on philosophical issues, both of truth and of meaning. At the same time, a belief shared by **Aquinas**, **Descartes** and **Berkeley** obviously has a certain chameleon-like quality.

The grounds on which the existence of the God of theism has been asserted are very various. There is first the Cartesian view that "God exists" is a necessary truth; "recurring to the examination of the idea of a Perfect Being, I found that the existence of the Being was comprised in the idea in the same way that the equality of its three angles to two right angles is comprised in the idea of a triangle . . . and that consequently it is at least as certain that God, who is this Perfect Being, is, or exists, as any demonstration of geometry can be". Descartes's mistake, which Aquinas had identified four centuries earlier, in thinking that any assertion of existence could be a necessary truth is not committed by those who have accepted either the cosmological or teleological arguments.

Both these arguments attempt to derive the conclusion that God exists from premises about the world. The cosmological argument takes as its premise the assertion that something exists, the teleological the assertion that the universe manifests traces of intelligent design. The cosmological argument then proceeds by way of the assertion that the existence of anything at all can only be explained by supposing that there exists an uncaused First Cause. The teleological argument passes from the assertion of design in nature to the assertion of a supernatural designer. Both arguments have been, perhaps over-frequently, pulverized by the charge that they attempt a causal inference from the universe to its maker; whereas **Hume** has shown that it only makes sense to speak of causal relations as holding between observable states of affairs, and, whatever God is, he is certainly not an observable state of affairs.

The Cartesian, or ontological, argument, the

cosmological and the teleological arguments became a standard triad in eighteenth century apologetics. The habit of reading the arguments of medieval theism as earlier versions of these may however be a questionable one. Clearly the chief difficulty in advancing a proof of, or argument for, the existence of God lies not in the difficulties over such concepts as those of causality, but in the elementary logical point that in a valid proof nothing can appear in the conclusion which was not already contained in the premises. A valid proof of God's existence could therefore be nothing other than the making explicit of a belief which was implicit in the premises. Those who are prepared to deny not only those premises which state, but also those which imply, divine existence must necessarily be left untouched by the theistic arguments. The concept of theistic proof as proceeding by unquestionable inferences from undeniable premises is ruled out not by any special difficulty in theism but by the prerequisites of proof in general. Aquinas, at least, was well aware of the central issues here (*Summa Theologica* I 1, 8). All that you can do, on a matter of first principles, such as theistic belief is, is to show that your opponent's position fails – *solvere rationes ipsius*.

The failure of the eighteenth century triad, however, led on not to a re-examination of the notion of proof but to an appeal to inner religious experience. This appeal became characteristic of Protestant philosophy of religion and led to the quest for an experience at once plainly identifiable as *the* religious experience by those who enjoyed it and as plainly witnessing to the existence of God. Schleiermacher's "feeling of absolute dependence" and Otto's "numinous" are the most notorious candidates in this field. This whole movement had fruitful consequences for the phenomenological study of religious experience. But as an attempt to provide grounds for theistic belief it fails, for it becomes either another version of the familiar and invalid causal inference, passing in this case from an alleged introspectible state of affairs to an unobserved author of this state of affairs, or a simple irrationalist affirmation that because I feel that it is so, it is so.

The latter alternative must be distinguished from another Protestants position which rests belief neither on argument nor on experience. For some Protestants the whole ground for belief is faith in a divine revelation; the belief that there is a God is from the standpoint of rational argument simply groundless. This is not to say that theistic belief lacks grounds which it might possess, but that it is held to be the logical character of theistic belief necessarily to lack grounds. Such a belief is not however invulnerable to rational argument even on its own assumptions. For, if God has revealed himself, it must be at some time and place to some specific person and the allegation that there was such a person is a purely historical affirmation which can be challenged on historical grounds. So the revealed belief of Islamic theism depends upon historical assertions about Mahomet and that of Christian theism depends on assertions about Jesus.

How in any case can the assertion that this or that event is revelatory of the divine be warranted? A necessary condition presumably is that the event in question should be a miraculous occurrence or be accompanied by such occurrences. In this way the problem of miracles arises for the theist, and since the assertion that God intervenes miraculously is essential to theism, as contrasted with **deism**, an *a priori* proof of the impossibility of miracles would be a disproof of theism. That Hume provides such a proof has often been asserted. Hume accepts the theological definition of a miracle as a breach of a law of nature, and he argues that when we speak of a law of nature we mean that a certain course of events has been uniformly experienced to occur. Now where such a sequence of events has been uniformly experienced by the whole of mankind it is of the highest degree of improbability that such a sequence should be interrupted. And when someone testifies that such a sequence has been interrupted, as the apostles testified that Jesus walked on the water, it is always more probable that the testimony is erroneous than that the hitherto observed regularity of nature should have been contravened. Of this argument it may be said that it is an argument against accepting reports of the miraculous rather than against believing in the possibility of miracles; and also it ignores one essential feature of claims about the miraculous.

What distinguishes a miraculous event is not just its apparent inexplicability; but also the fact that it appears as an answer to a human command or need. The concept that demands scrutiny is not that of a "miraculous event" but rather that of "doing a miracle".

This relationship between divine intervention and human life is characteristic of the religious content of theism and it is therefore not suprising that it should affect the conceptual problems which theism raises. It emerges notably in the difficulty posed for theistic belief by physical and moral evil. If God is all-powerful, then he must be able to prevent evil. If God is all-good, then he must wish to prevent evil. But evil occurs. So that God cannot be both all-powerful and all-good. And to assert that he is both these things and to allow that evils occur is to admit that theism involves the starkest contradiction. The Theistic answer to this charge is usually that God's willing some good end such as human freedom and the possibility of human moral achievement made it logically necessary that God should create a world with possible or actual evils in it. Among the difficulties which this answer encounters is the fact that so much animal suffering, for example, must have taken place before man ever appeared and must therefore be considered irrelevant to any divine purpose for human freedom. Theists however are normally disposed to admit that the facts of evil constitute at least a *prima facie* objection to theism. That they admit this perhaps assists them in meeting another type of problem.

Critics of the theistic proofs argue that there are no good reasons for believing that God exists; exponents of the problem of evil are apt to claim that there are good reasons for believing that God does not exist; neither scepticism cuts as deep as that which claims that it is equally meaningless to assert or to deny the existence of God. This may be asserted on the general positivist ground that the meaning of a statement is the method of its verification, and that there is no method of verifying theistic statements. But the same charge can also be made in a way that brings out the nature of theistic belief more strikingly. For to make an assertion is always to allow that one may be wrong, that there is some conceivable state of affairs incompatible with one's assertion which, if it occurs, shows that one's assertion is false. If one does not rule out anything by making what appears to be an assertion, then one simply has not succeeded in asserting anything. But the theist does not seem to allow that anything conceivable could falsify his assertion that

there is a good and all-powerful God. Whatever disasters happen, he claims that their occurrence is not incompatible with the care of an all-loving, all-powerful God. This seems to evacuate words like "loving" and "powerful" of all meaning. To this the theist will reply that his assertions would be falsified by the occurrence of pointless and irredeemable evil, but that no actual evils can be shown to be pointless and irredeemable, especially in the light of the possibilities of an after-life. Thus the theistic claim comes into logical connection with the claim that human beings are not mortal, a connection which is already made in most of the great religions on theological grounds.

What emerges from all this about the philosophical interest of theism? Simply that there is no one problem or group of problems which can be labelled "the theistic question". Proof, introspection, laws of nature, free-will, falsifiability – almost all the topics of philosophy arise in a theistic context. The conceptual problems of the theistic philosopher are thus for the most part the ordinary conceptual problems of philosophy raised from a particular point of view. (A.MACI.)

Theophrastus (c. 370–c. 286 B.C.), born in Lesbos, a Greek island in the Aegean, was **Aristotle**'s most famous pupil. He succeeded as head of the Lyceum when Aristotle left Athens in 323. Most of his many writings are lost and it is hard to get a true picture of his contributions to philosophy. He remained fundamentally an Aristotelian, but he criticized Aristotle on particular points and made useful additions to Aristotle's work, for example in logic. In some respects he paved the way for the teachings of stoicism and epicureanism. Three of his works may be mentioned. (*a*) The *De Plantis* (which we have) laid the foundations of scientific botany and introduced important botanical concepts. (*b*) The *Metaphysics* (also extant) raised problems about Aristotle's metaphysical doctrines, especially the doctrine of a Prime Mover. (*c*) Theophrastus compiled a large work containing the views of previous Greek philosophers on nature, God etc. This became the source for numerous later historians of Greek philosophy. It is not too much to say that until comparatively recent times historians of pre-Socratic philosophy were dominated by the influence of Theophrastus. This was

unfortunate because Theophrastus saw all earlier philosophers as mere precursors of Aristotle and forced their ideas into an Aristotelian framework.
(J.L.A.)

Thomism, *see* Aquinas and Neo-Thomism.

Thomas of Sutton. One of the Oxford Dominicans who rallied to the support of Thomas **Aquinas** after the Kilwardby and during the Peckham offensives from Canterbury. His early writings, which began from about 1286, centre on the soul as single substantial form of the body. His *Contra Pluralitatem Formarum* has been included by several editions among the works of Thomas Aquinas. His later writings, to about 1315, find him facing a new attack, from the developed Aristotelianism of **Scotus**, though the *Liber Propugnatorius*, ascribed to him, may be by another *Thomas Anglicus*, possibly the Dominican Jorz, or Joyce. He became a resolute defender of the distinction between essence and existence in finite beings, though perhaps he hardened existence into a "something", *aliquid reale, positivum et absolutum*, in answering Henry of Ghent to whom it was a *respectus* or relation to the Creator. (T.G.)

Toulmin, Stephen Edelston (1922–), an Englishman, was Professor of Philosophy in the University of Leeds. His *Place of Reason in Ethics* (1950) was the earliest book on ethics to present the viewpoint of modern linguistic analysis. He there maintains that the criteria of good reasons in ethical discussion can be elicited from the uses of such words as "ethics" and "ethical"; that ethical disagreement is essentially disagreement whether there is or is not good reason for some ethical conclusion; and that in ethics we proceed from grounds or reasons which are purely factual to normative ethical conclusions by a specifically ethical mode of argument which is neither deductive nor inductive in character. In *Philosophy of Science: An Introduction* (1953) Toulmin, with an eye especially on physics, gives an account of scientific theorising as being more like the making of maps to enable oneself to find one's way about than the process of generalization which is described in the classical theories of induction; he distinguishes between laws and principles, and shows how part of the understanding of a law is to know its scope of application. His *The Uses of Ar-*

gument (1958) is an attempt to redescribe the nature and function of arguments in terms more revealing than those traditionally used in logic textbooks.
(J.O.U.)

Truth. Philosophers have been concerned principally with two questions about truth; the first problem is concerned with the meaning of the word "true", the second with the criterion or criteria by which we can decide on the truth or falsity of statements. Most commonly philosophers have failed to distinguish these two questions and have offered as an answer to one of the questions what might be regarded as a possible answer to the other. But it is easy to see that there is such a distinction if we consider the views of a philosopher who does see and make the distinction; thus F. C. S. **Schiller** maintained that in meaning "true" was an evaluative term, meaning something like "good to believe", but as a **pragmatist** he maintained that the criterion of truth was utility.

The two most famous theories of truth, the correspondence theory and the coherence theory, have usually been represented as being theories about the meaning of "true"; so interpreted the correspondence theory asserts that "true" means "coheres with the facts" and the coherence theory asserts that "true" means "coheres with the body of accepted statements". The most obvious criticism of the coherence theory is that while it has considerable plausibility as a statement of one criterion of truth it hardly gives the meaning of "true"; we do treat the coherence of a statement with what we already believe as one reason, though not a sufficient reason, for accepting it as true, but if coherence is a test of truth it cannot be the same thing as truth. Criticism of the correspondence theory is more difficult and complex; from one point of view it seems that to say that truth is correspondence with fact is a mere platitude, but we get into difficulties when we try to give a clear meaning to "correspondence" and "fact". No doubt it is true that there are no centaurs, and we may say that the statement that there are no centaurs corresponds with the facts; but it is hard to see what sort of status the "fact" of there being no centaurs has and what sort of relation, called "correspondence", it can enter into with a statement. Thus the correspondence theory is liable to resolve itself into a mere metaphor.

A difficulty much noticed in recent years is that the phrase "it is true that" seems to add nothing to the meaning of sentences in which it occurs; it is hard to see what extra value is added if, instead of saying "the cat is on the mat", we say "it is true that the cat it on the mat". The real use of the word "true" appears to be in such expressions as "that is true", where it enables us to confirm a statement without repeating it. These points have led some philosophers, notably **Strawson**, to hold the view that the word "true" is rather a signal of assent, or concession, or admission, functioning more like the word "yes", than like a word signifying a quality or relation. Schiller's view, mentioned above, that "true" is a term of evaluation is closely related to this view.

Incautious pragmatists have sometimes spoken as though they identified the meaning of "true" with "useful to believe", though cautious pragmatists like Schiller avoided this trap. In putting forward utility as a criterion of truth, the pragmatists were not wishing to say that if it would be pleasant if something were true, we should count it as true; they rather wished to emphasize that systems of human beliefs and the concepts employed in them were man-made interpretations of the world to enable him to cope with it. If we thus think of statements as interpretations, we cannot divorce the question of their satisfactoriness from the question whether they do the job that they are intended to do.

Finally, a very celebrated paper by Tarski, "The Concept of Truth in Formalized Languages" should be mentioned. In this paper Tarski defines "truth" as a term in a calculus in a way that gives it a function in a calculus analogous to the function of "true" in ordinary language. It is quite certain that this definition cannot be applied directly to our ordinary notion of truth; whether it has any relevance to the philosophical problem of truth is a highly technical and disputable question. Such views as Tarski's are called semantic theories of truth. (J.O.U.)

U

Universals, in the first instance, are abstract objects such as qualities, relations and numbers, things which cannot be straightforwardly located in space and time. They are contrasted with particulars and are sometimes defined as the objects of thought, while particulars are the objects of perception or sensation. Particulars are sometimes identified with concrete objects in space and time, sometimes with that element of a concrete object which individuates it, that is, distinguishes it from everything else however similar in character. It is perhaps preferable to retain the term "particular" for the latter idea and to call concrete objects "individuals", as being made up of both a particular and universals. On this view a particular would be an uncharacterized spatio-temporal position, the bare possibility of an object. Some such idea is one of the roots of the traditional concept of substance.

Two main sorts of universals can be distinguished: predicative universals, the properties and relations that are the meaning of general terms or predicates, and formal universals, the abstract entities of **mathematics**. The difference is that while predicative universals can and usually do have instances, formal universals are rather ideal limits to which actual things more or less closely approximate. The existence of predicative universals (redness, justice, betweenness etc.) is argued for as a necessary condition of the predicative use of general terms. We cannot think or speak without general terms, every statement contains one such term as "red" or "earlier than", and we are never aware of anything except as having some property or standing in a relation. In other words, individual things fall into kinds, the world exhibits recurrences and similarities. Clearly there are general terms and they have meanings. But does it follow that there actually exist things which are the meanings of general terms? Could one not say that there is one set of things, namely concrete objects, to which singular terms are related in one way (each standing for one concrete thing) and general terms related in another (each applying to many)? The difficulty with this view (a form of **nominalism**) is that we can use general terms correctly without having been told in advance all the things to which they apply. There are, that is to say, sets of things in which a few members of the set are representative of the rest. Positive theories of universals are attempts to explain this peculiar and important fact. A predicative universal is what the members of a natural set of this kind have in common.

The existence of formal universals is argued for on two related grounds: abstract reference and necessary truth. Some true statements ("2 x 2 = 4" and "tuberculosis is decreasing") refer not to concrete things but to entities that are neither in space nor time. But what a true statement refers to must exist. Again, there are some truths which we know for certain simply by the use of reason and without any observation of the spatio-temporal world (such as "axb = bxa" and "Red is a colour"). Universals, then, may be thought of as the subject-matter of necessary or **a priori** knowledge; to use one's reason is to examine and elicit their invariable qualities and relations. The argument from predication is more emphasised at the present time than the argument from abstract reference and necessary knowledge. For it is widely held that all abstract reference is apparent and that the principle of reference does not apply to necessary truths. Contingent propositions with abstract subjects must refer to existing things if true. But what they refer to, and so presuppose the existence of, is ordinary concrete things. "Tuberculosis is decreasing" really refers to tuberculosis sufferers, not to the disease itself. It is an idiomatic, and potentially misleading, way of saying "fewer people suffer from tuberculosis nowadays". Necessary propositions refer to nothing, for they depend for their truth, not on the existence of anything, but on the meaning of the words used to express them. "Mary's husband is married to Mary" is a necessary truth whether Mary is married or single.

The most famous account of our ability to apply predicative general terms to things we have not come across before is **realism**, or, less confusingly, conceptual realism. On this view we can apply one general term to many things because we are aware of the common property they possess. This common property cannot be in space and time since, if it were, it would exhibit the logically insufferable characteristic of being in many different places at one and the same time. Furthermore there would be many such properties in many places at the same time. This theory suggests that universals are directly accessible to the mind in a way that is not easy to accept. It also has a formal defect common to all theories of universals in seeming to generate an infinite regress. I can tell that this particular thing is hard because I am aware of the abstract

universal Hardness and of the fact that the universal inheres in the thing. But to discern this fact of inherence I must be aware of the abstract universal Inherence and so on. This defect of platonism, first formulated in **Plato**'s own *Parmenides*, led **Aristotle** to say that universals were not abstract and "separated" from the things they inhered in but were to be found in the common world of space and time along with particular objects. What this presumably means is that Hardness is a vast fragmentary object, cropping up here and there all over the place. If so it would be little suited to its theoretical task, for people who know the meaning of the word *hard* perfectly well are acquainted with only a minute portion of this total object. They could only find out what the rest of it was composed of if they already knew the meaning of the word. Furthermore universals with no instances such as *Ghost* and *Female Pope* would be one and the same universal and the two terms would have one and the same meaning, which they plainly do not.

The two traditional alternatives to realism are **conceptualism**, which asserts that we apply general terms to new things through the use of some mental standard, a concept or image, and nominalism, the view that the things to which a general term applies have no more in common than the fact that men apply that general term to them. In practice neither of these theories is often held in its full rigour. Without some basis in the nature of the things in question, the general correspondence between different people's concepts and linguistic practices would be an unintelligible miracle. Thus conceptualists like **Abelard** and **Locke** say that concepts are based on the similarities of things; and nominalists like **Hobbes** and many contemporary philosophers explain the application of general terms by the similarity of the things they apply to either to one another or to some standard thing or group of things. Realists argue that since similarity is itself a universal these modifications are no more than realism in disguise.

Apart from absolutely pure nominalism all theories of universals are exposed to the regress argument. But this does not mean that what they say is false. It is rather that what is really a repetition in other words of the puzzling fact of the reapplicability of general terms has been misinterpreted as an explanation of it. To say that we can recognize hard things as hard because they all have the common property of being hard or fall under the concept of hardness is uninformative. To be aware of the common property or to possess the concept is simply and solely to know how to use the general term, above all in the recognition and classification of things. (A.Q.)

Urban, Wilbur Marshall (1873–1952), American philosopher, an advocate of philosophical **idealism**. His main interest was in theory of value and in linguistics. His principal publications were the following: *Valuation* (1909); *The Intelligible World; Metaphysics and Value* (1929); *Fundamentals of Ethics* (1930); *Language and Reality* (1939); and *Beyond Realism and Idealism* (1949). (J.W.S.)

Utilitarianism. The characteristic English empirical theory of ethics, which maintains:

(1) The *rightness* of an action is to be judged by the contribution it makes to the increase of human happiness or the decrease of human misery. The moral validity of a law or rule, the value of an institution, depends on the same considerations. Nothing else matters: e.g. conformity to revelation, authority, tradition, even "moral sense" or conscience: even perhaps, contract or history. An action may pass any of these tests, flatter the conscience of the doer, and yet bring deliberate misery and ruin. What matters is the contribution to happiness.

(2) Hence (on reflexion) pleasure is the only thing *good in itself* and pain the only thing evil in itself. Happiness includes pleasure and freedom from pain: perhaps such a balance of pleasures as itself produces further pleasure. For example, **Bentham**'s formulation in his *Principles of Morals and Legislation*, 1789, Chapter I (2) is: "By the principle of utility is meant that principle which approves or disapproves of every action whatsoever, according to the tendency which it appears to have to augment or diminish the happiness of the party whose interest is in question . . . if that party be the community in general, then the happiness of the community." If the tendency of an action to increase the happiness of the community (in so far as they are concerned in it) is greater than any tendency it has to diminish it, then it is "conformable to the principle of util-

ity". One may then say that it is a right action (one that ought to be done): or at least that it is not a wrong action.

The theory has its origins in Greek thought: in modern times it is derived from certain views of **Hobbes** and **Locke**: and was formulated by **Hutcheson** in 1726. A version of the theory was elaborated by **Hume** as a purely descriptive account of the way in which men make moral judgments: directly moralistic versions were given by Jospeh Priestley and William Paley; and practical applications in **jurisprudence** were worked out by Helvetius in France and Beccaria in Italy. Jeremy Bentham drew upon all these predecessors, setting out a clear and solid theory and making the widest possible use of it in his attacks upon the constitutional, economic, legal and social problems of his day. James **Mill**'s version is simpler and more egotistical. J. S. **Mill**'s *Utilitarianism* (1863), is a more complicated philosophy altogether and re-introduces many factors which Bentham had painstakingly eliminated. Henry **Sidgwick** and (with a difference) Herbert **Spencer** are in the tradition: G. E. **Moore** (*Principia Ethica*, 1903) made a fundamental modification. He accepted the view that the rightness of an action depends on the good or bad consequences that follow it: but held that many sorts of things (not pleasures and pains only, if at all) are good in themselves or bad in themselves. The view that pleasure alone is good, he traced to a fallacy and rejected. Moore's theory is not an expression of the original utilitarian point of view that what matters is human happiness or pleasure. What matters is what is *good*: and what kinds of things are good is to be learned by intuition.

"Pleasure and pleasure alone is good in itself." We may imagine a man tasting food, or settling himself to rest: even the malefactor zestfully attacking his victim. We may think of these pleasures as if they were a kind of sensation: and suppose that it is for the sake of this sensation that we eat, or rest, or do violence, so also for the sake of remote pleasures or for the sake of avoiding greater pains in the future, we work or save or suffer pains. It is the pleasure (or freedom from pain) that an object brings that makes us call it "good" – it is the pain or deprivation of expected pleasure that an object brings, that makes us call it "bad". In effect Bentham regards "good" and "bad" as expressive terms which in certain contexts we apply to things that bring pleasure or pain. And he is content to say that one pleasure is *better* than another only if it is (in one or more dimension) *a greater pleasure*. This ethical view (that pleasures are the only things good or desirable in themselves) is weakened by association with the metaphysical doctrine of psychological **hedonism**. For on that view all the objects that men aim at "for their own sakes" or "as ends not simply means", must be "pleasures". The ethical doctrine is weakened because the scope of "pleasure" is widened to include so many things one would expect a hedonist to repudiate (e.g. successfully completing a prolonged fast). Mill appeals to this metaphysical doctrine in order to establish the view that the man who aims at knowledge or virtue *for its own sake*, is still pursuing "pleasure". There are (he says) many objectives which were once pursued only as means to some pleasant end, but which (by association and by habit) have come to be pursued without reference to the original end. Saving money is one of Mill's examples: abiding by the rules of virtue at all costs, is another. So that "pleasure" now includes things that are desired only by a confusion of thought and things that are pursued by mere habit and without desire: nor is there any clear distinction between things desired as means and things desired for their own sake. Having widened "pleasure", Mill goes on to introduce a distinction between "lower" and "higher" pleasures. The higher pleasures are not known to be "greater" by Bentham's criteria: but nevertheless they are to be preferred. On this view it is a trivial point that only pleasure can be desired for its own sake: what really matters is that *some* of the objects of desires are higher pleasures. Mill's position is a half-way house on the road to the ideal or agathistic theory of G. E. Moore. "Pleasure and pleasure alone is good in itself" has some value as a war-cry: but so hospitable a doctrine is bound to include the *oddest* pleasures and ends up by counting as "pleasure", whatever is made the object of desire. The moral justification of this can hardly be that all these pleasures are good: it is rather that it is right or proper for *persons* to choose for themselves. This doctrine (wholly congenial to Bentham as to Mill) lacks the characteristic "scientific" features which the calculation of pains and pleasures was supposed to introduce.

"Actions are right in proportion as they tend to produce happiness, wrong as they tend to produce the reverse of happiness." G. E. Moore, in his account of utilitarianism, maintained that an action is right if its consequences would in fact be better than those of any other action which could be performed instead. Since we can never *know* what the consequences of an action will be (but can only judge what they are likely to be), it follows that when a man debates whether to do action A or action B, he can never *know* which action is right. The earlier utilitarians sometimes suggested this: but their real view seems to have been that "right" and "wrong" are to be attributed by reference to probable consequences. – (Compare Bentham: "the tendency which it appears to have to augment or diminish the happiness etc."). We think of the right act as what a man ought to do: and this has to be judged by reference to the probable consequences as they appear at the time of decision. So we may conclude that on this point Moore was mistaken. Moore also held that in deciding whether or not a given action would be right, it is the consequences (he should have said probable consequences) *of that action singly considered*, which are to be taken into account. (So also Bentham.) Such a view seems to offend against common-sense. We are accustomed to think of actions as falling into certain kinds: some of these kinds are never to be performed: other kinds always when opportunity arises; and that there are many other kinds of actions between which we are expected to choose by considering consequences. For example, in making choices for one's own life one has often to decide simply by reference to probable consequences. But one ought not even to consider cheating or lying as possible actions because all actions of those sorts are always wrong. On this point the Utilitarians will say (1) No doubt cheating and lying and killing have got a bad name because they almost always have very bad consequences. A moral rule against an action of a certain *kind*, may be regarded as a rule of thumb which shows us that such actions are to be avoided on almost all occasions; (2) Social Life is possible only if certain conventions are almost always followed, for example telling the truth. On a given occasion an immediate consequence of a lie may be good: but in almost all cases there is a further consequence to be considered. Any breach

368

[continued on p. 385

PLATE 81. SANTAYANA, George (1863–1952), photograph taken at Harvard University during his professorship there.

PLATE 82. SARTRE, Jean Paul (1905–), photographed August 2 1947.

PLATE 83. SCHOPENHAUER, Arthur (1788–1860), engraving.

PLATE 84. SCOTUS, John Duns (*c.* 1266–1308), painting by Justus van Ghent (*fl* 1446–1480/5).
(*Barberini Palace, Rome*)

PLATE 85. SENECA, Lucius Annaeus (c. 5 B.C.–65 A.D.), bronze head from Herculaneum.
(National Museum, Naples)

PLATE 86. SIDGWICK, Henry (1828–1900), photograph.

PLATE 87. SOCRATES (469–399 B.C.), bust of Roman date copied from a Greek original of 395–390 B.C. (*National Museum, Naples*)

PLATE 88. SPENCER, Herbert (1820–1903), photographed in about 1888.

PLATE 89. SPINOZA, Benedict de (1632–1677), portrait by an unknown artist.
(*Herzog August Bibliothek, Wolfenbüttel*)

PLATE 90.   SPINOZA, Benedict de (1632–1677): the house on the Paviljoensgracht at The Hague in which Spinoza lodged, is now commemorated by the statue in front of it.

378

Photo: Press and Information Office of the Federal Republic of Germany, London

PLATE 91. TÜBINGEN UNIVERSITY, founded in 1536, is a prominent centre of philosophical study and included Hegel among its pupils.

Photo : *Stearn and Sons*

PLATE 92.   WARD, James (1843–1925), photographed in 1892.
(*Trinity College, Cambridge*)

Photo: Radio Times Hulton Picture Library

PLATE 93. WHEWELL, William (1794–1866), painting.

PLATE 94. WHITEHEAD, Alfred North (1861–1947), pencil portrait drawn in 1928 by Paul Drury (1903–).
(*Trinity College, Cambridge*)

PLATE 95. WILSON, John Cook (1849–1915), photograph.

Photo: Anderson

PLATE 96. ZENO of Citium (c. 333–262 B.C.), bust found at Herculaneum. (National Museum, Naples) of the convention is likely to weaken it – chiefly by lowering public confidence in it. And although this consequence may touch the parties immediately concerned very lightly, it is not to be taken lightly, because it is an injury to "the general happiness". For this reason it is indeed *generally* wrong to lie even where the more obvious consequences are good. But if there should be a case where the consequence of a lie (even including the bad effect it has on public confidence) are not so bad as the consequences of not telling the lie – then the utilitarian would hold that the particular lie is right.

In this connexion, it has been argued that the utilitarianism put forward in Mill's essays is not the same theory as that of Bentham, Sidgwick and Moore. Mill's utilitarianism (it is said) is *restricted* in a most important way. For he recognizes that the test of the rightness or wrongness of individual actions is not normally the test of their consequences: the test lies in the application of a moral rule – or (as Mill calls it) a secondary principle. So that an act of theft is wrong because there is a rule against stealing: and morality consists of "rules and precepts for human conduct". But these rules may themselves be tested and found to be valid or invalid. The test is a utilitarian one: a rule is valid if the consequences of its being generally observed are better than the consequences of the rule's not being generally observed – and better also than the consequences of the general observance of any alternative rule on the same subject. According to this interpretation, Mill would hold it proper to follow the moral rule unless (1) one were prepared to question the validity of the rule in general on utilitarian grounds; or (2) there was a conflict of rules – the very same course of action being required by one rule and forbidden by another. In the latter case Mill clearly says that the proper procedure is to set aside both the "secondary principles" and appeal directly to "first principles" – i.e. to the test of the goodness or badness of the consequences of doing and of not doing the action in question.

Certainly Mill attaches great importance to following moral rules even at the greatest cost to oneself. But can a utilitarian hold that there is a virtue in following a rule *for its own sake*? The situation is complicated in the case of what Hume called the "Artificial Virtues" (justice, keeping promises, telling the truth etc.). As he showed, these virtues are possible only where certain institutions exist: and that means, where certain rules of conduct are generally followed. One cannot keep a promise or break a promise unless society has the institution of promising: just as one cannot defraud a residuary legatee in a society which has no law or custom of testation. In the case of the artificial virtues, then, it is true to say that one *could not* display them if one were guided simply by the First Principle of doing the action which promises the best consequences. The institutions which give rise to honesty in property, good faith in promises (and the reverse) presuppose that *most people* are bound by the rules of property and good faith and do *not* attempt to follow the course which seems to have the best consequences. All this shows that the artificial virtues are particularly liable to be undermined by *irregular* conduct: since *our chief reason* for observing them is the expectation that everyone else will always do the same. (This is not so in the case of kindness, generosity, saving life etc. – Hume's Natural Virtues which are worth practising whether or not *everybody* does so.) The argument cannot of course go so far as to show that such rules ought never to be broken. The question is: Does it succeed in explaining on utilitarian principles, why we feel that the rules about justice and promise-keeping are so important, and why it is always such a serious matter to break them? And it has to be borne in mind that the argument does not apply to the "Natural Virtues", some of which are taken at least as seriously as any of the artificial ones. It is argued by anti-utilitarians that we know that certain rules are binding: and know which of the rules are the most binding: and that we know this without having the information that would be necessary to infer it on utilitarian grounds. (K.B.)

V

Venn, John (1834–1923), born at Hull, England. After reading mathematics at Cambridge, where he was sixth wrangler in 1857, he was elected to a fellowship at Gonville and Caius College and took orders in the Church of England. (He later renounced his clerical status.) He returned to Cambridge in 1862 on his appointment as a college lecturer in moral science and the rest of his long career was spent in teaching and writing. From

1903 to his death, he was president of his college. He wrote three influential books on logic, *The Logic of Chance* (1866), *Symbolic Logic* (1881) and *Principles of Empirical or Inductive Logic* (1889). The first was the most important. It is a careful statement of the "frequency" theory of **probability** which was here expounded for the first time. His work is largely original though he worked from suggestions put forward by the mathematician, R. L. Ellis. Venn's account of probability has been extensively developed and criticised in the present century.

Symbolic Logic though containing little original work of importance is a thorough and readable survey of previous work in symbolic logic. It contains an extraordinarily full bibliography drawing attention among other important books to the long neglected but immensely fruitful work of **Frege**, *Begriffschrift*, then very recently published. Indeed, it is surprising in view of Venn's familiarity with the work of Frege, Schröder and **Peirce**, that he did not advance the development of logic far more than he did. *Principles of Empirical or Inductive Logic* is a less important book relying largely though not uncritically on the work of J. S. **Mill**. Curiously, Venn's own ideas on probability are little used there. (D.J.O'C.)

Vienna Circle was the group of logical **positivists** or, as they are sometimes called, logical **empiricists** who belonged to the University of Vienna in the nineteen-twenties and 'thirties. In 1895 a Chair of Philosophy of the Inductive Sciences had been founded in Vienna for Ernst **Mach**. Moritz **Schlick** was elected to this chair in 1922 and very soon an informal circle of colleagues and senior pupils formed about him; they were united by a common interest in the sciences and mathematics, a general acceptance of the positivistic outlook of Mach and a recognition of the importance of the developing science of mathematical logic. Among the more important of these are Friedrich Waismann, Rudolf **Carnap**, Otto Neurath, E. Zilsel, Herbert Feigl, B. von Juhos, Felix Kaufmann, Victor Kraft, Hans Hahn and Kurt Goedel. Though **Wittgenstein** was living in Austria at this time and was a personal friend of some of the members of this group he never was a member of it; but his *Tractatus Logico-philosophicus* greatly in-

fluenced it. In 1929 the Circle was given a more formal status and a pamphlet was issued setting out its basic tenets and aims. In 1930 the magazine *Erkenntnis* was founded to be the organ of publication of the group. Immense interest in the work of the Circle was aroused in the early 1930s both in Europe and in America; the group itself, however, was soon to be dispersed, because of the assassination of Schlick in 1936, the hostility of the Nazis after the *Anschluss* and finally the war in 1939. Many members of the group have subsequently led distinguished philosophical careers in other countries and the circle has had its greatest influence outside the German-speaking countries in which it originated; but Victor Kraft, a junior member of the circle is now Professor of Philosophy at Vienna. (J.O.U.)

Vitoria, Francis de, born between 1483 and 1486 in Old Castile, Spain. A Dominican Master of Paris, Valladolid, and Salamanca, he brought to the teaching of scholastic philosophy in his *Relectiones*, or published conferences, a new dignity and warmth. The founder of the great School of Spanish Thomists, he took a leading part in the university movement for promoting justice for the natives of Spanish America which earned the grateful admiration of Dr Johnson. He criticized the prevailing **nominalism** in philosophy, but above all is famous as the Father of International Law. He developed the jurisprudence of Thomas **Aquinas**, extending the *Jus Gentium* (law of nations) of the Roman legal texts into an organic instrument of concord for the whole *Respublica Humana* (community of mankind) which allows for pacts between States but also appeals to a higher sovereignty. (T.G.)

W

Ward, James (1843–1925), Englishman, Professor of Mental Philosophy and Logic 1879–1925, a Fellow of Trinity College, Cambridge, from 1875. He had entered the college in 1873, after resigning from the Congregational ministry, for which he had been educated at Spring Hill College, Birmingham, besides studying philosophy at Berlin and Göttingen. His interests were wide, ranging from biology to his elaborate **metaphysics**, set out in his two series of Gifford Lectures. The first series is mainly critical of **Spencer** and "physics treated as metaphysics", preferring history as a model of reality; the second develops under the influence of **Leibniz** and Lotze a pluralistic system of minds, (matter being composed of interacting mindlike monads), which is somehow to "leave room for" a unifying **theism**.

But it is his work as a philosophical psychologist which gives him historical importance. His *Encyclopaedia Britannica* article "Psychology" in 1886 brought about the downfall in Britain of the associationist psychology, which had attempted to reduce mental life to a system of experiences, or "presentations", mechanically interrelated by laws like those which relate bodies in physics. Most notably, Ward maintained that there must always be a *subject* to which these presentations occur. This psychological subject, or "Pure Ego", is not only aware of presentations, but feels pleased and pained in consequence, and has the power of variously distributing attention to the presentations, which form a continuum at any one moment (a "field of consciousness") and from one moment to another. Changes in this continuum occur objectively, but also by the selective attention of the subject; and it is a continuum precisely because an entirely new field of consciousness never arises but only a partial change within the preceding field. Indeed Ward denies that any presentation is ever "absolutely new". The bulk of the article was eventually incorporated in his book *Psychological Principles*. Ward's views in this field are extremely hard to classify, because they seem to continue the intermixture of philosophy with the empirical science of psychology, a confusion of which **Bradley** accused Ward at the time, and which is now generally anathema to philosophers and psychologists alike. Perhaps for this reason, Ward, in spite of changing the face of psychology, is now hardly read, and has had no lasting influence; among those he taught at Cambridge **Russell** and **Moore** owe nothing to his philosophy, while Stout, who does, has himself found little following. (R.HALL)

Plate 92, page 380.

Whewell, William (1794-1866), British philosopher, a graduate of Trinity College, Cambridge. He spent the rest of his life as a Fellow at the college, becoming Master in 1841. Elected F.R.S. in 1820, he was Professor of Mineralogy 1828-32, and Moral Philosophy 1838-55.

Whewell pioneered the study of scientific method, stressing the importance of induction in it; but in line with his general acceptance of Kantian Philosophy he regarded the "mysterious step" from the observation of particular facts to the discovery of general principles relating them as dependent on ideas formed by the understanding. That is to say, for the production of a scientific theory the mere collection of facts is inadequate; what is necessary is "a true *colligation* of facts by means of an exact and appropriate conception". Here and elsewhere he is in effect describing the hypothetico-deductive method: for example, "success seems to consist in framing several tentative hypotheses and selecting the right one". This emphasis on the value of hypotheses in science is his permanent contribution. It led directly to controversy with J. S. **Mill** because Whewell maintained that the formation of an explanatory hypothesis *was* the induction, and since the facts explained could then be deduced from the hypothesis, **induction** and **deduction** were not different kinds of reasoning as Mill thought, but each the other in reverse: "deduction justified by calculation what induction has happily guessed". The dispute was unreal, for Whewell was interested in, and undoubtedly right about, the method of discovery in science, whereas Mill was mainly concerned with the logic of induction as a method of proof, or "process of analysis", proceeding from particular premises and usually terminating in a general conclusion.

Whewell's views on induction and scientific method appeared in his *Philosophy of the Inductive Sciences*. They rested on the immense store of information in his earlier *History*, without which Mill, by his own confession, would have been unable to write the parts of his *Logic* dealing with induction and attacking the later book. Whewell also wrote on mathematical and moral philosophy, in both as an intuitionist, and in both Mill selected him for attack, accusing him of making all philosophy a support for "any opinions which happened to be established". Whewell was indeed the champion of the established order in every field.

Probably the most learned man of the early Victorian age, when he was famous, Whewell's voluminous works are now little read; but as a philosopher of science he deserves more attention than Mill. (R.HALL)

Plate 93, page 381.

Whitehead, Alfred North (1861–1947), born at Ramsgate in the Isle of Thanet in East Kent, England, where his father was vicar. His boyhood, spent first in Ramsgate and later in the country parish of St Peter's-in-Thanet, a countryside full of historical associations, gave him a strong sense of the continuity of the life of a society over the generations, and of religion as intimately bound up with its way of life. This impression was strengthened through his schooldays at Sherborne, an ancient public school in Dorset. Here he was taught history and classics in the Whig tradition, as conveying lessons in liberal principles and analogies with contemporary institutions and events. The historical reflections found in Whitehead's books shew that he kept this practical interest in history, as illustrating general ideas which could also be seen exemplified in contemporary ways of life. (For an account of his boyhood and education, see the biographical articles in *Essays in Science and Philosophy*). He also studied a good deal of mathematics, and went up to Trinity College Cambridge as a mathematical scholar in 1880, where he was subsequently elected to a fellowship in mathematics. Here he began the collaboration with **Russell** on the logical foundations of mathematics which led to the three volumes of *Principia Mathematica*. This interest was first shown in the *Treatise on Universal Algebra* (1903), and in *Mathematical Concepts of the Material World* (1905). The continuity of this early work with Whitehead's later philosophical interests has been shown by Dr V. Lowe in his contribution to the volume on A. N. Whitehead in the *Library of Living Philosophers* (Northwestern University), and the close resemblance between the view of schemes of mathematical postulates in *Mathematical Concepts of the Material World* and his later views on metaphysical theories has been shown by Dr. W. Mays *The Philosophy of Whitehead* (1959). In 1910 Whitehead moved to London, where he held the chair of Applied Mathematics at the Imperial College of Science in South Kensington until 1924, when he was invited to Harvard University as Professor of Philosophy, remaining in Cambridge, Massachusetts, until his death. With his wife (Evelyn Willoughby née Wade) he gained the reputation of a brilliant conversationalist, keeping open house to a succession of his pupils, colleagues and visitors. He was awarded the Order of Merit in 1945.

Whitehead's philosophy shows an attempt to combine (*a*) his logico-mathematical interest in abstract relational systems, (*b*) "cosmology" (not in the technical sense used in astro-physics, but in the broad sense of an interpretation of the world suggested by general notions underlying physical science); and (*c*) his moral and religious and also aesthetic interest in human relationships within societies. (Whitehead's interest in religion was not, however, merely sociological; he saw it also as concerned with man's relation to God thought of as the permanent ground of the world process). In his early logical work he pursued the suggestion, originating from **Frege**, that mathematics can be shown to be derivative from certain formal logical relationships. These make possible the development of deductive systems which supply, as it were, blank cheques of possible forms of relations, some of which may be filled in by "values" in empirical applications. In his interest in the general ideas underlying the physical science of his time, he was impressed chiefly by the field theories in physics, and the notion of energy as he learnt it from Sir J. J. Thompson, by whom it was presented as a vector magnitude, a measurable flux passing from one natural event to another. This notion, he thought, implied that the physical ultimates should be thought of as lines of force with a direction, not as particles of matter occupying points of space at instants of time. This led him, as early as the 1905 paper on *Mathematical Concepts of the Material World*, to an attack on the classical Newtonian concepts. The notion of lines of force overlapping one another in "fields" was seen as analogous to the logico-topological device of "Extensive Abstraction" a method he had devised by which geometrical elements such as points and lines are defined not as real or ideal entities, but relationally in terms of ways in which volumes of different kinds, such as circles rectangles or elipses, may systematically extend over or overlap one another (see *The Anatomy of Some Scientific Ideas*, republished in *The Organisation of Thought* and *The Aims of Education*).

The logical and epistemological notions connected with this way of regarding the physical world were developed in the three books of Whitehead's "middle" period, *The Principles of Natural Knowledge* (1919) *The Concept of Nature* (1920), and *The Principle of Relativity* (1922). Here he was concerned on the one hand with the framing of deductive systems of precise concepts, and on the other hand with the interpretation of these in the data of experience. "Experience", he believed, comes to us in the first instance in the form of vaguely interconnected *continua* of feelings, and not in the form of clear-cut sense-data. This led him to a repudiation of the Humean sense-datum analysis which started from the vaguer *continua* of organic sensation. Thus he considered that his basic logical notions of the relations of "Whole and Part", systematic overlapping, and "Extensive Connection" were more congenial than atomistic notions in the analysis of our basic experience; we should start, he believed, not from clear cut items; but from the sense of *something going on*, with a spatio-temporal spread. Whitehead at times claimed that his logical schemes could be reached by a process of idealizing and abstracting from the crude data of experience. This seems to underestimate the extent to which a notion such as the Method of Extensive Abstraction is a topological device for defining points and straight lines, and very unlike anything that can be derived from sense experience. But in seeing the need to devise logical and topological notions to deal with structures within an indeterminate continuum, he was fastening on a genuine problem, even if his own formulation of it was not sufficiently clearly developed to hold the attention and interest of his contemporaries or immediate post-contemporaries, most of whom have continued to work with logical notions related to the atomistic form of analysis.

In the books of his middle period Whitehead was concerned to give a general account of the "relatedness of nature" in terms of a logical scheme based on the notion of "Extensive Connection". In the books of his last period (*Science and the Modern World* (1926), *Process and Reality* (1929) and *Adventures of Ideas* (1933), he turned to the construction of a comprehensive metaphysical system, based on these notions, but centring in a speculative account of what it is to be an "actual entity" in process of development within nature as so related.

Here he presents a perspective view of structures within the continuum of natural events, each unified from its own centre, this centre being looked on as the locus of an active subject of experience, forming itself from its interrelations with the whole of its environment; in Whitehead's own terminology, it is a "concrescence of prehension". The nearest analogy among traditional metaphysical views would be **Leibniz**'s Monads; Whitehead's "actual entities" are, however, not "windowless", that is, undergoing purely internal development but they are in active interaction with each other throughout nature. Whitehead looked on this as a generalized notion of organic interconnection; indeed he described his later work as a "philosophy of organism". Its treatment in his later books is complicated by the use of terminology drawn not only from biology but from introspective psychology (for example the notion of "feelings" is used in a highly general sense). It is also complicated by his attempt to combine logical, mathematical, physical, biological, psychological, and indeed aesthetic and religious notions within the same scheme, looking on these as all in various ways descriptive of elements in real processes within nature, and also (he hoped) all finally to be seen as particular exemplifications of certain very general "metaphysical" principles. He acknowledged that the attempt to reach these completely general principles was unlikely finally to be successful, although he hoped metaphysical schemes might be produced which should approximate to them. His belief in the importance of aiming at a comprehensive system led him to try and produce such a scheme by generalizing principles derived from varied sources. These, however, may belong to different levels of abstraction or to different logical types, so that as Whitehead presents them they do not readily cohere in a single system. In the earlier work he had been concerned with logical devices by which orderly schemes of exact concepts could be connected with sensory experience, which is vague and fragmentary and also (he believed) qualitative, emotionally toned and teleologically directed. In this later work there is a gigantic attempt to bridge this gap by representing the scheme of general notions itself as derived by "descriptive generalization" from the kind of structure he believed we find in our actual experience. In this way he hoped to overcome the "bifurcation" between man and nature, and also the gap between general theory and actual experience. But in so doing he may have underestimated the artificial nature of general theories, and also his phenomenology of actual experience may at times be overinfluenced by his theoretical schemes.

Whitehead's work is many-sided, and has the faults as well as the virtues of a vast attempt to construct a comprehensive system which will "get everything in". It cannot be epitomized adequately, and those wishing to grasp it must be prepared for a sustained effort to enter into an unusual way of thinking, expressed in unusual terminology. Except for the great influence of the work on Symbolic Logic with Russell in *Principia Mathematica*, it has remained on the whole a self-contained form of thought with little direct effect on contemporary philosophy. Prophecy for the future is a gratuitous risk; venturing nonetheless, we suggest that even with a return of metaphysical interest his system as a whole is unlikely to be studied as are the systems of, say, **Spinoza**, or Leibniz, but that some of his seminal ideas may be taken up and developed, perhaps in other and more rigorous ways. Such might be (*a*) his attempt to relate symbolic logic to the study of *continua* instead of to discrete elements; (*b*) his belief in the primacy for a theory of knowledge of organic over visual sensation; and (*c*) his attempt to defend an "efficacious" as distinct from a "regularity" view of Causation, modelled on directly experienced transactions of a sentient agent within an environment. Some features of this view of organic interconnection, thought of in terms of overlapping fields of relationships, have already been drawn on in sociological theory. And certain of his books, notably *Science and the Modern World* and *Adventures of Ideas*, are likely to be read not only for the theoretical notions which they only partially present, but for their wealth of humane, and sometimes witty and penetrating, observations on the history of ideas and on man's life in society.

Plate 94, page 382. (D.M.E.)

William of Ockham (?–1347), English scholastic philosopher, a Friar Minor. He began to lecture at Oxford as a Bachelor about 1318 and since he never proceeded Master became known to his followers as *Venerabilis Inceptor*. In 1324 he was summoned to Avignon at the instigation of the Chan-cellor of his University, to reply to criticisms of his teaching before a Papal commission. After four years there he threw in his fortunes with the Emperor Lewis of Bavaria a few weeks after the latter had declared Pope John XXII deposed. Thenceforward till his death his pen was at the service of the Empire. He died at Munich while negotiations for his reconciliation with the Holy See were still in progress.

The dissolvent influence of Ockham and Ockhamism on previous ways of medieval thought was immense and lasting; many of his writings were political in purpose, but his logic (in a wide sense), developed at Oxford, was always basic and operative. Attempts to portray Ockham as some kind of modified Thomist or again Scotist are evidently mutually stultifying, and are not to be taken seriously. The "terminist" school which he founded knew itself, as it was known, to be wholly at odds with the representatives of the earlier syntheses. But all admit the extreme difficulty of summarizing a system which is in intention rigidly deductive but is not after all a mathematical one. The phrase "labyrinthine maze", of distinctions and sub-distinctions, has often recurred in the literature, and it is this feature which has been chiefly remembered by later ages to the neglect of much that could justly have been found sympathetic and even ancestral.

In **epistemology** Ockham propounded an intuitive knowledge of material singulars which he held to act directly, naturally and infallibly on the mind to produce a total impression of themselves. Theories of abstraction or of illumination are thus discarded. Direct and immediate, this intuition yet issues in concepts which are signs and representatives of their source, representatives with plenary powers so that their marshalling and analysis is a faithful presentation of their original. Here the by now traditional grammatical and logical treatises on modes of signification and the properties of terms, metaphysically neutral in the hands of earlier writers, acquire a definitely conceptualist tinge; Ockham himself cannot be said to have neglected the intuitive approach to singular reality, but his followers widely surrendered themselves to the technicalities of this conceptual reflection, so that logic and nominalism have been and still are often identified as by definition.

Ockham's *formal* logic was made the subject of a

classic paper by J. Salamucha in 1935, translated from Polish into German by J. Bendiek (*Die Aussagenlogik bei Wilhelm Ockham* in *Franziskanische Studien* No. 32, 1950). This argues that the chief stimulator of the vast logical activity towards the close of the Middle Ages was an accomplished though not faultless logician, with some idea of material implication and a preference for proposition logic which he understood to be more basic than the syllogistic. (At the same time we have to reckon with texts which show that his ideal of demonstration was explicitly syllogistic).

In ontology the singular object of intuition was for Ockham, often composite indeed, but always irreducibly singular. No common or universal nature is to be discovered in it, no distinction of essence and existence, no principles of change on the Aristotelian pattern, above all no relations. Matter and form he admitted, but conceived of no longer as incomplete principles of being, rather as themselves no less absolute and singular than the singulars composed of them. "I say then . . . that no natural reason can be found to prove that there is anything imaginable which is not absolute, and hence that no one thing depends on another or postulates another, and conversely that the fact that some things coexist does not prevent each being absolute" (In Sent. 1. d.3, q.2). "Plurality is never to be posited without need" (ibid. d. 27. q. 2) is one form of the principle known as "Ockham's razor", because he applied it frequently and thoroughly. Change is a mere re-shuffling of the singulars, and their origin in creation is a simple positing by God which remains wholly exterior to them. No more as for **Aquinas** does the causality of the first cause permeate their being and operations without exception; "creation" signifies the same thing, with connotation of a negation immediately preceding it; and "conservation" signifies the same thing, with connotation of continuance, and this is only to connote negation of interruption or destruction of its essence".

This atomistic theory of knowledge and being is faithfully reflected in the moral order. The obligatory law of right reason is in the last analysis imposed by an inexplicable divine command in no way rooted in the nature of God or the world. With regard to it every human will has the fullest autonomy, as indeed has God himself. For Ock-

ham the will is not essentially a power of choosing between goods, with which as goods it has a natural affinity, but a power of self-determination in face of isolated beings in respect of which it has been given some arbitrary rights and duties, such as it can further establish for itself. For the juridical and social consequences of this doctrine the reader should consult volumes IV to VI of G. de Lagarde's *La Naissance de l'Esprit Laique au Déclin du Moyen Age*, Paris, 1946. (I.T.)

Wilson, John Cook (1849–1915), British philosopher, Professor of Logic at Oxford. He published little in his lifetime; his one book *Statement and Inference* (1926) is a compilation from the lecture-notes of his pupils made after his death. But his personal influence in Oxford was immense; though brought up in the idealistic tradition of the late nineteenth century he was regarded as the leader of the Oxford realists, of whom **Prichard** and **Ross** are other notable examples, in their opposition to the hitherto supreme idealistic movement represented by F. H. **Bradley**. In particular he insisted that knowledge was a simple indefinable apprehension of the real in opposition to the idealistic contention that the given was inevitably affected by thought. He was also a notable Aristotelian scholar and was deeply interested in the philosophy of **mathematics** regarding which he bitterly opposed the logistical theory of **Russell**. (J.O.U.)

Plate 95, page 383.

Wisdom, (Arthur) John Terence Dibben (1904–), British philosopher, Professor of Philosophy in Cambridge University, and a Fellow of Trinity College. Though his work touches on an enormous variety of topics, it is remarkably consistent in method, following up the making of almost any philosophical assertion by saying just the opposite and seeing what comes to light. Even of one of his main theses, that philosophical statements are verbal recommendations, he is quite prepared to say the contradictory, since in this way *both* likenesses *and* differences between philosophers' statements and those of others will be brought out; and thus philosophy shows up the logic of different kinds of statement. He is heavily indebted to **Wittgenstein,** not least in rejecting traditional metaphysics regarded as dealing with strange entities but still finding it valuable because it expresses dissatisfaction with our ordinary linguistic usage where this contains conflicting conventions or none at all. It is these conflicts which are illuminating, says Wisdom, and he compares them to the obsessional doubts of the neurotic, which also have a point; indeed, philosophy, as a therapeutic value, in ridding us of perplexity, and is in some ways comparable to psychoanalysis. (R.HALL)

Wittgenstein, Ludwig Josef Johann (1889–1951), by birth an Austrian of Jewish descent. He studied engineering at Berlin and then, from 1908, at Manchester where he became especially interested in aeroplane engines and propellers. The mathematical aspects of this work led Wittgenstein to develop an interest in pure mathematics and the philosophy of mathematics and he thus became aware of the work of **Russell** and **Frege** on mathematical logic. Consequently he moved to Cambridge where he spent the greater part of 1912–13 working with Russell, first as a pupil but soon as a partner. Wittgenstein served in the Austrian army in the first world war, being captured in Italy at the end. By this time he had completed his *Tractatus Logico-Philosophicus* which was published in Germany in 1921 and in London in 1922. At this time Wittgenstein believed that this work was a definitive solution to the problems of philosophy; he had also undergone a deep mystical experience while on the Eastern front during the war, apparently as a result of reading Tolstoy. On his release after the war he consequently gave away the considerable fortune which he had inherited and went to work as an elementary schoolmaster in Austria; at this time also he began to lead the very simple life which he never abandoned. However, during the nineteen-twenties he began to re-establish contact with philosophy; under the auspices of J. M. Keynes he revisited Cambridge in 1925 and about the same time he established personal contact with **Schlick** and Waismann, two of the leaders of the positivist movement in Vienna. In 1929 he returned permanently to Cambridge; he became a British subject at the time of the *Anschluss*. During the next three or four years he was gradually led, largely through self-criticism, to his new position in philosophy, so influential on recent Anglo-Saxon thought, which was first stated in the Blue and Brown books,

which are notes of lectures dictated to pupils in 1933–35 and published posthumously in 1958. He became Professor of Philosophy at Cambridge in succession to G. E. **Moore** in 1939; but on the outbreak of war he went to work as a porter in a London hospital. In 1947 he resigned his chair in order to devote himself entirely to research; but his health soon deteriorated and he died of cancer in 1951.

He was an unusual man; even as a professor he invariably wore an open-neck shirt; his room in Trinity College, Cambridge, was furnished by little more than a few deck-chairs; he never dined at the High Table with the other dons; his candour was so extreme that it could easily be regarded as rudeness; to the philosophical world in general he often gave the impression of being the highpriest of a secret cult rather than a fellow-worker.

Wittgenstein's work as a philosopher divides clearly into two periods. The definitive account of his earlier views is contained in the *Tractatus Logico-Philosophicus*, written in 1914–1918; he himself published no account of his later views, but we have an earlier version of them in the Blue and Brown books, which date from 1933–35, and a later version in the *Philosophical Investigations*, which contain his thoughts, constantly revised, from the mid-thirties until his death. *Remarks on the Foundations of Mathematics*, posthumously published, contains his most mature views on the philosophy of mathematics. It is to be expected that other posthumous publications are still to follow.

The *Tractatus Logico-Philosophicus* is without doubt a modern classic of philosophy; but it is a very difficult work, written in aphoristic style. It presents a position in many ways similar to Russell's logical atomism; but it has been perhaps too frequently interpreted in Russellian terms, for Wittgenstein differed from Russell on important points and adopted a much more extreme and consistent **empiricism**. Wittgenstein first states a metaphysic according to which the world consists entirely of simple facts, none of which is in any way dependent on any other, these facts being the ultimate subject-matter of empirical science. Wittgenstein, unlike Russell, gives no examples of what he regarded as simple or elementary facts; there must be such in the last analysis but he is not prepared to claim that he has identified any. However he would presumably have regarded John's shooting at Johann as being more nearly a simple fact than Britain's being at war with Germany, and would have regarded most of what are usually called facts as being in truth mere assemblages of elementary facts. Language, he held in the *Tractatus*, the vehicle thought, has as its purpose the stating of facts, which it does by picturing the facts; by saying that language pictures facts Wittgenstein especially wanted to claim that language must have a structural similarity to what it describes; an informative statement will be a picture of some possible state of affairs in the same way as a sketch-map can picture a battle or the arrangement of the furniture in a room. This is true even though ordinary idiomatic language is so full of special conventions and *ad hoc* rules as to be hardly recognisable as a picture – just as a map of Australia might have such a queer projection that we would not recognise it intuitively as such; but a perfect language is imaginable and is in principle constructable in which, for example, the spatial relationship of objects will be pictured quite clearly by the spatial relationship of their names. The only fully significant use of language is thus to picture facts; beyond this there is a derivative but legitimate use of language for stating tautologies, of which a simple example would be "It is raining or it is not raining", but which Wittgenstein held to include the whole of logic and mathematics, which are vacuously true and tell us nothing. Beyond the fully-meaningful picture of fact and the legitimate but empty tautology there is no legitimate use of language and any attempt to use it otherwise will be nonsensical: in particular all ethical or metaphysical utterances will be but pseudo-propositions, nonsensical violations of the proper use of language, since they are neither empirical nor tautologies (here we have a clear glimpse of what the **Logical Positivists** were later to call the verification principle as a criterion of significance). By a famous paradox, but as consistency requires, Wittgenstein denounces his own metaphysics and theory of language in the *Tractatus* as meaningless nonsense; for to say, for example, that language pictures facts is to try to give a picture of the pictorial relation which holds between statement and fact, which is absurd; this pictorial relation shows itself and what shows itself cannot be said. Wittgenstein regarded his metaphysics as useful or impor-

tant nonsense which helped one to recognize it itself and all other nonsense as such. Our tendency to talk nonsense, particularly in philosophy, is caused by the complicated, untidy character of ordinary language, and Wittgenstein devotes a great deal of attention to the technical problem of constructing an ideal language which will never tempt anyone to talk nonsense. Finally, once one has understood the *Tractatus* there will be no temptation to concern oneself any more with philosophy, which is neither empirical like science nor tautological like mathematics; one will, like Wittgenstein in 1918, abandon philosophy, which, as traditionally understood, is rooted in confusion.

Wittgenstein's later philosophy was given its most simple, general and intelligible, though not its most mature and complete, statement in the *Blue Book* of 1933. It is largely directed, though not explicitly, to showing precisely why the whole way of thinking adopted in the *Tractatus* is mistaken, though it tends also to destroy all traditional approaches to philosophy. The basis of the new approach is a new view of language; the old view in the *Tractatus* that there is in principle the one perfect scientific language with the sole task of describing the world is abandoned and language is seen as an indefinite set of social activities, each serving a different kind of purpose. Each of these distinct ways of using language is called by Wittgenstein a language game. No doubt there is a use of language for describing the world, and there may be one way of so doing which may reasonably be called "picturing" as in the *Tractatus*; but there is a host of other uses of language for giving orders, asking, thanking, cursing, greeting, praying. Wittgenstein gives a considerable list of such different language games in paragraph 23 of *Philosophical Investigations* and ends with the remark: "It is interesting to compare the multiplicity of tools in language and of the ways they are used, the multiplicity of kinds of word and sentence with what logicians have said about the structure of language (including the author of the *Tractatus Logico-Philosophicus*)."

Though, in Wittgenstein's opinion, we learn to play all these language games correctly, by training in childhood rather than by theoretical instruction, we are liable to become over-impressed with one or two of the possible ways of using language, giving ourselves an over-simplified account even of these (as his own account of the language of science had been over-simplified). Thus we think of a word as being always the name of something, to be learnt by ostensive definition or pointing ("That is a cat"), and of sentences as typified by "The cat is on the mat" or "Tom is fat" – accounts of the way the world goes. It thus comes about that when we reflect on uses of language which are in fact quite different, and of which we are masters when we employ language unreflectingly in its proper context, we try to force them all into one pattern. We may for example reflect on the language game of wishing or hoping and try to force it into the pattern by taking is as "a description of my present mental state"; we may then introspectively attempt to isolate the special mental event of hoping or wishing. Wittgenstein sees here the main root of philosophical perplexity and metaphysical paradox; philosophical puzzlement arises when we utterly misunderstand the functioning of some of our conceptual tools. We may talk as though our problem is of precisely defining a hope or wish, as though we knew well enough roughly for ordinary purposes but needed in philosophy greater accuracy; whereas, Wittgenstein held, what we need philosophically is to see that we are utterly misconstruing the concept of hoping if we take "hoping" as the name of some psychic process. Therefore to have a philosophical problem is like not being able to find your way about a town through not understanding its plan, like being a fly in a bottle, buzzing against the side instead of flying out of the top; it is a bewitchment of the intelligence. What is needed in such a predicament is not a revelation of the hidden, a subtle theory or explanation, a fine-spun analysis, for these do not cure radical misunderstanding. These concepts which perplex us are one over which, out of our studies, we have complete mastery (in railway travel the notion of time does not perplex us). What we need, therefore, are simple reminders of the purposes for which, we make use of these concepts, of their proper employment, judiciously assembled so that we cease to be blind to what "already lies open to the view". A well-arranged selection of such reminders, to produce which requires philosophical gifts and is no automatic procedure, will make us see how we employ the concepts in question, the general nature

of the language game; having seen this we shall cease to be victims of philosophical puzzlement.

We have just observed that Wittgenstein found one source of philosophical puzzlement in our tendency to try to interpret all uses of language in terms of one over-simplified model, the attempt to assimilate the different. Another important source of philosophical perplexity he found in the search for the feature common to all things called by the same name. Thus we may try to find, and even invent, some feature common to all games, in virtue of which they are called games. But Wittgenstein held that there need be no such feature; if we call tennis a game it is easy to find similarities between it and bridge and between bridge and patience, and this is enough to explain the common name "game" without our looking for some feature common to both football and patience and possessed by all games and only games. In such a situation as this Wittgenstein spoke of a family resemblance. Thus we may tend to look for some psychic occurrence common to all cases of hoping or intending not only because we think that the verbs "hope" and "intend" must name some process but because we think that there must be a common feature to all cases of each; Wittgenstein will then suggest to us that there may be only a family resemblance between all the cases of intending.

The bulk of Wittgenstein's later work consists of the application of this method of philosophy to a wide variety of problems and tracing their interconnection. He will take a set of concepts, from mathematics or from ordinary conversation, set out the paradoxical things which we are inclined to say about them under the influence of philosophical puzzlement, and then attempt to banish the puzzlement by reminding us of the normal use of these concepts, by inventing new language games which will be both revealingly similar and revealingly different, always by description of actual and possible uses of language in various contexts.

Given this view of philosophy as being a fall into conceptual puzzlement from which one was rescued, or rescued oneself, by reminders of the use of these concepts in their natural context, Wittgenstein could find no place for any philosophical theories, doctrines or opinions. He conceived his task to be to remind us of what lay on the surface, not to express any opinions or offer deep explanations.

In his own words (*Investigations*, 126 and 129):
"Philosophy simply puts everything before us, and neither explains nor deduces anything... Since everything lies open to view there is nothing to explain ... The aspects of things that are most important for us are hidden because of their simplicity and familiarity". This makes the actual content of Wittgenstein's later work quite impossible to summarize; there is no doctrine and the method of description of conceptual matters that he employs has no theoretical rules of procedure: one must simply describe things in such a way as to end the intellectual bewitchment of the perplexed.

The influence of Wittgenstein on modern philosophy, particularly in the English-speaking countries, has been very great. His *Tractatus Logico-Philosophicus* was also of great importance for the growth of logical positivism in Continental countries, particularly in Austria; many of the modern logical empiricists who have been little affected by his later work are thus under a debt to his earlier views. The direct influence of the Tractatus on Anglo-Saxon philosophy was considerably lessened in earlier years by a tendency to think of it as being simply a rather extreme and paradoxical version of Russell's philosophy; it was also positively misinterpreted in the light of Russell's logical atomism and because of a translation which, as well as being inaccurate, made use of Russell's technical vocabulary (e.g. "atomic fact").

The influence of Wittgenstein's later work has however been very great in Britain, though it is still little known on the continent of Europe and has become widely known in America only comparatively recently. It is a mistake to see modern British philosophy as modelled entirely on Wittgenstein for this is to underestimate sadly the importance of Moore, Russell and **Ryle** specifically, very few modern analytic philosophers would accept Wittgenstein's view that the whole object of philosophy is to banish puzzlement. Moreover we can find other philosophers moving independently in the same direction as Wittgenstein at the same time; for all his great originality Wittgenstein like all men was of his time. But few would dispute that among analytic philosophers – between whom there is but a family resemblance – Wittgenstein stands out as a great and original philosophical genius. (J.O.U.)

X

Xenophanes, Greek poet and thinker lived at Colophon, 570–*c.* 475 B.C. Leaving Ionia when young, he travelled round the Greek world, particularly Sicily and the west, reciting his poems, which ranged from banqueting-songs to speculations on physics. He attacked the immoral gods of Homer and indeed the whole concept of anthropomorphism, stating that there was one single deity "in no way like men in body or in thought", but "shaking all things by the thought of his mind". Xenophanes was treated as the first **Eleatic** by later Greek historians because of the superficial resemblance of his one god (which according to **Aristotle**'s conjecture was coextensive with the world, though the truth here is obscure) to **Parmenides**' Being. Some of Xenophanes' physical ideas were also interesting: the heavenly bodies were ignited clouds; things were originally all mud, because fossils of sea-creatures are found inland; the sea will dry up, and then the process will be reversed. Other rather fantastic physical suggestions were perhaps intentional parodies of the excesses of Milesian dogmatism. Xenophanes certainly stated salutorily that positive philosophical certainty lay out of men's reach – "seeming is wrought over all things". *See also* **Pre-Socratics**. (G.S.K.)

Z

Zeno of Citium, Cyprus, (*c.* 333–262 B.C.), Greek philosopher, founder of **Stoicism**, which was so named from the Painted Stoa (colonnade) where Zeno taught. He came to Athens in 312/11, attended the lectures of Polemo, head of the Academy, studied dialectic under Stilpo and Diodorus of the Megaric School, but was most strongly influenced by Crates the **Cynic**. The immense literary output and authority of **Chrysippus**, the third head of the School, has made it difficult to penetrate to Zeno. But certainly the fundamental doctrines and the outline at least of the whole system are due to the founder. His philosophy proceeded from the Cynic base of the self-sufficiency of virtue, but he incorporated much from other sources into an original comprehensive system covering all departments of philosophy; besides the teachers mentioned, **Socrates** (probably through the works of **Antisthenes**) and the Peripatetic development of **ethics** most likely influenced his thinking. He declined the invitation of his admirer King Antigonus Gonatus, to advise him in Macedon, but sent his pupil Persaeus. Ancient authorities imply that he was of Phoenician origin, and many of his successors came from the eastern periphery of the Greek world; but eastern influences are problematic. Stoicism in thought and spirit was Hellenic. (I.G.K.)

Plate 96, page 384.

Zeno of Elea, Greek philosopher and follower of **Parmenides**, flourished in Greece *c.* 450 B.C. He wrote a book defending Parmenides' single motionless Being by showing that plurality and motion entailed logically contradictory consequences. Fragment 3 gives a typical argument against plurality: "(*a*) If there are many, there must be just as many as there are and neither more nor less. But if they are as many as they are, they must be limited. (*b*) If there are many, existing things are infinite; for there are always other things between the things that are, and again others between those. And thus the things that are are infinite". Against motion there were four related arguments, the stadium, Achilles and the tortoise, the flying arrow, and the moving rows. In the first, for example, Zeno argued that it is impossible to cross the stadium; for you must first reach half-way across, and before that quarter-way across, and so *ad infinitum*. Thus the distance is infinite. These arguments against motion assumed that space could be divided into portions which could be correlated with portions of time. The **Pythagoreans** believed that things were composed of discontinuous units, and many scholars think that Zeno was attacking their kind of plurality in particular. His arguments seemed, nevertheless, to be valid against other pluralistic systems in general.

Many of them were fallacious, since Zeno ignored the fact that the sum of an infinite geometrical progression is finite if the common ratio is less than 1. See also **Eleatics** and **Pre-Socratics**.

(G.S.K.)

NOTES ON THE CONTRIBUTORS

FOR FURTHER READING

Notes on the Contributors

J. L. ACKRILL, M.A.

Fellow, Tutor and Lecturer in Philosophy, Brasenose College, University of Oxford. Publications include contributions to *Bulletin of the Institute for Classical Studies of the University of London, Mind* and *Journal of Hellenic Studies.*

H. B. ACTON, M.A., D.PHIL.

Professor of Philosophy, Bedford College, University of London. Editor of *Philosophy.* Publications include: *The Illusion of the Epoch: Marxist-Leninism as a Philosophical Creed,* London, 1955, Boston, Mass., 1957; and contributions to *Mind, Philosophy* and *Proceedings of the Aristotelian Society.*

A. HILARY ARMSTRONG, M.A.

Gladstone Professor of Greek in the University of Liverpool. Publications include: *The Architecture of the Intelligible Universe in the Philosophy of Plotinus,* Cambridge, 1940; *An Introduction to Ancient Philosophy,* London, 1947, Westminster, Md, 1949; and *Plotinus,* London, 1953.

A. J. AYER, M.A., F.B.A.

Wykeham Professor of Logic in the University of Oxford, and Honorary Fellow of Wadham College, Oxford. Formerly Grote Professor of the Philosophy of the Mind, University College, London. Publications include: *Language, Truth and Logic,* London, 1936; *The Foundations of Empirical Knowledge,* London, 1940; *Thinking and Meaning* (Inaugural Lecture), London, 1947; *The Problem of Knowledge,* London, 1956; and *An Anthology of Logical Positivism,* Glencoe, Ill., 1959.

ERROL BEDFORD, B.A.

Lecturer in Moral Philosophy in the University of Edinburgh. Publications include contributions to *Proceedings of the Aristotelian Society* and *Proceedings of the XIth International Congress of Philosophy,* Amsterdam, 1953.

SIR ISAIAH BERLIN, C.B.E., M.A.

Professor of Social and Political Theory in the University of Oxford. Publications include: *Karl Marx,* Oxford, 1939; *The Inevitability of History,* London, 1954; *Two Concepts of Liberty,* Oxford, 1958; and contributions to *Mind* and *Proceedings of the Aristotelian Society.*

KARL BRITTON, M.A., A.M.

Professor of Philosophy, King's College, University of Durham. Publications include: *Communication. A Philosophical Study of Language,* London, 1939; *J. S. Mill,* London, 1953; and contributions to *Journal of Philosophy, Proceedings of the Aristotelian Society* and *Cambridge Review.*

JOSEPH G. DAWSON, B.A., PH.L.

Lecturer in Medieval Philosophy in the University of Glasgow. Publications include: *Aquinas: Selected Political Writings* (translation), Oxford, 1948; and contributions to *The Springs of Morality,* London, 1956, and *The Scots Philosophical Quarterly.*

M. A. E. DUMMETT, M.A.

Fellow of All Souls College, University of Oxford. Publications include contributions to *The Philosophical Review* and *Proceedings of the Aristotelian Society.*

DOROTHY M. EMMET, M.A.

Professor of Philosophy in the University of Manchester. Publications include: *Whitehead's Philosophy of Organism,* London, 1932; *The Nature of Metaphysical Thinking,* London, 1945; *Function, Purpose and Powers,* London, 1958; and contributions to *Mind, Philosophy* and *Proceedings of the Aristotelian Society.*

A. C. EWING, M.A., LITT.D., D.PHIL.

Reader in Philosophy in the University of Cambridge and Director of Studies in Moral Sciences, Trinity Hall, Cambridge. Publications include: *Idealism: a Critical Survey*, London, 1934; *The Individual, the State and World Government*, New York, 1947; *The Fundamental Questions of Philosophy*, London, 1951; and contributions to *Mind*, *Philosophy* and *Philosophy and Phenomenological Research*.

MARVIN FARBER, PH.D.

Chairman of the Department of Philosophy at Buffalo University. President of the International Phenomenological Society. Editor of *Quarterly Journal* and *Philosophy and Phenomenological Research*. Publications include: *Phenomenology as a Method and as a Philosophical Discipline*, Buffalo, 1928; *The Foundation of Phenomenology*, Harvard, 1943; *Husserl*, Buenos Aires, 1956; and *Philosophy for the Future* (Editor), New York, 1949.

J. N. FINDLAY, M.A., PH.D., F.B.A.

Professor of Philosophy, King's College, University of London. Publications include: *Meinong's Theory of Objects*, Oxford, 1933; *Hegel: a Re-examination*, London, 1958; and contributions to *Mind*, *Philosophy* and *Philosophy and Phenomenological Research*.

THOMAS GILBY, O.P., S.T.L., PH.D.

Publications include: *Phoenix and Turtle. The Unity of Knowing and Being*, London, 1950; *Between Community and Society, A Philosophy and Theology of the State*, London, 1953; and *Principality and Polity. Aquinas and the Rise of State Theory in the West*, London, 1958.

ROLAND HALL, B.A., B.PHIL.

Lecturer in Philosophy, Queen's College, Dundee, University of St Andrews. Publications include contributions to *The Philosophical Review* and *The Philosophical Quarterly*.

R. M. HARE, M.A.

Fellow of Balliol College, University of Oxford. Publications include: *The Language of Morals*, Oxford, 1952; and contributions to *Mind* and *Proceedings of the Aristotelian Society*.

R. HARRÉ, M.A., B.SC., B.PHIL.

Lecturer in Philosophy in the University of Leicester. Publications include contributions to *The Philosophical Review*, *Philosophy* and *Analysis*.

H. L. A. HART, M.A.

Professor of Jurisprudence in the University of Oxford and fellow of University College, Oxford.

D. J. B. HAWKINS, D.D., PH.D.

Publications include: *A Sketch of Mediaeval Philosophy*, London, 1946; *Essentials of Theism*, London, 1949; *Being and Becoming*, London, 1954; and *Crucial Problems of Modern Philosophy*, London, 1957.

P. L. HEATH, B.A.

Lecturer in Logic in the University of St Andrews. Publications include: *The Nature of Sympathy* by Max Scheler (translation), London and New York, 1954; *Dialectical Materialism* by Gustav Wetter (translation), London and New York, 1958; and contributions to *The Philosophical Quarterly* and *Proceedings of the Aristotelian Society*.

RONALD W. HEPBURN, M.A., PH.D.

Lecturer in Moral Philosophy in the University of Aberdeen. Publications include: *Metaphysical Beliefs* (with Alasdair Macintyre and Stephen Toulmin), London, 1957; *Christianity and Paradox*, London, 1958; and contributions to *Proceedings of the Aristotelian Society*, *The Philosophical Quarterly* and *Philosophy*.

EDMUND HILL, O.P., S.T.L., M.A.
  Tutor in philosophy to students of the Dominican Order. Publications include: *Nine Sermons of Saint Augustine on The Psalms* (translation), London, 1958; and contributions to *Blackfriars* and *Life of The Spirit*.

WALTER KAUFMANN, PH.D., M.A., B.A.
  Associate Professor of Philosophy in the University of Princeton. Publications include: *Nietzsche: Philosopher, Psychologist, Antichrist*, Princeton, 1950; *Existentialism from Dostoevsky to Sartre* (Editor), New York, 1956, London, 1957; *Critique of Religion and Philosophy*, Philadelphia, 1958; *From Shakespeare to Existentialism: Between Poetry, Religion, and Philosophy*, Boston, 1959; and contributions to *Commentary, Journal of the History of Ideas* and *The Philosophical Review*.

I. G. KIDD, M.A., B.A.
  Lecturer in Greek in the University of St Andrews. Publications include contributions to *Classical Quarterly* and *Classical Review*.

G. S. KIRK, M.A.
  Fellow of Trinity Hall, and Lecturer in Classics in the University of Cambridge. Publications include: *Heraclitus, the Cosmic Fragments*, Cambridge, 1954; and *The Presocratic Philosophers* (with J. E. Raven), Cambridge, 1957.

STEPHAN KÖRNER, JUR.DR., M.A., PH.D.
  Professor of Philosophy in the University of Bristol. Publications include: *Kant*, London, 1955; *Conceptual Thinking*, Cambridge, 1955, New York, 1958; *Observation and Interpretation* (Editor), London, 1957; and contributions to *Mind, Proceedings of the Aristotelian Society* and *The Philosophical Review*.

J. D. MABBOTT, C.M.G., B. LITT., M.A.
  Fellow and Tutor of St John's College, University of Oxford. Publications include: *The State and the Citizen*, London, 1948; and contributions to *Contemporary British Philosophy*, London, 1956; *Mind, Proceedings of the Aristotelian Society* and *Philosophy*.

ALASDAIR MACINTYRE, B.A., M.A.
  Lecturer in Philosophy in the University of Leeds. Publications include: *Marxism: An Interpretation*, London, 1953; *Metaphysical Beliefs* (with Ronald W. Hepburn and Stephen Toulmin), London, 1957; *The Unconscious*, London, 1958; and contributions to *Mind, Philosophy* and *The Philosophical Quarterly*.

D. M. MACKINNON, M.A.
  Regius Professor of Moral Philosophy in the University of Aberdeen. Stanton Lecturer in the Philosophy of Religion in the University of Cambridge, 1956–9. Publications include: *Christian Faith and Communist Faith*, London, 1953; *A Study in Ethical Theory*, London, 1957; and contributions to *Contemporary British Philosophy, Proceedings of the Aristotelian Society* and *The Philosophical Quarterly*.

D. G. C. MACNABB, M.A.
  Fellow, Senior Tutor and Lecturer in Philosophy, Pembroke College, University of Oxford. Publications include: *David Hume, His Theory of Knowledge*, London, 1951; and contributions to *Proceedings of the Aristotelian Society* and *Revue Internationale de Philosophie*.

PHILIP MERLAN, DR. IUR., DR.PHIL.
  Professor of Philosophy, Scripps College and Claremont Graduate School, California. Publications include: *From Platonism to Neoplatonism*, The Hague, 1953; and contributions to *Journal of the History of Ideas, Transactions of the American Philological Association* and *Philosophy and Phenomenological Research*.

ERNEST NAGEL, B.S. IN S.S., M.A., PH.D.
  John Dewey Professor in Philosophy at Columbia University in the City of New York. Past-President of the Association of Symbolic Logic and of the American Philosophical Association. Publications include: *Introduction to Logic and Scientific Method* (with M. R. Cohen), New York, 1934; *Principles of the Theory of Probability*, Chicago, 1939; *Sovereign Reason*, Glencoe, Ill., 1954; and *Logic without Metaphysics*, Glencoe, Ill., 1957.

P. H. NOWELL-SMITH, A.M., M.A.
> Professor of Philosophy in the University of Leicester. Publications include: *Ethics*, Oxford, 1957; and contributions to *Mind* and *Proceedings of the Aristotelian Society*.

JAMES O'CONNELL, M.A., PH. D.
> Lecturer, University College, Ibadan.

D. J. O'CONNOR, M.A., PH.D.
> Professor of Philosophy in the University of Exeter. Publications include: *John Locke*, London, 1952; *Introduction to Symbolic Logic*, 1953; *Introduction to the Philosophy of Education*, London, 1957; and contributions to *Mind* and *Philosophy*.

R. S. PETERS, B.A., PH.D.
> Reader in the Department of Philosophy and Psychology, Birkbeck College, University of London. Publications include: *Hobbes*, London, 1956; *The Concept of Motivation*, London, 1958; and contributions to *Mind*, *Philosophy* and *Analysis*.

ANTHONY QUINTON, M.A.
> Fellow and Tutor of New College, and Lecturer in Philosophy in the University of Oxford. Publications include contributions to *Philosophy, Politics and Society*, Oxford, 1956; *The Nature of Metaphysics*, London, 1957; *Mind, Proceedings of the Aristotelian Society* and *Victorian Studies*.

RICHARD ROBINSON, B. LITT., M.A., PH.D.
> Fellow of Oriel College, University of Oxford. Publications include: *The Province of Logic*, London, 1931; *Plato's Earlier Dialectic*, New York, 1941, Oxford, 1953; *Definition*, Oxford, 1950.

ERWIN I. J. ROSENTHAL, LITT. D., D. PHIL. M.A.
> Lecturer in Hebrew in the University of Cambridge. Publications include: *Averroes' Commentary on Plato's "Republic"*, Cambridge, 1956; and contributions to *Islamic Culture* and *The Listener*.

GILBERT RYLE, M.A.
> Waynflete Professor of Metaphysical Philosophy in the University of Oxford. Editor of *Mind*. Publications include: *The Concept of Mind*, London, 1949; and *Dilemmas*, Cambridge, 1954.

RUTH LYDIA SAW, B.A., PH.D.
> Head of the Department of Philosophy, Birkbeck College, and Reader in Philosophy in the University of London. Publications include: *The Vindication of Metaphysics*, London, 1951; *Leibniz*, London, 1954; and contributions to *Proceedings of the Aristotelian Society* and *Literary Guide*.

P. F. STRAWSON, M.A.
> Fellow of University College, and Lecturer in Philosophy in the University of Oxford. Publications include: *Introduction to Logical Theory*, London, 1952; *Individuals*, London, 1959; and contributions to *The Revolution in Philosophy*, London, 1956; *The Nature of Metaphysics*, London, 1957; *Philosophy, Mind* and *The Philosophical Review*.

F. A. TAYLOR, M.A., CHEVALIER DE LA LÉGION D'HONNEUR.
> Librarian, Christ Church, University of Oxford. Publications include: *Voltaire's Lettres Philosophiques*, Oxford, 1943.

IVO THOMAS, O.P., M.A., S.T.M.
> Visiting Professor in Logic in the University of Notre Dame, Indiana. Formerly Vice-Regent of Studies in the English Dominican Province. Publications include: *Aristotle's "De Anima" and the "Commentary" of St Thomas Aquinas* (translation), Yale, 1951; *A History of Formal Logic* by I. M. Bochenski (translation), Indiana, 1959; and contributions to *Mind, Blackfriars* and *Dominican Studies*.

J. O. URMSON, M.A.

Fellow of Corpus Christi College, University of Oxford. Formerly Professor of Philosophy in the University of St Andrews, and Visiting Associate Professor at Princeton University. Publications include *Philosophical Analysis*, Oxford, 1956; and contributions to *Logic and Language*, Oxford, 1953; *Essays in Conceptual Analysis*, London, 1956; and *Essays in Moral Philosophy*, Seattle, 1958.

JAMES WARD SMITH, PH.D.

Associate Professor of Philosophy at Princeton University. Publications include: *Theme for Reason*, Princeton, 1957; and contributions to *Mind, Journal of the History of Ideas* and *Journal of Philosophy*.

G. J. WARNOCK, M.A.

Fellow and Tutor in Philosophy, Magdalen College, University of Oxford. Publications include: *Berkeley*, London, 1953; *English Philosophy since 1900*, London, 1958; and contributions to *Logic and Language*, Oxford, 1953; *Essays in Conceptual Analysis*, London, 1956; and *The Nature of Metaphysics*, London, 1957.

ALAN R. WHITE, B.A.

Lecturer in Philosophy in the University of Hull. Publications include: *G. E. Moore*, Oxford, 1958; and contributions to *Mind, Proceedings of the Aristotelian Society* and *Philosophy and Phenomenological Research*.

B. A. O. WILLIAMS, M.A.

Lecturer, Department of Philosophy, University College, University of London. Publications include contributions to *The Nature of Metaphysics*, London. 1957; *Proceedings of the Aristotelian Society, Mind* and *Philosophy*.

For Further Reading

This list of books is far from comprehensive. Generally more difficult books have been excluded unless they have some claim to be classics; books in languages other than English have also been kept to a minimum.

Ancient Philosophy

GENERAL

Early Greek Philosophy by J. BURNET. Black, London and Macmillan, New York, 4th ed. 1930.

The Presocratic Philosophers by G. S. KIRK and J. E. RAVEN. C.U.P., Cambridge and New York, 1957.

The Theology of the Early Greek Philosophers by W. JAEGER. O.U.P., Oxford and New York, 1947.

The Physical World of the Greeks by S. SAMBURSKY, tr. M. DAGGUT. Routledge, London, 1956.

Socrates and the Socratic Schools by E. ZELLER, tr. O. J. REICHEL. Longmans, London, 1885.

Stoics, Epicureans and Sceptics by E. ZELLER, tr. O. J. REICHEL. Longmans, London, 1892.

The Greek Thinkers by T. GOMPERZ, tr. L. MAGNUS and G. G. BERRY. Murray, London, 1901–12; Humanities, New York.

Die Stoa by M. POHLENZ. Göttingen, 1948–9.

Stoics and Sceptics by E. BEVAN. O.U.P., Oxford, 1913.

History of Cynicism by D. R. DUDLEY. Methuen, London, 1937.

The Greek Cynics by F. SAYRE. 1948.

The Greek Atomists and Epicurus by C. BAILEY. O.U.P., Oxford, 1928.

Roman Stoicism by E. V. ARNOLD. O.U.P., Oxford, 1911, reprinted 1958.

Stoic and Epicurean by R. D. HICKS. Longmans, London and New York, 1910.

INDIVIDUAL PHILOSOPHERS

ARISTOTLE
The Works of Aristotle, Oxford translation. O.U.P., Oxford and New York, 1928–52.

Aristotle by W. D. ROSS. Methuen, London, 1923; Barnes & Noble, New York, 1955.

Aristotle by W. Jaeger, tr. R. ROBINSON. O.U.P., Oxford, 1934 and New York, 1948.

CICERO
De Officiis by CICERO, tr. W. MILLER. (Loeb Classical Library) Heinemann, London and Harvard U.P., Cambridge, Mass., 1896.

De Natura Deorum by CICERO, tr. F. BROOKS. Methuen, London, 1896.

De Finibus by CICERO, tr. H. RACKHAM. (Loeb Classical Library) Heinemann, London and Harvard U.P., Cambridge, Mass., 1937.

Academica by CICERO, tr. H. RACKHAM. (Loeb Classical Library) Heinemann, London and Harvard U.P., Cambridge, Mass., 1933.

EPICTETUS
Works by EPICTETUS, tr. A. OLDFATHER. (Loeb Classical Library) Heinemann, London and Harvard U.P., Cambridge, Mass., 1925–8.

EPICURUS
Epicurus and his Gods by A. J. FESTUGIERE, tr. C. W.

CHILTON. Blackwell, Oxford, 1955; Harvard U.P., Cambridge, Mass., 1956.

Extant Remains by EPICURUS, ed. and tr. C. BAILEY. O.U.P., Oxford, 1926.

LUCRETIUS
On the Nature of Things by LUCRETIUS, tr. W. H. ROUSE. (Loeb Classical Library) Heinemann, London and Harvard U.P., Cambridge, Mass., 1924.

MARCUS AURELIUS
Meditations etc. by MARCUS AURELIUS, ed. J. G. JENNINGS. Blackie, London, 1917.

PLATO
Dialogues by PLATO, tr. B. JOWETT. O.U.P., Oxford, 4th ed. (revised) 1953.

Plato, the Man and his Work by A. E. TAYLOR. Methuen, London, 1926; Humanities, New York.

PLOTINUS
Complete English Translations by S. MacKENNA, rev. B. S. PAGE. Warner, London, 1917–30.

Selections in Translation. Introduction and notes by A. H. ARMSTRONG. Allen & Unwin, London, 1953.

The Philosophy of Plotinus by W. R. INGE. Longmans, London and New York, rev. ed. 1948.

The Architecture of the Intelligible Universe in the Philosophy of Plotinus by A. H. ARMSTRONG. C.U.P., Cambridge, 1940.

SENECA
Moral Essays by SENECA, tr. J. W. BASORE. (Loeb Classical Library) Heinemann, London and Harvard U.P., Cambridge, Mass., 1935.

For translations of works of other Greek philosophers, see especially the above-mentioned works of Burnet and of Kirk and Raven.

Medieval Philosophy

GENERAL

History of Christian Philosophy in the Middle Ages by E. GILSON. Sheed & Ward, London and Random, New York, 1955.

A Sketch of Medieval Philosophy by D. J. B. HAWKINS. Sheed & Ward, London, 1946; New York, 1947.

Medieval Thought from St Augustine to Ockham by G. LEFF. Penguin, London and Baltimore, 1958.

Selections from Medieval Philosophers ed. R. McKEON. Scribner's, London, 1930–1 and New York, 1929.

Encyclopedia of Islam ed. J. H. KRAMERS and Sir H. A. R. GIBB. Luzac, London, 1954–9.

A Library of Fathers ed. E. B. PUSEY and others. O.U.P., Oxford, 1838–85.

A History of Philosophy, Vols. 2 and 3, by F. C. COPLESTON. Burns & Oates, London, 1953; Newman, Westminster, Maryland, 1950–3.

INDIVIDUAL PHILOSOPHERS

ABELARD
Selections from Medieval Philosophy, Vol. I, ed. R. McKEON. Scribner's, London 1930–1 and New York, 1926.
Peter Abailard by J. K. SIKES. C.U.P., Cambridge, and Macmillan, New York, 1932.

AQUINAS
Philosophical Texts by AQUINAS, ed. T. GILBY. O.U.P., Oxford and New York, 1951.
The Christian Philosophy of St Thomas Aquinas by E. GILSON (with a catalogue of his works by I. T. ESCHMANN). Sheed & Ward, London, 1957.
Aquinas by F. C. COPLESTON. Penguin, London and Baltimore, 1955.
The Life of St Thomas Aquinas by K. FOSTER.

AUGUSTINE
Confessions by AUGUSTINE, tr. Sir T. MATTHEW, rev. R. HUDDLESTON. Burns & Oates, London, 1954; Regnery, Chicago, Ill., 1956.
The City of God by AUGUSTINE, tr. J. HEALEY, ed. R. TASKER. (Everyman) Dent, London and Dutton, New York, 1957.
On Christian Doctrine and Enchiridion by AUGUSTINE, tr. J. S. F. LAW. Clark, Edinburgh, 1892.
A Guide to the City of God by M. VERSFELD. Sheed & Ward, London, 1958.
Saint Augustine by H. MARROU. Longmans, London, 1957

AVERROES
Tahafut al-tahafut by AVERROES, tr. S. VAN DEN BERGH. Luzac, London, 1955.
Commentary on Plato's Republic by AVERROES, ed. and tr. E. I. J. ROSENTHAL. C.U.P., Cambridge, 1956.
Political Thought in Medieval Islam, Ch. IX, by E. I. J. ROSENTHAL. C.U.P., Cambridge, 1958.
Ibn Rushd (Averroes) by L. GAUTHIER. Paris, 1948.

AVICENNA
Avicenna on Theology by A. J. ARBERRY. Murray, London, 1951.
Avicenna's Psychology by F. RAHMAN. O.U.P., Oxford, 1952.
Avicenna: Scientist and Philosopher ed. G. N. WICKENS. Luzac, London, 1952.
Avicenna. His life and works by S. N. AFNAN. London, 1958.

BACON, ROGER
The Opus Maius by ROGER BACON, tr. R. B. BURKE. Pennsylvania U.P., Philadelphia, 1928.
Roger Bacon and His Search for a Universal Science by STEWART EASTON. Blackwell, Oxford and Columbia U.P., New York, 1952.

BOETHIUS
Works by BOETHIUS, tr. H. F. STEWART. (Loeb Classical Library) Heinemann, London and Harvard U.P., Cambridge, Mass., 1918.

BONAVENTURA
The Philosophy of St Bonaventure by E. GILSON, tr. Dom I. TRETHOWAN. Sheed & Ward, London, 1938.

CAJETAN
The Analogy of Names by CAJETAN, tr. E. A. BUSHINSKI. Duquesne U.P., Pittsburgh, Pa.

The Concept of Being by CAJETAN, tr. E. A. BUSHINSKI. Duquesne U.P., Pittsburgh, Pa.
Existence and Analogy, pp. 92–121, by E. L. MASCALL. Longmans, London and New York, 1949.
The Analogy between God and the World, pp. 205–475, by H. LYTTKENS, tr. A. POIGNANT. Lundequist, Uppsala and Harrasowitz, Wiesbaden, 1953.

SCOTUS, DUNS
Duns Scotus by S. R. S. HARRIS. O.U.P., Oxford, 1927; Humanities, New York.

ERIGENA
Selections from Medieval Philosophers, Vol. I, by JOHANNES SCOTUS ERIGENA, ed. R. McKEON. Scribner's, London, 1930–1 and New York, 1926.
Johannes Scotus Erigena, a Study in Mediaeval Philosophy by H. BETT. C.U.P., Cambridge, 1925.

MAIMONIDES
The Guide of the Perplexed by MAIMONIDES, tr. M. FRIED-LÄNDER. Routledge, London and Dutton, New York, 1947.
The Eight Chapters on Ethics by MAIMONIDES, tr. J. I. GORFINKLE. Columbia U.P., New York, 1912.
The Teachings of Maimonides by A. COHEN. Routledge, London, 1927.

PETER OF SPAIN
Petri Hispani Summulae Logicales by PETER OF SPAIN, ed. I. M. BOCHENSKI. Turin, 1947.

WILLIAM OF OCCAM
Selections from Medieval Philosophy, Vol. II, by WILLIAM OF OCCAM, ed. R. McKEON. Scribner's, London, 1930–1 and New York, 1926.
Philosophical Writings by WILLIAM OF OCCAM, tr. P. BOEHNER. Nelson, Edinburgh and New York, 1957.
The Logic of William of Ockam by E. A. MOODY. Sheed & Ward, London, 1935.

Many of the earlier medieval philosophers have had none of their works translated; they are to be found in the original, especially in the *Patrologia Graeca* and the *Patrologia Latina*, both edited by Migne (Paris).

Modern Philosophy
(Some introductory and classical works on main topics)

HISTORY OF PHILOSOPHY

History of Philosophy by F. C. COPLESTON. Burns & Oates, London, 1947; Newman Press, New York.
History of Western Philosophy by H. HØFFDING, reprinted 1956.
History of Western Philosophy by B. A. W. RUSSELL. Allen & Unwin, London, 1946; Simon & Schuster, New York, 1947.
History of Modern Philosophy by H. HØFFDING, tr. B. MEYER. Macmillan, London, reprinted 1956; Dover, New York, 1955.
A History of Philosophy by C. C. J. WEBB. O.U.P., Oxford and New York, 1915.
Contemporary European Philosophy by I. M. BOCHENSKI, tr. DONALD NICHOLL and KARL ASCHENBRENNER. California U.P., California, 1957.
English Philosophy since 1900 by G. J. WARNOCK. O.U.P., Oxford and New York, 1958.

THEORY OF KNOWLEDGE AND METAPHYSICS

(i) *Some easier classics*

Meditations on the First Philosophy by R. DESCARTES, tr. J. VEITCH. Simpkin & Marshall, London, 1853.

Essay concerning Human Understanding by J. LOCKE, ed. R. WILBURN. (Everyman) Dent, London and Dutton, New York, 1947.

Dialogues between Hylas and Philonous by G. BERKELEY. Collier, (Harvard Classics, Vol. 37), New York, 1910.

Principles of Human Knowledge by G. BERKELEY, ed. C. SIMON. Routledge, London, 1907.

Inquiry concerning the Human Understanding by D. HUME, ed. L. SELBY-BIGGE. O.U.P., Oxford, 1902; Collier (Harvard Classics, Vol. 37), New York, 1910.

Essay on the Intellectual Powers of Man by T. REID, ed. A. WOOZLEY. Macmillan, London, 1941.

Prolegomena to any Future Metaphysics by I. KANT, ed. and tr. P. LUCAS. Manchester U.P., Manchester, 1953; ed. and tr. P. CARUS. Open Court, La Salle, Ill.

(ii) *Some useful contemporary works*

The Problems of Philosophy by B. A. W. RUSSELL. O.U.P., Oxford, 1912.

The Revolution in Philosophy by A. J. AYER, D. PEARS and others. Macmillan, London, 1955; Yale, New Haven, Conn.

The Foundation of Phenomenology by M. FARBER. Harvard U.P., Cambridge, Mass., 1943.

Logic and Language (first and second series) ed. A. G. N. FLEW. Blackwell, Oxford, 1951-3.

New Essays in Philosophical Theology ed. A. G. N. FLEW and A. MACINTYRE. S.C.M., London, 1955; Macmillan, New York, 1956.

Readings in Philosophical Analysis ed. H. FEIGL and W. SELLARS. Appleton-Century-Crofts, New York, 1949.

Theory of Knowledge by A. WOOZLEY. Hutchinson, London, 1949.

Readings in the Philosophy of Science ed. H. FEIGL and BRODRICK. Appleton-Century-Crofts, New York, 1953.

Introduction to the Philosophy of Science by S. TOULMIN. Hutchinson, London, 1953; Rinehart, New York.

Fundamentals of Symbolic Logic by A. AMBROSE and M. LAZEROVITZ. Rinehart, New York, 1948.

Introduction to Symbolic Logic by A. H. BASSON and D. J. O'CONNOR. University Tutorial Press, London, 3rd ed. 1959.

A Handbook of Logic by BRENNAN. New York, 1957.

Introduction to Logic and Scientific Method by M. R. COHEN and E. NAGEL. Routledge, London and Harcourt, New York, 1934.

Scientific Method and Probability by P. H. NIDDITCH. London, 1958.

Symbolic Logic by I. COPI. Macmillan, London and New York, 1954.

Probability and Induction by W. KNEALE. O.U.P., Oxford and New York, 1949.

The Logical Problem of Induction by G. VON WRIGHT. Blackwell, Oxford, rev. ed. 1957.

See also under: BOOLE, FREGE, JEVONS, RUSSELL, POPPER, QUINE and VENN, *below.*

AESTHETICS

Philosophies of Beauty (selections) by E. F. CARRITT. O.U.P., Oxford and New York, 1931.

Beauty and other Forms of Value by S. ALEXANDER. Macmillan, London, 1933.

Breviary of Aesthetics by B. CROCE, tr. D. AINSLIE. Houston, 1915.

Aesthetic by B. CROCE, tr. D. AINSLIE. Owen & Vision, London, 1953; Noonday, New York, 1956.

Feeling and Form by S. LANGER. Routledge, London, 1953.

Critique of Judgement by I. KANT, tr. J. C. MEREDITH. O.U.P., Oxford, 1952.

Principles of Art by R. G. COLLINGWOOD. O.U.P., Oxford, 1938.

The History of Aesthetic by B. BOSANQUET. Allen & Unwin, London, 1892; Macmillan, New York.

Essays in Aesthetics and Language ed. W. ELTON and others. Blackwell, Oxford, 1954.

ETHICS

(i) *General Introductions*

Ethics by P. H. NOWELL-SMITH. Blackwell, Oxford, 1957.

Ethics by G. E. MOORE. O.U.P., Oxford and New York, 1947.

The Language of Morals by R. HARE. O.U.P., Oxford, 1952.

The Logic of Moral Discourse by P. EDWARDS. Free Press, Glencoe, Ill., 1955.

A Modern Introduction to Moral Philosophy by A. MONTE-FIORE. Routledge, London, 1958.

(ii) *Some classical works*

The Republic by PLATO, ed. F. M. CORNFORD. O.U.P., Oxford, 1941.

The Nicomachaean Ethics by ARISTOTLE, tr. H. JOACHIM, ed. D. A. REES. O.U.P., Oxford and New York, 1951.

Ethics by B. DE SPINOZA, tr. BOYLE. (Everyman) Dent, London and Dutton, New York, 1955.

Inquiry concerning the Principles of Morals by D. HUME. O.U.P., Oxford, 1902; Liberal Arts Press, New York, 1955.

Fundamental Principles of the Metaphysics of Ethics by I. KANT, tr. T. ABBOTT. Longmans, London, 3rd ed. 1907.

Review of the Principal Questions in Morals by R. PRICE, ed. D. D. RAPHAEL. O.U.P., Oxford, 1948.

The Philosophy of Right by G. HEGEL, tr. T. M. KNOX. O.U.P., Oxford and New York, 1942.

Utilitarianism by J. S. MILL. (Everyman) Dent, London and Dutton, New York.

Prolegomena to Ethics by T. H. GREEN, ed. A. C. BRADLEY. O.U.P., Oxford, 1883.

Principia Ethica by G. E. MOORE. C.U.P., Cambridge, 1903.

See also under: BENTHAM, BRAITHWAITE, BROAD, BUTLER, CLARKE, DEWEY, EDWARDS, GROTIUS, GREEN, HARTMANN, HOBBES, HUTCHESON, MARX, NIETZSCHE, PRICHARD, ROSS, ROUSSEAU, SCHLICK, SIDGWICK, SPENCER, STEVENSON, TAYLOR and TOULMIN, *below.*

Individual Philosophers

AYER

Language Truth and Logic by A. J. AYER. Gollancz, London, 2nd ed. 1946; Dover, New York, 2nd rev. ed. 1952.

The Foundations of Empirical Knowledge by A. J. AYER. Macmillan, London, 1940.

407

Thinking and Meaning (Inaugural Lecture at London) by A. J. AYER. Lewis, London, 1947.

Philosophical Essays by A. J. AYER. Macmillan, London, 1954; St Martins, New York, 1955.

The Problem of Knowledge by A. J. AYER. Penguin, London and Baltimore, 1956.

BACON, FRANCIS
Works by F. BACON, ed. J. SPEDDING, R. L. ELLIS and D. D. HEATH. Longmans, London, 1857–74.

Philosophical Works by F. BACON, ed. J. M. ROBERTSON. Routledge, London, 1905.

The Philosophy of Francis Bacon by F. H. ANDERSON. Chicago U.P., Chicago, 1948.

Francis Bacon by J. NICHOL. Blackwood, London, 1907.

The Philosophy of Francis Bacon in *Ethics and the History of Philosophy* by C. D. BROAD. Kegan Paul, London, 1952.

Francis Bacon by A. E. TAYLOR. British Academy, London, 1927.

BENTHAM
Works by J. BENTHAM, ed. J. BOWRING. Tait, Edinburgh, 1838–43.

Introduction to the Principles of Morals and Legislation by J. BENTHAM, ed. L. LAFLEUR. Hafner, London and New York, 1948.

Theory of Fictions by J. BENTHAM, ed. C. K. OGDEN. Routledge, London, 1932.

Fragment on Government and Introduction to the Principles of Morals by J. BENTHAM, ed. W. HARRISON. Blackwell, Oxford and Macmillan, New York, 1948.

The English Utilitarians by L. STEPHEN. London School of Economics, London, 1950; Peter Smith, Gloucester, Mass.

The Growth of Philosophical Radicalism by E. HALÉVY, tr. M. MORRIS. Faber & Faber, London, 1928.

Bentham and the Ethics of Today by DAVID BAUMGARDT. Princeton U.P., Princeton, N.J., 1952.

Philosophical Essays (No. II) by A. J. AYER. Macmillan, London, 1954; St Martins, New York, 1955.

BERGSON
Time and Free Will by H. BERGSON, tr. F. G. POGSON. Allen & Unwin, London, 1910.

Matter and Memory by H. BERGSON, tr. N. M. PAUL and W. S. PALMER. Allen & Unwin, London, 1911.

Laughter by H. BERGSON, tr. C. BRERETON and F. ROTHWELL. Macmillan, London.

Introduction to Metaphysics by H. BERGSON, tr. T. E. HULME. Macmillan, London, 1913.

Creative Evolution by H. BERGSON, tr. A. MITCHELL. Macmillan, London, 1954.

The Two Sources of Morality and Religion by H. BERGSON, tr. R. ANDRA and C. BRERETON. Macmillan, London, 1935.

BERKELEY
Works by G. BERKELEY, ed. A. A. LUCE and T. E. JESSOP. Nelson, Edinburgh and New York, 1948–57.

New Theory of Vision, etc. by G. BERKELEY. (Everyman) Dent, London and Dutton, New York, 1954.

Philosophical Writings by G. BERKELEY, sel. T. E. JESSOP. Texas U.P., Austin, Texas, 1953.

Berkeley by G. J. WARNOCK. Penguin, London and Baltimore, 1953.

BLACK
The Nature of Mathematics by M. BLACK. Routledge, London, 1953.

Language and Philosophy by M. BLACK. Cornell U.P., Ithaca, N.Y., 1949.

Problems of Analysis (Philosophical Essays) by M. BLACK. Routledge, London, 1954.

BOOLE
The Mathematical Analysis of Logic by G. BOOLE. Blackwell, Oxford, 1948 (reprint).

Investigation of the Laws of Thought by G. BOOLE. Dover, New York, 1953 (reprint).

BOSANQUET
Knowledge and Reality by B. BOSANQUET. Kegan Paul, London, 1885.

Logic by B. BOSANQUET. O.U.P., Oxford, 2nd ed. 1931.

A History of Aesthetic by B. BOSANQUET. Allen & Unwin, London, 1904; Macmillan, New York.

The Philosophical Theory of the State by B. BOSANQUET. Allen & Unwin, London, 4th ed. 1923.

The Principle of Individuality and Value by B. BOSANQUET. Macmillan, London, 1912.

The Value and Destiny of the Individual by B. BOSANQUET. Macmillan, London, 1913.

Some Suggestions in Ethics by B. BOSANQUET. Macmillan, London, 1918.

Implication and Linear Inference by B. BOSANQUET. Macmillan, London, 1920.

BRADLEY
Ethical Studies by F. BRADLEY. O.U.P., Oxford, 2nd ed. with notes, 1927.

Principles of Logic by F. BRADLEY. O.U.P., Oxford, 2nd ed. with notes and essays, 1922 and New York, 1927.

Appearance and Reality by F. BRADLEY. O.U.P., Oxford, rev. ed. 1930.

Essays on Truth and Reality by F. BRADLEY. O.U.P., Oxford, 1914.

Collected Essays (containing articles not republished in *Essays on Truth and Reality*) by F. BRADLEY. O.U.P., Oxford, 1935.

BRAITHWAITE
Moral Principles and Inductive Policies (*Proc. Brit. Acad.*) by R. BRAITHWAITE. O.U.P., Oxford, 1950.

Scientific Explanation by R. BRAITHWAITE. C.U.P., Cambridge, 1953.

An Empiricist's View of the Nature of Religious Belief (Eddington Memorial Lecture) by R. BRAITHWAITE. C.U.P., Cambridge, 1955.

The Theory of Games as a Tool for the Moral Philosopher by R. BRAITHWAITE. C.U.P., Cambridge, 1955.

BROAD
Perception, Physics and Reality by C. D. BROAD. C.U.P., Cambridge, 1914.

Scientific Thought by C. D. BROAD. Kegan Paul, London, 1923.

The Mind and its Place in Nature by C. D. BROAD. Kegan Paul, London, 1925.

Five Types of Ethical Theory by C. D. BROAD. Kegan Paul, London, 1930; Humanities, New York.

An Examination of McTaggart's Philosophy by C. D. BROAD. C.U.P., Cambridge, 1933–8.

Ethics and the History of Philosophy (Essays) by C. D. BROAD. Routledge, London, 1952.

Religion, Philosophy and Psychical Research (Essays) by C. D. BROAD. Routledge, London, 1953.

The Philosophy of C. D. Broad ed. P. A. SCHILPP. (Library of Living Philosophers) Northwestern U.P., Evanston, Ill., (forthcoming).

Sense-Perception and Matter by M. LEAN. Routledge, London, 1953.

BUTLER

Fifteen Sermons by J. BUTLER. Knapton, London, 1726.

The Analogy of Religion by J. BUTLER. Knapton, London, 1736.

Butler's Moral Philosophy by A. DUNCAN-JONES. Penguin, London and Baltimore, 1952.

Cambridge Platonists: *see* WHICHCOTE, GLANVILL *and* MORE.

CARNAP

Logical Syntax of Language by R. CARNAP, tr. A. SMEATON. Kegan Paul, London, 1937.

Introduction to Semantics by R. CARNAP. O.U.P., Oxford and Harvard U.P., Cambridge, Mass., 1942.

Formalization of Logic by R. CARNAP. Harvard U.P., Cambridge, Mass., 1947.

Meaning and Necessity by R. CARNAP. Chicago U.P., Chicago, Ill., 2nd ed. 1956.

The Logical Foundations of Probability by R. CARNAP. Routledge, London, 1950.

Introduction to Symbolic Logic and its Applications by R. CARNAP. 1958.

CASSIRER

Language and Myth by E. CASSIRER, tr. S. K. LANGER. Harper, London and New York, 1946.

An Essay on Man by E. CASSIRER. O.U.P., Oxford and Yale U.P., New Haven, Conn., 1944.

The Philosophy of Symbolic Forms by E. CASSIRER, tr. C. HENDEL. O.U.P., Oxford and Yale U.P., New Haven, Conn., 1953-5.

The Myth of the State by E. CASSIRER. O.U.P., Oxford and Yale U.P., New Haven, Conn., 1946.

Determinism and Indeterminism in Modern Physics by E. CASSIRER, tr. O. BENFEY. O.U.P., Oxford and New York, 1956.

The Problem of Knowledge by E. CASSIRER, tr. W. WOGLOM and C. HENDEL. O.U.P., Oxford and Yale U.P., New Haven, Conn., 1950.

The Philosophy of Ernst Cassirer ed. P. A. SCHILPP. (Library of Living Philosophers) C.U.P., Cambridge and Northwestern U.P., Evanston, Ill., 1949.

CLARKE

A Demonstration of the Being and Attributes of God (Boyle Lectures 1704-5) by S. CLARKE. Knapton, London, 1705.

Leibniz-Clarke Correspondence ed. H. ALEXANDER. Manchester U.P., Manchester, 1956.

COHEN

Reason and Nature by M. R. COHEN. Kegan Paul, London, 1931; Free Press, Chicago, 1953.

An Introduction to Logic and Scientific Method by M. R. COHEN (with E. NAGEL). Routledge, London and Harcourt, New York, 1934.

Law and the Social Order by M. R. COHEN. Harcourt Brace, New York, 1933.

A Preface to Logic by M. R. COHEN. Routledge, London, 1946; Meridian, New York.

The Meaning of Human History by M. R. COHEN. Open Court, La Salle, Ill., 1947.

Studies in Philosophy and Science by M. R. COHEN. Holt, New York, 1949.

Reason and Law by M. R. COHEN. Free Press, Chicago, 1950.

COLLINGWOOD

Religion and Philosophy by R. G. COLLINGWOOD. Macmillan, London, 1916.

Speculum Mentis by R. G. COLLINGWOOD. O.U.P., Oxford, 1924.

Idea of Nature by R. G. COLLINGWOOD. O.U.P., Oxford, 1944.

Idea of History by R. G. COLLINGWOOD, ed. T. M. KNOX. O.U.P., Oxford and New York, 1946.

Autobiography by R. G. COLLINGWOOD. O.U.P., Oxford, 1951.

Essay on Metaphysics by R. G. COLLINGWOOD. O.U.P., Oxford and New York, 1940.

Principles of Art by R. G. COLLINGWOOD. O.U.P., Oxford and New York, 1938.

The New Leviathan by R. G. COLLINGWOOD. O.U.P., Oxford, 1942.

COMTE

Early Essays on Social Philosophy by A. COMTE, H. D. HUTTON. Routledge, London, 1911.

Cours de Philosophie Positive by A. COMTE. Paris, 1830-42.

Condensed translation of *Cours de Philosophie Positive*, entitled *The Positive Philosophy of Auguste Comte* by A. COMTE, tr. H. MARTINEAU. Bell, London, 3rd ed. 1896.

A Discourse on the Positive Spirit by A. COMTE, tr. S. BEESLEY. Reeves, London, 1903.

A General View of Positivism by A. COMTE, tr. J. H. BRIDGES. Routledge, London, 1910; Speller, New York.

The Catechism of Positive Religion by A. COMTE, tr. R. CONGREVE. Kegan Paul, London, 3rd ed. 1891.

CONDORCET

Sketch of the Historical Picture of the Human Mind by A. N. DE CONDORCET, tr. J. BARRACLOUGH. Weidenfeld & Nicholson, London, and Philosophical Library, New York, 1956.

CROCE

Aesthetic by B. CROCE, tr. D. AINSLIE. Owen & Vision, London, 1953; Noonday, New York, 1956.

Philosophy of the Practical by B. CROCE. Macmillan, London, 1913.

Logic as the Science of the True Concept by B. CROCE. Macmillan, London, 1917.

Theory and History of Historiography by B. CROCE. Macmillan, London, 1921.

My Philosophy, and other Essays by B. CROCE, sel. R. KLIBANSKY, tr. E. F. CARRITT. Allen & Unwin, London, 1949.

CUDWORTH

The True Intellectual System of the Universe, etc. by R. CUDWORTH. Royston, London, 1678.

A Treatise Concerning Eternal and Immutable Morality by R. CUDWORTH. Knapton, London, 1731.

DESCARTES
Philosophical Works by R. DESCARTES, tr. E. S. HALDANE and G. R. T. ROSS. C.U.P., Cambridge, 1931.
Philosophical Writings, a Selection by R. DESCARTES, tr. and ed. E. ANSCOMBE and P. GEACH. Nelson, Edinburgh and New York, 1954.

DEWEY
Experience and Nature by J. DEWEY. Open Court, London and Chicago, 1925.
The Quest for Certainty by J. DEWEY. Allen & Unwin, London, 1930; New York, 1929.
Logic, the Theory of Enquiry by J. DEWEY. Allen & Unwin, London and New York, 1939.
Human Nature and Conduct by J. DEWEY. Allen & Unwin, London, 1922.
Philosophy of John Dewey ed. P. A. SCHILPP. (Library of Living Philosophers) Northwestern U.P., Evanston and Chicago, Ill., 2nd ed. 1951.
John Dewey, an Intellectual Portrait by S. HOOK. Day, New York, 1939.

DIDEROT
Selected Philosophical Writings by D. DIDEROT, ed. LOUGH. C.U.P., Cambridge and New York, 1953.

DUCASSE
Philosophy as a Science by C. DUCASSE. Hafner, London and New York, 1941.
Nature, Mind and Death by C. DUCASSE. Open Court, La Salle, Ill., 1951.

ENGELS
Anti-Dühring by F. ENGELS. Lawrence & Wishart, London, 1955.
Ludwig Feuerbach by F. ENGELS, tr. C. DUTT. Lawrence & Wishart, London, 1936; Int. Publishers, New York.
Dialectics of Nature by F. ENGELS, tr. C. DUTT. Lawrence & Wishart, London 1955; Int. Publishers, New York, 1940.

EDWARDS
Enquiry into the Modern Notion of the Freedom of the Will by J. EDWARDS. Boston, 1754.

FREGE
Philosophical Writings by G. FREGE, tr. P. GEACH and M. BLACK. Blackwell, Oxford, 1952.
Foundations of Aesthetic by G. FREGE, tr. J. AUSTIN. Blackwell, Oxford, 2nd ed. 1953.

GASSENDI
Syntagma Philosophiae Epicuri by P. GASSENDI. Amsterdam, 1684.
The Philosophy of Gassendi (English précis) by G. S. BRETT. Macmillan, London, 1908.

GILSON
God and Philosophy by E. GILSON. O.U.P., Oxford and Yale U.P., New Haven, Conn., 1941.
History of Christian Philosophy in the Middle Ages by E. GILSON. Sheed & Ward, London, 1955.

GLANVILL
The Vanity of Dogmatising by J. GLANVILL. London, 1661.
Philosophical Considerations by J. GLANVILL. London, 1666.

GOODMAN
The Structure of Appearance by N. GOODMAN. O.U.P., Oxford and Harvard U.P., Cambridge, Mass., 1951.
Fact, Fiction and Forecast by N. GOODMAN. Athlone, London, 1954.

GREEN
Prolegomena to Ethics by T. H. GREEN, ed. A. C. BRADLEY. O.U.P., Oxford, 1883.
Works of T. H. Green (excluding the above), ed. R. L. NETTLESHIP. Longmans, London, 1885-8.

GROTIUS
De Jure Belli et Pacis Libri Tres (with-abridged tr.) by H. GROTIUS, tr. W. WHEWELL. C.U.P., Cambridge, 1854.
The Social and Political Idea of Some Great Thinkers of the 16th and 17th Centuries by F. J. C. HEARNSHAW. Harrap, London, 1926.

HAMILTON
Lectures on Metaphysics and Logic by Sir W. HAMILTON, ed. H. L. MANSEL and J. VEITCH. Edinburgh, 1859-60.
An Examination of Sir William Hamilton's Philosophy by J. S. MILL. Longmans, London, 1889.

HARE
The Language of Morals by R. HARE. O.U.P., Oxford and New York, 1952.

HARTMANN, C. R. E. VON
The Philosophy of the Unconscious by C. R. E. VON HARTMANN, tr. W. C. COUPLAND. Routledge, London, 1931.

HARTMANN, N.
Ethics by N. HARTMANN, tr. S. COIT. Allen & Unwin, London, 1932; Macmillan, New York.

HEGEL
Philosophy of Right by G. HEGEL, tr. T. M. KNOX. O.U.P., Oxford, 1942.
Lectures on the History of Philosophy by G. HEGEL, tr. J. HALDANE and SIMPSON. Routledge, London, 1955 (reissue); Humanities, New York, 1954.
Lectures on the Philosophy of History by G. HEGEL, tr. J. SIBREE. Bell, London, 1878; Dover, New York, 1956.
Phenomenology of the Mind by G. HEGEL, tr. J. B. BAILLIE. Allen & Unwin, London and Macmillan, New York, 1931.
Philosophy of Hegel by W. T. STACE. Macmillan, London, 1924.
Hegel: A Re-examination by J. N. FINDLAY. London, 1958.

HEIDEGGER
Being and Time by M. HEIDEGGER. 1958.
What is Philosophy? by M. HEIDEGGER, tr. W. KLUBACK and J. T. WILDE. Vision Press, London and New York, 1958.

HICKS
Thought and Real Existence by G. D. HICKS. O.U.P., Oxford, 1936.
The Philosophical Bases of Theism (Hibbert Lectures) by G. D. HICKS. Allen & Unwin, London, 1937.
Critical Realism by G. D. HICKS. Macmillan, London, 1938.

HOBBES
English Works by T. HOBBES, ed. Sir W. MOLESWORTH. London, 1839–45.
Latin Works by T. HOBBES, ed. Sir W. MOLESWORTH. London, 1839–45.
Leviathan by T. HOBBES, ed. M. OAKESHOTT. Blackwell, Oxford, 1946.
Hobbes by E. S. PETERS. Penguin, London and Baltimore, 1956.

HOCKING
Lasting Elements of Individualism by W. E. HOCKING. Yale U.P., New Haven, Conn., 1937.
Types of Philosophy by W. E. HOCKING. Scribner's, London, 1929.
Thoughts of Death and Life by W. E. HOCKING. Harper, London and New York, 1937.
The Meaning of God in Human Experience by W. E. HOCKING. O.U.P., Oxford and Yale U.P., New Haven, Conn., 1912.
Human Nature and its Remaking by W. E. HOCKING. Yale U.P., New Haven, Conn., 1929.
Rethinking Missions by W. E. HOCKING.

HOOK
The Metaphysics of Pragmatism by S. HOOK. Open Court, London and Chicago, Ill., 1927.
From Hegel to Marx by S. HOOK. Gollancz, London, 1936.
Education for Modern Man by S. HOOK. Dial, New York, 1946.
Reason, Social Myths and Democracy by S. HOOK. Humanities, New York.

HUME
Treatise of Human Nature by D. HUME. (Everyman) Dent, London and Dutton, New York, 1956.
Inquiry concerning the Human Understanding and Inquiry concerning the Principles of Morals by D. HUME, ed. L. SELBY-BIGGE. O.U.P., Oxford, 1895.
Dialogues concerning Natural Religion by D. HUME, ed. N. KEMP SMITH. O.U.P., Oxford, 1935.
David Hume, His Theory of Knowledge by D. G. C. McNABB. Hutchinson, London, 1951.
The Life of David Hume by E. C. MOSSNER. Nelson, Edinburgh, 1954.

HUSSERL
Logische Untersuchungen by E. HUSSERL. Halle, rev. ed. 1913.
Ideen zu einer reinen Phänomenologie, Vol. I, tr. as *Ideas: General Introduction to Pure Phenomenology* by E. HUSSERL, tr. W. R. BOYCE GIBSON. Allen & Unwin, London and Macmillan, New York, 1931–52.

HUTCHESON
Inquiry into the Original of our Ideas of Beauty and Virtue by F. HUTCHESON. London, 1720.
Essay on the Nature and Conduct of our Passions by F. HUTCHESON. Knapton, London, 1730.
A System of Moral Philosophy (posthumous) by F. HUTCHESON. Glasgow and London, 1755.
Extracts in *British Moralists* ed. L. SELBY-BIGGE. O.U.P., Oxford, 1897.

JAMES
The Will to Believe by W. JAMES. Dover, New York.
Principles of Psychology by W. JAMES. Macmillan, London, 1901; Holt, New York.

Pragmatism by W. JAMES. Longmans, London and New York, 1943.
The Varieties of Religious Experience by W. JAMES. Longmans, London, 1952; Modern Library, New York, 1936.
A Pluralistic Universe by W. JAMES. Longmans, London and New York, 1943.
The Meaning of Truth by W. JAMES. Longmans, London and New York, 1909.
Some Problems of Philosophy by W. JAMES. Longmans, London and New York, 1940.
Memories and Studies by W. JAMES. Longmans, New York, 1911.
Collected Essays and Reviews by W. JAMES. Longmans, London and New York, 1920.

JASPERS
Perennial Scope of Philosophy by K. JASPERS, tr. R. MANHEIM. Routledge, London, 1950.
Man in the Modern Age by K. JASPERS, tr. E. and C. PAUL. Routledge, London, 1951.
Reason and Anti-Reason in our Time by K. JASPERS, tr. S. GODMAN. S.C.M., London, 1952.
Reason and Existenz by K. JASPERS, tr. W. EARL. Routledge, London, 1956.
The Philosophy of K. Jaspers ed. P. A. SCHILPP. (Library of Living Philosophers) Tudor, New York, 1957.

JEVONS
The Principles of Science by F. JEVONS. O.U.P., Oxford, 1874.
Studies in Deductive Logic by F. JEVONS. London, 1880.

KANT
Critique of Pure Reason by I. KANT, tr. N. KEMP SMITH. Macmillan, London, 1929; St Martins, New York.
Critique of Practical Reason, etc. by I. KANT, tr. T. ABBOTT. Longmans, London and New York, 1909.
Critique of Judgment by I. KANT, tr. J. MEREDITH. O.U.P., Oxford and New York, 1952.
Prolegomena to any Future Metaphysics by I. KANT, ed. and tr. P. LUCAS. Manchester U.P., Manchester, 1953; ed. and tr. P. CARUS. Open Court, La Salle, Ill.
The Moral Law by I. KANT, tr. H. J. PATON. Hutchinson, London, 1948.
The Categorical Imperative by H. J. PATON. Hutchinson, London, 2nd ed. 1953; Chicago U.P., Chicago, Ill., 1948.
Kant's Metaphysic of Experience by H. J. PATON. Allen & Unwin, London and Macmillan, New York, 1936.
Kant by S. KÖRNER. Penguin, London and Baltimore, 1955.

KIERKEGAARD
Concept of Dread by S. KIERKEGAARD, tr. W. LOWRIE. O.U.P., Oxford and Princeton U.P., Princeton, N.J., 1944.
Fear and Trembling by S. KIERKEGAARD, tr. W. LOWRIE. O.U.P., Oxford and Princeton U.P., Princeton, N.J., 1944.
For Self-Examination by S. KIERKEGAARD, tr. W. LOWRIE and D. F. SWENSON. O.U.P., Oxford and Princeton U.P., Princeton, N.J., 1941.
Concluding Unscientific Postscript by S. KIERKEGAARD, tr. D. F. SWENSON, ed. W. LOWRIE. O.U.P., Oxford and Princeton U.P., Princeton, N.J., 1941.
Sören Kierkegaard by J. HOHLENBERG, tr. T. H. CROXALL. Routledge, London and Pantheon, New York, 1954.

LEIBNIZ

New Essays Concerning the Human Understanding by
G. LEIBNIZ, tr. LANGLEY. 1896.

The Monadology, etc. by G. LEIBNIZ, tr. R. LATTA.
O.U.P., Oxford, 1898.

Theodicy by G. LEIBNIZ, tr. E. M. HUGGARD. Routledge,
London, 1952.

Discourse on Metaphysics by G. LEIBNIZ, tr. P. LUCAS and
GRINT. Manchester U.P., Manchester, 1953; Barnes &
Noble, New York, 1954.

Leibniz-Clarke Correspondence ed. H. ALEXANDER. Manchester U.P., Manchester, 1956.

A Critical Exposition of the Philosophy of Leibniz by
B. A. W. RUSSELL. Allen & Unwin, London, 2nd ed.
1937; Humanities, New York.

Leibniz by R. L. SAW. Penguin, London and Baltimore,
1954.

LEWIS

Survey of Symbolic Logic by C. I. LEWIS. California U.P.,
Berkeley, Calif., 1918.

Mind and the World Order by C. I. LEWIS. Scribner's,
London and New York, 1928.

Symbolic Logic by C. I. LEWIS (with C. H. LANGFORD).
Dover, London and New York, 1932.

An Analysis of Knowledge and Valuation by C. I. LEWIS.
Open Court, La Salle, Ill., 1946.

The Ground and Nature of Right by C. I. LEWIS. Columbia
U.P., New York, 1955.

LOCKE

Two Treatises of Government by J. LOCKE, ed. T. COOK.
Hafner, London and New York, 1956.

Essay Concerning Human Understanding (abridged) by
J. LOCKE, ed. R. WILBURN. (Everyman) Dent, London
and Dutton, New York, 1947.

Some Thoughts concerning Education by J. LOCKE, ed.
R. H. QUICK. C.U.P., Cambridge, 1899; ed. C. W.
ELIOT. Harvard U.P. (Harvard Classics, Vol. 37), Cam-
bridge, Mass., 1910.

John Locke by D. J. O'CONNOR. Penguin, London and
Baltimore, 1952.

MALEBRANCHE

De la Recherche de la Vérité by N. MALEBRANCHE. Paris,
1674–8.

A Treatise of Morality by N. MALEBRANCHE, tr. J. SHIP-
TON. London, 1699.

Dialogues on Metaphysics and Religion by N. MALE-
BRANCHE, tr. M. GINSBERG. Macmillan, London and
New York, 1923.

MACH

Contributions to the Analysis of Sensations by E. MACH.
Dover, New York, 1897.

The Science of Mechanics by E. MACH, tr. T. MCCORMACK.
Open Court, London and La Salle, Ill., 4th ed. 1919.

MARCEL

Philosophy of Existence by G. MARCEL, tr. M. HARARI.
Harvill, London, 1949.

Le Mystère de l'Être (Gifford Lectures) by G. MARCEL, tr.
G. S. FRASER and R. HAGUE. Harvill, London, 1951.

MCTAGGART

The Nature of Existence by J. MCTAGGART. C.U.P., Cambridge and Macmillan, New York, 1927.

Studies in the Hegelian Dialectic by J. MCTAGGART. C.U.P.,
Cambridge, 2nd ed. 1922.

Some Dogmas of Religion by J. MCTAGGART. Arnold,
London, 1930.

Philosophical Studies by J. MCTAGGART, ed. S. KEELING.
Arnold, London, 1934.

An Examination of McTaggart's Philosophy by C. D.
BROAD. C.U.P., Cambridge and New York, 1933–8.

MARITAIN

Introduction to Philosophy by J. MARITAIN, tr. E. WATKIN.
Sheed & Ward, London and New York, 2nd ed. 1947.

Existence and the Existent by J. MARITAIN. Doubleday,
New York, 1957.

The Degrees of Knowledge by J. MARITAIN, tr. G. PHELAN.
Bles, London, 1937; Scribner's, New York, 1958.

MARX

Manifesto of the Communist Party by K. MARX (with
F. ENGELS). Reeves, London, 1888.

Theses on Feuerbach (in Engels' *Ludwig Feuerbach*, q.v.).

Marx by I. BERLIN. O.U.P., Oxford, 1948.

The Critique of the Hegelian Philosophy of Right by K. MARX.

The Jewish Question by K. MARX. 1843.

Political Economy and Philosophy (notebooks of 1844) by
K. MARX.

The Holy Family by K. MARX (with F. ENGELS). Moscow,
1956; Lawrence & Wishart, London, 1956.

The German Ideology by K. MARX (with F. ENGELS).
Lawrence & Wishart, London, 1953; Int. Publishers,
New York.

The Poverty of Philosophy by K. MARX. Lawrence &
Wishart, London, 1956.

Preface to *Critique of Political Economy* by K. MARX, tr.
N. I. STONE. Kegan Paul, London and Int. Library
Publishing Co., New York, 2nd ed. 1904.

Preface to *Capital* (2nd edition) by K. MARX. Hamburg,
1872.

MEINONG

Meinong's Theory of Objects by J. N. FINDLAY. O.U.P.,
Oxford, 1933.

MILL, JAMES

Essay on Government by JAMES MILL. C.U.P., Cambridge
and New York, 1937.

Analysis of the Phenomena of the Human Mind by JAMES
MILL, ed. JOHN S. MILL, London, 1869.

James Mill, A Biography by A. BAIN. London, 2nd ed. 1887.

MILL, JOHN, S.

A System of Logic by JOHN S. MILL. Longmans, London,
1884 and New York, 1929.

On Liberty; Representative Government and *Utilitarianism*
by JOHN S. MILL. (Everyman) Dent, London and
Dutton, New York, 1954.

An Examination of Sir William Hamilton's Philosophy by
JOHN S. MILL. Longmans, London, 1889.

Autobiography by JOHN S. MILL. O.U.P., Oxford and
Columbia U.P., New York, 1924.

Nature; The Utility of Religion and *Theism* by JOHN S. MILL.
Watts, London, 1904.

The English Utilitarians by L. STEPHEN. London School of
Economics, London, 1950; Peter Smith, Gloucester,
Mass.

The Philosophy of J. S. Mill by R. P. ANSCHUTZ. O.U.P., Oxford and New York, 1953.

J. S. Mill by K. BRITTON. Penguin, London and Baltimore, 1953.

MISES

Probability, Statistics and Truth by R. VON MISES, tr. J. NEYMAN and others. Hodge, London, 1939.

Positivism by R. VON MISES. O.U.P., Oxford and Braziller, New York, 1956.

MOORE

Principia Ethica by G. E. MOORE. C.U.P., Cambridge and New York, 1954.

Some Main Problems of Philosophy by G. E. MOORE. Allen & Unwin, London and Macmillan, New York, 1953.

Ethics by G. E. MOORE. O.U.P., Oxford and New York, 1947.

Philosophical Studies by G. E. MOORE. Routledge, London, 1922; Humanities, New York, 1921.

Philosophical Papers by G. E. MOORE. Allen & Unwin, London and Macmillan, New York, 1959.

The Philosophy of G. E. Moore ed. P. SCHILPP. (Library of Living Philosophers) Tudor, New York, 1952.

G. E. Moore, A Critical Exposition by A. R. WHITE. Blackwell, Oxford, 1958.

MORE

Works by H. MORE. London, 1675–9.

MORRIS

Six Theories of Mind by C. W. MORRIS. Chicago U.P., Chicago, Ill., 1932.

Foundations of the Theory of Signs by C. W. MORRIS. Chicago U.P., Chicago, Ill., 1938.

Paths of Life by C. W. MORRIS. New York, 1942.

Signs, Language and Behaviour by C. W. MORRIS. Prentice-Hall, New York, 1946.

Varieties of Human Value by C. W. MORRIS. Chicago U.P., Chicago, Ill., 1956.

NAGEL

Introduction to Logic and Scientific Method by E. NAGEL (with M. R. COHEN). Routledge, London and Harcourt, New York, 1934.

Sovereign Reason (Essays) by E. NAGEL. Glencoe, Ill., 1954.

Logic without Metaphysics by E. NAGEL. Glencoe, Ill., 1957.

NIETZSCHE

A Nietzsche Reader ed. W. A. KAUFMANN. O.U.P., Oxford and Princeton U.P., Princeton, N.J., 1950.

Nietzsche: Philosopher, Psychologist, Antichrist by W. A. KAUFMANN. Princeton U.P., Princeton, N.J., 1950.

The Tragic Philosopher by F. A. LEA. Methuen, London, 1957.

PEIRCE

Collected Papers by C. S. PEIRCE, ed. C. HARTSHORNE and P. WEISS. Harvard U.P., Cambridge, Mass., 1931–5.

Philosophy of Peirce (Selected Writings) ed. J. BUCHLER. Kegan Paul, London, 1940.

Values in a Universe of Chance by C. S. PEIRCE, ed. WIENER. Dover, New York, 1958.

Peirce and Progenatism by W. B. GALLIE. Penguin, London and Baltimore, 1952.

POPPER

The Open Society and its Enemies by K. POPPER. Routledge, London, 3rd ed. 1957.

Poverty of Historicism by K. POPPER. Routledge, London, 1957.

Logic of Scientific Discovery by K. POPPER. Routledge, London, 1959.

PRICE, H. H.

Perception by H. H. PRICE. Methuen, London, 1954.

Hume's Theory of the External World by H. H. PRICE. O.U.P., Oxford and New York, 1940.

Thinking and Experience by H. H. PRICE. Hutchinson, London, 1953.

PRICE, R.

A Review of the Principal Questions in Morals by R. PRICE ed. D. D. RAPHAEL. O.U.P., Oxford and New York, 1948.

PRICHARD

Kant's Theory of Knowledge by H. PRICHARD. O.U.P., Oxford, 1909.

Knowledge and Perception (Posthumous essays) by H. PRICHARD. O.U.P., Oxford and New York, 1950.

Moral Obligation (Posthumous essays) by H. PRICHARD. O.U.P., Oxford and New York, 1949.

QUINE

Mathematical Logic by W. QUINE. O.U.P., Oxford and Harvard U.P., Cambridge, Mass., 1951.

Methods of Logic by W. QUINE. Routledge, London, 1952; Holt, New York, 1950.

From a Logical Point of View by W. QUINE. O.U.P., Oxford and Harvard U.P., Cambridge, Mass., 1953.

REID

An Inquiry into the Human Mind, on the Principles of Common Sense by T. REID. Edinburgh, 1764.

Essays on the Intellectual Powers of Man by T. REID, abr. ed. A. D. WOOZLEY. Macmillan, London, 1941; St Martins, New York.

ROSS

The Right and the Good by Sir W. ROSS. O.U.P., Oxford, 1930.

The Foundations of Ethics by Sir W. ROSS. O.U.P., Oxford and New York, 1939.

ROUSSEAU

Du Contrat Social by J.-J. ROUSSEAU, tr. and ed. G. D. H. COLE. (Everyman) Dent, London and Dutton, New York, 1955.

Political Writings by J.-J. ROUSSEAU, tr. F. WATKINS. Nelson, Edinburgh, 1953.

ROYCE

The Religious Aspect of Philosophy by J. ROYCE. Peter Smith, Gloucester, Mass., 1958.

The Conception of God by J. ROYCE. Macmillan, New York, 1897.

Study of Good and Evil by J. ROYCE. Macmillan, New York, 1898.

The World and the Individual by J. ROYCE. Macmillan, New York, 1900–2.

The Philosophy of Loyalty by J. ROYCE. Macmillan, New York, 1908.

W. James and Other Essays by J. ROYCE. Macmillan, New York, 1911.

The Sources of Religious Insight by J. ROYCE. Clark, Edinburgh and Scribner's, New York, 1912.

The Problem of Christianity by J. ROYCE. Macmillan, New York, 1913.

Lectures on Modern Idealism by J. ROYCE. Yale U.P., New Haven, Conn., 1919.

Fugitive Essays by J. ROYCE. Harvard U.P., Cambridge, Mass., 1920.

RUSSELL

A Critical Exposition of the Philosophy of Leibniz by B. A. W. RUSSELL. Allen & Unwin, London, 2nd ed. 1937; Humanities, New York.

The Principles of Mathematics by B. A. W. RUSSELL. Allen & Unwin, London, 2nd ed. 1950; Norton, New York, 1938.

Philosophical Essays by B. A. W. RUSSELL. Longmans, London and New York, 1910.

Principia Mathematica by B. A. W. RUSSELL (with A. N. WHITEHEAD). C.U.P., Cambridge, 2nd ed. 1927.

The Problems of Philosophy by B. A. W. RUSSELL. Williams & Norgate, London and Holt, New York, 1912.

Our Knowledge of the External World by B. A. W. RUSSELL. Allen & Unwin, London, 2nd ed. 1949; Humanities, New York.

Principles of Social Reconstruction by B. A. W. RUSSELL. Allen & Unwin, London, 2nd ed. 1920; Century, New York, 1916.

Mysticism and Logic, and Other Essays by B. A. W. RUSSELL. Allen & Unwin, London, 1917; Barnes & Noble, New York, 1954.

Introduction to Mathematical Philosophy by B. A. W. RUSSELL. Allen & Unwin, London, 2nd ed. 1949; Macmillan, New York, 1924.

The Practice and Theory of Bolshevism by B. A. W. RUSSELL. Allen & Unwin, London, 1921; Macmillan, New York, 1949.

The Analysis of Mind by B. A. W. RUSSELL. Allen & Unwin, London and Macmillan, New York, 1921.

On Education Especially in Early Childhood by B. A. W. RUSSELL. Allen & Unwin, London and Liveright, New York, 1926.

An Analysis of Matter by B. A. W. RUSSELL. Allen & Unwin, London 1955; Dover, New York, 1954.

An Outline of Philosophy by B. A. W. RUSSELL. Allen & Unwin, London and Meridian, New York, 1927.

Power: A New Social Analysis by B. A. W. RUSSELL. Allen & Unwin, London and Norton, New York, 1938.

An Inquiry into Meaning and Truth by B. A. W. RUSSELL. Allen & Unwin, London, 1940; Humanities, New York.

The Philosophy of Bertrand Russell ed. P. A. SCHILPP. (Library of Living Philosophers) C.U.P., Cambridge and Northwestern University, Evanston, Ill., 1944.

History of Western Philosophy by B. A. W. RUSSELL. Allen & Unwin, London and Simon & Schuster, New York, 1946.

Human Knowledge, its Scope and Limits by B. A. W. RUSSELL. Allen & Unwin, London and Simon & Schuster, New York, 1948.

Authority and the Individual by B. A. W. RUSSELL. Allen & Unwin, London and Simon & Schuster, New York, 1949.

Human Society in Ethics and Politics by B. A. W. RUSSELL. Allen & Unwin, London, 1954; Simon & Schuster, New York, 1955.

Logic and Knowledge (Essays, 1901–50) by B. A. W. RUSSELL, ed. R. MARSH. Allen & Unwin, London, 1956; Macmillan, New York.

My Philosophical Development by B. A. W. RUSSELL. Simon & Schuster, New York, 1959.

RYLE

The Concept of Mind by G. RYLE. Hutchinson, London, 1949; Barnes & Noble, New York, 1950.

Dilemmas by G. RYLE. C.U.P., Cambridge, 1954.

SANTAYANA

The Life of Reason by G. SANTAYANA. Constable, London and Scribner's, New York, 1954.

The Sense of Beauty by G. SANTAYANA. Black, London, 1896; Dover, New York, 1955.

Realms of Being by G. SANTAYANA. Constable, London, 1928–40; Scribner's, New York, 1942.

The Philosophy of G. Santayana ed. P. SCHILPP. (Library of Living Philosophers). C.U.P., Cambridge and Tudor, New York, 1943.

SARTRE

Being and Nothingness by J.-P. SARTRE, tr. H. E. BARNES; Methuen, London and Philosophical Library, New York, 1957.

Existentialism and Humanism by J.-P. SARTRE, tr. P. MAIRET. Methuen, London, 1955; Philosophical Library, New York.

Literary and Philosophical Essays by J.-P. SARTRE, tr. A. MICHELSON. Rider, London, 1955.

Transcendence of the Ego by J.-P. SARTRE, tr. F. WILLIAMS and R. KIRKPATRICK. Vision Press, London, 1958; Noonday, New York, 1957.

SCHILLER

Humanism: Philosophical Essays by F. C. S. SCHILLER. Macmillan, London, 2nd ed. 1912.

Studies in Humanism by F. C. S. SCHILLER. Macmillan, London, 2nd ed. 1912.

Formal Logic by F. C. S. SCHILLER. Macmillan, London, 2nd ed. 1931.

Logic for Use by F. C. S. SCHILLER. Bell, London, 1929.

SCHLICK

Space and Time in Contemporary Physics by F. SCHLICK, tr. H. L. BROSE. O.U.P., Oxford, 1920.

Problems of Ethics by F. SCHLICK. New York, 1939.

Gesammelte Aufsätze (1926–36) by F. SCHLICK. Vienna, 1938.

Philosophy of Nature by F. SCHLICK. New York, 1949.

SCHOPENHAUER

Essays from the Parerga and Paralipomena by A. SCHOPENHAUER, tr. T. B. SAUNDERS. Allen & Unwin, London, 1951.

The World as Will and Idea by A. SCHOPENHAUER, tr. R. B. HALDANE and J. KEMP. Routledge, London, 1883.

SIDGWICK

The Methods of Ethics by H. SIDGWICK. London, 1930 (reissue).

Lectures on the Ethics of Green, Spencer and Martineau by H. SIDGWICK, ed. E. C. JONES. Macmillan, London, 1902.

SPENCER

A System of Synthetic Philosophy by H. SPENCER. Williams & Norgate, London, 1862–92.

Data of Ethics by H. SPENCER. Williams & Norgate, London, 1879.

SPINOZA

Ethics by B. DE SPINOZA, tr. A. BOYLE. (Everyman) Dent, London and Dutton, New York, 1955.

Political Works by B. DE SPINOZA, with tr. A. WERNHAM. O.U.P., Oxford and New York, 1958.

Spinoza by S. HAMPSHIRE. Penguin, London and Baltimore, 1952.

Vindication of Metaphysics: A Study in the Philosophy of Spinoza by R. L. SAW. Macmillan, London, 1951; St Martins, New York.

STEVENSON

Ethics and Language by C. STEVENSON. Yale U.P., New Haven, Conn., 1944.

TAYLOR

The Problem of Conduct by A. E. TAYLOR. Macmillan, London, 1901.

Elements of Metaphysics by A. E. TAYLOR. Methuen, London, 1903.

The Faith of a Moralist by A. E. TAYLOR. Macmillan, London, 1951; St Martins, New York.

Philosophical Studies by A. E. TAYLOR. Macmillan, London, 1934.

TOULMIN

Examination of the Place of Reason in Ethics by S. TOULMIN. C.U.P., Cambridge and New York, 1950.

Philosophy of Science, an Introduction by S. TOULMIN. Hutchinson, London and Rinehart, New York, 1953.

The Uses of Argument by S. TOULMIN. C.U.P., Cambridge and New York, 1958.

URBAN

The Intelligible World, Metaphysics and Value by W. URBAN Allen & Unwin, London, 1929.

Language and Reality: the Philosophy of Language and the Principles of Symbolism by W. URBAN. Allen & Unwin, London, 1939; Macmillan, New York.

Beyond Realism and Idealism by W. URBAN. Allen & Unwin, London and Macmillan, New York, 1949.

VENN

The Logic of Chance by J. VENN. Macmillan, London, 3rd ed. 1888.

Symbolic Logic by J. VENN. Macmillan, London, 2nd ed. 1894.

Principles of Empirical or Inductive Logic by J. VENN. Macmillan, London, 1889.

WARD

Naturalism and Agnosticism by J. WARD. London, 1899.

The Realm of Ends, or Pluralism and Theism by J. WARD. C.U.P., Cambridge and New York, 3rd ed. 1920.

Psychological Principles by J. WARD. C.U.P., Cambridge and New York, 1920.

Essays in Philosophy by J. WARD. C.U.P., Cambridge and New York, 1927.

WHEWELL

History of the Inductive Sciences by W. WHEWELL. London, 3rd ed. 1857.

The Mechanical Euclid by W. WHEWELL. Cambridge, 5th ed. 1849.

Philosophy of the Inductive Sciences by W. WHEWELL. Parker, London, 1837.

The Elements of Morality by W. WHEWELL. Cambridge, 4th ed. 1864.

Lectures on Systematic Morality by W. WHEWELL. London, 1846.

William Whewell by I. TODHUNTER. London, 1876.

WHICHCOTE

Selections in: *The Cambridge Platonists* ed. E. T. CAMPAGNAC. O.U.P., Oxford, 1901.

WHITEHEAD

Principia Mathematica by A. N. WHITEHEAD (with B. A. W. RUSSELL). C.U.P., Cambridge, 2nd ed. 1927.

The Principles of Natural Knowledge by A. N. WHITEHEAD. C.U.P., Cambridge, 1919.

The Concept of Nature by A. N. WHITEHEAD. C.U.P., Cambridge and New York, 1919.

The Principle of Relativity by A. N. WHITEHEAD. C.U.P., Cambridge, 1922.

Science and the Modern World by A. N. WHITEHEAD. C.U.P., Cambridge, 2nd ed. 1926; Macmillan, New York, 1925.

Religion in the Making (Lowell Lectures) by A. N. WHITEHEAD. C.U.P., Cambridge, 1929; Macmillan, New York, 1926.

Process and Reality (Gifford Lectures) by A. N. WHITEHEAD. C.U.P., Cambridge, 1929.

Adventures of Ideas by A. N. WHITEHEAD. C.U.P., Cambridge, 1938; Macmillan, New York, 1933.

Modes of Thought by A. N. WHITEHEAD. C.U.P., Cambridge and Macmillan, New York, 1938.

Whitehead's Metaphysics by I. LECLERC. Allen & Unwin, London and Macmillan, New York, 1958.

The Philosophy of Whitehead by W. MAYS. 1959.

WISDOM

Problems of Mind and Matter by J. WISDOM. C.U.P., Cambridge, 1934.

Other Minds by J. WISDOM. Blackwell, Oxford, 1952.

Philosophy and Psycho-Analysis by J. WISDOM. Blackwell, Oxford, 1953.

WITTGENSTEIN

Tractatus Logico-Philosophicus by L. WITTGENSTEIN, tr. C. K. OGDEN. Routledge, London, 1922; Humanities, New York.

Philosophical Investigations by L. WITTGENSTEIN, tr. G. E. M. ANSCOMBE, Blackwell, Oxford, 2nd ed. 1958.

Remarks on the Foundations of Mathematics by L. WITTGENSTEIN, ed. G. VON WRIGHT, tr. G. E. M. ANSCOMBE. Blackwell, Oxford and Macmillan, New York, 1956.

The Blue and Brown Books by L. WITTGENSTEIN, ed. G. E. M. ANSCOMBE. Blackwell, Oxford, 1958.

Introduction to Wittgenstein's Tractatus by G. E. M. ANSCOMBE. 1959.

Wittgenstein's Tractatus, A Critical Exposition by E. STENIUS. Blackwell, Oxford, 1959.

Ludwig Wittgenstein: A Memoir by N. MALCOLM. 1958.